Diagnosis, Pathogenesis and Treatment of CNS Tumors

Diagnosis, Pathogenesis and Treatment of CNS Tumors

Guest Editor

Dimitrios Kanakis

MDPI

Basel • Beijing • Wuhan • Barcelona • Belgrade • Novi Sad • Cluj • Manchester

Guest Editor
Dimitrios Kanakis
Pathology
University of Nicosia Medical School
Nicosia
Cyprus

Editorial Office
MDPI AG
Grosspeteranlage 5
4052 Basel, Switzerland

This is a reprint of the Special Issue, published open access by the journal *Biomedicines* (ISSN 2227-9059), freely accessible at: https://www.mdpi.com/journal/biomedicines/special_issues/E2XQVEV38J.

For citation purposes, cite each article independently as indicated on the article page online and as indicated below:

Lastname, A.A.; Lastname, B.B. Article Title. *Journal Name* **Year**, *Volume Number*, Page Range.

ISBN 978-3-7258-7733-1 (Hbk)
ISBN 978-3-7258-7734-8 (PDF)
https://doi.org/10.3390/books978-3-7258-7734-8

Contents

About the Editor

Dimitrios Kanakis

Dimitrios Kanakis is Professor of Pathology and Neuropathology at the University of Nicosia Medical School, Cyprus, and Honorary Senior Lecturer at St George's, University of London, UK. He holds an MD from the University of Novi Sad and a PhD, magna cum laude, from Otto von Guericke University Magdeburg, Germany. He also holds specialist certification in neuropathology from the Medical Association of North Rhine, Germany (2011), and in general pathology from the General Directorate of Public Health and Social Welfare of the Region of Thessaly, Greece (2013).

At the University of Nicosia, he established the MD pathology course in 2016 and helped refine the MBBS curriculum. He teaches lectures, tutorials, and laboratory practicals, and contributes to the assessment, quality assurance, and mentoring of junior faculty and students. Previously, he was Lecturer in Pathology at the Democritus University of Thrace from 2013 to 2016 and Scientific Associate at the Aristotle University of Thessaloniki in 2013, following residency training in pathology and neuropathology in Germany and Greece from 2001 to 2012.

His academic work covers general pathology and neuropathology. He edited "Pituitary Adenoma: Pathophysiology, Diagnosis and Treatment Options" (NOVA, 2016), the *Biomedicines* Special Issue "Establishment of State-of-the-Art Methods/Techniques and Identification of Novel Biomarkers in Brain Tumor Diagnosis", later published as a reprint volume (2026), and co-edited the *Frontiers in Neurology* Research Topic "Recent Advances in Diagnosis and Treatment of Brain Tumors: From Pediatrics to Adults", published as an e-book (2025). He has also guest-edited seven additional Special Issues, authored four book chapters, published peer-reviewed papers, and serves as a reviewer and Editorial Board Member for several journals.

Preface

Remarkable breakthroughs in molecular pathology, genomics, neuroimaging, and computational analysis have substantially reshaped the field of neuro-oncology. Given the rapid pace of medical research, the diagnostic and therapeutic frameworks for central nervous system (CNS) tumors continue to evolve, with increasing emphasis on integrated approaches that connect histopathology with tumor-defining molecular, and when appropriate, epigenetic and radiologic features.

The Special Issue "Diagnosis, Pathogenesis and Treatment of CNS Tumors", was developed to highlight advances that improve how CNS tumors are classified, understood, and managed across the care pathway. In particular, the collection reflects current priorities in the field: refining diagnosis in line with contemporary WHO-aligned principles, advancing biomarker discovery and validation, and supporting the translation of new technologies into clinically workable protocols.

The main objective was to bring together studies and reviews that combine methodological rigor with clinical relevance, while also encouraging clear reporting of methods, cohorts, and implementation considerations. By emphasizing approaches that strengthen accuracy and feasibility, this Special Issue aims to help narrow the gap between technical innovation and measurable patient benefit.

After a meticulous peer review, twelve articles were accepted, including original research, methodological contributions, reviews, and case-based reports. Topics encompass integrated molecular profiling in gliomas (with clinically relevant markers and outcome associations), advanced imaging and radiotracer-based assessment, intraoperative and tissue-based diagnostic technologies, cytogenomic approaches for structural variant detection, liquid biopsy-related biology, artificial intelligence for MRI segmentation and classification, and emerging perspectives on mechanisms and therapeutic opportunities in high-grade disease.

This Special Issue is aimed at physicians involved in the care of patients with CNS tumors, as well as molecular biologists and clinical laboratory scientists, and it will also be relevant to computational researchers developing tools for diagnostic support.

We extend our appreciation to all contributing authors and to the reviewers for their careful evaluations. We anticipate that the articles collected in this Special Issue will help guide practice and inspire ongoing research toward integrated diagnostic approaches and better treatment options for CNS tumors.

Dimitrios Kanakis
Guest Editor

biomedicines

MDPI

Article

Cortical Origin-Dependent Metabolic and Molecular Heterogeneity in Gliomas: Insights from ^{18}F-FET PET

Huantong Diao [1,2,†], Xiaolong Wu [1,2,†], Xiaoran Li [1,3], Siheng Liu [1,2], Bingyang Shan [1,2], Ye Cheng [1,2,*], Jie Lu [1,3,*] and Jie Tang [1,2,*]

1 Department of Neurosurgery, Xuanwu Hospital, Capital Medical University, Beijing 100053, China
2 Department of Neurosurgery, China International Neuroscience Institute, Beijing 100053, China
3 Department of Radiology and Nuclear Medicine, Xuanwu Hospital, Capital Medical University, Beijing 100053, China
* Correspondence: chengye@xwhosp.org (Y.C.); imaginglu@hotmail.com (J.L.); tangjiett@163.com (J.T.)
† These authors contributed equally to this work.

Abstract: Objectives: The objective of this study is to explore the potential variations in metabolic activity across gliomas originating from distinct cortical regions, as assessed by O-(2-^{18}F-fluoroethyl)-L-tyrosine positron emission tomography (^{18}F-FET PET). Also, this study seeks to elucidate whether these metabolic disparities correlate with the molecular characteristics and clinical prognoses of the tumors. Specifically, this research aims to determine whether variations in ^{18}F-FET PET uptake are indicative of underlying genetic or biochemical differences that could influence patients' outcomes. **Methods**: The researchers retrospectively included 107 patients diagnosed with gliomas from neocortex and mesocortex, all of whom underwent hybrid PET/MR examinations, including ^{18}F-FET PET and diffusion weighted imaging (DWI), prior to surgery. The mean and maximum tumor-to-background ratio (TBR) and apparent diffusion coefficient (ADC) values were calculated based on whole tumor volume segmentations. Comparisons of TBR, ADC values, and survival outcomes were performed to determine statistical differences between groups. **Results**: Among glioblastomas (GBMs, WHO grade 4) originating from the two cortical regions, there was a significant difference in the human Telomerase Reverse Transcriptase (*TERT*) promoter mutation rate, while no difference was observed in O^{6}-Methylguanine-DNA Methyltransferase (*MGMT*) promoter methylation status. For WHO grade 3 gliomas, significant differences were found in the *TERT* promoter mutation rate and the proportion of 1p/19q co-deletion between the two cortical regions, whereas no difference was noted in *MGMT* methylation status. For WHO grade 2 gliomas, no molecular phenotypic differences were observed between the two cortical regions. In terms of survival, only GBMs originating from the mesocortex demonstrated significantly longer survival compared to those from the neocortex, while no statistically significant differences were found in survival for the other two groups. **Conclusions**: Gliomas originating from different cortical regions exhibit variations in metabolic activity, molecular phenotypes, and clinical outcomes.

Keywords: gliomas; ^{18}F-FET PET; neocortex; mesocortex; molecular phenotyping

1. Introduction

Gliomas are among the most common primary intracranial tumors. According to the World Health Organization (WHO) classification, gliomas are categorized into four grades (1–4) based on histological and molecular features [1]. Glioblastoma (GBM, WHO grade 4), in particular, is associated with a poor prognosis, with a median overall survival of only

14.6 to 20 months [2,3]. Gliomas can originate from various locations in the brain, with the frontal lobe being the most commonly affected region, followed by the temporal lobe and other brain areas [4]. Previous studies have demonstrated that tumor location is a critical prognostic factor, influencing tumorigenesis and tumor-specific genetic alterations. Supratentorial gliomas, for instance, exhibit worse overall survival compared to infratentorial gliomas and show significant differences in molecular and imaging biomarkers [4–6]. Recent findings further indicate that gliomas originating from different brain regions, such as the neocortex, mesocortex, and cerebellum, present distinct clinical profiles and molecular landscapes [4]. Notably, neocortical gliomas are more aggressive, with higher Ki67 indices and Telomerase Reverse Transcriptase (*TERT*) promoter mutation rates, compared to mesocortical gliomas, which exhibit longer survival and distinct molecular alterations, including lower Epidermal Growth Factor Receptor (*EGFR*) amplification and a higher prevalence of 1p/19q co-deletion [4].

O-(2-^{18}F-fluoroethyl)-L-tyrosine positron emission tomography (^{18}F-FET PET) has demonstrated significant advantages in metabolic imaging of gliomas [7,8]. Unlike conventional Contrast-Enhanced MRI (CE-MRI), it is not affected by the integrity of the blood–brain barrier and provides a more comprehensive depiction of metabolically active tumor regions [9]. This enables greater specificity and sensitivity in tumor grading, subtyping, and treatment target delineation. Hybrid imaging that combines ^{18}F-FET PET with multi-parametric MRI has shown to improve the spatial delineation of tumor distribution, revealing metabolically active regions often exceeding those defined by MRI alone [9,10]. These regions have been validated through biopsy, emphasizing the potential of ^{18}F-FET PET in guiding biopsy, gross total resection, and radiotherapy planning [9]. Moreover, ^{18}F-FET uptake correlates strongly with molecular markers such as Ki67, reflecting tumor proliferation and heterogeneity. This makes it an invaluable tool in understanding glioma biology and optimizing individualized treatment strategies [9,10].

Despite advancements in glioma imaging, systematic investigations on the metabolic characteristics of gliomas originating from different cortical regions remain scarce. Moreover, it is unclear whether the metabolic features are linked to tumor molecular features and clinical outcomes. This study aims to provide new insights into their biological behavior and clinical management by elucidating the metabolic heterogeneity of gliomas from neocortex and mesocortex, integrating molecular characteristics and clinical outcomes.

2. Materials and Methods

2.1. Patients

From July 2019 to August 2019, of the initial 260 patients, by the end a total of 107 patients with newly diagnosed or recurrent gliomas proven by pathology who underwent hybrid PET/MRI imaging prior to biopsy or surgical resection were retrospectively recruited into this study (Table 1). The study workflow is presented in Figure 1. Figure 1a shows the patient enrolment process. Based on brain MRI, gliomas involving the frontal, temporal, parietal, and occipital lobes are classified as the neocortex group, while those involving the cingulate gyrus and insular cortex are classified as the mesocortex group (Figure 1b). Written informed consent was obtained from all the patients before PET/MRI examinations. This study was conducted in accordance with the Declaration of Helsinki. This study was approved by the Medical Research Ethics Committee of Xuanwu Hospital, Capital Medical University. In accordance with the 2021 WHO classification, we collaborated with pathologists to reclassify glioma patients diagnosed prior to 2021 by integrating histopathological and molecular pathological results [1]. The inclusion criteria for this study were as follows: (1) adult-type diffuse gliomas pathologically diagnosed according to the 2021 WHO standards, (2) a tracer for PET examination of ^{18}F-FET, (3) gliomas only involving the neocortex or mesocortex of the patient's brain.

Table 1. Patient data.

Characteristic	Data
Total patients	107
Age	51.7 ± 14.7
Sex	
female	43 (40.2%)
male	64 (59.8%)
Neocortex	79 (73.8%)
frontal lobe	32 (29.9%)
temporal lobe	25 (23.4%)
parietal lobe	12 (11.2%)
occipital lobe	10 (9.3%)
Mesocortex	28 (26.2%)
insular lobe	27 (25.2%)
cingulate gyrus	1 (1.0%)

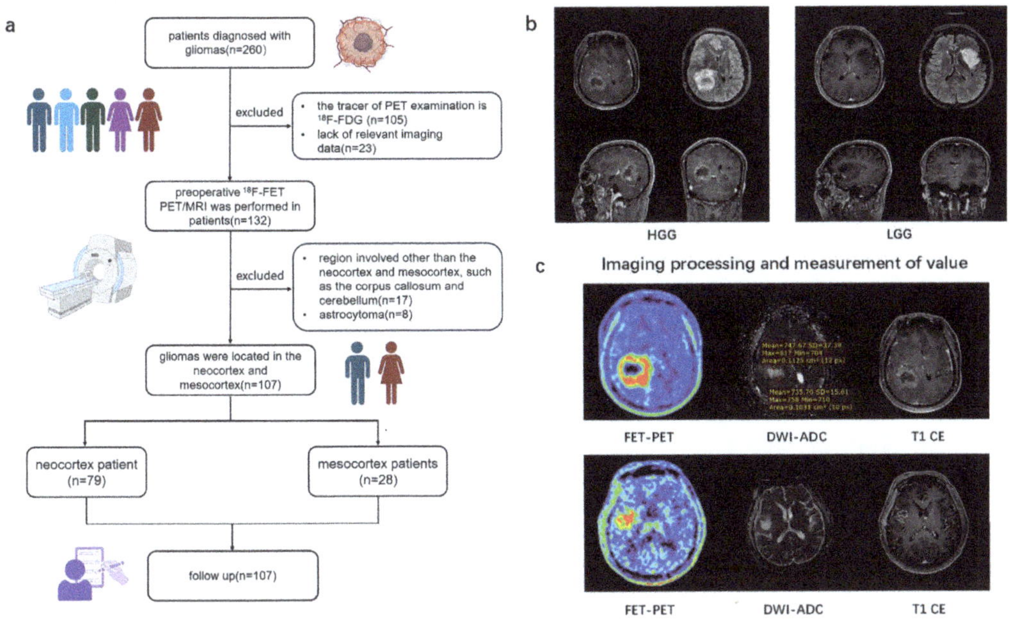

Figure 1. Study flow chart. (**a**) A flowchart of inclusion and exclusion criteria for glioma patients in the retrospective study. (**b**) Typical imaging of glioma originating from different cortical regions. (**c**) The value of TBR and ADC values measured from 3D ROI of tumors. ^{18}F-FDG (2-[^{18}F]-fluoro-2-deoxy-D-glucose); ^{18}F-FET (O-(2-^{18}F-fluoroethyl)-L-tyrosine positron emission tomography); HGG (high-grade glioma); LGG (low-grade glioma); DWI (diffusion weighted imaging); ADC (apparent diffusion coefficient); TBR (Tumor-to-brain ratio).

RNA sequencing data (Transcripts Per Million, TPM) correlated clinical information of patients with glioma (WHO grade 2–4) and were downloaded from TCGA (https://cancergenome.nih.gov/, accessed on 4 December 2024) database.

2.2. PET/MRI Imaging Acquisition and Reconstruction

All patients underwent integrated preoperative PET and MRI examinations using a 3-T time-of-flight (TOF) hybrid PET/MRI scanner (GE Signa, GE Healthcare, Chicago, IL, USA) equipped with a 19-channel head and neck coil. Accurate attenuation correction in PET/MRI scanning was based on MRI. A 3.0T brain MRI scan was performed to process the attenuation correction of PET images. The MRI sequences included a contrast-enhanced T1-weighted sequence (T1 CE), an axial T2-weighted (T2) sequence, a T2-weighted fluid-attenuated inversion recovery (T2 FLAIR; repetition time/echo time = 9000/maximum) sequence, and an axial diffusion-weighted imaging (DWI) sequence. All patients were required to fast for at least 4 h prior to intravenous injection of ^{18}F-FET at a dose recommended for adult brain imaging (185–200 MBq). Image acquisition for FET-PET and multiparametric MRI scanning was performed simultaneously 20 min after the injection, with a total acquisition time of 20 min [11].

We used another 3.0-T PET/MRI hybrid scanner (uPMR790, United Imaging Healthcare, Shanghai, China) to conduct the PET image reconstruction. Image reconstruction utilized the TOF point-spread function-ordered subset expectation maximization (TOF-PSF-OSEM) method with four iterations and 20 subsets [12]. The parameters were as follows: matrix = 256 $\times$ 256, axial field of view = 30 cm, and slice thickness = 1.40 mm. The emission data were corrected for scatter, random effects, and dead-time coincidences [12].

2.3. Quantitative Analysis of Cerebral Metabolism and DWI

All images were post-processed and analyzed using MM BrainAnalysis software (version 2.1.3, United Imaging Intelligence, Shanghai, China). FET uptake was normalized using the standardized uptake value (SUV), which was calculated by dividing the radioactivity in the tissue (kBq/mL) by the injected radioactivity per gram of body weight. A banana-shaped or crescent-shaped volume of interest (VOI) was placed in the healthy cortex (gray and white matter) on the contralateral hemisphere of the lesion to serve as a reference for calculating the tumor-to-background ratio (TBR) (Figure 1c) [11]. Any voxels within the VOI with SUV exceeding the threshold due to vessels or other non-tumor structures were excluded. The biological tumor volume (BTV) was determined using a three-dimensional automatic contouring process with a TBR threshold of 1.6 or higher [13]. Mean Tumor-to-Background Ratio (TBRmean) was calculated by dividing the mean SUV of the tumor VOI by the mean SUV of normal brain tissue. Maximum Tumor-to-Background Ratio (TBRmax) was calculated by dividing the maximum SUV of the tumor VOI by the mean SUV of normal brain tissue. Apparent diffusion coefficient (ADC) maps were generated from DWI sequences. The ADC value for each tumor was obtained through region of interest (ROI) analysis, with ROIs carefully drawn to exclude areas of hemorrhage, cysts, and necrosis. The mean value of multiple ROIs was used to calculate the mean ADC (meanADC) (Figure 1c) [14].

2.4. Molecular Phenotypes

The included gliomas were pathologically diagnosed based on the 2021 World Health Organization (WHO) classification of central nervous system (CNS) tumors, incorporating histological subtypes, and relevant molecular markers. The mutation status of isocitrate dehydrogenase 1 (*IDH1*), Ki67 index, O^6-Methylguanine-DNA Methyltransferase (*MGMT*) promoter methylation status, *TERT* promoter mutation status, and 1p/19q codeletion status were assessed using immunohistochemistry, Sanger sequencing, pyrosequencing, next-generation sequencing (NGS), and fluorescence in situ hybridization (FISH), respectively. Pathological results were jointly confirmed by two neuropathologists.

2.5. Statistical Analysis

Statistical analyses were performed using SPSS version 26 (IBM) and GraphPad Prism version 10.1.0. All quantitative data were expressed as mean ± standard deviation. The Shapiro–Wilk test was used to assess the normality of continuous variables. For continuous variables, Student's t test or the Mann–Whitney U test (two-tailed) were used to evaluate statistical differences between groups. For categorical variables, Pearson's chi-square test or Fisher's exact test were applied. Descriptive statistics were presented as a mean with standard deviation or a median with range. To determine the accuracy of PET imaging in predicting *TERT* promoter mutation status, receiver operating characteristic (ROC) analysis was conducted. Imaging measurements were used as the diagnostic test, with histopathological analysis serving as the reference standard. The area under the ROC curve (AUC) and its 95% confidence interval were calculated. A p-value of less than 0.05 was considered statistically significant.

3. Results

3.1. Patient Enrollment and Tumor Characteristics

A total of 260 glioma patients who underwent preoperative integrated PET/MRI examinations were retrospectively reviewed at the beginning of this study. After excluding 153 patients, 107 eligible patients from July 2019 to August 2024 were included in the analysis. This cohort consisted of 64 males and 43 females, with a mean age of 51.7 ± 14.7 years (Table 1). In the neocortex group, there were 54 GBM patients, 12 WHO grade 3 and 13 WHO grade 2 glioma patients. Gliomas originating from the frontal lobe accounted for the highest proportion in this group (32 cases, 40.5%), followed by those from the temporal lobe (25 cases, 31.6%), parietal lobe (12 cases, 15.2%), and occipital lobe (10 cases, 12.7%). In the mesocortex group, there were nine GBM patients, eight WHO grade 3 and eleven WHO grade 2 glioma patients. The majority of gliomas in this group originated from the insula (27 cases, 96.4%), with only a small proportion arising from the cingulate gyrus (1 case, 3.6%). The mean age of patients in the neocortex group was 53.3 years (SD: 14.0), while the mean age in the mesocortex group was 47.3 years (SD: 16.1) (Table 2). There were no significant differences in age or sex between the two groups ($p > 0.05$). However, a significant difference was observed in the tumor composition between the two groups (a higher proportion of high-grade gliomas in the neocortex group compared to the mesocortex group, $p < 0.01$) (Table 2). Therefore, we further divided gliomas involving the neocortex and mesocortex into three groups based on WHO grading and conducted statistical comparisons between groups of the same grade.

Table 2. Distribution.

	Neocortex	Mesocortex	p Value
Age	53.3 ± 14.0	47.3 ± 16.1	$p > 0.05$
Sex			$p > 0.05$
female	33 (41.8%)	10 (35.7%)	
male	46 (58.2%)	18 (64.3%)	
WHO grade			$p < 0.01$
GBM	54 (68.3%)	9 (32.1%)	
WHO grade 3	12 (15.2%)	8 (28.6%)	
WHO grade 2	13 (16.5%)	11 (39.3%)	

Student's t test for comparing the difference in age between two cortices. Chi-square test for comparing the distribution of gender and tumor between two cortices.

3.2. Metabolic Differences in GBM Originating from Different Cortexs

There were significant differences in TBR values and molecular testing results between GBMs originating from the two cortical regions. GBMs originating from the neocortex had higher TBRmax and TBRmean values compared to those from the mesocortex (4.46 ± 1.51 vs. 2.92 ± 1.12, $p < 0.01$; 2.57 ± 0.65 vs. 1.96 ± 0.67, $p < 0.05$) (Figure 2b) (Table 3). Additionally, the *TERT* promoter mutation rate and Ki67 index were significantly higher in neocortical GBMs (*TERT* promoter-mutant: 77.8% vs. 22.2%, $p < 0.01$; Ki67: $38.0\% \pm 15.5\%$ vs. $20.9\% \pm 12.2\%$, $p < 0.01$) (Figure 2c) (Table 3). Meanwhile, we also observed that GBMs originating from the mesocortex had a better prognosis compared to those in the neocortex (Overall Survival (OS) 30 months vs. 18 months, $p < 0.05$; Progression-Free Survival (PFS) 25 months vs. 11 months $p < 0.01$) (Figure 2d) (Table 3).

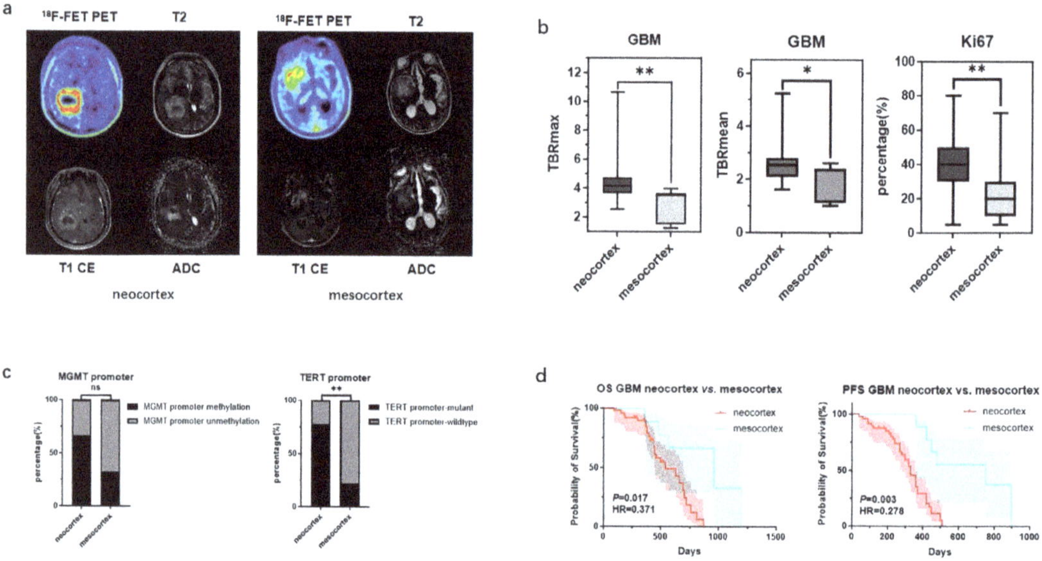

Figure 2. Mutation landscapes, clinical and imaging characteristics of GBMs originating from the neocortex and mesocortex. (**a**) The ^{18}F-FET metabolic range of gliomas determined by semi-automatically segmenting the 3D ROI with a TBR > 1.6. (**b**) Comparison of TBRmax and TBRmean values in GBMs originating from different cortices (Student's *t* test, $p < 0.01$, $p < 0.05$). Ki67 percentage in GBMs originating from the neocortex and mesocortex (Student's *t* test, $p < 0.01$). (**c**) Comparison of mutation rates of key genes in GBMs originating from different cortices (Fisher's exact test, $p > 0.05$, $p < 0.05$) (*, $p < 0.05$; **, $p < 0.01$; ns, not significant). (**d**) Comparison of OS and PFS between GBMs of neocortex and mesocortex origins (Kaplan Maier). ^{18}F-FET PET, O-(2-^{18}F-fluoroethyl)-L-tyrosine positron emission tomography; ADC, apparent diffusion coefficient; T1 CE, contrast-enhanced T1-weighted sequence; TBR, tumor-to-background ratio; TBRmax, maximum tumor-to-background ratio; TBRmean, mean tumor-to-background ratio; GBM, glioblastoma; OS, overall survival; PFS, progression-free survival; *TERT*, telomerase reverse transcriptase; *MGMT*, O^6-Methylguanine-DNA Methyltransferase.

3.3. Metabolic Differences in WHO Grade 3 and 2 Gliomas Originating from Different Cortexs

For WHO grade 3 gliomas, significant differences in TBR values and molecular testing results were also observed between samples originating from the neocortex and the mesocortex. The determination of glioma location and the processing of PET images can be seen in Figure 3a. WHO grade 3 gliomas from the neocortex had higher TBRmax and TBRmean values compared to those from the mesocortex (3.94 ± 1.39 vs. 2.72 ± 0.83, $p < 0.05$; 2.55 ± 0.88 vs. 1.79 ± 0.32 $p < 0.05$) (Figure 3b) (Table 4). Moreover, neocortical

WHO grade 3 gliomas exhibited higher rates of *TERT* promoter mutation and 1p/19q co-deletion (*TERT* promoter-mutant: 66.7% vs. 12.5%, $p < 0.05$; 1p/19q-codeleted: 66.7% vs. 12.5%, $p < 0.05$) (Figure 3c) (Table 4). However, there was no statistically significant difference in prognosis between the two groups (Figure 3d).

Table 3. GBM neocortex vs. mesocortex.

Characteristic	Neocortex	Mesocortex	*p* Value
TBRmax	4.46 ± 1.51	2.92 ± 1.12	$p < 0.01$ [1]
TBRmean	2.57 ± 0.65	1.96 ± 0.67	$p < 0.05$ [1]
TERT promoter			$p < 0.01$ [2]
mutant	42 (77.8%)	2 (22.2%)	
wildtype	12 (22.2%)	7 (77.8%)	
MGMT promoter			$p > 0.05$ [2]
methylation	35 (64.8%)	3 (33.3%)	
unmethylation	19 (35.2%)	6 (66.7%)	
Ki67	38.0% ± 15.5%	20.9% ± 12.2%	$p < 0.01$ [1]
OS, month	18	30	$p < 0.05$ [3]
PFS, month	11	25	$p < 0.01$ [3]

[1] Student's *t* test; [2] Fisher's exact test; [3] Kaplan Maier. TBR, tumor-to-background ratio; TBRmax, maximum tumor-to-background ratio; TBRmean, mean tumor-to-background ratio; *TERT*, telomerase reverse transcriptase; *MGMT*, O^6-Methylguanine-DNA Methyltransferase; OS, overall survival; PFS, progression-free survival.

Table 4. WHO grade 3 neocortex vs. mesocortex.

Characteristic	Neocortex	Mesocortex	*p* Value
TBRmax	3.94 ± 1.39	2.72 ± 0.83	$p < 0.05$ [1]
TBRmean	2.55 ± 0.88	1.79 ± 0.32	$p < 0.05$ [1]
TERT promoter			$p < 0.05$ [2]
mutant	8 (66.7%)	1 (12.5%)	
wildtype	4 (33.3%)	7 (87.5%)	
MGMT promoter			$p > 0.05$ [2]
methylation	10 (83.3%)	6 (75.0%)	
unmethylation	2 (16.7%)	2 (25.0%)	
1p/19q			$p < 0.05$ [2]
codeleted	8 (66.7%)	1 (12.5%)	
intact	4 (33.3%)	7 (87.5%)	

[1] Student's *t* test; [2] Fisher's exact test. TBR, tumor-to-background ratio; TBRmax, maximum tumor-to-background ratio; TBRmean, mean tumor-to-background ratio; *TERT*, telomerase reverse transcriptase; *MGMT*, O^6-Methylguanine-DNA Methyltransferase.

In contrast, for WHO grade 2 gliomas originating from different cortical regions, differences were observed only in TBRmax and TBRmean values (2.86 ± 0.78 vs. 2.05 ± 0.50, $p < 0.01$; 1.78 ± 0.36 vs. 1.47 ± 0.30 $p < 0.05$), while no significant statistical differences were found in their molecular phenotypes and prognosis (Figure 4) (Table 5).

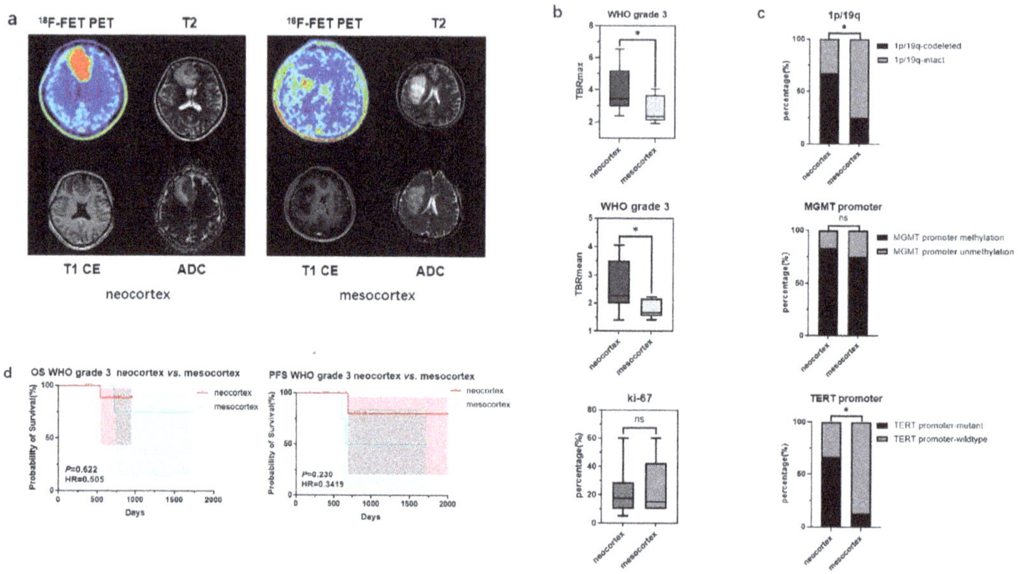

Figure 3. Mutation landscapes, clinical, and imaging characteristics of WHO grade 3 gliomas originating from the neocortex and mesocortex. (**a**) The ^{18}F-FET metabolic range of gliomas determined by semi-automatically segmenting the 3D ROI with a TBR > 1.6. (**b**) Comparison of TBRmax and TBRmean values in WHO grade 3 gliomas originating from different cortices (Student's t test, $p < 0.05$, $p < 0.05$). Ki67 percentage in WHO grade 3 gliomas originating from the neocortex and mesocortex (Student's t test, $p > 0.05$). (**c**) Comparison of mutation rates of key genes in WHO grade 3 gliomas originating from different cortices (Fisher's exact test, $p < 0.05$, $p > 0.05$, $p < 0.05$) (*, $p < 0.05$; ns, not significant). (**d**) Comparison of OS and PFS between WHO grade 3 gliomas of neocortex and mesocortex origins (Kaplan Maier). ^{18}F-FET PET, O-(2-^{18}F-fluoroethyl)-L-tyrosine positron emission tomography; ADC, apparent diffusion coefficient; T1 CE, contrast-enhanced T1-weighted sequence; TBR, tumor-to-background ratio; TBRmax, maximum tumor-to-background ratio; TBRmean, mean tumor-to-background ratio; OS, overall survival; PFS, progression-free survival; *TERT*, telomerase reverse transcriptase; *MGMT*, O^6-Methylguanine-DNA Methyltransferase.

Table 5. WHO grade 2 neocortex vs. mesocortex.

Characteristic	Neocortex	Mesocortex	p Value
TBRmax	2.86 ± 0.78	2.05 ± 0.50	$p < 0.01$ [1]
TBRmean	1.78 ± 0.36	1.47 ± 0.30	$p < 0.05$ [1]
TERT promoter			$p > 0.05$ [2]
mutant	8(61.5%)	3(27.3%)	
wildtype	5(38.5%)	8(72.3%)	
MGMT promoter			$p > 0.05$ [2]
methylation	10(76.9%)	10(90.9%)	
unmethylation	3(23.1%)	1(0.91%)	
1p/19q			$p > 0.05$ [2]
codeleted	7(53.8%)	6(54.5%)	
intact	6(46.2%)	5(45.5%)	

[1] Student's t test; [2] Fisher's exact test. TBR, tumor-to-background ratio; TBRmax, maximum tumor-to-background ratio; TBRmean, mean tumor-to-background ratio; *TERT*, telomerase reverse transcritase; *MGMT*, O^6-Methylguanine-DNA Methyltransferase.

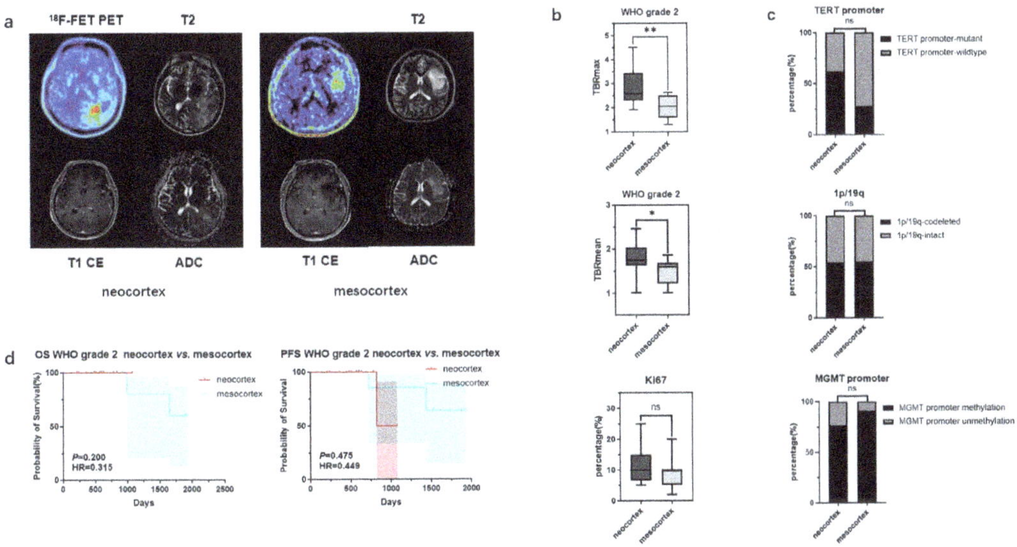

Figure 4. Mutation landscapes, clinical, and imaging characteristics of WHO grade 2 gliomas originating from the neocortex and mesocortex. (**a**) The ^{18}F-FET metabolic range of gliomas determined by semi-automatically segmenting the 3D ROI with a TBR > 1.6. (**b**) Comparison of TBRmax and TBRmean values in WHO grade 2 gliomas originating from different cortices (Student's *t* test, $p < 0.01$, $p < 0.05$). Ki67 percentage in WHO grade 2 gliomas originating from the neocortex and mesocortex (Student's *t* test, $p > 0.05$). (**c**) Comparison of mutation rates of key genes in WHO grade 2 gliomas originating from different cortices (Fisher's exact test, $p > 0.05$, $p > 0.05$, $p > 0.05$) (*, $p < 0.05$; **, $p < 0.01$; ns, not significant). (**d**) Comparison of OS and PFS between WHO grade 2 gliomas of neocortex and mesocortex origins (Kaplan Maier). ^{18}F-FET PET, O-(2-^{18}F-fluoroethyl)-L-tyrosine positron emission tomography; ADC, apparent diffusion coefficient; T1 CE, contrast-enhanced T1-weighted sequence; TBR, tumor-to-background ratio; TBRmax, maximum tumor-to-background ratio; TBRmean, mean tumor-to-background ratio; OS, overall survival; PFS, progression-free survival; *TERT*, telomerase reverse transcriptase; *MGMT*, O^6-Methylguanine-DNA Methyltransferase.

3.4. FET Uptake Levels and Prognosis Are Influenced by the Status of TERT Promoter and Ki67

We further divided GBMs into two groups based on the status of the *TERT* promoter and compared the TBR values and prognosis between the two groups. The results showed that GBMs with *TERT* promoter mutations had higher TBR values (4.62 ± 1.65 vs. 3.39 ± 0.99 $p < 0.01$; 2.64 ± 0.75 vs. 2.12 ± 0.55 $p < 0.01$) and poorer prognosis (OS 18 months vs. 27 months $p < 0.05$; PFS 11 months vs. 15 months $p < 0.05$) compared to those with wild-type *TERT* promoters (Figure 5) (Table 6). Subsequently, we applied the same criteria to classify WHO grade 3 and WHO grade 2 gliomas. The results were consistent with those observed in glioblastomas, showing that gliomas with *TERT* promoter mutations exhibited higher metabolic activity than *TERT* wild-type gliomas (Supplementary Figure S2). Additionally, we conducted a correlation analysis between TBR values and Ki67 and found a positive correlation between them (Ki67 and TBRmax, $R^2 = 0.1318$, $p = 0.0001$; Ki67 and TBRmean, $R^2 = 0.1482$, $p < 0.0001$) (Supplementary Figure S3). Then, we used the receiver operating characteristic (ROC) curve for evaluation and obtained an area under the curve (AUC) of 0.763 (TBRmax) and 0.723 (TBRmean). Additionally, we found that the combination of TBR and ADC values yielded the highest AUC when predicting the status of the *TERT* promoter (TBRmax 0.763, meanADC 0.723, combination 0.863; TBRmean 0.723, meanADC 0.723, combination 0.865) (Figure 6).

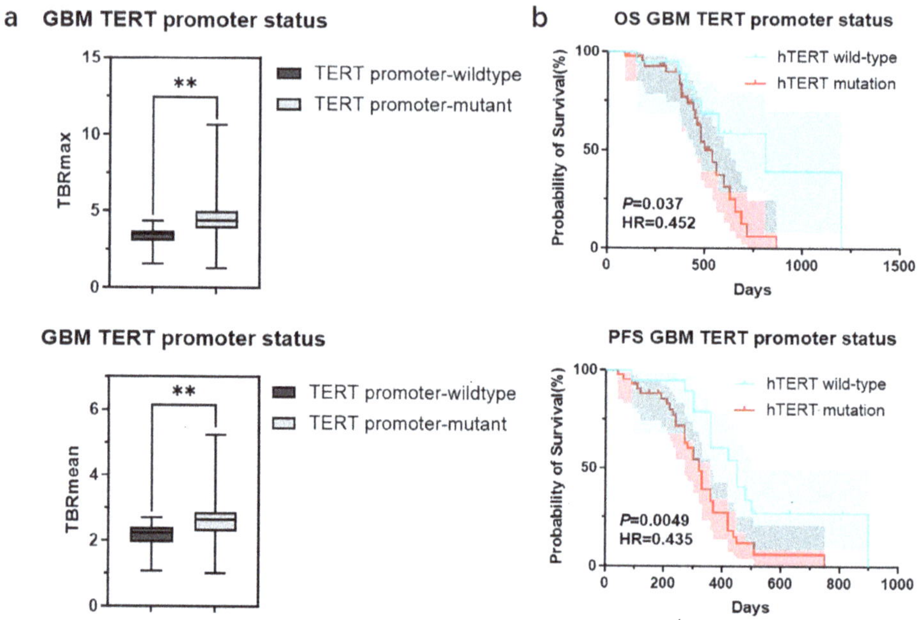

Figure 5. TBR values and clinical outcomes of GBMs divided into groups according to the status of *TERT* promoter. (**a**) Comparison of TBRmax and TBRmean values in GBMs with different *TERT* promoter status (Student's *t* test, $p < 0.01$, $p < 0.01$) (**, $p < 0.01$). (**b**) Comparison of OS and PFS between GBMs with different *TERT* promoter status (Kaplan Maier). GBM, Glioblastoma; *TERT*, telomerase reverse transcriptase; TBR, tumor-to-background ratio; TBRmax, maximum tumor-to-background ratio; TBRmean, mean tumor-to-background ratio; OS, overall survival; PFS, progression-free survival.

Table 6. *TERT* promoter status in GBM.

Status	*TERT* Promoter		*p* Value
	Mutation	Wildtype	
TBRmax	4.21 ± 1.65	2.97 ± 0.99	$p < 0.01$ [1]
TBRmean	2.48 ± 0.75	1.91 ± 0.55	$p < 0.01$ [1]
OS, month	18	27	$p < 0.05$ [2]
PFS, month	11	15	$p < 0.01$ [2]

[1] Student's *t* test; [2] Kaplan Maier; *TERT*, telomerase reverse transcriptase; GBM, glioblastoma; TBR, tumor-to-background ratio; TBRmax, maximum tumor-to-background ratio; TBRmean, mean tumor-to-background ratio; OS, overall survival; PFS, progression-free survival.

We downloaded transcriptomic data of gliomas (WHO grade 2–4) from the TCGA database and divided the samples into two groups based on *TERT* promoter status. Comparing the two groups, we found that *SLC7A5* (solute carrier family 7 member 5) expression was higher in gliomas with *TERT* promoter mutations (Supplementary Figure S4).

3.5. Metabolic Differences Between Neocortical and Mesocortical Gliomas

Finally, we analyzed the metabolic and molecular phenotypic differences between neocortical and mesocortical gliomas without stratifying by tumor grade. There were significant differences in TBR values and molecular testing results between gliomas originating from the two cortical regions. Gliomas originating from the neocortex had a significantly higher mean TBRmax and TBRmean value compared to those from the mesocortex

(4.17 ± 1.53 vs. 2.54 ± 0.93, $p < 0.001$; 2.44 ± 0.71 vs. 1.72 ± 0.49, $p < 0.001$). Moreover, the proportions of *IDH1* and *TERT* promoter mutations were higher in neocortical gliomas than in mesocortical gliomas (67.9% vs. 31.6%, $p < 0.01$ and 68.4% vs. 25.0%, $p < 0.001$, respectively). In addition, the Ki67 index was significantly higher in neocortical gliomas compared to mesocortical gliomas (30.8% ± 18.0% vs. 17.6% ± 14.2%, $p < 0.001$). These findings suggest that gliomas originating from the neocortex exhibit significantly higher metabolic activity compared to those from the mesocortex (Supplementary Figure S1) (Supplementary Table S1).

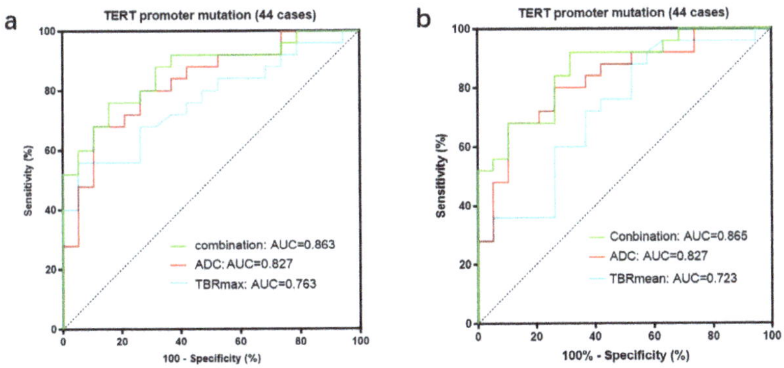

Figure 6. A total of 44 patients had both FET-PET and DWI-ADC imaging data. (**a**) The accuracy of predicting the TERT promoter status was evaluated using receiver operating characteristic (ROC) curves for TBRmax, ADC values, and their combination. The results showed that the area under the ROC curve was largest when both parameters were combined, indicating the highest accuracy (TBRmax: AUC = 0.763, ADC: AUC = 0.827, Conbination: AUC = 0.863). (**b**) The accuracy of predicting the TERT promoter status was evaluated using receiver operating characteristic (ROC) curves for TBRmean, ADC values, and their combination. The results showed that the area under the ROC curve was largest when both parameters were combined, indicating the highest accuracy (TBRmean: AUC = 0.723, ADC: AUC = 0.827, Conbination: AUC = 0.865). ROC curve for TBRmax, TBRmean and meanADC, in differentiating *TERT* promoter mutation from wildtype in gliomas. *TERT*, telomerase reverse transcriptase; TBR, tumor-to-background ratio; TBRmax, maximum tumor-to-background ratio; TBRmean, mean tumor-to-background ratio; ADC, apparent diffusion coefficient; AUC, area under the curve.

4. Discussion

In this study, we analyzed 107 glioma cases treated at our institution, which originated from the neocortex and meso-cortex. All patients underwent pre-operative FET-PET/MRI imaging. Similarly to a previous study [4], gliomas originating from the neocortex and mesocortex may differ in terms of age at onset, with patients having neocortical gliomas tending to be older. However, no significant difference was observed, and future studies should focus on larger sample sizes. Grade heterogeneity of gliomas originating from the neocortex and mesocortex was found in the current study. Approximately 68.35% of gliomas from the neocortex and 32.14% of gliomas from the mesocortex were GBM. The percentage of GBM in gliomas of the neocortex is similar to the results of a previous study, which found that about 60% gliomas from the neocortex were GBM [4]. Additionally, Mackintosh et al. reported that 84% of gliomas in the temporal lobe were GBM [15].

Our study findings were the first to confirm that different neocortical gliomas (including GBM, WHO grade 3 and 2 glioma) exhibited significantly higher TBRmax and TBRmean values, indicating higher metabolic activity. Additionally, neocortical gliomas (including GBM, WHO grade 3 glioma) had significantly higher *TERT* promoter mutation rates and Ki67. Accordingly, survival analysis showed that neocortical GBMs had worse clinical outcomes, with shorter OS and PFS, suggesting greater proliferative potential and aggressiveness. Similar results could be found in a previous study [4], which reported that the *TERT* mutation rate in neocortical high-grade gliomas (WHO grade 3–4) was higher than that in mesocortical and the gliomas originating from the neocortex had significantly shorter OS and PFS compared to those from the mesocortex. Notably, this study is the first to reveal that gliomas of the same grade originating from the neocortex have significantly higher TBR values compared to those of the same grade originating from the meso-cortex. Although the TBR value alone cannot determine the exact malignancy of gliomas and requires a comprehensive evaluation incorporating pathological and molecular analyses, studies have shown that a higher TBR value is generally associated with a higher degree of malignancy in gliomas [8,9,16,17]. This correlation is mainly reflected in the fact that gliomas with higher TBR values often exhibit increased metabolic activity, greater proliferative and invasive potential, and are associated with higher-grade gliomas and poorer survival outcomes [16]. Specifically, gliomas with higher TBR values tend to have higher Ki67 and *TERT* promoter mutation rates, indicating increased tumor proliferative activity [9], this may be related to a higher number of active tumor cells, leading to increased FET uptake. As an imaging biomarker, the TBR value serves as an important reference for the comprehensive assessment of glioma malignancy and the formulation of treatment strategies. This study revealed significant clinical, metabolic, and molecular differences between gliomas originating from the neocortex and mesocortex.

In most tumors, including gliomas, *TERT* expression is associated with poor prognosis [18–20]. Typically, *TERT* promoter mutations are predictive of GBM survival and serve as an independent prognostic factor for poor outcomes [21]. Therefore, the worse clinical outcomes observed in GBMs originating from the neocortex compared to those from the mesocortex may be explained by the higher *TERT* promoter mutation rate. L-type amino acid transporter 1 (LAT1) is an essential neutral amino acid transporter that is highly expressed in tissues with high metabolic demands, including cancer cells [7,8,16]. Studies have shown that LAT1 is overexpressed in various malignant tumors, including GBM, and is closely associated with tumor invasiveness, proliferation, and treatment response [16]. Compared to normal brain tissue, LAT1 expression is significantly elevated in glioma tissues, with expression levels increasing in correlation with tumor grade, indicating a positive association with tumor malignancy. Furthermore, tumors with high LAT1 expression typically exhibit higher Ki67, reflecting enhanced cellular proliferative capacity [16]. The high expression of LAT1 is also associated with increased metabolic activity in ^{18}F-FET-PET (^{18}F-fluoroethyl-L-tyrosine PET) imaging, suggesting that LAT1 may play a crucial role in mediating amino acid uptake and promoting tumor cell metabolism and growth. Kaplan–Meier survival analysis reveals that patients with high LAT1 expression have significantly shorter OS and PFS compared to those with low LAT1 expression, further indicating that LAT1 could serve as a potential prognostic marker for poor outcomes in gliomas [7,8,16]. The high expression of LAT1 is usually accompanied by a high accumulation of FET in tumor tissue. This accumulation is reflected in PET imaging as higher TBR values [7,8]. Therefore, based on previous research findings [7,16], it may be inferred that the higher the expression level of LAT1, the higher the corresponding TBR values in gliomas. In this study, the TBR values of gliomas of the same grade originating from the neocortex were significantly higher than those from the mesocortex, which seems to suggest that the expression levels of LAT1 in neocortical gliomas are significantly higher than those in mesocortical gliomas. In this research, we found that gliomas originating from the neocortex have a higher *TERT* promoter mutation rate and higher TBR values compared to those originating from the mesocortex. Additionally, our analysis of glioma transcriptomic data from the TCGA database revealed that gliomas with *TERT* promoter mutations exhibit higher expression levels of SLC7A5. Since LAT1 is the protein encoded by the SLC7A5 gene [22], we hypothesize that the higher *TERT* promoter mutation rate in neocortical gliomas may lead to increased LAT1 expression, which in turn enhances FET uptake and consequently increases metabolic activity. The high expression of LAT1 in tumor cells and its differential expression in gliomas of different cortical origins may become a key focus for future research.

Our study has preliminarily found some differences in clinical outcomes and molecular phenotypes between gliomas originating from the neocortex and mesocortex. In particular, it was found that patients with glioblastoma originating from the mesocortex had a better prognosis than those with tumors arising from the neocortex. Several mechanistic hypotheses can be considered to explain this phenomenon: First, During the development of the cerebral cortex, the mesocortex develops earlier and consists of three to six layers, mainly responsible for processing emotions and feelings. In contrast, the neocortex develops later and consists of six layers, primarily responsible for higher cognitive functions [23,24]. The complexity of the neocortex implies greater plasticity in its cellular composition and a higher likelihood of mutations, which may contribute to more aggressive tumor characteristics [25–28]. Secondly, neurons and glial cells in the neocortex originate from the neuroepithelium and undergo complex migration and layering processes, whereas the mesocortex develops earlier and maintains a more conserved structure. The high plasticity and neural stem cell reservoir in the neocortex may provide tumors with greater adaptability for rapid progression and treatment resistance [27–29]. In addition, the neocortex has a richer vascular supply and higher metabolic demand, which may explain why gliomas originating from the neocortex exhibit higher TBR values on ^{18}F-FET PET. This hypermetabolic state may enable tumor cells to grow more rapidly and invade more aggressively, potentially influencing their response to treatments such as radiotherapy and chemotherapy [25,29,30]. Finally, neurons in the neocortex form extensive connections across multiple brain regions, whereas the mesocortex has more restricted connectivity. Since gliomas tend to infiltrate along white matter fiber tracts, the widespread connections of the neocortex may provide tumor cells with more efficient pathways for dissemination, accelerating disease progression [25,26,31]. Although speculative, these hypotheses are based on the previous literature regarding the anatomy of the cerebral cortex, structure–function relationships, brain networks, energy metabolism, and neuron–glia interactions, making them appear credible. Therefore, we speculate that the differences in tissue structure and microenvironment between the neocortex and mesocortex during development may contribute to the differences in molecular mutations and clinical outcomes. In future studies, we will integrate genomics, proteomics, and metabolomics to further explore the molecular mechanisms underlying the metabolic activity differences between the neocortex and mesocortex. Additionally, we plan to expand the sample size and strive to conduct large-scale, multicenter studies to enhance the generalizability and clinical applicability of our findings. On this basis, we aim to develop more precise radiotherapy, chemotherapy, and targeted therapy protocols based on metabolic imaging and molecular characteristics.

5. Conclusions

Gliomas originating from the neocortex and mesocortex exhibit differences in clinical prognosis, cellular metabolism, and molecular phenotypes, which may assist neurosurgeons in preoperative planning and treatment decision-making.

Supplementary Materials: The following supporting information can be downloaded at: https://www.mdpi.com/article/10.3390/biomedicines13030657/s1, Figure S1: TBR values of WHO grade 3 and 2 gliomas divided into groups according to the status of *TERT* promoter. (a). Comparison of TBRmax and TBRmean values in WHO grade 3 gilomas with different *TERT* promoter status (Student's t test, $p < 0.05$, $p < 0.05$). (b) Comparison of TBRmax and TBRmean values in WHO grade 2 gilomas with different *TERT* promoter status (Student's t test, $p > 0.05$, $p < 0.01$); Figure S2: Correlation analysis between TBR and Ki-67 (Simple linear regression, $R^2 = 0.1318$, $p = 0.0001$; $R^2 = 0.1482$, $p < 0.0001$); Figure S3: Comparison of SLC7A5 expression in gilomas with different *TERT* promoter status (Student's t test, $p < 0.05$); Figure S4 Mutation landscapes, clinical and imaging characteristics of gliomas originating from the neocortex and mesocortex. (a) The 18F-FET metabolic range of gliomas determined by semi-automatically segmenting the 3D ROI with a TBR > 1.6. (b) Comparison of TBRmax and TBRmean values in gliomas originating from different cortices (Student's t test, $p < 0.0001$, $p < 0.0001$). Ki-67 percentage in gliomas originating from the neocortex and mesocortex (Student's t test, $p < 0.001$). (c) Comparison of mutation rates of key genes in gliomas originating from different cortices(chi-square test, $p < 0.01$, $p > 0.05$, $p > 0.05$, $p < 0.001$). (d) Comparison of OS and PFS between GBMs of neocortex and mesocortex origins (Kaplan Maier); Table S1: All neocortex vs. mesocortex.

Author Contributions: Conceptualization, J.T., J.L., Y.C. and H.D.; methodology, H.D., X.W. and X.L.; data curation, H.D., X.W., S.L., B.S. and Y.C.; writing—original draft preparation, H.D. and X.W.; writing—review and editing, all authors; visualization, H.D., X.W. and Y.C. All authors have read and agreed to the published version of the manuscript.

Funding: This study has received funding from the National Key Research and Development Program of China (No. 2022YFC2406905), the National Natural Science Foundation of China (No. 82373403 to Y.C.), and the Beijing Natural Science Foundation (No. L222022).

Institutional Review Board Statement: This study was conducted in accordance with the Declaration of Helsinki. This study was approved by the Medical Research Ethics Committee of Xuanwu Hospital, Capital Medical University (protocol number: [2023]044, 23 April 2023).

Informed Consent Statement: Written informed consent was obtained from all subjects (patients) in this study.

Data Availability Statement: Dates of this research are available from the corresponding author upon reasonable request.

Acknowledgments: This work was supported by Xiaoran Li and Leiming Wang. The writing of this English translation was supported by Jie Tang and Ye Cheng.

Conflicts of Interest: The authors declare no competing interests.

Abbreviations

The following abbreviations are used in this manuscript:

^{18}F-FET PET	O-(2-^{18}F-fluoroethyl)-L-tyrosine positron emission tomography
DWI	Diffusion weighted imaging
TERT	Telomerase Reverse Transcriptase
MGMT	O^6-Methylguanine-DNA Methyltransferase
TBR	Tumor-to-brain ratio
ADC	Apparent diffusion coefficient
WHO	World Health Organization
GBM	Glioblastoma
EGFR	Epidermal growth factor receptor
TOF	Time-of-flight

T1 CE	Contrast-enhanced T1-weighted
T1 FLAIR	T1-weighted fluid-attenuated inversion recovery
T2 FLAIR	T2-weighted fluid-attenuated inversion recovery
SUV	Standardized uptake value
BTV	Biological tumor volume
VOI	Volume of interest
ROI	Region of interest
IDH	Isocitrate Dehydrogenase
NGS	next-generation sequencing
ROC	Receiver operating characteristic
OS	Overall survival
PFS	Progression-Free Survival
LAT1	L-type amino acid transporter 1

References

1. Louis, D.N.; Perry, A.; Wesseling, P.; Brat, D.J.; Cree, I.A.; Figarella-Branger, D.; Hawkins, C.; Ng, H.K.; Pfister, S.M.; Reifenberger, G.; et al. The 2021 WHO Classification of Tumors of the Central Nervous System: A summary. *Neuro-Oncol.* **2021**, *23*, 1231–1251. [CrossRef] [PubMed]
2. Stupp, R.; Taillibert, S.; Kanner, A.; Read, W.; Steinberg, D.; Lhermitte, B.; Toms, S.; Idbaih, A.; Ahluwalia, M.S.; Fink, K.; et al. Effect of Tumor-Treating Fields Plus Maintenance Temozolomide vs Maintenance Temozolomide Alone on Survival in Patients With Glioblastoma: A Randomized Clinical Trial. *JAMA* **2017**, *318*, 2306–2316. [CrossRef] [PubMed]
3. Bale, T.A.; Rosenblum, M.K. The 2021 WHO Classification of Tumors of the Central Nervous System: An update on pediatric low-grade gliomas and glioneuronal tumors. *Brain Pathol.* **2022**, *32*, e13060. [CrossRef] [PubMed]
4. Cheng, Y.; Zhang, L.; Wu, X.; Wakimoto, H.; Geng, H.; Wei, Y.; Xu, G.; Xiao, X.; Bai, J.; Wang, Y.; et al. Distinct clinical profiles and mutation landscapes of gliomas originating from the neocortex, mesocortex, and cerebellum. *Genes. Dis.* **2024**, *11*, 53–56. [CrossRef]
5. Sayegh, E.T.; Aranda, D.; Kim, J.M.; Oh, T.; Parsa, A.T.; Oh, M.C. Prognosis by tumor location in adults with intracranial ependymomas. *J. Clin. Neurosci.* **2014**, *21*, 2096–2101. [CrossRef]
6. Lopci, E.; Riva, M.; Olivari, L.; Raneri, F.; Soffietti, R.; Piccardo, A.; Bizzi, A.; Navarria, P.; Ascolese, A.M.; Ruda, R.; et al. Prognostic value of molecular and imaging biomarkers in patients with supratentorial glioma. *Eur. J. Nucl. Med. Mol. Imaging* **2017**, *44*, 1155–1164. [CrossRef]
7. Habermeier, A.; Graf, J.; Sandhöfer, B.F.; Boissel, J.P.; Roesch, F.; Closs, E.I. System L amino acid transporter LAT1 accumulates O-(2-fluoroethyl)-L-tyrosine (FET). *Amino Acids* **2015**, *47*, 335–344. [CrossRef]
8. Langen, K.J.; Hamacher, K.; Weckesser, M.; Floeth, F.; Stoffels, G.; Bauer, D.; Coenen, H.H.; Pauleit, D. O-(2-[^{18}F]fluoroethyl)-L-tyrosine: Uptake mechanisms and clinical applications. *Nucl. Med. Biol.* **2006**, *33*, 287–294. [CrossRef]
9. Song, S.; Cheng, Y.; Ma, J.; Wang, L.; Dong, C.; Wei, Y.; Xu, G.; An, Y.; Qi, Z.; Lin, Q.; et al. Simultaneous FET-PET and contrast-enhanced MRI based on hybrid PET/MR improves delineation of tumor spatial biodistribution in gliomas: A biopsy validation study. *Eur. J. Nucl. Med. Mol. Imaging* **2020**, *47*, 1458–1467. [CrossRef]
10. Li, X.; Cheng, Y.; Han, X.; Cui, B.; Li, J.; Yang, H.; Xu, G.; Lin, Q.; Xiao, X.; Tang, J.; et al. Exploring the association of glioma tumor residuals from incongruent [^{18}F]FET PET/MR imaging with tumor proliferation using a multiparametric MRI radiomics nomogram. *Eur. J. Nucl. Med. Mol. Imaging* **2024**, *51*, 779–796. [CrossRef]
11. Law, I.; Albert, N.L.; Arbizu, J.; Boellaard, R.; Drzezga, A.; Galldiks, N.; la Fougère, C.; Langen, K.J.; Lopci, E.; Lowe, V.; et al. Joint EANM/EANO/RANO practice guidelines/SNMMI procedure standards for imaging of gliomas using PET with radiolabelled amino acids and [^{18}F]FDG: Version 1.0. *Eur. J. Nucl. Med. Mol. Imaging* **2019**, *46*, 540–557. [CrossRef] [PubMed]
12. Spangler-Bickell, M.G.; Khalighi, M.M.; Hoo, C.; DiGiacomo, P.S.; Maclaren, J.; Aksoy, M.; Rettmann, D.; Bammer, R.; Zaharchuk, G.; Zeineh, M.; et al. Rigid Motion Correction for Brain PET/MR Imaging using Optical Tracking. *IEEE Trans. Radiat. Plasma Med. Sci.* **2019**, *3*, 498–503. [CrossRef] [PubMed]
13. Pauleit, D.; Floeth, F.; Hamacher, K.; Riemenschneider, M.J.; Reifenberger, G.; Müller, H.W.; Zilles, K.; Coenen, H.H.; Langen, K.J. O-(2-[^{18}F]fluoroethyl)-L-tyrosine PET combined with MRI improves the diagnostic assessment of cerebral gliomas. *Brain* **2005**, *128 Pt 3*, 678–687. [CrossRef]
14. Caravan, I.; Ciortea, C.A.; Contis, A.; Lebovici, A. Diagnostic value of apparent diffusion coefficient in differentiating between high-grade gliomas and brain metastases. *Acta Radiol.* **2018**, *59*, 599–605. [CrossRef]

15. Mackintosh, C.; Butterfield, R.; Zhang, N.; Lorence, J.; Zlomanczuk, P.; Bendok, B.R.; Zimmerman, R.S.; Swanson, K.; Porter, A.; Mrugala, M.M. Does location matter? Characterisation of the anatomic locations, molecular profiles, and clinical features of gliomas. *Neurol. I Neurochir. Pol.* **2020**, *54*, 456–465. [CrossRef]
16. Nawashiro, H.; Otani, N.; Uozumi, Y.; Ooigawa, H.; Toyooka, T.; Suzuki, T.; Katoh, H.; Tsuzuki, N.; Ohnuki, A.; Shima, K.; et al. High expression of L-type amino acid transporter 1 in infiltrating glioma cells. *Brain Tumor Pathol.* **2005**, *22*, 89–91. [CrossRef]
17. Cappoli, N.; Jenkinson, M.D.; Dello Russo, C.; Dickens, D. LAT1, a novel pharmacological target for the treatment of glioblastoma. *Biochem. Pharmacol.* **2022**, *201*, 115103. [CrossRef]
18. Tabori, U.; Ma, J.; Carter, M.; Zielenska, M.; Rutka, J.; Bouffet, E.; Bartels, U.; Malkin, D.; Hawkins, C. Human telomere reverse transcriptase expression predicts progression and survival in pediatric intracranial ependymoma. *J. Clin. Oncol.* **2006**, *24*, 1522–1528. [CrossRef]
19. Ducrest, A.L.; Szutorisz, H.; Lingner, J.; Nabholz, M. Regulation of the human telomerase reverse transcriptase gene. *Oncogene* **2002**, *21*, 541–552. [CrossRef]
20. Mao, J.; Zhang, Q.; Wang, Y.; Zhuang, Y.; Xu, L.; Ma, X.; Guan, D.; Zhou, J.; Liu, J.; Wu, X.; et al. TERT activates endogenous retroviruses to promote an immunosuppressive tumour microenvironment. *EMBO Rep.* **2022**, *23*, e52984. [CrossRef]
21. Aldape, K.; Zadeh, G.; Mansouri, S.; Reifenberger, G.; von Deimling, A. Glioblastoma: Pathology, molecular mechanisms and markers. *Acta Neuropathol.* **2015**, *129*, 829–848. [CrossRef] [PubMed]
22. Fotiadis, D.; Kanai, Y.; Palacín, M. The SLC3 and SLC7 families of amino acid transporters. *Mol. Asp. Med.* **2013**, *34*, 139–158. [CrossRef] [PubMed]
23. Patestas, M.A.; Gartner, L.P. *A Textbook of Neuroanatomy*; WILEY: Hoboken, NJ, USA, 2016.
24. Gogolla, N. The insular cortex. *Curr. Biol.* **2017**, *27*, R580–R586. [CrossRef] [PubMed]
25. Lui, J.H.; Hansen, D.V.; Kriegstein, A.R. Development and evolution of the human neocortex. *Cell* **2011**, *146*, 18–36. [CrossRef]
26. Shura, R.D.; Hurley, R.A.; Taber, K.H. Insular cortex: Structural and functional neuroanatomy. *J. Neuropsychiatry Clin. Neurosci.* **2014**, *26*, 276–282. [CrossRef]
27. Hatten, M.E. New directions in neuronal migration. *Science* **2002**, *297*, 1660–1663. [CrossRef]
28. Granger, B.; Tekaia, F.; Le Sourd, A.M.; Rakic, P.; Bourgeois, J.P. Tempo of neurogenesis and synaptogenesis in the primate cingulate mesocortex: Comparison with the neocortex. *J. Comp. Neurol.* **1995**, *360*, 363–376. [CrossRef]
29. Duffau, H.; Capelle, L. Preferential brain locations of low-grade gliomas. *Cancer* **2004**, *100*, 2622–2626. [CrossRef]
30. Aubert, A.; Costalat, R.; Duffau, H.; Benali, H. Modeling of pathophysiological coupling between brain electrical activation, energy metabolism and hemodynamics: Insights for the interpretation of intracerebral tumor imaging. *Acta Biotheor.* **2002**, *50*, 281–295. [CrossRef]
31. Fields, R.D.; Stevens-Graham, B. New insights into neuron-glia communication. *Science* **2002**, *298*, 556–562. [CrossRef]

biomedicines

MDPI

Article

Enhancing Brain Tumor Diagnosis with L-Net: A Novel Deep Learning Approach for MRI Image Segmentation and Classification

Lehel Dénes-Fazakas [1,2,3], Levente Kovács [1,2], György Eigner [1,2] and László Szilágyi [1,2,4,*]

1 Physiological Controls Research Center, University Research and Innovation Center, Obuda University, 1034 Budapest, Hungary; denes-fazakas.lehel@uni-obuda.hu (L.D.-F.); kovacs@uni-obuda.hu (L.K.); eigner.gyorgy@uni-obuda.hu (G.E.)

2 Biomatics and Applied Artificial Intelligence Institute, John von Neumann Faculty of Informatics, Obuda University, 1034 Budapest, Hungary

3 Doctoral School of Applied Informatics and Applied Mathematics, Obuda University, 1034 Budapest, Hungary

4 Computational Intelligence Research Group, Sapientia Hungarian University of Transylvania, 547367 Târgu Mureș, Romania

* Correspondence: szilagyi.laszlo@uni-obuda.hu

Abstract: Background: Brain tumors are highly complex, making their detection and classification a significant challenge in modern medical diagnostics. The accurate segmentation and classification of brain tumors from MRI images are crucial for effective treatment planning. This study aims to develop an advanced neural network architecture that addresses these challenges. **Methods:** We propose L-net, a novel architecture combining U-net for tumor boundary segmentation and a convolutional neural network (CNN) for tumor classification. These two units are coupled such a way that the CNN classifies the MRI images based on the features extracted by the U-net while segmenting the tumor, instead of relying on the original input images. The model is trained on a dataset of 3064 high-resolution MRI images, encompassing gliomas, meningiomas, and pituitary tumors, ensuring robust performance across different tumor types. **Results:** L-net achieved a classification accuracy of up to 99.6%, surpassing existing models in both segmentation and classification tasks. The model demonstrated effectiveness even with lower image resolutions, making it suitable for diverse clinical settings. **Conclusions:** The proposed L-net model provides an accurate and unified approach to brain tumor segmentation and classification. Its enhanced performance contributes to more reliable and precise diagnosis, supporting early detection and treatment in clinical applications.

Keywords: brain tumors; MRI; segmentation; classification; neural networks; L-net; U-net; convolutional neural network (CNN); glioma; meningioma; pituitary tumor; automated diagnosis; medical imaging; deep learning

1. Introduction

Every year, hundreds of thousands of individuals receive a brain tumor diagnosis, with the United States alone recording approximately 18,000 fatal cases annually [1]. The likelihood of survival significantly improves with early detection. Nonetheless, factors such as the specific tumor type also play a pivotal role [2]. Detecting tumors in their early stages does not necessarily require precise tumor segmentation; rather, it is crucial that the detection process is sensitive enough to consistently identify even the smallest brain lesions. Brain tumors can exhibit a vast array of sizes, shapes, positions, and visual characteristics, making detection challenging due to deformations in normal brain structures and various forms of noise interference [3].

Over the past decade, there has been a remarkable surge in the development of methods for segmenting brain tumors, a surge largely catalyzed and sustained by the brain tumor segmentation (BraTS) Challenge, an annual event initiated in 2012 [4,5]. In the initial years of the BraTS initiative, researchers explored the entire classical spectrum of machine learning theories and practices [6]. More recently, the landscape of medical image analysis has witnessed a profound transformation, with deep learning techniques and an array of convolutional neural networks (CNNs) emerging as the predominant forces in this domain [7,8]. This paradigm shift underscores the remarkable progress and ongoing evolution in brain tumor segmentation methodologies.

While the brain tumor segmentation (BraTS) challenge primarily focused on gliomas, it is imperative to recognize the existence of diverse brain tumor lesions that necessitate precise classification for the establishment of a comprehensive brain tumor diagnostic pipeline. Consequently, the brain tumor segmentation problem can be regarded as an offshoot of the BraTS challenges, which has gained significant momentum in recent years. Numerous cutting-edge solutions, predominantly based on convolutional neural networks (CNNs), have emerged, boasting remarkable achievements, often attaining an accuracy of 97–98% in the challenging three-class brain tumor classification problem.

These state-of-the-art approaches not only leverage deep learning and convolutional networks but also incorporate various advanced techniques: Neelima et al. [9] introduced generative adversarial networks (GANs) into the domain of brain tumor segmentation. Kanchanamala et al. [10] proposed a deep hybrid representation learning approach, further enhancing the accuracy of brain tumor classification. Rajeev et al. [11] combined deep learning with Gabor wavelets to address brain tumor segmentation challenges. Mishra et al. [12] and Reddy et al. [13] introduced adaptive attention mechanisms to improve the segmentation of brain tumors. Mehnatkesh et al. [14] proposed a deep residual learning framework for robust brain tumor segmentation. Vankdothu et al. [15] explored recurrent CNNs to address the intricacies of brain tumor segmentation. Rahman et al. [16] introduced parallel deep CNNs as a promising approach to enhance brain tumor segmentation. Isunuri et al. [17] devised a multi-path convolution and multi-head attention network for accurate brain tumor segmentation.

These recent advancements underline the dynamic and rapidly evolving landscape of brain tumor segmentation research, bringing us closer to more accurate and effective diagnostic pipelines.

Baseline and Background

The starting point of this work is represented by a previous study [18], where we deployed two different CNN networks based on VGG with a modified architecture, consisting of 14 and 17 layers, respectively. The main modification consisted of using MaxPooling layers with a 4×4 kernel. The convolution layers were Conv2D ones, with a kernel size of 3×3 in most of the cases, but we also studied versions with a 9×9 kernel in the first convolution layer. Batch normalization and MaxPooling were used after each convolution layer. The convolution blocks were followed by a flatten layer and three dense layers, where the last one performed the classification. The larger architecture also included a dropout layer placed in front of the dense layers, with a dropout rate set to 0.2. The number of filters in the first convolutional layer represented a relevant hyperparameter, whose value was chosen from the set $\{64, 128, 256, 512\}$. The input image size was also used as a hyperparameter; we performed tests with image sizes of 128×128, 256×256 and 512×512. The number of neurons in the first two dense layers was set equal, and we tested network variants with 32, 256, 1024, 2048 and 4096 neurons in both layers. Also, we deployed two different learning strategies. Those strategies concerned the condition under which we save the weights of the model during learning. In one case, the strategy was to save for the smallest possible cost function. In the other case, it was if we increased the precision value on the TRAINING set by observing that metric during training. Tests were performed according to the five-fold cross-validation technique, meaning that the available data were divided into five equal groups, and each group took its turn to serve as testing data while the other four groups were used for training the chosen model. The average and standard deviation of the five runs were extracted. Since all available images received a prediction during the five runs, we also evaluated the network versions based of the sum of the five confusion matrices. The same five groups of images were used for all networks. In addition running thorough tests using various hyperparameter settings, we compared the classification outcome with state-of-the-art models like VGG with 16 layers and Resnet with 50 and 30 layers. Based on these tests, we proved that our architectures were able to be better adjusted to this classification problem than the state-of-the-art models. Our best achieved global accuracy was 98.27%, with a standard deviation of 0.66%. The best-performing model was running with 256 × 256 images. In addition, the neuron numbers in the dense layers were 256, the dropout layer was present, and the learning strategy was set to maximum accuracy.

In this study, we propose a more complex neural network to classify different brain tumors. Our solution was created by coupling a U-net and a CNN network. The data and the network architecture are discussed in detail in Section 2. We also report therein on our past results. In addition, we describe the teaching and testing methods we used. The metrics we use are also mentioned here. In Section 3, we describe our results with this more complex mesh structure. Finally, in Section 4, we summarize the results and set future plans.

2. Materials and Methods

2.1. Data

The dataset used for training and evaluating all CNN models involve in this study were originally compiled and made available for the public by Cheng et al. [19,20]. This dataset was meticulously assembled from 233 patients who received medical treatment at two distinct state-owned hospitals in Guangzhou and Tianjin, China, spanning the years 2005 to 2010. It comprises a total of 3064 T1-weighted contrast-enhanced brain MRI scans, each boasting a high resolution of 512 × 512 pixels per image, with a pixel size of 0.49 mm in both dimensions.

The dataset is rich and diverse, encompassing three distinct categories of brain tumors, specifically Pituitary, Meningioma, and Glioma, and covers three different image planes: axial, coronal, and sagittal views. These varied perspectives offer comprehensive insights into the structural characteristics and localization of these brain tumors. The dataset's distribution is as follows: it contains 930 instances of Pituitary tumors, 708 instances of Meningioma tumors, and 1426 instances of Glioma tumors, ensuring a balanced representation of these different brain tumor types.

Each image in the dataset is provided in MATLAB (.mat) format, offering a comprehensive set of associated information. This includes a detailed description, a tumor mask delineating the tumor's boundaries, a tumor class label indicating the specific tumor type, a tumor border to precisely demarcate the tumor region, and a unique patient identifier (ID) for traceability.

For a more comprehensive understanding of the dataset's structural characteristics, Table 1 provides a detailed summary of its key attributes.

This dataset, with its rich and comprehensive attributes, serves as a valuable resource for the development and evaluation of brain tumor classification models, such as the L-net model proposed in the following.

Table 1. The structure of the image dataset involved in the study.

Tumor Type	Patient Count	Section Plane			Total Images
		Coronal	Sagittal	Transversal	
Glioma	89	437	495	494	1426
Meningioma	82	268	231	209	708
Pituitary	62	319	320	291	930
Total	233	1024	1046	994	3064

2.2. U-Net: A Versatile Semantic Segmentation Framework

The U-net architecture, introduced by Ronneberger et al. in 2015 [21], is a deep learning model that has gained significant popularity in the field of semantic image segmentation. It was originally designed for biomedical image segmentation tasks, particularly for segmenting neuronal structures in microscopy images, but its versatility has led to its adoption in various domains beyond medical imaging.

2.2.1. Architecture Overview

The U-net architecture derives its name from its distinctive U-shaped design. It consists of an encoder and a decoder, with a contracting path on the left side of the U and an expansive path on the right side.

The encoder, often referred to as the "downsampling" path, is responsible for capturing contextual information from the input image. It typically consists of multiple convolutional and pooling layers, which gradually reduce the spatial dimensions of the input while increasing the depth of feature representations.

The decoder, or the "upsampling" path, is responsible for generating the final segmentation mask. It consists of a series of up-convolutional (transposed convolutional) layers that gradually increase the spatial resolution of the feature map [22]. Skip connections are a key component of the U-net architecture, connecting corresponding layers in the encoder and decoder. These skip connections enable the model to retain fine-grained details from the input image.

2.2.2. Skip Connections and Semantic Segmentation

The use of skip connections [23] in the U-net architecture is crucial for semantic segmentation tasks. These connections allow the decoder to access high-resolution feature maps from the encoder, which helps in preserving spatial information and capturing fine details. As a result, U-net excels at segmenting objects with well-defined boundaries in images, making it particularly suitable for tasks like medical image segmentation, where the precise delineation of structures is essential.

2.2.3. Applications

The U-net architecture has found widespread use in various applications, including:

- Medical Image Segmentation: U-net has been extensively applied to segment various anatomical structures and abnormalities in medical images, such as tumors, organs, and blood vessels [24,25].
- Satellite Image Analysis: U-net is employed to segment land use, identify objects, and monitor environmental changes in satellite and aerial imagery [26–28].
- Industrial Quality Control: It is used for detecting and classifying defects in manufacturing processes, such as identifying defects in semiconductor wafers [29,30].
- Autonomous Vehicles: U-net assists in road scene understanding, enabling autonomous vehicles to identify objects and navigate safely [31–33].
- Biomedical Image Analysis: Beyond neuronal structures, U-net has been applied to segment cell nuclei, histological structures, and various biological objects [34].

The adaptability and effectiveness of the U-net in diverse domains have made it a go-to architecture for semantic segmentation tasks, and it continues to be a subject of research and innovation in the field of deep learning.

2.3. L-Net: U-Net Plus CNN

In our current study, we propose a complex model, depicted in Figure 1, which is based on the observation that neural networks can learn better when trained on multiple problems simultaneously. The architecture consists of a U-net and a CNN connected in a special cascade. The input MR image is presented to the U-net, which provides at its output a predicted brain mask. The result provided by the U-net at the penultimate layer (just before the output layer) is fed to the input of the CNN instead of the original image, and thus the CNN predicts the tumor type from the information received from the U-net. The U-net is trained to predict segmentation result, based on the available tumor masks. The second part of the cascade, namely the CNN, is trained the provide an accurate prediction of the tumor type using the available annotation of images. The training of the two parts is performed simultaneously, not one after the other, so that each batch of images in each training epoch changes the weights in both parts of the architecture. The figures we use are similar to other manuscripts we have already written, since we have already dealt with segmentation and classification several times. However, they have been adapted to the current parameters used in the research [18,35–37].

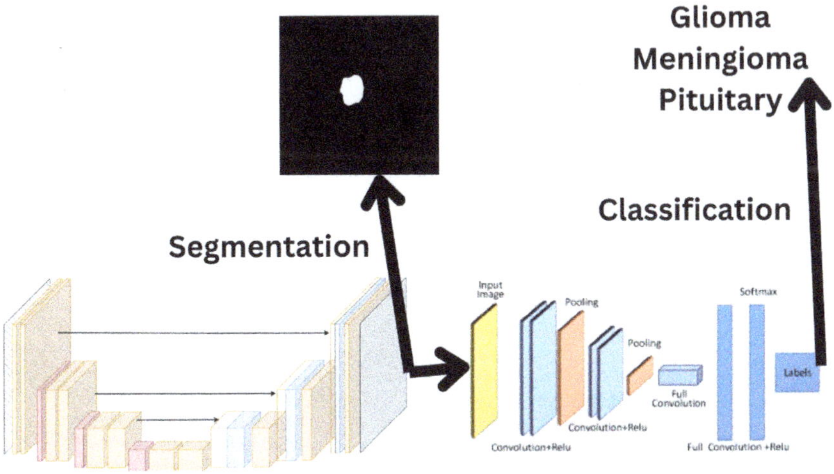

Figure 1. An overview of the L-net architecture, combining segmentation and classification tasks. The model first segments the tumor region using a U-net structure (**left**), where the black image represents the segmentation mask as the output. It then classifies the tumor, based on the features extracted by the U-net, into one of three categories: Glioma, Meningioma, or Pituitary (**right**), using a CNN.

2.3.1. The U-Net Part of the L-Net

Our U-net, shown in Figure 2, contains four encoder blocks and four decoder blocks. These blocks are connected at the bottom by a bridge, as well as the skip connection at each level. As a difference in comparison to the original U-net, our model contains an extra convolution block with nine filters right before the output layer consisting of two filters marked in green, whose two filters give the predicted segmentation outcome. The filter numbers for the encoder blocks are 64, 32, 16 and 8, respectively, while the decoder blocks have the same filter numbers in reversed order. The bridge contains the smallest number of four filters as this is the smallest representation within U-net. Image sizes are not indicated in Figure 2, since multiple image resolutions were involved in the evaluation process. Each encoder block halves the image size in both directions, while each decoder doubles it to return to the original size at the output of the U-net. The CNN part of the L-net is connected after the layer marked in green, and uses it as input.

The structure of the encoder blocks is given in Figure 3, four such blocks are built in the encoder branch of the U-net network. These blocks consist of six layers, including two Conv2D layers, two batch normalization layers, a dropout layer, and a MaxPooling2D layer. The data progression within the block is shown in Figure 3. Data arriving to the block first pass through a Conv2D layer [38], whose output is fed into the batch normalization to obtain normalized data. After that comes a dropout layer that helps avoid overfitting [39]. The dropout rate is set to 0.2. Then comes the second Convd2D layer, whose output again is connected to a batch normalization layer. Finally, the MaxPooling2D [40] layer reduces the image dimensions. The matrix of the MaxPooling2D layer is 2 × 2, so the size of the images is halved compared to the input image. The skip connection obtains the output of the second batch normalization layer. That reduced-size output of the MaxPooling2D layer is wired into the subsequent decoder block. The Conv2D layers use an ELU [41] activation function. The filter numbers for each encoder block is indicated in Figure 2. The size of the convolution kernels is 3 × 3 and their fill factor is set. Thus, the size of the data does not change in the convolution layers.

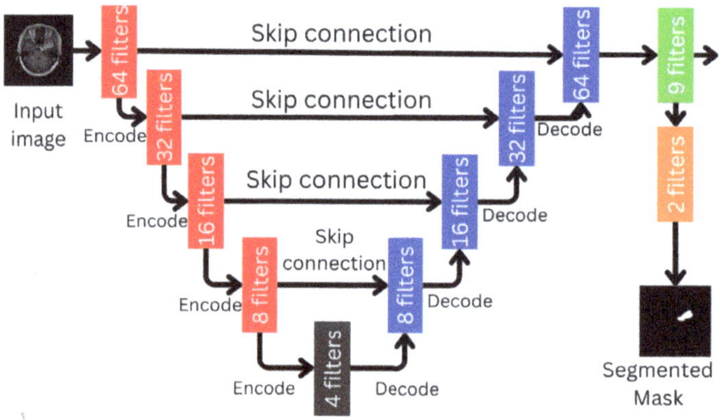

Figure 2. The U-net module, which forms a key part of the overall L-net architecture.

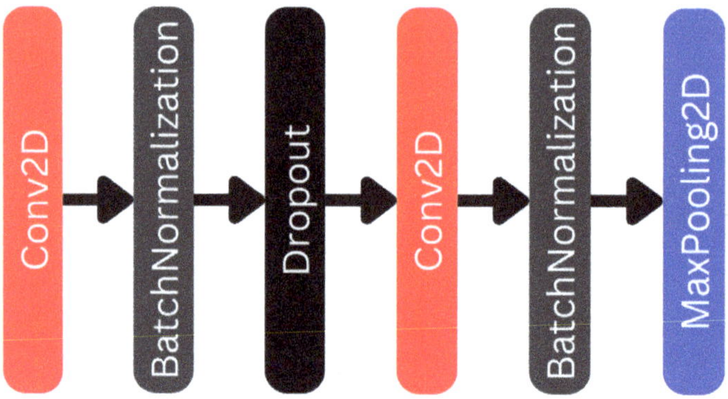

Figure 3. Encoder blocks of the U-net part of the L-net.

The bridge part of our U-net network is shown in Figure 4. The bridge connects the encoder and decoder branches of the U-net network. Its structure is almost the same as the one of the encoder blocks, but there is no MaxPooling2D at the end of the bridge, and the image size is not reduced further.

The blocks of the decoder branch on the U-net part are built as indicated in Figure 5. These are the most complex blocks of the U-net, as they receive the output of the bridge or the output of the previous decoder, and after an upscaling of this lower-level data performed by the Conv2DTranspose layer, it is concatenated with the data received from the skip connection situated at the same level. The latter is performed by the Concatenate layer. The data then go through two Conv2D layers, each followed by a batch normalization, and with a dropout layer in between, with its dropout rate set to 0.2. The Conv2DTranspose layer uses a 2 × 2 kernel matrix, as well as a 2 × 2 stride, so it can double the size of the data it receives from the previous block. The filter number is the same as in the Conv2D layers situated within the given block. Similar to the encoder blocks, the Conv2D layers use kernels of size 3 × 3 and activation function ELU. The last decoder block outputs images that correspond in size with the original input of the U-net.

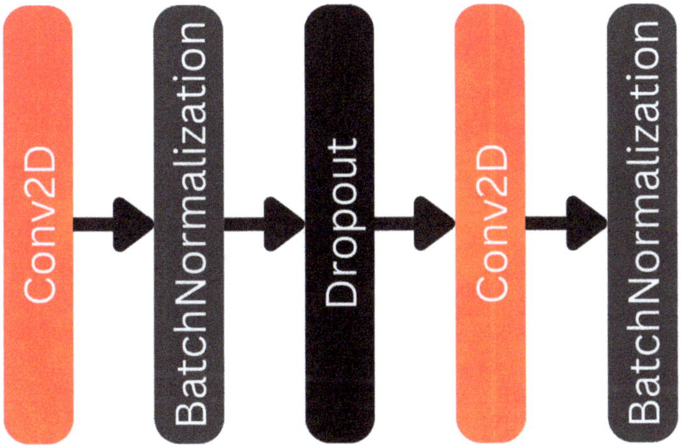

Figure 4. The bridge section within the U-net component of the L-net architecture.

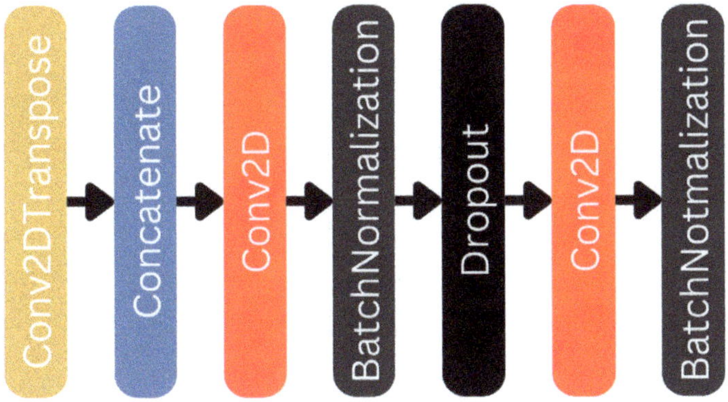

Figure 5. The decoder blocks within the U-net component of the L-net architecture.

2.3.2. The CNN Part of the L-Net

The convolutional part of the L-net architecture is responsible for classification. Its structure is shown in Figure 6. As already shown in Figure 1, the CNN is connected after the U-net. More precisely, Figure 2 indicates the exact connection point: the output of the penultimate layer of the U-net, consisting of nine filters, is fed to the input of the CNN. The CNN consists of a convolutional part responsible for feature extraction, and a classifier part which performs the actual classification. The blocks of the CNN network are shown in the Figure 7. The convolutional part consists of four convolutional blocks. The number of filters in the convolutional blocks are 64, 128, 256 and 512, respectively. The classifier part starts with a flatten layer that expands the elements in a column vector, which is then followed by three dense blocks. These dense blocks contain different number of neurons. The first two blocks contain 256 neurons, while the last one, which does the actual classification, contains three neurons corresponding to the three tumor classes that need to be distinguished.

These blocks, as mentioned above, come after the flatten layer, i.e., they only work with column vectors. The first layer of these blocks is the dropout layer with its rate set to 0.2, which was added to avoid overfitting. After that comes the dense layer, which represents a vector neuron set. The number of neurons per block is equal to the number of neurons in the corresponding layer, as shown in Figure 6. In addition, their activation function for this block is ReLU [42], with the exception of the last layer, which uses SoftMax activation [43] to predict probabilities for the actual classification.

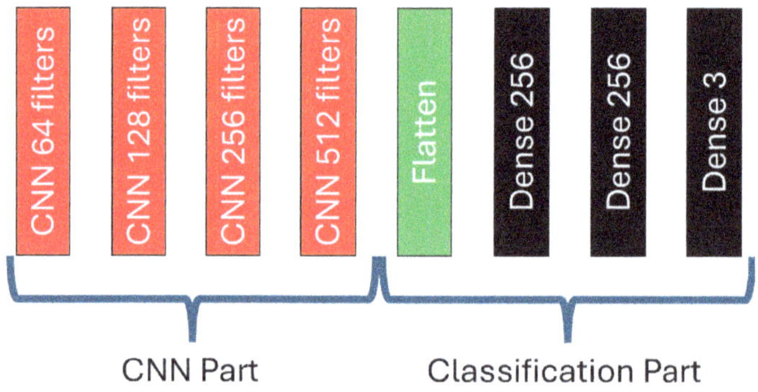

Figure 6. The detailed architecture of the CNN component that forms a crucial part of the overall L-net structure.

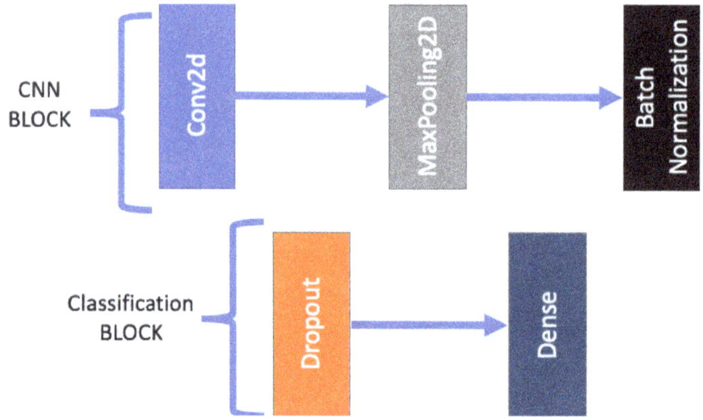

Figure 7. The individual blocks of the CNN component within the broader L-net architecture.

2.4. Training and Testing

In this study we involved images in various resolutions, aiming to establish which resolution leads to the best classification accuracy. Due to the complexity of the proposed network, we had to limit the input image size. Training and testing sessions were separately performed at image resolutions of 16×16, 32×32, 64×64, and 128×128 pixels.

To ensure the fair circumstances for comparison with previous solutions, the training and testing was performed using the very same five groups of images described in Section 1. For each run of the evaluation process, training was performed in 1000 epochs using the Adam optimizer [44].

Our cost function was a complex one, since the network has two outputs. For segmentation, we employed a Dice loss function that we have successfully used in a previous work [36]. The essence of this cost function is to use sparse categorical cross-entropy (SCCE) [45], and, in addition, it computes the Dice score for each class. This Dice score is averaged and subtracted from 1. Then, weighted by 0.5, it is added to the SCCE cost, which is also weighted by 0.5. In the second output, the cost function was only SCCE. The total cost was the sum of these two cost functions. This was the basis on which our optimizer worked.

2.5. Performance Metrics

The performance of the classification methods used in this study is assessed through statistical indicators. Let us define $\Psi = \{M, G, P\}$ as the set of tumor classes, where M, G, and P correspond to the Meningioma, Glioma, and Pituitary tumors, respectively. The set of all images in class $i \in \Psi$, as identified by the ground truth, is denoted by Γ_i, while the set of images predicted to belong to the three classes is denoted by Λ_i, for any $i \in \Psi$. Let Γ represent the entire set of images used in the evaluation. Then, we have $\Gamma = \Gamma_M \cup \Gamma_G \cup \Gamma_P$ and also $\Gamma = \Lambda_M \cup \Lambda_G \cup \Lambda_P$.

Using the variables presented above, we can derive the following statistical metrics for any class $i \in \Psi$: sensitivity (also known as true positive rate, TPR, or recall), specificity (true negative rate, TNR), precision (positive predictive value, PPV), and the Dice similarity coefficient (DSC) or F1-score. Their formal definitions are provided in the upper part of Table 2. Additionally, the proportion of correct decisions across all tumor classes is referred to as accuracy (ACC), with its definition found in the lower part of Table 2.

Furthermore, we utilized the area under the receiver operating characteristic curve (AUC) as an additional benchmark to evaluate the classification performance.

All statistical accuracy indicators range between 0 and 1, with higher values indicating better accuracy.

Table 2. Accuracy indicators with respect to tumor class $i \in \Psi$ (upper part), and overall accuracy (ower part).

Indicator	Definition
Sensitivity	$\mathrm{TPR}_i = \frac{\lvert\Gamma_i \cap \Lambda_i\rvert}{\lvert\Gamma_i\rvert}$
Specificity	$\mathrm{TNR}_i = \frac{\lvert(\Gamma \setminus \Gamma_i) \cap (\Gamma \setminus \Lambda_i)\rvert}{\lvert\Gamma \setminus \Gamma_i\rvert}$
Precision	$\mathrm{PPV}_i = \frac{\lvert\Gamma_i \cap \Lambda_i\rvert}{\lvert\Lambda_i\rvert}$
F1 score	$\mathrm{F1}_i = \frac{2 \cdot \lvert\Gamma_i \cap \Lambda_i\rvert}{\lvert\Gamma_i\rvert + \lvert\Lambda_i\rvert}$
Accuracy	$\mathrm{ACC} = \frac{1}{\lvert\Gamma\rvert} \sum_{i \in \Psi} \lvert\Gamma_i \cap \Lambda_i\rvert$

2.6. Development Environments

During our research, we used the Python 3.8 environment, which was developed in the cloud using Google Colab. This Colab cloud service is useful because it has pre-installed libraries, which are important when building a neural network. The libraries that we used in the development—and can be found in Colab's libraries—are Tensorflow 2.0.0 [46], Numpy [47], Scikit-learn [48] and Pandas [49]. Colab provided us with a Jupyter Notebook [50] environment for development, so the code was written in Jupyter Notebook. For our virtual environment, we also had resources provided by Colab. These resources are usually around 12 GB of video card memory. However, there is also the possibility of adding Google Drive, which is around 110 GB. We had 30 GB of RAM available. We also had four VCPUs.

3. Results and Discussion

The whole set of 3064 images was involved in a five-fold cross-validation process, using the very same five (almost) equal groups of images, which served as testing data in turns for the architecture trained on the other four groups of images. The proposed L-net model was evaluated with various hyperparameter settings and the classification outcome was compared with the baseline models. The segmentation results were not examined, as the L-net was working with a smaller image size than the original 512 × 512 resolution of the dataset. Under these circumstances, the segmentation results would be deceptive.

Although the model provides a segmentation of the tumor in the input image, we focused only on the classification outcome, just like in our previous test described in Section 1. The results are exhibited in the following tables and figures.

Table 3 presents the precision, recall, F1 score and accuracy values obtained by the L-net model, and the mean and standard deviation of each metric obtained in the five folds of the cross-validation. In the case of the first three metrics, the average of the values obtained for the three different classes were averaged, and then the average and standard deviation of the five means values are presented in the table. In case of the accuracy, there is only one overall value in each fold which reflects the rate of correct decisions. The last row of the table also shows the best benchmarks obtained by the baseline model. One may notice that even with the lowest image resolution, the proposed L-net model provides a better classification outcome than the previous modified VGG model running at its optimal settings. The higher the image resolution, the better the obtained benchmarks, and the differences are relevant, as all benchmark values intensively tends towards 1 as the image resolution grows. We may also remark that the L-net models seems to be more stable than the previous VGG architecture, as the standard deviation of its accuracy indicators is much lower. At its best performance, L-net produces four times less misclassifications than the VGG model.

Table 3. Precision and recall values obtained by the L-net model.

Image Size	Precision Mean ± Std	Recall Mean ± Std	F1 Score Mean ± Std	Accuracy Mean ± Std
16 × 16	0.986743 ± 0.002653	0.986622 ± 0.002665	0.986633 ± 0.002656	0.986622 ± 0.002665
32 × 32	0.989924 ± 0.002099	0.989884 ± 0.002121	0.989888 ± 0.002106	0.989884 ± 0.002121
64 × 64	0.991222 ± 0.001860	0.991189 ± 0.001853	0.991187 ± 0.001865	0.991189 ± 0.001853
128 × 128	0.996761 ± 0.001155	0.996737 ± 0.001153	0.996738 ± 0.001154	0.996737 ± 0.001153
Baseline	0.9817 ± 0.0068	0.9838 ± 0.0063	0.9827 ± 0.0066	0.9827 ± 0.0066

Figure 8 depicts the boxplots for the different metrics at various image sizes. As the image resolution increases, all observed benchmarks increase, making large steps towards 1. A step-like increase is observed: the median value rises and the inter quartile (IQR) range narrows. At the lowest resolution, L-net provides slightly better results than the previously modified VGG model's best performance. As the image resolution doubles, the minimum value of benchmarks become higher or equal to the median obtained with the previous smaller resolution. As the resolution increases, the range between the quartiles gradually narrows. This trend results in a decreasing variance across the five test cases, indicating that the network's generalization ability becomes increasingly stable. However, a notable and sudden decrease in the interquartile range occurs at the 128 resolution. This sharp decline suggests that, at this resolution, the network achieves a level of accuracy and consistency that significantly reduces the variability in test results. Consequently, there is less disparity between the tests, allowing for more reliable and precise outcomes. In other cases, there is already very little variance in the tests. Even in the 64 case, the variance is between 0.990 and 0.992. In the case of IQR 128 I show that three test cases are very close to each other around 0.997. Also, there are the two outliers below and above, which reach values below 0.996 and above 0.998.

Table 4 presents the AUC values obtained for each class of tumors, with the mean and standard deviation extracted from the five folds. Each row of the table represents a certain image resolution, and they are ordered in ascending order of the image size. In each case, it is obvious that very high AUC values are obtained for the Pituitary tumor class. Lower resolutions lead to AUC of 1. This proves that the Pituitary class is the one that the models can learn best, i.e., it is the least confused with other classes. It also has the lowest values for variance. Between the Meningioma and Glioma classes, there is no relevant difference in mean AUC values, as any of the two can be larger than the other in different rows. We can also observe that the AUC value of the Glioma class is obtained higher that the baseline model's benchmark only at resolutions greater or equal to 64 × 64.

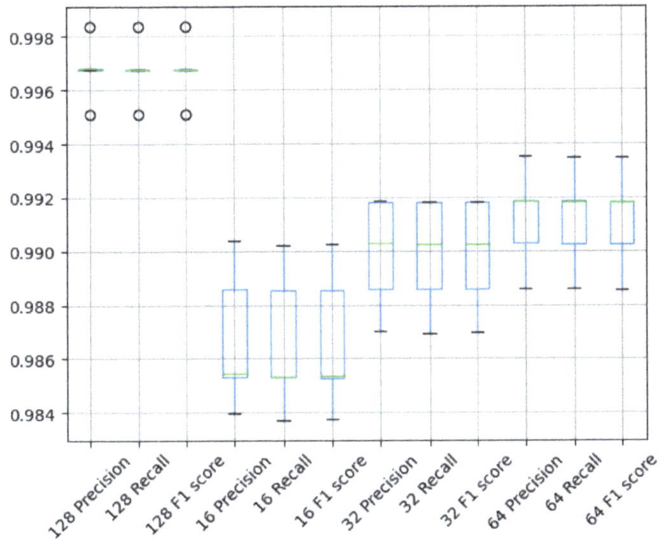

Figure 8. A boxplot for the precision, recall, and F1 score metrics. Lower axis indicates the image size and metric as well.

Table 4. AUC benchmarks obtained for different tumor classes.

Image Size	AUC Meningioma Mean ± Std	AUC Glioma Mean ± Std	AUC Pituitary Mean ± Std
16 × 16	0.996590 ± 0.001485	0.997482 ± 0.001324	1.000000 ± 0.000000
32 × 32	0.998341 ± 0.000495	0.997849 ± 0.000825	1.000000 ± 0.000000
64 × 64	0.997923 ± 0.001722	0.998192 ± 0.001595	0.999766 ± 0.000524
128 × 128	0.999646 ± 0.000229	0.999554 ± 0.000664	0.999992 ± 0.000017
Baseline	0.9961 ± 0.0008	0.9981 ± 0.0013	0.9987 ± 0.0013

Figure 9 exhibits the boxplots of AUC metrics listed in Table 4. The Pituitary class, in all test cases, can be seen to hover around an AUC of 1. This class can be easily distinguished by any other image class. In the case of the Glioma class, the lowest benchmarks are achieved at 16 × 16 resolution, with the minimum AUC value reaching 0.9955. The median value is close to but not reaching 0.998. Thus, it can be said that half of the tests fail to achieve an AUC value of 0.998 for Glioma classification at the lowest resolution. At an image size of 32 × 32 pixels, it is interesting to note that Glioma's were less accurately detected than Meningioma tumors, which is not the case at other resolutions. At the 64 × 64 resolution, the median value rises to almost 0.999. However, its minimum is very close to the minimum reached in the smallest resolution case. At the highest tested resolution, namely 128 × 128, we can observe much higher AUC scores as the ones obtained at lower resolution, but there is an outlier among the five folds, affecting most the Glioma class and least the Pituitary tumor class.

Table 5 presents the overall confusion matrices obtained with the baseline VGG model using its four best-performing settings, and also those obtained by the L-net architecture at image sizes varying from 16 × 16 to 128 × 128. It can be easily noticed that the L-net model produces 40, 32, 20 and 10 misclassifications, respectively, in the four-image-size case, while the best baseline model made 53 mistakes while classifying the total number of 3064 tumor images. The number of correctly detected Meningioma cases achieved by the best set baseline model is equal to that obtained by L-net at 32 × 32 resolution, while at higher resolutions L-net makes less mistakes. In case of the other two classes, L-net deployed at any tested image resolutions correctly detects more tumors than the baseline model using any settings.

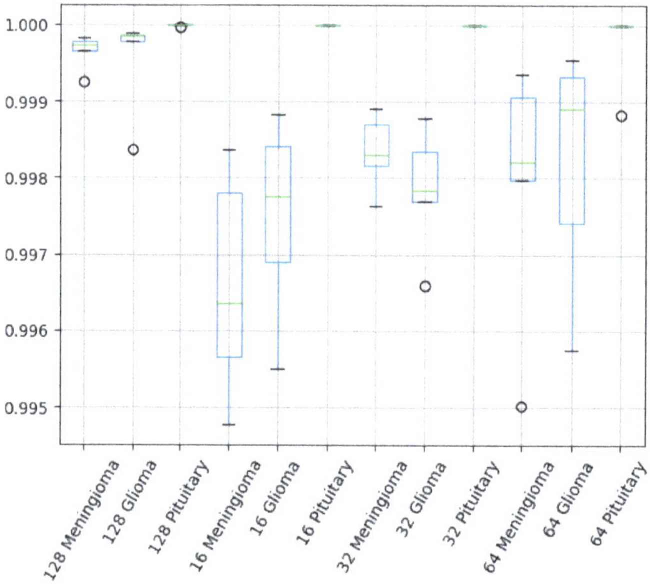

Figure 9. Boxplot for AUC metrics obtained for different tumor types and various image sizes.

Table 5. Overall confusion matrices obtained by the best four VGG models [18] (upper row), and the proposed L-net architecture at various image resolutions.

		Predicted			Predicted			Predicted			Predicted		
	Class	Meningioma	Glioma	Pituitary	Meningioma	Glioma	Pituitary	Meningioma	Glioma	Pituitary	Meningioma	Glioma	Pituitary
Actual	Meningioma	691	10	7	681	17	10	681	19	8	685	13	10
	Glioma	24	1399	3	25	1401	0	25	1401	0	29	1396	1
	Pituitary	5	4	921	3	2	925	3	2	925	3	3	924
		VGG first			VGG second			VGG third			VGG fourth		
		Predicted			Predicted			Predicted			Predicted		
	Class	Meningioma	Glioma	Pituitary	Meningioma	Glioma	Pituitary	Meningioma	Glioma	Pituitary	Meningioma	Glioma	Pituitary
Actual	Meningioma	683	21	4	691	12	5	695	9	4	704	4	0
	Glioma	12	1414	0	11	1415	0	5	1421	0	4	1422	0
	Pituitary	1	2	927	3	1	926	1	1	928	1	1	928
		16 × 16			32 × 32			64 × 64			128 × 128		

Figure 10 shows some examples of input images, one for each case of the overall confusion matrix where available, reflecting the classification outcome of the best performing L-net network working at an 128 × 128 resolution.

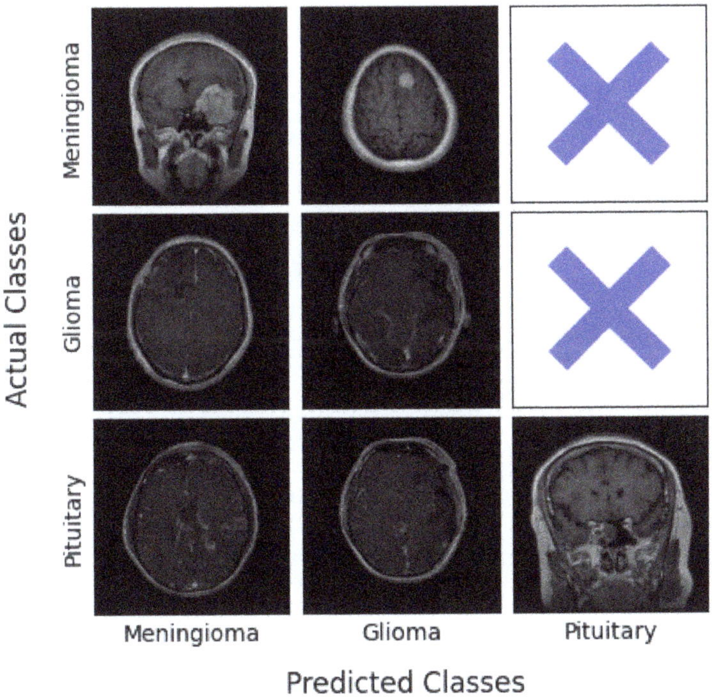

Figure 10. Some examples of correct and mistaken decisions made by the L-net architecture at the image size 128 × 128, organized in the format of a confusion matrix. The Pituitary class has no false positives.

Overall, we have proved that the idea can work, as employing a U-net to preprocess or to transform the input images into some intermediate data and feeding it to classification can greatly improve the accuracy of the decision. This is demonstrated by the previously presented evaluation results. Furthermore, we also proved that the proposed L-net model can work fine with even smaller images than a CNN-based classification. Table 3 shows the average results obtained with different metrics and their standard deviations. From the table, we can see that even for the 64 × 64 resolution, the average F1-score is higher than 0.99. Moreover, we can also see that even at the 16 × 16 resolution, we achieved better results than our previous solution. Additionally, it can be observed that the variance values are consistently decreasing with the proposed architecture. This decrease is well represented in Figure 8, which contains the boxplots. The higher the resolution, the smaller the variance of benchmarks, signifying that the learning process is much more stable. Table 4 gives the AUC metrics for each class. Very outstanding results are obtained for the Pituitary class. However, for this class, the best results are not obtained at the highest resolution of the input image. On the other hand, for the other classes, the 128 × 128 resolution performs the best. The most important results are represented by the confusion matrices; it is clear to see in Table 5 how much better the proposed L-net model classifies the images. The total number of misclassification reduced by up to 80%, in comparison to previous solutions. With our best L-net model, the Pituitary tumor class has no false positives at all, only a couple of false negatives. For the other two classes there are more misclassification, but still significantly less than in earlier solutions. The big step forward is clear, and we can assert that it makes sense to use a U-net to extract features for a CNN network model deployed for classification. The results of our method demonstrate that this network can be effectively used for tumor classification with high accuracy. Additionally, it offers the capability for segmentation. This network structure allows for the classification and detection of various types of diseases, particularly in cases where there may be multiple output classes within a segmentation region. For instance, the segmented region can include Glioma, Meningioma, and Pituitary tumors. However, to adapt the network for other datasets, retraining will be necessary, and modifications to the cost function may also be required.

4. Conclusions

In this paper, we proposed a novel architecture for the classification of MRI tumor images, which is performed simultaneously with a segmentation of the tumor. The proposed network has two main parts. First, a slightly modified U-net is deployed to segment the tumor from the input image, but the output of the penultimate layer in the U-net is used as an extracted feature, which is then fed to the second part of the architecture consisting of a modified VGG network. Compared to previous solutions, we achieved an improvement of classification accuracy from 98.3% to 99.6%, which represents a reduction to up to 80% of the misclassified cases. According to our previous findings, a classical VGG model best classifies these images at 256×256 resolution, while our model can surpass the accuracy of previous models even when using images at a 16×16 resolution. However, using a 128×128 image size is still recommendable, as it is beneficial with respect to the classification outcome. L-net is an excellent example to support the idea that training a neural network on two problems simultaneously can yield better results than performing the two works separately. In our case, the L-net learned both classification and segmentation. The results faithfully reflect that the error rate is now very low, as can be seen mainly from the confusion matrix. Also, the tables and boxplots show that the training is very stable at 128×128 resolution, with no large fluctuations. However, outliers occur for some metrics.

Further works will aim at the validation of the L-net architecture on various medical image datasets. This process presents the most difficulty, as few public image collections include both annotated segmentation and classification labels.

Author Contributions: Methodology, L.D.-F.; Software, L.D.-F.; Validation, L.D.-F. and L.S.; Formal analysis, G.E. and L.S.; Data curation, L.S.; Writing—original draft, L.D.-F.; Writing—review & editing, L.D.-F. and L.S.; Visualization, L.D.-F.; Supervision, L.K., G.E. and L.S.; Project administration, L.K., G.E. and L.S.; Funding acquisition, L.K., G.E. and L.S. All authors have read and agreed to the published version of the manuscript.

Funding: Project no. 2019-1.3.1-KK-2019-00007 has been implemented with the support provided from the National Research, Development and Innovation Fund of Hungary, financed under the 2019-1.3.1-KK funding scheme. This project has been supported by the National Research, Development, and Innovation Fund of Hungary, financed under the TKP2021-NKTA-36 funding scheme. The work of L. Szilágyi and Gy. Eigner were partially supported by the Researcher Program of Óbuda University.

Institutional Review Board Statement: Not applicable.

Informed Consent Statement: Not applicable.

Data Availability Statement: Access to the data is available upon request. Access to the data can be requested via e-mail to the corresponding author.

Acknowledgments: On behalf of the AI development for diabetic and brain MRI scans project, we are grateful for the opportunity to use ELKH Cloud (see Héder et al. 2022 [51]), which helped us achieve the results published in this paper.

Conflicts of Interest: The authors declare no conflicts of interest.

Abbreviations

The following abbreviations are used in this manuscript:

BraTS	Brain Tumor Segmentation
GANs	Generative Adversarial Networks
MRI	Magnetic resonance imaging
AI	Artificial Intelligence
CNN	Convolutional neural network
CNNs	Convolutional neural networks
ELU	Exponential Linear Unit
SCCE	Sparse categorical cross-entropy
TPR	Sensitivity or True Positive Rate
TNR	Specificity or True Negative Rate
PPV	Precision or Positive Predictive Value
DSC	Dice Similarity Score
ACC	Accuracy

References

1. Feigin, V.L.; Nichols, E.; Alam, T.; Bannick, M.S.; Beghi, E.; Blake, N.; Culpepper, W.J.; Dorsey, E.R.; Elbaz, A.; Ellenbogen, R.G.; et al. Global, regional, and national burden of neurological disorders, 1990–2016: A systematic analysis for the Global Burden of Disease Study 2016. *Lancet Neurol.* **2019**, *18*, 459–480. [CrossRef] [PubMed]
2. Mohan, G.; Subashini, M.M. MRI based medical image analysis: Survey on brain tumor grade classification. *Biomed. Signal Process. Control* **2018**, *39*, 139–161. [CrossRef]
3. Gordillo, N.; Montseny, E.; Sobrevilla, P. State of the art survey on MRI brain tumor segmentation. *Magn. Reson. Imaging* **2013**, *31*, 1426–1438. [CrossRef] [PubMed]
4. Menze, B.H.; Jakab, A.; Bauer, S.; Kalpathy-Cramer, J.; Farahani, K.; Kirby, J.; Burren, Y.; Porz, N.; Slotboom, J.; Wiest, R.; et al. The Multimodal Brain Tumor Image Segmentation Benchmark (BRATS). *IEEE Trans. Med. Imaging* **2015**, *34*, 1993–2024. [CrossRef] [PubMed]
5. Bakas, S.; Reyes, M.; Jakab, A.; Bauer, S.; Rempfler, M.; Crimi, A.; Shinohara, R.T.; Berger, C.; Ha, S.M.; Rozycki, M.; et al. Identifying the Best Machine Learning Algorithms for Brain Tumor Segmentation, Progression Assessment, and Overall Survival Prediction in the BRATS Challenge. *arXiv* **2019**, arXiv:1811.02629. [CrossRef]
6. Győrfi, A.; Szilágyi, L.; Kovács, L. A Fully Automatic Procedure for Brain Tumor Segmentation from Multi-Spectral MRI Records Using Ensemble Learning and Atlas-Based Data Enhancement. *Appl. Sci.* **2021**, *11*, 564. [CrossRef]
7. Macsik, P.; Pavlovicova, J.; Goga, J.; Kajan, S. Local binary CNN for diabetic retinopathy classification on fundus images. *Acta Polytech. Hung.* **2022**, *19*, 27–45. [CrossRef]
8. Szepesi, P.; Szilágyi, L. Detection of pneumonia using convolutional neural networks and deep learning. *Biocybern. Biomed. Eng.* **2022**, *42*, 1012–1022. [CrossRef]
9. Neelima, G.; Chigurukota, D.R.; Maram, B.; Girirajan, B. Optimal DeepMRSeg based tumor segmentation with GAN for brain tumor classification. *Biomed. Signal Process. Control* **2022**, *74*, 103537. [CrossRef]
10. Kanchanamala, P.; Revathi, K.G.; Ananth, M.B.J. Optimization-enabled hybrid deep learning for brain tumor detection and classification from MRI. *Biomed. Signal Process. Control* **2023**, *84*, 104955. [CrossRef]
11. Rajeev, S.K.; Pallikonda Rajasekaran, M.; Vishnuvarthanan, G.; Arunprasath, T. A biologically-inspired hybrid deep learning approach for brain tumor classification from magnetic resonance imaging using improved gabor wavelet transform and Elmann-BiLSTM network. *Biomed. Signal Process. Control* **2022**, *78*, 103949. [CrossRef]
12. Mishra, L.; Verma, S. Graph attention autoencoder inspired CNN based brain tumor classification using MRI. *Neurocomputing* **2022**, *503*, 236–247. [CrossRef]
13. Rasool Reddy, K.; Dhuli, R. Segmentation and classification of brain tumors from MRI images based on adaptive mechanisms and ELDP feature descriptor. *Biomed. Signal Process. Control* **2022**, *76*, 103704. [CrossRef]
14. Mehnatkesh, H.; Jalali, S.M.J.; Khosravi, A.; Nahavandi, S. An intelligent driven deep residual learning framework for brain tumor classification using MRI images. *Expert Syst. Appl.* **2023**, *213*, 119087. [CrossRef]
15. Vankdothu, R.; Hameed, M.A. Brain tumor MRI images identification and classification based on the recurrent convolutional neural network. *Meas. Sens.* **2022**, *24*, 100412. [CrossRef]
16. Rahman, T.; Islam, M.S. MRI brain tumor detection and classification using parallel deep convolutional neural networks. *Meas. Sens.* **2023**, *26*, 100694. [CrossRef]
17. Isunuri, B.V.; Kakarla, J. EfficientNet and multi-path convolution with multi-head attention network for brain tumor grade classification. *Comput. Electr. Eng.* **2023**, *108*, 108700. [CrossRef]
18. Dénes-Fazekas, L.; Kovács, L.; Eigner, G.; Szilágyi, L. Brain Tumor Segmentation from Multi-Spectral MRI Records Using a U-Net Cascade Architecture. In Proceedings of the 2023 IEEE International Conference on Systems, Man, and Cybernetics (SMC), Honolulu/Oahu, HI, USA, 1–4 October 2023; pp. 3003–3008. [CrossRef]

19. Cheng, J.; Huang, W.; Cao, S.; Yang, R.; Yang, W.; Yun, Z.; Wang, Z.; Feng, Q. Enhanced Performance of Brain Tumor Classification via Tumor Region Augmentation and Partition. *PLoS ONE* **2015**, *10*, e0140381. [CrossRef]
20. Cheng, J. *Brain Tumor Dataset*; Figshare: London, UK, 2017. [CrossRef]
21. Ronneberger, O.; Fischer, P.; Brox, T. U-Net: Convolutional Networks for Biomedical Image Segmentation. *Med. Image Comput. Comput.-Assist. Interv. (MICCAI)* **2015**, *9351*, 234–241. [CrossRef]
22. Cao, F.; Yao, K.; Liang, J. Deconvolutional neural network for image super-resolution. *Neural Netw.* **2020**, *132*, 394–404. [CrossRef]
23. Oyedotun, O.K.; Ismaeil, K.A.; Aouada, D. Training very deep neural networks: Rethinking the role of skip connections. *Neurocomputing* **2021**, *441*, 105–117. [CrossRef]
24. Azad, R.; Aghdam, E.K.; Rauland, A.; Jia, Y.; Avval, A.H.; Bozorgpour, A.; Karimijafarbigloo, S.; Cohen, J.P.; Adeli, E.; Merhof, D. Medical Image Segmentation Review: The success of U-Net. *arXiv* **2022**, arXiv:2211.14830. [CrossRef] [PubMed]
25. Huang, H.; Lin, L.; Tong, R.; Hu, H.; Zhang, Q.; Iwamoto, Y.; Han, X.; Chen, Y.W.; Wu, J. UNet 3+: A Full-Scale Connected UNet for Medical Image Segmentation. In Proceedings of the ICASSP 2020—2020 IEEE International Conference on Acoustics, Speech and Signal Processing (ICASSP), Barcelona, Spain, 4–8 May 2020; pp. 1055–1059. [CrossRef]
26. Ayushi; Buttar, P.K. Satellite Imagery Analysis for Crop Type Segmentation Using U-Net Architecture. *Procedia Comput. Sci.* **2024**, *235*, 3418–3427. [CrossRef]
27. Kong, H.; Ling, C.; Zhang, K. Satellite Image Parcel Segmentation and Extraction Based on U-Net Convolution Neural Network Model. In Proceedings of the 2023 IEEE International Conference on Control, Electronics and Computer Technology (ICCECT), Jilin, China, 28–30 April 2023; pp. 95–100. [CrossRef]
28. Ulmas, P.; Liiv, I. Segmentation of Satellite Imagery using U-Net Models for Land Cover Classification. *arXiv* **2020**, arXiv:2003.02899. [CrossRef]
29. Kim, T.Y.; Park, S.; Lim, C.K.; Choi, J.H.; An, C.H.; Song, L.H.; Kim, D.N. Deep Learning-Based Detection of Defects in Wafer Buffer Zone During Semiconductor Packaging Process. *Multiscale Sci. Eng.* **2024**, *6*, 25–32. [CrossRef]
30. Ma, J.; Zhang, T.; Yang, C.; Cao, Y.; Xie, L.; Tian, H.; Li, X. Review of Wafer Surface Defect Detection Methods. *Electronics* **2023**, *12*, 1787. [CrossRef]
31. Bouzidi, W.; Bouaafia, S.; Hajjaji, M.A.; Bergasa, L.M. Enhanced U-Net Approach: Semantic Segmentation for Self-Driving Cars Applications. In Proceedings of the 2023 20th International Multi-Conference on Systems, Signals & Devices (SSD), Mahdia, Tunisia, 20–23 February 2023; pp. 387–392. [CrossRef]
32. Thayalan, S.; Muthukumarasamy, S. Semantic Segmentation using Modified U-Net for Autonomous Driving. In Proceedings of the IEEE International IOT, Electronics and Mechatronics Conference (IEMTRONICS), Toronto, ON, Canada, 1–4 June 2022; pp. 1–7. [CrossRef]
33. Hussain, S.; Hamza, S.; Samad, A. Image Segmentation for Autonomous Driving Using U-Net Inception. In Proceedings of the IEEE International Conference on Signal and Image Processing, Toronto, ON, Canada, 1–4 June 2022; pp. 426–429. [CrossRef]
34. Punn, N.S.; Agarwal, S. Modality specific U-Net variants for biomedical image segmentation: A survey. *Artif. Intell. Rev.* **2022**, *55*, 5845–5889. [CrossRef]
35. Dénes-Fazakas, L.; Csaholczi, S.; Eigner, G.; Kovács, L.; Szilágyi, L. Using Resizing Layer in U-Net to Improve Memory Efficiency. In *System Dependability–Theory and Applications*; Zamojski, W., Mazurkiewicz, J., Sugier, J., Walkowiak, T., Kacprzyk, J., Eds.; Springer: Cham, Switzerland, 2024; pp. 38–48.
36. Dénes-Fazakas, L.; Eigner, G.; Kovács, L.; Szilágyi, L. Two U-net Architectures for Infant Brain Tissue Segmentation from Multi-Spectral MRI Data. *IFAC-PapersOnLine* **2023**, *56*, 5637–5642. [CrossRef]
37. Dénes-Fazakas, L.; Eigner, G.; Szilágyi, L. Segmentation of 6-month infant brain tissues from multi-spectral MRI records using a U-Net neural network architecture. In Proceedings of the 2022 IEEE 10th Jubilee International Conference on Computational Cybernetics and Cyber-Medical Systems (ICCC), Reykjavík, Iceland, 6–9 July 2022; pp. 000077–000082. [CrossRef]
38. O'Shea, K.; Nash, R. An Introduction to Convolutional Neural Networks. *arXiv* **2015**, arXiv:1511.08458. [CrossRef]
39. Srivastava, N.; Hinton, G.; Krizhevsky, A.; Sutskever, I.; Salakhutdinov, R. Dropout: A simple way to prevent neural networks from overfitting. *J. Mach. Learn. Res.* **2014**, *15*, 1929–1958.
40. Zafar, A.; Aamir, M.; Mohd Nawi, N.; Arshad, A.; Riaz, S.; Alruban, A.; Dutta, A.K.; Almotairi, S. A Comparison of Pooling Methods for Convolutional Neural Networks. *Appl. Sci.* **2022**, *12*, 8643. [CrossRef]
41. Clevert, D.A.; Unterthiner, T.; Hochreiter, S. Fast and Accurate Deep Network Learning by Exponential Linear Units (ELUs). *arXiv* **2016**, arXiv:1511.08458. [CrossRef]
42. Agarap, A.F. Deep Learning using Rectified Linear Units (ReLU). *arXiv* **2019**, arXiv:1803.08375. [CrossRef]
43. Kouretas, I.; Paliouras, V. Simplified Hardware Implementation of the Softmax Activation Function. In Proceedings of the 2019 8th International Conference on Modern Circuits and Systems Technologies (MOCAST), Thessaloniki, Greece, 13–15 May 2019; pp. 1–4. [CrossRef]
44. Kingma, D.P.; Ba, J. Adam: A Method for Stochastic Optimization. *arXiv* **2017**, arXiv:1412.6980. [CrossRef]
45. Chatterjee, S.; Keprate, A. Predicting Remaining Fatigue Life of Topside Piping Using Deep Learning. In Proceedings of the International Conference on Applied Artificial Intelligence (ICAPAI), Halden, Norway, 19–21 May 2021. [CrossRef]
46. TensorFlow Core v2.4.0. Available online: https://www.tensorflow.org/api_docs (accessed on 21 September 2024).
47. NumPy Documentation. Available online: https://numpy.org/doc/ (accessed on 21 September 2024).

48. Scikit-Learn User Guide. Available online: https://scikit-learn.org/0.18/_downloads/scikit-learn-docs.pdf (accessed on 21 September 2024).
49. Pandas Documentation. Available online: https://pandas.pydata.org/docs/ (accessed on 21 September 2024).
50. Jupyter Notebook Documentation. Available online: https://docs.jupyter.org/en/latest/ (accessed on 21 September 2024).
51. HUN-REN Cloud. Available online: https://science-cloud.hu/ (accessed on 21 September 2024).

biomedicines

MDPI

Article

Tumor-Promoted Changes in Pediatric Brain Histology Can Be Distinguished from Normal Parenchyma by Desorption Electrospray Ionization Mass Spectrometry Imaging

Ana L. Seidinger [1,2,*], Felipe L. T. Silva [1,2], Mayara F. Euzébio [1,2], Anna C. Krieger [3], João Meidanis [1,4], Junier M. Gutierrez [5], Thais M. S. Bezerra [1,6], Luciano Queiroz [1,6], Alex A. Rosini. Silva [5], Iva L. Hoffmann [1], Camila M. M. Daiggi [1], Helder Tedeschi [1,7], Marcos N. Eberlin [8], Livia S. Eberlin [9], José A. Yunes [1,2], Andreia M. Porcari [5] and Izilda A. Cardinalli [1]

1 Boldrini Children's Center, Campinas 13083-210, Brazil; felipeluztorres@outlook.com (F.L.T.S.); ma.euzebio@gmail.com (M.F.E.); meidanis@unicamp.br (J.M.); t243567@dac.unicamp.br (T.M.S.B.); gradanat@yahoo.com.br (L.Q.); iva@boldrini.org.br (I.L.H.); camis.maia@icloud.com (C.M.M.D.); htedeschi@hotmail.com (H.T.); andres@boldrini.org.br (J.A.Y.); izilda@boldrini.org.br (I.A.C.)

2 Graduate Program in Genetics and Molecular Biology, Institute of Biology, State University of Campinas, Campinas 13083-970, Brazil

3 Department of Chemistry, The University of Texas at Austin, Austin, TX 78712, USA; akrieger@utexas.edu

4 Institute of Computing, State University of Campinas, Campinas 13083-852, Brazil

5 MS4Life Laboratory of Mass Spectrometry, Health Sciences Postgraduate Program, São Francisco University, Bragança Paulista 12916-900, Brazil; juniermarreroguti@gmail.com (J.M.G.); alexrosinisilva@hotmail.com (A.A.R.S.); andreia.porcari@usf.edu.br (A.M.P.)

6 Faculty of Medical Sciences, State University of Campinas, Campinas 13083-887, Brazil

7 Department of Neurology, Division of Neurosurgery, State University of Campinas, Campinas 13083-888, Brazil

8 MackMass Laboratory for Mass Spectrometry, School of Engineering, PPGEMN & Mackenzie Institute of Research in Graphene and Nanotechnologies, Mackenzie Presbyterian University, São Paulo 01302-907, Brazil; marcos.eberlin@mackenzie.br

9 Department of Surgery, Baylor College of Medicine, Houston, TX 77030, USA; livia.eberlin@bcm.edu

* Correspondence: analuseidinger@gmail.com; Tel.: +55-19-37879096

Abstract: Background: Central nervous system (CNS) tumors are the second most frequent type of neoplasm in childhood and adolescence, after leukemia. Despite the incorporation of molecular classification and improvement of protocols combining chemotherapy, surgery, and radiotherapy, CNS tumors are still the most lethal neoplasm in this age group. Mass spectrometry imaging (MSI) is a powerful tool to map the distribution of molecular species in tissue sections. Among MSI techniques, desorption electrospray ionization (DESI-MSI) has been demonstrated to enable reliable agreement with the pathological evaluation of different adult cancer types, along with an acceptable time scale for intraoperative use. **Methods:** In the present work, we aimed to investigate the chemical profile obtained by DESI-MSI as an intraoperative surgical management tool by profiling 162 pediatric brain biopsies and reporting the results according to the histopathology and molecular profile of the tumors. **Results:** The 2D chemical images obtained by DESI-MSI allowed us to distinguish tumor-transformed tissue from non-tumor tissue with an accuracy of 96.8% in the training set and 94.3% in the validation set after statistical modeling of our data using Lasso. In addition, high-grade and low-grade tumors also displayed a distinct chemical profile when analyzed by DESI-MSI. We also provided evidence that the chemical profile of brain tumors obtained by DESI-MSI correlates with methylation-based molecular classes and specific immunophenotypes found in brain biopsies. **Conclusions:** The results presented herein support the incorporation of DESI-MSI analysis as an intraoperative assistive tool in prospective clinical trials for pediatric brain tumors management in the near future.

Keywords: pediatric oncology; brain tumor; intraoperative tool; mass spectrometry imaging; DESI

1. Introduction

Among all childhood solid tumors, those originating from the central nervous system (CNS) are the most frequent. Despite advances in pediatric neoplasm treatment due to protocol development guided by molecular classification, brain tumors remain the leading cause of cancer mortality and morbidity in children [1].

Brain tumors may vary from benign to highly malignant entities and can emerge in a diversity of anatomical regions in both infra- and supratentorial compartments [2]. Surgical handling plays a central role in CNS tumor management and occurs by fine-needle biopsy for histological diagnosis, cytoreduction, or complete excision [3]. Intraoperative histopathological diagnosis improves the surgical procedure, assisting the surgeon in the assessment of margins of excision and evaluation of the adequacy of the submitted tissue for downstream diagnostic procedures. Additionally, intrasurgical analysis enables the detection of suspicious lesions uncovered by clinical or radiological imaging, thus reducing the need for a second invasive procedure [4,5]. The current gold-standard technique for intraoperative diagnosis is the frozen tissue sectioning followed by the hematoxylin and eosin (H&E) staining protocol, developed in 1905 [6]. Despite its wide use, robustness, and affordability, there are important limitations imposed by this technique, such as the formation of water crystals that cause distortion of the tissue's architectural detail, harming a reliable diagnosis [5]. Folding, crushing, and overstretching artifacts, as well as cautery from the surgery procedure can also affect the tissue's architecture significantly [5]. Aside from these technical aspects, there is also the requirement of a trained neuropathologist, a good clinical history, neuroimaging, and specialized staff to provide higher intraoperative diagnostic accuracy [7]. Due to these difficulties, the overall concordance between intraoperative frozen section consultation and final diagnosis for brain lesions falls between 67% and 97% [8–13]. Agreement is lower in low-grade gliomas (82.5%) than in high-grade gliomas (93.2%) [13], and in 5% of cases, misdiagnosis of tumor versus non-tumor conditions may happen [12]. Noteworthy, it may take up to four biopsy analyses to increase the accuracy in diagnostic yield from 67% to 89% [8].

Cancer cells acquire functional capabilities that are crucial for their ability to form malignant tumors as they make their way from healthy to neoplastic growth states. Amongst these changes, altered abundance and types of lipids play a role in each of the hallmarks of cancer [14,15]. For example, ceramides with long-chain fatty acids are reported to have pro-apoptotic properties, whilst very long-chain fatty acid-containing ceramides are anti-apoptotic [16]. Several studies found lipid alteration in cancer, e.g., lysophospholipids in ovarian cancer [17], glycerophospholipids in hepatocellular carcinoma [18], acylcarnitines and glycerophospholipids in prostate cancer [19], sphingolipids in glioma [20] and breast cancer [21]. Evidence also suggests that choline-containing lipids and phospholipids increase in abundance during the metastasis process [22]. Once lipid classes show significative differences between tumor and non-tumor samples, changes in the lipid profile have been exploited for biomarker development, with the mass spectrometry-based approach emerging as a valuable tool in the field.

Mass spectrometry (MS) has gained attention from clinical audiences, as it can provide quantification of multiple biomarkers at a time, as well as enable discovery of molecules that pinpoint to novel biological processes related to disease development [23,24]. MS techniques encompasses multiple instrumentation types according to the choice of the inlet method, ionization source, and mass analyzer. One specific subset of MS techniques is defined by the analysis of samples in their native state, aiming to speed up the assay and minimize or eliminate sample preparation [25]. This subset is called ambient ionization MS (AIMS) and was introduced in 2004, with the invention of the Desorption Electrospray Ionization Technique (DESI-MS) and DART [26,27]. There are a variety of related AIMS techniques being used for intrasurgical tissue analysis such as rapid evaporative ionization MS (REIMS) [28,29], SpiderMass [30,31], the MasSpec Pen [32–34], and the Picosecond Infrared Laser MS (PIRL-MS) [35,36].

DESI-MS offers the possibility of profiling the molecules present on the surface of the tissue as a function of their spatial distribution, thus generating an MS image that maps the molecule's location without the need to use antibodies or markers. Although DESI has lower spatial resolution than other MSI techniques, it has advantages in the minimal need for sample preparation and open air analysis. DESI-MS imaging (DESI-MSI) of tissue sections is conducted under ambient conditions using nondestructive histologically compatible solvent systems that preserve the tissue architecture and allow subsequent analyses on tissue sections already screened by DESI, adding and correlating molecular and biological information retained from other techniques on the very same section [37]. The tissue section placed on a glass slide is mapped on the x and y-axis while it is sprayed with a charged solvent at high speed provided by a high-pressure flow of N_2. The spray microdroplets extract biomolecules (mainly lipids and metabolites) from the tissue. The secondary microdroplets carrying the extracted molecules are further converted into gaseous ions through ESI-like mechanisms, allowing their detection and quantification in the mass spectrometer [38–40]. The molecular profile obtained for each x- and y-coordinates are converted into a 2D chemical image from the tissue. Ion intensities are displayed by using a false-color scale with the relative ion abundance reflected by the intensity of the color [41].

DESI-MSI has been successfully applied to identify different cancer types, such as liver [42], breast [43], kidney [44], prostate [45], bladder [46], gastric [47], pancreatic [48], thyroid [49], lung [50], and colorectal cancer tissues [51]. Different types of brain tumors have also been assessed using DESI-MS or DESI-MSI approaches. This research was led by Cooks et al. and evolved from demonstrating the ability of DESI-MSI to discriminate between types of brain tumor in adults, such as oligodendroglioma, astrocytoma, and oligoastrocytoma, up to the validation of DESI-MS for target detection of 2-hydroxyglutarate (2-HG) in a large human glioma cohort of adult subjects, for intraoperative isocitrate dehydrogenase (IDH) mutation assessment [52–57]. With a focus on pediatric patients, Woolman et al. (2024) recently applied PIRL-MS to differentiate between medulloblastoma and pilocytic astrocytoma, as well as two ependymoma molecular subtypes, using a set of 18 metabolic lipid markers [36]. Based on the molecular changes associated with the tumorigenesis processes and focusing on developing reliable surgical devices that can improve and refine the intraoperative consultation tools, we aimed at investigating the use of DESI-MSI, especially for intrasurgical margin evaluation, in a large pediatric brain tumor cohort. Our results show that DESI coupled to low-resolution mass spectrometry imaging allows for robust classification of pediatric brain biopsies specimens and may serve as an assistive tool for pathology diagnosis during the intraoperative analysis of frozen sections. Furthermore, the profile obtained by DESI-MSI in this pediatric cohort showed correlation with the methylation-based molecular classification of tumors and specific immunophenotypes, illustrating that the approach has the potential to be used to deliver real-time molecular information intraoperatively thusimproving the decision-making process in pediatric neuro-oncology.

2. Materials and Methods

2.1. Study Design

A retrospective/prospective study was carried out encompassing tissue samples from patients diagnosed with primary or metastatic CNS tumors in our institution, submitted to a neurosurgical procedure aiming at diagnostic and/or therapeutic purposes. Retrospective tissue samples were collected between the years 2000 and 2003 and the prospective ones were collected between the years 2019 and 2021. The samples were snap frozen and long-term (if retrospective) stored at −80 °C. The exclusion criteria to assign a sample ineligible for downstream analysis included the following: (i) samples presenting low signal intensity after ionization, (ii) low tissue adhesion to the glass slide, or (iii) very small sample size, preventing the accurate assessment of its histological characteristics for further annotation.

2.2. Patients and Clinical Data

A total of 162 samples were obtained from 132 patients. The age of patients at diagnosis ranged from 6.2 months to 21.4 years, with a mean of 7.3 years and a median of 6.8 years. The diagnoses of patients included in this study are detailed in Supplementary Table S1. The tumor biopsies were diagnosed according to the WHO 2016 classification [58] by two medical pathologists. Data regarding sex, age, clinical manifestations, images, staging and clinical evolution were collected by clinical oncologists from the patient's medical records.

2.3. Sample Preparation

Tissue specimens were sectioned using a CM 1850 Leica cryostat (Leica® Microsystems, Wetzlar, Germany) with the chamber at −20 °C. Sections measuring 14 μm thick were mounted onto silanized glass slides and stored at −80 °C until the DESI-MSI analysis.

2.4. DESI-MSI

MS measurements were performed by using a 2D Omni Spray DESI imaging platform (Prosolia Inc., Indianapolis, IN, USA) coupled to a linear ion trap mass spectrometer (LTQ XL, Thermo Fisher Scientific, Waltham, MA, USA). Lab-built sprayers were adapted to the commercial Omni Spray DESI imaging stages [59]. DESI-MSI was performed on mounted tissue slides using dimethylformamide-acetonitrile (1:1 v/v), in the negative-ion mode. Solvent flow rate was 1.1 μL/min and N_2 pressure was 150 psi. Ions over the mass range *m/z* 180–1200 (which we will refer to as the lipid profile) were acquired in the profile mode, performed with the sum of 2 microscans and an injection time of 350 ms. The automatic gain control was deactivated.

The raw data obtained by the mass spectrometer were grouped and converted into a 2D image using the software FireFly version 2.1.05 (Prosolia, Inc.), with a bin size of 0.083 Da, generating 12,240 values of *m/z* for each coordinate scanned. The generated images were later visualized with the Biomap software version 3.8.0.4 (Novartis, Basel, Switzerland).

2.5. Histopathological Analyses and Spectra Annotation

The same tissue sections which underwent DESI-MSI were subjected to standard H&E staining and visualized under a light microscope by the medical pathologist (I. A. Cardinalli). The regions of interest (ROI) in each biopsy were labeled according to their histological characteristics as normal tissue, necrosis, inflammation, keratin, calcification, grade I, II, III or IV malignant tumors, metastases, benign tumors, and malignant mesenchymal neoplasia. The corresponding MS spectra from each ROI were extracted using MSiReader software version 1.0 (North Carolina State University) with a *m/z* tolerance of 5 ppm. Both raw data for each pixel and averaged *m/z* abundance in the ROI were exported.

2.6. Statistical Analysis

The averaged mass spectra were normalized to the total ion current (TIC), log-transformed (base 10), and auto-scaled (mean-centered and divided by the standard deviation of each variable) [60–62]. The unsupervised clustering analyses were based in *t*-test/ANOVA and were conducted by using the MetaboAnalyst 5.0 platform [63]. The clustering method and distance measure are indicated for each analysis in the respective figure captions. To identify differentially abundant ions between groups, a non-parametric *t*-test was employed, using an FDR (false discovery rate) adjusted p-value ≤ 0.05, and at least 2× fold change cutoff. Due to the high number of variables (*m/z* values) considered in the analysis (>1000), 40% of the variables presenting near constant values between the groups were filtered out through the interquantile range filter.

2.7. Data Modeling

Data obtained from each pixel was compiled into an .xlsx file and the *m/z* values that were not detected in more than 10% of the pixels were removed. The mass spectra were normalized by log-transformed median ion intensity. Median normalization adjusts the log intensity values based on the global median value [64]. Data were grouped according to the nominal value of the masses. The spreadsheets containing the *m/z* values per pixel were processed using the Lasso regression analysis method (Least Absolute Shrinkage and Selection Operator) [65]. Inverse probability weighting was used to minimize the imbalance between classes. The Lasso model performance was evaluated using 5-fold cross-validation on the training dataset, as well as assessing performance on a withheld validation dataset comprising samples not included in model generation.

2.8. Collision Induced Dissociation Tandem Mass Spectrometry (CID-MS/MS)

CID-MS/MS was performed following the same conditions as the DESI-MSI for the initial acquisition. The precursor ion selection mode was used, and sufficient fragmentation energy was applied to fragment the ion of interest keeping its intensity at ~30% of the base peak. The acquired spectra were integrated for at least 30 s, using the average spectrum obtained for the assignment. The resulting fragmentation profiles were compared to the information present in the Lipid Maps database [66]

2.9. Immunohistochemistry Staining

After deparaffinization and rehydration, 5 µm-thick histological sections of primary CNS tumors (n = 50) were mounted on silanized slides, treated with H_2O_2, and then subjected to heat-mediated antigen retrieval. The sections were incubated with the primary antibodies according to Supplementary Table S2. The visualization system used was the EnVision FLEX Mini Kit, High pH (Agilent, Santa Clara, CA, USA). Positive controls were used in all batches.

Vascular micro density was evaluated through the average number of micro vessels in selected areas of the tumor. Slides labeled with the anti-CD34 antibody were initially examined at a lower magnification (40× or 100×) to identify areas of higher vascular concentration ("hotspots") i.e., areas with higher intensity of CD34 expression. Ten high power fields (400×) were examined. The micro vessel count was expressed as the average of all evaluated fields.

2.10. Methylation-Based Molecular Classification of Tumors

Genomic DNA was extracted from tumor samples using the GenElute™ Mammalian Genomic DNA Miniprep Kit (Merck, Rahway, NJ, USA) according to the manufacturer's instructions and quantified using the Qubit dsDNA HS Assay Kit (Thermo Fisher Scientific). A total of 200 ng of genomic DNA were converted by sodium bisulfite treatment with the EZ DNA Methylation-Gold Kit (Zymo Research, Irvine, CA, USA) as per the manufacturer's instructions. The samples were hybridized with the Infinium MethylationEPIC Kit array, according to the manufacturer's specifications (Illumina, San Diego, CA, USA).

Molecular classification of tumors was performed using a molecular neuropathology platform (MNP), jointly developed by the University Hospital of Heidelberg, the German Center for Cancer Research (DKFZ), and the German Consortium for Translational Research in Cancer (DKTK) [67]; it has been used for molecular classification of CNS tumors in Germany since 2015. The platform is based on the random forest algorithm and performs a prediction based on comparison with data from a reference cohort containing more than 2800 tumors of neural origin of almost all known entities (currently, more than 80 tumor classes or subclasses are included). The main result is a classification-calibrated score that indicates the similarity of the sample of interest to one of the included CNS tumor classes. A calibrated score between 0 and 1 is generated for each class. All class prediction scores theoretically add up to 1. For a reliable prediction, a methylation class score must be above the cutoff of 0.84 [68].

3. Results

3.1. 2D Ion Images Obtained by DESI-MSI Consistently Agree with Histological Architecture of the Tissue

The results obtained after analysis of the 162 pediatric brain tissue biopsies demonstrate that 2D chemical images generated by DESI-MSI agree with the histologic information observed, as illustrated in Figure 1, where normal and tumoral tissue findings were represented, and Figure 2, where analysis of a tissue section containing necrosis and tumoral tissue is depicted. The chemical image reproduces the architecture of the tissue analyzed, evidencing uneven distribution of ions throughout the sample, according to the tissue regions with different histological characteristics. In addition, the results of prospective (n = 76) and retrospective (n = 86) DESI-MSI analyses showed that no biases were identified due to the type of recruitment (prospective vs. retrospective samples), as shown in Supplementary Figure S1.

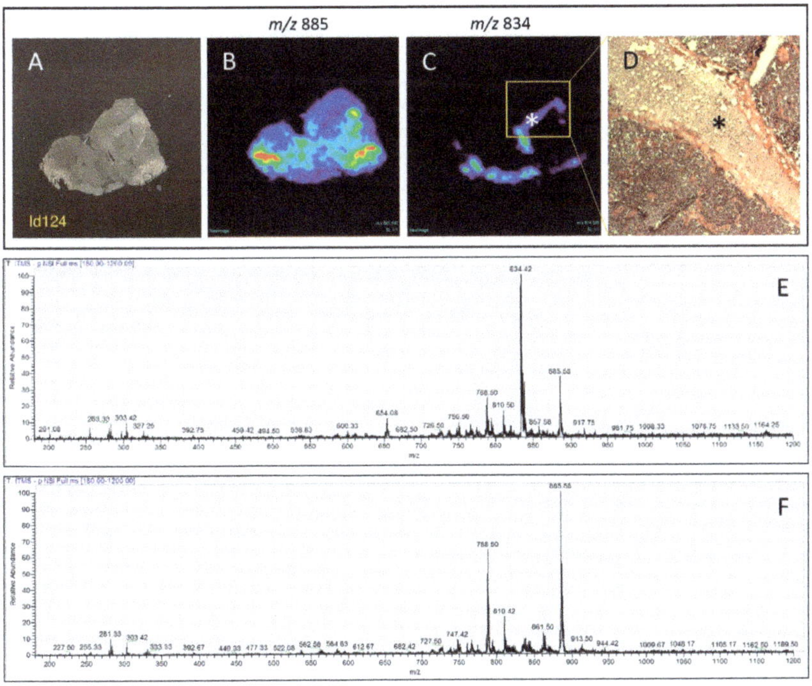

Figure 1. DESI-MSI analysis of a tissue section containing non-tumor and tumor tissue in the same biopsy. (**A**) Frozen section before DESI-MSI analysis. (**B**) Distribution of the ion *m/z* 885 across the tissue. (**C**) Uneven distribution of the ion *m/z* 834; the asterisk indicates the tissue region corresponding to the non-tumor brain parenchyma. (**D**) Histological examination of the section after analysis by DESI-MSI, stained with hematoxylin-eosin (40×). The asterisk corresponds to the same non-tumor brain parenchyma region seen in panel (**C**). (**E**) Mass spectrum corresponding to the non-tumor tissue region. (**F**) Mass spectrum corresponding to the tumor tissue region.

A subset of samples (n = 37; 23%) was excluded from the subsequent steps of this study due to the exclusion criteria (Supplementary Figure S2). The percentage of exclusion in the retrospective group was higher than in the prospective group, but not statistically significant (26% vs. 20%, respectively; $\chi 2$ test (1, N = 162) = 0.7, p = 0.37).

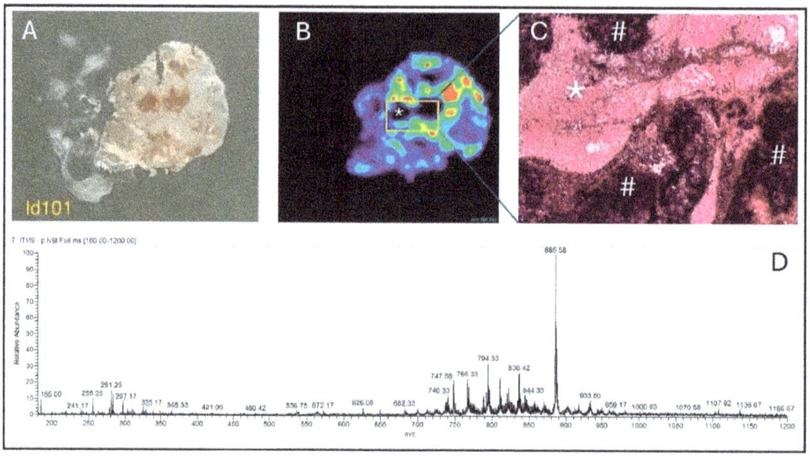

Figure 2. DESI-MSI analysis of a tissue section containing tumor tissue and necrosis in the same biopsy. (**A**) Frozen section before DESI-MSI analysis. (**B**) Uneven distribution of the ion *m/z* 885 across the tissue; the asterisk indicates the tissue region corresponding to necrosis. (**C**) Histological examination of the section stained with hematoxylin-eosin, after the analysis by DESI-MSI (40×). The photograph is equivalent to the region detailed by the yellow rectangle in panel (**B**). The asterisk corresponds to the same necrosis region seen in panel (**B**). The # symbol refers to regions of high cellularity, corresponding to tumoral cells. (**D**) Mass spectrum relative to the tumor tissue region.

3.2. DESI-MSI Data Can Be Used to Distinguish Tumor Tissue from Normal Parenchyma in Pediatric Brain Biopsies

To investigate putative differences between the lipid profile from normal brain tissue and tumor brain tissue in the pediatric age group, 21 sets of mass spectra from normal brain parenchyma and 98 sets of mass spectra from tumor tissue were analyzed, regardless of diagnosis and/or staging.

We identified 119 variables (ions) with a significantly different abundance between the two tissue classes analyzed (non-parametric *t*-test; FDR adjusted *p*-value: 0.05; Fold change > 2×) (Figure 3A). The list of the 119 differentially abundant ions found between normal and tumor tissues and the respective fold-change is presented in Supplementary Table S3. The hierarchical clustering analysis shows that the two categories of tissues present a different abundance of ions, and can be distinguished through their chemical profile, as illustrated in Figure 3B. There are only 5 of 98 tumors grouped with normal tissues, and 2 of 21 normal tissues grouped with tumors (Figure 3B).

To further explore if the differences found in the lipid profile of samples allowed distinguishing between normal and tumor-transformed brain parenchyma by using mass spectrometry data, we used the Lasso method [65] to build and validate a model (or classifier) that can predict the tissue type based on the DESI-MSI profile. The Lasso method can effectively select a model that includes only the most important predictors, making it simpler to interpret the selected metabolites' contribution to the model [69]. This is particularly useful in high-dimensional datasets, such as the one produced by DESI-MSI, since the spectrum of each pixel produces a large number of ion signal features. The Lasso method has been employed in many DESI-MSI applications [40,43,48,70,71] and presents robustness to overfitting because the penalty term helps ensure that the model generalizes well to new data. Data modeling followed these general steps: (i) split data into training and validation sets; (ii) generate a model with the training data; and, (iii) insert test data in the model and compare the prediction to real labels. The whole dataset used for Lasso modeling comprised 36,408 pixels, from which 25,674 pixels labeled as non-normal (tumor-transformed) or normal were used to train the model, and 10,734 pixels were withheld from model generation and used to assess model performance.

The Lasso method identified *m/z* values that are predictive of the two classes considering the lipid profile *m/z* > 700 from normal brain tissue (tissue with no histological evidence of tumor transformation) and those from the remaining eleven histological categories associated with tumor transformation (necrosis, inflammation, keratin, calcification, grade I, II, III or IV malignant tumors, metastasis, benign tumors or malignant mesenchymal neoplasia). By using this approach, the cross-validation analysis of all samples from the training set achieved an accuracy of 96.2%, and 94.3% in the validation set, compared with standard histopathologic evaluation (H&E) (AUC = 0.96) (Table 1). As a result of the combination approach DESI-MSI/Lasso modeling, we were able to identify molecules that are common to the tissue transformation process, allowing us to discriminate against the complexity of tumor-associated changes in brain histology when compared to normal brain parenchyma, regardless of tumor histology.

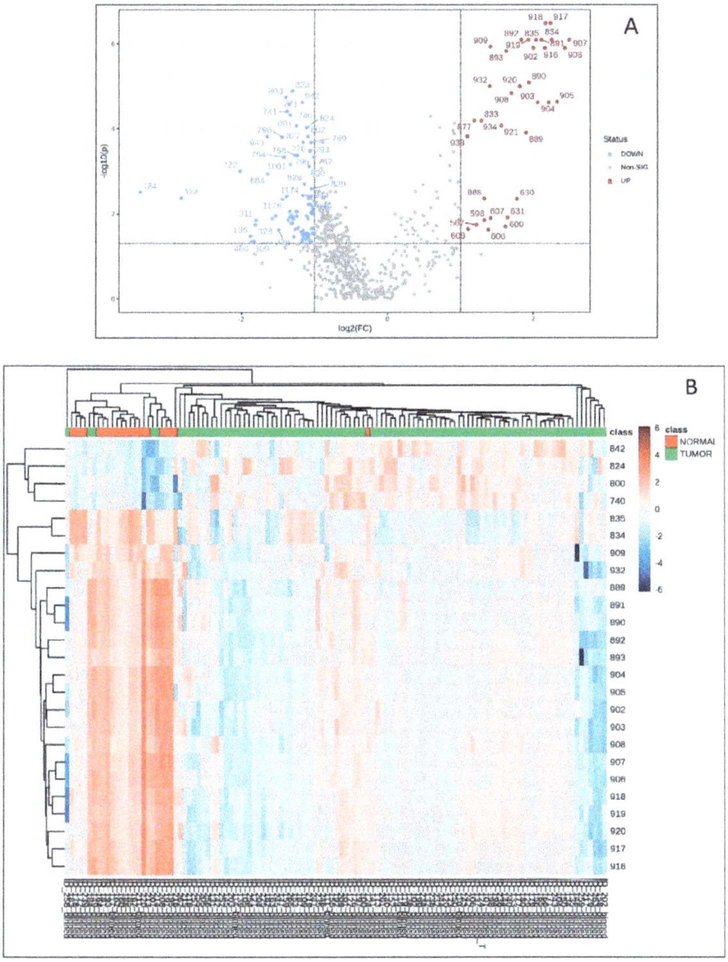

Figure 3. (**A**) Volcano plot depicting downregulated variables in the normal tissue in blue, upregulated variables in red, and non-significant variables in gray. Each dot represents one ion. (**B**) Hierarchical clustering analysis based on the average and Euclidean distance measure depicting the main 25 variables responsible for unsupervised grouping of samples according to their lipid profile into the normal parenchyma and tumoral tissue categories. The color bar represents the data values across the samples, where blue means lower ion abundance and red means higher ion abundance.

Table 1. DESI-MSI/Lasso prediction results for 25,674 pixels in the training set and 10,734 pixels in the validation set, in comparison with histopathological analyses.

	Pathology	DESI-MSI prediction		Agreement
Training set performance		Normal	non-Normal	
	Normal	1285	146	90%
	non-Normal	830	23,413	97%
		Overall Accuracy: 96.3%		
	Pathology	DESI-MSI prediction		Agreement
Validation set performance		Normal	non-Normal	
	Normal	364	124	75%
	non-Normal	493	9753	95%
		Overall Accuracy: 94.2%		

3.3. DESI-MSI Reveals Differences Between the Lipid Profile Found in Low-Grade Tumors Compared to High-Grade Tumors

CNS WHO grading relates to the clinical-biological behavior of tumors, which ultimately leads to differences in prognosis of patients. Treatment strategies, including surgical resection, are very different for low-grade and high-grade tumors [2]. Therefore, it is crucial to accurately assign tumor grade as soon as possible in the clinical management process. We investigated putative differences in the lipid profile between low-grade and high-grade tumors by analyzing 52 sets of mass spectra from low-grade tumors and 35 sets of mass spectra from high-grade tumors. For these analyses, only primary CNS tumors were considered. We identified 104 variables (ions) with significantly different abundances between the two groups and analyzed and built a volcano plot to depict the results (Figure 4) (Fold change > 2×; non-parametric t-test FDR-adjusted p-value 0.01). Our results showed that low-grade and high-grade tumors present a distinct lipid profile. The output list containing the 104 ions differentially abundant between the two groups (Supplementary Table S4) may serve as a basis for investigating the signaling pathways and mechanisms underlying acquisition of aggressiveness of brain tumors, especially in those cases in which a given tumor can evolve and be classified into different degrees of malignancy, such as astrocytoma, which can be classified as grade I (pilocytic astrocytoma), grade II (diffuse astrocytoma), grade III (anaplastic astrocytoma), or grade IV (glioblastoma).

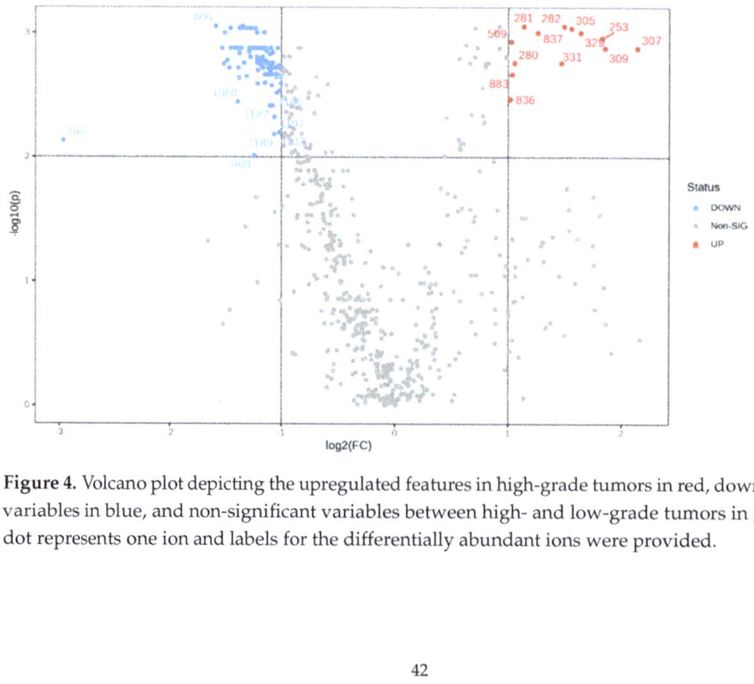

Figure 4. Volcano plot depicting the upregulated features in high-grade tumors in red, downregulated variables in blue, and non-significant variables between high- and low-grade tumors in gray. Each dot represents one ion and labels for the differentially abundant ions were provided.

3.4. Tandem Mass Spectrometry Allowed the Identification of Molecular Species Associated with Tumor Transformation in Pediatric Brain Tissue

The Lasso modelling of our data identified the ions of *m/z* 794, *m/z* 722, *m/z* 760, *m/z* 796, *m/z* 810, *m/z* 816, *m/z* 768, *m/z* 885, *m/z* 734, and *m/z* 772 as the top 10 features most predictive of tumor transformation in pediatric brain tissue, while the ions of *m/z* 834 and *m/z* 835 were predictive ofnormal brain parenchyma, according to their absolute value of the weight coefficient in the model (Table 1). In order to link specific molecular entities to the ions selected by the Lasso method, we conducted tandem mass spectrometry (MS/MS) utilizing collision-induced dissociation (CID) with a linear ion trap mass spectrometer for the five most relevant features of our model. CID involves the fragmentation of selected precursor ions in a reaction cell by colliding them with an inert gas. After the collision step, product ions are generated and then are subsequently analyzed by a second cycle of mass analysis, providing the fragmentation profile of the selected precursor ion based on its chemical structure. The resulting fragmentation profile is then queried against public databases, making it possible to identify ions of interest [72]. Although the LTQ-XL has nominal precision, our tentative ion identification allowed us to putatively identify the ion of *m/z* 794 as the chlorinated adduct of phosphatidylcholine (PC 34:1) and the ion most strongly associated with tumor transformation. The ion of *m/z* 834, [PS 40:6 –H]- was the most strongly associated with normal brain parenchyma (Table 2).

Table 2. Molecular identification of features selected by Lasso as significant contributors to the model for discrimination between tumor-transformed and normal pediatric brain tissue, with attributed statistical weights.

	Feature (Nominal *m/z*)	MS/MS Matched Fragments (Delta)	Putative Lipid Assignment	Proposed Formula	Exact *m/z*	Lasso Weight
Features associated with tumor-promoted changes	794	744.55 (0.48) 506.33 (0.91) 480.31 (0.11)	PC(34:1)	$C_{42}H_{82}ClNO_8P$	794.5472	0.118
	722	436.25 (0.02) 303.23 (0.07) 259.24 (0.23)	PE(35:5) or PE(P-36:4)	$C_{40}H_{70}NO_8P$ or $C_{41}H_{74}NO_7P$	722.4766	0.077
	760	673.48 (0.11) 281.25 (0.04) 255.23 (0.09)	PS(34:1)	$C_{40}H_{76}NO_{10}P$	760.5129	0.073
Features associated with histologically normal brain parenchyma	834	747.50 (0.17) 419.26 (0.26) 283.26 (0.04)	PS(40:6)	$C_{46}H_{78}NO_{10}P$	834.5285	−0.282
	835	579.29 (0.07) 553.28 (0.12) 417.24 (0.22) 391.23 (0.13) 281.25 (0.01) 255.23 (0.06) 241.01 (0.03)	PI(34:1)	$C_{43}H_{81}O_{13}P$	835.5342	−0.236

3.5. Mass Spectra Profile According to the Expression of Clinically Relevant Phenotype and Proliferation Biomarkers in Pediatric Brain Tumors

Immunohistochemistry (IHC) utilizes antibodies for the detection of specific antigens in tissue sections and it is widely used to refine the diagnosis of tumors because specific tumor antigens show marked alteration in cancer. It can help to define tumors of uncertain histogenesis and predict the prognosis of tumors by identification of biomarkers, such as enzymes, tumor-specific antigens, oncogenes, tumor suppressor genes, and tumor cell proliferation markers [73]. We interrogated the lipid profile of pediatric brain tumors according to the expression of clinically relevant phenotype and proliferation biomarkers determined by IHC in brain cancer. We found differentially abundant ions in pediatric CNS tumors immunopositive for CD34, BCL2, P53, B-catenin, EGFR, IGF1R, PDGFR-a, and VEGF when compared to immunonegative tumors (Nonparametric *t*-test, p-value ≤ 0.05). Although we have not found any differentially abundant ions when adjusting the p-value for FDR (q value 0.05), the unsupervised analysis showed that tumors immunopositive for CD34, BCL2, P53, EGFR, IGF1R, and VEGF clustered together based on their lipid profile when compared to tumors negative to the expression of these markers (Supplementary Figures S3–S8).

3.6. Mass Spectra Profile of Pediatric Brain Tumors According to Its Methylation-Based Classification

Genome-wide DNA methylation patterns have emerged as a promising tool to precisely define tumor classes and to improve diagnostic accuracy. The development of a CNS tumor classifier based on a DNA methylation array acts as a diagnostic adjunct in neuropathology, increasing diagnostic precision and reliable prognostic evaluation. For instance, for medulloblastomas and ependymomas, therapy decisions in University Hospitals of Heidelberg were often more heavily influenced by methylation class rather than morphological WHO diagnosis [74]. To understand how the lipid profile of brain tumors is related to their molecular classification, we obtained the global methylation profile for 128 tumor samples. Considering the cut-off of 0.84 [68], 97 samples (76%) were assigned into a known methylation class through the MNP classifier v.12.3 [67] and 81% of proposed classifications were in agreement with the histopathological diagnosis (n = 79).

To verify whether there is a correlation between the lipid profile of pediatric brain tumors and their methylation-based molecular classification, the samples were grouped according to the methylation class to which they belong, according to Table 3. Only groups containing more than three samples per group were included, totalizing 46 sets of chemical spectra of tumors.

Table 3. Distribution of tumor samples analyzed according to their methylation-based molecular classification.

Methylation Classes	N. Patients
Low grade glioma, pilocytic astrocytoma subtype	20
Atypical teratoid rhabdoid tumor	4
Choroid plexus tumor, subtype pediatric B	4
Posterior fossa ependymoma, subtype A	4
Medulloblastoma, Group 4 subtype	4
Medulloblastoma, SHH subtype	4
Control tissue, cerebellum	3
Schwannoma	3
Total	**46**

An unsupervised hierarchical clustering analysis based on the lipid profile allowed the identification of a cluster of glioma tumors at the left side of the panel, with subsequent division between pilocytic astrocytoma and ependymoma subtype A. Medulloblastoma tumors clustered together, with a further split into Group 4 and SHH-activated subgroups. Choroid plexus tumors subtype B and atypical teratoid rhabdoid tumors (ATRT) also clustered accordingly, at the right side of the panel. Control tissue clustered at the center of the panel, displaying a higher abundance of the ions of m/z 888 and 834, typically found in white and gray matter of normal brain parenchyma, respectively (Figure 5).

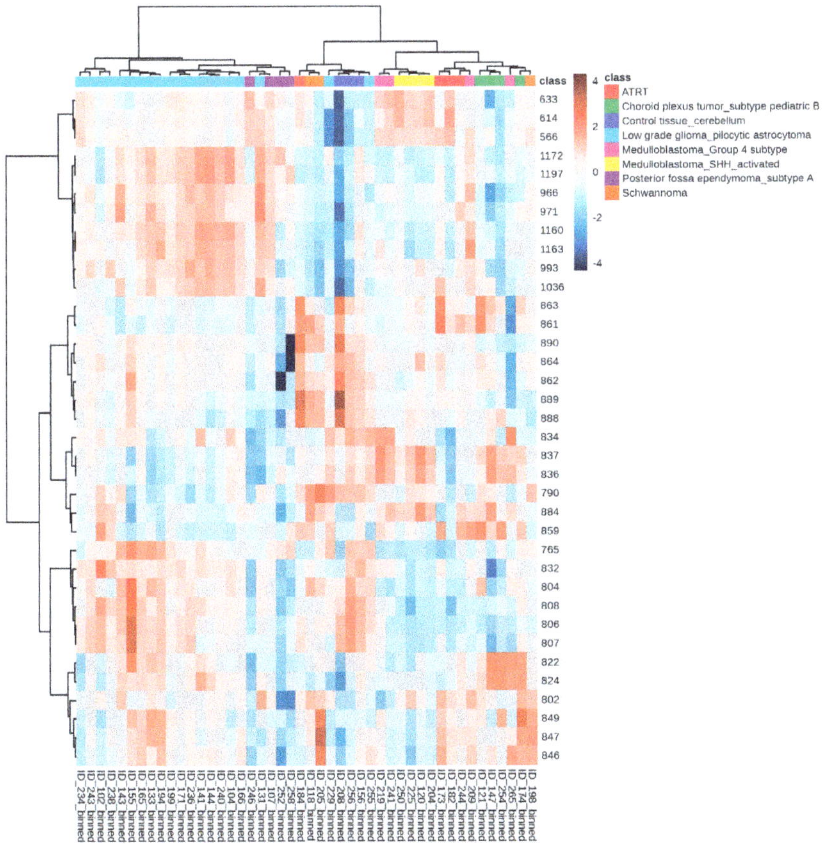

Figure 5. Hierarchical clustering analysis based on the Ward linkage method and Pearson distance depicting the unsupervised grouping of samples based on their lipid profile, according to their respective methylation classes. The color bar represents the data values across the samples, where blue means lower ion abundance and red means higher ion abundance.

Despite the clear clustering trend, the number of molecular classes is very large (currently more than 80 classes) and, therefore, our cohort has few representatives in each class. Nevertheless, our results suggest that larger cohorts can potentially reveal distinct chemical profiles for each molecular class of pediatric brain tumors.

4. Discussion

In this study, we used DESI-MSI to investigate molecular differences between tumor-transformed tissue and non-tumor tissue in a large cohort of diverse pediatric brain tumors. The 2D chemical images obtained by DESI-MSI were highly correlated to the histological findings present in the brain tumor biopsies. This enabled us to build correlation models between the chemical composition and the tissue histology of the samples. Such models can be trained, allowing a lipid profile to be used as a classifier of samples based on the presence of molecules such as fatty acids or glycerophospholipids [41]. Lasso modeling of our data indicated that it is possible to distinguish tumor-transformed tissue from non-tumor tissue by using DESI-MSI with an accuracy of 96.2% in the training set and 94.3% in the validation set (AUC = 0.96).

Precise brain tumor resection is a fundamental prognostic factor in pediatric neuro-oncology, in association with histology. In general, resection aims at safe gross total resection, and intraoperative imaging tools and intraoperative pathology play a substantial role during the surgical procedure [75]. Friable, fat-rich tissues in the brain are difficult to cut and produce good quality cryosections, which may affect the interpretation of the slides. Regarding suspected intracranial lesions, the agreement between intraoperative frozen section pathology diagnoses and final section diagnoses is variable. Considering a single dataset from a single-center study, agreement was seen in 90.3% of cases (n = 558 biopsies). However, agreement is lower in low-grade gliomas (82.5%) than in high-grade gliomas (93.2%) and even lower in re-do operations (81.5%) [13]. Data presented here suggest that incorporation of DESI-MSI analysis as an assistive intraoperative tool in prospective clinical trials for pediatric brain tumors could be useful to the pathologist's decision-making process during the intraoperative analysis of frozen sections and, ultimately, may improve the accuracy of surgical handling.

Eberlin et al. (2012) used DESI-MSI to classify gliomas based on their lipid composition and discriminated between oligodendroglioma, astrocytoma, and oligoastrocytoma, demonstrating DESI's potential in providing diagnosis and information on tumor margins [57]. Santagata et al. (2014) highlighted the role of metabolites like 2-hydroxyglutarate (2-HG) in distinguishing between glioma subtypes and its ability to identify isocitrate dehydrogenase 1-mutant (IDH) tumors, by mapping tissue sections of surgically resected gliomas with DESI-MSI [76]. Cooks and co-workers advanced by testing negative and positive ionization modes of DESI-MS [55] and then opted for the use of negative mode to profile lipids and metabolites from the brain to differentiate gray and white matter, gliomas, meningiomas, and pituitary tumors [52].

Aiming at speeding up the analysis time, DESI-MS was tested for rapid profiling of tissue smears. In this respect, Cooks and co-workers compared the performance of DESI-MSI and DESI-MS rapid analysis of tissue smears for glioma and normal brain tissue and showed the equivalence of the results [54]. They also validated the capability of DESI-MS to differentiate the IDH mutation status of the tumor via detection of 2-HG and to examine the resection cavity walls for residual tumor, estimating tumor cell percentage (TCP) at surgical margins with 93% sensitivity and 83% specificity [53]. The same authors performed DESI-MS in tissue smears to identify IDH mutation status, glioma diagnosis, and estimation of tumor cell infiltration intraoperatively in a large human glioma cohort [56]. Other AIMS techniques, such as PIRL-MS, were also demonstrated as valuable for brain tumor diagnosis. Woolman et al. (2024), while inspecting pediatric brain tumor samples, differentiated between medulloblastoma and pilocytic astrocytoma, as well as two ependymoma molecular subtypes with high sensitivity (94%) and specificity (99%), indicating a significant advancement in cancer classification precision [36].

One of the major gaps in research addressed by our study is the lack of robust evidence to support the incorporation of novel approaches, like DESI-MSI, in molecular margin assessment of pediatric brain tumors. Given the relative lower incidence when compared to adult cancer, pediatric brain series are usually (i) small in numbers [77], (ii) biased towards medulloblastoma, one of the most common pediatric CNS tumors [35,36], or (iii) based on cell line xenografts [78], weakening the power of findings and hindering advancements in the field, since biomarkers relevant for adult cancers and prediction models generated for these patients cannot be automatically transposed to pediatric cancer patients [79].

Our results also demonstrate that prospective and retrospective samples can be jointly analyzed by DESI-MSI, with no apparent bias. In the present study, we included a retrospective clinical case who had disease recurrence at the time of collection of the prospective cohort, allowing us to analyze his tumor at diagnosis and at recurrence, 17 years apart (Supplementary Figure S9). This finding not only opens the possibility of designing specific studies to assess the chemical profile of tumors at diagnosis and at recurrence, aiming at uncovering drug resistance mechanisms and new therapeutic targets, but allows studies to be designed using fresh and banked tissue in the same batch analysis, strengthening the power of analysis.

Although chemical identification of the lipid species is not necessary for a correlation to histopathology data, the identification of these compounds is an important step to gain a deeper understanding of the biochemical processes associated with malignant transformation. Tentative lipid attribution here was based on nominal mass, but previous findings support our data. The ion of *m/z* 794, strongly associated with the tissue changes accompanying tumor transformation, was identified as the chloride adduct of phosphatidylcholine (PC 34:1). Increase in the abundance of *m/z* 794 (PC 34:1) was also reported in other cancers, notably in glioma samples when compared to normal brain tissue from adult patients and prostate cancer [55,80]. An increase in the abundance of *m/z* 885 was also noted in tumor tissue from our series (Figure 1B,F). Our tentative identification of this ion as phosphatidylinositol (PI 38:4) is in accordance with previous DESI studies, which also described higher abundance of *m/z* 885 (PI 38:4) in glioma samples from adult patients, as well in the glioblastoma U87 xenograft model [52,57,81]. The notable increase in the abundance of *m/z* 794 and *m/z* 885 in pediatric brain tissue modified by tumor growth was accompanied by a suppression of *m/z* 834, (PS 40:6) (Table 1, Figure 1C,F), characteristic of normal parenchyma gray matter [52,55]. As per the evidence collected in our study, we observed an overlap between the relevant ions identified by Lasso modeling in our cohort and those previously identified in adult brain tumor patients [52,55]. Such correlation supports the hypothesis of a common panel of biomarkers to be used in neuro-oncology surgery facilities for brain tissue assignment. However, to fully address whether a single model could be employed for both adult and pediatric brain biopsy categorization, a joint clinical study should be conducted.

Brain tumors harboring mutations in genes IDH1 or IDH2 can be identified by DESI-MS due to the accumulation of the oncometabolite 2-hydroxyglutarate (2-HG) [56,76]. Likewise, our evidence suggests that pediatric brain tumors expressing known clinically relevant phenotype biomarkers present a distinct lipid profile. Tumors immunopositive for CD34, BCL2, P53, EGFR, IGF1R, and VEGF showed a typical clusterization pattern based on their lipid profile when compared to negative tumors. In order to precisely identify those lipids differentially abundant between the categories, a large number of tumors should be analyzed. This information is not only relevant for patient prognosis and therapy assessment, but might add up information to the discrimination models based in DESI-MSI data.

In 2021, the WHO adopted the methylation profile as the gold standard method for the molecular classification of CNS tumors [2]. After profiling 128 tumors from our cohort, we found that the lipid profile of tumors showed a clear tendency to cluster according to their methylation-based molecular profile, though the study of a larger number of tumors belonging to each of the different molecular classes will be necessary to definitively establish this association. To our knowledge, this is the first time that DESI-MSI has revealed that the lipid profile of CNS tumors is related to its methylation-based molecular classification. This finding is of utmost clinical relevance and supports further advance in multi-omics studies combining methylome and metabolome datasets to provide real-time intraoperative molecular information from tumors.

In summary, our results strongly suggest that tumor-promoted histology changes can be distinguished from non-tumor tissue in pediatric brain biopsies by using DESI-MSI, irrespective of the tumor diagnosis. Our findings not only made a valuable contribution to the concept of molecular margin assessment, supporting the incorporation of DESI-MSI as an intraoperative assistive tool in prospective clinical trials for management of pediatric neuro-oncology, but positioned these tumors into the vanguard of technical development together with adult glioma, oral squamous cell carcinoma, pancreas, and gastric cancer, for which the value of DESI-MSI as an intraoperative assistive tool was already proved [47,48,57,71].

Supplementary Materials: The following supporting information can be downloaded at: https://www.mdpi.com/article/10.3390/biomedicines12112593/s1, Supplementary Figure S1A. DESI-MSI analysis of two tumor samples diagnosed as medulloblastoma. The left panels show the frozen section before the DESI-MSI analysis. The right panels show the 2D chemical image generated from the DESI-MSI analysis, evidencing the distribution of ion 885. The comparison between the prospective and retrospective sample shows that there is no significant difference in the ionization and resolution of the image generated when the two forms of collection are compared. Supplementary Figure S1B. Unsupervised analysis (Principal Component Analysis, PCA) of the data obtained from the prospective and retrospective samples. Supplementary Figure S1C. The nonlinear dimensionality reduction analysis using the t-SNE algorithm shows that it is not possible to distinguish the two groups of samples in relation to the type of recruitment; Supplementary Figure S2. Representative results of ionization failures. In the two left panels, it is observed a lack of correlation between the chemical image generated and the frozen section analyzed. On the right panels, it is possible to observe the chemical spectra obtained demonstrating the relative abundance of ions between m/z 180 and m/z 1200. As a result of inadequate ionization, nonspecific ions can significantly interfere with the interpretation of results, evidenced by the background noise observed in the spectra; Supplementary Figure S3. Hierarchical clustering analysis based on complete clustering method and Euclidean distance representing the 25 main variables responsible for grouping the samples into the respective groups: tumors with CD34-positive vessels below and above the median; Supplementary Figure S4. Hierarchical clustering analysis based on complete-linkage clustering and Euclidean distance representing the 25 main variables responsible for grouping the samples into the respective groups: positive and negative tumors for BCL2 immunoexpression; Supplementary Figure S5. Hierarchical clustering analysis based on Ward clustering method and Pearson distance representing 25 variables responsible for grouping the samples into the respective groups: positive and negative tumors for p53 immunoexpression; Supplementary Figure S6. Hierarchical clustering analysis based on Ward clustering method and Euclidean distance representing the main 20 variables responsible for grouping the samples into the respective groups: positive and negative tumors for EGFR immunoexpression; Supplementary Figure S7. Hierarchical clustering analysis representing the main 25 variables responsible for grouping the samples into the respective groups: positive and negative tumors for IGF1R immunoexpression; Supplementary Figure S8. Hierarchical clustering analysis based on complete-linkage clustering and Euclidean distance representing the 25 main variables responsible for grouping the samples into the respective groups: positive and negative tumors for VEGF immunoexpression; Supplementary Figure S9. DESI-MSI analysis of tumor samples from the same patient, at the time of initial diagnosis (year 2003) and at tumor recurrence (year 2020). The left panels depict the chemical images generated from DESI-MSI analysis of frozen sections, evidencing the distribution of the m/z 788 ion in the tissue. The right panels show the chemical spectra of representative areas of the analyzed tissues, evidencing a high similarity between the chemical profile of the samples, with slight alterations in the relative abundances of the ions. X axis: m/z range 180–1200. Y axis: relative abundance of ions. The pathology diagnosis confirmed tumor recurrence; Supplementary Table S1: Histopathology diagnosis of patients included in the study; Supplementary Table S2: List of primary antibodies used in the immunohistochemical studies; Supplementary Table S3: List of 119 differentially abundant ions found between normal and tumor tissues; Supplementary Table S4: List of 104 differentially abundant ions found between low- and high-grade tumors.

Author Contributions: A.L.S.: conceptualization; methodology; data curation; investigation; validation; formal analysis; supervision; project administration; writing—original draft. F.L.T.S.: methodology; data curation; formal analysis; writing—original draft; investigation. M.F.E.: methodology; data curation; formal analysis; writing—original draft; investigation. A.C.K.: methodology; formal analysis; writing—original draft. J.M.: methodology; software; formal analysis; writing—original draft. J.M.G.: methodology; software; formal analysis; writing—original draft. T.M.S.B.: methodology; software; formal analysis; writing—original draft. L.Q.: methodology; formal analysis; writing—original draft. A.A.R.S.: methodology; formal analysis; writing—original draft. I.L.H.: methodology; formal analysis; writing—original draft. C.M.M.D.: methodology; formal analysis; writing—original draft. H.T.: methodology; resources; writing—original draft. M.N.E.: conceptualization; funding acquisition; writing—original draft. L.S.E.: conceptualization; writing—original draft; supervision. J.A.Y.: supervision; funding acquisition; resources; writing—original draft; conceptualization. A.M.P.: methodology; investigation; formal analysis; supervision; writing—original draft; conceptualization; validation. I.A.C.: conceptualization; supervision; funding acquisition; resources; writing—original draft; project administration. All authors have read and agreed to the published version of the manuscript.

Funding: This research was funded by Brazilian Health Ministry—PRONON grant number 25.000.069610/2015-43; São Paulo Research Foundation (FAPESP), grant numbers 2019/04314-6;

Coordination of Improvement of Higher Education Personnel (CAPES)—Brazil, grant number 88887.504805/2020-00, 88887.511153/2020-00 and 88887.636093/2021-00; NIH/NCI grant number R33CA229068; Welch Foundation, grant number Q-1895-20220331; Eli Lilly Research Award.

Institutional Review Board Statement: This study was conducted in accordance with the ethical standards laid down in the revised version of the 1964 Declaration of Helsinki and approved by the Institutional Review Board of Boldrini Children's Center (CAAE: 38849614.2.0000.5376).

Informed Consent Statement: The Institutional Review Board of Boldrini Children's Hospital waived the signature of the Informed Consent given the samples followed the storage workflow of the institution's Biobank (CAAE: 25574714.9.0000.5376), which previously obtained the consent of patients and/or guardians to store the biological material and later use in research.

Data Availability Statement: The data presented in this study are available upon request from the corresponding author, given the ethics committee approval to execute the study does not apply to making raw data and related clinical and demographic information publicly available.

Conflicts of Interest: L.S. Eberlin: Chief Scientific Officer, MS Pen Technologies Inc. (unpaid), Board Member and shareholder MS Pen Technologies Inc., royalties received from Purdue Research Foundation, officer and shareholder for Inspectra Diagnostics (unpaid), received honorarium from Merck for a research lecture. Co-inventor in patents owned by UT Austin and Baylor College of Medicine related to the MS Pen Technology; Co-inventor in patents owned by UT Austin and Baylor College of Medicine related to DESI-MS imaging of thyroid biopsies; Co-inventor in patents owned by Purdue University related to DESI-MS imaging.

References

1. Pollack, I.F.; Agnihotri, S.; Broniscer, A. Childhood Brain Tumors: Current Management, Biological Insights, and Future Directions. *J. Neurosurg. Pediatr.* **2019**, *23*, 261–273. [CrossRef] [PubMed]
2. Louis, D.N.; Perry, A.; Wesseling, P.; Brat, D.J.; Cree, I.A.; Figarella-Branger, D.; Hawkins, C.; Ng, H.K.; Pfister, S.M.; Reifenberger, G.; et al. The 2021 WHO Classification of Tumors of the Central Nervous System: A Summary. *Neuro-Oncology* **2021**, *23*, 1231–1251. [CrossRef] [PubMed]
3. Silva, A.H.D.; Aquilina, K. Surgical Approaches in Pediatric Neuro-Oncology. *Cancer Metastasis Rev.* **2019**, *38*, 723–747. [CrossRef] [PubMed]
4. Adesina, A.M. Frozen Section Diagnosis of Pediatric Brain Tumors. *Surg. Pathol. Clin.* **2010**, *3*, 769–796. [CrossRef] [PubMed]
5. Jaafar, H. Intra-Operative Frozen Section Consultation: Concepts, Applications and Limitations. *Malays. J. Med. Sci.* **2006**, *13*, 4–12.
6. Gal, A.A. The 100-Year Anniversary of the Description of the Frozen Section Procedure. *JAMA* **2005**, *294*, 3135. [CrossRef]
7. Mat Zin, A.A.; Zulkarnain, S. Diagnostic Accuracy of Cytology Smear and Frozen Section in Glioma. *Asian Pac. J. Cancer Prev.* **2019**, *20*, 321–325. [CrossRef]
8. Brainard, J.A.; Prayson, R.A.; Barnett, G.H. Frozen Section Evaluation of Stereotactic Brain Biopsies: Diagnostic Yield at the Stereotactic Target Position in 188 Cases. *Arch. Pathol. Lab. Med.* **1997**, *121*, 481–484.
9. Kobayashi, K.; Ando, K.; Ito, K.; Tsushima, M.; Morozumi, M.; Tanaka, S.; Machino, M.; Ota, K.; Ishiguro, N.; Imagama, S. Accuracy of Intraoperative Pathological Diagnosis Using Frozen Sections of Spinal Cord Lesions. *Clin. Neurol. Neurosurg.* **2018**, *167*, 117–121. [CrossRef]
10. Uematsu, Y.; Owai, Y.; Okita, R.; Tanaka, Y.; Itakura, T. The Usefulness and Problem of Intraoperative Rapid Diagnosis in Surgical Neuropathology. *Brain Tumor Pathol.* **2007**, *24*, 47–52. [CrossRef]
11. Plesec, T.P.; Prayson, R.A. Frozen Section Discrepancy in the Evaluation of Central Nervous System Tumors. *Arch. Pathol. Lab. Med.* **2007**, *131*, 1532–1540. [CrossRef]
12. Nouri Obeidat, F.; Adnan Awad, H.; Talal Mansour, A.; Hussein Hajeer, M.; Asem Al-jalabi, M.; Emad Abudalu, L. Accuracy of Frozen-Section Diagnosis of Brain Tumors: An 11-Year Experience from a Tertiary Care Center. *Turk. Neurosurg.* **2018**, *29*, 242–246. [CrossRef]
13. Tofte, K.; Berger, C.; Torp, S.; Solheim, O. The Diagnostic Properties of Frozen Sections in Suspected Intracranial Tumors: A Study of 578 Consecutive Cases. *Surg. Neurol. Int.* **2014**, *5*, 170. [CrossRef]
14. Molendijk, J.; Robinson, H.; Djuric, Z.; Hill, M.M. Lipid Mechanisms in Hallmarks of Cancer. *Mol. Omics* **2020**, *16*, 6–18. [CrossRef]
15. Hanahan, D. Hallmarks of Cancer: New Dimensions. *Cancer Discov.* **2022**, *12*, 31–46. [CrossRef]
16. Stiban, J.; Perera, M. Very Long Chain Ceramides Interfere with C16-Ceramide-Induced Channel Formation: A Plausible Mechanism for Regulating the Initiation of Intrinsic Apoptosis. *Biochim. Biophys. Acta (BBA)-Biomembr.* **2015**, *1848*, 561–567. [CrossRef]
17. Sutphen, R.; Xu, Y.; Wilbanks, G.D.; Fiorica, J.; Grendys, E.C.; LaPolla, J.P.; Arango, H.; Hoffman, M.S.; Martino, M.; Wakeley, K.; et al. Lysophospholipids Are Potential Biomarkers of Ovarian Cancer. *Cancer Epidemiol. Biomark. Prev.* **2004**, *13*, 1185–1191. [CrossRef]

18. Lin, L.; Ding, Y.; Wang, Y.; Wang, Z.; Yin, X.; Yan, G.; Zhang, L.; Yang, P.; Shen, H. Functional Lipidomics: Palmitic Acid Impairs Hepatocellular Carcinoma Development by Modulating Membrane Fluidity and Glucose Metabolism. *Hepatology* **2017**, *66*, 432–448. [CrossRef]
19. Giskeødegård, G.F.; Hansen, A.F.; Bertilsson, H.; Gonzalez, S.V.; Kristiansen, K.A.; Bruheim, P.; Mjøs, S.A.; Angelsen, A.; Bathen, T.F.; Tessem, M.-B. Metabolic Markers in Blood Can Separate Prostate Cancer from Benign Prostatic Hyperplasia. *Br. J. Cancer* **2015**, *113*, 1712–1719. [CrossRef]
20. Abuhusain, H.J.; Matin, A.; Qiao, Q.; Shen, H.; Kain, N.; Day, B.W.; Stringer, B.W.; Daniels, B.; Laaksonen, M.A.; Teo, C.; et al. A Metabolic Shift Favoring Sphingosine 1-Phosphate at the Expense of Ceramide Controls Glioblastoma Angiogenesis. *J. Biol. Chem.* **2013**, *288*, 37355–37364. [CrossRef]
21. Nagahashi, M.; Tsuchida, J.; Moro, K.; Hasegawa, M.; Tatsuda, K.; Woelfel, I.A.; Takabe, K.; Wakai, T. High Levels of Sphingolipids in Human Breast Cancer. *J. Surg. Res.* **2016**, *204*, 435–444. [CrossRef]
22. Yan, F.; Zhao, H.; Zeng, Y. Lipidomics: A Promising Cancer Biomarker. *Clin. Transl. Med.* **2018**, *7*, 21. [CrossRef]
23. Zhang, J.; Sans, M.; Garza, K.Y.; Eberlin, L.S. Mass spectrometry technologies to advance care for cancer patients in clinical and intraoperative use. *Mass Spectrom. Rev.* **2021**, *40*, 692–720. [CrossRef]
24. King, M.E.; Lin, M.; Spradlin, M.; Eberlin, L.S. Advances and Emerging Medical Applications of Direct Mass Spectrometry Technologies for Tissue Analysis. *Annu. Rev. Anal. Chem.* **2023**, *16*, 1–25. [CrossRef]
25. Rankin-Turner, S.; Sears, P.; Heaney, L.M. Applications of Ambient Ionization Mass Spectrometry in 2022: An Annual Review. *Anal. Sci. Adv.* **2023**, *4*, 133–153. [CrossRef]
26. Takáts, Z.; Wiseman, J.M.; Gologan, B.; Cooks, R.G. Mass Spectrometry Sampling Under Ambient Conditions with Desorption Electrospray Ionization. *Science* **2004**, *306*, 471–473. [CrossRef]
27. Morato, N.M.; Cooks, R.G. Desorption Electrospray Ionization Mass Spectrometry: 20 Years. *Acc. Chem. Res.* **2023**, *56*, 2526–2536. [CrossRef]
28. Tzafetas, M.; Mitra, A.; Paraskevaidi, M.; Bodai, Z.; Kalliala, I.; Bowden, S.; Lathouras, K.; Rosini, F.; Szasz, M.; Savage, A.; et al. The Intelligent Knife (IKnife) and Its Intraoperative Diagnostic Advantage for the Treatment of Cervical Disease. *Proc. Natl. Acad. Sci. USA* **2020**, *117*, 7338–7346. [CrossRef]
29. Van Hese, L.; De Vleeschouwer, S.; Theys, T.; Larivière, E.; Solie, L.; Sciot, R.; Siegel, T.P.; Rex, S.; Heeren, R.M.A.; Cuypers, E. Towards Real-Time Intraoperative Tissue Interrogation for REIMS-Guided Glioma Surgery. *J. Mass Spectrom. Adv. Clin. Lab.* **2022**, *24*, 80–89. [CrossRef]
30. Ogrinc, N.; Kruszewski, A.; Chaillou, P.; Saudemont, P.; Lagadec, C.; Salzet, M.; Duriez, C.; Fournier, I. Robot-Assisted SpiderMass for In Vivo Real-Time Topography Mass Spectrometry Imaging. *Anal. Chem.* **2021**, *93*, 14383–14391. [CrossRef]
31. Ogrinc, N.; Attencourt, C.; Colin, E.; Boudahi, A.; Tebbakha, R.; Salzet, M.; Testelin, S.; Dakpé, S.; Fournier, I. Mass Spectrometry-Based Differentiation of Oral Tongue Squamous Cell Carcinoma and Nontumor Regions With the SpiderMass Technology. *Front. Oral Health* **2022**, *3*, 827360. [CrossRef]
32. DeHoog, R.J.; King, M.E.; Keating, M.F.; Zhang, J.; Sans, M.; Feider, C.L.; Garza, K.Y.; Bensussan, A.; Krieger, A.; Lin, J.Q.; et al. Intraoperative Identification of Thyroid and Parathyroid Tissues During Human Endocrine Surgery Using the MasSpec Pen. *JAMA Surg.* **2023**, *158*, 1050. [CrossRef]
33. Garza, K.Y.; King, M.E.; Nagi, C.; DeHoog, R.J.; Zhang, J.; Sans, M.; Krieger, A.; Feider, C.L.; Bensussan, A.V.; Keating, M.F.; et al. Intraoperative Evaluation of Breast Tissues During Breast Cancer Operations Using the MasSpec Pen. *JAMA Netw. Open* **2024**, *7*, e242684. [CrossRef]
34. Challen, B.; Cramer, R. Advances in Ionisation Techniques for Mass Spectrometry-based Omics Research. *Proteomics* **2022**, *22*, e2100394. [CrossRef]
35. Woolman, M.; Kuzan-Fischer, C.M.; Ferry, I.; Kiyota, T.; Luu, B.; Wu, M.; Munoz, D.G.; Das, S.; Aman, A.; Taylor, M.D.; et al. Picosecond Infrared Laser Desorption Mass Spectrometry Identifies Medulloblastoma Subgroups on Intrasurgical Timescales. *Cancer Res.* **2019**, *79*, 2426–2434. [CrossRef]
36. Woolman, M.; Kiyota, T.; Belgadi, S.A.; Fujita, N.; Fiorante, A.; Ramaswamy, V.; Daniels, C.; Rutka, J.T.; McIntosh, C.; Munoz, D.G.; et al. Lipidomic-Based Approach to 10 s Classification of Major Pediatric Brain Cancer Types with Picosecond Infrared Laser Mass Spectrometry. *Anal. Chem.* **2024**, *96*, 1019–1028. [CrossRef]
37. Eberlin, L.S.; Liu, X.; Ferreira, C.R.; Santagata, S.; Agar, N.Y.R.; Cooks, R.G. Desorption Electrospray Ionization Then MALDI Mass Spectrometry Imaging of Lipid and Protein Distributions in Single Tissue Sections. *Anal. Chem.* **2011**, *83*, 8366–8371. [CrossRef]
38. Fenn, J.B.; Mann, M.; Meng, C.K.; Wong, S.F.; Whitehouse, C.M. Electrospray Ionization for Mass Spectrometry of Large Biomolecules. *Science* **1989**, *246*, 64–71. [CrossRef]
39. Banerjee, S.; Mazumdar, S. Electrospray Ionization Mass Spectrometry: A Technique to Access the Information beyond the Molecular Weight of the Analyte. *Int. J. Anal. Chem.* **2012**, *2012*, 282574. [CrossRef]
40. Banerjee, S.; Zare, R.N.; Tibshirani, R.J.; Kunder, C.A.; Nolley, R.; Fan, R.; Brooks, J.D.; Sonn, G.A. Diagnosis of Prostate Cancer by Desorption Electrospray Ionization Mass Spectrometric Imaging of Small Metabolites and Lipids. *Proc. Natl. Acad. Sci. USA* **2017**, *114*, 3334–3339. [CrossRef]
41. Wu, C.; Dill, A.L.; Eberlin, L.S.; Cooks, R.G.; Ifa, D.R. Mass Spectrometry Imaging under Ambient Conditions. *Mass Spectrom. Rev.* **2013**, *32*, 218–243. [CrossRef]

42. Nagai, K.; Uranbileg, B.; Chen, Z.; Fujioka, A.; Yamazaki, T.; Matsumoto, Y.; Tsukamoto, H.; Ikeda, H.; Yatomi, Y.; Chiba, H.; et al. Identification of Novel Biomarkers of Hepatocellular Carcinoma by High-definition Mass Spectrometry: Ultrahigh-performance Liquid Chromatography Quadrupole Time-of-flight Mass Spectrometry and Desorption Electrospray Ionization Mass Spectrometry Imaging. *Rapid Commun. Mass Spectrom.* **2020**, *34*, e8551. [CrossRef]
43. Porcari, A.M.; Zhang, J.; Garza, K.Y.; Rodrigues-Peres, R.M.; Lin, J.Q.; Young, J.H.; Tibshirani, R.; Nagi, C.; Paiva, G.R.; Carter, S.A.; et al. Multicenter Study Using Desorption-Electrospray-Ionization-Mass-Spectrometry Imaging for Breast-Cancer Diagnosis. *Anal. Chem.* **2018**, *90*, 11324–11332. [CrossRef]
44. Dill, A.L.; Eberlin, L.S.; Zheng, C.; Costa, A.B.; Ifa, D.R.; Cheng, L.; Masterson, T.A.; Koch, M.O.; Vitek, O.; Cooks, R.G. Multivariate Statistical Differentiation of Renal Cell Carcinomas Based on Lipidomic Analysis by Ambient Ionization Imaging Mass Spectrometry. *Anal. Bioanal. Chem.* **2010**, *398*, 2969–2978. [CrossRef]
45. Eberlin, L.S.; Dill, A.L.; Costa, A.B.; Ifa, D.R.; Cheng, L.; Masterson, T.; Koch, M.; Ratliff, T.L.; Cooks, R.G. Cholesterol Sulfate Imaging in Human Prostate Cancer Tissue by Desorption Electrospray Ionization Mass Spectrometry. *Anal. Chem.* **2010**, *82*, 3430–3434. [CrossRef]
46. Dill, A.L.; Eberlin, L.S.; Costa, A.B.; Zheng, C.; Ifa, D.R.; Cheng, L.; Masterson, T.A.; Koch, M.O.; Vitek, O.; Cooks, R.G. Multivariate Statistical Identification of Human Bladder Carcinomas Using Ambient Ionization Imaging Mass Spectrometry. *Chem.—A Eur. J.* **2011**, *17*, 2897–2902. [CrossRef]
47. Eberlin, L.S.; Tibshirani, R.J.; Zhang, J.; Longacre, T.A.; Berry, G.J.; Bingham, D.B.; Norton, J.A.; Zare, R.N.; Poultsides, G.A. Molecular Assessment of Surgical-Resection Margins of Gastric Cancer by Mass-Spectrometric Imaging. *Proc. Natl. Acad. Sci. USA* **2014**, *111*, 2436–2441. [CrossRef]
48. Eberlin, L.S.; Margulis, K.; Planell-Mendez, I.; Zare, R.N.; Tibshirani, R.; Longacre, T.A.; Jalali, M.; Norton, J.A.; Poultsides, G.A. Pancreatic Cancer Surgical Resection Margins: Molecular Assessment by Mass Spectrometry Imaging. *PLoS Med.* **2016**, *13*, e1002108. [CrossRef]
49. DeHoog, R.J.; Zhang, J.; Alore, E.; Lin, J.Q.; Yu, W.; Woody, S.; Almendariz, C.; Lin, M.; Engelsman, A.F.; Sidhu, S.B.; et al. Preoperative Metabolic Classification of Thyroid Nodules Using Mass Spectrometry Imaging of Fine-Needle Aspiration Biopsies. *Proc. Natl. Acad. Sci. USA* **2019**, *116*, 21401–21408. [CrossRef]
50. Bensussan, A.V.; Lin, J.; Guo, C.; Katz, R.; Krishnamurthy, S.; Cressman, E.; Eberlin, L.S. Distinguishing Non-Small Cell Lung Cancer Subtypes in Fine Needle Aspiration Biopsies by Desorption Electrospray Ionization Mass Spectrometry Imaging. *Clin. Chem.* **2020**, *66*, 1424–1433. [CrossRef]
51. Gerbig, S.; Golf, O.; Balog, J.; Denes, J.; Baranyai, Z.; Zarand, A.; Raso, E.; Timar, J.; Takats, Z. Analysis of Colorectal Adenocarcinoma Tissue by Desorption Electrospray Ionization Mass Spectrometric Imaging. *Anal. Bioanal. Chem.* **2012**, *403*, 2315–2325. [CrossRef]
52. Jarmusch, A.K.; Pirro, V.; Baird, Z.; Hattab, E.M.; Cohen-Gadol, A.A.; Cooks, R.G. Lipid and Metabolite Profiles of Human Brain Tumors by Desorption Electrospray Ionization-MS. *Proc. Natl. Acad. Sci. USA* **2016**, *113*, 1486–1491. [CrossRef]
53. Pirro, V.; Alfaro, C.M.; Jarmusch, A.K.; Hattab, E.M.; Cohen-Gadol, A.A.; Cooks, R.G. Intraoperative Assessment of Tumor Margins during Glioma Resection by Desorption Electrospray Ionization-Mass Spectrometry. *Proc. Natl. Acad. Sci. USA* **2017**, *114*, 6700–6705. [CrossRef]
54. Pirro, V.; Jarmusch, A.K.; Alfaro, C.M.; Hattab, E.M.; Cohen-Gadol, A.A.; Cooks, R.G. Utility of Neurological Smears for Intrasurgical Brain Cancer Diagnostics and Tumour Cell Percentage by DESI-MS. *Analyst* **2017**, *142*, 449–454. [CrossRef]
55. Jarmusch, A.K.; Alfaro, C.M.; Pirro, V.; Hattab, E.M.; Cohen-Gadol, A.A.; Cooks, R.G. Differential Lipid Profiles of Normal Human Brain Matter and Gliomas by Positive and Negative Mode Desorption Electrospray Ionization—Mass Spectrometry Imaging. *PLoS ONE* **2016**, *11*, e0163180. [CrossRef]
56. Brown, H.M.; Alfaro, C.M.; Pirro, V.; Dey, M.; Hattab, E.M.; Cohen-Gadol, A.A.; Cooks, R.G. Intraoperative Mass Spectrometry Platform for IDH Mutation Status Prediction, Glioma Diagnosis, and Estimation of Tumor Cell Infiltration. *J. Appl. Lab. Med.* **2021**, *6*, 902–916. [CrossRef]
57. Eberlin, L.S.; Norton, I.; Dill, A.L.; Golby, A.J.; Ligon, K.L.; Santagata, S.; Cooks, R.G.; Agar, N.Y.R. Classifying Human Brain Tumors by Lipid Imaging with Mass Spectrometry. *Cancer Res.* **2012**, *72*, 645–654. [CrossRef]
58. Louis, D.N.; Perry, A.; Reifenberger, G.; von Deimling, A.; Figarella-Branger, D.; Cavenee, W.K.; Ohgaki, H.; Wiestler, O.D.; Kleihues, P.; Ellison, D.W. The 2016 World Health Organization Classification of Tumors of the Central Nervous System: A Summary. *Acta Neuropathol.* **2016**, *131*, 803–820. [CrossRef]
59. Eberlin, L.S. DESI-MS Imaging of Lipids and Metabolites from Biological Samples. In *Mass Spectrometry in Metabolomics: Methods and Protocols*; Humana Press: New York, NY, USA, 2014; pp. 299–311.
60. Xia, J.; Wishart, D.S. Web-Based Inference of Biological Patterns, Functions and Pathways from Metabolomic Data Using MetaboAnalyst. *Nat. Protoc.* **2011**, *6*, 743–760. [CrossRef]
61. van den Berg, R.A.; Hoefsloot, H.C.; Westerhuis, J.A.; Smilde, A.K.; van der Werf, M.J. Centering, Scaling, and Transformations: Improving the Biological Information Content of Metabolomics Data. *BMC Genom.* **2006**, *7*, 142. [CrossRef]
62. Li, B.; Tang, J.; Yang, Q.; Cui, X.; Li, S.; Chen, S.; Cao, Q.; Xue, W.; Chen, N.; Zhu, F. Performance Evaluation and Online Realization of Data-Driven Normalization Methods Used in LC/MS Based Untargeted Metabolomics Analysis. *Sci. Rep.* **2016**, *6*, 38881. [CrossRef]

63. Pang, Z.; Chong, J.; Zhou, G.; de Lima Morais, D.A.; Chang, L.; Barrette, M.; Gauthier, C.; Jacques, P.-É.; Li, S.; Xia, J. MetaboAnalyst 5.0: Narrowing the Gap between Raw Spectra and Functional Insights. *Nucleic Acids Res.* **2021**, *49*, W388–W396. [CrossRef]
64. Kultima, K.; Nilsson, A.; Scholz, B.; Rossbach, U.L.; Fälth, M.; Andrén, P.E. Development and Evaluation of Normalization Methods for Label-Free Relative Quantification of Endogenous Peptides. *Mol. Cell. Proteom.* **2009**, *8*, 2285–2295. [CrossRef]
65. Tibshirani, R. The Lasso Method for Variable Selection in the Cox Model. *Stat. Med.* **1997**, *16*, 385–395. [CrossRef]
66. Fahy, E.; Sud, M.; Cotter, D.; Subramaniam, S. LIPID MAPS Online Tools for Lipid Research. *Nucleic Acids Res.* **2007**, *35*, W606–W612. [CrossRef]
67. Capper, D.; Jones, D.T.W.; Sill, M.; Hovestadt, V.; Schrimpf, D.; Sturm, D.; Koelsche, C.; Sahm, F.; Chavez, L.; Reuss, D.E.; et al. DNA Methylation-Based Classification of Central Nervous System Tumours. *Nature* **2018**, *555*, 469–474. [CrossRef]
68. Wu, Z.; Abdullaev, Z.; Pratt, D.; Chung, H.-J.; Skarshaug, S.; Zgonc, V.; Perry, C.; Pack, S.; Saidkhodjaeva, L.; Nagaraj, S.; et al. Impact of the Methylation Classifier and Ancillary Methods on CNS Tumor Diagnostics. *Neuro-Oncology* **2022**, *24*, 571–581. [CrossRef]
69. Shankar, V.; Tibshirani, R.; Zare, R.N. MassExplorer: A Computational Tool for Analyzing Desorption Electrospray Ionization Mass Spectrometry Data. *Bioinformatics* **2021**, *37*, 3688–3690. [CrossRef]
70. Margulis, K.; Chiou, A.S.; Aasi, S.Z.; Tibshirani, R.J.; Tang, J.Y.; Zare, R.N. Distinguishing Malignant from Benign Microscopic Skin Lesions Using Desorption Electrospray Ionization Mass Spectrometry Imaging. *Proc. Natl. Acad. Sci. USA* **2018**, *115*, 6347–6352. [CrossRef]
71. Yang, X.; Song, X.; Zhang, X.; Shankar, V.; Wang, S.; Yang, Y.; Chen, S.; Zhang, L.; Ni, Y.; Zare, R.N.; et al. In Situ DESI-MSI Lipidomic Profiles of Mucosal Margin of Oral Squamous Cell Carcinoma. *EBioMedicine* **2021**, *70*, 103529. [CrossRef]
72. Kind, T.; Tsugawa, H.; Cajka, T.; Ma, Y.; Lai, Z.; Mehta, S.S.; Wohlgemuth, G.; Barupal, D.K.; Showalter, M.R.; Arita, M.; et al. Identification of Small Molecules Using Accurate Mass MS/MS Search. *Mass Spectrom. Rev.* **2018**, *37*, 513–532. [CrossRef] [PubMed]
73. Duraiyan, J.; Govindarajan, R.; Kaliyappan, K.; Palanisamy, M. Applications of Immunohistochemistry. *J. Pharm. Bioallied Sci.* **2012**, *4*, 307. [CrossRef]
74. Capper, D.; Stichel, D.; Sahm, F.; Jones, D.T.W.; Schrimpf, D.; Sill, M.; Schmid, S.; Hovestadt, V.; Reuss, D.E.; Koelsche, C.; et al. Practical Implementation of DNA Methylation and Copy-Number-Based CNS Tumor Diagnostics: The Heidelberg Experience. *Acta Neuropathol.* **2018**, *136*, 181–210. [CrossRef] [PubMed]
75. Giussani, C.; Trezza, A.; Ricciuti, V.; Di Cristofori, A.; Held, A.; Isella, V.; Massimino, M. Intraoperative MRI versus Intraoperative Ultrasound in Pediatric Brain Tumor Surgery: Is Expensive Better than Cheap? A Review of the Literature. *Child's Nerv. Syst.* **2022**, *38*, 1445–1454. [CrossRef]
76. Santagata, S.; Eberlin, L.S.; Norton, I.; Calligaris, D.; Feldman, D.R.; Ide, J.L.; Liu, X.; Wiley, J.S.; Vestal, M.L.; Ramkissoon, S.H.; et al. Intraoperative Mass Spectrometry Mapping of an Onco-Metabolite to Guide Brain Tumor Surgery. *Proc. Natl. Acad. Sci. USA* **2014**, *111*, 11121–11126. [CrossRef]
77. Clark, A.R.; Calligaris, D.; Regan, M.S.; Pomeranz Krummel, D.; Agar, J.N.; Kallay, L.; MacDonald, T.; Schniederjan, M.; Santagata, S.; Pomeroy, S.L.; et al. Rapid Discrimination of Pediatric Brain Tumors by Mass Spectrometry Imaging. *J. Neuro-Oncol.* **2018**, *140*, 269–279. [CrossRef]
78. Woolman, M.; Ferry, I.; Kuzan-Fischer, C.M.; Wu, M.; Zou, J.; Kiyota, T.; Isik, S.; Dara, D.; Aman, A.; Das, S.; et al. Rapid Determination of Medulloblastoma Subgroup Affiliation with Mass Spectrometry Using a Handheld Picosecond Infrared Laser Desorption Probe. *Chem. Sci.* **2017**, *8*, 6508–6519. [CrossRef]
79. Kattner, P.; Strobel, H.; Khoshnevis, N.; Grunert, M.; Bartholomae, S.; Pruss, M.; Fitzel, R.; Halatsch, M.-E.; Schilberg, K.; Siegelin, M.D.; et al. Compare and Contrast: Pediatric Cancer versus Adult Malignancies. *Cancer Metastasis Rev.* **2019**, *38*, 673–682. [CrossRef]
80. Kerian, K.S.; Jarmusch, A.K.; Pirro, V.; Koch, M.O.; Masterson, T.A.; Cheng, L.; Cooks, R.G. Differentiation of Prostate Cancer from Normal Tissue in Radical Prostatectomy Specimens by Desorption Electrospray Ionization and Touch Spray Ionization Mass Spectrometry. *Analyst* **2015**, *140*, 1090–1098. [CrossRef]
81. Henderson, F.; Jones, E.; Denbigh, J.; Christie, L.; Chapman, R.; Hoyes, E.; Claude, E.; Williams, K.J.; Roncaroli, F.; McMahon, A. 3D DESI-MS Lipid Imaging in a Xenograft Model of Glioblastoma: A Proof of Principle. *Sci. Rep.* **2020**, *10*, 16512. [CrossRef]

biomedicines

MDPI

Review

The 2021 World Health Organization Central Nervous System Tumor Classification: The Spectrum of Diffuse Gliomas

Racine Gue [1] and Dhairya A. Lakhani [1,2,*]

1 Department of Neuroradiology, West Virginia University, Morgantown, WV 26506, USA
2 Department of Radiology and Radiological Sciences, Johns Hopkins University, Baltimore, MD 21218, USA
* Correspondence: dhairyalakhani@gmail.com

Abstract: The 2021 edition of the World Health Organization (WHO) classification of central nervous system tumors introduces significant revisions across various tumor types. These updates, encompassing changes in diagnostic techniques, genomic integration, terminology, and grading, are crucial for radiologists, who play a critical role in interpreting brain tumor imaging. Such changes impact the diagnosis and management of nearly all central nervous system tumor categories, including the reclassification, addition, and removal of specific tumor entities. Given their pivotal role in patient care, radiologists must remain conversant with these revisions to effectively contribute to multidisciplinary tumor boards and collaborate with peers in neuro-oncology, neurosurgery, radiation oncology, and neuropathology. This knowledge is essential not only for accurate diagnosis and staging, but also for understanding the molecular and genetic underpinnings of tumors, which can influence treatment decisions and prognostication. This review, therefore, focuses on the most pertinent updates concerning the classification of adult diffuse gliomas, highlighting the aspects most relevant to radiological practice. Emphasis is placed on the implications of new genetic information on tumor behavior and imaging findings, providing necessary tools to stay abreast of advancements in the field. This comprehensive overview aims to enhance the radiologist's ability to integrate new WHO classification criteria into everyday practice, ultimately improving patient outcomes through informed and precise imaging assessments.

Keywords: WHO classification; brain tumor; glioma

1. Introduction

Since its inception in 1956, the WHO Classification of Tumors, commonly referred to as the WHO Blue Books, has evolved from a simple list of terms to a comprehensive resource that integrates diverse information including histological, immunohistochemical, genetic, epidemiological, and clinical data [1,2]. This series has become the global standard, essential for establishing uniform nomenclature for human cancers. Each edition has expanded to reflect the growing understanding of cancer biology, employing a systematic approach to the multifaceted nature of tumor classification [3]. Tumor types are meticulously detailed based on their localization, clinical features, epidemiology, etiology, pathogenesis, histopathology, diagnostic molecular pathology, staging, prognosis, and prediction [4]. This detailed and systematic approach is crucial for radiologists to accurately help diagnose, stage, and predict tumor behavior, ensuring consistent and informed patient care.

In this review, we aim to present the evolution of the latest updates on adult diffuse gliomas, highlighting the most relevant aspects for radiologists, along with genetic information that aids in understanding their classification, behavior, and imaging findings. Additionally, we provide pertinent information on some newly classified entities and pediatric-type diffuse high-grade gliomas, recognizing the overlap between these categories.

2. Significance and Context

The standardized terminology adopted by the WHO Blue Books has profound implications across various medical disciplines, in the case of CNS Tumors, enhancing communication among multidisciplinary teams that include neurosurgeons, neurologists, neuro-oncologists, neuropathologists, and neuroradiologists [5]. For neuroradiologists, this consistent language is critical, as it ensures that imaging findings are interpreted in alignment with global standards, enabling accurate correlations with clinical and pathological data [5]. This facilitates seamless collaboration in treatment planning and decision-making, allowing for clear discussions about tumor types, subtypes, and characteristics [6,7].

Furthermore, the use of standardized terminology in the classification supports accurate data collection for population-based cancer registries [5]. This meticulous approach empowers researchers to conduct comprehensive analyses of histological and genetic variations, thus enriching our understanding of cancer epidemiology and informing the development of targeted public health interventions [5,8].

Additionally, the advocacy for standardized terminology by the WHO Blue Books promotes consistency in documentation practices. This ensures precise recording and reporting of CNS tumor cases across healthcare systems and registries, enhancing data integrity and facilitating comparative analyses [5]. Such detailed documentation not only supports the accurate representation of clinical cases, but also underpins research efforts aimed at unraveling tumor biology, identifying prognostic factors, and advancing innovative therapeutic strategies [3,5–7].

This comprehensive approach helps maintain the highest standards of clinical practice and research.

2.1. *Innovation in Molecular Diagnostics Prompts Necessary Revisions*

The landscape of CNS tumor classification has dramatically transformed with the integration of molecular medicine techniques, marking a significant departure from the traditional reliance solely on histological findings. Historically, the foundation of tumor classification has been built on histological examination, utilizing tools such as light microscopy, immunohistochemistry, and various tissue staining methods. These techniques have provided essential insights into the cellular characteristics and structures of tumors, facilitating initial diagnostic assessments [1].

However, the last century has witnessed the introduction of groundbreaking technologies, notably DNA and RNA sequencing, which have revolutionized the approach to tumor diagnosis and classification. These molecular methods allow for a more detailed analysis of the genetic and molecular blueprints of tumors, offering a deeper understanding of their origins and behaviors [3,9].

Among the most significant recent advances is methylome profiling, a technique that analyzes DNA methylation patterns across the entire genome [10]. Over the past decade, methylome profiling has emerged as a critical tool for CNS tumor classification [11]. It has proven especially adept at identifying a wide range of tumor types and subtypes, providing a level of precision that surpasses traditional methods [10,12]. This technology not only enhances the accuracy of tumor classification, but also proves invaluable in diagnosing complex, challenging neoplasms and rare tumor forms that might elude conventional diagnostic approaches [11,13].

While the availability of methylome profiling is not yet universal due to its associated technological and cost considerations, the advantages it brings are undeniable [4,12]. This technique enhances diagnostic precision and specificity significantly, setting the stage for more tailored therapeutic approaches and more accurate prognostic assessments [13]. As the accessibility of this technology improves, it promises to refine the diagnostic landscape of CNS tumors further [13]. With more detailed molecular profiles at their disposal, clinicians can offer more personalized and effective care to patients, ensuring that treatments are well-aligned with the unique genetic makeup of each tumor [9].

2.2. *Overview of Updates*

2.2.1. Rising Importance of Molecular Diagnostics

This evolution in diagnostic capabilities was utilized in the 2016 WHO classification of CNS tumors, which marked a significant shift by incorporating molecular markers into tumor classification [14]. This integration allowed for a more precise identification of tumor subtypes, leveraging cutting-edge molecular diagnostics to enhance classification accuracy [4]. The 2021 update to the WHO classification built on this foundation, capitalizing on the broader availability of advanced diagnostics to expand their use further [12]. This ongoing development in CNS tumor standards continues to improve the alignment between clinical practice and the latest scientific insights, ensuring that patient care keeps pace with technological advancements in the field [7,9,15].

Furthermore, molecular markers now play a pivotal role in both the grading and prognosis estimation of various tumors [16]. For example, cyclin-dependent kinase inhibitor A/B (CDKN2A/B) homozygous deletion in isocitrate dehydrogenase (IDH)-mutant astrocytomas and the presence of telomerase reverse transcriptase (TERT) promoter mutations, epidermal growth factor receptor (EGFR) amplification, and +7/−10 chromosomal copy-number changes in the IDH-wildtype glioblastoma are critical for accurate classification and prognosis [16,17]. These molecular parameters take precedence over histological findings when assigning a tumor grade [9,14].

As our understanding of the molecular underpinnings of CNS tumors deepens, the task of classifying these tumors becomes increasingly intricate. While some tumors fit neatly into newly established molecular classifications, others align inconsistently or not at all, prompting an evolving hybrid approach to taxonomy [3]. This transition reflects the dynamic nature of the current landscape and reinforces a shift towards a future classification system that may rely more heavily on molecular diagnostics than traditional methods [3,4].

2.2.2. Update: Not Otherwise Specified and Not Elsewhere Classified

The 2021 WHO classification acknowledges these complexities by introducing categories like "Not Otherwise Specified" (NOS) and "Not Elsewhere Classified" (NEC) [18,19]. These categories serve to differentiate between well-characterized WHO diagnoses and those cases where diagnostic or molecular information is lacking or inconclusive. The designation of "NOS" is used when specific criteria for a definitive WHO diagnosis are not met due to the absence or incomplete nature of molecular analysis. This indicates that while some diagnostic efforts have been made, they do not provide enough information to precisely categorize the tumor under existing WHO classifications [18,19].

Conversely, the "NEC" category is applied when, despite comprehensive diagnostic efforts, including successful pathological and molecular testing, the tumor does not fit any established WHO diagnostic criteria. This suggests that the tumor presents unique or atypical features that do not conform to the current understanding [18,19].

2.2.3. Update: Types and Subtypes

Continuing its historical commitment to systematic organization, the 2021 WHO classification updates strive to standardize tumor diagnosis across various organ systems, enhancing consistency, and clarity [1,3]. This iteration incorporates advanced molecular insights gained from recent technological progress, structuring the classification by starting with the tumor's site of origin [3]. From there, tumors are grouped based on shared characteristics, and are further categorized at the family or class level. Subsequent divisions into "types" and "subtypes" provide more detail, reflecting distinctions based on molecular and histopathological features [12]. Notably, the terminology has evolved, transitioning from "entity" to "type" and from "variant" to "subtype", a change that better captures the heterogeneity of tumors and emphasizes the increasing role of molecular details in their classification [3,10].

2.2.4. Update: Tumor Grading

With these updates, the grading system for CNS tumors has also undergone significant changes, including the adoption of Arabic numerals instead of Roman numerals [10]. This adjustment aims to minimize typographical errors and ensure consistency across different organ systems [10]. Furthermore, while previous WHO classifications applied a uniform grading system across various CNS tumor types, the 2021 WHO classification of CNS tumors introduces a within-type grading approach [10]. This method offers greater flexibility and emphasizes the biological similarities within specific tumor types. Such a targeted approach aligns CNS tumor grading more closely with the grading systems used for neoplasms in other organ systems [2,10]. Despite these extensive revisions, the term "CNS WHO Grade" remains unchanged, serving as a consistent marker to denote the assigned grade within the updated classification system [3].

2.2.5. Update: Continued Integration of Histological and Molecular Markers

The 2021 WHO classification of CNS tumors introduces new types and updates the nomenclature to clarify molecular features, aligning it with the cIMPACT guidelines [20]. The updates in these areas are outlined below, reflecting the latest scientific understanding and aiming to enhance diagnostic precision and treatment approaches [4,12].

2.3. Broad Categorization Overview

The 2021 WHO classification of CNS tumors organizes tumors into several broad categories, including gliomas, glioneuronal, and neuronal tumors; choroid plexus tumors; embryonal tumors; pineal tumors; cranial and paraspinal nerve tumors; meningiomas; mesenchymal, non-meningothelial tumors involving the CNS; melanocytic tumors; hematolymphoid tumors involving the CNS; germ cell tumors; tumors of the sellar region; metastases to the CNS; and genetic tumor syndromes involving the CNS [3,4].

2.3.1. Gliomas, Glioneuronal Tumors and Neuronal Tumors

The chapter dedicated to gliomas, glioneuronal, and neuronal tumors covers a substantial portion of primary intra-axial CNS tumors [3,12]. Within this chapter, these tumors are further classified into six distinct families, a division that reflects their significant differences in underlying biology, growth patterns, and typical patient demographics [12,14].

2.3.2. Update: Gliomas, Glioneuronal Tumors and Neuronal Tumors

A notable refinement in the latest edition involves distinguishing gliomas primarily occurring in adults from those typically found in children [9,14]. This is further propelled by heightened molecular insights [14]. For instance, within pediatric-type diffuse gliomas, the classification now encompasses specific molecular subtypes such as Diffuse pediatric-type high-grade glioma, categorized as either H3-wildtype or IDH-wildtype, and Diffuse hemispheric glioma, characterized by H3 G34-mutation. Furthermore, the transition from "H3 K27-mutant" to "H3 K27-altered" within pediatric gliomas marks a significant development, indicative of deeper understandings into the genetic mechanisms underpinning these tumors [3,20,21].

While this review primarily delves into adult-type diffuse gliomas, it is essential to briefly mention Diffuse Midline Glioma, H3 K27-altered and newly recognized tumors due to overlapping imaging features and affected populations [22]. These include Diffuse Hemispheric Glioma, H3 G34-mutation, Diffuse Pediatric-Type High-Grade Glioma, H3-wildtype or IDH-wildtype, and High-Grade Astrocytoma with Piloid Features [14]. These examples highlight the expanding spectrum of gliomas and underscore the importance of comprehensive diagnostic approaches across age groups.

2.3.3. Adult-Type Diffuse Gliomas

Adult-type diffuse gliomas have been significantly simplified in the 2021 WHO classification, going from fifteen entities to just three: Astrocytoma, IDH-mutant; Oligodendroglioma, IDH-mutant and 1p/19q codeleted; and Glioblastoma, IDH-wildtype. Grading within these types now considers molecular markers alongside histology [3].

3. Astrocytoma, IDH-Mutant

3.1. Epidemiology and Localization

IDH-mutant astrocytoma, often arising in adults aged thirty to forty, predominantly develops in the frontal lobes, but can occur throughout the central nervous system, including the cerebral hemispheres, brainstem, and spinal cord [23].

3.2. Brief Genetic Overview

The most defining feature of IDH-mutant astrocytoma is the mutation in either the IDH1 or IDH2 gene [23]. IDH1 mutations are more common, especially the R132H mutation [24,25]. These mutations are critical because they result in the production of an abnormal enzyme that converts a normal cellular metabolite, alpha-ketoglutarate, into an abnormal product, 2-hydroxyglutarate (2-HG) [26]. This byproduct is not typically found in high concentrations in normal cells and has significant implications for tumor biology [27,28]. The accumulation of 2-HG in tumor cells is particularly harmful because it mimics the shape and function of alpha-ketoglutarate but disrupts normal processes [29]. 2-HG is a competitive inhibitor of several alpha-ketoglutarate-dependent dioxygenases, which are crucial for proper cell function [30]. These enzymes include histone demethylases and the Ten-Eleven Translocation (TET) enzymes involved in DNA demethylation [29,30]. By inhibiting these enzymes, 2-HG causes widespread changes in the methylation landscape of both histones (proteins around which DNA is wrapped) and DNA itself [30]. This interference results in the abnormal methylation or "silencing" of DNA in certain regions [28,31]. In turn, this abnormal methylation changes the activity of genes in ways that can promote tumor growth [32–35].

In addition to IDH mutations, astrocytomas often exhibit other genetic alterations, including tumor protein p53 (TP53) and alpha-thalassemia/mental retardation, and X-linked (ATRX) mutations [35,36]. TP53 mutations compromise the protein's ability to regulate cell growth and initiate apoptosis, thereby allowing cells with damaged DNA to continue dividing [37]. ATRX mutations disrupt chromatin remodeling, which is crucial for DNA replication and repair, and are associated with a phenotype that enables cancer cells to maintain telomere length and avoid senescence, contributing to their classification as CNS WHO grades 2–4 [7,37–39].

Relevance

The IDH mutation serves as a critical diagnostic and prognostic marker [33]. Testing for IDH status is now a standard part of the pathological assessment of gliomas [24]. Specific inhibitors targeting the mutant IDH enzymes are in development and clinical trials, offering a new avenue for targeted therapy in managing these tumors [31].

3.3. Update

A notable change in the 2021 WHO CNS classification involves the inclusion of CDKN2A/B homozygous deletion as a marker. This genetic anomaly allows for the classification of the IDH-mutant astrocytoma as CNS WHO grade 4, regardless of histological features such as microvascular proliferation or necrosis [39].

Brief Genetic Overview of Relevance of CDKN2A/B Homozygous Deletion as a Marker

The CDKN2A and CDKN2B genes are critical in cell-cycle regulation, acting as tumor suppressors by encoding proteins that prevent unchecked cell proliferation, a hallmark of cancer [40]. Cyclin-dependent kinase inhibitor 2A (CDKN2A) is a gene located at chromosome 9, band p21.3. p14ARF and p15INK4b are proteins encoded by the CDKN2A and CDKN2B genes, respectively, and play crucial roles in cell-cycle regulation and tumor suppression [41,42].

p14ARF (alternate reading frame protein) functions primarily by activating the p53 tumor suppressor pathway, crucial for inducing cell-cycle arrest and apoptosis in response to oncogenic stress [37]. It achieves this by inhibiting mouse double minute 2 homolog (MDM2), a protein that targets p53 for degradation [37]. By binding to MDM2, p14ARF prevents the degradation of p53, allowing it to accumulate and activate genes that lead to apoptosis or cell-cycle arrest, thus preventing damaged cells from proliferating and potentially forming tumors [42].

On the other hand, p15INK4b is involved in regulating the cell cycle at the G1 checkpoint by inhibiting the activity of cyclin-dependent kinases CDK4 and CDK6 [43]. p15INK4b prevents the phosphorylation of the retinoblastoma protein (RB), maintaining RB in its active state, which binds to and sequesters E2F transcription factors, thus blocking the transition from G1 to S phase of the cell cycle [41,44–46].

Both proteins are vital in maintaining cellular integrity; mutations or deletions in the genes encoding these proteins can lead to uncontrolled cell division and contribute to the progression of various cancers [42,47]. Molecular insights are pivotal in exploiting specific weaknesses in a tumor's genetic profile [48].

3.4. *Imaging*

The retention of functional CDKN2A and CDKN2B genes contributes to a more controlled cell cycle, and typically correlates with a less aggressive tumor behavior.As such, the slow-growing nature of CNS WHO grade 2 or 3 IDH-mutant astrocytomas, coupled with the brain's ability to adapt and compensate, can make their presence less apparent until symptoms become more pronounced or the tumor is incidentally discovered during medical evaluation for other reasons, such as epilepsy [48].

On CT scans, IDH-mutant astrocytomas of CNS WHO grade 2 usually present as poorly defined, homogeneous, low-density masses without contrast enhancement [49]. As the tumor grade increases, features such as midline deviation, extensive edema (including peritumoral edema), contrast enhancement, and central hypodensity due to necrosis become more pronounced [49]. These changes reflect the progression of the tumor and the associated increase in aggressiveness and disruption of surrounding brain tissue. On CT scans, peritumoral edema can appear as areas of low density surrounding the tumor mass [50]. Peritumoral edema is an important radiological feature to identify, as it provides valuable information about the extent of tumor involvement and its impact on surrounding brain structures.

On MRI, IDH-mutant astrocytomas exhibit certain characteristic features. These include T1 hypointensity and T2 hyperintensity, along with enlargement and distortion of involved areas [3,12]. Grade 2 IDH-mutant astrocytomas typically exhibit homogeneous T1-hypointense and T2-hyperintense masses without enhancement [51]. The T2- FLAIR mismatch sign, when seen, is highly suggestive of grade 2 and grade 3 IDH-mutant astrocytoma (Figures 1 and 2) [52–54]. Signal characteristics of the T2-FLAIR mismatch sign include homogenous hyperintensity on T2-weighted images with a central hypointense signal and a thin rim of residual hyperintensity on fluid-attenuated inversion recovery (FLAIR) images. However, it is important to note that this sign may not be equally sensitive, and has been reported to result in false-positive findings [55].

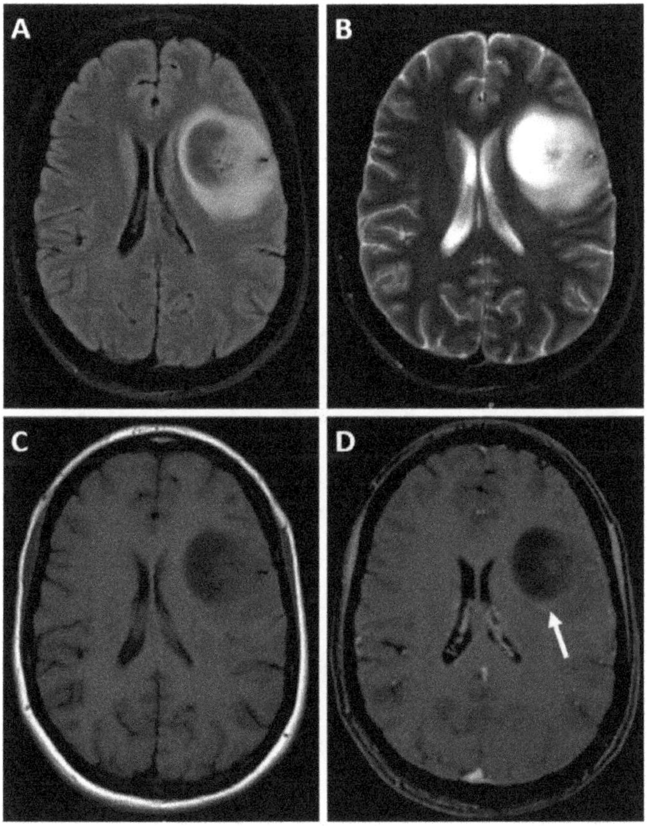

Figure 1. MR images derived from a 31 year old female with astrocytoma, Isocitrate dehydrogenase (IDH)-mutant, harboring a canonical IDH-1 mutation as well as alpha-thalassemia/mental retardation, X-linked (ATRX), and tumor protein p53 mutation. There was no cyclin-dependent kinase inhibitor 2A/B (CDKN2A/B) homozygous deletion. No increased mitotic activity was evident on histopathology; hence, it was classified as CNS WHO grade 2 IDH-mutant astrocytoma. (**A**) Axial T2-weighted fluid-attenuated inversion recovery (FLAIR) and (**B**) axial T2-weighted axial MRI scans demonstrate the presence of the T2-FLAIR mismatch sign, suggestive of WHO grade 2 and 3 IDH-mutant astrocytomas. (**C**) Axial T1-weighted image and (**D**) axial postcontrast T1-weighted fat-suppressed images demonstrate subtle peripheral enhancement (arrow). Note that the presence of contrast is uncommon in grade 2 IDH-mutant astrocytomas.

Contrast enhancement, indicating increased vascularity, is uncommon in grade 2 tumors, but becomes more frequent in grade 3 and grade 4 tumors [48]. As the tumor grade increases, features such as T2 heterogeneity and elevated maximum relative cerebral blood volume (CBV) on perfusion imaging, in addition to contrast enhancement, become more prominent [48,56]. Rim enhancement around central necrosis can be observed in WHO grade 4 tumors [29]. Moreover, higher-grade lesions typically display more extensive surrounding edema On MRI scans, peritumoral infiltrative edema appears as areas of increased signal intensity surrounding the tumor on T2-weighted and FLAIR sequences. These areas typically appear brighter than normal brain tissue [57].

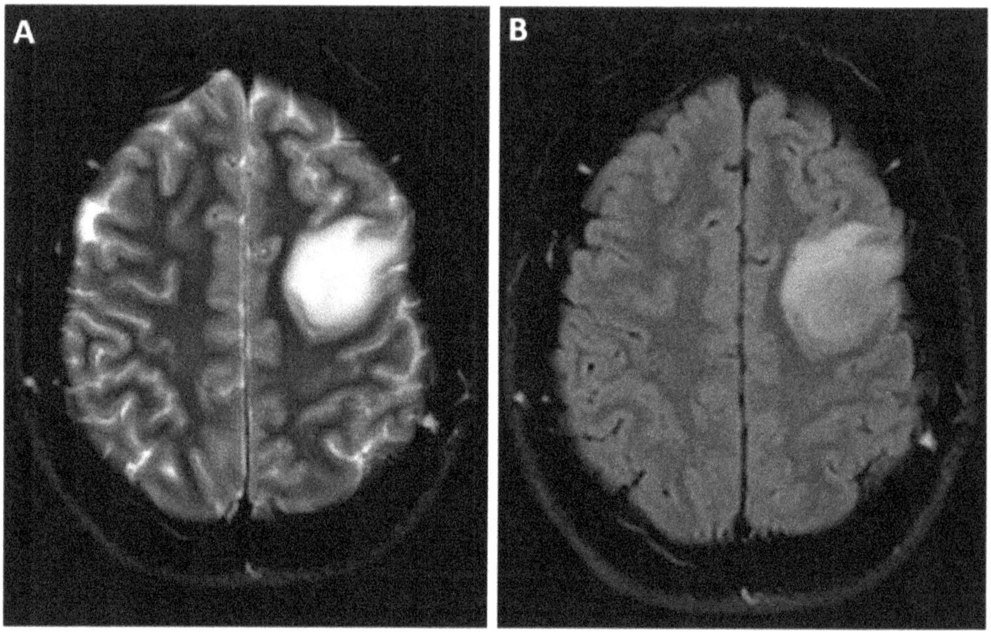

Figure 2. MR images derived from a 21 year old man with astrocytoma, isocitrate dehydrogenase (IDH)-mutant, WHO grade 2, harboring a canonical IDH1 mutation as well as loss of alpha-thalassemia/mental retardation, X-linked (ATRX), and tumor protein p53 mutation. No increased mitotic activity was evident on histopathology. There was nocyclin-dependent kinase inhibitor 2A/B (CDKN2A/B) homozygous deletion. (**A**) Axial T2-weighted fluid-attenuated inversion recovery (FLAIR) and (**B**) axial T2-weighted axial MRI images demonstrate left frontal lobe mass. T2-FLAIR mismatch sign is less conspicuous in this case.

4. Oligodendrioglioma, IDH-Mutant and 1p/19q-Codeleted

4.1. Epidemiology and Localization

Both IDH-mutant astrocytomas and oligodendrogliomas share similarities in their epidemiology. They predominantly affect adults, with a typical age range of onset in the third to fifth decades of life [3]. Furthermore, both IDH-mutant astrocytomas and oligodendrogliomas exhibit a preference for the frontal lobes of the brain [3,14,58,59]. This shared anatomical predilection suggests potential commonalities in the microenvironment or cellular factors that contribute to tumorigenesis in this region [60–62]. Despite their distinct histopathological and genetic features, these similarities underscore overlapping characteristics in the clinical presentation and localization of these primary brain tumors [3].

4.2. Brief Genetic Overview

Oligodendrogliomas are characterized by a distinctive molecular profile that significantly influences their diagnosis, treatment, and prognosis [48,63]. Central to their molecular identity is the co-deletion of chromosome arms 1p and 19q, a predictor of a favorable response to chemotherapy and radiation, as well as a positive overall prognosis [63]. The co-deletion of chromosome arms 1p and 19q in oligodendrogliomas results in the loss of several genes that might be involved in DNA repair processes [64]. When these genes are missing, the tumor cells have a reduced ability to repair DNA damage caused by radiation or chemotherapy. As a result, these treatments may be more effective because the damaged tumor cells are less likely to survive and continue dividing [65].

Oligodendrogliomas are distinguished not only by their typical 1p/19q co-deletion and IDH mutations, but also by mutations in other specific genesleading to alterations in CIC (Capicua Transcriptional Repressor) and FUBP1 (Far Upstream Element Binding Protein 1) [66,67]. CIC is a transcriptional repressor that is involved in the regulation of gene expression within the MAPK signaling pathway [63,68]. Mutations in the CIC gene lead to a loss of function of this repressor. This eventually results in deregulated gene expression [68].

Oligodendrogliomas, unlike astrocytomas, rarely exhibit mutations in ATRX [63]. However, mutations in the telomerase reverse transcriptase (TERT) promotor are common [36]. While TERT promoter mutations generally enhance the expression of telomerase, helping tumor cells to maintain telomere length and survive longer, the presence of these mutations in the context of other vulnerabilities (like 1p/19q co-deletion and IDH mutation) might still contribute to a context where the overall DNA repair capabilities are compromised, rendering these cells more sensitive to treatments that cause DNA damage [7,37]. The presence of these molecular alterations—1p/19q co-deletion, IDH mutation, and TERT-promoter mutation—provides a robust framework for the classification of oligodendrogliomas [36,69].

Oligodendrogliomas are often classified into CNS WHO grades 2 or 3, primarily based on histological criteria, with additional consideration of CDKN2A/B homozygous deletion, which may serve as a molecular marker for assigning CNS WHO grade 3 status in certain instances [11,70].

4.3. Clinical Features

Oligodendroglioma, like IDH-mutant astrocytoma, could be described as insidious. The tumor might slowly grow without causing any noticeable symptoms until it has reached a significant size or has started to affect brain function [3]. The clinical presentation can vary significantly, but often includes seizures, which are the most common initial symptom due to the tumor's frequent cortical involvement [48]. Other symptoms might include headaches, which can range from mild to severe depending on the tumor's size and location, as well as personality changes and cognitive impairments when the frontal lobes are affected [63].

4.4. Imaging

On CT scans, IDH-mutant and 1p/19q-codeleted oligodendrogliomas commonly display as areas of decreased density (hypodense) or similar density (isodense) compared to surrounding brain tissue [59]. These lesions are often situated in the cortex and the underlying white matter of the brain. While the presence of calcifications is a frequent finding, it is important to note that calcifications alone are not sufficient for a definitive diagnosis of oligodendroglioma [59]. Additionally, some oligodendrogliomas may exhibit intratumoral hemorrhages or areas of cystic degeneration, further adding to the complexity of their appearance on imaging (Figures 3 and 4) [51,59,71].

On MRI scans, oligodendrogliomas often appear as masses with low signal intensity on T1-weighted images and high signal intensity on T2-weighted images [59]. However, their margins may not be well-defined, leading to a blurred appearance [12]. Additionally, the signal intensities within the tumor can be heterogeneous, indicating variations in tissue composition and density [51,59,71].

When gadolinium-based contrast agents are administered, oligodendrogliomas may exhibit enhancement in some cases [51,59]. This enhancement, seen in less than 20% of grade 2 tumors but in over 70% of grade 3 tumors, is associated with increased microvascular proliferation within the tumor [71].

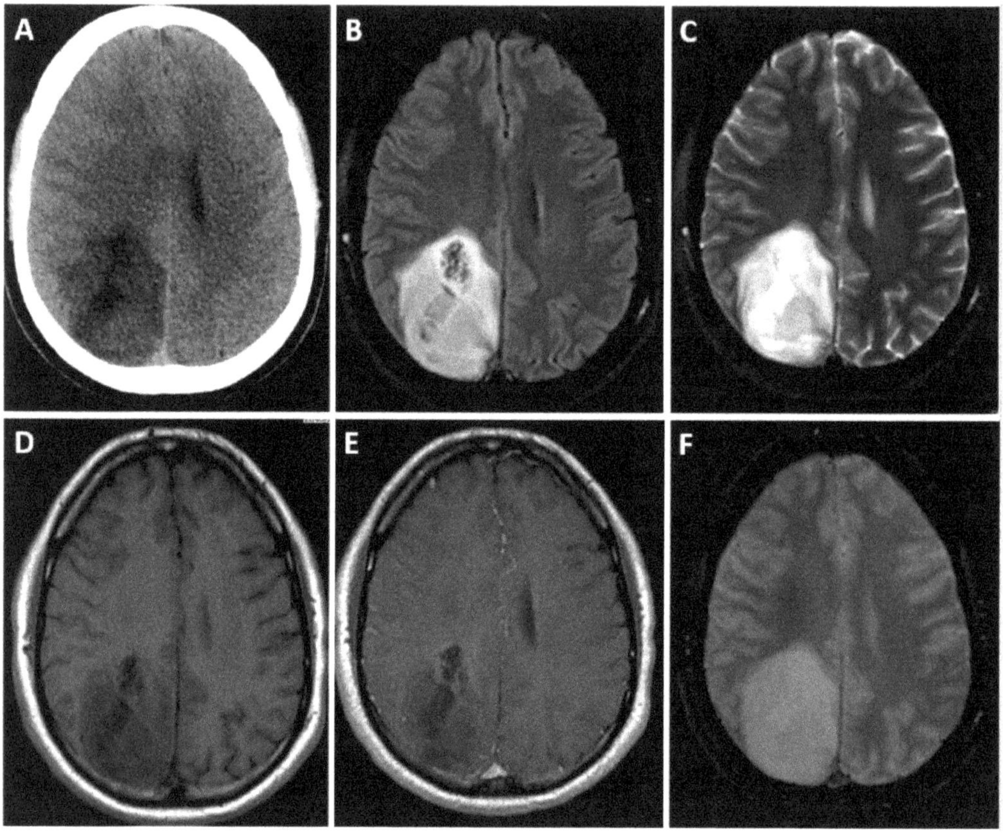

Figure 3. Axial unenhanced CT head (**A**), axial T2-weighted fluid-attenuated inversion recovery (FLAIR) (**B**), axial T2-weighted (**C**), axial T1-weighted (**D**), axial postcontrast T1-weighted (**E**), and multi-echo gradient recalled echo (GRE) (**F**) images in a 28 year old man with oligodendroglioma, isocitrate dehydrogenase (IDH)-mutant, and 1p/19q codeletion. Images demonstrate a heterogeneous right parieto-occipital region mass. This mass has indistinct margins and subtle contrast enhancement. Note: no calcification or hemorrhage on GRE or CT.

Comparing oligodendrogliomas to IDH-mutant diffuse astrocytomas reveals differences in vascular characteristics [59]. Oligodendrogliomas, in general, tend to demonstrate higher microvascularity and vascular heterogeneity [59]. These features can be observed on perfusion imaging techniques, indicating differences in blood flow patterns within the tumor vasculature [59].

Detecting IDH-mutant gliomas, including oligodendrogliomas, non-invasively is an area of active research. Magnetic resonance spectroscopy (MRS) is a specialized imaging technique that provides information about the chemical composition of tissues based on the signals emitted by atoms in different molecules [48,59,72]. In the context of gliomas, MRS can detect specific metabolic markers associated with tumor cells. In IDH-mutant gliomas, including oligodendrogliomas, there is a characteristic alteration in cellular metabolism that leads to the accumulation of a metabolite called 2-hydroxyglutarate (2-HG) [72,73]. This metabolite serves as a potential biomarker for the presence of IDH mutations in gliomas [73].

MRS allows researchers and clinicians to non-invasively measure the levels of 2-HG within the tumor tissue [73]. By analyzing the spectroscopic data obtained from MRS scans, it is theoretically possible to detect elevated levels of 2-HG, which indicate the presence of IDH mutations in the glioma cells [74]. However, implementing MRS for the detection of IDH-mutant gliomas in clinical practice presents several challenges [72]. The technique requires specialized equipment and expertise to acquire and interpret the spectroscopic data accurately. Additionally, factors such as tumor heterogeneity and variations in imaging protocols can affect the reliability of MRS measurements [48]. Its utility is also currently constrained by sensitivity and specificity issues. These limitations mean that MRS cannot fully replace the need for molecular diagnostics, which offer more precise and accurate information about tumor genetics and classification [74].

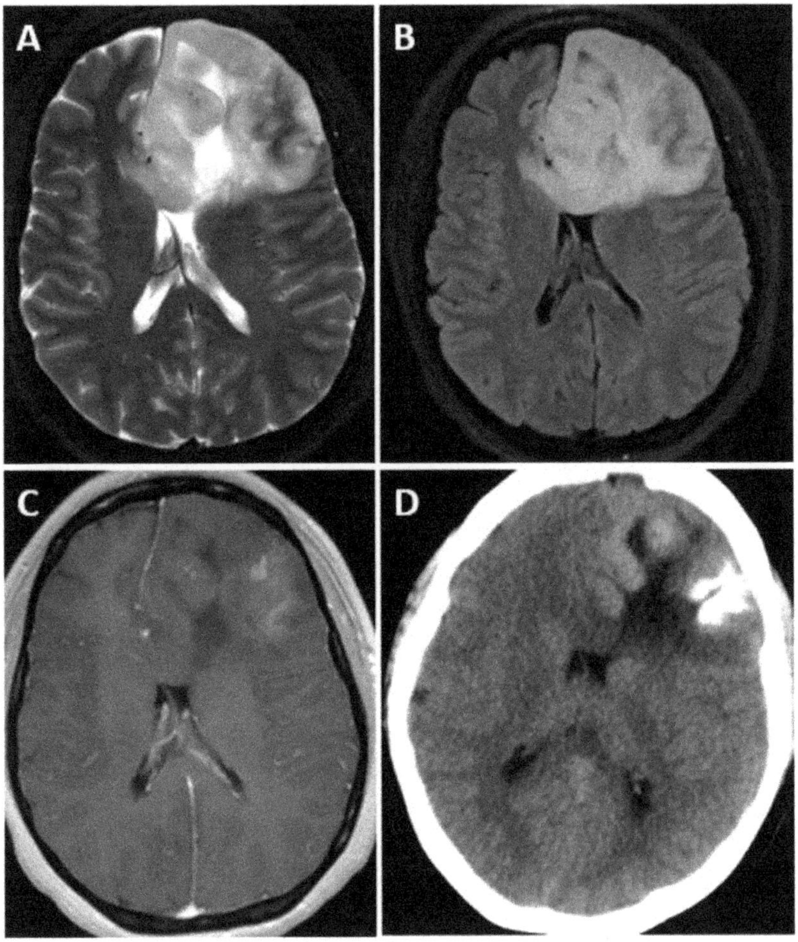

Figure 4. Axial T2-weighted (**A**), axial T2-weighted fluid-attenuated inversion recovery (FLAIR) (**B**), axial T1-weighted post-contrast(**C**), and unenhanced CT (**D**) through the level of the lateral ventricles in a 39 year old woman with oligodendroglioma, isocitrate dehydrogenase (IDH)-mutant and 1p/19q codeletion. Images demonstrate a heterogeneous left frontal lobe mass extending towards the right frontal lobe via the genu and proximal body of the corpus callosum. The mass demonstrates heterogeneous contrast enhancement and coarse calcifications.

5. Glioblastoma, IDH-Wildtype

5.1. Update

The 2021 update to the WHO classification of brain tumors has refined the criteria for diagnosing glioblastoma, placing greater emphasis on molecular features over traditional histopathological signs [3]. In this updated classification, a glioblastoma is now defined not only by the presence of IDH-wildtype status, which indicates the absence of mutations in IDH1 or IDH2 genes, but also by the presence of one or more of the following features: microvascular proliferation, necrosis, TERT-promoter mutation, EGFR gene amplification, or +7/−10 chromosome copy number changes. This shift reflects an increased understanding of the molecular drivers behind glioblastoma's aggressive behavior [17,75].

Brief Genetic Overview of Relevance of Molecular Markers

Glioblastomas are notoriously heterogeneous, with genetic and phenotypic variation, leading to significant therapeutic challenges [76]. Some of the alterations noted above portend a more aggressive course, and include TERT-promoter mutation, which allows cancer cells to bypass normal cellular aging and continue dividing indefinitely [36]. EGFR gene amplification results in the overexpression of the epidermal growth factor receptor, enhancing multiple downstream signaling pathways that promote cell proliferation, survival, and angiogenesis, characteristics central to the aggressive nature of glioblastoma [77,78]. Furthermore, chromosomal changes, specifically the gain of chromosome 7 and the loss of chromosome 10, introduce additional layers of complexity [79]. The gain of chromosome 7 often includes the EGFR gene, enhancing its oncogenic effects, while the loss of chromosome 10 frequently impacts the phosphatase and tensin homolong (PTEN) tumor-suppressor gene, leading to unregulated activation of growth pathways [17,75,79].

5.2. Clinical Features and Localization

Clinically, glioblastomas typically present with symptoms that reflect their fast growth, location, and high degree of malignancy [80]. Common symptoms include persistent headaches, nausea, and vomiting, which often are worse in the morning [81]. These symptoms are usually a result of increased intracranial pressure caused by the tumor mass [82]. Seizures can be an initial symptom due to the involvement of the tumor in the cerebral cortex. Depending on the tumor's location in the brain, patients may experience a range of neurological deficits, such as weakness on one side of the body, speech difficulties, and vision problems [83]. Cognitive and personality changes are also sometimes observed, affecting the patient's behavior and cognitive functions [3]. The rapid deterioration in neurological function is a hallmark of the disease, often leading to diagnosis at an advanced stage [83].

5.3. Imaging

Glioblastomas, known for their aggressive behavior, present a spectrum of imaging features (Figures 5 and 6) [84]. These tumors can infiltrate all areas of the brain, extending along white matter tracts and the corpus callosum to involve the contralateral hemisphere. Imaging manifestations of glioblastomas are inherently diverse, typically showcasing irregular ring enhancement around central necrosis, surrounding white matter tumor infiltration, and vasogenic edema [57]. The tumor typically has enhancing and non-enhancing components [85]. The rim of enhancing tissue is hypercellular and exhibits high cell turnover; on imaging, this is depicted by diffusion restriction, contrast enhancement, and high relative cerebral blood volume on perfusion. Patchy or no enhancement may also occur [85–87]. Moreover, glioblastomas have the capability to spread into adjacent lobes and deeply infiltrate the brainstem [88].

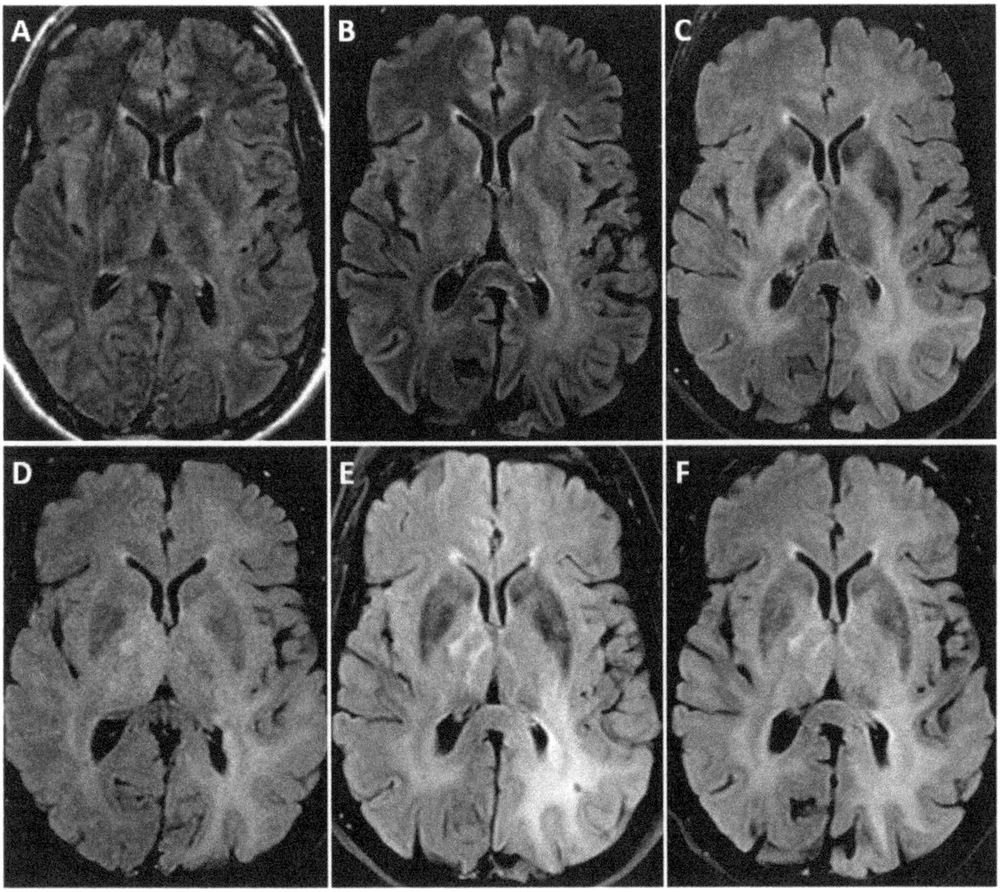

Figure 5. Imaging over the span of 10 years in a 71 year old man, demonstrating gradual progressive infiltrative changes diffusely throughout the left greater than right cerebral hemispheres, as depicted by T2/FLAIR hyperintensity. Axial T2-weighted fluid-attenuated inversion recovery (FLAIR) image at baseline (**A**), axial T2-weighted FLAIR image two years after baseline (**B**), axial T2-weighted FLAIR image four years after baseline (**C**), axial T2-weighted FLAIR image six years after baseline (**D**), axial T2 weighted FLAIR image obtained seven years after baseline and after left parietal biopsy (**E**), and axial T2 weighted FLAIR image obtained nine years after baseline and two years after biopsy (**F**). Histopathology showed no necrosis or microvascular proliferation. Immunohistochemistry was negative for isocitrate dehydrogenase (IDH) mutation, and next-generation sequencing identified an isolated reverse transcriptase telomerase (TERT)-promoter mutation, meeting 2021 CNS WHO criteria for glioblastoma (CNS WHO grade 4).

Despite the limitations of MRI in distinguishing morphological subtypes, subtle variations contribute to their overall diversity on imaging. For instance, giant cell glioblastomas and gliosarcomas can present with more circumscribed lesions located subcortically, resembling metastasis or meningiomas [89–92].

Moreover, assessing the extent of the tumor via imaging also poses challenges due to the presence of infiltrating tumor cells identified several centimeters from the tumor epicenter, even in the absence of T2/FLAIR changes, a likely site of recurrence [57,93,94].

Additionally, although less frequent, multifocal glioblastomas appear radiographically as multiple enhancing lesions on a background of T2-weighted signal changes, indicating a clear pathological connection [95,96]. Multicentric glioblastomas have also been described which can emerge in different lobes or hemispheres without a discernible connection [95–97].

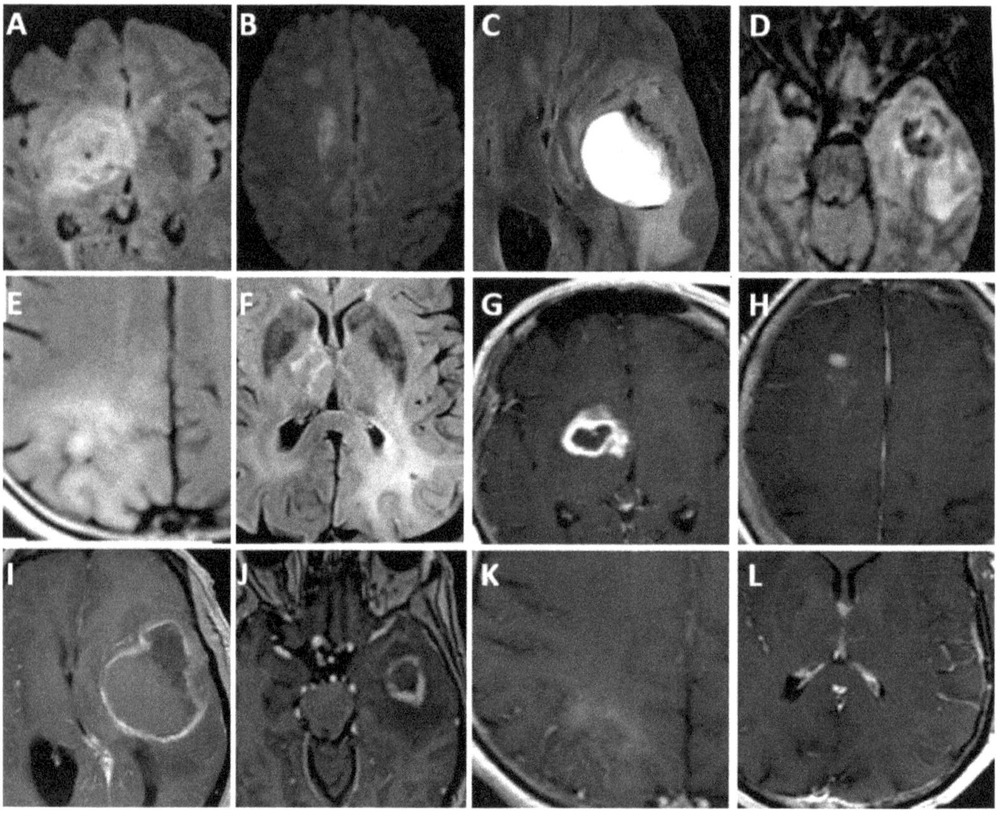

Figure 6. Spectrum of imaging found in five patients with WHO grade 4 glioblastoma, isocitrate dehydrogenase (IDH)-wildtype. Figures (**A–F**) are T2-weighted FLAIR, and (**G–L**) are post-contrast T1-weighted images. Figure components (**A**,**B**,**G**,**H**) are derived from a 74 year old woman with IDH-wildtype, +7/−10 chromosomal copy number changes. Images demonstrate a lesion centered in the right basal ganglia/ thalamocapsular region with ring enhancement (**G**), surrounding tumor infiltration, and vasogenic edema (**A**). Note the additional lesions with enhancement in the right frontal lobe (**H**). Figure components (**C**,**I**) are derived from a 55 year old man with left frontal IDH-wildtype glioblastoma, harboringtelomerase reverse transcriptase (TERT)-promoter mutation, epidermal growth factor receptor (EGFR) amplification, and +7/−10 chromosomal copy-number changes. Figure components (**D**,**J**) are derived from a 72 year old woman with left temporal IDH-wildtype glioblastoma, harboring TERT-promoter mutation, EGFR amplification, and +7/−10 chromosomal copy-number changes. Figure components (**E**,**K**) are derived from a 66 year old woman with IDH-wildtype glioblastoma with TERT-promoter mutation, demonstrating intrinsic T1 hyperintense signal (**K**), without enhancement. Note the presence of the surrounding FLAIR hyperintense signal (**E**). Figure components (**F**,**L**), derived from a 72 year old man originally diagnosed with "low-grade" glioma, but IDH-wildtype with TERT-promoter mutation, show infiltrative FLAIR signal (**F**) and no associated enhancement (**L**).

6. Reiterated Update: Age Demographics in Glioma Classification

As mentioned above, in the 2021 WHO classification, gliomas are categorized into "adult-type" and "pediatric-type" based on age demographics, recognizing some overlap [3]. Age-related variations in glioma presentation are recognized, highlighting the importance of tailored diagnostic approaches for each patient population [22]. For example, for individuals under 55 or with a history of lower-grade glioma, negative IDH1 staining prompts DNA sequencing for rare IDH1 or IDH2 mutations [14]. The absence of IDH mutations leads to the classification of glioblastoma as an IDH-wildtype. Midline tumors require testing for the H3 p.K28M (K27M) mutation, while hemispheric tumors, especially in younger patients, necessitate examination for H3 G34-mutant diffuse hemispheric gliomas [98]. Also, it is important to acknowledge overlap, i.e., adult-type gliomas mainly affect adults, but may also occur in children, whereas pediatric-type tumors, commonly found in children, may occasionally present in adults [14].

Pediatric-Type Diffuse High-Grade Glioma

This family includes Diffuse midline glioma, H3, K27-altered, Diffuse hemispheric glioma, H3 G34-mutant, Diffuse pediatric-type high-grade glioma, H3-wildtype and IDH-wildtype, and Infant-type hemispheric glioma [3].

7. Diffuse Midline Glioma, H3 K27-Altered

7.1. Epidemiology and Localization

Diffuse midline glioma, H3 K27-altered, represents a distinct category of brain tumors characterized by their aggressive nature and poor prognosis [20]. These tumors primarily affect children and young adults, although they can occur at any age [99]. They are most commonly located in the brainstem, thalamus, and spinal cord—regions critical for vital functions—which complicates treatment efforts [20].

7.2. Clinical Features

These aggressive brain tumors can have a rapid and severe onset due to their critical locations within the central nervous system. Most patients present with symptoms characterized by a classic triad: cranial nerve palsy, long tract signs, and ataxia [100]. Specifically, studies suggest that about 82% of patients experience cranial nerve palsy, which may manifest as facial weakness, double vision, or difficulty swallowing [101]. Long tract signs, including pyramidal tract impairment such as weakness, reflex abnormalities, and increased muscle tone, are observed in approximately 51% of cases [100]. Ataxia, which involves a lack of voluntary coordination of muscle movements, affects about 62% of these patients [101].

On the other hand, thalamic lesions commonly present with symptoms related to intracranial hypertension and motor or sensory deficits [101,102]. The increased intracranial pressure can lead to headaches, nausea, vomiting, blurred vision, and altered mental status [102]. Motor or sensory deficits due to the tumor's impact on the thalamic region, a critical area for sensory and motor signal relay, can result in varying degrees of paralysis or abnormal sensations [103].

Given their location in the brainstem and other midline structures, these tumors often impact the function of surrounding nervous tissue, leading to progressive and multifaceted symptoms. Seizures are less common in diffuse midline gliomas compared to other brain tumors due to their deep location away from the cerebral cortex [102].

7.3. Brief Genetic Overview

Chromatin is made up of nucleosomes, which are histone octamers wrapped by DNA. It helps regulate key cellular processes like transcription, replication, DNA repair, and genomic stability. This regulation is achieved through post-translational modifications of DNA and histones [104]. In humans, different histone H3 variants exist. H3.3 proteins are expressed continuously, whereas H3.1 and H3.2 are only expressed during the S phase of the cell cycle [104]. H3.3 is encoded by two genes, H3F3A and H3F3B [104]. Diffuse Midline Glioma, H3 K27-altered, harbors a mutation primarily of the of the H3F3A gene, leading to amino acid substitution where a lysine side chain, the 27th residue, is typically replaced by methionine [105].

The presence of the H3 K27M mutation initiates a series of molecular events that significantly alter the epigenetic landscape of the affected cells. H3K27 can undergo mono-methylation (H3K27me1), di-methylation (H3K27me2), tri-methylation (H3K27me3), or acetylation (H3K27ac) [104]. This mutation results in a hypomethylated state of H3K27me2 and H3K27me3 across the genome [106]. In vitro, H3K27M appears to affect the enzymatic activity of EZH2, a part of the Polycomb Repressive Complex 2 (PRC2) that typically adds methyl groups to H3K27 [107]. This interference results in a substantial decrease in H3K27me3 levels and presumed transcription dysregulation with derepression, contributing to the abnormal gene expression patterns observed in these tumors [104,108,109].

Diffuse midline gliomas, H3 K27-altered can be classified into distinct subclassifications based on the histone H3 variant [110–112]. The first subtype encompasses H3.3 - mutant cases [112]. The H3.3 p.K28M (K27M)-mutant involves mutations in the H3F3A gene encoding the H3.3 histone variant, predominantly affecting children and typically found in vital brain regions like the brainstem and thalamus [112]. The H3.1 or H3.2 p.K28M (K27M)-mutant subtype includes mutations in the HIST1H3B or HIST1H3C genes; these might exhibit distinct biological behavior, occurring in the pons of younger patients [3,111,112]. The third subtype is characterized by H3-wildtype tumors with overexpression of EZHIP, which mimics the effects of the K27M mutation by inhibiting the PRC2 complex. This leads to similar epigenetic deregulation [107,108,113,114]. Lastly, the EGFR-mutant subtype is driven by mutations in the EGFR gene, and is associated with varying tumor behaviors compared to histone-mutated gliomas [115,116]. Thus, given recognition of alternative mechanisms, the name has been changed from H3 K27-mutant to H3 K27-altered.

7.4. Imaging

These tumors have variable imaging characteristics, but can appear on MRI as ill-defined, infiltrative masses primarily located within the brainstem, thalamus, or spinal cord, frequently with no enhancement [112]. The H3.1 subtype reportedly has an increased propensity to demonstrate edema and necrosis with ring enhancement [111]. On T1-weighted MRI sequences, they usually present as hypointense or isointense, whereas on T2-weighted and Fluid-Attenuated Inversion Recovery (FLAIR) sequences, they are hyperintense. Contrast enhancement in general can vary, but many diffuse midline gliomas show a patchy or heterogeneous pattern after the administration of gadolinium-based contrast agents, which may correlate with areas of higher tumor cell density or a disrupted blood–brain barrier (Figure 7) [117].

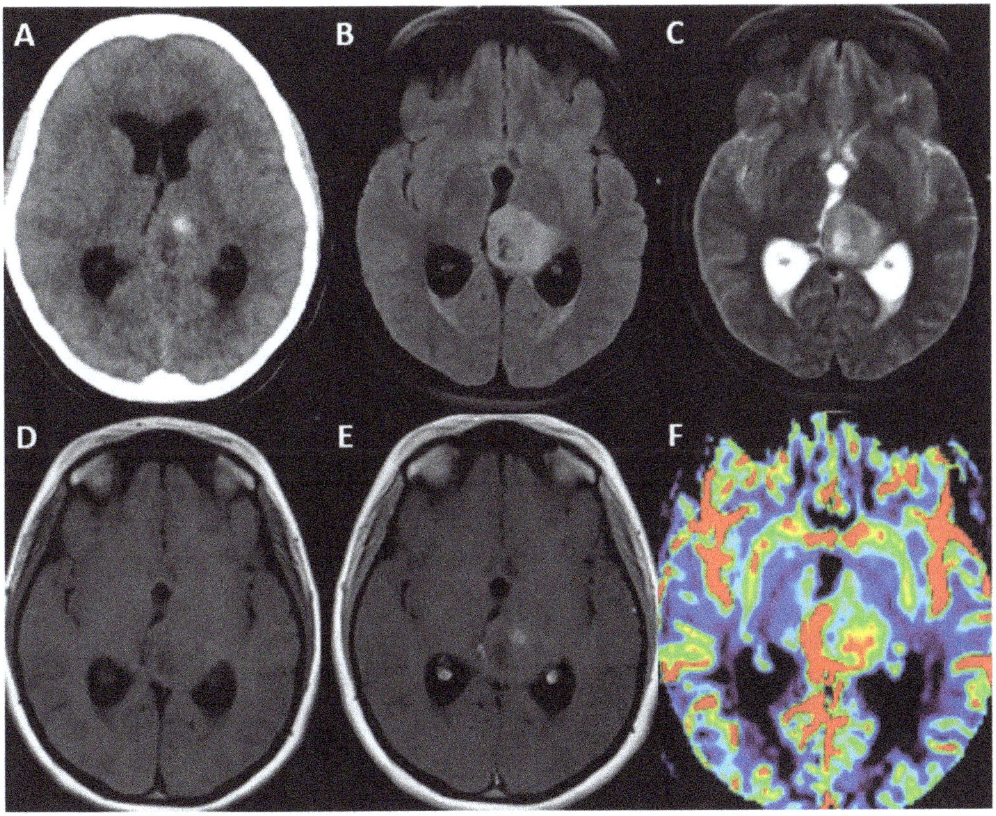

Figure 7. Axial unenhanced CT head (**A**), axial T2-weighted fluid-attenuated inversion recovery (FLAIR) (**B**), axial T2-weighted (**C**), axial T1-weighted (**D**), axial T1-weighted fat suppressed post-contrast (**E**), and cerebral blood volume (CBV) perfusion map (**F**) through the level of the thalamus in a 17 year old woman with diffuse midline glioma, H3K27-altered. Images illustrate an expansile, hyperintense left thalamic mass, more typical of adolescents/adults. This mass demonstrates heterogeneous contrast enhancement and increased perfusion. Histopathological diagnosis and grade were consistent with diffuse astrocytoma, WHO grade 2, by morphology. The patient had multiple recurrences with resections and radiation necrosis, eventually succumbing to the disease three years after presentation.

8. Diffuse Hemispheric Glioma, H3 G34-Mutant

In the 2021 WHO classification, a newly recognized tumor is Diffuse Hemispheric Glioma, H3 G34-mutant [118]. This tumor is characterized by mutations in H3F3A, leading to substitution at position G34, which influences both the biological behavior of the tumor and its response to therapy [111,119].

8.1. Clinical Features

Clinically, patients with H3 G34-mutant gliomas may present with symptoms related to increased intracranial pressure, such as headaches, nausea, and vomiting, or with seizures, focal neurological deficits, and cognitive or behavioral changes depending on the location of the tumor within the cerebral hemispheres [120].

8.2. Epidemiology and Localization

The epidemiology of diffuse hemispheric glioma with H3 G34 mutation shows a slight male predominance and a typically more aggressive course than other pediatric brain tumors [119]. This mutation is less common than the H3 K27M mutation found in midline gliomas, with specific genetic and clinical features that differentiate them from other glioma subtypes [121].

8.3. Brief Genetic Overview

Driving mutation here is a missense mutation of the H3F3A gene, eventually causing glycine 34 to be replaced by arginine or valine in the mature protein [121]. While G34 is not subject to methylation, this particular mutation leads to changes that inhibit binding of regulatory proteins and ultimately causes transcriptional reprograming [3,105]. Often, this mutation is found alongside alterations in Alpha Thalassemia/Mental Retardation Syndrome X-linked (ATRX) and mutations in TP53 [119].

8.4. Imaging

These lesions can present on MRI scans as contrast-enhancing tumors causing mass effect in cortical areas, commonly in the parietal or temporal lobe, with features that may include necrosis, cystic changes, hemorrhage, and calcifications [122]. They have been described as unifocal lesions with a propensity for ependymal and leptomeningeal contact [112,120].

9. Diffuse Pediatric-Type High-Grade Glioma, H3-Wildtype and IDH-Wildtype

Diffuse pediatric-type high-grade glioma H3-wildtype and IDH-wildtype is a heterogeneous group of tumors characterized by a combination of high-grade morphology, which can be either glial or primitive/undifferentiated [112].

9.1. Brief Genetic Overview

These tumors lack mutations in the IDH1 or IDH2 genes, and do not exhibit histone H3 alterations. Instead, they align with one of three pediatric high-grade glioma (pHGG) methylation groups: pHGG receptor tyrosine kinase 1 (RTK1), pHGG receptor tyrosine kinase 2 (RTK2), or pHGG V-Myc Avian Myelocytomatosis Viral Oncogene Neuroblastoma-Derived Homolog (MYCN) [112]. Alternatively, these tumors may be identified by the genetic alterations that are characteristic of these methylation groups, involving Platelet-Derived Growth Factor Receptor Alpha (PDGFRA) for the RTK1 group, EGFR for the RTK2 group, or MYCN for the MYCN group [112,123,124].

Relevance

The molecular pathology often involves the activation of RTKs like PDGFRA and EGFR, which trigger critical downstream signaling pathways including PI3K/AKT/mTOR and RAS/MAPK [21]. These pathways are essential for cell proliferation and survival, making them attractive targets for therapeutic intervention. For instance, the use of MEK inhibitors, which act on the MAPK pathway, has demonstrated potential in preclinical trials to curb tumor growth [125].

Furthermore, specific clinical scenarios, such as gliomas that develop after therapeutic radiation or those associated with germline mismatch repair deficiencies, often exhibit molecular characteristics, particularly the RTK1 subtype involving PDGFRA amplification [126,127].

9.2. Imaging

MRI characteristics typically resemble those of other high-grade gliomas, presenting as T2 hyperintense tumors with varying degrees of contrast enhancement and mass effect (Figures 8 and 9) [120,124].

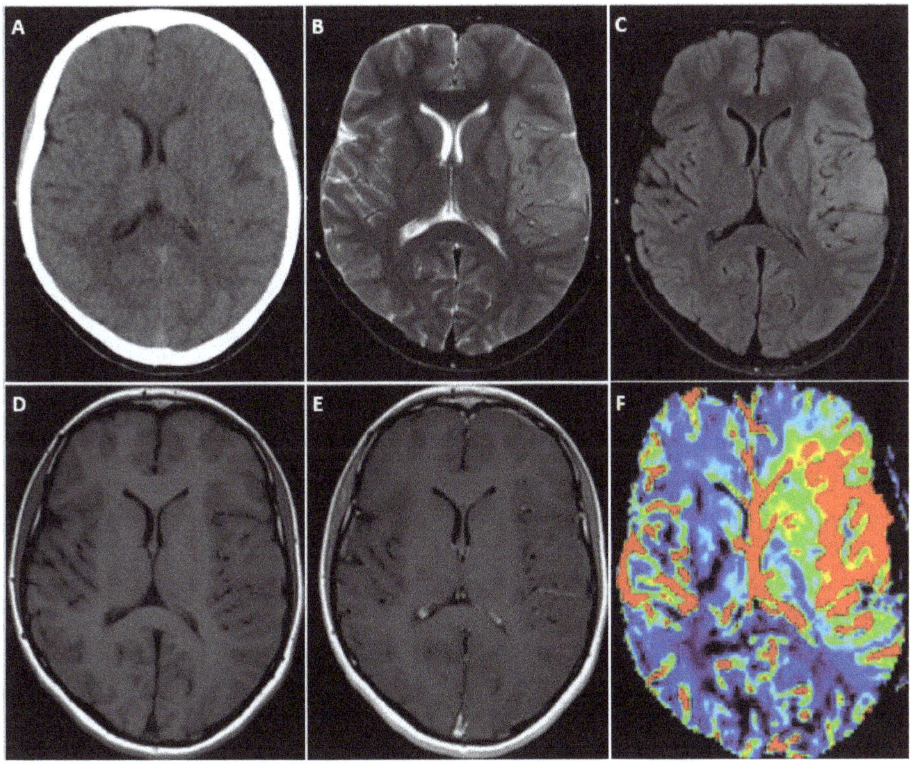

Figure 8. Axial unenhanced CT (**A**), axial T2- weighted (**B**), axial T2 fluid-attenuated inversion recovery (FLAIR) (**C**), axial T1-weighted (**D**), axial T1-weighted post-contrast (**E**), and cerebral blood volume map from dynamic susceptibility contrast (DSC) perfusion images (**F**) through the level of the lateral ventricles in a 22 year old female with diffuse hemispheric glioma, H3 G34-mutant and IDH-wildtype tumor, who presented with first-time seizure. The images demonstrate an infiltrative left frontal and left temporal operculum mass, as depicted by abnormal T2 FLAIR hyperintensity, with associated increased perfusion and no abnormal contrast enhancement. Lesion is unifocal with leptomeningeal contact at its lateral aspect. There was no diffusion abnormality. Note that this was initially misdiagnosed as acute encephalitis.

Figure 9. Sagittal T1-weighted (**A**), sagittal T2-weighted (**B**), and coronal T2-weighted short tau inversion recovery (STIR) cervical spine images (**C**) in a 32 year old woman with previously treated intracranial germinoma who presented with left sensorineural deficits. Images demonstrate an expansile, T1 hypointense and T2 hyperintense central pontine mass. This was diffuse pediatric-type high-grade glioma, H3-wildtype, receptor tyrosine kinase (RTK1) subtype, subclass C. RTK1 subtypes typically involve the supratentorial brain, with approximately 18% located in infratentorial/brainstem structures. Gliomas arising after therapeutic radiation, as in this patient, are predominantly of the RTK1 molecular subtype.

10. High-Grade Astrocytoma with Piloid Features

High-grade astrocytoma with piloid features (HGAP) represents a distinct category within the spectrum of brain tumors, newly recognized for its unique DNA methylation patterns that set it apart from other gliomas [3,128].

Epidemiologically, HGAP remains rare, and its exact incidence is still being delineated as the medical community gains a better understanding of its distinct molecular characteristics [3].

HGAP tumors can occur anywhere in the central nervous system (CNS), but they have a predilection for the cerebellum, where they can cause symptoms related to increased intracranial pressure, cerebellar dysfunction, or cranial nerve deficits, depending on their size and exact location [128,129] (Figure 10). They can be seen in the brain or spine, often midline or paramedian in location [130]. Imaging suggests a propensity for rim enhancement and central necrosis [129,130].

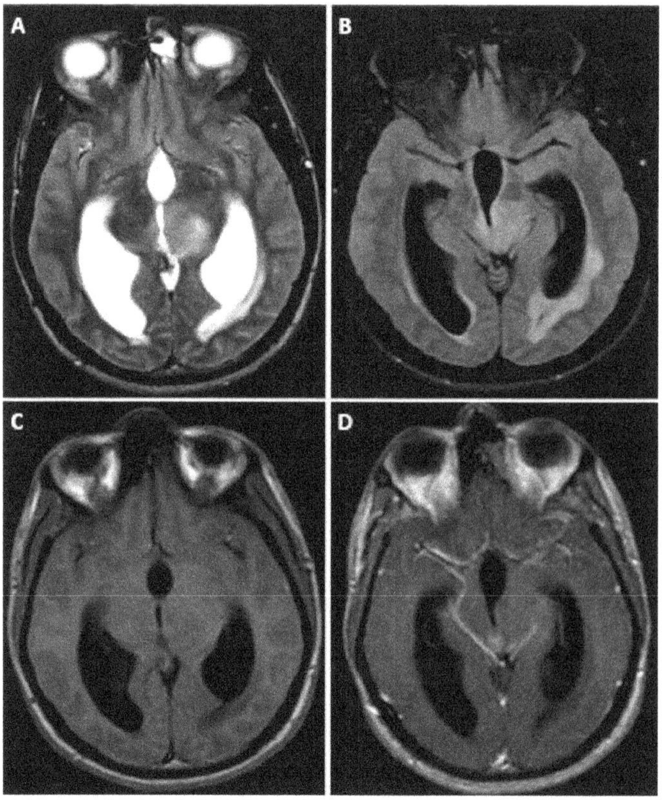

Figure 10. Axial T2-weighted (**A**), axial T2 fluid-attenuated inversion recovery (FLAIR) (**B**), axial T1-weighted (**C**), and axial T1-weighted post-contrast (**D**) images in 27 year old man with high-grade astrocytoma with piloid features (HGAP). Images demonstrate a heterogeneous T2 hyperintense mass centered in the left thalamus, extending into the tectal plate. There were some areas of heterogeneous enhancement. Local mass effect and obstruction at the level of the cerebral aqueduct resulted in upstream obstructive hydrocephalus. Molecular profiling showed isocitrate dehydrogenase (IDH) wildtype, alpha-thalassemia/mental retardation, X-linked (ATRX), Neurofibromin 1 (NF1) mutation, and cyclin-dependent kinase inhibitor 2A/B (CDKN2A/B) homozygous deletion. Collective molecular features suggest high-grade astrocytoma with piloid features (HGAP), according to WHO CNS5 tumor classification.

Brief Genetic Overview

From a genetic standpoint, HGAP commonly exhibits alterations in genes associated with the mitogen-activated protein kinase (MAPK) pathway, which is pivotal in cell growth and differentiation [128,129]. Additionally, this tumor type frequently shows homozygous deletion of the CDKN2A/B genes, which are crucial tumor suppressors regulating the cell cycle [129]. Loss or mutation of ATRX, a gene involved in chromatin remodeling, is another hallmark of HGAP, contributing to its distinct molecular profile [129].

11. Discussion

The 2021 World Health Organization (WHO) classification of central nervous system (CNS) tumors has ushered in a paradigm shift. This update underscores the increasing importance of genetic and molecular markers in the management of gliomas.

This molecular approach allows for deeper insights into tumor behavior, enabling more accurate prognostication and guiding treatment decisions, thus allowing for the development of personalized treatment plans tailored to the specific genetic profile of each tumor. As insight increases, the aim would be to maximize therapeutic efficacy and minimize adverse effects, ultimately improving patient outcomes.

Furthermore, the 2021 WHO classification is expected to drive significant advancements in research by providing a clearer framework for studying tumor biology. This, in turn, will likely accelerate the translation of research findings into clinical applications, hopefully fostering the development of innovative treatments that improve survival rates and quality of life for patients.

Ultimately, the standardized terminology and classification criteria introduced by the WHO update promotes consistency in diagnosis and treatment across healthcare systems. This enhances the comparability of clinical trial results, supports global treatment guidelines, and fosters international collaboration in research. Aligning clinical practice with the latest scientific insights ensures that patients worldwide benefit from advanced diagnostic and therapeutic strategies.

The updates and some imaging findings are summarized in Tables 1 and 2.

Table 1. Adult-type diffuse gliomas, alterations, imaging characteristics, and updates from 2016 WHO classification of CNS tumors.

Adult-Type Diffuse Glioma	Some Common Genetic/Molecular Alterations	Interval Update	Typical Imaging Characteristics
Astrocytoma, IDH-mutant	IDH1, IDH2, ATRX, TP53	CDKN2A/B homozygous deletion designated grade 4, no IDH-wildtype	Homogenous, circumscribed, T2-FLAIR mismatch sign
Oligodendroglioma, IDH-mutant and 1p/19q-codeleted	IDH1, IDH2, 1p/19q, TERT Promotor, CIC, FUBP1	CDKN2A/B homozygous deletion indicates a CNS WHO grade 3	Heterogeneity, calcification, variable enhancement, possible increased rCBV
Glioblastoma, IDH-wildtype	IDH-wildtype, TERT promotor, +7/−10 chromosome copy number changes, EGFR	Only IDH-wildtype no IDH-mutant, IDH-wildtype astrocytic tumors with 1 of following: Microvascular proliferation or necrosis, TERT promotor mutation, or EGFR gene amplification, +7/−10 chromosome copy number changes.	Inherent heterogeneity, heterogeneously enhancing, sometimes ring- enhancing around central necrosis, surrounding T2/FLAIR signal, edema and mass effect, increased rCBV, surrounding infiltration.

Table 2. Pediatric-type diffuse high-grade gliomas, alterations, imaging characteristics, and updates from 2016 WHO classification of CNS tumors.

Pediatric-Type Diffuse High-grade Gliomas	Some Common Alterations	Interval Update	Imaging Characteristics
Diffuse midline glioma, H3 K27-altered	H3 K27, TP53, ACVR, PDGFRA, EGFR, EZHIP	Name changed from H3K27-mutant, Subgroups recognized	Variable, ill-defined, infiltrative masses, in brainstem, thalamus, or spinal cord, frequently no enhancement, H3.1 subgroup-necrosis and edema likely.
Diffuse hemispheric glioma, H3 G34-mutant	H3 G34, TP53, ATRX	Newly recognized	Unifocal, cortex, ependymal and/or leptomeningeal contact.
Diffuse pediatric-type high-grade glioma, H3-wildtype, and IDH-wildtype	No IDH or H3 mutations, PDGFRA, MYCN, EGFR	Newly recognized	Heterogeneous, akin to other high-grade gliomas.
Infant-type hemispheric glioma (not discussed in this review)	NRTK family, ALK, ROS, MET	Newly recognized	Large masses with frequent superficial involvement including leptomeninges.

12. Conclusions

In conclusion, the 2021 WHO classification of CNS tumors represents a significant advancement in the field of medicine. By incorporating molecular diagnostics into the classification and grading of gliomas, the update enhances diagnostic precision and aligns clinical practice with the latest scientific insights. This integration of genetic and molecular data into routine diagnostic protocols is pivotal for accurate classification, prognosis, treatment, and follow-up strategies.

Radiologists and other healthcare professionals involved in the care of patients with CNS tumors must stay abreast of these updates to effectively contribute to multidisciplinary tumor boards and collaborate with peers in neuro-oncology, neurosurgery, radiation oncology, and neuropathology. The comprehensive understanding of molecular underpinnings provided by these updates facilitates personalized treatment approaches, ultimately improving patient outcomes through informed and precise imaging assessments.

Overall, the 2021 WHO classification marks a significant step forward in the understanding and management of CNS tumors. By further emphasizing molecular diagnostics, it promises to significantly advance the field, driving improvements in research, therapy, and global collaboration, ultimately leading to better patient outcomes. This review aims to simplify these changes and provide illustrative case examples to enhance understanding and application in clinical practice.

Author Contributions: R.G.: Writing—original draft; D.A.L.: Writing—review and editing. All authors have read and agreed to the published version of the manuscript.

Funding: This research received no external funding.

Conflicts of Interest: The authors declare no conflict of interest.

References

1. Scheithauer, B.W. Development of the WHO classification of tumors of the central nervous system: A historical perspective. *Brain Pathol.* **2009**, *19*, 551–564. [CrossRef]
2. Cree, I.A. The WHO Classification of Haematolymphoid Tumours. *Leukemia* **2022**, *36*, 1701–1702. [CrossRef]
3. WHO Classification of Tumours Editorial Board. Central Nervous System Tumours [Internet]. In *WHO Classification of Tumours Series*, 5th ed.; International Agency for Research on Cancer: Lyon, France, 2021; Volume 6. Available online: https://tumourclassification.iarc.who.int/chapters/45 (accessed on 4 May 2024).
4. Louis, D.N.; Perry, A.; Wesseling, P.; Brat, D.J.; Cree, I.A.; Figarella-Branger, D.; Hawkins, C.; Ng, H.K.; Pfister, S.M.; Reifenberger, G.; et al. The 2021 WHO Classification of Tumors of the Central Nervous System: A summary. *Neuro-Oncology* **2021**, *23*, 1231–1251. [CrossRef]

5. Saracci, R.; Wild, C.P. *International Agency for Research on Cancer: The First 50 Years, 1965–2015*; International Agency for Re-search on Cancer: Lyon, France, 2015.
6. Santanam, L.; Hurkmans, C.; Mutic, S.; van Vliet-Vroegindeweij, C.; Brame, S.; Straube, W.; Galvin, J.; Tripuraneni, P.; Michalski, J.; Bosch, W. Standardizing naming conventions in radiation oncology. *Int. J. Radiat. Oncol.* **2012**, *83*, 1344–1349. [CrossRef]
7. Gritsch, S.; Batchelor, T.T.; Castro, L.N.G. Diagnostic, therapeutic, and prognostic implications of the 2021 World Health Organization classification of tumors of the central nervous system. *Cancer* **2022**, *128*, 47–58. [CrossRef]
8. Cree, I.A.; Ruiz, B.I.I.; Zavadil, J.; McKay, J.; Olivier, M.; Kozlakidis, Z.; Lazar, A.J.; Hyde, C.; Holdenrieder, S.; Hastings, R.; et al. The International Collaboration for Cancer Classification and Research. *Int. J. Cancer* **2021**, *148*, 560–571. [CrossRef]
9. Berger, T.R.; Wen, P.Y.; Lang-Orsini, M.; Chukwueke, U.N. World Health Organization 2021 Classification of Central Nervous System Tumors and Implications for Therapy for Adult-Type Gliomas: A Review. *JAMA Oncol.* **2022**, *8*, 1493–1501. [CrossRef]
10. Louis, D.N.; Wesseling, P.; Aldape, K.; Brat, D.J.; Capper, D.; Cree, I.A.; Eberhart, C.; Figarella-Branger, D.; Fouladi, M.; Fuller, G.N.; et al. cIMPACT-NOW update 6: New entity and diagnostic principle recommendations of the cIMPACT-Utrecht meeting on future CNS tumor classification and grading. *Brain Pathol.* **2020**, *30*, 844–856. [CrossRef]
11. Capper, D.; Jones, D.T.W.; Sill, M.; Hovestadt, V.; Schrimpf, D.; Sturm, D.; Koelsche, C.; Sahm, F.; Chavez, L.; Reuss, D.E.; et al. DNA methylation-based classification of central nervous system tumours. *Nature* **2018**, *555*, 469–474. [CrossRef]
12. Johnson, D.R.; Giannini, C.; Vaubel, R.A.; Morris, J.M.; Eckel, L.J.; Kaufmann, T.J.; Guerin, J.B. A Radiologist's Guide to the 2021 WHO Central Nervous System Tumor Classification: Part I—Key Concepts and the Spectrum of Diffuse Gliomas. *Radiology* **2022**, *304*, 494–508. [CrossRef]
13. Jaunmuktane, Z.; Capper, D.; Jones, D.T.W.; Schrimpf, D.; Sill, M.; Dutt, M.; Suraweera, N.; Pfister, S.M.; von Deimling, A.; Brandner, S. Methylation array profiling of adult brain tumours: Diagnostic outcomes in a large, single centre. *Acta Neuropathol. Commun.* **2019**, *7*, 24. [CrossRef]
14. Osborn, A.; Louis, D.; Poussaint, T.; Linscott, L.; Salzman, K. The 2021 World Health Organization Classification of Tumors of the Central Nervous System: What Neuroradiologists Need to Know. *Am. J. Neuroradiol.* **2022**, *43*, 928–937. [CrossRef]
15. Bent, M.J.v.D.; Weller, M.; Wen, P.Y.; Kros, J.M.; Aldape, K.; Chang, S. A clinical perspective on the 2016 WHO brain tumor classification and routine molecular diagnostics. *Neuro-Oncology* **2017**, *19*, 614–624. [CrossRef]
16. Brat, D.J.; Aldape, K.; Colman, H.; Figrarella-Branger, D.; Fuller, G.N.; Giannini, C.; Holland, E.C.; Jenkins, R.B.; Kleinschmidt-DeMasters, B.; Komori, T.; et al. cIMPACT-NOW update 5: Rec-ommended grading criteria and terminologies for IDH-mutant astrocytomas. *Acta Neuropathol.* **2020**, *139*, 603–608. [CrossRef]
17. Brat, D.J.; Aldape, K.; Colman, H.; Holland, E.C.; Louis, D.N.; Jenkins, R.B.; Kleinschmidt-DeMasters, B.K.; Perry, A.; Reifenberger, G.; Stupp, R.; et al. cIMPACT-NOW update 3: Recommended diagnostic criteria for "Diffuse astrocytic glioma, IDH-wildtype, with molecular features of glioblastoma, WHO grade IV". *Acta Neuropathol.* **2018**, *136*, 805–810. [CrossRef]
18. Louis, D.N.; Wesseling, P.; Paulus, W.; Giannini, C.; Batchelor, T.T.; Cairncross, J.G.; Capper, D.; Figarella-Branger, D.; Lopes, M.B.; Wick, W.; et al. cIMPACT-NOW update 1: Not Otherwise Specified (NOS) and Not Elsewhere Classified (NEC). *Acta Neuropathol.* **2018**, *135*, 481–484. [CrossRef]
19. Louis, D.N.; Ellison, D.W.; Brat, D.J.; Aldape, K.; Capper, D.; Hawkins, C.; Paulus, W.; Perry, A.; Reifenberger, G.; Figarella-Branger, D.; et al. cIMPACT-NOW: A practical summary of diagnostic points from Round 1 updates. *Brain Pathol.* **2019**, *29*, 469–472. [CrossRef]
20. Louis, D.N.; Giannini, C.; Capper, D.; Paulus, W.; Figarella-Branger, D.; Lopes, M.B.; Batchelor, T.T.; Cairncross, J.G.; van den Bent, M.; Wick, W.; et al. cIMPACT-NOW update 2: Diagnostic clarifications for diffuse midline glioma, H3 K27M-mutant and diffuse astrocytoma/anaplastic astrocytoma, IDH-mutant. *Acta Neuropathol.* **2018**, *135*, 639–642. [CrossRef]
21. Buczkowicz, P.; Hoeman, C.; Rakopoulos, P.; Pajovic, S.; Letourneau, L.; Dzamba, M.; Morrison, A.; Lewis, P.; Bouffet, E.; Bartels, U.; et al. Genomic analysis of diffuse in-trinsic pontine gliomas identifies three molecular subgroups and recurrent activating ACVR1 mutations. *Nat. Genet.* **2014**, *46*, 451–456. [CrossRef]
22. Roux, A.; Pallud, J.; Saffroy, R.; Edjlali-Goujon, M.; Debily, M.-A.; Boddaert, N.; Sanson, M.; Puget, S.; Knafo, S.; Adam, C.; et al. High-grade gliomas in adolescents and young adults highlight histomolecular differences from their adult and pediatric counterparts. *Neuro-Oncology* **2020**, *22*, 1190–1202. [CrossRef]
23. Balss, J.; Meyer, J.; Mueller, W.; Korshunov, A.; Hartmann, C.; von Deimling, A. Analysis of the IDH1 codon 132 mutation in brain tumors. *Acta Neuropathol.* **2008**, *116*, 597–602. [CrossRef]
24. Capper, D.; Zentgraf, H.; Balss, J.; Hartmann, C.; von Deimling, A. Monoclonal antibody specific for IDH1 R132H mutation. *Acta Neuropathol.* **2009**, *118*, 599–601. [CrossRef]
25. Yan, H.; Parsons, D.W.; Jin, G.; McLendon, R.; Rasheed, B.A.; Yuan, W.; Kos, I.; Batinic-Haberle, I.; Jones, S.; Riggins, G.J.; et al. *IDH1* and *IDH2* Mutations in Gliomas. *N. Engl. J. Med.* **2009**, *360*, 765–773. [CrossRef]
26. Du, X.; Hu, H. The Roles of 2-Hydroxyglutarate. *Front. Cell Dev. Biol.* **2021**, *9*, 651317. [CrossRef]
27. Ward, P.S.; Patel, J.; Wise, D.R.; Abdel-Wahab, O.; Bennett, B.D.; Coller, H.A.; Cross, J.R.; Fantin, V.R.; Hedvat, C.V.; Perl, A.E.; et al. The common feature of leukemia-associated IDH1 and IDH2 mutations is a neomorphic enzyme activity converting alpha-ketoglutarate to 2-hydroxyglutarate. *Cancer Cell* **2010**, *17*, 225–234. [CrossRef]
28. Noushmehr, H.; Weisenberger, D.J.; Diefes, K.; Phillips, H.S.; Pujara, K.; Berman, B.P.; Pan, F.; Pelloski, C.E.; Sulman, E.P.; Bhat, K.P.; et al. Identification of a CpG island methylator phenotype that defines a distinct subgroup of glioma. *Cancer Cell* **2010**, *17*, 510–522. [CrossRef]

29. Chowdhury, R.; Yeoh, K.K.; Tian, Y.-M.; Hillringhaus, L.; Bagg, E.A.; Rose, N.R.; Leung, I.K.H.; Li, X.S.; Woon, E.C.Y.; Yang, M.; et al. The oncometabolite 2-hydroxyglutarate inhibits histone lysine demethylases. *EMBO Rep.* **2011**, *12*, 463–469. [CrossRef]
30. Xu, W.; Yang, H.; Liu, Y.; Yang, Y.; Wang, P.; Kim, S.-H.; Ito, S.; Yang, C.; Wang, P.; Xiao, M.-T.; et al. Oncometabolite 2-hydroxyglutarate is a competitive inhibitor of alpha-ketoglutarate-dependent dioxygenases. *Cancer Cell* **2011**, *19*, 17–30. [CrossRef]
31. Ozair, A.; Bhat, V.; Alisch, R.S.; Khosla, A.A.; Kotecha, R.R.; Odia, Y.; McDermott, M.W.; Ahluwalia, M.S. DNA Methylation and Histone Modification in Low-Grade Gliomas: Current Understanding and Potential Clinical Targets. *Cancers* **2023**, *15*, 1342. [CrossRef]
32. Ye, D.; Guan, K.-L.; Xiong, Y. Metabolism, Activity, and Targeting of D- and L-2-Hydroxyglutarates. *Trends Cancer* **2018**, *4*, 151–165. [CrossRef]
33. Dang, L.; White, D.W.; Gross, S.; Bennett, B.D.; Bittinger, M.A.; Driggers, E.M.; Fantin, V.R.; Jang, H.G.; Jin, S.; Keenan, M.C.; et al. Cancer-associated IDH1 mutations produce 2-hydroxyglutarate. *Nature* **2010**, *465*, 966. [CrossRef]
34. Zhang, L.; Sorensen, M.D.; Kristensen, B.W.; Reifenberger, G.; McIntyre, T.M.; Lin, F. D-2-Hydroxyglutarate Is an Intercellular Mediator in IDH-Mutant Gliomas Inhibiting Complement and T Cells. *Clin. Cancer Res.* **2018**, *24*, 5381–5391. [CrossRef]
35. Modrek, A.S.; Golub, D.; Khan, T.; Bready, D.; Prado, J.; Bowman, C.; Deng, J.; Zhang, G.; Rocha, P.P.; Raviram, R.; et al. Low-Grade Astrocytoma Mutations in IDH1, P53, and ATRX Cooperate to Block Differentiation of Human Neural Stem Cells via Repression of SOX2. *Cell Rep.* **2017**, *21*, 1267–1280. [CrossRef]
36. Eckel-Passow, J.E.; Lachance, D.H.; Molinaro, A.M.; Walsh, K.M.; Decker, P.A.; Sicotte, H.; Pekmezci, M.; Rice, T.; Kosel, M.L.; Smirnov, I.V.; et al. Glioma Groups Based on 1p/19q, IDH, and TERT Promoter Mutations in Tumors. *N. Engl. J. Med.* **2015**, *372*, 2499–2508. [CrossRef]
37. Negrini, S.; Gorgoulis, V.G.; Halazonetis, T.D. Genomic instability--an evolving hallmark of cancer. *Nat. Rev. Mol. Cell Biol.* **2010**, *11*, 220–228. [CrossRef]
38. Kannan, K.; Inagaki, A.; Silber, J.; Gorovets, D.; Zhang, J.; Kastenhuber, E.R.; Heguy, A.; Petrini, J.H.; Chan, T.A.; Huse, J.T. Whole exome sequencing identifies ATRX mutation as a key molecular determinant in lower-grade glioma. *Oncotarget* **2012**, *3*, 1194–1203. [CrossRef]
39. Appay, R.; Dehais, C.; Maurage, C.-A.; Alentorn, A.; Carpentier, C.; Colin, C.; Ducray, F.; Escande, F.; Idbaih, A.; Kamoun, A.; et al. CDKN2A homozygous deletion is a strong adverse prognosis factor in diffuse malignant IDH-mutant gliomas. *Neuro-Oncology* **2019**, *21*, 1519–1528. [CrossRef]
40. Ming, Z.; Lim, S.Y.; Rizos, H. Genetic Alterations in the INK4a/ARF Locus: Effects on Melanoma Development and Progression. *Biomolecules* **2020**, *10*, 1447. [CrossRef]
41. Malumbres, M.; Carnero, A. Cell cycle deregulation: A common motif in cancer. *Prog. Cell Cycle Res.* **2003**, *5*, 5–18.
42. Ichimura, K.; Bolin, M.B.; Goike, H.M.; Schmidt, E.E.; Moshref, A.; Collins, V.P. Deregulation of the p14ARF/MDM2/p53 pathway is a prerequisite for human astrocytic gliomas with G1-S transition control gene abnormalities. *Cancer Res.* **2000**, *60*, 417–424.
43. Xia, Y.; Liu, Y.; Yang, C.; Simeone, D.M.; Sun, T.-T.; DeGraff, D.J.; Tang, M.-S.; Zhang, Y.; Wu, X.-R. Dominant role of CDKN2B/p15INK4B of 9p21.3 tumor suppressor hub in inhibition of cell-cycle and glycolysis. *Nat. Commun.* **2021**, *12*, 2047. [CrossRef] [PubMed]
44. Wang, J.; Xi, Y.-F.; Zhao, Q.; Guo, J.-H.; Zhang, Z.; Zhang, M.-B.; Chang, J.; Wu, Y.-Q.; Su, W. CDKN2A promoter methylation enhances self-renewal of glioblastoma stem cells and confers resistance to carmustine. *Mol. Biol. Rep.* **2024**, *51*, 385. [CrossRef] [PubMed]
45. Dick, F.A.; Rubin, S.M. Molecular mechanisms underlying RB protein function. *Nat. Rev. Mol. Cell Biol.* **2013**, *14*, 297–306. [CrossRef] [PubMed]
46. Schmidt, E.E.; Ichimura, K.; Messerle, K.R.; Goike, H.M.; Collins, V.P. Infrequent methylation of CDKN2A(MTS1/p16) and rare mutation of both CDKN2A and CDKN2B(MTS2/p15) in primary astrocytic tumours. *Br. J. Cancer* **1997**, *75*, 2–8. [CrossRef]
47. Andersson, N.; Saba, K.H.; Magnusson, L.; Nilsson, J.; Karlsson, J.; Nord, K.H.; Gisselsson, D. Inactivation of RB1, CDKN2A, and TP53 have distinct effects on genomic stability at side-by-side comparison in karyotypically normal cells. Genes. *Chromo-somes Cancer* **2023**, *62*, 93–100. [CrossRef] [PubMed]
48. Schiff, D.; Bent, M.V.D.; Vogelbaum, M.A.; Wick, W.; Miller, C.R.; Taphoorn, M.; Pope, W.; Brown, P.D.; Platten, M.; Jalali, R.; et al. Recent developments and future directions in adult lower-grade gliomas: Society for Neuro-Oncology (SNO) and European Association of Neuro-Oncology (EANO) consensus. *Neuro-Oncology* **2019**, *21*, 837–853. [CrossRef] [PubMed]
49. Tans, J.; de Jongh, I. Computed tomography of supratentorial astrocytoma. *Clin. Neurol. Neurosurg.* **1978**, *80*, 156–168. [CrossRef] [PubMed]
50. Ikeda, Y.; Nakazawa, S. Analysis of peritumoral edema--with special reference to the value of contrast-enhanced CT scan and dynamic CT scan. *No Shinkei* **1984**, *36*, 1055–1062.
51. Zhao, K.; Sun, G.; Wang, Q.; Xue, Z.; Liu, G.; Xia, Y.; Yao, A.; Zhao, Y.; You, N.; Yang, C.; et al. The Diagnostic Value of Conventional MRI and CT Features in the Identification of the IDH1-Mutant and 1p/19q Co-Deletion in WHO Grade II Gliomas. *Acad. Radiol.* **2021**, *28*, e189–e198. [CrossRef]
52. Patel, S.H.; Poisson, L.M.; Brat, D.J.; Zhou, Y.; Cooper, L.; Snuderl, M.; Thomas, C.; Franceschi, A.M.; Griffith, B.; Flanders, A.E.; et al. T2–FLAIR Mismatch, an Imaging Biomarker for IDH and 1p/19q Status in Lower-grade Gliomas: A TCGA/TCIA Project. *Clin. Cancer Res.* **2017**, *23*, 6078–6085. [CrossRef]

53. Mohammed, S.; Ravikumar, V.; Warner, E.; Patel, S.; Bakas, S.; Rao, A.; Jain, R. Quantifying T2-FLAIR Mismatch Using Geographically Weighted Regression and Predicting Molecular Status in Lower-Grade Gliomas. *Am. J. Neuroradiol.* **2022**, *43*, 33–39. [CrossRef]
54. van Garderen, K.A.; Vallentgoed, W.R.; Lavrova, A.; Niers, J.M.; de Leng, W.W.; Hoogstrate, Y.; de Heer, I.; Ylstra, B.; van Dijk, E.; Klein, S.; et al. Longitudinal char-acteristics of T2-FLAIR mismatch in IDH-mutant astrocytomas: Relation to grade, histopathology, and overall survival in the GLASS-NL cohort. *Neuro-Oncol. Adv.* **2023**, *5*, vdad149. [CrossRef]
55. Juratli, T.A.; Tummala, S.S.; Riedl, A.; Daubner, D.; Hennig, S.; Penson, T.; Zolal, A.; Thiede, C.; Schackert, G.; Krex, D.; et al. Radiographic assessment of contrast en-hancement and T2/FLAIR mismatch sign in lower grade gliomas: Correlation with molecular groups. *J. Neuro-Oncol.* **2019**, *141*, 327–335. [CrossRef] [PubMed]
56. Doig, D.; Kachramanoglou, C.; Dumba, M.; Tona, F.; Gontsarova, A.; Limbäck, C.; Jan, W. Characterisation of isocitrate dehydrogenase gene mutant WHO grade 2 and 3 gliomas: MRI predictors of 1p/19q co-deletion and tumour grade. *Clin. Radiol.* **2021**, *785.e9*, 785.e16. [CrossRef] [PubMed]
57. Lasocki, A.; Gaillard, F. Non-Contrast-Enhancing Tumor: A New Frontier in Glioblastoma Research. *Am. J. Neuroradiol.* **2019**, *40*, 758–765. [CrossRef]
58. Bent, M.J.v.D.; Smits, M.; Kros, J.M.; Chang, S.M. Diffuse Infiltrating Oligodendroglioma and Astrocytoma. *J. Clin. Oncol.* **2017**, *35*, 2394–2401. [CrossRef]
59. Smits, M. Imaging of oligodendroglioma. *Br. J. Radiol.* **2016**, *89*, 20150857. [CrossRef]
60. Chen, R.; Nishimura, M.C.; Kharbanda, S.; Peale, F.; Deng, Y.; Daemen, A.; Forrest, W.F.; Kwong, M.; Hedehus, M.; Hatzivassiliou, G.; et al. Hominoid-specific enzyme GLUD2 promotes growth of IDH1 R132H glioma. *Proc. Natl. Acad. Sci. USA* **2014**, *111*, 14217–14222. [CrossRef] [PubMed]
61. Ghisai, S.A.; van Hijfte, L.; Vallentgoed, W.R.; Tesileanu, C.M.S.; de Heer, I.; Kros, J.M.; Sanson, M.; Gorlia, T.; Wick, W.; Vogelbaum, M.A.; et al. Epigenetic landscape reorgan-ization and reactivation of embryonic development genes are associated with malignancy in IDH-mutant astrocytoma. *bioRxiv* **2024**. [CrossRef]
62. Lai, A.; Kharbanda, S.; Pope, W.B.; Tran, A.; Solis, O.E.; Peale, F.; Forrest, W.F.; Pujara, K.; Carrillo, J.A.; Pandita, A.; et al. Evidence for Sequenced Molecular Evolution of *IDH1* Mutant Glioblastoma From a Distinct Cell of Origin. *J. Clin. Oncol.* **2011**, *29*, 4482–4490. [CrossRef]
63. Wesseling, P.; Bent, M.v.D.; Perry, A. Oligodendroglioma: Pathology, molecular mechanisms and markers. *Acta Neuropathol.* **2015**, *129*, 809–827. [CrossRef] [PubMed]
64. Tang, L.; Deng, L.; Bai, H.X.; Sun, J.; Neale, N.; Wu, J.; Wang, Y.; Chang, K.; Huang, R.Y.; Zhang, P.J.; et al. Reduced expression of DNA repair genes and chemosensitivity in 1p19q codeleted lower-grade gliomas. *J. Neuro-Oncol.* **2018**, *139*, 563–571. [CrossRef] [PubMed]
65. Cairncross, J.G.; Wang, M.; Jenkins, R.B.; Shaw, E.G.; Giannini, C.; Brachman, D.G.; Buckner, J.C.; Fink, K.L.; Souhami, L.; Laperriere, N.J.; et al. Benefit from procarbazine, lomustine, and vincristine in oligodendroglial tumors is associated with mutation of IDH. *J. Clin. Oncol.* **2014**, *32*, 783–790. [CrossRef] [PubMed]
66. Bettegowda, C.; Agrawal, N.; Jiao, Y.; Sausen, M.; Wood, L.D.; Hruban, R.H.; Rodriguez, F.J.; Cahill, D.P.; McLendon, R.; Riggins, G.; et al. Mutations in *CIC* and *FUBP1* Contribute to Human Oligodendroglioma. *Science* **2011**, *333*, 1453–1455. [CrossRef]
67. Halani, S.H.; Yousefi, S.; Vega, J.V.; Rossi, M.R.; Zhao, Z.; Amrollahi, F.; Holder, C.A.; Baxter-Stoltzfus, A.; Eschbacher, J.; Griffith, B.; et al. Multi-faceted computational assessment of risk and progression in oligodendroglioma implicates NOTCH and PI3K pathways. *NPJ Precis. Oncol.* **2018**, *2*, 24. [CrossRef] [PubMed]
68. Park, J.-W.; Kilic, O.; Deo, M.; Jimenez-Cowell, K.; Demirdizen, E.; Kim, H.; Turcan, S. CIC reduces xCT/SLC7A11 expression and glutamate release in glioma. *Acta Neuropathol. Commun.* **2023**, *11*, 13. [CrossRef] [PubMed]
69. Sahm, F.; Brandner, S.; Bertero, L.; Capper, D.; French, P.J.; Figarella-Branger, D.; Giangaspero, F.; Haberler, C.; Hegi, M.E.; Kristensen, B.W.; et al. Molecular diagnostic tools for the World Health Organization (WHO) 2021 classification of gliomas, glioneuronal and neuronal tumors; an EANO guideline. *Neuro-Oncology* **2023**, *25*, 1731–1749. [CrossRef] [PubMed]
70. Weller, M.; van den Bent, M.; Preusser, M.; Le Rhun, E.; Tonn, J.C.; Minniti, G.; Bendszus, M.; Balana, C.; Chinot, O.; Dirven, L.; et al. EANO guidelines on the diagnosis and treatment of diffuse gliomas of adulthood. *Nat. Rev. Clin. Oncol.* **2021**, *18*, 170–186. [CrossRef]
71. Khalid, L.; Carone, M.; Dumrongpisutikul, N.; Intrapiromkul, J.; Bonekamp, D.; Barker, P.B.; Yousem, D.M. Imaging Characteristics of Oligodendrogliomas That Predict Grade. *Am. J. Neuroradiol.* **2012**, *33*, 852–857. [CrossRef]
72. Kumar, M.; Nanga, R.P.R.; Verma, G.; Wilson, N.; Brisset, J.C.; Nath, K.; Chawla, S. Emerging MR Imaging and Spectroscopic Methods to Study Brain Tumor Metabolism. *Front. Neurol.* **2022**, *13*, 789355. [CrossRef]
73. de Godoy, L.L.; Lim, K.C.; Rajan, A.; Verma, G.; Hanaoka, M.; O'rourke, D.M.; Lee, J.Y.K.; Desai, A.; Chawla, S.; Mohan, S. Non-Invasive Assessment of Isocitrate Dehydrogenase-Mutant Gliomas Using Optimized Proton Magnetic Resonance Spectroscopy on a Routine Clinical 3-Tesla MRI. *Cancers* **2023**, *15*, 4453. [CrossRef] [PubMed]
74. Serkova, N.J.; Brown, M.S. Quantitative analysis in magnetic resonance spectroscopy: From metabolic profiling to in vivo biomarkers. *Bioanalysis* **2012**, *4*, 321–341. [CrossRef] [PubMed]

75. Stichel, D.; Ebrahimi, A.; Reuss, D.; Schrimpf, D.; Ono, T.; Shirahata, M.; Reifenberger, G.; Weller, M.; Hänggi, D.; Wick, W.; et al. Distribution of *EGFR* amplification, combined chromosome 7 gain and chromosome 10 loss, and *TERT* promoter mutation in brain tumors and their potential for the reclas-sification of IDHwt astrocytoma to glioblastoma. *Acta Neuropathol.* **2018**, *136*, 793–803. [CrossRef] [PubMed]
76. Qazi, M.A.; Vora, P.; Venugopal, C.; Sidhu, S.S.; Moffat, J.; Swanton, C.; Singh, S.K. Intratumoral heterogeneity: Pathways to treatment resistance and relapse in human glioblastoma. *Ann. Oncol.* **2017**, *28*, 1448–1456. [CrossRef] [PubMed]
77. Auffinger, B.; Spencer, D.; Pytel, P.; Ahmed, A.U.; Lesniak, M.S. The role of glioma stem cells in chemotherapy resistance and glioblastoma multiforme recurrence. *Expert Rev. Neurother.* **2015**, *15*, 741–752. [CrossRef] [PubMed]
78. Vivanco, I.; Rohle, D.; Versele, M.; Iwanami, A.; Kuga, D.; Oldrini, B.; Tanaka, K.; Dang, J.; Kubek, S.; Palaskas, N.; et al. The phosphatase and tensin homolog regulates epidermal growth factor receptor (EGFR) inhibitor response by targeting EGFR for degradation. *Proc. Natl. Acad. Sci. USA* **2010**, *107*, 6459–6464. [CrossRef] [PubMed]
79. Verhaak, R.G.W.; Hoadley, K.A.; Purdom, E.; Wang, V.; Wilkerson, M.D.; Miller, C.R.; Ding, L.; Golub, T.; Jill, P.; Alexe, G.; et al. Integrated genomic analysis identifies clinically relevant subtypes of glioblastoma characterized by abnormalities in PDGFRA, IDH1, EGFR, and NF1. *Cancer Cell* **2010**, *17*, 98–110. [CrossRef] [PubMed]
80. Hansen, A.L.; Desai, S.M.; Cooper, A.N.; Steinbach, M.A.; Gosselin, K.; Wanebo, J.E. The clinical progression of patients with glioblastoma. *Interdiscip. Neurosurg.* **2023**, *32*, 101756. [CrossRef]
81. McKinnon, C.; Nandhabalan, M.; Murray, S.A.; Plaha, P. Glioblastoma: Clinical presentation, diagnosis, and management. *BMJ* **2021**, *374*, n1560. [CrossRef]
82. Hanif, F.; Muzaffar, K.; Perveen, K.; Malhi, S.M.; Simjee, S.U. Glioblastoma Multiforme: A Review of its Epidemiology and Pathogenesis through Clinical Presentation and Treatment. *Asian Pac. J. Cancer Prev.* **2017**, *18*, 3–9.
83. Grochans, S.; Cybulska, A.M.; Simińska, D.; Korbecki, J.; Kojder, K.; Chlubek, D.; Baranowska-Bosiacka, I. Epidemiology of Glioblastoma Multiforme–Literature Review. *Cancers* **2022**, *14*, 2412. [CrossRef]
84. Neftel, C.; Laffy, J.; Filbin, M.G.; Hara, T.; Shore, M.E.; Rahme, G.J.; Richman, A.R.; Silverbush, D.; Shaw, M.L.; Hebert, C.M.; et al. An Integrative Model of Cellular States, Plasticity, and Genetics for Glioblastoma. *Cell* **2019**, *178*, 835–849. [CrossRef]
85. Carrillo, J.; Lai, A.; Nghiemphu, P.L.; Kim, H.J.; Phillips, H.S.; Kharbanda, S.; Moftakhar, P.; Lalaezari, S.; Yong, W.; Ellingson, B.M.; et al. Relationship between Tumor En-hancement, Edema, IDH1 Mutational Status, MGMT Promoter Methylation, and Survival in Glioblastoma. *Am. J. Neuroradiol.* **2012**, *33*, 1349–1355. [CrossRef]
86. Fan, H.; Yu, Y.; Du, J.; Liu, L.; Luo, Y.; Yu, H.; Liao, X. Computed Tomography, Magnetic Resonance Imaging, and Pathological Features of Gliosarcoma. *Neuropsychiatr. Dis. Treat.* **2022**, *18*, 2577–2589. [CrossRef] [PubMed]
87. Melhem, J.M.; Detsky, J.; Lim-Fat, M.J.; Perry, J.R. Updates in IDH-Wildtype Glioblastoma. *Neurotherapeutics* **2022**, *19*, 1705–1723. [CrossRef] [PubMed]
88. Drumm, M.R.; Dixit, K.S.; Grimm, S.; Kumthekar, P.; Lukas, R.V.; Raizer, J.J.; Stupp, R.; Chheda, M.G.; Kam, K.-L.; McCord, M.; et al. Extensive brainstem infiltration, not mass effect, is a common feature of end-stage cerebral glioblastomas. *Neuro-Oncology* **2020**, *22*, 470–479. [CrossRef] [PubMed]
89. Matute-González, M.; Mosteiro-Cadaval, A.; Vidal-Robau, N.; Páez-Carpio, A.; Valduvieco, I.; Pineda, E.; González, J.J.; Aldecoa, I.; Oleaga, L. Clinico-pathological and Neuroimaging Features of Primary Gliosarcoma: A Case Series and Review of Literature. *World Neurosurg.* **2023**, *178*, e480–e488. [CrossRef]
90. Peckham, M.E.; Osborn, A.G.; Palmer, C.A.; Tsai, A.; Salzman, K.L. Gliosarcoma: Neuroimaging and Immunohistochemical Findings. *J. Neuroimaging* **2019**, *29*, 126–132. [CrossRef]
91. Weis, S.; Sonnberger, M.; Dunzinger, A.; Voglmayr, E.; Aichholzer, M.; Kleiser, R.; Strasser, P. Gliosarcoma WHO Grade IV-Giant Cell Glioblastoma WHO Grade IV. In *Imaging Brain Diseases*; Springer: Vienna, Austria, 2019.
92. Zipp, L.; Schwartz, K.M.; Hewer, E.; Yu, Y.; Stippich, C.; Slopis, J.M. Magnetic Resonance Imaging and Computed Tomography Findings in Pediatric Giant Cell Glioblastoma. *Clin. Neuroradiol.* **2012**, *22*, 359–363. [CrossRef]
93. Giese, A.; Bjerkvig, R.; Berens, M.; Westphal, M. Cost of Migration: Invasion of Malignant Gliomas and Implications for Treatment. *J. Clin. Oncol.* **2003**, *21*, 1624–1636. [CrossRef]
94. Niyazi, M.; Brada, M.; Chalmers, A.J.; Combs, S.E.; Erridge, S.C.; Fiorentino, A.; Grosu, A.L.; Lagerwaard, F.J.; Minniti, G.; Mirimanoff, R.O.; et al. ESTRO-ACROP guideline "target de-lineation of glioblastomas". *Radiother. Oncol.* **2016**, *118*, 35–42. [CrossRef] [PubMed]
95. Thomas, R.P.; Xu, L.W.; Lober, R.M.; Li, G.; Nagpal, S. The incidence and significance of multiple lesions in glioblastoma. *J. Neuro-Oncol.* **2013**, *112*, 91–97. [CrossRef]
96. Farhat, M.; Fuller, G.N.; Wintermark, M.; Chung, C.; Kumar, V.A.; Chen, M. Multifocal and multicentric glioblastoma: Imaging signature, molecular characterization, patterns of spread, and treatment. *Neuroradiol. J.* **2023**. [CrossRef]
97. Paulsson, A.K.; Holmes, J.A.; Peiffer, A.M.; Miller, L.D.; Liu, W.; Xu, J.; Hinson, W.H.; Lesser, G.J.; Laxton, A.W.; Tatter, S.B.; et al. Comparison of clinical outcomes and genomic characteristics of single focus and multifocal glioblastoma. *J. Neuro-Oncol.* **2014**, *119*, 429–435. [CrossRef]
98. Korshunov, A.; Ryzhova, M.; Hovestadt, V.; Bender, S.; Sturm, D.; Capper, D.; Meyer, J.; Schrimpf, D.; Kool, M.; Northcott, P.A.; et al. Integrated analysis of pediatric glio-blastoma reveals a subset of biologically favorable tumors with associated molecular prognostic markers. *Acta Neuropathol.* **2015**, *129*, 669–678. [CrossRef]

99. Meyronet, D.; Esteban-Mader, M.; Bonnet, C.; Joly, M.-O.; Uro-Coste, E.; Amiel-Benouaich, A.; Forest, F.; Rousselot-Denis, C.; Burel-Vandenbos, F.; Bourg, V.; et al. Characteristics of H3 K27M-mutant gliomas in adults. *Neuro-Oncology* **2017**, *19*, 1127–1134. [CrossRef]
100. Damodharan, S.; Lara-Velazquez, M.; Williamsen, B.C.; Helgager, J.; Dey, M. Diffuse Intrinsic Pontine Glioma: Molecular Landscape, Evolving Treatment Strategies and Emerging Clinical Trials. *J. Pers. Med.* **2022**, *12*, 840. [CrossRef] [PubMed]
101. Hoffman, L.M.; van Zanten, S.E.V.; Colditz, N.; Baugh, J.; Chaney, B.; Hoffmann, M.; Lane, A.; Fuller, C.; Miles, L.; Hawkins, C.; et al. Clinical, Radiologic, Pathologic, and Molecular Characteristics of Long-Term Survivors of Diffuse Intrinsic Pontine Glioma (DIPG): A Collaborative Report From the International and European Society for Pediatric Oncology DIPG Registries. *J. Clin. Oncol.* **2018**, *36*, 1963–1972. [CrossRef] [PubMed]
102. Steinbok, P.; Gopalakrishnan, C.V.; Hengel, A.R.; Vitali, A.M.; Poskitt, K.; Hawkins, C.; Drake, J.; Lamberti-Pasculli, M.; Ajani, O.; Hader, W.; et al. Pediatric thalamic tumors in the MRI era: A Canadian perspective. *Child's Nerv. Syst.* **2015**, *32*, 269–280. [CrossRef]
103. Cao, L.; Li, C.; Zhang, Y.; Gui, S. Surgical resection of unilateral thalamic tumors in adults: Approaches and outcomes. *BMC Neurol.* **2015**, *15*, 229. [CrossRef]
104. Lowe, B.R.; Maxham, L.A.; Hamey, J.J.; Wilkins, M.R.; Partridge, J.F. Histone H3 Mutations: An Updated View of Their Role in Chromatin Deregulation and Cancer. *Cancers* **2019**, *11*, 660. [CrossRef]
105. Schwartzentruber, J.; Korshunov, A.; Liu, X.-Y.; Jones, D.T.W.; Pfaff, E.; Jacob, K.; Sturm, D.; Fontebasso, A.M.; Quang, D.-A.K.; Tönjes, M.; et al. Erratum: Corrigendum: Driver mutations in histone H3.3 and chromatin remodelling genes in paediatric glioblastoma. *Nature* **2012**, *482*, 226–231. [CrossRef] [PubMed]
106. Kfoury-Beaumont, N.; Prakasam, R.; Pondugula, S.; Lagas, J.S.; Matkovich, S.; Gontarz, P.; Yang, L.; Yano, H.; Kim, A.H.; Rubin, J.B.; et al. The H3K27M mutation alters stem cell growth, epigenetic regulation, and differentiation potential. *BMC Biol.* **2022**, *20*, 124. [CrossRef] [PubMed]
107. Harutyunyan, A.S.; Krug, B.; Chen, H.; Papillon-Cavanagh, S.; Zeinieh, M.; De Jay, N.; Deshmukh, S.; Chen, C.C.; Belle, J.; Mikael, L.G.; et al. H3K27M induces defective chromatin spread of PRC2-mediated repressive H3K27me2/me3 and is essential for glioma tumorigenesis. *Nat. Commun.* **2019**, *10*, 1262. [CrossRef]
108. Lewis, P.W.; Müller, M.M.; Koletsky, M.S.; Cordero, F.; Lin, S.; Banaszynski, L.A.; Garcia, B.A.; Muir, T.W.; Becher, O.J.; Allis, C.D. Inhibition of PRC2 Activity by a Gain-of-Function H3 Mutation Found in Pediatric Glioblastoma. *Science* **2013**, *340*, 857–861. [CrossRef] [PubMed]
109. Filbin, M.; Monje, M. Developmental origins and emerging therapeutic opportunities for childhood cancer. *Nat. Med.* **2019**, *25*, 367–376. [CrossRef]
110. Auffret, L.; Ajlil, Y.; Tauziède-Espariat, A.; Kergrohen, T.; Puiseux, C.; Riffaud, L.; Blouin, P.; Bertozzi, A.-I.; Leblond, P.; Blomgren, K.; et al. A new subtype of diffuse midline glioma, H3 K27 and BRAF/FGFR1 co-altered: A clinico-radiological and histomolecular characterisation. *Acta Neuropathol.* **2023**, *147*, 2. [CrossRef]
111. Castel, D.; Philippe, C.; Calmon, R.; Le Dret, L.; Truffaux, N.; Boddaert, N.; Pagès, M.; Taylor, K.R.; Saulnier, P.; Lacroix, L.; et al. Histone *H3F3A* and *HIST1H3B* K27M mu-tations define two subgroups of diffuse intrinsic pontine gliomas with different prognosis and phenotypes. *Acta Neuropathol.* **2015**, *130*, 815–827. [CrossRef]
112. Gianno, F.; Giovannoni, I.; Cafferata, B.; Diomedi-Camassei, F.; Minasi, S.; Barresi, S.; Buttarelli, F.R.; Alesi, V.; Cardoni, A.; Antonelli, M.; et al. Paediatric-type diffuse high-grade gliomas in the 5th CNS WHO Classification. *Pathologica* **2022**, *114*, 422–435. [CrossRef]
113. Elsässer, S.J.; Allis, C.D.; Lewis, P.W. New Epigenetic Drivers of Cancers. *Science* **2011**, *331*, 1145–1146. [CrossRef]
114. Castel, D.; Kergrohen, T.; Tauziede-Espariat, A.; Mackay, A.; Ghermaoui, S.; Lechapt, E.; Pfister, S.M.; Kramm, C.M.; Boddaert, N.; Blauwblomme, T.; et al. Histone H3 wild-type DIPG/DMG overexpressing EZHIP extend the spectrum diffuse midline gliomas with PRC2 inhibition beyond H3-K27M mutation. *Acta Neuropathol.* **2020**, *139*, 1109–1113. [CrossRef]
115. Vallero, S.G.; Bertero, L.; Morana, G.; Sciortino, P.; Bertin, D.; Mussano, A.; Ricci, F.S.; Peretta, P.; Fagioli, F. Pediatric diffuse midline glioma H3K27- altered: A complex clinical and biological landscape behind a neatly defined tumor type. *Front. Oncol.* **2022**, *12*, 1082062. [CrossRef]
116. Mondal, G.; Lee, J.C.; Ravindranathan, A.; Villanueva-Meyer, J.E.; Tran, Q.T.; Allen, S.J.; Barreto, J.; Gupta, R.; Doo, P.; Van Ziffle, J.; et al. Pediatric bithalamic gliomas have a distinct epigenetic signature and frequent EGFR exon 20 insertions resulting in potential sensitivity to targeted kinase inhibition. *Acta Neuropathol.* **2020**, *139*, 1071–1088. [CrossRef]
117. Aboian, M.; Solomon, D.; Felton, E.; Mabray, M.; Villanueva-Meyer, J.; Mueller, S.; Cha, S. Imaging Characteristics of Pediatric Diffuse Midline Gliomas with Histone H3 K27M Mutation. *Am. J. Neuroradiol.* **2017**, *38*, 795–800. [CrossRef] [PubMed]
118. Mackay, A.; Burford, A.; Carvalho, D.; Izquierdo, E.; Fazal-Salom, J.; Taylor, K.R.; Bjerke, L.; Clarke, M.; Vinci, M.; Nandhabalan, M.; et al. Integrated Molecular Meta-Analysis of 1,000 Pediatric High-Grade and Diffuse Intrinsic Pontine Glioma. *Cancer Cell* **2017**, *32*, 520–537. [CrossRef]
119. Korshunov, A.; Capper, D.; Reuss, D.; Schrimpf, D.; Ryzhova, M.; Hovestadt, V.; Sturm, D.; Meyer, J.; Jones, C.; Zheludkova, O.; et al. Histologically distinct neuroepithelial tumors with histone 3 G34 mutation are molecularly similar and comprise a single nosologic entity. *Acta Neuropathol.* **2016**, *131*, 137–146. [CrossRef]

120. Kurokawa, R.; Baba, A.; Kurokawa, M.; Pinarbasi, E.S.; Makise, N.; Ota, Y.; Kim, J.; Srinivasan, A.; Moritani, T. Neuroimaging features of diffuse hemispheric glioma, H3 G34-mutant: A case series and systematic review. *J. Neuroimaging* **2022**, *32*, 17–27. [CrossRef] [PubMed]
121. Nguyen, A.V.; Soto, J.M.; Gonzalez, S.-M.; Murillo, J.; Trumble, E.R.; Shan, F.Y.; Huang, J.H. H3G34-Mutant Gliomas—A Review of Molecular Pathogenesis and Therapeutic Options. *Biomedicines* **2023**, *11*, 2002. [CrossRef] [PubMed]
122. Vettermann, F.J.; Felsberg, J.; Reifenberger, G.; Hasselblatt, M.; Forbrig, R.; Berding, G.; la Fougère, C.; Galldiks, N.; Schittenhelm, J.; Weis, J.; et al. Characterization of Diffuse Gliomas With Histone H3-G34 Mutation by MRI and Dynamic 18F-FET PET. *Clin. Nucl. Med.* **2018**, *43*, 895–898. [CrossRef]
123. Korshunov, A.; Schrimpf, D.; Ryzhova, M.; Sturm, D.; Chavez, L.; Hovestadt, V.; Sharma, T.; Habel, A.; Burford, A.; Jones, C.; et al. H3-/IDH-wild type pediatric glio-blastoma is comprised of molecularly and prognostically distinct subtypes with associated oncogenic drivers. *Acta Neuropathol.* **2017**, *134*, 507–516. [CrossRef]
124. Tauziède-Espariat, A.; Debily, M.-A.; Castel, D.; Grill, J.; Puget, S.; Sabel, M.; Blomgren, K.; Gareton, A.; Dangouloff-Ros, V.; Lechapt, E.; et al. An integrative radiological, histopathological and molecular analysis of pediatric pontine histone-wildtype glioma with MYCN amplification (HGG-MYCN). *Acta Neuropathol. Commun.* **2019**, *7*, 87. [CrossRef] [PubMed]
125. Jones, C.; Karajannis, M.A.; Jones, D.T.W.; Kieran, M.W.; Monje, M.; Baker, S.J.; Becher, O.J.; Cho, Y.-J.; Gupta, N.; Hawkins, C.; et al. Pediatric high-grade glioma: Biologically and clinically in need of new thinking. *Neuro-Oncology* **2017**, *19*, 153–161. [CrossRef] [PubMed]
126. López, G.Y.; Van Ziffle, J.; Onodera, C.; Grenert, J.P.; Yeh, I.; Bastian, B.C.; Clarke, J.; Bush, N.A.O.; Taylor, J.; Chang, S.; et al. The genetic landscape of gliomas arising after therapeutic radiation. *Acta Neuropathol.* **2019**, *137*, 139–150. [CrossRef] [PubMed]
127. Trkova, K.; Sumerauer, D.; Bubenikova, A.; Krskova, L.; Vicha, A.; Koblizek, M.; Zamecnik, J.; Jurasek, B.; Kyncl, M.; Malinova, B.; et al. Clinical and molecular study of radiation-induced gliomas. *Sci. Rep.* **2024**, *14*, 3118. [CrossRef] [PubMed]
128. Bender, K.; Perez, E.; Chirica, M.; Onken, J.; Kahn, J.; Brenner, W.; Ehret, F.; Euskirchen, P.; Koch, A.; Capper, D.; et al. High-grade astrocytoma with piloid features (HGAP): The Charité experience with a new central nervous system tumor entity. *J. Neuro-Oncol.* **2021**, *153*, 109–120. [CrossRef] [PubMed]
129. Reinhardt, A.; Stichel, D.; Schrimpf, D.; Sahm, F.; Korshunov, A.; Reuss, D.E.; Koelsche, C.; Huang, K.; Wefers, A.K.; Hovestadt, V.; et al. Anaplastic astrocytoma with piloid features, a novel molecular class of IDH wildtype glioma with recurrent MAPK pathway, CDKN2A/B and ATRX alterations. *Acta Neuropathol.* **2018**, *136*, 273–291. [CrossRef]
130. Soni, N.; Agarwal, A.; Ajmera, P.; Mehta, P.; Gupta, V.; Vibhute, M.; Gubbiotti, M.; Mark, I.T.; Messina, S.A.; Mohan, S.; et al. High-Grade Astrocytoma with Piloid Features: A Dual Institutional Review of Imaging Findings of a Novel Entity. *Am. J. Neuroradiol.* **2024**, *45*, 468–474. [CrossRef]

biomedicines

MDPI

Article

Association of IDH1 Mutation and MGMT Promoter Methylation with Clinicopathological Parameters in an Ethnically Diverse Population of Adults with Gliomas in England

Hiba A. Wanis [1], Henrik Møller [1,2], Keyoumars Ashkan [3] and Elizabeth A. Davies [1,*]

[1] Cancer Epidemiology and Cancer Services Research, Centre for Cancer, Society & Public Health, Bermondsey Wing, King's College London, 3rd Floor, Guy's Hospital, Great Maze Pond, London SE1 9RT, UK

[2] Danish Centre for Health Services Research, Aalborg University, 9220 Aalborg, Denmark

[3] Department of Neurosurgery, King's College Hospital NHS Trust, Denmark Hill, London SE5 9RS, UK

* Correspondence: elizabeth.davies@kcl.ac.uk; Tel.: +44-(0)20-718-88414

Abstract: Background: Molecular profiles can predict which patients will respond to current standard treatment and new targeted therapy regimens. Using data from a highly diverse population of approximately three million in Southeast London and Kent, this study aims to evaluate the prevalence of IDH1 mutation and MGMT promoter methylation in the gliomas diagnosed in adult patients and to explore correlations with patients' demographic and clinicopathological characteristics. **Methods:** Anonymised data on 749 adult patients diagnosed with a glioma in 2015–2019 at King's College Hospital were extracted. Univariable and multivariable logistic regressions were used to estimate odds ratios (ORs) for expressing IDH1 mutation and MGMT promoter methylation, based on each patient's age, sex, ethnicity, histology, tumour location and extent of resection. The Kaplan–Meier method was used to estimate the overall survival functions. **Results:** A total of 19.5% of cases were IDH1-mutated. Being 39 years and younger (OR 5.48, 95% CI 3.17–9.47), from Asian/Asian British background (OR 3.68, 95% CI 1.05–12.97), having MGMT methylation (OR 15.92, 95% CI 7.30–34.75), an oligodendroglioma diagnosis (OR 7.45, 95% CI 2.90–19.13) and receiving a gross total/total microscopic resection (OR 1.95, 95% CI 1.24–3.08) were each univariately correlated with IDH1 mutation. MGMT methylation association persisted on adjustment (OR 14.13, 95% CI 3.88–51.43). MGMT promoter methylation was seen in 54.3% of gliomas. In the univariate adjusted ORs, being younger than 39 years (OR 2.56, 95% CI 1.48–4.43), female (OR 1.52, 95% CI 1.11–2.08), having IDH1 mutation (OR 15.92, 95% CI 7.30–34.75) and an oligodendroglioma diagnosis (OR 6.20, 95% CI 1.33–28.88) were associated with MGMT methylation. Being female (OR 1.75, 95% CI 1.22–2.51) and having an IDH1 mutation (OR 15.54, 95% CI 4.73–51.05) persisted after adjustment for age, sex, ethnicity, histology, tumour location and extent of resection. IDH1 mutant and MGMT methylated gliomas were associated with frontal lobe location. Survival analysis showed that patients with both IDH1 mutation and MGMT methylation had significantly better survival than those with either molecular marker alone. Over a 3-year period, women with unmethylated MGMT promoters generally had better survival than men with unmethylated MGMT. **Conclusion:** This study showed that the molecular markers of IDH1 mutation and MGMT promoter methylation were associated with age, sex, Asian/Asian British ethnic group, tumour histology, anatomical location and extent of resection. This study has demonstrated the importance of assessing glioma molecular markers in the clinical setting and the need to stratify patients according to their clinicopathological characteristics.

Keywords: brain tumours; IDH1 mutation; MGMT promoter methylation; odds ratio; clinicopathological parameters; health inequalities

1. Introduction

The classification term glioma includes a broad range of tumours originating from the glial brain cells. Gliomas occur mostly in adults, most frequently in the frontal lobe, and have a higher incidence in males [1,2]. The most common glioma subtypes are glioblastoma, followed by grade II and III astrocytoma and oligodendroglioma [2]. Their diagnosis, treatment and prognosis depend on several key variables, including the patient's age, the tumour subtype and its location, with new findings indicating the significance of certain molecular biomarkers [1]. Understanding the molecular characteristics of glioma has improved our knowledge of disease progression and response to treatment and opened up new opportunities for prognostication [3]. With the introduction of the 2016 and, more recently, the 2021 WHO Central Nervous System (CNS) tumour classification, both molecular and histopathologic features have now been incorporated into classification schemes. By integrating genetic and epigenetic information to define tumour entities, these molecular biomarkers may give patients a more precise diagnosis and prognosis of their tumours [4,5].

The main biomarkers that are now routinely tested for in clinical practice are isocitrate dehydrogenase (IDH) gene mutations (mainly IDH1), O6-methylguanine-DNA methyltransferase (MGMT) promoter methylation and the co-deletion of 1p/19q. An IDH1-R132H point mutated enzyme (mutation in IDH1 at R132) is seen in 80–90% of grade II-III gliomas. Much less commonly, in less than 1% of IDH mutant gliomas, is IDH2 (mutation at R172). IDH1/2 are key enzymes in the tricarboxylic cycle and glutamine metabolism. Although histologically indistinguishable, primary and secondary glioblastomas are genetically and epigenetically different. Mutations in IDH1 and, less frequently, IDH2 now define a secondary glioblastoma (low-grade gliomas that eventually underwent a malignant transformation) [3,6], whereas the IDH1 wild-type is considered to be a primary glioblastoma that arose as a higher-grade tumour.

Equally important to the biomarker IDH1 mutation is MGMT gene silencing by methylation, which is found in about 50% of all newly diagnosed glioblastoma [7]. MGMT is a DNA repair enzyme that removes alkyl groups from the O6 position of guanine nucleotide, which is the critical site modified by alkylating chemotherapeutics [8]. This repair activity allows MGMT to reverse the damage induced by temozolomide (TMZ). Approximately 40% of gliomas exhibit MGMT methylation, leading to decreased MGMT expression i.e., decreased DNA repair and therefore to an enhanced sensitivity to TMZ, which significantly prolongs survival compared to patients without the methylation of this site [8]. Thus, IDH1 mutations and MGMT methylation are recognised as independent prognostic factors affecting overall survival [8,9].

The association between molecular biomarkers and progression-free survival and overall survival has been well investigated, particularly for glioblastoma. This paper concentrates on the IDH1 mutation and MGMT promoter methylation and their associations with various clinicopathological characteristics in low-grade and high-grade glioma. The patient population is those living in Southeast London and Kent and seen at King's College Hospital.

2. Material and Methods

2.1. Study Population

Data on all patients aged 18 years or over, diagnosed with a glioma between 1 January 2015 and 31 December 2019 and discussed in the Multi-Disciplinary Team meeting (MDT) at King's College Hospital NHS Trust were extracted. These data included information on demographic characteristics, tumour type, referral and surgery details.

2.2. Selection of Cases

Patients were given a histologically confirmed diagnosis using ICD-10 and morphology codes according to the WHO classification of CNS tumours. The brain tumour morphological subtypes considered in this analysis were glioblastoma (morphology codes: 9440–9442, 9445), astrocytoma that excludes glioblastoma (morphology codes: 9381, 9384, 9400–9411, 9420–9421, 9424, 9425) and oligodendroglioma (morphology codes: 9450–9451). The 2016 WHO classification was used to categorise tumour morphology. The WHO CNS classification was updated in 2021, but these changes have minimal effect on the analysis of the extracted data. Data were then cross-checked against the patients' MDT reports and neuropathology records for accuracy and validity.

These records include self-assigned ethnicity data provided by patients upon admission to King's College Hospital Neurosciences Department. Due to the small numbers of patients in some of the ethnicity categories the following groups were used for analysis: White British, Asian/Asian British, Black/Black British, Mixed Ethnic Groups, Any Other White, Any Other Ethnic Group and Unknown/Not Stated.

The Neuropathology Department at King's College Hospital carries out nearly 400 molecular pathology tests per year [10]. For all molecular pathology tests, ten 4–5 μm thick unstained formalin-fixed paraffin-embedded (FFPE) tissue sections are required. DNA testing of MGMT promoter methylation status and the sequencing of IDH1 and IDH2 are carried out using pyrosequencing. Co-deletion of 1p/19q test is performed using fluorescence in situ hybridisation (FISH). The MGMT methylation status is reported as the percentage of methylation (<5% = unmethylated, 5–10% = borderline methylated and >10% = methylated). Following a similar survival outcome between methylated and borderline methylated, and due to the low number of tumours in the borderline group, these two categorisations of methylation were combined to form one group: 'MGMT-methylated'.

The initial extraction comprised 770 records. We then cleaned the data to exclude duplicated cases, metastatic tumours (18 cases) as well as those originating in the spine (2 cases) from the analysis. Survival time was calculated from the date of diagnosis until date of death with a period of observation of up to one year. Data on one patient who died before their date of diagnosis were removed. In order to retain those who died on their date of diagnosis, we added half a day to their survival time (4 patients were retained). The final study population included 749 patients.

2.3. Data Analysis

Firstly, we began by examining the distribution of patients by person-level characteristics (age, sex, ethnicity and performance status at referral), tumour morphology, tumour WHO grade, tumour location, molecular characteristics (IDH1 mutation, MGMT promoter methylation and 1p19q co-deletion) and extent of resection. The Kaplan–Meier (KM) method was used to estimate the overall survival functions. Data for patients who did not experience death were censored on the study end date (30 July 2021) or the last MDT date available in the database, whichever occurred first. Logistic regression was used to estimate odds ratios (OR) (and their 95% confidence intervals (CI)) for IDH1 mutation and then for MGMT promoter methylation and their associations with age, sex, ethnicity, tumour location, tumour histology and extent of resection. ORs were adjusted sequentially for age, sex, performance status at referral, molecular biomarkers, tumour histology, tumour location and extent of resection. $\chi 2$ tests were performed to estimate the p-values for trend and heterogeneity, excluding unknown categories. All analyses were performed using Stata Software, version 16 (StataCorp, College Station, TX, USA).

2.4. Ethical Approval

This study involved anonymised information about the patients and received Health Research Authority (HRA) approval (IRAS Number 228103) and was approved by the local Neurosciences Research Advisory Group Meeting at King's College Hospital NHS Foundation Trust.

3. Results

Table 1 summarises the characteristics of glioma patients, their tumour anatomical locations and molecular profiles. Most patients diagnosed with a glioma were male (60.5%), and approximately half were aged 50–69 years. The majority of cases were high-grade glioma, i.e., WHO grade III/IV (89.7%), and of those, 76.1% were classified as a glioblastoma. The most frequent location within the brain was the frontal lobe (31.6%). Further breakdown of glioma histology by molecular characteristics is shown in Table 2. The proportion of tumours tested for IDH1 mutations and MGMT promoter methylation were high (97.9% and 92.3%, respectively). For a confirmed oligodendroglioma diagnosis, testing for 1p/19q co-deletion along with IDH1 mutation is required, and hence, molecular information for both biomarkers is available.

Table 1. Patient and tumour characteristics of 749 patients diagnosed with a glioma during 2015–2019.

	Variables	Groups	No. of Patients	(%)
Patient characteristics	**Sex**	Female	296	(39.5)
		Male	453	(60.5)
	Age at diagnosis	Mean (SD)	56.4 (14.7)	
	Age group	≤39	119	(15.9)
		40–49	95	(12.7)
		50–59	165	(22.0)
		60–69	225	(30.0)
		≥70	145	(19.4)
	Year of diagnosis	2015	151	(20.2)
		2016	136	(18.2)
		2017	163	(218)
		2018	147	(19.6)
		2019	152	(20.3)
	Ethnic group	White British	484	(64.6)
		Asian/Asian British	11	(1.5)
		Black/Black British	23	(3.1)
		Mixed Ethnic Group	10	(1.3)
		Any Other White	30	(4.1)
		Any Other Ethnic Group	19	(2.5)
		Not Stated/Specified	172	(23.0)
	Performance status at referral	0	312	(41.7)
		1	244	(32.6)
		2	63	(8.4)
		3/4	27	(3.6)
		Unknown	103	(13.8)
	Vital status (on 30 July 2021)	Alive	210	(28.0)
		Dead	539	(72.0)
Tumour characteristics	**Histology**	Glioblastoma	570	(76.1)
		Astrocytoma	98	(13.1)
		Oligodendroglioma	81	(10.8)
	WHO grade	I/II	77	(10.3)
		III/IV	672	(89.7)
	Tumour location	Frontal Lobe	237	(31.6)
		Occipital Lobe	27	(3.6)
		Parietal Lobe	116	(15.5)
		Temporal Lobe	176	(23.5)
		Overlapping Lesion of Brain	131	(17.5)
		Cerebrum	31	(4.1)
		Ventricle	10	(1.3)
		Brain, other	21	(2.8)

Table 1. *Cont.*

	Variables	Groups	No. of Patients	(%)
Tumour characteristics	**IDH1 mutation**	Mutated	146	(19.5)
		Wild-type	587	(78.4)
		Not Tested/Unknown	16	(2.1)
	MGMT promoter methylation	Methylated	407	(54.3)
		Unmethylated	291	(38.9)
		Not Tested/Unknown	51	(6.8)
	1p19q co-deletion	Co-deleted	86	(11.5)
		Not Co-deleted	50	(6.7)
		Not Tested/Unknown	613	(81.8)
	Resection type	Total/Total Macroscopic	149	(19.9)
		Gross Subtotal/Partial	192	(25.6)
		Extent Uncertain	408	(54.5)

Table 2. Frequency of molecular biomarkers by tumour histology for 749 glioma cases diagnosed during 2015–2019.

	Glioblastoma N = 570 (76.1%)		**Astrocytoma N = 98 (13.1%)**		**Oligodendroglioma N = 81 (10.8%)**		**Total**		***p*-Value**
IDH Mutation									
IDH1Mutated	19	(3.3%)	52	(53.1%)	75	(92.6%)	146	(19.5%)	*<0.001*
Wildtype	550	(96.5%)	31	(31.6%)	6	(7.4%)	587	(78.4%)	
Not Tested/Unknown	1	(0.2%)	15	(15.3%)	0	(0.0%)	16	(2.1%)	
MGMT Promoter Methylation									
MGMT methylated	285	(50.0%)	60	(61.2%)	62	(76.5%)	407	(54.3%)	*<0.001*
Unmethylated	277	(48.6%)	12	(12.2%)	2	(2.5%)	291	(38.9%)	
Not Tested/Unknown	8	(1.4%)	26	(26.5%)	17	(21%)	51	(6.8%)	
1p19q Co-deletion									
Co-deleted	6	(1.0%)	4	(4.1%)	76	(93.8%)	86	(11.5%)	*<0.001*
Not Co-deleted	21	(3.7%)	24	(24.5%)	5	(6.2%)	50	(6.7%)	
Not Tested/Unknown	543	(95.3%)	70	(71.4%)	0	(0.0%)	613	(81.8%)	

3.1. Significance of IDH1 Mutation

Table 3 shows that in the unadjusted analyses, each of the covariates except for sex was correlated with having an IDH1 mutation. There were higher odds of expressing IDH1 mutation for younger patients (OR 5.48, 95% CI 3.17–9.47, in the $\leq$39 years group), those from an Asian/Asian British background (OR 3.68, 95% CI 1.05–12.97) or those with MGMT promoter methylation (OR 15.92, 95% CI 7.30–34.75) or an oligodendroglioma diagnosis (OR 7.45, 95% CI 2.90–19.13) and those receiving a gross total/total microscopic resection (OR 1.95, 95% CI 1.24–3.08). Having a glioblastoma diagnosis was less likely to be associated with IDH1 mutation (OR 0.02, 95% CI 0.01–0.04). In the adjusted model, the associations with MGMT methylated promoter (OR 14.13, 95% CI 3.88–51.43), receiving a gross total/total microscopic resection (OR 2.73, 95% CI 1.01–7.33) and a glioblastoma diagnosis (OR 0.03, 95% CI 0.01–0.09) persisted. IDH1 mutation was also associated with frontal lobe tumour location. Table 3 shows the odds ratios for IDH1 mutation in glioma cancer patients diagnosed at King's College Hospital between 2015 and 2019.

Table 3. Odds ratios for IDH1 mutation in glioma cancer patients diagnosed during 2015–2019.

	Unadjusted			Adjusted for Age, Sex, PS, Ethnicity			and Tumour Biomarkers			and Tumour Histology, Tumour Location			and Extent of Resection		
	OR	95% CI		OR	95% CI		OR	95% CI		OR	95% CI		OR	95% CI	
Age at diagnosis															
≤39	5.48	3.17	9.47	4.86	2.77	8.54	6.04	2.48	14.73	2.18	0.75	6.39	1.83	0.61	5.50
40–49	2.45	1.35	4.42	2.34	1.27	4.30	3.78	1.42	10.08	2.63	0.80	8.60	2.29	0.70	7.51
50–59	1.00			1.00			1.00			1.00			1.00		
60–69	0.45	0.25	0.84	0.48	0.26	0.89	0.53	0.21	1.37	0.60	0.18	1.95	0.51	0.15	1.72
≥70	0.20	0.08	0.51	0.20	0.08	0.51	0.46	0.14	1.53	0.61	0.16	2.38	0.65	0.16	2.60
χ2 and p-value	*χ2 (4) = 103.85; p < 0.001*			*χ2 (4) = 86.56; p < 0.001*			*χ2 (4) = 40.42; p < 0.001*			*χ2 (4) = 9.03; p = 0.0603*			*χ2 (4) = 7.54; p = 0.1098*		
Sex															
Male	1.00			1.00			1.00			1.00			1.00		
Female	1.11	0.76	1.60	0.99	0.65	1.50	0.66	0.35	1.24	0.72	0.33	1.55	0.72	0.33	1.58
χ2 and p-value	*χ2 (1) = 0.29; p = 0.5913*			*χ2 (1) = 0.00; p = 0.9456*			*χ2 (1) = 1.65; p = 0.1984*			*χ2 (1) = 0.70; p = 0.4012*			*χ2 (1) = 0.65; p = 0.4193*		
Ethnic groups															
White British	1.00			1.00			1.00			1.00			1.00		
Any Other Ethnic Group	1.70	0.63	4.58	1.08	0.36	3.27	1.50	0.36	6.19	3.00	0.57	15.63	2.61	0.50	13.58
Any Other White	1.84	0.84	4.06	1.43	0.58	3.54	1.75	0.39	7.90	1.23	0.18	8.60	1.38	0.20	9.50
Asian/Asian British	3.68	1.05	12.97	2.30	0.49	10.78	1.56	0.13	18.47	1.20	0.03	54.51	1.11	0.03	39.17
Black/Black British	0.55	0.16	1.90	0.42	0.11	1.64	0.93	0.17	4.96	0.65	0.08	5.17	0.68	0.09	5.39
Mixed Ethnic Group	0.41	0.05	3.27	0.17	0.02	1.47	0.03	0.00	0.55	0.11	0.00	2.64	0.14	0.01	2.95
Not Stated/Specified	0.50	0.30	0.83	0.57	0.33	1.01	0.59	0.26	1.33	0.60	0.22	1.61	0.59	0.22	1.60
χ2 and p-value	*χ2 (6) = 17.87; p = 0.0066*			*χ2 (6) = 9.90; p = 0.1288*			*χ2 (6) = 8.34; p = 0.2140*			*χ2 (6) = 5.02; p = 0.5414*			*χ2 (6) = 4.46; p = 0.6148*		
MGMT methylation status															
Unmethylated	1.00			1.00			1.00			1.00			1.00		
Methylated	15.92	7.30	34.75	19.73	8.64	45.08	18.74	6.31	55.68	13.33	3.78	47.08	14.13	3.88	51.43
χ2 and p-value	*χ2 (1) = 48.33; p < 0.001*			*χ2 (1) = 50.18; p < 0.001*			*χ2 (1) = 27.56; p < 0.001*			*χ2 (1) = 16.31; p = 0.0001*			*χ2 (1) = 16.21; p = 0.0001*		
Tumour location															
Frontal	1.00			1.00			1.00			1.00			1.00		
Brain, other	0.54	0.17	1.68	0.30	0.09	1.03	0.64	0.07	5.52	1.32	0.14	12.52	2.30	0.22	23.84
Cerebrum	0.08	0.01	0.58	0.05	0.01	0.40	0.11	0.01	1.26	0.06	0.00	0.85	0.08	0.00	1.82
Occipital Lobe	0.17	0.04	0.73	0.16	0.03	0.77	0.26	0.04	1.65	0.33	0.03	3.19	1.02	0.10	10.57
Overlapping Brain Lesions	0.48	0.29	0.81	0.68	0.37	1.23	1.12	0.47	2.67	1.33	0.47	3.74	1.69	0.56	5.08
Parietal Lobe	0.28	0.15	0.52	0.38	0.19	0.77	0.53	0.19	1.46	0.50	0.15	1.65	0.62	0.17	2.25
Temporal Lobe	0.28	0.17	0.48	0.35	0.19	0.63	0.44	0.18	1.06	0.41	0.15	1.17	0.67	0.23	1.99
Ventricle	0.29	0.03	2.39	0.20	0.02	1.92	0.16	0.01	3.57	0.09	0.00	1.83	0.08	0.00	2.19
χ2 and p-value	*χ2 (7) = 39.34; p < 0.001*			*χ2 (7) = 27.16; p = 0.0003*			*χ2 (7) = 9.60; p = 0.2122*			*χ2 (7) = 11.04; p = 0.1370*			*χ2 (7) = 7.84; p = 0.3466*		

Table 3. *Cont.*

	Unadjusted			Adjusted for Age, Sex, PS, Ethnicity			and Tumour Biomarkers			and Tumour Histology, Tumour Location			and Extent of Resection		
	OR	95% CI		OR	95% CI		OR	95% CI		OR	95% CI		OR	95% CI	
Tumour histology															
Astrocytoma	1.00			1.00			1.00			1.00			1.00		
Glioblastoma	0.02	0.01	0.04	0.03	0.01	0.07	0.05	0.02	0.12	0.04	0.02	0.11	0.03	0.01	0.09
Oligodendroglioma	7.45	2.90	19.13	10.54	3.73	29.78	2.49	0.40	15.56	2.47	0.37	16.61	3.73	0.47	29.79
χ2 and p-value	*χ2 (2) = 215.81; p < 0.001*			*χ2 (2) = 154.87; p < 0.001*			*χ2 (2) = 55.46; p < 0.001*			*χ2 (2) = 55.89; p < 0.001*			*χ2 (2) = 53.13; p < 0.001*		
Extent of resection															
Extent Uncertain	1.00			1.00			1.00			1.00			1.00		
Gross Total/Total Macroscopic	1.95	1.24	3.08	1.87	1.11	3.17	1.92	0.88	4.20	2.73	1.01	7.33	2.73	1.01	7.33
Subtotal/Partial	1.13	0.71	1.80	1.33	0.78	2.26	1.09	0.49	2.42	1.77	0.63	5.00	1.77	0.63	5.00
χ2 and p-value	*χ2 (2) = 8.59; p = 0.0136*			*χ2 (2) = 5.50; p = 0.0638*			*χ2 (2) = 2.86; p = 0.2387*			*χ2 (2) = 4.08; p = 0.1299*			*χ2 (2) = 4.08; p = 0.1299*		

Abbreviations: OR = Odds ratio, CI = Confidence interval, PS = Performance status.

3.2. Significance of MGMT Promoter Methylation

Table 4 shows the factors correlated with the MGMT promoter methylation group (the combined group of methylation and borderline methylation). In the unadjusted ORs, each of the covariates was associated with MGMT promoter methylation except for ethnicity and extent of resection. The methylation of the MGMT promoter was correlated with younger patients who were aged less than 39 years (OR 2.56, 95% CI 1.48–4.43), female (OR 1.52, 95% CI 1.11–2.08) or had an IDH1 mutation (OR 15.92, 95% CI 7.30–34.75) and an oligodendroglioma diagnosis (OR 6.20, 95% CI 1.33–28.88). Being female (OR 1.75, 95% CI 1.22–2.51) and having an IDH1 mutation (OR 15.54, 95% CI 4.73–51.05) persisted on adjustment. There are higher odds in older patients (60–69 years) (OR 1.76, 95% CI 1.11–2.78) with this epigenetic alteration. MGMT promoter methylation was also associated with frontal lobe tumour location.

Table 4. Odds ratios for MGMT methylated promoter in glioma cancer patients diagnosed during 2015–2019.

	Unadjusted			Adjusted for Age, Sex, PS, Ethnicity			and Tumour Biomarkers			and Tumour Histology, Tumour Location			and Extent of Resection		
	OR	95% CI		OR	95% CI		OR	95% CI		OR	95% CI		OR	95% CI	
Age at diagnosis															
≤39	2.56	1.48	4.43	2.54	1.45	4.45	1.42	0.73	2.77	1.15	0.54	2.45	1.20	0.56	2.56
40–49	1.32	0.77	2.27	1.29	0.75	2.24	0.83	0.44	1.57	0.82	0.42	1.57	0.82	0.43	1.59
50–59	1.00			1.00			1.00			1.00			1.00		
60–69	1.35	0.90	2.05	1.45	0.95	2.21	1.69	1.08	2.67	1.73	1.09	2.73	1.76	1.11	2.78
≥70	1.11	0.70	1.75	1.18	0.74	1.88	1.56	0.95	2.55	1.56	0.95	2.57	1.53	0.93	2.53
χ2 and p-value	*χ2 (4) = 12.41; p = 0.0145*			*χ2 (4) = 11.42; p = 0.0223*			*χ2 (4) = 9.01; p = 0.0608*			*χ2 (4) = 9.26; p = 0.0550*			*χ2 (4) = 9.28; p = 0.0544*		
Sex															
Male	1.00			1.00			1.00			1.00			1.00		
Female	1.52	1.11	2.08	1.54	1.11	2.12	1.72	1.22	2.44	1.72	1.20	2.46	1.75	1.22	2.51
χ2 and p-value	*χ2 (1) = 6.76; p = 0.0093*			*χ2 (1)= 6.77; p = 0.0093*			*χ2 (1) = 9.39; p = 0.0022*			*χ2 (1) = 8.88; p = 0.0029*			*χ2 (1) = 9.38; p = 0.0022*		
Ethnic groups															
White British	1.00			1.00			1.00			1.00			1.00		
Any Other Ethnic Group	0.94	0.37	2.39	0.78	0.30	2.03	0.82	0.27	2.48	0.90	0.29	2.76	0.92	0.30	2.82
Any Other White	0.86	0.39	1.87	0.73	0.33	1.63	0.59	0.24	1.48	0.52	0.20	1.36	0.49	0.19	1.28
Asian/Asian British	0.69	0.17	2.78	0.62	0.14	2.66	0.38	0.06	2.37	0.47	0.07	2.90	0.44	0.07	2.78
Black/Black British	0.69	0.28	1.68	0.69	0.27	1.74	0.79	0.30	2.10	0.76	0.28	2.04	0.75	0.28	2.01
Mixed Ethnic Group	1.60	0.41	6.27	1.17	0.29	4.76	1.53	0.36	6.50	1.36	0.32	5.84	1.37	0.32	5.90
Not Stated/Specified	0.90	0.63	1.29	0.93	0.64	1.35	1.01	0.68	1.50	1.00	0.67	1.50	1.00	0.67	1.48
χ2 and p-value	*χ2 (6) = 1.79; p = 0.9379*			*χ2 (6) = 1.80; p = 0.9373*			*χ2 (6) = 3.01; p = 0.8070*			*χ2 (6) = 2.95; p = 0.8156*			*χ2 (6) = 3.36; p = 0.7631*		
IDH1 mutation															
Unmutated	1.00			1.00			1.00			1.00			1.00		
Mutated	15.92	7.30	34.75	19.88	8.72	45.33	16.71	6.15	45.43	12.61	4.14	38.41	15.54	4.73	51.05
χ2 and p-value	*χ2 (1) = 48.33; p < 0.001*			*χ2 (1) = 50.56; p < 0.001*			*χ2 (1) = 30.46; p < 0.001*			*χ2 (1) = 19.88; p < 0.001*			*χ2 (1) = 20.42; p < 0.001*		
Tumour location															
Frontal	1.00			1.00			1.00			1.00			1.00		
Brain, other	0.46	0.17	1.23	0.38	0.14	1.07	0.62	0.21	1.82	0.65	0.22	1.94	0.60	0.20	1.82
Cerebrum	0.34	0.15	0.80	0.28	0.12	0.67	0.43	0.17	1.07	0.43	0.17	1.07	0.40	0.16	1.01
Occipital Lobe	0.61	0.26	1.42	0.66	0.27	1.62	0.88	0.34	2.27	0.86	0.33	2.25	0.75	0.28	2.02
Overlapping Brain Lesions	0.81	0.52	1.28	0.83	0.51	1.33	0.93	0.56	1.55	0.95	0.57	1.58	0.93	0.55	1.58
Parietal Lobe	0.62	0.39	0.98	0.67	0.41	1.08	0.88	0.53	1.48	0.90	0.53	1.52	0.87	0.51	1.47
Temporal Lobe	0.55	0.36	0.82	0.56	0.37	0.87	0.71	0.45	1.13	0.71	0.45	1.13	0.68	0.42	1.09
Ventricle	3.08	0.36	26.06	1.80	0.20	15.93	3.40	0.38	30.69	3.08	0.34	27.96	3.03	0.33	27.55
χ2 and p-value	*χ2 (7) = 15.90; p = 0.0261*			*χ2 (7) = 15.37; p = 0.0316*			*χ2 (7) = 6.80; p = 0.4499*			*χ2 (7) = 6.59; p = 0.4732*			*χ2 (7) = 7.48; p = 0.3805*		

Table 4. *Cont.*

	Unadjusted			Adjusted for Age, Sex, PS, Ethnicity			and Tumour Biomarkers			and Tumour Histology, Tumour Location			and Extent of Resection		
	OR	95% CI		OR	95% CI		OR	95% CI		OR	95% CI		OR	95% CI	
Tumour histology															
Astrocytoma	1.00			1.00			1.00			1.00			1.00		
Glioblastoma	0.21	0.11	0.39	0.19	0.09	0.39	0.45	0.19	1.08	0.46	0.19	1.12	0.44	0.18	1.09
Oligodendroglioma	6.20	1.33	28.88	7.01	1.45	33.91	0.21	0.02	2.45	0.22	0.02	2.51	0.10	0.01	1.80
χ2 and p-value	*χ2 (2) = 44.17; p < 0.001*			*χ2 (2) = 40.62; p < 0.001*			*χ2 (2) = 4.34; p = 0.1141*			*χ2 (2) = 4.05; p = 0.1318*			*χ2 (2) = 5.03; p = 0.0808*		
Extent of resection															
Extent Uncertain	1.00			1.00			1.00			1.00			1.00		
Gross Total/Total Macroscopic	0.95	0.64	1.40	0.84	0.56	1.26	0.70	0.44	1.10	0.68	0.43	1.08	0.68	0.43	1.08
Subtotal/Partial	0.95	0.66	1.37	0.97	0.66	1.41	0.93	0.62	1.40	0.93	0.61	1.40	0.93	0.61	1.40
χ2 and p-value	*χ2 (2) = 0.11; p = 0.9450*			*χ2 (2) = 0.72; p = 0.6994*			*χ2 (2) = 2.47; p = 0.2903*			*χ2 (2) = 0.11; p = 0.9450*			*χ2 (2) = 0.11; p = 0.9450*		

Abbreviations: OR = Odds ratio, CI = Confidence interval, PS = Performance status.

3.3. Survival Analysis

The results of this study have shown that there is an association between IDH1 mutation and MGMT promoter methylation. The combined effect of these two important biomarkers on overall survival is observed in the Kaplan–Meier survival curve (Figure 1). Glioma patients with both the IDH1 mutation and MGMT methylation (3.0% of all patients) had the best overall survival, followed by patients with an IDH1 mutation and unmethylated MGMT promoter (1.0%), then by patients with MGMT promoter methylation and IDH1 wildtype (55.4%). Those without an IDH1 mutation or MGMT methylation (40.6%) had the worst overall survival. Patients with only an IDH1 mutation did not have significantly different survival from patients with only MGMT promoter methylation.

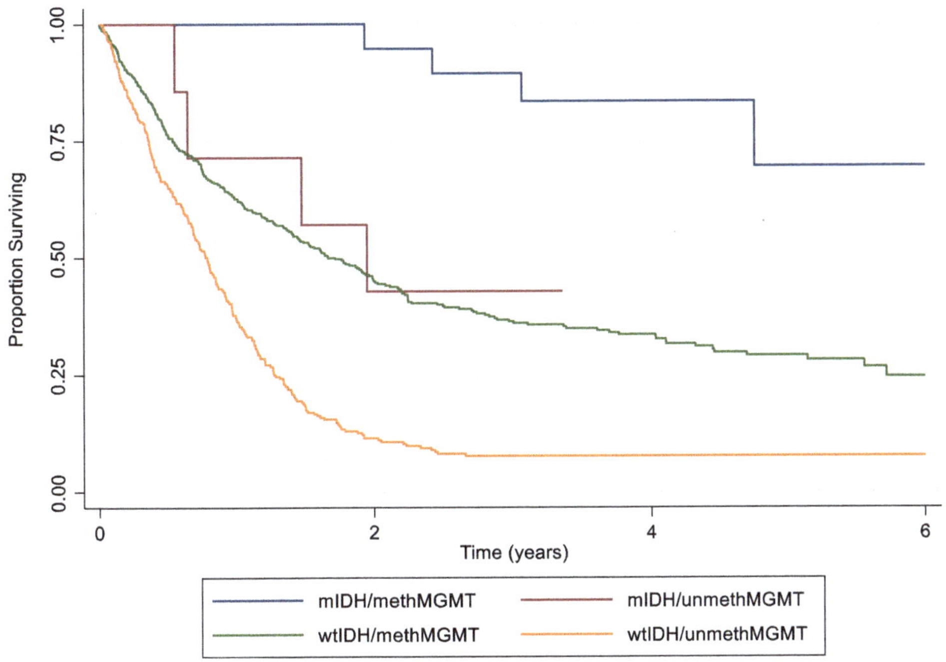

Figure 1. Kaplan–Meier survival curves of 749 King's College Hospital glioma patients comparing IDH1 wild-type and unmethylated MGMT promoter (wtIDH/unmethMGMT); IDH1 wild-type and methylated MGMT promoter (wtIDH/methMGMT); IDH1 mutation and unmethylated MGMT promoter (mIDH/unmethMGMT); IDH1 mutation and methylated MGMT promoter (mIDH/methMGMT) ($p < 0.001$). p-values were calculated by the log-rank test.

Figure 2a shows the survival by sex for the patient cohort ($p = 0.5215$) and when it is stratified by MGMT methylation status as presented in Figure 2b. For the unmethylated MGMT promoter group, the survival for women was still better than for the unmethylated group of men over a longer period of time.

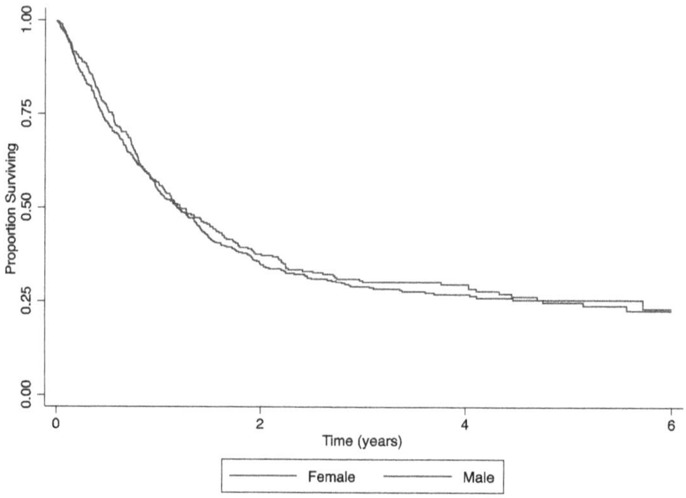

(a)

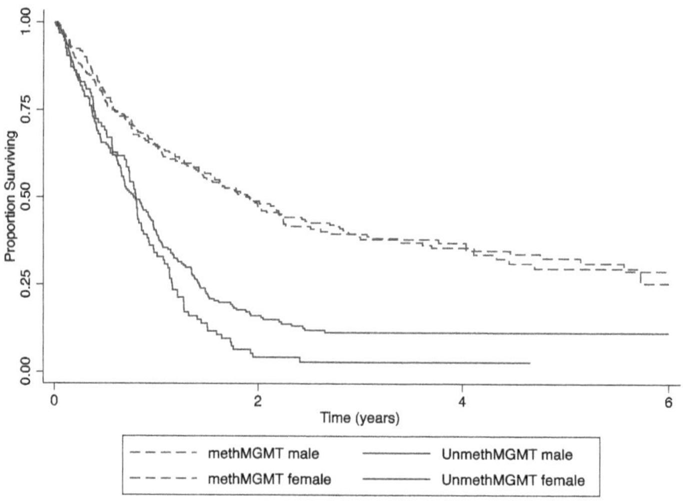

(b)

Figure 2. Kaplan–Meier survival curves of the King's College Hospital glioma patient cohort (**a**) for males (n = 453) vs. females (n = 296) (p = 0.521). (**b**) according to MGMT promoter methylation status for males (methMGMT = 171; unmethMGMT = 94) vs. females (methMGMT = 236; unmethMGMT = 197) (p < 0.001). p-values were calculated by the log-rank test.

4. Discussion

4.1. Main Findings

Using information extracted from a highly diverse population of around three million in Southeast London and Kent, we investigated data on 749 adult patients diagnosed with a glioma at King's College Hospital between 2015 and 2019. This study's aim was to explore factors associated with IDH1 mutation and/or MGMT promoter methylation. We found that 19.5% of cases were IDH1-mutated. Being young (OR 5.48, 95% CI 3.17–9.47), from an Asian/Asian British background (OR 3.68, 95% CI 1.05–12.97), having MGMT promoter methylation (OR 15.92, 95% CI 7.30–34.75), an oligodendroglioma diagnosis (OR 7.45, 95% CI 2.90–19.13) and receiving a gross total/total microscopic resection (OR 1.95, 95% CI 1.24–3.08) were univariately correlated with IDH1 mutation. MGMT methylation association persisted on adjustment (OR 14.13, 95% CI 3.88–51.43). MGMT promoter methylation was seen in 54.3% of gliomas. In the univariate adjusted ORs, being young (OR 2.56, 95% CI 1.48–4.43), being female (OR 1.52, 95% CI 1.11–2.08), having IDH1 mutation (OR 15.92, 95% CI 7.30–34.75) and an oligodendroglioma diagnosis (OR 6.20, 95% CI 1.33–28.88) were associated with MGMT methylation. Being female (OR 1.75, 95% CI 1.22–2.51) and having IDH1 mutation (OR 15.54, 95% CI 4.73–51.05) persisted after adjustment. IDH1 mutant and MGMT promoter methylated gliomas were also associated with a frontal lobe location. Survival analysis showed that patients with both IDH1 mutation and MGMT promoter methylation had significantly better survival than those with either molecular biomarker. Over a longer period, women with unmethylated MGMT promoters generally had better survival than men with unmethylated promoters.

4.2. Comparison to Other Findings

There have been several population-based studies investigating molecular biomarkers and glioma subtypes; however, only a few have considered the associations of such biomarkers and patients' clinicopathological characteristics that could play an important role in determining prognosis.

One study by Pandith et al. (2020) evaluated the associations of IDH1/IDH2 and MGMT promoter methylation with clinical variables in glioma patients [11]. They reported IDH1 mutation as being also associated with oligodendrogliomas and astrocytomas ($p = 0.005$) and being more frequent in males ($p = 0.0002$) but not significant among age groups [11]. IDH1 mutation was correlated with MGMT promoter methylation (OR = 3.6, 95% CI 1.1–11.1). Multivariate survival analysis showed better survival rates in patients with MGMT methylation following adjustment for age, sex, grade and IDH1/2 mutation. By comparison, our new results showed an association between IDH1 mutation and age. These findings can be compared to previous work by Molenaar et al. (2014) who presented an independent two-gene predictive and prognostic factor for glioblastoma based on IDH1 mutation and MGMT methylation status [12]. Patients with IDH1 mutation as well as MGMT methylation had the longest survival compared to either IDH1 mutations or MGMT methylation alone. Here, similar results are found where the combination of IDH1 mutation and MGMT promoter methylation predicts an improved survival compared to the remaining three combinations, with the worst prognostic group being those with wild-type IDH1 plus an unmethylated promoter. A study by Aurora et al. (2018) has also reported that the MGMT methylation group did not show a statistically significant correlation with age, sex or tumour location, but it was associated with IDH1 mutation (OR 4.3 CI 1.3–13.8) [13].

4.3. Interpretation and Implications

Low-grade glioma typically occurs more commonly in younger people than high-grade glioma [14]. In glioblastoma, IDH1 mutations are more common in younger patients and in those diagnosed with a secondary glioblastoma [15]. Our study showed that younger patients are more likely to be diagnosed with an IDH1-mutated glioma than with a wild-type form and that this mutation is rarely found in the elderly patient population. Previous work has shown that patients with grade II–IV gliomas harbouring IDH1 or IDH2 mutation had significantly longer overall survival than those without IDH mutation [16]. These findings are therefore consistent with previous studies that reveal the prognostic importance of IDH mutation independently of other known prognostic factors such as age, grade and MGMT methylation status [16]. In the analysis undertaken for MGMT methylation status in this study, patients under the age of 39 years were more likely to have MGMT methylated promoter in the unadjusted model. However, after sequentially adjusting for tumour characteristics as well as surgery, there was a stronger correlation with this among older patients. It would be of interest to investigate the association between older patients and increased odds of MGMT methylation, in IDH1 mutant astrocytomas.

Glioblastoma occurs more frequently in the male population (male-to-female ratio 1.6:1) [17], with less of a sex difference being found for low-grade astrocytomas [18,19]. Reports show that being female is also associated with a better outcome [20,21]; thus, sex differences in glioma progression have received more interest, particularly at a molecular level, and there is accumulating evidence that gliomas display sex-specific methylation patterns [22]. In glioblastoma, MGMT promoter methylation is common in females, with a subsequent better outcome after treatment with TMZ. This study has confirmed previous findings correlating females with methylated MGMT promoter status. The results also show that even without MGMT methylation, females still have a better survival than males. Taken together, our data illustrates the need for stratification by sex in clinical cohorts of patients with gliomas, where an unequal frequency of gliomas between males and females may disguise sex-specific association with prognosis.

The multivariate analysis found no significant associations between either IDH1 mutation or MGMT methylation and anatomic location in the brain. However, in the unadjusted analysis, both IDH1 mutation and MGMT promoter methylation were associated with frontal lobe gliomas. In other studies, the MGMT methylation was seen predominately in the parietal and occipital lobes [23], temporal lobe [24] or independent from tumour location [25]. Unmethylated cases were commonly located in the temporal lobe [13,23]. Paldor et al. (2016) suggested that glioblastomas arising in the frontal lobe are more prone to exhibiting IDH mutation ($p = 0.006$) and MGMT methylation ($p = 0.005$) than glioblastomas arising in other lobes [26].

In this study, the incidence of IDH1 mutation and MGMT promoter methylation were comparable to figures found globally. A study by Ang et al. (2020) based on a Southeast Asian cohort, includes an ethnically diverse population of Chinese, Malays and Indians. Indians were found to have the highest incidence of positive MGMT methylation and IDH1 mutation results (50% and 30%, respectively) [27]. Our previous work (Wanis et al. 2023) found better survival for those of Indian background after adjusting for patient characteristics, tumour morphology and route to diagnosis and treatment, compared to British White people [28]. Here in this study, the results have shown that individuals from the Asian/British Asian Ethnic Group have higher odds of DH1 mutation compared with the White British Group in the univariate analysis. We suggested a possible explanation for this is that there might be a correlation between those from an Indian background and having an IDH1 mutation [28]. In one study based in India, Indian patients with glioma were revealed as more likely to be diagnosed with a low-grade glioma and to have a higher prevalence of IDH1 mutation, giving them an improved outcome [29]. Other Indian studies also showed a greater IDH1 mutation prevalence reaching as high as 84% of Indian patients tested [30]—assuming that all aggressive tumours are being given a confirmed diagnosis. To address this interesting question, larger and more detailed analyses are needed to determine if there are genetic or other relationships between British-based, Indian-based ethnic groups and IDH1 mutation prevalence.

It has become increasingly evident that IDH mutation status accounts for much of the prognostic knowledge previously characterised by histological subtype and grade [31]. As replicated in our study, most glioblastomas are IDH wild-type, and most lower grade diffuse gliomas are IDH-mutant. IDH mutant status therefore offers the basis for an alternative method of classification. Since the 2016 WHO CNS tumour classification, the presence of IDH mutation is required to diagnose oligodendroglioma, along with 1p/19q co-deletion [4]. While nearly all oligodendrogliomas are MGMT-methylated, this routine testing might not be necessary. IDH mutation increases overall genomic methylation and is associated with MGMT promoter methylation. Additionally, in one study, the MGMT methylation was also seen in nearly all IDH-mutated astrocytomas and oligodendrogliomas [32]. However, this has also been questioned [12], and a detailed analysis is needed to obtain a better understanding of these associations, particularly for grade II–III astrocytomas and oligodendrogliomas.

The methylation of the MGMT promoter was apparent in approximately 50% of newly diagnosed glioblastomas in a few studies as well as this [33–35]. Studies have also demonstrated that patients with MGMT promoter methylated glioblastomas have a significantly longer overall survival regardless of treatment [24]. Associations between IDH1 mutation, MGMT promoter methylation and survival outcomes have also been analysed [36]. MGMT methylation is also associated with IDH1 mutant tumours and therefore is more common in secondary than in primary glioblastoma (75% vs. 36% respectively) [23,37]. This molecular biomarker is associated with better response to TMZ as well as radiotherapy [38], and its prognostic and predictive significance in glioblastoma patients remains irrespective of treatment choices. Regarding the extent of resection, studies have shown no benefit of gross total resection and MGMT promoter methylation [39–41]. In our study, there was also no association between MGMT promoter methylation and the extent of resection.

Surgery is the first crucial phase in classifying and managing gliomas. Neuro-oncologists and neurosurgeons now face the challenge of incorporating these new molecular biomarkers into the treatment of glioma patients, as evidence for using them in clinical decision-making is evolving. A review by Li et al. (2020) highlighted the potential effect of molecular biomarkers on informing surgical resection decisions for diffuse astrocytomas [42]. Surgical decisions are usually made as a result of a biopsy's pathology and molecular analyses; however, real-time molecular analyses as tumours are resected could inform surgical decision-making, balancing potential harm from surgical procedures against benefit. It could be determined from this work that IDH1-mutated gliomas are less diffuse and therefore easier to resect than IDH1 wild-type gliomas, and hence, a correlation between IDH1-mutated gliomas and gross total/total microscopic resection type was found. The use of additional treatment data to explore whether the IDH mutation also influences survival in patients receiving radiation or chemotherapy following resection would add useful information. In the NOA-04 phase III trial, comparing radiotherapy with alkylating chemotherapy as an initial treatment of grade III glioma showed an association of IDH mutation with improved overall survival in both treatment groups approximately equally [43]. Conclusions from our study also included that IDH1 mutation is a new positive prognostic factor in anaplastic gliomas, with the extent of resection being an important prognosticator [44]. MGMT promoter methylation was also associated with prolonged PFS in the chemotherapy and radiotherapy arm [43].

4.4. Strengths and Limitations

The hospital data used in our study has both strengths and limitations. In addition to the data covering a highly diverse population in Kent and Southeast London of approximately 3 million [45], robustness following an audit of the database was a major strength. Compared to the National Cancer Registry—NDRS, this MDT database has much more extensive information on the extent of resection and surgery type. One major limitation, however, is the absence of linked chemotherapy and radiotherapy data, which could potentially be obtained by data linkage to other hospital treatment databases. Previous work has also considered how molecular markers may be used in clinical decision-making for recurrent surgery for high-grade gliomas particularly for unmethylated MGMT promoter and wildtype IDH1 gliomas—since no other treatment option has demonstrated a survival benefit for these subgroups. Even though this database does not gather information on recurrences, these could be traced using medical history and MDT reports. Tracing could also be used to distinguish between primary and secondary glioblastoma with their differing genetic alteration profiles and prognostic significance. For example, secondary glioblastomas have a far better prognosis with longer median survivals than IDH wild-type primary glioblastomas [6]. Ideally, these data should include a longer duration of follow-up for mortality to consider long-term survival, particularly for low-grade astrocytomas. Furthermore, the study population is limited by relatively small sample sizes for some subgroups, particularly for ethnicity and tumour histology. These variables were broadly grouped making it difficult to draw significant conclusions for smaller populations and limiting the comparison of molecular alterations between defined ethnic groups and astrocytoma specified by WHO grade. Having more data could also give insight into rarer tumour histologies and locations within the brain. Finally, due to the significant genetic heterogeneity within each tumour subtype, the analysis would be strengthened if other genetic alterations, for example, p53 and ATRX mutation, were considered, as these might play a role in IDH1 mutation associations. The absence of the ATRX protein and the abundance of p53 protein are required for classifying low-grade astrocytomas [46–48]. Other emerging molecular biomarkers that are more specific to younger adults would also be of interest to investigate such as H3G34 mutation and histone H3K27M mutation. In addition to considering detailed molecular data, a larger study sample will therefore maximise the clinical relevance of these findings if the updated 2021 WHO CNS classifications are implemented (e.g., reassigned IDH-mutated glioblastoma to IDH-mutant astrocytoma).

5. Conclusions

Our study has demonstrated the importance of assessing glioma molecular biomarkers in the clinical setting, and the need to stratify patients according to their clinicopathological characteristics. Of the glioma patients diagnosed and treated at King's College Hospital, 19.5% had IDH1-mutated tumours and 54.3% were MGMT promoter methylated. This analysis showed these molecular biomarkers being associated with sex, age, ethnicity, tumour histology, anatomical location and extent of resection. The results of these analyses substantiate and support recent efforts to increase the extent of resection in gliomas particularly for those tumours with IDH1 mutation and for considering sex-specific associations. Such reports may encourage clinical trials to consider including molecular biomarker characteristics either when allocating patients to trial arms or by stratifying the analysis. These findings can also assist the selection of treatment options for patients based on their clinicopathological characteristics.

Simple Summary: Using hospital data that cover a highly diverse population of around three million in Southeast London and Kent, this study showed the associations of the glioma molecular markers of IDH1 mutation and MGMT promoter methylation with a patient's age, sex, ethnicity, tumour histology, brain location and extent of resection. These results should galvanise efforts to better understand the molecular characteristics of gliomas in order to detect these tumours earlier and maximise treatment management. This study also demonstrated the importance of assessing the translation of these molecular markers in the clinical setting. Not only do they inform prognosis, but they are also predictive in helping the selection of treatment options for glioma patients based on their clinicopathological characteristics.

Author Contributions: Conceptualization, H.A.W., H.M., K.A. and E.A.D.; methodology, H.A.W. and H.M.; software, H.A.W.; validation, H.A.W., H.M., K.A. and E.A.D.; formal analysis, H.A.W.; investigation, H.A.W.; resources, K.A.; data curation, H.A.W.; writing—original draft preparation, H.A.W.; writing—review and editing, H.A.W., H.M., K.A. and E.A.D.; visualization, H.A.W., H.M., K.A. and E.A.D.; supervision, H.M., K.A. and E.A.D.; project administration, K.A. and E.A.D.; funding acquisition, not funded. All authors have read and agreed to the published version of the manuscript.

Funding: This research received no external funding.

Institutional Review Board Statement: The study was conducted in accordance with the Declaration of Helsinki, and approved by the Health Research Authority (HRA) Approval (IRAS Number 228103) as well as the local Neurosciences Research Advisory Group Meeting at King's College Hospital NHS Foundation Trust. Ethical review and approval were waived for this study due to the use of anonymised information about the patients.

Informed Consent Statement: Not applicable.

Data Availability Statement: The data are collated, maintained, and quality assured by the Neurosciences Department within King's College Hospital NHS Foundation Trust.

Acknowledgments: We thank Amadou Barry from the Neurosciences Data Team for assisting with extracting and verifying the data.

Conflicts of Interest: The authors declare no conflicts of interest.

References

1. Schwartzbaum, J.A.; Fisher, J.L.; Aldape, K.D.; Wrensch, M. Epidemiology and molecular pathology of glioma. *Nat. Clin. Pract. Neurol.* **2006**, *2*, 494–503, quiz 1 p following 516. [CrossRef] [PubMed]
2. Larjavaara, S.; Mäntylä, R.; Salminen, T.; Haapasalo, H.; Raitanen, J.; Jääskeläinen, J.; Auvinen, A. Incidence of gliomas by anatomic location. *Neuro-Oncology* **2007**, *9*, 319–325. [CrossRef] [PubMed]
3. Yan, H.; Parsons, D.W.; Jin, G.; McLendon, R.; Rasheed, B.A.; Yuan, W.; Kos, I.; Batinic-Haberle, I.; Jones, S.; Riggins, G.J.; et al. IDH1 and IDH2 Mutations in Gliomas. *N. Engl. J. Med.* **2009**, *360*, 765–773. [CrossRef] [PubMed]
4. Louis, D.N.; Perry, A.; Reifenberger, G.; von Deimling, A.; Figarella-Branger, D.; Cavenee, W.K.; Ohgaki, H.; Wiestler, O.D.; Kleihues, P.; Ellison, D.W. The 2016 World Health Organization Classification of Tumors of the Central Nervous System: A summary. *Acta Neuropathol.* **2016**, *131*, 803–820. [CrossRef] [PubMed]
5. Louis, D.N.; Perry, A.; Wesseling, P.; Brat, D.J.; Cree, I.A.; Figarella-Branger, D.; Hawkins, C.; Ng, H.K.; Pfister, S.M.; Reifenberger, G.; et al. The 2021 WHO Classification of Tumors of the Central Nervous System: A summary. *Neuro-Oncology* **2021**, *23*, 1231–1251. [CrossRef]
6. Han, S.; Liu, Y.; Cai, S.J.; Qian, M.; Ding, J.; Larion, M.; Gilbert, M.R.; Yang, C. IDH mutation in glioma: Molecular mechanisms and potential therapeutic targets. *Br. J. Cancer* **2020**, *122*, 1580–1589. [CrossRef]
7. Hegi, M.E.; Diserens, A.-C.; Gorlia, T.; Hamou, M.-F.; de Tribolet, N.; Weller, M.; Kros, J.M.; Hainfellner, J.A.; Mason, W.; Mariani, L.; et al. MGMT gene silencing and benefit from temozolomide in glioblastoma. *N. Engl. J. Med.* **2005**, *352*, 997–1003. [CrossRef]
8. Esteller, M.; Garcia-Foncillas, J.; Andion, E.; Goodman, S.N.; Hidalgo, O.F.; Vanaclocha, V.; Baylin, S.B.; Herman, J.G. Inactivation of the DNA-repair gene MGMT and the clinical response of gliomas to alkylating agents. *N. Engl. J. Med.* **2000**, *343*, 1350–1354. [CrossRef]
9. Lamborn, K.R.; Chang, S.M.; Prados, M.D. Prognostic factors for survival of patients with glioblastoma: Recursive partitioning analysis. *Neuro-Oncology* **2004**, *6*, 227–235. [CrossRef]
10. King's College Hospital NHS Trust Molecular Pathology Test Protocol. 2021. Available online: https://www.kch.nhs.uk/gps-and-referrers/neuropathology-guides-for-referrers/molecular-neuropathology-service/ (accessed on 1 July 2022).
11. Pandith, A.A.; Qasim, I.; Baba, S.M.; Koul, A.; Zahoor, W.; Afroze, D.; Lateef, A.; Manzoor, U.; Bhat, I.A.; Sanadhya, D.; et al. Favorable role of IDH1/2 mutations aided with MGMT promoter gene methylation in the outcome of patients with malignant glioma. *Future Sci. OA* **2020**, *7*, FSO663. [CrossRef]
12. Molenaar, R.J.; Verbaan, D.; Lamba, S.; Zanon, C.; Jeuken, J.W.M.; Boots-Sprenger, S.H.E.; Wesseling, P.; Hulsebos, T.J.M.; Troost, D.; van Tilborg, A.A.; et al. The combination of IDH1 mutations and MGMT methylation status predicts survival in glioblastoma better than either IDH1 or MGMT alone. *Neuro-Oncology* **2014**, *16*, 1263–1273. [CrossRef] [PubMed]
13. Arora, I.; Gurav, M.; Rumde, R.; Dhanavade, S.; Kadam, V.; Kurani, H.; Shetty, O.; Goda, J.S.; Shetty, P.; Moiyadi, A.; et al. MGMT gene promoter methylation and its correlation with clinicopathological parameters in glioblastomas. *Neurol. India* **2018**, *66*, 1106–1114. [CrossRef] [PubMed]
14. Ostrom, Q.T.; Gittleman, H.; Fulop, J.; Liu, M.; Blanda, R.; Kromer, C.; Wolinsky, Y.; Kruchko, C.; Barnholtz-Sloan, J.S. CBTRUS Statistical Report: Primary Brain and Central Nervous System Tumors Diagnosed in the United States in 2008–2012. *Neuro-Oncology* **2015**, *17* (Suppl. S4), iv1–iv62. [CrossRef] [PubMed]
15. Bleeker, F.E.; Atai, N.A.; Lamba, S.; Jonker, A.; Rijkeboer, D.; Bosch, K.S.; Tigchelaar, W.; Troost, D.; Vandertop, W.P.; Bardelli, A.; et al. The prognostic IDH1(R132) mutation is associated with reduced NADP+-dependent IDH activity in glioblastoma. *Acta Neuropathol.* **2010**, *119*, 487–494. [CrossRef]
16. Sanson, M.; Marie, Y.; Paris, S.; Idbaih, A.; Laffaire, J.; Ducray, F.; El Hallani, S.; Boisselier, B.; Mokhtari, K.; Hoang-Xuan, K.; et al. Isocitrate dehydrogenase 1 codon 132 mutation is an important prognostic biomarker in gliomas. *J. Clin. Oncol. Off. J. Am. Soc. Clin. Oncol.* **2009**, *27*, 4150–4154. [CrossRef]
17. Wanis, H.A.; Møller, H.; Ashkan, K.; Davies, E.A. The incidence of major subtypes of primary brain tumors in adults in England 1995-2017. *Neuro-Oncology* **2021**, *23*, 1371–1382. [CrossRef]
18. Ostrom, Q.T.; Gittleman, H.; Xu, J.; Kromer, C.; Wolinsky, Y.; Kruchko, C.; Barnholtz-Sloan, J.S. CBTRUS Statistical Report: Primary Brain and Other Central Nervous System Tumors Diagnosed in the United States in 2009–2013. *Neuro-Oncology* **2016**, *18*, v1–v75. [CrossRef]
19. Sun, T.; Warrington, N.M.; Rubin, J.B. Why does Jack, and not Jill, break his crown? Sex disparity in brain tumors. *Biol. Sex Differ.* **2012**, *3*, 3. [CrossRef]
20. Trifiletti, D.M.; Alonso, C.; Grover, S.; Fadul, C.E.; Sheehan, J.P.; Showalter, T.N. Prognostic Implications of Extent of Resection in Glioblastoma: Analysis from a Large Database. *World Neurosurg.* **2017**, *103*, 330–340. [CrossRef]

21. Ostrom, Q.T.; Rubin, J.B.; Lathia, J.D.; Berens, M.E.; Barnholtz-Sloan, J.S. Females have the survival advantage in glioblastoma. *Neuro-Oncology* **2018**, *20*, 576–577. [CrossRef]
22. Smits, A.; Lysiak, M.; Magnusson, A.; Rosell, J.; Söderkvist, P.; Malmström, A. Sex Disparities in MGMT Promoter Methylation and Survival in Glioblastoma: Further Evidence from Clinical Cohorts. *J. Clin. Med.* **2021**, *10*, 556. [CrossRef] [PubMed]
23. Eoli, M.; Menghi, F.; Bruzzone, M.G.; De Simone, T.; Valletta, L.; Pollo, B.; Bissola, L.; Silvani, A.; Bianchessi, D.; D'Incerti, L.; et al. Methylation of O6-methylguanine DNA methyltransferase and loss of heterozygosity on 19q and/or 17p are overlapping features of secondary glioblastomas with prolonged survival. *Clin. Cancer Res. Off. J. Am. Assoc. Cancer Res.* **2007**, *13*, 2606–2613. [CrossRef] [PubMed]
24. Ellingson, B.M.; Cloughesy, T.F.; Pope, W.B.; Zaw, T.M.; Phillips, H.; Lalezari, S.; Nghiemphu, P.L.; Ibrahim, H.; Naeini, K.M.; Harris, R.J.; et al. Anatomic localization of O6-methylguanine DNA methyltransferase (MGMT) promoter methylated and unmethylated tumors: A radiographic study in 358 de novo human glioblastomas. *NeuroImage* **2012**, *59*, 908–916. [CrossRef] [PubMed]
25. Kickingereder, P.; Bonekamp, D.; Nowosielski, M.; Kratz, A.; Sill, M.; Burth, S.; Wick, A.; Eidel, O.; Schlemmer, H.-P.; Radbruch, A.; et al. Radiogenomics of Glioblastoma: Machine Learning-based Classification of Molecular Characteristics by Using Multiparametric and Multiregional MR Imaging Features. *Radiology* **2016**, *281*, 907–918. [CrossRef] [PubMed]
26. Paldor, I.; Drummond, K.J.; Kaye, A.H. IDH1 mutation may not be prognostically favorable in glioblastoma when controlled for tumor location: A case-control study. *J. Clin. Neurosci. Off. J. Neurosurg. Soc. Australas.* **2016**, *34*, 117–120. [CrossRef]
27. Ang, S.Y.L.; Lee, L.; See, A.A.Q.; Ang, T.Y.; Ang, B.T.; King, N.K.K. Incidence of biomarkers in high-grade gliomas and their impact on survival in a diverse SouthEast Asian cohort—A population-based study. *BMC Cancer* **2020**, *20*, 79. [CrossRef]
28. Wanis, H.A.; Møller, H.; Ashkan, K.; Davies, E.A. The Influence of Ethnicity on Survival from Malignant Primary Brain Tumours in England: A Population-Based Cohort Study. *Cancers* **2023**, *15*, 1464. [CrossRef]
29. Das, B.R.; Tangri, R.; Ahmad, F.; Roy, A.; Patole, K. Molecular investigation of isocitrate dehydrogenase gene (IDH) mutations in gliomas: First report of IDH2 mutations in Indian patients. *Asian Pac. J. Cancer Prev. APJCP* **2013**, *14*, 7261–7264. [CrossRef]
30. Rajmohan, K.S.; Sugur, H.S.; Shwetha, S.D.; Ramesh, A.; Thennarasu, K.; Pandey, P.; Arivazhagan, A.; Santosh, V. Prognostic significance of histomolecular subgroups of adult anaplastic (WHO Grade III) gliomas: Applying the "integrated" diagnosis approach. *J. Clin. Pathol.* **2016**, *69*, 686–694. [CrossRef]
31. Juratli, T.A.; Cahill, D.P.; McCutcheon, I.E. Determining optimal treatment strategy for diffuse glioma: The emerging role of IDH mutations. *Expert Rev. Anticancer Ther.* **2015**, *15*, 603–606. [CrossRef]
32. Mulholland, S.; Pearson, D.M.; Hamoudi, R.A.; Malley, D.S.; Smith, C.M.; Weaver, J.M.J.; Jones, D.T.W.; Kocialkowski, S.; Bäcklund, L.M.; Collins, V.P.; et al. MGMT CpG island is invariably methylated in adult astrocytic and oligodendroglial tumors with IDH1 or IDH2 mutations. *Int. J. Cancer* **2012**, *131*, 1104–1113. [CrossRef] [PubMed]
33. Mellai, M.; Monzeglio, O.; Piazzi, A.; Caldera, V.; Annovazzi, L.; Cassoni, P.; Valente, G.; Cordera, S.; Mocellini, C.; Schiffer, D. MGMT promoter hypermethylation and its associations with genetic alterations in a series of 350 brain tumors. *J. Neurooncol.* **2012**, *107*, 617–631. [CrossRef] [PubMed]
34. Ohka, F.; Natsume, A.; Motomura, K.; Kishida, Y.; Kondo, Y.; Abe, T.; Nakasu, Y.; Namba, H.; Wakai, K.; Fukui, T.; et al. The global DNA methylation surrogate LINE-1 methylation is correlated with MGMT promoter methylation and is a better prognostic factor for glioma. *PLoS ONE* **2011**, *6*, e23332. [CrossRef] [PubMed]
35. Preusser, M.; Charles Janzer, R.; Felsberg, J.; Reifenberger, G.; Hamou, M.-F.; Diserens, A.-C.; Stupp, R.; Gorlia, T.; Marosi, C.; Heinzl, H.; et al. Anti-O6-methylguanine-methyltransferase (MGMT) immunohistochemistry in glioblastoma multiforme: Observer variability and lack of association with patient survival impede its use as clinical biomarker. *Brain Pathol. Zurich Switz.* **2008**, *18*, 520–532. [CrossRef] [PubMed]
36. Minniti, G.; Scaringi, C.; Arcella, A.; Lanzetta, G.; Di Stefano, D.; Scarpino, S.; Bozzao, A.; Pace, A.; Villani, V.; Salvati, M.; et al. IDH1 mutation and MGMT methylation status predict survival in patients with anaplastic astrocytoma treated with temozolomide-based chemoradiotherapy. *J. Neurooncol.* **2014**, *118*, 377–383. [CrossRef]
37. Horbinski, C. What do we know about IDH1/2 mutations so far, and how do we use it? *Acta Neuropathol.* **2013**, *125*, 621–636. [CrossRef]
38. Yang, P.; Zhang, W.; Wang, Y.; Peng, X.; Chen, B.; Qiu, X.; Li, G.; Li, S.; Wu, C.; Yao, K.; et al. IDH mutation and MGMT promoter methylation in glioblastoma: Results of a prospective registry. *Oncotarget* **2015**, *6*, 40896–40906. [CrossRef]
39. McGirt, M.J.; Chaichana, K.L.; Gathinji, M.; Attenello, F.J.; Than, K.; Olivi, A.; Weingart, J.D.; Brem, H.; Quiñones-Hinojosa, A.R. Independent association of extent of resection with survival in patients with malignant brain astrocytoma. *J. Neurosurg.* **2009**, *110*, 156–162. [CrossRef]
40. Stummer, W.; Pichlmeier, U.; Meinel, T.; Wiestler, O.D.; Zanella, F.; Reulen, H.-J. Fluorescence-guided surgery with 5-aminolevulinic acid for resection of malignant glioma: A randomised controlled multicentre phase III trial. *Lancet Oncol.* **2006**, *7*, 392–401. [CrossRef]
41. Sanai, N.; Polley, M.-Y.; McDermott, M.W.; Parsa, A.T.; Berger, M.S. An extent of resection threshold for newly diagnosed glioblastomas. *J. Neurosurg.* **2011**, *115*, 3–8. [CrossRef]
42. Li, L.; Wang, Y.; Li, Y.; Fang, S.; Jiang, T. Role of molecular biomarkers in glioma resection: A systematic review. *Chin. Neurosurg. J.* **2020**, *6*, 18. [CrossRef] [PubMed]

43. Wick, W.; Hartmann, C.; Engel, C.; Stoffels, M.; Felsberg, J.; Stockhammer, F.; Sabel, M.C.; Koeppen, S.; Ketter, R.; Meyermann, R.; et al. NOA-04 randomized phase III trial of sequential radiochemotherapy of anaplastic glioma with procarbazine, lomustine, and vincristine or temozolomide. *J. Clin. Oncol. Off. J. Am. Soc. Clin. Oncol.* **2009**, *27*, 5874–5880. [CrossRef] [PubMed]
44. Nuño, M.; Birch, K.; Mukherjee, D.; Sarmiento, J.M.; Black, K.L.; Patil, C.G. Survival and prognostic factors of anaplastic gliomas. *Neurosurgery* **2013**, *73*, 458–465, quiz 465. [CrossRef] [PubMed]
45. Panesar, S.; Tailor, J.; Bhangoo, R.; Ashkan, K. Multidisciplinary Team Management of Cerebral Metastases: Recent Trends and Future Implications. *Clin. Oncol.* **2016**, *28*, 343–344. [CrossRef] [PubMed]
46. The Cancer Genome Atlas Research Network Comprehensive genomic characterization defines human glioblastoma genes and core pathways. *Nature* **2008**, *455*, 1061–1068. [CrossRef]
47. Brat, D.J.; Verhaak, R.G.W.; Aldape, K.D.; Yung, W.K.A.; Salama, S.R.; Cooper, L.A.D.; Rheinbay, E.; Miller, C.R.; Vitucci, M.; Morozova, O.; et al. Comprehensive, Integrative Genomic Analysis of Diffuse Lower-Grade Gliomas. *N. Engl. J. Med.* **2015**, *372*, 2481–2498. [CrossRef]
48. Modrek, A.S.; Golub, D.; Khan, T.; Bready, D.; Prado, J.; Bowman, C.; Deng, J.; Zhang, G.; Rocha, P.P.; Raviram, R.; et al. Low-Grade Astrocytoma Mutations in IDH1, P53, and ATRX Cooperate to Block Differentiation of Human Neural Stem Cells via Repression of SOX2. *Cell Rep.* **2017**, *21*, 1267–1280. [CrossRef]

biomedicines

MDPI

Article

Clinical Utility of Optical Genome Mapping for Improved Cytogenomic Analysis of Gliomas

Harmanpreet Singh [1,†], Nikhil S. Sahajpal [2,†], Ashis K. Mondal [1], Stephanie L. Burke [3], Jaspreet Farmaha [1], Ahmet Alptekin [1], Ashutosh Vashisht [1], Kimya Jones [1], Vishakha Vashisht [1] and Ravindra Kolhe [1,*]

1 Department of Pathology, Medical College of Georgia, Augusta University, Augusta, GA 30912, USA; hsingh1@augusta.edu (H.S.); amondal@augusta.edu (A.K.M.); jfarmaha@augusta.edu (J.F.); avashisht@augusta.edu (A.V.); kjones2@augusta.edu (K.J.); vvashisht@augusta.edu (V.V.)
2 Greenwood Genetic Center, Greenwood, SC 29646, USA; nsahajpal@ggc.org
3 Clinical and Scientific Affairs, Bionano Genomics, San Diego, CA 92121, USA
* Correspondence: rkolhe@augusta.edu; Tel.: +1-(706)-721-2771; Fax: +1-(706)-434-6053
† These authors contributed equally to this work.

Abstract: A glioma is a solid brain tumor which originates in the brain or brain stem area. The diagnosis of gliomas based on standard-of-care (SOC) techniques includes karyotyping, fluorescence in situ hybridization (FISH), and chromosomal microarray (CMA), for detecting the pathogenic variants and chromosomal abnormalities. But these techniques do not reveal the complete picture of genetic complexity, thus requiring an alternative technology for better characterization of these tumors. The present study aimed to evaluate the clinical performance and feasibility of using optical genome mapping (OGM) for chromosomal characterization of gliomas. Herein, we evaluated 10 cases of gliomas that were previously characterized by CMA. OGM analysis showed concordance with the results of CMA in identifying the characterized Structural Variants (SVs) in these cases. More notably, it also revealed additional clinically relevant aberrations, demonstrating a higher resolution and sensitivity. These clinically relevant SVs included cryptic translocation, and SVs which are beyond the detection capabilities of CMA. Our analysis highlights the unique capability of OGM to detect all classes of SVs within a single assay, thereby unveiling clinically significant data with a shorter turnaround time. Adopting this diagnostic tool as a standard of care for solid tumors like gliomas shows potential for improving therapeutic management, potentially leading to more personalized and timely interventions for patients.

Keywords: optical genome mapping; structural variants; solid tumor; glioma; chromosomal microarray

1. Introduction

Gliomas originating from the glial or supporting cells in the Central Nervous System (CNS), constitute a diverse spectrum of neuroepithelial tumors. According to the latest Surveillance, Epidemiology, and End Results (SEER) report, the incidence rate of brain cancer was 5.9 per 100,000 people in 2021, and in 2024, it is estimated that there will be 25,400 new cases of brain cancer, which constitutes the 1.3% of all new cancer cases in the U.S. [1]. Gliomas constitute the most common form of malignant tumor of the CNS, exhibiting a wide histological spectrum, from benign ependymomal tumors to aggressive and deadly grade IV glioblastoma (GBM) with a median survival rate of 15 months [2,3]. These solid tumors were traditionally classified using histological features only. However, in 2016, the World Health Organization (WHO) introduced molecular markers to classify CNS tumors (CNS WHO 4). This molecular characterization was further reinforced by the latest WHO Classification of Tumors of the CNS (WHO-2021) guidelines, by advocating for integrated diagnosis that combines genetic markers, molecular profiles, and histology for precise sub-typing of these solid tumors [4]. In addition to genetic alterations in isocitrate dehydrogenase (*IDH1/2*) and 1p/19q-codeletion, WHO-2021 guidelines include additional molecular markers such as *H3-3A*, *ATRX*, *CDKN2A/B*, *TERT*, *MGMT*, and *EGFR* to classify gliomas.

While acknowledging the importance of precise molecular aberrations in prognosis determination, treatment response, and personalized therapy, WHO-2021 guidelines also include a NEC (Not Elsewhere Classified) diagnosis for cases where conventional diagnostic testing fails to yield a specific diagnosis [4]. The current cytogenetic analysis of gliomas relies on conventional methods that include karyotyping, fluorescence in situ hybridization (FISH), and chromosomal microarray (CMA). Karyotyping, while proficient in detecting copy number variations (CNVs) and balanced/unbalanced structural variations (SVs), encounters limitations due to its banding resolution (5–10 Mb), necessity for cell culturing, and sensitivity to the technical skills of the technicians [5]. FISH has higher resolution in detecting chromosome abnormalities but is not capable of unraveling novel SV events. CMA has a higher resolution of approximately 50–100 kb for the detection of CNVs; however, it has limited utility in detecting balanced rearrangements or the orientation of duplicated segments, identifying the location of inserted segments, and is unable to detect low-frequency allelic changes. Thus, a more robust technique that overcomes these conventional drawbacks is needed for a more detailed molecular characterization of the gliomas to further refine their sub-typing and hence improve patient outcomes.

Optical genome mapping (OGM), a high-resolution imaging approach that combines optical microscopy with computational algorithms, has recently emerged as a next-generation cytogenomic technology for molecular diagnosis in cancer and non-cancer diseases. With its resolution of 500 bp, OGM helps in the detection of complex rearrangements and different classes of SVs (inversions, translocations, insertions, deletions, duplications) in a single step, providing a detailed picture of the genome in a timely manner [6]. Our recent publications highlight the use of this state-of-art cytogenomic technology in clinical diagnosis of hematological malignancy [7], acute myeloid leukemia [8], and for prenatal genomic analysis [9]. In this study, we present the first use of OGM as a complementary approach for the detection of various cryptic and complex rearrangements and SVs involved in gliomas beyond the limit of detection of the SOC testing.

2. Materials and Methods

2.1. Sample Collection

This study included 10 deidentified, frozen, glioma brain tumors obtained from the tumor bank at Georgia Cancer Center, Augusta University. These archived, residual biopsy samples were previously characterized using chromosomal microarray for clinical diagnosis purposes at Augusta University Medical Center and were subsequently reanalyzed using OGM as part of the current comparative study. The diagnostic reports, devoid of any patient identifiers, were obtained with the samples.

2.2. Optical Genome Mapping: DNA Isolation, Labeling, and Data Collection

DNA Isolation from solid tissue samples: Ultra-high-molecular-weight (UHMW) DNA was isolated from the solid tumor tissue samples using the Bionano Prep SP Tissue and Tumor DNA Isolation kit (Bionano Genomics, San Diego, CA, USA, Cat. No. 80038) per the manufacturer's protocol. The protocol is described in greater detail in the Bionano support document [10]. The isolated UHMW DNA was labeled and processed for analysis on the Bionano Genomics Saphyr® platform following the manufacturer's protocols (Bionano Genomics Inc., San Diego, CA, USA). Briefly, the frozen tissue samples were weighed, and approximately 30 mg of brain tissue was used for the DNA isolation. DNA isolation was performed as per the standard protocol optimized for solid tumors. Finally, isolated DNA was eluted in the elution buffer and homogenized overnight at room temperature, followed by quantification using Qubit broad-range double-stranded DNA assay kits (ThermoFisher Scientific, San Francisco, CA, USA).

Direct Label and Staining (DLS): 750 ng of UHMW DNA was labeled using the Bionano Direct Label and Stain (DLS) kit (Bionano Genomics, San Diego, CA, USA, Cat. No. 80005) as per the manufacturer's protocol for DNA labeling and quantified using Qubit High Sensitivity (HS) double-stranded DNA assay kits. The fluorescently labeled UHMW DNA was then loaded onto flowcells of a Saphyr® chip, electrophoretically linearized within the nanochannel arrays, and imaged using the Bionano Saphyr® instrument.

OGM Variant Calling and Data Analysis: Genome analysis was performed using the rare variant pipeline included in the Bionano Access v.1.7.2/Bionano Solve (v.3.7.2) software (Bionano Genomics, San Diego, CA, USA). Briefly, the DNA molecules from each sample were directly aligned against the reference human genome assembly (hg19), and the SVs were detected based on the differences in the alignment of the labels between the reference assembly and samples. Consensus genome maps were assembled, and final SVs were called, having reported a minimum of five molecules. SVs and CNVs generated by the rare variant pipeline were then annotated and analyzed using known hg19 pan-cancer bed files to determine clinical relevance. Analytical quality control (QC) targets were set to achieve >300× effective coverage of the genome, >70% mapping rate, 13 to 17 label density (labels per 100 kbp), and >220 kbp N50 (of molecules >150 kbp).

2.3. *Chromosomal Microarray*

UHMW DNA was isolated from tumor tissue following manufacturer's protocol. OGM and CMA were performed using the same DNA to remove tumor/tissue-dependent bias. The genomic DNA (gDNA) for SNP microarray was analyzed using the CytoScan HD assay following the manufacturer's protocol (ThermoFisher Scientific, Waltham, MA USA) using hg19 reference assembly.

3. Results

3.1. *Quality Control Metrics of the Samples*

All 10 samples passed the quality control metrics and achieved the minimum average parameter required to run the rare variant pipeline (RVP) analysis with an average N50 (>150 kb) of 260 kb (±46.2), map rate of 86.4% (±3.7%), label density of 15.1/100 kb (±0.82), and average coverage of 413.8X (±30.5) (Supplementary File Table S1).

3.2. *OGM Showed Concordance with the Results of CMA*

OGM demonstrated concordance with CMA results, excluding those results related to the loss of heterozygosity calls. For instance, in one case, CMA identified multiple aneuploidies and CNVs, including +2, 6q−, +7, −10, −14, 19q−, and −22. These SVs were also identified by OGM, as shown in Figure 1, which shows the overlapping copy number variations between OGM and CMA. In another case, CMA identified chromothripsis involving chromosome 8 (Figure 2), with the different breakpoints visible in an enlarged view of the call. OGM detected the same chromothryptic event in chromosome 8 (Figure 3). By enlarging the OGM calls on chromosome 8, various breakpoints and fusion events involved in the chromothripsis were visualized. This finding was further confirmed in the whole genome view, with a visualization of the highlighted segmental changes.

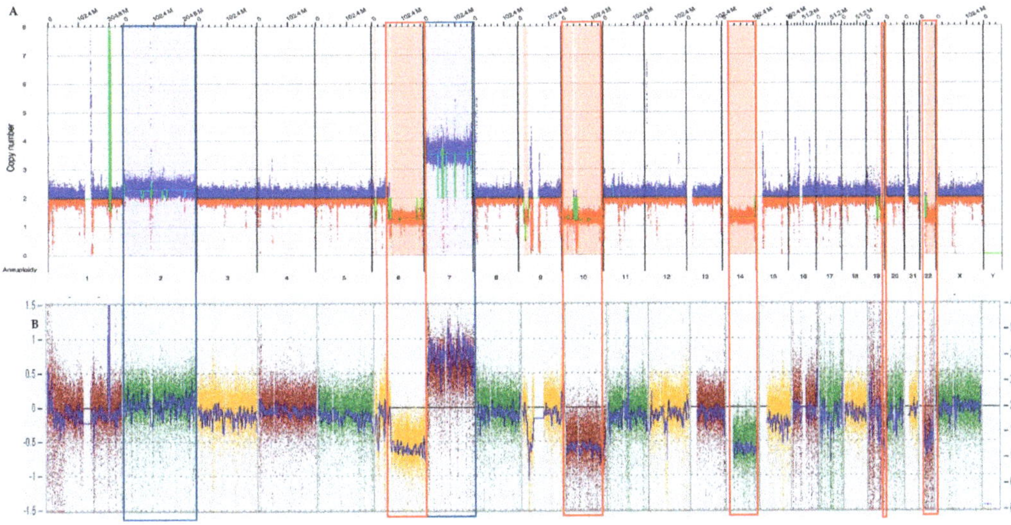

Figure 1. Whole genome view showing the concordance of the copy number variations detected +2, 6q-, +7, -10, -14, 19q-, and -22 by OGM (**A**) and CMA (**B**).

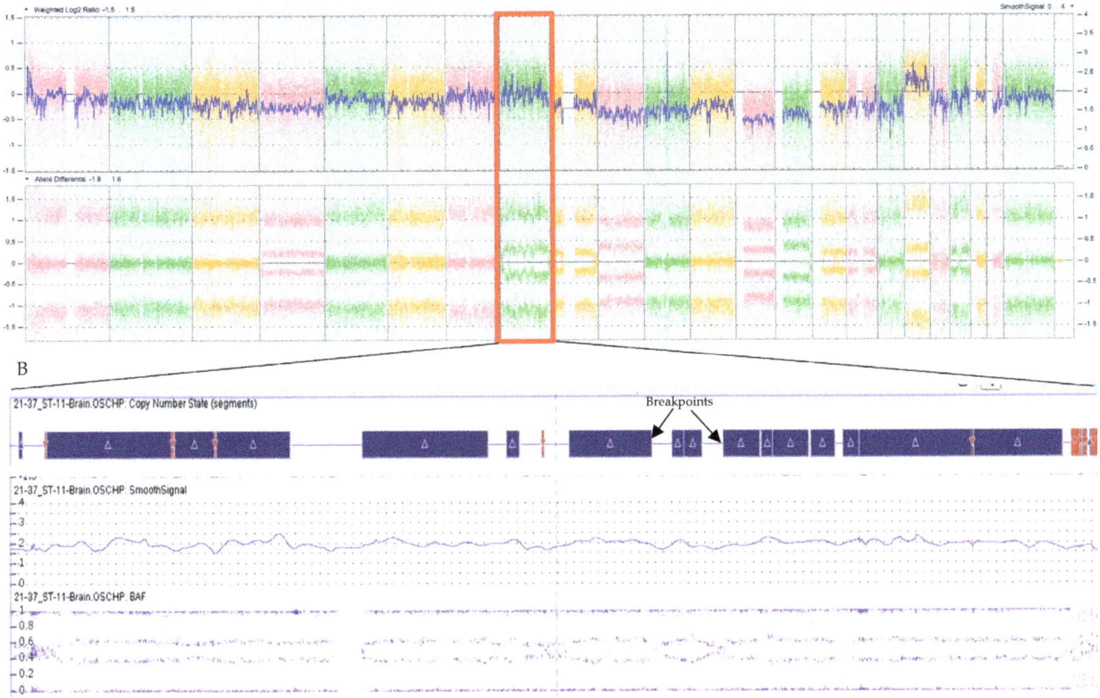

Figure 2. (**A**) The chromothripsis event detected on chromosome 8 in microarray, (**B**) the enlarged view of the same event indicating the various breakpoints by microarray where blue is gain and red is loss of CN.

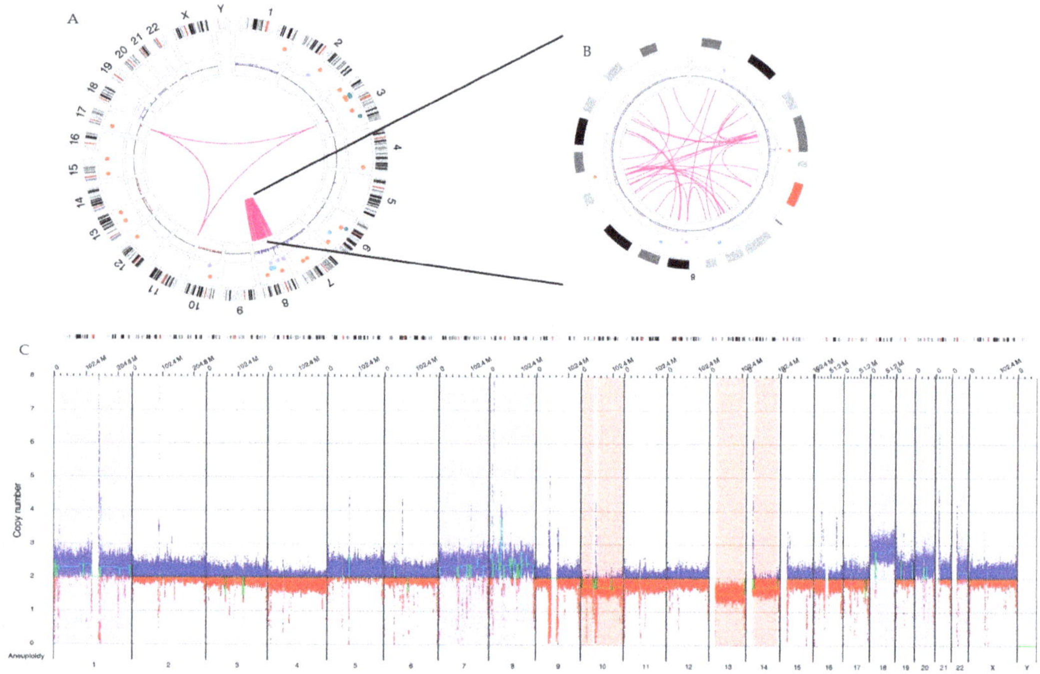

Figure 3. The OGM circus plot (**A**) showing the chromothripsis event observed on chromosome 8 with an enlarged view of chromosome 8 and (**B**) showing the SV events related to the chromothripsis call. On the bottom (**C**) is the OGM whole genome view as a secondary visualization confirming the chromothripsis event in this case, blue color indicates CMV gain segment and red color indicates CNV loss in chromosomes.

3.3. OGM Clearly Defined an SV Event

In one case, OGM clearly defined an SV event that was detected with microarray analysis. In this case, a homozygous deletion of the cyclin-dependent kinase inhibitor 2A (*CDKN2A)* and cyclin-dependent kinase inhibitor 2B (*CDKN2B)* genes was detected in the microarray, as shown in Figure 4. OGM not only detected this event (Figure 5A) but also provided a more detailed insight into how the homozygous deletion happened. In this event, the microarray showed the copy number loss in the region p21.3 on chromosome 9 with a nested deletion, resulting in the biallelic loss of both copies of *CDKN2A* and *CDKN2B* genes. In contrast, OGM analysis uncovered an unbalanced translocation between chromosomes 7 and 9, resulting in a loss of regions between 15.91 M and 32.90 M on chromosome 9, with no loss or gain on chromosome 7 (Figures 5A and 6A). There is trisomy of chromosome 7, which is an independent event. The resulting derivative chromosomes are shown in Figure 6B. This translocation ended up with the monoallelic loss of both *CDKN2A* and *CDKN2B* genes. But the second allele of chromosome 9 was not involved in this translocation event, as confirmed by a secondary/nested deletion on chromosome 9, leading to loss of *CDKN2A* and *CDKN2B* genes (Figure 5B).

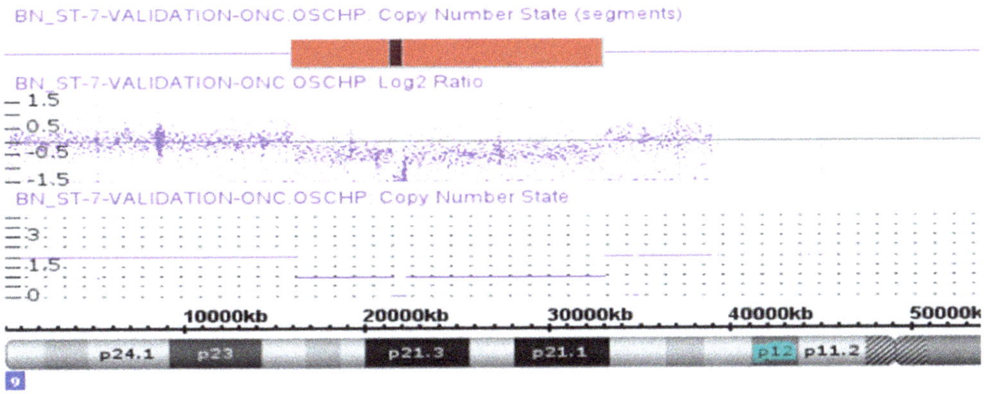

Figure 4. The copy number loss and the nested deletion involving the *CDKN2A* and CDKN2*B* genes identified by CMA analysis in one of the glioma cases. Light red is the CNV event and dark red is the nested deleted present in the CNV loss event which contain the *CDKN2A* and CDKN2*B* genes.

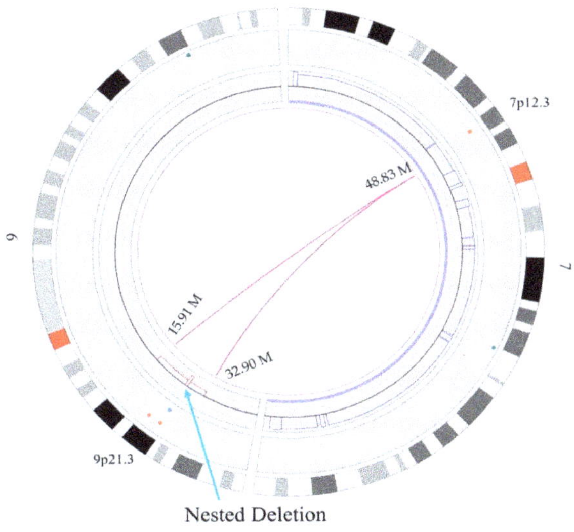

(A)

Figure 5. *Cont.*

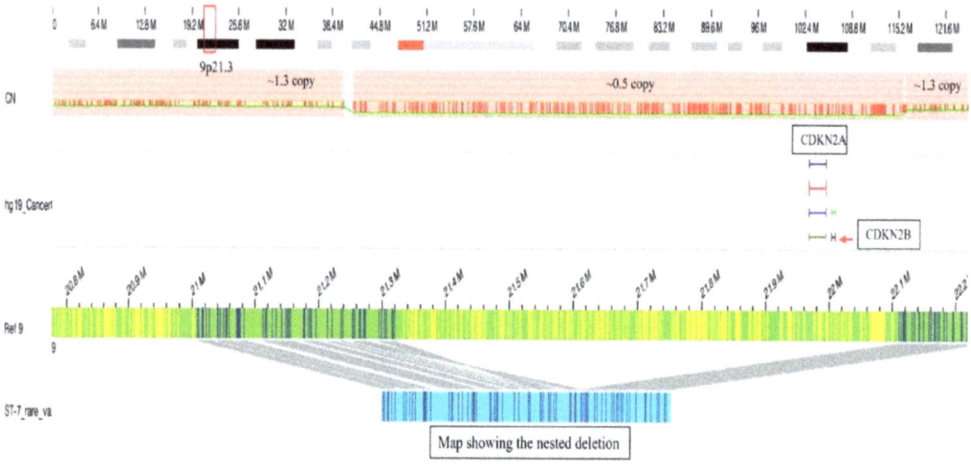

(**B**)

Figure 5. OGM reveals additional details for a glioma case presented in Figure 4. (A) unbalanced translocation event between chromosome 9 and 7 which resulted in the CN loss on chromosome 9, and the nested deletion present on chromosome 9, (**B**) shows the enlarge view of nested deletion having the CN state of approximately 0.5 surrounded by CN state of 1.3 which contain *CDKN2A* and *CDKN2B* genes. Green map shows the reference map and blue map shows the nested deletion detected in this case.

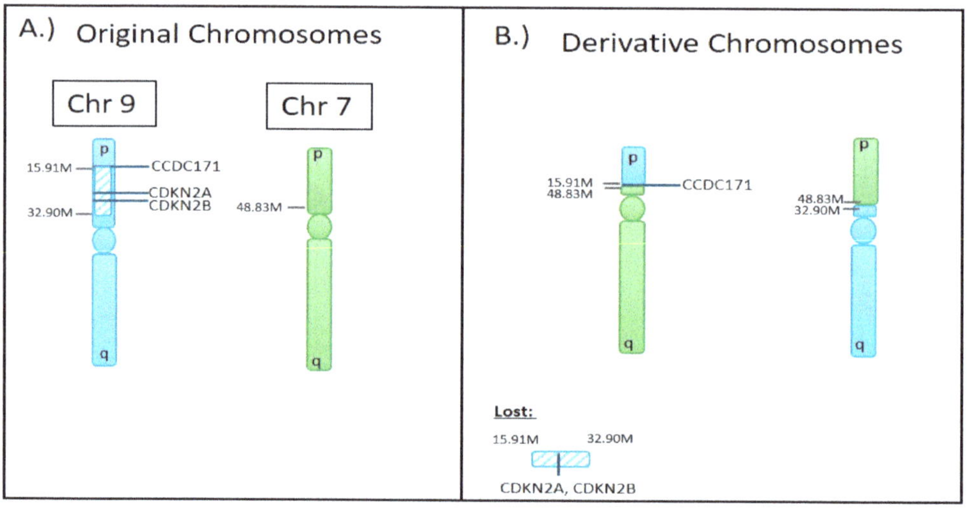

Figure 6. Graphic depiction of (**A**) the original chromosome involved in the translocation event between chromosome 7 and chromosome 9, (**B**) the resulting derivative chromosomes, including the lost section of chromosome 9 that encompasses *CDKN2A* and *CDKN2B* for the glioma case examined by CMA in Figure 4 and OGM in Figure 5.

3.4. OGM Detected the Cryptic SV Events

In addition to identifying the previously characterized SVs, OGM also detected some additional cryptic SV events (Supplementary File Table S2). Some of the examples are presented here.

3.4.1. A Complex Translocation Event

OGM identified a complex translocation event t(3,5)(p12.1;q22.1) in another glioma case in which the portion of p-arm of chromosome 3 was lost, and a copy number gain was observed on chromosome 5, as shown in Figure 7. This event involved three translocation breakpoints, resulting in the derivative chromosome depicted in Figure 8. The first translocation breakpoint on chromosome 3 at ~86.88 M joins with q-arm of chromosome 5 at 114.3 M, causing a loss of the p-arm of chromosome 3. The second breakpoint on chromosome 3 at 88.57 M joins to a second copy of the q-arm of chromosome 5 at 110.54 M. This results in a derivative chromosome containing a portion of the p-arm of chromosome 3 (86.88 M to 88.57 M) flanked between two q-arms of chromosome 5, as shown in 8B. The presence of two 5q-arms creates a duplication from 5q22.3 to the q-terminus. Due to the non-homologous breaking of the two q-arms of chromosome 5, a section slightly upstream (110.54–113.90 M) has been duplicated and was present on both derivative chromosomes, as shown in Figure 8B. The end result is a duplication of the adenomatous polyposis coli (*APC*), a tumor suppressor gene. The third breakpoint results in the fusion of the q-arm of chromosome 3 with a single p-arm of chromosome 5 at 89.3 M and 113.9 M, respectively. As a result of this event, Ephrin type-A receptor 3 (*EPHA3*) on chromosome 3 was disrupted. The second half of the gene has been attached to chromosome 5, while the first half was lost due to a small segmental loss involved in the translocation of a small section of chromosome 3 (88.57–89.30 M) between two breakpoints on chromosome 3.

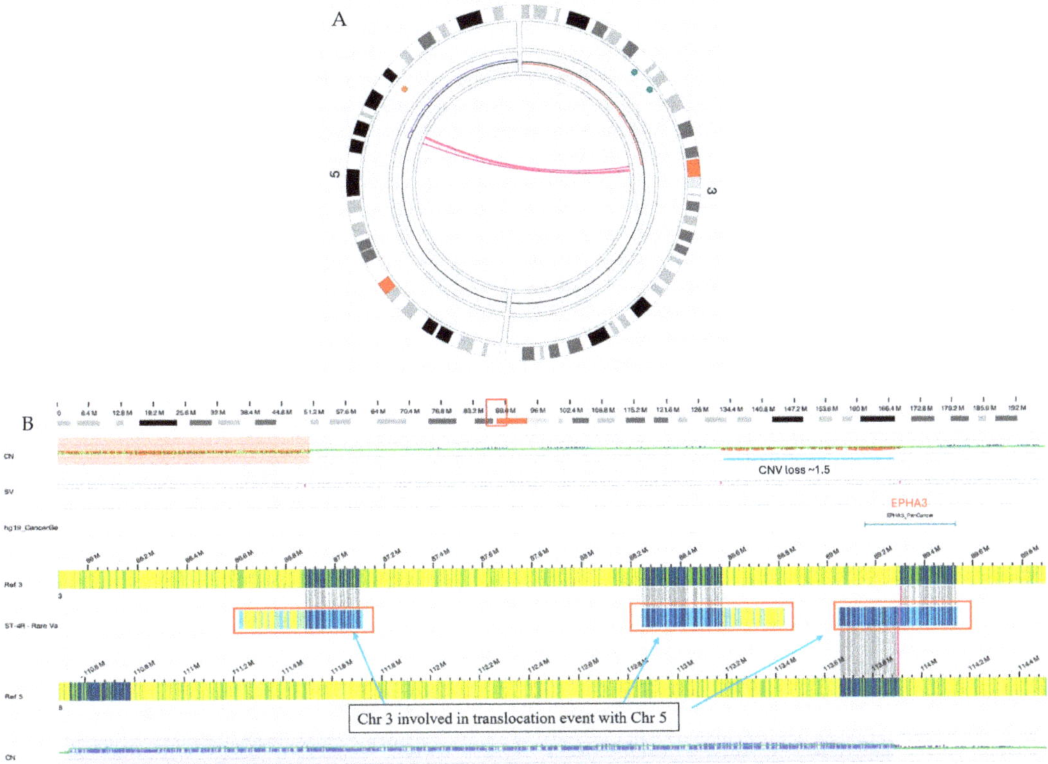

Figure 7. An unbalanced, complex translocation was detected in glioma case. (**A**) Circos plot showing the loss of p-arm on chromosome 3 and a copy number gain on chromosome 5 in SV track. (**B**) Enlarged view of the SV track showing three breakpoints on chromosome 3 involved in the translocation with

chromosome 5, labeled with red rectangular boxes. One breakpoint at position 89.23 M on chromosome 3 results in the disruption of the *EPHA3* gene. In CN track, red is loss of copy number state and blue is copy number gain.

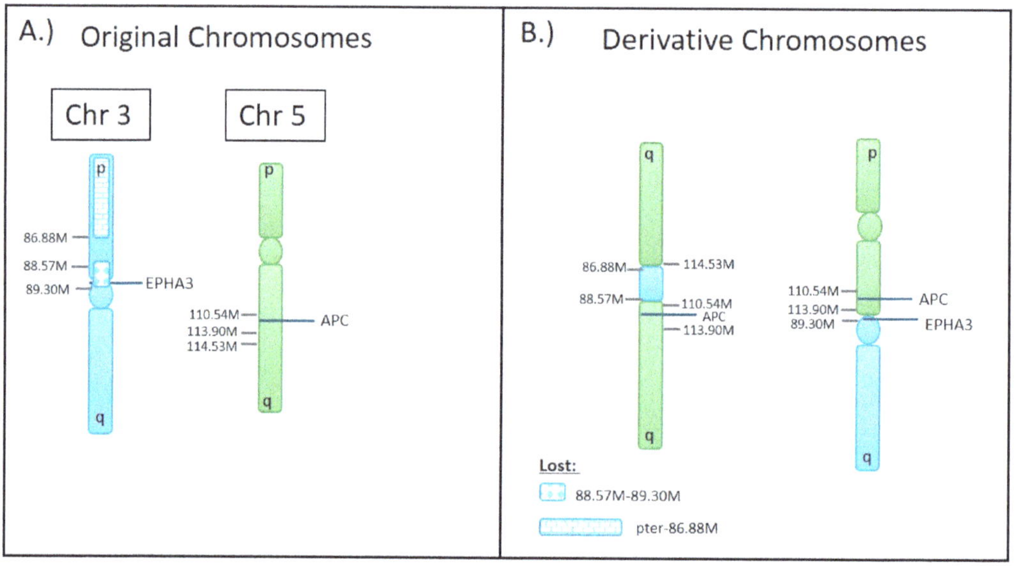

Figure 8. Graphic depiction of (**A**) the original chromosomes involved, (**B**) the movement of genetic material between chromosome 3 and chromosome 5 in the translocation identified by OGM. This translocation results in a loss of genetic material on 3p, a disruption of *EPHA3* on chromosome 3, a duplication on chromosome 5q (110.54–113.90 M), and a gain of chromosome 5q from 5q22.3/114.5 to the q-terminus.

3.4.2. Three-Way Translocation Event

OGM identified a three-way translocation t(17,3,11)(q24.3;q13.33;p15.3), which was not revealed previously by CMA analysis (Figure 9). In this complex translocation, the q24.3 region of chromosome 17 attached to an inverted p-arm of chromosome 11 at p15.3, bringing the gene *ZBED5-AS1* in contact with q24.3 on chromosome 17 in a region with no genes present (68.65 M). A portion of chromosome 17, including the pan-cancer gene *SOX9*, was deleted at q24.3 and q25.1 due to the translocation. The remaining q-arm of chromosome 17 was inverted, partially deleted, and reattached upstream from 70.08 M to an 81 kb section of chromosome 3 (119.55–119.63 M). The breakpoint on the other side of the 81 kb section of chromosome 3 is the remaining chromosome 11 with no immediate genes involved in the breakpoint from either chromosome. The 81 kb section of chromosome 3 (119.55–119.63 M) involved in the translocation was accompanied by flanking deletions identified by OGM, spanning the region of 118.74 M to 120.76 M, that involve many genes, including *GSK3B*, a pan-cancer gene. The derivative chromosomes are shown in Figure 10B.

3.5. OGM Detected a Balanced Translocation Event

OGM analysis detected a balanced translocation SV event in another case between chromosome 12 and 9, in which the fusion of *ETNK1*, a pan-cancer gene, and *ADAMTSL1* was observed in this event, as shown in Figure 11A. In this balanced translocation event, no gain or loss of a chromosome segment was observed on either chromosome, and fusion of these two genes was observed. In the CMA analysis, no change in the copy number state of either gene was observed, as shown in Figure 11B,C.

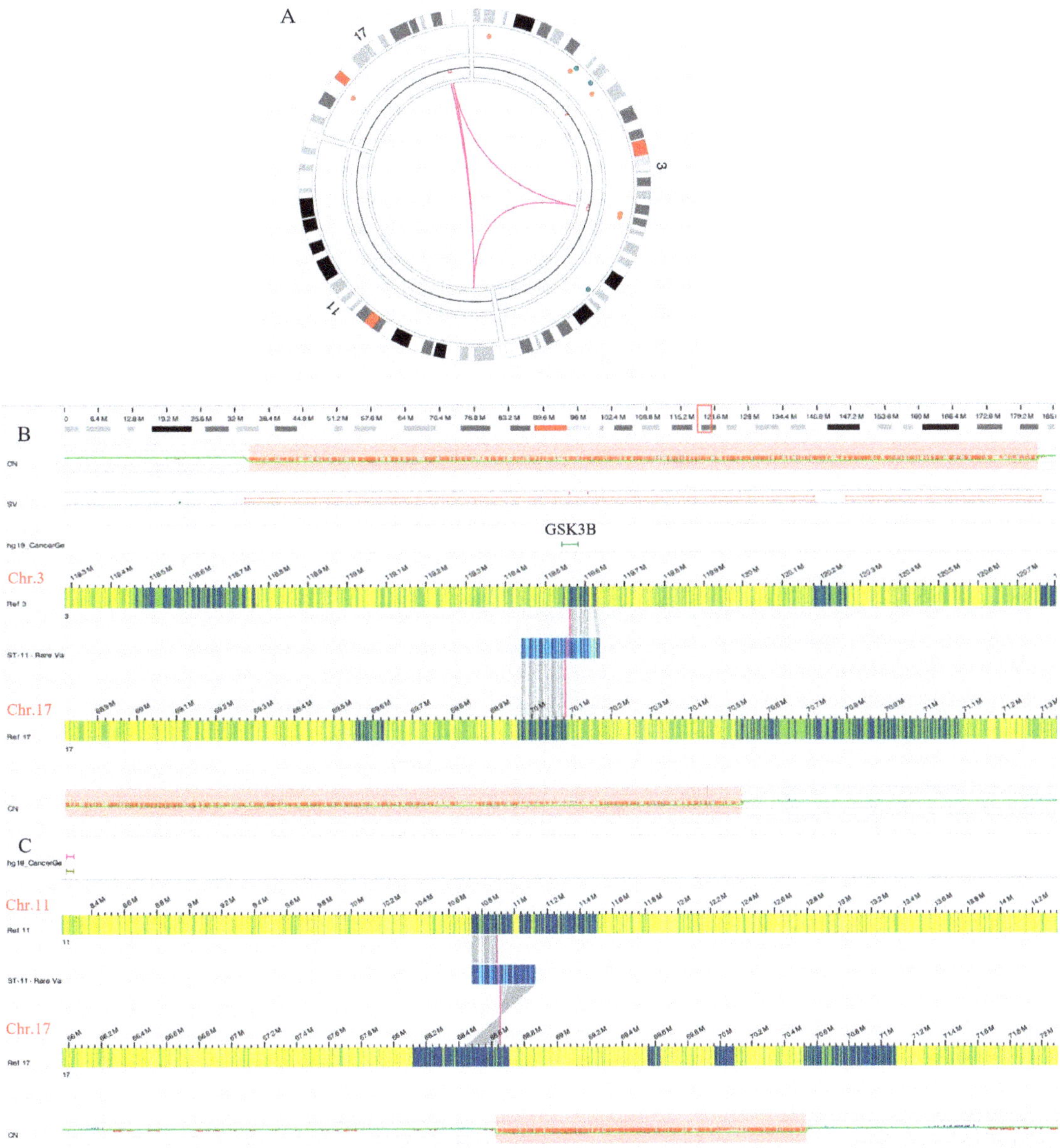

Figure 9. A three-way translocation between chromosomes 3, 11, and 17, as revealed by OGM in glioma case. (**A**) Circos plot of the translocation event, (**B**) enlarged SV view of a breakpoint between chromosome 3 and chromosome 17 involving gene *GSK3B*, and (**C**) enlarged SV view of a breakpoint between chromosome 11 and the inverted chromosome 17.

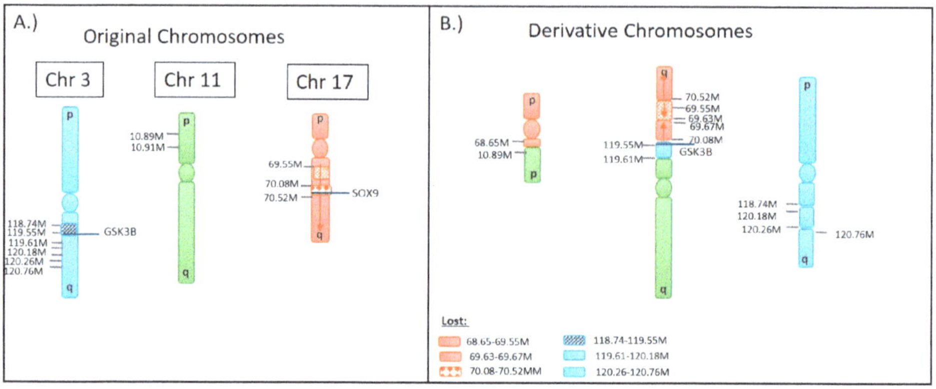

Figure 10. (**A**) Graphic depiction of the original chromosomes involved in the 3-way translocations and the original location of the genes that are affected by the translocation. (**B**) The derivative chromosomes identified by OGM and formed as a result of the 3-way translocation.

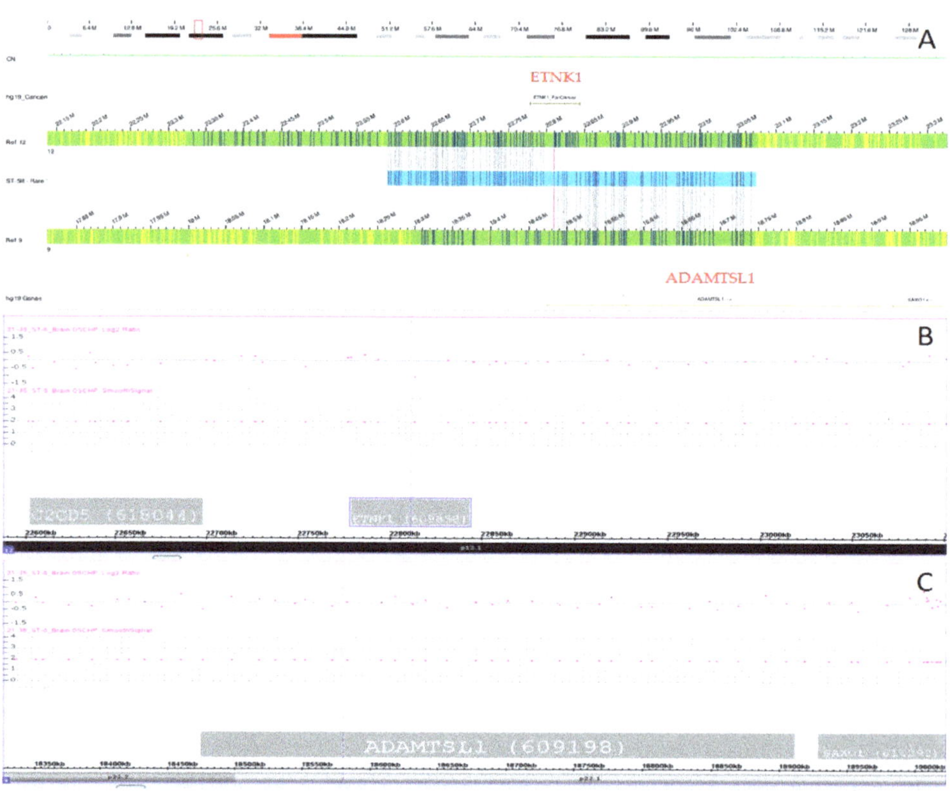

Figure 11. (**A**) OGM showing the balanced translocation event in which gene fusion was observed between *ETNK1* and *ADAMTSL1* gene. (**B**,**C**) No change in either of gene was observed in the CMA analysis.

4. Discussion

The 2021 World Health Organization (WHO-2021) guidelines for gliomas emphasize the importance of precise molecular characterization for accurate diagnosis, prognosis, and treatment planning. Optical Genome Mapping (OGM) is revolutionizing the clinical practice of cytogenomic characterization, currently obtained through a combination of technologies such as karyotyping, FISH, and CMA. Recent reports, including those from our lab, have demonstrated the utility of OGM in the detection of clinically significant cytogenomic abnormalities in hematological malignancies and constitutional cases [11,12]. We show here that OGM analysis of gliomas can provide a comprehensive picture of the whole genome, enabling detailed analysis of different SVs, unraveling complex/cryptic rearrangements, and reliably identifying translocation events in a single step, potentially decreasing the turnaround time for the start of tailored treatment.

OGM data were found to be concordant with CMA in identifying previously characterized SVs and CNVs. In addition, OGM identified additional clinically relevant aberrations and demonstrated higher resolution and sensitivity in accurately defining different SV events. While CMA can detect CNVs as small as 50–100 kb, OGM can detect SVs down to 500 bp. Furthermore, CMA cannot detect translocations, inversions, smaller imbalances, or low-level mosaicism.

Chromothripsis is a catastrophic event in which chromosomal segments are shattered, reshuffled, and randomly stitched together, producing complex derivative chromosomes. Ramos-Campoy et al. described that OGM provides a more detailed description of this event than microarray in chronic lymphocytic leukemia (CLL) cases, due to better characterization of translocations, distinct rearrangement patterns, and breakpoints [13]. Similarly, in our study, CMA presented the results of a particular case as a simple deletion of a region of chromosome 9 involving *CDKN2A* and *CDKN2B*. OGM, however, provided a clear presentation of the SV events involved in an unbalanced translocation coupled with a secondary deletion. In this event, the deletion on one allele was supported by a translocation, while the deletion on the other allele was due to a secondary deletion on chromosome 9. OGM accurately identified the breakpoints involved in these events, supporting both gene deletions, whereas microarray could only define the presence of the deletion without identifying the translocation pattern. In a similar study, microarray failed to detect unbalanced chromosome abnormalities in six postnatal cases, which were detected by chromosome analysis [14]. These cases exhibited low-level mosaicism, ranging between 2% and 7.5%, below CMA's detection limit. OGM, with a detection capability down to 5%, demonstrates higher resolution in detecting low-level mosaic events [7].

OGM also showed the disruption of the *EPHA3* gene, which is implicated in gliomas and overexpressed in 60% of cases, making it a target for glioma therapy [15]. Although *EPHA3* is associated with tumor initiation and infiltration in gliomas, no correlation between its disruption/rearrangement and gliomas has been reported in the literature. Additionally, in a three-way translocation, the *GSK3* gene was found to be disrupted. This gene is involved in the differentiation of malignant glial cells via critical downstream signaling protein pathways. This gene was found to be disrupted and deleted by OGM analysis, but only copy number change/deletion of *GSK3* was observed in CMA. OGM provided the better resolution of an SV event here, with correct position of a translocated gene and its possible interactions with other genes, when compared with CMA. OGM detected a balanced translocation event which was not detected in the CMA analysis. This event leads to a gene fusion between the *ETNK1* and *ADAMTSL1* genes. *ADAMTSL1* is involved in promoting the progression of gliomas [16] and is a potential prognostic biomarker for malignant invasion in glioma.

Microarray assays are limited to detecting genome-wide copy number changes, and their capacity depends on the number of probes used. In contrast, OGM can detect various types of SVs genome-wide in a single run, providing detailed information about translocated partners, inverted regions, and gene fusions to help understand an SV event, which can be helpful for the sub-typing of gliomas. This capability is critical for cancer diagnosis and will help in making better diagnostic and therapeutic decisions, resulting in better patient outcomes.

5. Conclusions

This OGM approach helps in the detection of all classes of SVs in a single assay and generates clinically actionable high-resolution genomic data. OGM can be incorporated in the laboratory workflow and will facilitate precise diagnosis and better prognostication of gliomas. This would help with making better therapeutic decisions, establishing new insight for this class of solid tumors by uncovering additional clinically relevant SVs.

Supplementary Materials: The following supporting information can be downloaded at: https://www.mdpi.com/article/10.3390/biomedicines12081659/s1, Supplementary Table S1: Showing the quality control metrics of the tumor samples for OGM, Supplementary Table S2: Showing the findings of OGM in different tumor samples.

Author Contributions: Conceptualization, H.S., N.S.S., A.K.M. and R.K.; Methodology, H.S., N.S.S. and A.K.M.; Software, H.S. and N.S.S.; Validation, H.S., N.S.S. and S.L.B.; Formal Analysis, H.S., N.S.S. and S.L.B.; Investigation, H.S. and N.S.S.; Resources, R.K.; Data Curation, H.S., N.S.S., S.L.B. and A.A.; Writing—Original Draft Preparation, H.S; Writing—Review and Editing, A.K.M., S.L.B., J.F., A.A., A.V., K.J., V.V. and R.K.; Visualization, J.F.; Supervision, R.K. All authors have read and agreed to the published version of the manuscript.

Funding: This research received no external funding.

Institutional Review Board Statement: The study was performed under the Institutional Review Board (IRB) A: BIOMEDICAL I (IRB REGISTRATION #00000150), Augusta University. IRB number 611298. Based on the IRB approval, the need for consent was waived; all protected health information was removed, and all data was anonymized before accessing the clinical validation study.

Informed Consent Statement: The study was performed on left-over material after testing and the need for consent was waived under the IRB-as given in IRB statement.

Data Availability Statement: The original contributions presented in the study are included in the article/supplementary material, further inquiries can be directed to the corresponding author/s.

Conflicts of Interest: R.K. has received honoraria, and/or travel funding, and/or research support from Illumina, ALDA, OCDdx, Roche, Novartis, AbbVie, Bionano Genomics, Agena, PGDx, Cepheid. SLB was an employee of Bionano Genomics, a company commercializing optical genome mapping technology. All other authors have no competing interests to disclose.

References

1. Cancer Stat Facts: Brain and Other Nervous System Cancer. Available online: https://seer.cancer.gov/statfacts/html/brain.html (accessed on 15 May 2024).
2. Liang, J.; Lv, X.; Lu, C.; Ye, X.; Chen, X.; Fu, J.; Luo, C.; Zhao, Y. Prognostic factors of patients with gliomas–an analysis on 335 patients with glioblastoma and other forms of gliomas. *BMC Cancer* **2020**, *20*, 35. [CrossRef] [PubMed]
3. McNeill, K.A. Epidemiology of brain tumors. *Neurol. Clin.* **2016**, *34*, 981–998. [CrossRef] [PubMed]
4. Louis, D.N.; Perry, A.; Wesseling, P.; Brat, D.J.; Cree, I.A.; Figarella-Branger, D.; Hawkins, C.; Ng, H.K.; Pfister, S.M.; Reifenberger, G.; et al. The 2021 WHO classification of tumors of the central nervous system: A summary. *Neuro-Oncology* **2021**, *23*, 1231–1251. [CrossRef] [PubMed]
5. Mantere, T.; Neveling, K.; Pebrel-Richard, C.; Benoist, M.; van der Zande, G.; Kater-Baats, E.; Baatout, I.; van Beek, R.; Yammine, T.; Oorsprong, M.; et al. Optical genome mapping enables constitutional chromosomal aberration detection. *Am. J. Hum. Genet.* **2021**, *108*, 1409–1422. [CrossRef] [PubMed]
6. Garcia-Heras, J. Optical Genome Mapping: A Revolutionary Tool for "Next Generation Cytogenomics Analysis" with a Broad Range of Diagnostic Applications in Human Diseases. *J. Assoc. Genet. Technol.* **2021**, *47*, 191–200. [PubMed]
7. Sahajpal, N.S.; Mondal, A.K.; Tvrdik, T.; Hauenstein, J.; Shi, H.; Deeb, K.K.; Saxe, D.; Hastie, A.R.; Chaubey, A.; Savage, N.M.; et al. Clinical validation and diagnostic utility of optical genome mapping for enhanced cytogenomic analysis of hematological neoplasms. *J. Mol. Diagn.* **2022**, *24*, 1279–1291. [CrossRef] [PubMed]
8. Levy, B.; Baughn, L.B.; Akkari, Y.; Chartrand, S.; LaBarge, B.; Claxton, D.; Lennon, P.A.; Cujar, C.; Kolhe, R.; Kroeger, K.; et al. Optical genome mapping in acute myeloid leukemia: A multicenter evaluation. *Blood Adv.* **2023**, *7*, 1297–1307. [CrossRef] [PubMed]

9. Sahajpal, N.S.; Barseghyan, H.; Kolhe, R.; Hastie, A.; Chaubey, A. Optical Genome Mapping as a Next-Generation Cytogenomic Tool for Detection of Structural and Copy Number Variations for Prenatal Genomic Analyses. *Genes* **2021**, *12*, 398. [CrossRef] [PubMed]
10. SP Tissue and Tumor DNA Isolation Kit. Available online: https://bionano.com/sp-tissue-and-tumor-dna-isolation-kit (accessed on 15 May 2022).
11. Neveling, K.; Mantere, T.; Vermeulen, S.; Oorsprong, M.; van Beek, R.; Kater-Baats, E.; Pauper, M.; van der Zande, G.; Smeets, D.; Weghuis, D.O.; et al. Next-generation cytogenetics: Comprehensive assessment of 52 hematological malignancy genomes by optical genome mapping. *Am. J. Hum. Genet.* **2021**, *108*, 1423–1435. [CrossRef] [PubMed]
12. Xie, M.; Zheng, Z.J.; Zhou, Y.; Zhang, Y.X.; Li, Q.; Tian, L.Y.; Cao, J.; Xu, Y.T.; Ren, J.; Yu, Q.; et al. Prospective Investigation of Optical Genome Mapping for Prenatal Genetic Diagnosis. *Clin. Chem.* **2024**, *70*, hvae031. [CrossRef] [PubMed]
13. Ramos-Campoy, S.; Puiggros, A.; Kamaso, J.; Beà, S.; Bougeon, S.; Larráyoz, M.J.; Costa, D.; Parker, H.; Rigolin, G.M.; Blanco, M.L.; et al. TP53 abnormalities are underlying the poor outcome associated with chromothripsis in chronic lymphocytic leukemia patients with complex karyotype. *Cancers* **2022**, *14*, 3715. [CrossRef] [PubMed]
14. Bi, W.; Borgan, C.; Pursley, A.N.; Hixson, P.; Shaw, C.A.; Bacino, C.A.; Lalani, S.R.; Patel, A.; Stankiewicz, P.; Lupski, J.R.; et al. Comparison of chromosome analysis and chromosomal microarray analysis: What is the value of chromosome analysis in today's genomic array era. *Genet. Med.* **2013**, *15*, 450–457. [CrossRef] [PubMed]
15. Ferluga, S.; Tomé, C.M.L.; Herpai, D.M.; D'Agostino, R.; Debinski, W. Simultaneous targeting of Eph receptors in glioblastoma. *Oncotarget* **2016**, *7*, 59860. [CrossRef] [PubMed]
16. Wang, S.; Zhang, J.; Wang, K.; Zhao, Y.; Liu, D. ADAMTS1 as potential prognostic biomarker promotes malignant invasion of glioma. *Int. J. Clin. Oncol.* **2023**, *28*, 52–68. [CrossRef] [PubMed]

biomedicines

MDPI

Case Report

A High-Grade Glioma, Not Elsewhere Classified in an Older Adult with Discordant Genetic and Epigenetic Analyses

Carlen A. Yuen [1,*], Silin Bao [2], Xiao-Tang Kong [1], Merryl Terry [3], Alexander Himstead [4], Michelle Zheng [5] and Melike Pekmezci [3]

1 Neuro-Oncology Division, Department of Neurology, University of California, Irvine, CA 92868, USA
2 Neurosciences Division, Department of Internal Medicine, Community Regional Medical Center, Fresno, CA 93721, USA
3 Department of Pathology, University of California, San Francisco, CA 94143, USA
4 Department of Neurosurgery, University of California, Irvine, CA 92868, USA
5 UC Irvine Charlie Dunlop School of Biological Sciences, University of California, Irvine, CA 92697, USA
* Correspondence: carleny@hs.uci.edu

Abstract: The World Health Organization's (WHO) classification of central nervous system (CNS) tumors is continually being refined to improve the existing diagnostic criteria for high-grade gliomas (HGGs), including glioblastoma. In 2021, advances in molecular analyses and DNA methylation profiling were incorporated to expand upon the diagnostic criteria for HGG, including the introduction of high-grade astrocytoma with piloid features (HGAP), a new tumor entity for which a match to the HGAP class in DNA methylation profiling is an essential criterion. We present an equivocal case of a 72-year-old male with an HGG exhibiting features of both HGAP and glioblastoma, but which did not conform to any existing 2021 WHO classification of CNS tumor entities. This "no match" in DNA methylation profiling resulted in a final diagnosis of HGG not elsewhere classified (NEC), for which standard treatment options do not exist.

Keywords: high-grade astrocytoma with piloid features; HGAP; HGG NEC; pilocytic astrocytoma; DNA methylation; classification; glioblastoma; high-grade glioma; not elsewhere classified; WHO classification; central nervous system tumors

1. Introduction

The World Health Organization's (WHO) classification of central nervous system (CNS) tumors has undergone multiple revisions to improve the diagnostic accuracy of high-grade gliomas (HGGs). The prior classification schemes relied solely on histopathologic features. The more recent classification schemes have been updated to integrate molecular features with the existing histologic criteria. Each iteration of the WHO classification refines and expands the diagnostic categories, reflecting the exponential increase in our understanding of genetic and epigenetic mechanisms driving CNS tumors. More recently, DNA methylation profiling has emerged as a formidable diagnostic tool for CNS tumor classification [1–4]. Methylation involves the addition of a methyl group to a cytosine nucleotide, predominantly occurring within CpG sites (sites wherein a cytosine nucleotide precedes a guanine nucleotide) [5]. Methylation profiles are DNA methylation patterns defined across the genome [6,7] and are fingerprints that identify the cell of origin [1,8–10]. These DNA methylation patterns are grouped into classifiers that are utilized for the distinct classification of tumors [1,8–10]. Methylation profiling is increasingly being used as an ancillary diagnostic tool to reliably diagnose otherwise equivocal high-grade glioma (HGG) tumor cases and to identify new CNS tumor entities, such as high-grade astrocytoma with piloid features (HGAP) [6,11,12].

HGAP is a described high-grade astrocytoma that is exclusively diagnosed by its distinct global DNA methylation signature [13,14]. Most commonly occurring in the posterior fossa, the morphology of HGAPs is diverse, with some overlapping features between glioblastoma and pilocytic astrocytoma [14,15]. However, characteristic histologic features of pilocytic astrocytomas, such as Rosenthal fibers, are often lacking despite the "piloid" designation [14]. HGAPs typically behave more aggressively than benign pilocytic astrocytomas but reportedly have a better prognosis compared to IDH-wild-type glioblastomas [11]. HGAPs frequently harbor alterations in the mitogen-activated protein kinase (MAPK) pathway, such as *NF1* mutations (40.4%), *FGFR1* mutations or fusions (19.1% and 14%, respectively), and *BRAF* mutations or fusions (2.3% and 18.6%, respectively), accompanied by *CDKN2A* and *ATRX* gene alterations [14]. HGAPs do not harbor *EGFR* amplification, polysomy 7/monosomy 10, and rarely harbor *TERT* promoter mutations (1.1%), which define molecular alterations for glioblastoma [6]. Along with these biological differences, which remain under investigation, divergence in treatment options between pilocytic astrocytoma and glioblastoma also remains. Intervention for this new CNS tumor entity, which lies amidst a benign and malignant tumor, is challenging. Evidence for HGAP is scant, with few reported cases and a tenuous association between treatment and patient outcomes [13,14,16].

Herein, we present a case of a 72-year-old male with a challenging HGG not elsewhere classified (NEC), showing characteristics of both HGAP and glioblastoma that did not fit neatly with any of the existing tumor entities in the 2021 WHO classification of CNS tumors, despite molecular profiling and DNA methylation analysis. We report on his response to standard-of-care glioblastoma treatment for his HGG NEC.

2. Detailed Case Description

A 72-year-old male presented with a two-day history of altered mental status and emesis secondary to a 4.3 cm enhancing mass in the left temporal region, detected on a brain MRI with and without contrast (Figure 1A). His neurological exam was notable for memory impairment. Following a subtotal resection, which left a residual 1 cm nodule at the medial aspect of the resection cavity, histopathology revealed a high-grade glial neoplasm. In some areas, tumor cells with spindled hyperchromatic nuclei showed a compact growth pattern, interspersed with intervening areas (Figure 2A,B). Rosenthal fibers and eosinophilic granular bodies were absent. Scattered in these regions were bizarre, multinucleated cells with smudgy chromatin. In other areas, tumor cells with round-to-oval nuclei and scant-to-moderate amounts of cytoplasm were embedded in a fibrillary, neuropil-like background, associated with entrapped neurons, increased mitotic activity (at least 6 mitoses per 2 mm^2), and incipient microvascular proliferation (Figure 2C). In these infiltrative high-grade areas, geographic necrosis and viable tumor cells surrounding vasculature formed a pseudopapillary architecture (Figure 2D). Tumor cells were positive for GFAP, OLIG2, and synaptophysin (weak, diffuse in high-grade areas, focal in compact areas). Neurofilament staining was negative in compact areas and highlighted entrapped axons in infiltrative high-grade areas. The p53 stain was patchy, suggestive of the wild-type *TP53* gene. ATRX was retained in compact areas but was lost in infiltrative high-grade areas. P16 was absent from both regions. The Ki-67 labeling index was low in the compact areas but was estimated at 40% in high-grade areas (Figure 3).

We performed targeted DNA-based next-generation sequencing (NGS) evaluating all exons of 479 cancer genes and select introns and upstream regulatory regions of 47 genes, including genes critical for glioma diagnosis, e.g., *IDH1, IDH2, EGFR, PDGFRA, MET, FGFR1, FGFR2, FGFR3, NF1, BRAF, PIK3CA, PIK3R1, PTEN, CDKN2A, CDK4, CDK6, RB1, TP53, MDM2, MDM4, H3F3A, HIST1H3B, CIC, FUBP1, ATRX*, and *TERT* (including the promoter region) [17,18]. NGS results from our case demonstrated an activating hotspot mutation in the *FGFR1* oncogene (NM_023110.2; p.N546K, variant allele frequency of 82%) and homozygous deletion of the *CDKN2A* and *CDKN2B* tumor suppressor genes on chromosome 9p21.3 in the background of additional copy number changes (Figure 4). In addition, alterations in *DNMT3A* and *TET2* were also noted, at low variant allele frequencies (7% and 5%, respectively, suggestive of clonal hematopoiesis of indeterminate potential (CHIP) [19]. No other alterations were detected, including *TERT, EGFR, PTEN, TP53, BRAF*, and *ATRX* genes, as well as polysomy 7/monosomy 10 involving the whole chromosome arms. While sequencing did not show an *ATRX* alteration, the loss of *ATRX* immunohistochemical staining (in the presence of an internal positive control) suggested either a cryptic genetic alteration or epigenetic inactivation of *ATRX*.

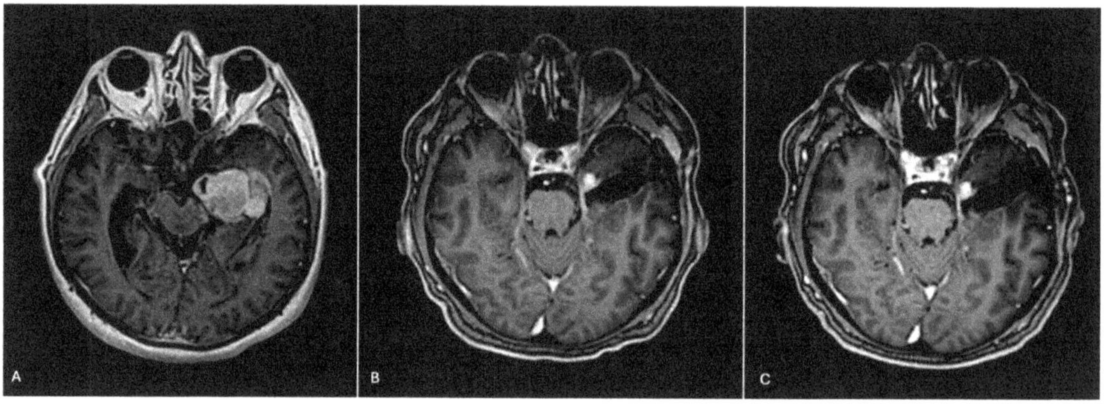

Figure 1. Pre-surgical, post-surgical, and post-2 cycles of temozolomide imaging. (**A**) Pre-surgical axial T1 brain MRI with contrast reveals a 4.3 cm enhancing mass. (**B**) Post-radiation axial T1 brain MRI with contrast reveals a residual 1 cm enhancing nodule at the medial aspect of the resection cavity. (**C**) Following two cycles of adjuvant temozolomide, axial T1 brain MRI with contrast reveals a stable residual 1 cm enhancing nodule at the medial aspect of the resection cavity.

In addition, genome-wide methylation analysis was performed at the National Institutes of Health (NIH, Bethesda, MD, USA) after DNA extraction and bisulfite conversion (EZ DNA Methylation kit, Zymo Research, Irvine, CA, USA) using the Infinium MethylationEPIC kit (Illumina, San Diego, CA, USA). Our patient's tumor was compared to an existing database of known CNS tumors using machine learning algorithms, including random forest and uniform manifold approximation and projection (UMAP) for dimension reduction. The class prediction was reported with a calibrated confidence score ranging from 0 to 1, with a score > 0.9, considered a "match". This case was analyzed using versions 11b6 and 12b6 of the DKFZ Classifier (The German Cancer Research Center-Deutsches Krebsforschungszentrum, Heidelberg, Germany) and the National Cancer Institute (NCI)/Bethesda Classifier (NIH, Bethesda, MD, USA). On the Heidelberg/DKFZ classifiers, versions 11b6 and 12b6, this tumor matched to methylation class (MC)-anaplastic astrocytoma with piloid features, which is the name this classifier uses for HGAP, with a confidence score of 0.25, and to MC-pilocytic astrocytoma with a confidence score of 0.35, respectively. These matches were considered "no match" due to low confidence scores. On the NCI/Bethesda Classifier, which uses 10 different classification algorithms, this tumor matched to MC-HGAP on 8 of the 10 classifiers with high confidence scores (ranging from 0.96 to 0.99), but it matched to MC-pilocytic astrocytoma on the remaining two classifiers and on the UMAP embedding of DNA methylation array data. While the histological and molecular features of this astrocytic glioma fulfill all of the desirable criteria for HGAP, given the lack of concordance between the classifiers, an integrated diagnosis of HGG and NEC was favored. NEC is an indicator that this tumor does not conform to a specific, well-defined diagnostic entity in WHO 2021 despite adequate genetic and epigenetic testing [20].

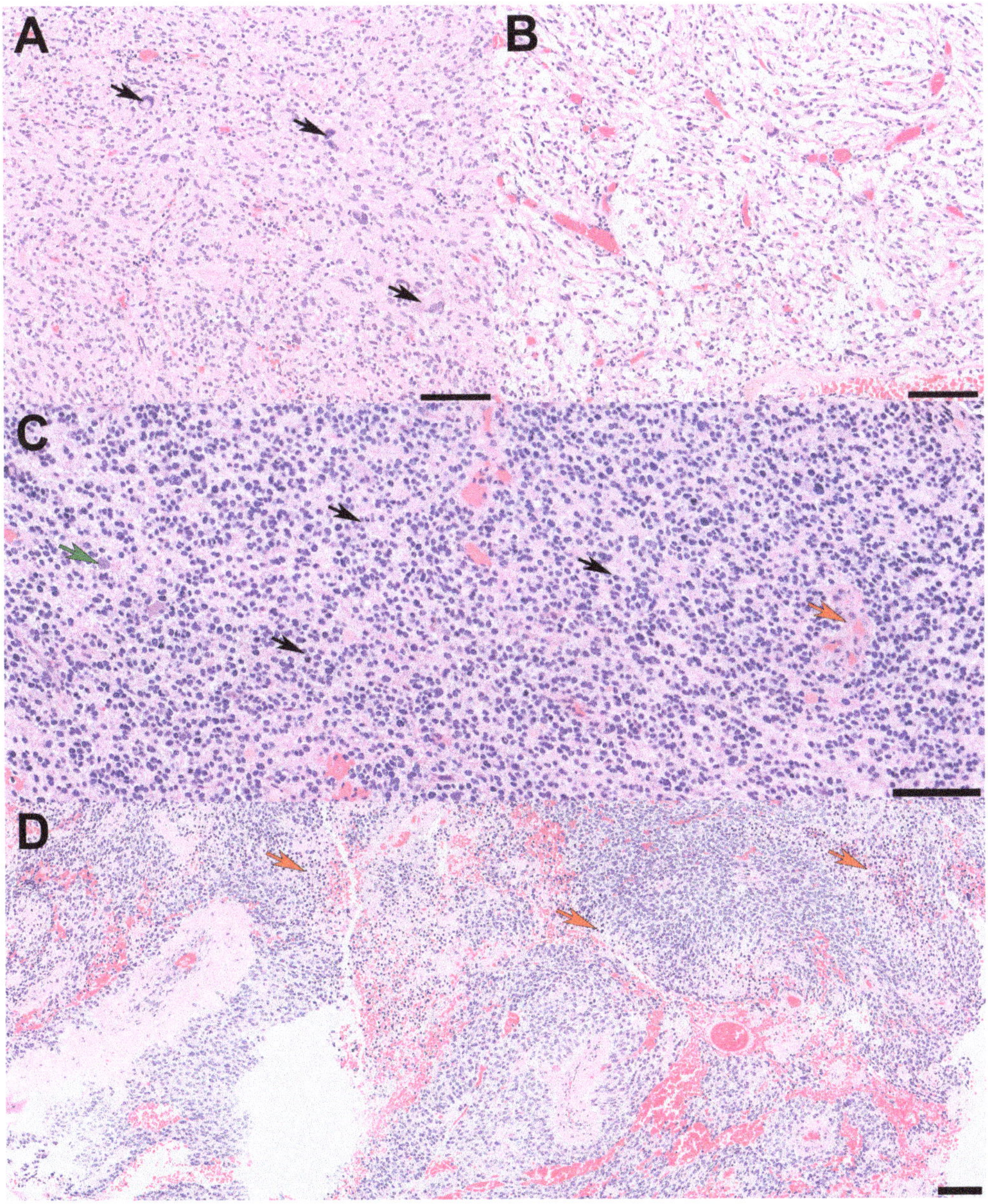

Figure 2. Histopathologic features. All scale bars are 100 microns. (**A**) Sections reveal glial cells with spindled and hyperchromatic nuclei with a compact growth pattern and (**B**) intervening areas of the microcystic background. Note the pleomorphic, bizarre cells with smudgy chromatin in panel (**A**) (arrows); (**C**) in other areas, tumor cells with round nuclei and scant chromatin show infiltrative growth patterns and high-grade features. Note the entrapped cortical neuron (green arrow), mitotic figures (black arrows), and incipient microvascular proliferation (red arrow); (**D**) some high-grade areas show pseudopapillary architecture due to geographic necrosis (red arrows) and viable tumor cells clinging around vessels.

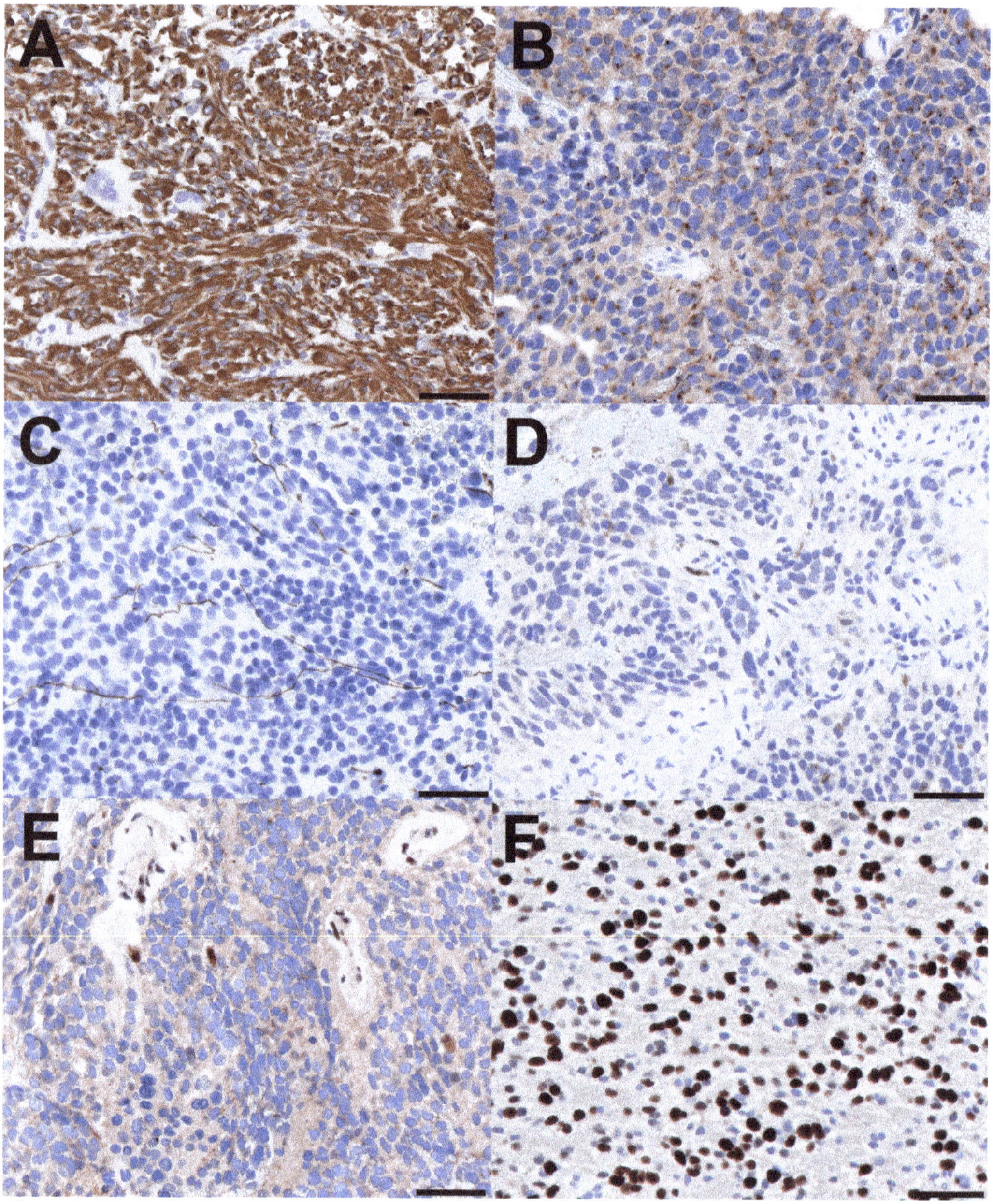

Figure 3. Immunohistochemical features. All scale bars are 50 microns. (**A**) Tumor cells are positive with GFAP and (**B**) weakly positive with synaptophysin; (**C**) neurofilament stain highlights entrapped axons in the high-grade areas; (**D**) p16 is essentially negative, which can be interpreted as a "loss" in tumor cells; (**E**) ATRX is lost in tumor cells in the high-grade areas and retained in endothelial cells; (**F**) Ki-67 labeling index is approximately 40% in high-grade areas.

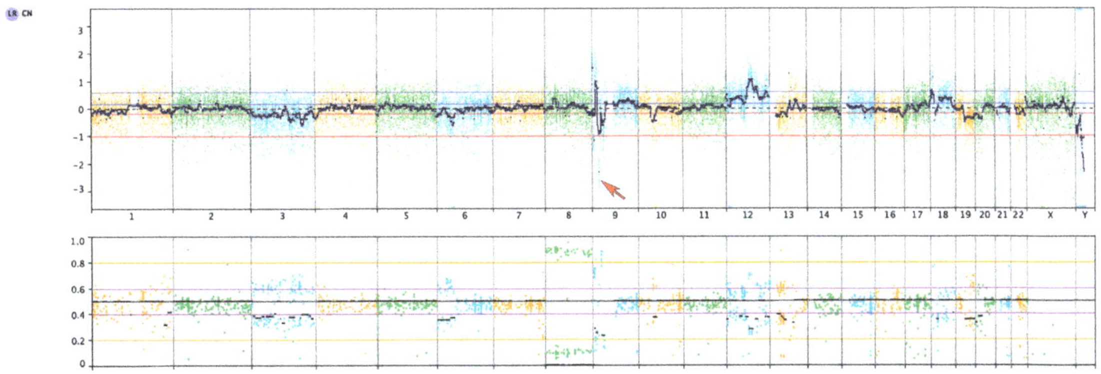

Figure 4. Copy number profile showed gains and losses of multiple chromosomes, and homozygous deletion of CDKN2A/CDKN2B (red arrow).

The patient was treated with radiation and concomitant temozolomide. Post-radiation brain MRI showed a stable residual 1 cm enhancing nodule at the medial aspect of the resection cavity (Figure 1B). At the time of publication, he completed 6 cycles of adjuvant temozolomide and remains stable both clinically and radiographically (Figure 1C). Ethical guidelines set out by the Declaration of Helsinki were followed in the preparation of this report, and the patient provided written consent.

3. Discussion

The most recent WHO classification of CNS tumors incorporates histologic, genetic, and epigenetic features into an integrated diagnosis, which is expected to increase the accuracy and reproducibility of the diagnoses [3]. Morphologic features in this case, including infiltrative growth patterns, frequent mitoses, necrosis, and microvascular proliferation, were consistent with an aggressive astrocytoma. In the pre-integrative diagnosis era, prior to the 2016 WHO classification, these features may have been sufficient to diagnose this tumor as glioblastoma [21]. However, the tumor lacked *TERT* promoter mutation, *EGFR* amplification, and polysomy 7/monosomy 10, which are the characteristic genetic alterations of IDH-wild-type glioblastoma in adult patients [6,22–24]. Given the "glioblastoma IDH-wild-type" is defined by what it is lacking (i.e., lack of *IDH1* and *IDH2* hotspot mutations) rather than what it is harboring, many opportunities exist to identify new CNS tumor entities with unique genetic and epigenetic features within this HGG group. HGAP is one newly identified tumor type among HGGs, wherein a match to methylation class HGAP on DNA methylation profiling is an essential criterion [11,13,14,25].

Our case demonstrated unusual histologic features, including a relatively lower-grade region with a compact growth pattern. A pilocytic astrocytoma with high-grade progression designation was considered, given the combination of MAPK pathway alteration (*FGFR1* hotspot mutation) and ATRX loss in the high-grade areas [15]. However, the lower-grade regions did not fit neatly into characteristic pilocytic astrocytoma morphology. The presence of scattered pleomorphic cells as well as a pseudopapillary architecture also raised the possibility of high-grade glioma with pleomorphic and pseudopapillary features (HPAP), a recently proposed tumor entity with frequent *TP53* alterations and monosomy 13q [12], which were absent from our case. The histologic and molecular features also raised the possibility of HGAP [13,14,26], prompting DNA methylation profiling.

Clinical data garnered from limited existing literature for HGAP corroborated with our patient's tumor to a limited extent. HGAP predominantly affects males with a mean age of 44 years at the time of surgery [14]. Our patient was male but was significantly older at the age of 72 at the time of surgery. Although HGAP has a predilection for the posterior fossa (62%), 26% of cases occur in the supratentorial region [14,27], as in our case where the tumor was located in the temporal lobe. An infiltrative glioblastoma-like morphology is observed in 86.7% of HGAP cases [14], substantiated by the morphology observed in our patient's tumor. Necrosis and/or microvascular proliferation are observed in 62.3% of HGAP cases (and were present in our case) [14]. While some foci showed a compact growth pattern, Rosenthal fibers and classic pilocytic astrocytoma morphology were absent, keeping with the lack of piloid features in the majority of HGAPs [11,12,14]. Mitotic activity ranges from 0 to 6 mitoses/mm^2 in HGAP tumors [14], which was validated by the mitotic count of 6 per HPF in our patient's tumor. The Ki-67 proliferative index of HGAP ranges from 1 to 30%, but the Ki-67 proliferation index in our patient's tumor was significantly elevated at 40% [14].

DNA methylation profiling was contributory, but insufficient to establish a definitive diagnosis in our case. While some of the classification algorithms used in the NCI/Bethesda Classifier matched to the methylation class "HGAP", others, including UMAP embedding, matched to the methylation class "pilocytic astrocytoma", while the DKFZ classifier resulted in a no-match to "anaplastic pilocytic". Collectively, the lack of concordance and a "no match" on DNA methylation profiling yielded a final descriptive integrated diagnosis of HGG NEC.

The recent discovery of HGAP highlights the role of DNA methylation profiling in uncovering new CNS tumor entities [12,14]. Our case may represent either a new emerging CNS tumor type or subtype that has yet to be defined, or more likely, it is an unusual variant that has yet to be incorporated into the existing databases [20]. Nevertheless, using "an astrocytic glioma with DNA methylation profile of HGAP" as the sole diagnostic criterion of HGAP is not fully integrative of histologic, genetic, and epigenetic features of a tumor. Furthermore, it poses challenges to issue a specific diagnosis in cases such as this one. Accordingly, refraining from forcing a diagnosis is imperative. To our knowledge, there is only one other reported case of a suspected HGAP, with no match on DNA methylation profiling resulting in a diagnosis of HGG NEC, but treatment was not reported and remains a knowledge gap to be explored [28]. Additional cases with similar clinical, histologic, molecular, and epigenetic features are required for confirmation. Nonetheless, substantial data remain to be uncovered for HGAP, including its affiliation with pilocytic astrocytoma or glioblastoma and therapeutic options (Table 1).

Table 1. High-grade astrocytoma with piloid features: confirmed or suspected reported cases.

Author/Year	Age/Sex	Location	Molecular Alterations	Surgery (s)	RT (Gy)	PFS (m)	OS (m)
Yuen et al., 2024	72/M	Temporal lobe	*CDKN2A*/B homozygous deletion *FGFR1* p.N546K ATRX loss (on IHC) *BRAF, NF1, KRAS, IDH1, IDH2, H3-3A, TERT, EGFR, PTEN, PDGFRA*–wild-type	NTR	60	15	alive at 15 m follow-up
Bender et al., 2021 [13]	71/M	Spinal cord	*CDKN2A*/B deletion ATRX loss (on IHC) *FGFR1* complex rearrangement *IDH* 1/2 wild-type *MGMT* unmethylated	STR → GTR	50.4	3.6	alive at 14.6 m follow-up
	49/F	Pons Cerebellar peduncle	*CDKN2A*/B deletion ATRX loss (on IHC) IDH1 R132H IHC negative *MGMT* unmethylated	biopsy	54	7.6	9.1

Table 1. *Cont.*

Author/Year	Age/Sex	Location	Molecular Alterations	Surgery (s)	RT (Gy)	PFS (m)	OS (m)
	67/M	Spinal cord	*CDKN2A*/B deletion ATRX loss (on IHC) *IDH* 1/2 wild-type *MGMT* unmethylated	STR	n/a	n/a	n/a
	53/M	Brainstem	*CDKN2A*/B deletion ATRX retained (on IHC) *IDH* 1/2 wild-type *H3-3A* wild-type *BRAF* V600 hotspot-wild-type *MGMT* methylated	STR	54	n/a	18.6
	47/M	Mesencephalon—diencephalon	NF1 syndrome *CDKN2A*/B deletion ATRX loss (on IHC) *MGMT* unmethylated	bx	n/a	n/a	1.8
	44/M	Parieto-occipital	*NF1* mutation in the setting of NF1 syndrome *CDKN2A*/B deletion ATRX retained (on IHC) *IDH1* R132H IHC negative H3 K27M IHC negative *BRAF* V600 wild-type, *MGMT* methylated	STR → STR	59.2	5.4	14.8
Cimino et al., 2023 [14] (*n* = 144)	43 (mean)/ F (*n* = 59), M (*n* = 85)	Posterior fossa (81/130, 62%) Supratentorial (34/130, 26%) Spinal Cord (13/130, 10%)	*CDKN2A* deletion (84.1%) ATRX mutation or loss on IHC (58.6%) *NF1* alterations (40.4%) *FGFR1* alterations (33.1%) *BRAF* alterations (20.9%) *KRAS* (1.1%)	n/a	n/a	n/a	n/a
Reinhardt et al., 2018 [11] (*n* = 102)	41.5 (median)/ F (*n* = 40), M (*n* = 43)	Posterior fossa (74%)	*CDKN2A*/B deletion (66/83, 80%) ATRX mutations/loss on IHC (33/74, 45%) *NF1* alterations (20/67, 30%) *BRAF* fusion (15/74, 20%) *FGFR1* alterations (12/64, 19%) *KRAS* mutation (2/64, 3%) *IDH* 1/2 wild-type (100%) *MGMT* methylated (38/83, 46%)	n/a	n/a	n/a	n/a
Nawa et al., 2024 [29]	34/M	Cerebellum/pons	*CDKN2A/B* homozygous deletion	STR	54	16	n/a
	37/F	Cerebellum, spinal cord	*CDKN2A/B* homozygous deletion	STR	60	12	n/a

Table 1. *Cont.*

Author/Year	Age/Sex	Location	Molecular Alterations	Surgery (s)	RT (Gy)	PFS (m)	OS (m)
Gareton et al., 2020 [30]	8/F	Supratentorial Parietal lobe	ATRX retained (on IHC) *CDKN2A* intact *FGFR1* p.K678E *RAD50* p.R365Q *MDM2* amplification Monosomy 10q	GTR	RT dose n/a	13.4	37
Zander et al., 2024 [28]	68/M	Cerebellum	*NF1* truncating mutation *CDKN2A* deletion (likely not homozygous) ATRX retained (on IHC) *BRAF, IDH1, IDH2, H3-3A, TERT* wild-type	GTR	n/a	n/a	n/a

ATRX = alpha thalassemia/mental retardation syndrome X-linked; *BRAF* = B-Raf proto-oncogene; *CDKN2A* = cyclin-dependent kinase inhibitor 2A; *FGFR1* = fibroblast growth factor receptor 1, GTR = gross total resection, Gy = Gray; *H3-3A* = H3 histone family member 3A; *IDH* isocitrate dehydrogenase; m = months; *MGMT* = O6-methylguanine-DNA-methyltransferase, n/a = not available, OS = overall survival, *NF1* = neurofibromatosis type 1; *PTEN* = Phosphatase and TENsin homolog deleted on chromosome 10; PFS = progression-free survival; RT = radiotherapy; STR = subtotal resection, IHC: Immunohistochemistry.

Treatment for HGGs that do not conform to existing tumor entities in the WHO classification is challenging and remains a knowledge gap in literature today [14]. While standard-of-care treatment exists for glioblastoma, treatment for HGAP has not been established [29]. Treatments with the Stupp regimen, neurosurgical resection, radiation therapy, temozolomide, and targeted therapy have been reported with minimal evidence to support efficacy and with unreported long-term patient outcomes [13,14,16]. Targeted therapy, including *FGFR* inhibition, is an emerging treatment intervention for tumors with these mutations or fusions [31,32]. Preliminary evidence shows that single-agent FGFR inhibitors in recurrent gliomas with *FGFR1* mutations can achieve durable response [31]. However, our patient's activating *FGFR1* p.N546K mutation has been reported to carry therapeutic resistance to FGFR inhibitors [33]. The lack of uniform treatment options for the genetically distinct HGAP and the lack of data on treatment for an unmatched HGG NEC posed challenges for treatment decision-making in our case. Although our patient's tumor was not classified as either HGAP or glioblastoma, both have a poor prognosis and arguably necessitate aggressive therapy [13,34,35]. Our patient was treated with standard-of-care chemoradiation following the Stupp regimen [34]. At the time of publication, he remains clinically and radiographically stable fifteen months from the initial diagnosis.

Our case provides insights into the diagnostic challenges associated with discordant histological, molecular, and methylation results for individual patients. Our case contributes to the growing body of evidence for the treatment of HGG NEC. Further investigations are needed to better understand the clinical behavior and treatment of HGAP and to validate if this applies to our exceptional case and other similar cases [13,36,37]. As recognition and understanding of HGG NEC and HGAP improve, the treatment paradigm may also begin to diverge from standard-of-care glioblastoma treatment.

4. Conclusions

DNA methylation profiling is a powerful tool for uncovering new CNS tumor types and subtypes and can be used as an ancillary diagnostic tool to accurately classify challenging cases. Nevertheless, unusual cases that do not fit into established diagnostic classes exist. While some of these cases may potentially represent novel unidentified CNS tumor types, certainly all of them pose challenges in treatment decision-making for individual patients. Future investigations should be directed at understanding the therapeutic options and their associated patient outcomes for newly defined high-grade glioma entities.

Author Contributions: C.A.Y.—study concept, data collection, analysis, interpretation, manuscript drafting, revision, and final approval. S.B.—data collection, manuscript drafting, and final approval. X.-T.K.—manuscript revision and final approval. M.T.—data collection, manuscript revision, and final approval. A.H.—manuscript revision and final approval. M.Z.—manuscript revision and final approval. M.P.—data collection, analysis, interpretation, manuscript drafting, revision, and final approval. All authors have read and agreed to the published version of the manuscript.

Funding: This research received no external funding.

Institutional Review Board Statement: This study was conducted in accordance with the Declaration of Helsinki and approved by the Institutional Review Board of Community Regional Medical Center.

Informed Consent Statement: Informed consent was obtained from all subjects involved in the study.

Data Availability Statement: Data are unavailable due to privacy.

Conflicts of Interest: Xiao-Tang Kong: Received honorarium from Zai Lab for invited symposium presentations prior to July 2021. There are no financial interests or conflicts with the subject matter or materials discussed in the manuscript.

Abbreviations

ATRX	alpha thalassemia/mental retardation syndrome X-linked
BRAF	B-Raf proto-oncogene
CDKN2A	cyclin-dependent kinase inhibitor 2A
CNS	central nervous system
EGFR	epidermal growth factor receptor
FGFR1	fibroblast growth factor receptor 1
GTR	gross total resection
H3-3A	H3 histone family member 3
HGAP	high-grade astrocytoma with piloid features
IDH	isocitrate dehydrogenase
HGG	high-grade gliomas
IHC	immunohistochemistry
MAPK	mitogen-activated protein kinase
MGMT	O6-methylguanine-DNA-methyltransferase
NEC	not elsewhere classified
NF1	neurofibromatosis type 1
OS	overall survival
PTEN	Phosphatase and TENsin homolog deleted on chromosome 10
RT	radiation therapy
STR	subtotal resection
TERT	telomerase reverse transcriptase
WHO	World Health Organization

References

1. Capper, D.; Jones, D.T.W.; Sill, M.; Hovestadt, V.; Schrimpf, D.; Sturm, D.; Koelsche, C.; Sahm, F.; Chavez, L.; Reuss, D.E.; et al. DNA methylation-based classification of central nervous system tumours. *Nature* **2018**, *555*, 469–474. [CrossRef] [PubMed]
2. Capper, D.; Stichel, D.; Sahm, F.; Jones, D.T.W.; Schrimpf, D.; Sill, M.; Schmid, S.; Hovestadt, V.; Reuss, D.E.; Koelsche, C.; et al. Practical implementation of DNA methylation and copy-number-based CNS tumor diagnostics: The Heidelberg experience. *Acta Neuropathol.* **2018**, *136*, 181–210. [CrossRef]
3. Jaunmuktane, Z.; Capper, D.; Jones, D.T.W.; Schrimpf, D.; Sill, M.; Dutt, M.; Suraweera, N.; Pfister, S.M.; von Deimling, A.; Brandner, S. Methylation array profiling of adult brain tumours: Diagnostic outcomes in a large, single centre. *Acta Neuropathol. Commun.* **2019**, *7*, 24. [CrossRef]
4. Tran, S.; Bielle, F. WHO 2021 and beyond: New types, molecular markers and tools for brain tumor classification. *Curr. Opin. Oncol.* **2022**, *34*, 670–675. [CrossRef] [PubMed]
5. Moore, L.D.; Le, T.; Fan, G. DNA methylation and its basic function. *Neuropsychopharmacology* **2013**, *38*, 23–38. [CrossRef]
6. Louis, D.N.; Perry, A.; Wesseling, P.; Brat, D.J.; Cree, I.A.; Figarella-Branger, D.; Hawkins, C.; Ng, H.K.; Pfister, S.M.; Reifenberger, G.; et al. The 2021 WHO Classification of Tumors of the Central Nervous System: A summary. *Neuro-Oncology* **2021**, *23*, 1231–1251. [CrossRef]

7. Wenger, A.; Caren, H. Methylation Profiling in Diffuse Gliomas: Diagnostic Value and Considerations. *Cancers* **2022**, *14*, 5679. [CrossRef]
8. Noushmehr, H.; Weisenberger, D.J.; Diefes, K.; Phillips, H.S.; Pujara, K.; Berman, B.P.; Pan, F.; Pelloski, C.E.; Sulman, E.P.; Bhat, K.P.; et al. Identification of a CpG island methylator phenotype that defines a distinct subgroup of glioma. *Cancer Cell* **2010**, *17*, 510–522. [CrossRef]
9. Turcan, S.; Rohle, D.; Goenka, A.; Walsh, L.A.; Fang, F.; Yilmaz, E.; Campos, C.; Fabius, A.W.; Lu, C.; Ward, P.S.; et al. IDH1 mutation is sufficient to establish the glioma hypermethylator phenotype. *Nature* **2012**, *483*, 479–483. [CrossRef] [PubMed]
10. Fernandez, A.F.; Assenov, Y.; Martin-Subero, J.I.; Balint, B.; Siebert, R.; Taniguchi, H.; Yamamoto, H.; Hidalgo, M.; Tan, A.C.; Galm, O.; et al. A DNA methylation fingerprint of 1628 human samples. *Genome Res.* **2012**, *22*, 407–419. [CrossRef]
11. Reinhardt, A.; Stichel, D.; Schrimpf, D.; Sahm, F.; Korshunov, A.; Reuss, D.E.; Koelsche, C.; Huang, K.; Wefers, A.K.; Hovestadt, V.; et al. Anaplastic astrocytoma with piloid features, a novel molecular class of IDH wildtype glioma with recurrent MAPK pathway, CDKN2A/B and ATRX alterations. *Acta Neuropathol.* **2018**, *136*, 273–291. [CrossRef] [PubMed]
12. Pratt, D.; Abdullaev, Z.; Papanicolau-Sengos, A.; Ketchum, C.; Panneer Selvam, P.; Chung, H.J.; Lee, I.; Raffeld, M.; Gilbert, M.R.; Armstrong, T.S.; et al. High-grade glioma with pleomorphic and pseudopapillary features (HPAP): A proposed type of circumscribed glioma in adults harboring frequent TP53 mutations and recurrent monosomy 13. *Acta Neuropathol.* **2022**, *143*, 403–414. [CrossRef]
13. Bender, K.; Perez, E.; Chirica, M.; Onken, J.; Kahn, J.; Brenner, W.; Ehret, F.; Euskirchen, P.; Koch, A.; Capper, D.; et al. High-grade astrocytoma with piloid features (HGAP): The Charite experience with a new central nervous system tumor entity. *J. Neuro-Oncol.* **2021**, *153*, 109–120. [CrossRef] [PubMed]
14. Cimino, P.J.; Ketchum, C.; Turakulov, R.; Singh, O.; Abdullaev, Z.; Giannini, C.; Pytel, P.; Lopez, G.Y.; Colman, H.; Nasrallah, M.P.; et al. Expanded analysis of high-grade astrocytoma with piloid features identifies an epigenetically and clinically distinct subtype associated with neurofibromatosis type 1. *Acta Neuropathol.* **2023**, *145*, 71–82. [CrossRef] [PubMed]
15. Rodriguez, F.J.; Brosnan-Cashman, J.A.; Allen, S.J.; Vizcaino, M.A.; Giannini, C.; Camelo-Piragua, S.; Webb, M.; Matsushita, M.; Wadhwani, N.; Tabbarah, A.; et al. Alternative lengthening of telomeres, ATRX loss and H3-K27M mutations in histologically defined pilocytic astrocytoma with anaplasia. *Brain Pathol.* **2019**, *29*, 126–140. [CrossRef] [PubMed]
16. Soni, N.; Agarwal, A.; Ajmera, P.; Mehta, P.; Gupta, V.; Vibhute, M.; Gubbiotti, M.; Mark, I.T.; Messina, S.A.; Mohan, S.; et al. High-Grade Astrocytoma with Piloid Features: A Dual Institutional Review of Imaging Findings of a Novel Entity. *AJNR Am. J. Neuroradiol.* **2024**, *45*, 468–474. [CrossRef]
17. Kline, C.N.; Joseph, N.M.; Grenert, J.P.; van Ziffle, J.; Talevich, E.; Onodera, C.; Aboian, M.; Cha, S.; Raleigh, D.R.; Braunstein, S.; et al. Targeted next-generation sequencing of pediatric neuro-oncology patients improves diagnosis, identifies pathogenic germline mutations, and directs targeted therapy. *Neuro-Oncology* **2017**, *19*, 699–709. [CrossRef]
18. Zhang, Y.; Lucas, C.G.; Young, J.S.; Morshed, R.A.; McCoy, L.; Oberheim Bush, N.A.; Taylor, J.W.; Daras, M.; Butowski, N.A.; Villanueva-Meyer, J.E.; et al. Prospective genomically guided identification of "early/evolving" and "undersampled" IDH-wildtype glioblastoma leads to improved clinical outcomes. *Neuro-Oncology* **2022**, *24*, 1749–1762. [CrossRef]
19. Jaiswal, S.; Fontanillas, P.; Flannick, J.; Manning, A.; Grauman, P.V.; Mar, B.G.; Lindsley, R.C.; Mermel, C.H.; Burtt, N.; Chavez, A.; et al. Age-related clonal hematopoiesis associated with adverse outcomes. *N. Engl. J. Med.* **2014**, *371*, 2488–2498. [CrossRef]
20. Louis, D.N.; Wesseling, P.; Paulus, W.; Giannini, C.; Batchelor, T.T.; Cairncross, J.G.; Capper, D.; Figarella-Branger, D.; Lopes, M.B.; Wick, W.; et al. cIMPACT-NOW update 1: Not Otherwise Specified (NOS) and Not Elsewhere Classified (NEC). *Acta Neuropathol.* **2018**, *135*, 481–484. [CrossRef]
21. Aldape, K.; Zadeh, G.; Mansouri, S.; Reifenberger, G.; von Deimling, A. Glioblastoma: Pathology, molecular mechanisms and markers. *Acta Neuropathol.* **2015**, *129*, 829–848. [CrossRef] [PubMed]
22. Stichel, D.; Ebrahimi, A.; Reuss, D.; Schrimpf, D.; Ono, T.; Shirahata, M.; Reifenberger, G.; Weller, M.; Hanggi, D.; Wick, W.; et al. Distribution of EGFR amplification, combined chromosome 7 gain and chromosome 10 loss, and TERT promoter mutation in brain tumors and their potential for the reclassification of IDHwt astrocytoma to glioblastoma. *Acta Neuropathol.* **2018**, *136*, 793–803. [CrossRef] [PubMed]
23. Brat, D.J.; Aldape, K.; Colman, H.; Holland, E.C.; Louis, D.N.; Jenkins, R.B.; Kleinschmidt-DeMasters, B.K.; Perry, A.; Reifenberger, G.; Stupp, R.; et al. cIMPACT-NOW update 3: Recommended diagnostic criteria for "Diffuse astrocytic glioma, IDH-wildtype, with molecular features of glioblastoma, WHO grade IV". *Acta Neuropathol.* **2018**, *136*, 805–810. [CrossRef] [PubMed]
24. Tesileanu, C.M.S.; Dirven, L.; Wijnenga, M.M.J.; Koekkoek, J.A.F.; Vincent, A.; Dubbink, H.J.; Atmodimedjo, P.N.; Kros, J.M.; van Duinen, S.G.; Smits, M.; et al. Survival of diffuse astrocytic glioma, IDH1/2 wildtype, with molecular features of glioblastoma, WHO grade IV: A confirmation of the cIMPACT-NOW criteria. *Neuro-Oncology* **2020**, *22*, 515–523. [CrossRef]
25. WHO Classification of Tumours Editorial Board. *Central Nervous System Tumours*; International Agency for Research on Cancer, World Health Organization: Lyon, France, 2021.
26. Cancer Genome Atlas Research, N.; Brat, D.J.; Verhaak, R.G.; Aldape, K.D.; Yung, W.K.; Salama, S.R.; Cooper, L.A.; Rheinbay, E.; Miller, C.R.; Vitucci, M.; et al. Comprehensive, Integrative Genomic Analysis of Diffuse Lower-Grade Gliomas. *N. Engl. J. Med.* **2015**, *372*, 2481–2498. [CrossRef]
27. Raghu, A.L.B.; Chen, J.A.; Valdes, P.A.; Essayed, W.; Claus, E.; Arnaout, O.; Smith, T.R.; Chiocca, E.A.; Peruzzi, P.P.; Bernstock, J.D. Cerebellar High-Grade Glioma: A Translationally Oriented Review of the Literature. *Cancers* **2022**, *15*, 174. [CrossRef]

28. Zander, C.; Diebold, M.; Shah, M.J.; Malzkorn, B.; Prinz, M.; Urbach, H.; Erny, D.; Taschner, C.A. Freiburg Neuropathology Case Conference: 68-Year-Old Patient with Slurred Speech, Double Vision, and Increasing Gait Disturbance. *Clin. Neuroradiol.* **2024**, *34*, 279–286. [CrossRef]
29. Nawa, S.; Ohka, F.; Motomura, K.; Takeuchi, K.; Nagata, Y.; Yamaguchi, J.; Saito, R. Obstructive Hydrocephalus Due to Aggressive Posterior Fossa Tumor Exhibiting Histological Characteristics of Pilocytic Astrocytoma in Two Adult Neurofibromatosis Type 1 (NF1) Cases. *Cureus* **2024**, *16*, e58697. [CrossRef]
30. Gareton, A.; Tauziede-Espariat, A.; Dangouloff-Ros, V.; Roux, A.; Saffroy, R.; Castel, D.; Kergrohen, T.; Fina, F.; Figarella-Branger, D.; Pages, M.; et al. The histomolecular criteria established for adult anaplastic pilocytic astrocytoma are not applicable to the pediatric population. *Acta Neuropathol.* **2020**, *139*, 287–303. [CrossRef]
31. Lassman, A.B.; Sepulveda-Sanchez, J.M.; Cloughesy, T.F.; Gil-Gil, M.J.; Puduvalli, V.K.; Raizer, J.J.; De Vos, F.Y.F.; Wen, P.Y.; Butowski, N.A.; Clement, P.M.J.; et al. Infigratinib in Patients with Recurrent Gliomas and FGFR Alterations: A Multicenter Phase II Study. *Clin. Cancer Res.* **2022**, *28*, 2270–2277. [CrossRef]
32. Loilome, W.; Joshi, A.D.; ap Rhys, C.M.; Piccirillo, S.; Vescovi, A.L.; Gallia, G.L.; Riggins, G.J. Glioblastoma cell growth is suppressed by disruption of Fibroblast Growth Factor pathway signaling. *J. Neuro-Oncol.* **2009**, *94*, 359–366. [CrossRef]
33. Yoza, K.; Himeno, R.; Amano, S.; Kobashigawa, Y.; Amemiya, S.; Fukuda, N.; Kumeta, H.; Morioka, H.; Inagaki, F. Biophysical characterization of drug-resistant mutants of fibroblast growth factor receptor 1. *Genes Cells* **2016**, *21*, 1049–1058. [CrossRef]
34. Stupp, R.; Mason, W.P.; van den Bent, M.J.; Weller, M.; Fisher, B.; Taphoorn, M.J.; Belanger, K.; Brandes, A.A.; Marosi, C.; Bogdahn, U.; et al. Radiotherapy plus concomitant and adjuvant temozolomide for glioblastoma. *N. Engl. J. Med.* **2005**, *352*, 987–996. [CrossRef] [PubMed]
35. Whitfield, B.T.; Huse, J.T. Classification of adult-type diffuse gliomas: Impact of the World Health Organization 2021 update. *Brain Pathol.* **2022**, *32*, e13062. [CrossRef]
36. Cimmino, F.; Montella, A.; Tirelli, M.; Avitabile, M.; Lasorsa, V.A.; Visconte, F.; Cantalupo, S.; Maiorino, T.; De Angelis, B.; Morini, M.; et al. FGFR1 is a potential therapeutic target in neuroblastoma. *Cancer Cell Int.* **2022**, *22*, 174. [CrossRef] [PubMed]
37. Sabbagh, M.F.; Janovitz, T.; Dias-Santagata, D.; Siegmund, S.E.; Nardi, V.; Wirth, L.J.; Randolph, G.W.; Lennerz, J.K.; Decker, B.; Nose, V.; et al. FGFR Alterations in Thyroid Carcinoma: A Novel Class of Primary Drivers with Significant Therapeutic Implications and Secondary Molecular Events Potentially Mediating Resistance in Thyroid Malignancy. *Thyroid* **2024**. [CrossRef] [PubMed]

biomedicines

MDPI

Article

Extracellular Vesicles from Plasma of Patients with Glioblastoma Promote Invasion of Glioblastoma Cells Even After Tumor Resection

Ekaterina N. Lyukmanova [1,2,3,4,*], Artem V. Kirichenko [2,3], Igor A. Medyanik [5], Konstantin S. Yashin [5], Mikhail P. Kirpichnikov [2,4] and Maxim L. Bychkov [2,*]

1 Faculty of Biology, Shenzhen MSU-BIT University, Shenzhen 518172, China
2 Shemyakin-Ovchinnikov Institute of Bioorganic Chemistry, Russian Academy of Sciences, 119997 Moscow, Russia; bittert@mail.ru (A.V.K.); kirpichnikov@inbox.ru (M.P.K.)
3 Moscow Center for Advanced Studies, 123592 Moscow, Russia
4 Interdisciplinary Scientific and Educational School of Moscow University «Molecular Technologies of the Living Systems and Synthetic Biology», Faculty of Biology, Lomonosov Moscow State University, 119234 Moscow, Russia
5 Department of Neurosurgery, Privolzhsky Research Medical University, 603005 Nizhny Novgorod, Russia; med_neuro@inbox.ru (I.A.M.); jashinmed@gmail.com (K.S.Y.)
* Correspondence: lyukmanova_ekaterina@smbu.edu.cn (E.N.L.); maksim.bychkov@gmail.com (M.L.B.)

Abstract: Background: Glioblastoma (GB) is a highly aggressive tumor, whose progression is mediated by secretion of extracellular vesicles (EVs), which can pass the brain–blood barrier and be found in the plasma. Here, we performed a comparative analysis of the effects of EVs from the plasma of healthy donors (hEVs) and GB patients before (bEVs) and after (aEVs) tumor surgical resection on invasion of normal astrocytes and GB cells. **Methods**: We performed the transwell invasion assay, analyzed MAP kinases activation by Western blotting, studied SNAI1/SNAI2 cellular localization by confocal microscopy, measured cadherins expression by flow cytometry, and analyzed secretion of cytokines, which regulate migration and inflammation, by immunoassay. **Results**: hEVs did not affect invasion of astrocytes and GB cells, there was down-regulated cadherins expression in astrocytes, while there was increased E- and N-cadherin expression in GB cells. hEVs increased the secretion of inflammation and adhesion regulators both in astrocytes and GB cells. bEVs enhanced the invasion of GB cells but not of astrocytes via MAP AKT, JNK1/2/3, and p38 kinases activation, stimulated the clasterization of SNAI1 in the GB cell nucleus, promoted an E/N cadherin switch, and caused the secretion of inflammation and adhesion regulators in astrocytes and GB cells. aEVs exhibited the most of pro-oncogenic effects of bEVs (stimulation of GB cell invasion, SNAI1 nuclear localization, JNK1/2/3 activation, E/N cadherin switch, and secretion of inflammation and adhesion regulators in astrocytes and GB cells). However, aEVs effects were less pronounced than those of bEVs. **Conclusions**: In our study, we revealed common and different effects of plasma-derived hEVs, aEVs, and bEVs. hEVs can stimulate some pro-oncogenic effects in GB cells. Being less tumorigenic then bEVs, aEVs are still able to promote invasion of GB cells, probably remaining after tumor resection.

Keywords: glioblastoma; extracellular vesicles; astrocytes; invasion; AKT; JNK; p38; E/N cadherin switch; cytokines; adhesion molecules; inflammatory molecules

1. Introduction

Glioblastoma (GB) is the most aggressive brain tumor characterized by rapid growth, metastasis, establishment of an inflammatory microenvironment and high heterogeneity [1]. To support tumor progression, GB cells secrete into the environment numerous pro-oncogenic cytokines and adhesion molecules [2], as well as extracellular vesicles (EVs) containing pro-oncogenic factors [3]. The transport of these vesicles through the body allows tumor cells to 'communicate' with each other and to promote tumor growth, metastasis, and chemoresistance [4]. GB-derived EVs (GDEVs) influence the cells surrounding a tumor [5], promote tumor vascularization [6], and transfer pro-oncogenic factors into the tumor endothelium [6].

EVs from cultured GB cells promote various effects in the brain cells: disruption of neuronal synchronization [7], regulation of proliferation and activation of immune cells in the brain [5,8,9], induction of malignant transformation of normal astrocytes [10], enhancement of proliferation, migration and invasion of GB cells [11,12], and stimulation of angiogenesis [12]. GDEVs also regulate secretion of various cytokines and adhesion molecules by immune cells [13,14] and normal astrocytes [15]. EVs are the central players in regulation of the inflammatory microenvironment of GB [13]. GDEVs can cross through the blood–brain barrier (BBB) in both directions [6], so they can be detected in the bloodstream [16,17] and cerebrospinal fluid (CSF) [18–20] of patients. In addition, GDEVs can disrupt the BBB function by activation of endothelial permeability regulator semaphorin-3A [21]. EV concentration in the plasma of GB patients is higher than in the plasma of healthy donors, and decreases upon tumor resection and radiation/temozolomide therapy [22,23]. GDEVs from the plasma can transport different pro-oncogenic proteins and RNAs, for example, mRNA encoding alkylpurine-DNA-N-glycosylase (*APNG*) and O^6-methylguanine DNA methyltransferase (*MGMT*), which mediate a resistance to the temozolomide therapy in GB patients and GB cells [24]. GDEVs from the plasma and CSF also contain a high level of pro-oncogenic miRNA-21, which mediates GB growth and invasion [25]. Moreover, in comparison with EVs derived from the plasma of healthy donors, plasma GDEVs contain a higher level of hypoxia-regulated proteins (such as VEGF and metalloprotease inhibitor TIMP), which regulate GB vascularization [26], pro-oncogenic integrin β1, hyaluronic acid receptor CD44, cytoskeleton protein CD146, complement protein C1Qa, and histone H3 [27]. Another aspect of the effects of plasma GDEVs is immunosuppression by the down-regulation of proliferation of tumor-inhibitory T cells [13]. Plasma GDEVs contain immunosuppressive miRNAs (miR-1246, miR-29a, miR-10a, etc.) [28] and high levels of PD-L1, which drives differentiation of monocytes towards the non-classical immunosuppressive phenotype [29]. On the other hand, EVs secreted by tumor-surrounding microglia cells can restrict GB cells' metabolism via miR-124 and reduce GB growth in vivo [30]. Factors delivered by GDEVs from CSF (mutated variant of EGFR, -EGFR vIII, and pro-oncogenic miR-21, miR-24, miR-103, and miR-125) can stimulate GB proliferation, invasion, and angiogenesis [31]. Similar to plasma GDEVs, GDEVs from CSF suppress the presentation of GB antigens by DC cells via transfer of adhesion protein galectin 9 [32].

GDEVs from both plasma and CSF can be used for tumor diagnosis or serve as biomarkers of its progression [8,33–35]. Several clinical trials have been conducted to explore the potential of GDEVs as markers of GB progression and response to the therapy. For example, the mRNA level of IL8 and TGFβ in plasma GDEVs correlates with the immunological response of GB patients to dendritic cell-based vaccines [36]. Some molecules from GDEVs of CSF (cytoskeletal protein MYO1C, IDH1-mutant mRNA, miR-9, miR-30-3p, and miR-1298-5p) can serve as markers for GB diagnostics and monitoring [37]. Another recent clinical trial showed the perceptiveness of the serum GDEVs analysis for the classification and monitoring of CNS tumors [38]. Furthermore, due to their low immunogenicity, EVs secreted by mesenchymal stem cells [39] or EVs loaded with therapeutic agents [40] can be used for targeted delivery of therapeutic substances to GB. However, presently there is no information about ongoing trials of EVs as therapeutic agents on ClinicalTrials.gov. Additionally, EVs can be loaded with fluorescent agents and serve as tracking tools [41].

Thus, GDEVs are the central transmitters of pro-oncogenic signals both into the tumor itself, surrounding tissues, and through the body. While many aspects of the action of EVs from cultured cells in GB are known, the effects of EVs from the plasma of healthy and GB patients on glial cells have not been compared. Moreover, although secretion of various inflammatory adhesion factors by GB cells is recognized as an important mechanism of tumor progression [2], the effect of EVs on the secretion of these molecules by GB cells also remains unclear.

Here, we investigated the influence of EVs isolated from the plasma of healthy donors and patients with GB (before and after tumor resection) on invasion of the normal astrocytes and GB cells, and revealed the mechanisms mediating these effects.

2. Materials and Methods

2.1. Patients

The plasma from healthy donors (n = 8) and patients with GB (n = 8, clinically assessed as histological grade IV, *IDH* wild-type) was obtained from patients of the Clinic of Privolzhsky Research Medical University (Nizhny Novgorod, Russia) after informed consent and approval of the ethics committee (protocol № 12 from 25 June 2019). The plasma before and after resection was collected from the same patient on the previous and next days after tumor resection, respectively.

2.2. Isolation and Characterization of EVs

EVs were isolated from the plasma of patients using the Total Exosome Isolation kit (4484450, Thermo Fisher Scientific, Waltham, CA, USA) according to the manufacturer instructions. An amount of 0.5 mL of the plasma was centrifuged 2 times (2000× *g* and 10,000× *g* for 20 min, RT), diluted 2 times with PBS, and the exosome precipitation reagent was added. After that, plasma was incubated at 37 °C for 1 h. Then, precipitated EVs were washed from the resting plasma by centrifugation (10,000× *g*, RT). The supernatant was aspirated and discarded, while the EV-containing pellet was resuspended in PBS and centrifugated (10,000× *g*, RT). The EV-containing supernatant was collected, filtered through 0.2 μm PVDF syringe filter (Merck, Darmstadt, Germany), EVs were aliquoted, frozen at −150°C, and used for characterization and assays. EVs were not subjected to freeze–thaw cycles.

EVs were characterized using dynamic light scattering (DynaPro Titan, Wyatt Technology, Golata, CA, USA) with 828 nm laser and scattering angle 90°. Particles with diameters in the range of 20–120 nm were detected in EV suspension (Figure 1a). The size of EVs was in agreement with the previously published data [42]. It should be noted that plasma-derived EVs are smaller than those from cultured cells [43] and have the higher size distribution [44]. EVs were visualized using scanning electron microscope REM 200 (Moscow, Russia) under 15 kW power. Mainly, EVs with an average diameter ~50 nm were observed (Figure 1b). Expression of vesicular molecular markers in EVs were accessed using the ProcartaPlex™ Human Exosome Characterization Panel (EPX060-15845-901, Thermo Fisher Scientific). All samples contained CD9, CD63, CD81, syntenin-1, and VLA4, but not cytochrome C (Figure 1c). No statistical differences in the protein content were observed between the samples. All experiments were performed at the EV concentration of 50 μg/mL, which was in a range of that found in the plasma of patients with GB (20–100 μg/mL) [45].

To confirm a relevance of the Total Exosome Isolation kit for EV isolation, we compared the properties of EVs derived from the plasma of three patients and isolated them by the method described above and by widely used ultracentrifugation [46]. In both batches, we did not find a statistically significant difference in EVs' marker expression including CD9 (Figure S1). Nevertheless, similar to [47], some difference in the size distribution of EVs isolated by different techniques was observed (Figure S1). We speculate that this difference may be due to high plasma EV heterogeneity. The choice of the Total Exosome Isolation Kit is also supported by the previous reports on EV isolation by its use for different in vitro [48–51] and in vivo [52,53] assays. Notably, the main study was performed using EVs isolated from the plasma of other patients.

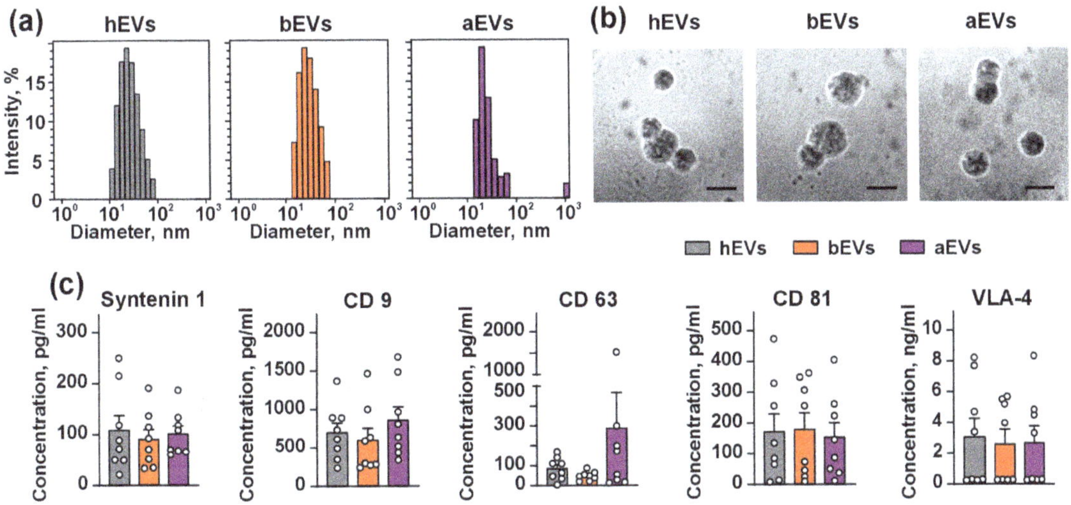

Figure 1. Characterization of EVs from the plasma of healthy donors and GB patients before and after tumor resection: (**a**) representative distribution of EVs according to the size determined by dynamic light scattering; (**b**) representative pictures of EVs according to scanning EM (scale = 50 nm); (**c**) expression of EV markers, no cytochrome C was detected in all studied EVs. Data presented as protein concentration ± SEM (n = 8).

2.3. Cell Cultivation and Isolation of Primary Astrocytes

Authenticated human GB U251 MG cells obtained from the Russian vertebrate cell culture collection (Institute of Cytology RAS, St. Petersburg, Russia) were grown in the IMDM medium (PanEco, Moscow, Russia) supplemented with 10% of FCS (Corning Corp., Corning, CA, USA). GB cell line GBM 011 was kindly provided by M.S. Pavlyukov (IBCH RAS, Moscow, Russia). GBM 011 cells were obtained from the patient of N.N. Burdenko National Medical Research Center of Neurosurgery (Moscow, Russia) after informed consent and were characterized previously [54]. GBM 011 cells were cultured for no longer than 10 passages in the DMEM/F12 medium supplemented with MACS NeuroBrew-21 supplement (Miltenyi Biotec, Gladbach, Germany, 10 mL of supplement per 500 mL of cell medium), 2.5 µg/mL heparin, 20 ng/mL bFGF, and 20 ng/mL EGF (all compounds were from Sigma-Aldrich, St. Louis, MO, USA). EGF and bFGF were added twice a week and the culture medium was changed every 7 days.

Rat cortical astrocytes were isolated as in [55] and grown in the DMEM/F12 (PanEco)/10% FCS medium with addition of MACS NeuroBrew-21 supplement. Forty-two-day-old astrocytes were used for the experiments. GFAP expression in the astrocytes was confirmed by flow cytometry.

All cells were monthly tested for mycoplasma contamination (Mycoreport kit, Evrogen, Moscow, Russia).

2.4. Transwell Invasion Assay

The transwell assay, in which cells migrate through 8 µm pores of polystyrene membrane, was used to study cell invasion. Cells were seeded in migration chambers in 24-well plates (SPL Lifesciences, Pocheon, Republic of Korea; 2×10^5 cells/well), immediately treated with 50 µg/mL of EVs and incubated for 72 h without media change (the incubation time was chosen so that the cells did not die at the end of the experiment). Then, the cells migrating through the pores were photographed (100× magnification, CloneSelect Imager, Molecular Devices, San Jose, CA, USA). The number of invaded cells was quantified using the find maxima option of the ImageJ 1.54f software (NIH, Bethesda, MD, USA). For comparison of action of EVs from U251 MG cells (isolated as in [46]) and plasma EVs on U251 MG cells, the Cell Migration/Chemotaxis assay (ab235673Abcam, Cambridge, UK) was performed according to the manufacturer instructions.

2.5. Western Blotting

Cells (3×10^5 cells per well of a 6-well plate) were treated with EVs (50 μg/mL) for 72 h, lysed in the RIPA buffer containing SIGMAFAST protease inhibitor cocktail (Sigma-Aldrich), diluted in the PAGE loading buffer and subjected to gel electrophoresis. The proteins were then transferred to nitrocellulose membranes (Bio-Rad, Hercules, CA, USA) which then were blocked for 1 h with 5% BSA in TBST. After that, the membranes were incubated with the rabbit primary antibodies to pAKT (S473) (1:4000, GB150002, Service-Bio, Wuhan, China), pERK1/2 (T202/204; T185/Y187) (1:1000, GB113492, ServiceBio), pJNK1/2/3 (T183/Y185) (1:1000, GB12018, ServiceBio), and pp38 (T180/Y182) (1:1000, GB1133880, ServiceBio) overnight at 4 °C. Note that pJNK and pp38 were assayed on the same membranes: pJNK was the first, and pp38 followed after membrane stripping. For antibodies' wash-out, the membranes were incubated in the buffer (50 mM Tris, pH 6.8, 1% SDS, 0.8% β-mercaptoethanol) at 55 °C for 45 min, washed under running tap water for 5 min, incubated with TBST for 5 min, and processed from the blocking stage. Expression of pAKT and pERK was analyzed on one membrane, which was cut near 50 kDa. After incubation with the primary antibodies, the membranes were washed 3 times in TBST and incubated with anti-rabbit HRP-conjugated antibodies (1:5000, 711-035-152, Jackson Immunoresearch, West Grove, PA, USA) for 1 h. Then, the membranes were washed 3 times in TBST, and the HRP signal was detected by the ECL substrate (Bio-Rad) using the ImageQuant LAS 500 imaging system (GE Healthcare, Chicago, IL, USA). After analysis of phosphorylation of target proteins, membranes were stripped and re-probed for GAPDH with the rabbit anti-GAPDH antibody (1:1000, GB15004, ServiceBio) as described above. The results were analyzed using the ImageQuant TL 8.0 software (GE Healthcare) and the level of phosphorylated proteins was normalized to the GAPDH level. Absence of the HRP signal after membrane stripping was confirmed by imaging after 1 h of incubation with the secondary antibodies.

2.6. Flow Cytometry

To analyze GFAP expression in the primary astrocytes, the cells seeded on glasses in a 6-well plate (10×10^3 cells per well) for 24 h were detached by the Versene solution (PanEco), fixed in 4% paraformaldehyde (PanEco) and incubated with the rabbit primary antibodies to GFAP (1:500, ABIN3043832, Antibodies-online, Aachen, Germany) for 1 h, then washed with PBS and incubated with anti-rabbit Alexa-488-conjugated antibodies (1:1000, 611-545-215, Jackson Immunoresearch).

To determine the effect of EVs on expression of cadherins on the glial cells' membrane, cells (3×10^5 cells per well of a 6-well plate) were treated with EVs (50 μg/mL) for 72 h, detached by the Versene solution, fixed in 4% paraformaldehyde, and incubated for 1 h with the rabbit primary antibodies to E cadherin (1:2000, 3195, Cell Signaling, Danvers, MA, USA), N cadherin (1:2000, 13116, Cell Signaling), or P cadherin (1:2000, 2189, Cell Signaling). The cells were then washed with PBS and incubated with the anti-rabbit Alexa-488-conjugated antibodies (1:1000, 611-545-215, Jackson Immunoresearch).

Cells stained only with the secondary antibodies were used as a negative control. All cells were analyzed by the Attune NxT flow cytometer (Life Technologies, Waltham, CA, USA) using the Attune NxT 2.3. Software (Life Technologies). The gating strategy is shown in Figure S2a.

2.7. Confocal Microscopy

Cells were seeded on glasses in a 24-well plate (3×10^3 cells per well), incubated with EVs (50 μg/mL) for 72 h, blocked with 3% BSA for 16 h, stained with the rabbit antibodies to SNAI1 (1:200, FNab08051, FineTest, Wuhan, China) for 6 h, washed 3 times with PBS, and stained with the anti-rabbit Alexa-488-conjugated antibodies (1:1000, 611-545-215, Jackson Immunoresearch) for 1 h. After that, the glasses were blocked with 3% BSA for 16 h, stained with the rabbit antibodies to SNAI2 (1:200, FNab08052, FineTest) for 6 h, washed 3 times and stained with the anti-rabbit Alexa-647-conjugated antibodies (1:1000, 611-605-215, Jackson Immunoresearch) for 1 h. The cells were then washed 3 times, and nuclei were stained with Hoechst 33342. Glasses were embedded in the Mowiol-DABCO and examined under ×60 (1.4) objective of the Carl Zeiss LSM 710 confocal microscope (Carl Zeiss, Jena, Germany). The % of laser power and detector voltage were maintained constant. The number of SNAI clusters in the nuclei was analyzed using the Focinator 2.31 tool [56] in the ImageJ 1.54f software.

2.8. Analysis of Inflammation and Adhesion Regulators Secretion

To investigate the effect of EVs on the secretion of cytokines and adhesion factors by the astrocytes and GB cells, the 13-plex adhesion molecule panel immunoassay kit (740946, BioLegend, San Diego, CA, USA) was used. Cells were seeded on glasses in a 24-well plate (3×10^3 cells per well), incubated with EVs (50 μg/mL) for 72 h, then 25 μL of cell media was collected from the untreated cells (control) or from the astrocytes incubated with EVs, GBM 011 and U251 MG cells and assayed in accordance with the manufacturer's protocol. The results were analyzed by the Attune NxT flow cytometer (Life Technologies) using the Attune NxT Software 2.3. (Life Technologies). The calibration curve (5-parameter non-linear regression) built in the GraphPad 8.0 software (San Diego, CA, USA) was used to determine the concentration of substances. The calibration curves were obtained from [57]. The gating strategy is shown in Figure S2b.

2.9. Statistical Analysis

Data are presented as mean ± SEM. The number of samples (biological replicates, n) and statistical tests are indicated in the figure legends. Biological replicates were chosen by availability of the plasma for isolation of EVs. No exclusion criteria were applied to the experimental data, except for Western blotting. For Western blotting experiments, some bands were excluded due to technical failure. Before comparisons, the data were tested for normality (Shapiro–Wilk test, at $p = 0.05$). Differences in the data were considered statistically significant at $p < 0.05$. Analysis was performed using the GraphPad Prism 8.0 software.

3. Results

3.1. aEVs and bEVs from the Plasma of GB Patients Enhance Invasion of GB Cells

Since EVs from the cultured GB cells enhance invasion of GB cells [11], we studied whether EVs derived from GB patients crossing the BBB and circulating in the bloodstream influence invasion of GB cells. For this purpose, we used EVs from the plasma of GB patients isolated before and after tumor resection (bEVs and aEVs, respectively) and EVs isolated from the plasma of healthy donors (hEVs) as a control for the 'general' effect of plasma EVs. Analysis of the EV effects was performed on the normal rat primary cortical astrocytes and two GB cell lines: patient-derived glioblastoma GBM 011 cells and U251 MG cells.

The transwell assay showed that all types of EVs did not alter the motility of the normal astrocytes in comparison to the untreated cells, and no influence of hEVs on invasion of both astrocytes and GB cells was found (Figure 2). In the case of GBM 011 cells, bEVs increased cell invasion in comparison to the untreated cells, and bEVs and aEVs increased cell invasion by ~70% and 40% in comparison to hEVs, respectively (Figure 2). Also, bEVs increased the invasion of U251 MG cells in comparison to the cells treated with hEVs and untreated cells. Unlike GBM 011 cells, aEVs did not influence U251 MG cell invasion (Figure 2). We also compared the effect of aEVs, bEVs, and hEVs with EVs isolated from U251 MG cells on the invasion of U251 MG cells. We found that, similar to bEVs, EVs secreted by U251 MG cells increased the invasion of U251 MG cells (Figure S3). This points to the specific action of EVs on GB cell's invasion.

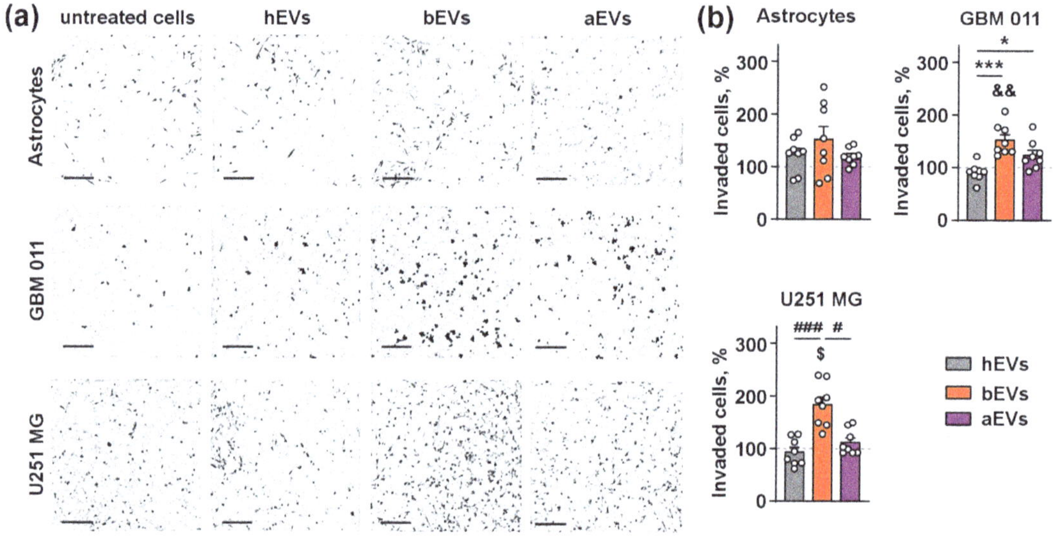

Figure 2. Influence of EVs on invasion of astrocytes, GBM 011, and U251 MG cells. (**a**) Representative images showing the cells migrated through 8 μM pore to the bottom of the migration chamber upon incubation with EVs (×100 magnification, scale bar = 100 μm); (**b**) number of the invaded cells. Data are shown as the number of invaded cells upon incubation with EVs normalized to the number of invaded untreated cells (100%, dashed line) ± SEM (n = 8); && ($p < 0.01$) indicates significant difference from the untreated cells according to one-sample t-test followed by post hoc Holm–Sidak's test; $ ($p < 0.05$) indicates significant difference from the untreated cells according to one-sample Wilcoxon test, followed by post hoc Holm–Sidak's test; * ($p < 0.05$) and *** ($p < 0.001$) indicate significant difference between the data groups according to one-way ANOVA followed by post hoc Tukey's test; # ($p < 0.05$) and ### ($p < 0.001$) indicate significant difference between the data groups according to Kruskal–Wallis test followed by post hoc Dunn's test.

3.2. aEVs and bEVs Activate MAP Kinases in GB Cells

To investigate the molecular mechanisms underlying the effect of EVs on the invasion of GB cells, we examined the phosphorylation of key pro-migratory MAP kinases: AKT, ERK, JNK, and p38 by Western blotting. In the astrocytes, no type of EVs influenced the phosphorylation of MAP kinases (Figure 3a,b). In GBM 011 cells, bEVs up-regulated the phosphorylation of AKT (S437) by ~three-fold compared to hEVs. Furthermore, bEVs up-regulated the phosphorylation of AKT in relation to the untreated cells (Figure 3c,d). In U251 MG cells, bEVs significantly up-regulated the phosphorylation of JNK1/2/3 (T183/Y185) and p38 (T180/Y182) compared both to the untreated cells and cells treated with hEVs, while aEVs increased the phosphorylation only of JNK1/2/3 (T183/Y185) in comparison with hEVs (Figure 3e,f). hEVs did not activate any MAP kinases in any of the cell types studied.

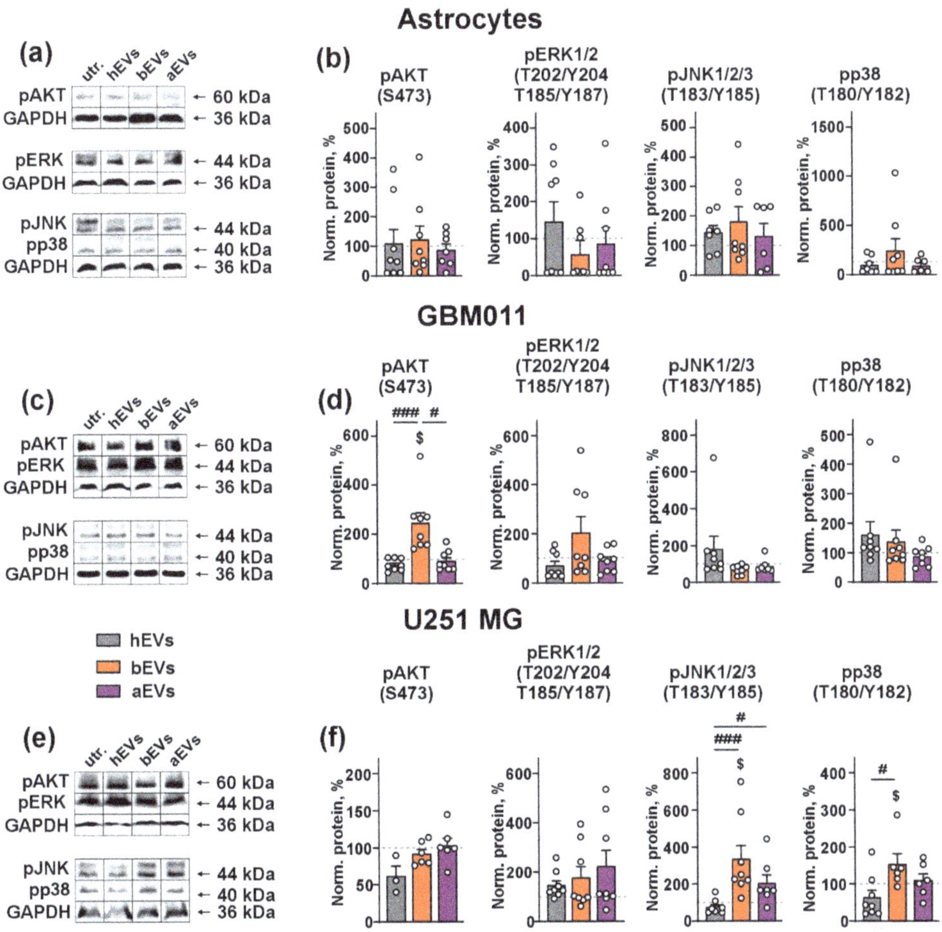

Figure 3. Analysis of influence of EVs on the MAP kinases phosphorylation in astrocytes (**a**,**b**), GBM 011 cells (**c**,**d**), and U251 MG cells (**e**,**f**). The following phosphorylation sites were assayed: pAKT (S473), pERK1/2 (T202/204; T185/Y187), pJNK1/2/3 (T183/Y185), and pp38 (T180/Y182). (**a**,**c**,**e**) Cut representative membranes with the bands (marked by frames); (**b**,**d**,**f**) quantification of the band intensity reflecting expression of different MAP kinases in the phosphorylated form. Please note that MAP kinases were assayed on the same (pJNK and pp38) or cut (pAKT and pERK) membranes, so they 'share' GAPDH. Whole Western blotting membranes are shown in Figures S4–S6. The quantification data are presented as band intensity (relative to GAPDH) normalized to that of the untreated cells (100%, dashed line) ± SEM (n = 3–8); $ ($p < 0.05$) indicates significant difference from the untreated cells according to one-sample Wilcoxon test, followed by post hoc Holm–Sidak's test; # ($p < 0.05$) and ### ($p < 0.001$) indicate significant difference between the data groups according to Kruskal–Wallis test followed by post hoc Dunn's test.

3.3. aEVs and bEVs Drive Localization of SNAI1 to the Nuclei in GB Cells

Previous studies proposed that the activation of AKT [58,59], JNK [59], and p38 [60] MAP kinases is associated with the activity of SNAI1 or SNAI2 zinc fingers, —the transcriptional factors that up-regulate cell migration and induce EMT in GB cells [61,62]. To study whether these factors are involved in the pro-invasive activity of aEVs and bEVs, we analyzed the localization of SNAI1 and SNAI2 in the nuclei of glial cells using confocal microscopy. hEVs were used as a control because they did not affect invasion of the astrocytes and GB cells and did not influence the activity of MAP kinases (Figures 2 and 3). We found that all types of EVs did not affect the number of SNAI1 and SNAI2 clusters in the nuclei of the normal astrocytes (Figure 4a,b). However, we observed a significant increase in the number of the SNAI1 clusters in the nuclei of GBM 011 and U251 MG cells treated by bEVs (more than two times in both cases, Figure 4c–f). Treatment by aEVs led to an increase in the number of SNAI1 clusters in the nuclei of GBM 011 but not of U251 MG cells, although some non-significant increase was observed in the last case too (Figure 4c–f). A significant increase in the SNAI2 level in the nuclei was observed only for hEVs in U251 MG cells (Figure 4a–f).

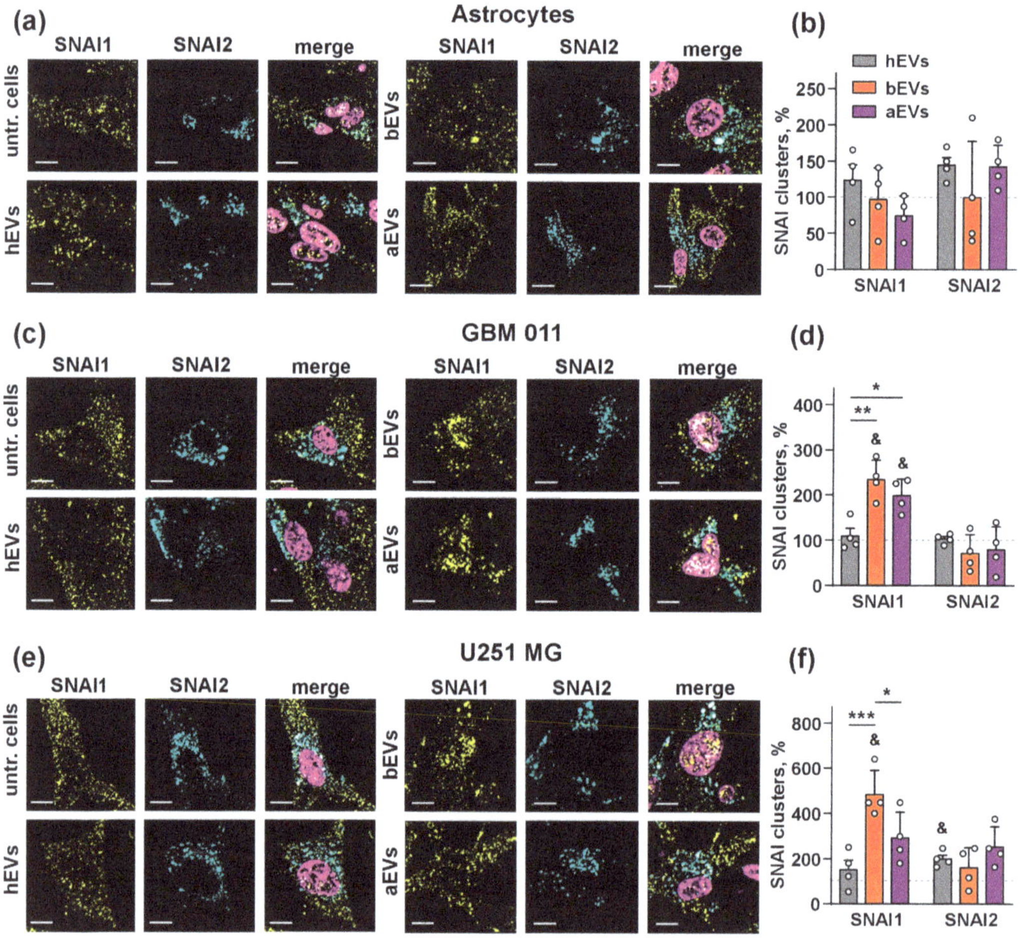

Figure 4. Influence of EVs on nuclear localization of SNAI1 and SNAI2 in astrocytes (**a**,**b**), GBM 011 cells (**c**,**d**), and U251 MG cells (**e**,**f**). Representative images of EV-treated astrocytes (**a**), GBM 011 cells (**c**), and U251 MG cells (**e**). Scale bar = 10 μm. (**b**,**d**,**f**) Number of SNAI clusters in the nuclei of studied cells. Data presented as a number of the clusters per the nuclei normalized to that of the untreated cells (100%, dashed line) ± SEM (n = 4 glasses, 3–4 cells from each glass were analyzed and averaged). & ($p < 0.05$) indicates significant difference from the untreated cells according to one-sample *t*-test followed by post hoc Holm–Sidak's test; * ($p < 0.05$), ** ($p < 0.01$), and *** ($p < 0.001$) indicate significant difference between the data groups according to two-way ANOVA followed by post hoc Bonferroni's test.

3.4. aEVs and bEVs Induce E/N Cadherin Switch in GB Cells

Different cadherin isoforms regulate epithelial-mesenchymal transition (EMT) and invasion of GB cells [63]. Here, we investigated the influence of EVs on expression of different cadherins on the surface of the astrocytes and GB cells.

In the astrocytes, hEVs dramatically down-regulated expression of anti-migratory E cadherin to the zero level, while bEVs and aEVs did not affect its expression compared to the untreated cells (Figure 5a). The level of pro-migratory N cadherin in the astrocytes treated by hEVs and aEVs was lower by ~20–30% in relation to the untreated astrocytes, while bEVs did not demonstrate any effect (Figure 5a). All types of EVs significantly down-regulated by ~60–70% pro-invasive P cadherin expression in the astrocytes compared to the untreated cells, while no difference between the action of different EVs was found (Figure 5a).

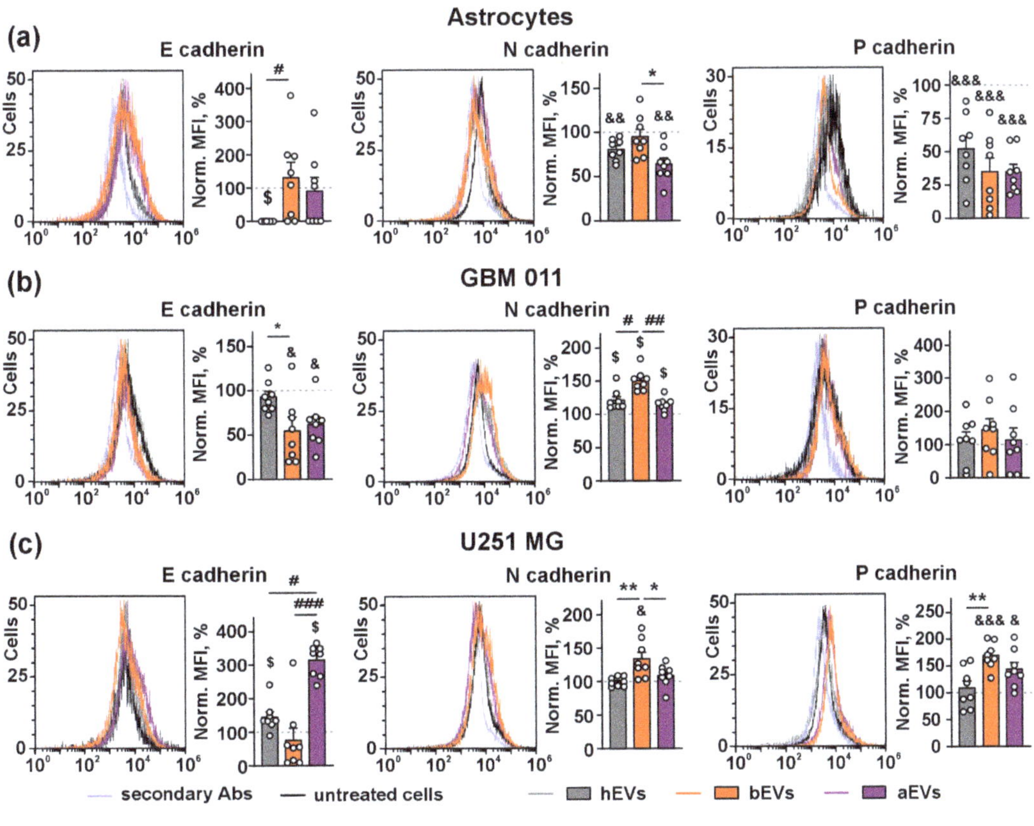

Figure 5. Influence of EVs on expression of E, N, and P cadherins on the surface of astrocytes (**a**), GBM 011 cells (**b**), and U251 MG cells (**c**). Representative cell distribution histograms and quantification of expression are shown on the left and right panels of the figures, respectively. The data are presented as background-subtracted MFI normalized to that of the untreated cells (100%, dashed line) ± SEM (n = 8). & ($p < 0.05$), && ($p < 0.01$), and &&& ($p < 0.001$) indicate significant difference from the untreated cells according to one-sample *t*-test followed by post hoc Holm–Sidak's test; $ ($p < 0.05$) indicates significant difference from the untreated cells according to one-sample Wilcoxon test, followed by post hoc Holm–Sidak's test; * ($p < 0.05$) and ** ($p < 0.01$) indicate significant difference between the data groups according to one-way ANOVA followed by post hoc Tukey's test; # ($p < 0.05$), ## ($p < 0.01$), and ### ($p < 0.001$) indicate significant difference between the data groups according to Kruskal–Wallis test followed by post hoc Dunn's test.

In GBM 011 cells, both bEVs and aEVs down-regulated E cadherin expression in comparison to the untreated or hEV-treated cells (by ~50% in both cases, Figure 5b). At the same time, all types of EVs significantly increased expression of N cadherin in comparison to the untreated cells, and bEVs additionally up-regulated N cadherin expression by ~20% in comparison to the hEV-treated cells (Figure 5b). No effect of any types of EVs on P cadherin expression compared to the untreated cells was observed (Figure 5b).

In the U251 MG cells, hEVs and aEVs both up-regulated E cadherin expression compared to the untreated cells, and aEVs increased E cadherin expression 3-fold in comparison to hEV treated cells. No effect of bEVs on E cadherin expression was revealed (Figure 5c), while bEVs slightly but significantly up-regulated N-cadherin expression (by ~15%) in comparison to the hEV-treated, aEV-treated, and untreated cells. Similar to hEVs, aEVs did not affect N-cadherin expression (Figure 5c). Both bEVs and aEVs but not hEVs increased P cadherin expression in U251 MG cells (by ~40–50%, Figure 5c).

3.5. aEVs and bEVs Stimulate Secretion of Inflammation and Adhesion Regulators by GB Cells

EMT in GB is mediated by an establishment of immunosuppressive milieu, which is promoted by secretion of different cytokines and adhesion factors [13–15]. Using the multiplex immunoassay, we studied secretion of 13 cytokines and adhesion molecules by the astrocytes, GBM 011 cells, and U251 MG cells upon incubation with EVs and found that all types of them (hEVs, aEVs, and bEVs) affect secretion of many of the regulatory molecules by GB cells (Table S1).

In the astrocytes, all studied EVs up-regulated by ~50% secretion of pro-inflammatory factor ALCAM-1 (activated leukocyte cell adhesion molecule), and pro-migratory hyaluronic acid receptor CD44 (by ~25% Figure 6a, Table S1). hEVs slightly but significantly up-regulated secretion of EpCAM (epithelial cell adhesion molecule), which serves as a pro-inflammatory and pro-migratory cell junction protein. aEVs up-regulated by ~25% secretion of adhesion molecule NCAM-1 (neural cell adhesion molecule 1, and down-regulated by 3 times secretion of pro-migratory and anti-inflammatory factor VCAM-1 (vascular cell adhesion molecule 1). Both aEVs and hEVs slightly increased secretion of E-selectin (GB angiogenic modulator) by astrocytes (Figure 6a, Table S1). Untreated astrocytes did not secrete pro-inflammatory factor L-selectin, but all types of EVs caused secretion of this molecule (Figure 6a, Table S1).

In GBM011 cells, all types of studied EVs further up-regulated secretion of ALCAM-1 by 4-fold, CD44 (by ~20–25%), dramatically increased level of pro-inflammatory factor ICAM-1 (intercellular adhesion molecule 1), as well as E- and L-selectins (Figure 6b, Table S1). E-selectin was up-regulated by ~40–50% upon incubation with all types of EVs, while the effect of aEVs was lower than that of hEVs (Figure 6b). Secreted L-selectin was not detected in the media of the untreated cells, but all EVs dramatically up-regulated its secretion. Notably, the aEVs effect was significantly lower than that of bEVs (Figure 6b). Similar to the astrocytes, the level of secreted EpCAM in GBM011 cells was slightly increased upon incubation only with hEVs (Figure 6b). All types of EVs caused down-regulation of NCAM-1 secretion by ~15–25% (Figure 6b). Untreated GBM 011 cells secreted non-detectable amounts of VCAM-1, while all types of EVs caused dramatic up-regulation of its secretion, and hEVs demonstrated the stronger effect than bEVs (Figure 6b, Table S1).

In U251 MG cells, secretion of ALCAM-1 was significantly up-regulated upon incubation with aEVs and bEVs in comparison with the untreated cells. hEVs also stimulated secretion of this factor, although the difference with the untreated cells did not reach statistical significance. Notably, effect of aEVs was significantly higher in comparison to hEVs (Figure 6c). bEVs up-regulated by 20 CD44 secretion in comparison to the untreated cells (Figure 6c, Table S1). hEVs and bEVs increased secretion of ICAM-1 (by ~150–200%) and down-regulated the level of NCAM-1 (by ~25%) in comparison to untreated cells. aEVs also diminished secretion of NCAM-1, but the difference with the untread cells did not reach the significance (Figure 6c, Table S1). bEVs increased by 5-fold secretion of pro-inflammatory apoptosis inhibitor ICAM-3 (intercellular adhesion molecule 3), while hEVs down-regulated secretion of this molecule up to the zero level and aEVs did not affect its secretion (Figure 6c, Table S1). Moreover, aEVs and bEVs dramatically decreased secretion of VCAM-1 (Figure 6c, Table S1). Unlike to bEVs and hEVs, aEVs slightly decreased the E-selectin secreted level, while hEVs down-regulated secretion of adhesion regulator P-selectin (Figure 6c, Table S1).

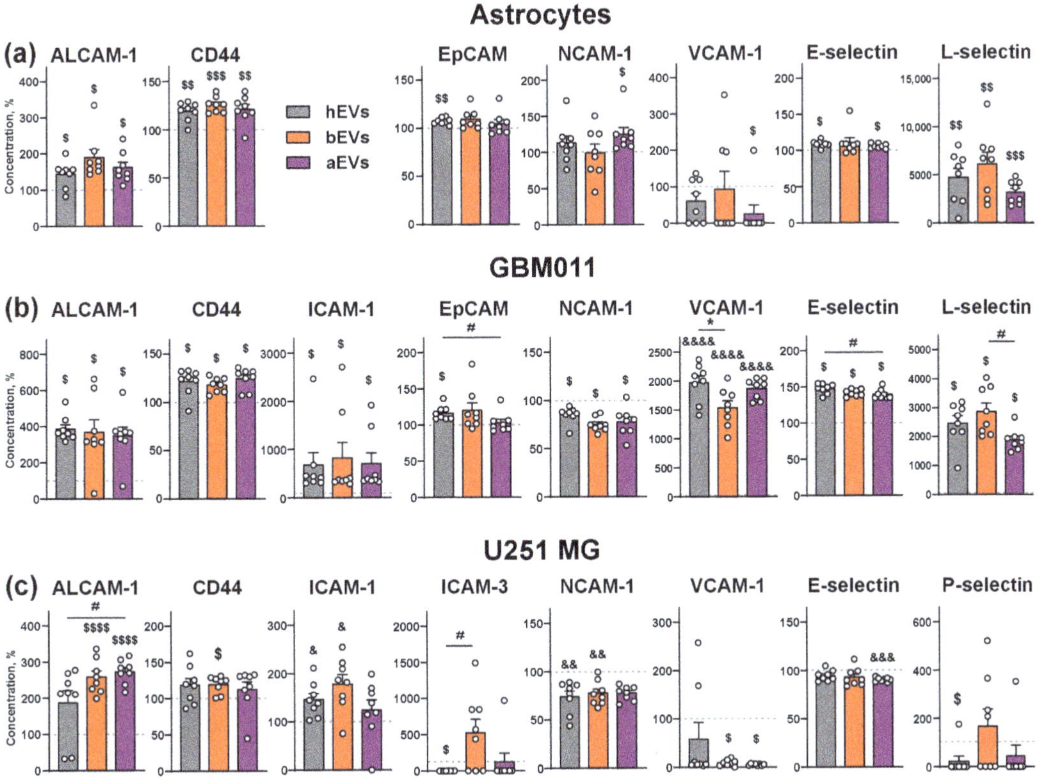

Figure 6. Influence of EVs on secretion of inflammation and adhesion regulators by astrocytes (**a**), GBM 011 cells (**b**), and U251 MG cells (**c**). The data are presented as molecules' concentration in the cell growth media normalized to that of the untreated cells (100%, dashed line) ± SEM (n = 8). & ($p < 0.05$), && ($p < 0.01$), &&& ($p < 0.001$), and &&&& ($p < 0.0001$) indicate significant difference from the untreated cells according to one-sample t-test followed by post hoc Holm–Sidak's test; $ ($p < 0.05$), $$ ($p < 0.01$), $$$ ($p < 0.001$), and $$$$ ($p < 0.0001$) indicate significant difference from the untreated cells according to one-sample Wilcoxon test, followed by post hoc Holm–Sidak's test; * ($p < 0.05$) indicates significant difference between the data groups according to one-way ANOVA followed by post hoc Tukey's test; # ($p < 0.05$) indicates significant difference between the data groups according to Kruskal–Wallis test followed by post hoc Dunn's test.

4. Discussion

GDEVs are the main molecule carriers between tumors and their microenvironment [5]. Despite an ability of EVs to cross the BBB and circulate in the bloodstream [6], little is known about the influence of GB vesicles from the bloodstream on homeostasis of the normal astrocytes and GB cells. To fill this gap, we performed a comparative analysis of the effects of EVs from the plasma of healthy donors (hEVs) and GB patients (bEVs and aEVs) in the normal astrocytes and GB cells.

First, we analyzed the influence of the vesicles on cell invasion and found that hEVs did not affect the invasion of either astrocytes or GB cells. At the same time, bEVs increased the invasion both of GBM 011 and U251 MG cells, and aEVs increased the invasion of GBM 011 cells (Figure 2). It has previously been shown that EVs secreted by model GB cells stimulate invasion of GB cells [4,64], but here we showed for the first time that EVs isolated from the bloodstream of GB patients also stimulate invasion of the GB cells. The fact that aEVs induce GB cell invasion shows that even after tumor resection, residual GB cells can be re-stimulated to spread along the body by aEVs remaining in the bloodstream. Thus, GDEVs may mediate the formation of secondary cancers in the GB patients, which are known to occur in long-term GB survivors [65].

We showed that bEVs activate in the GB cells several MAP kinases: AKT and ERK in GBM 011 cells and JNK with p38 in U251 MG cells, while aEVs increase the phosphorylation level only of JNK in U251 MG cells in comparison with hEVs (Figure 3). JNK activation promotes GB stem cell invasion [66], while p38 phosphorylation promotes invasion of glioma cells [67]. Thus, their activation in U251 MG cells is consistent with the pro-invasive activity of aEVs and bEVs. Notably, no influence on the activity of MAP kinases was observed for all EVs studied here in the normal astrocytes (Figure 3). Interestingly, in spite of absence of the broad effect on the kinase activity, aEVs still retain their pro-invasive activity in GBM 011 cells. This means that aEVs and bEVs may mediate their pro-invasive effect through different molecular mechanisms.

Here we detected the increased number of the SNAI1 but not of SNAI2 clusters in the nuclei of the GB cells upon incubation with aEVs and bEVs, and this effect was not observed in the normal astrocytes (Figure 4). It should be noted that SNAI1 is the transcriptional repressor [68], and its localization to the cell nucleus is required to inhibit expression of the anti-migratory factors, such as the cell junction protein E cadherin [69]. In line with this, we showed that aEVs and bEVs induce the E/N cadherin switch: down-regulation of surface expression of E cadherin with simultaneous up-regulation of N cadherin expression in the GB cells (Figure 5). The E/N cadherin switch is the common marker of EMT [70], which is required for GB metastasis and invasion [71]. EMT can be influenced by the GB–astrocyte communication [71], and our data propose that aEVs and bEVs may modulate the GB–astrocyte interaction via the E/N cadherin switch. Induction of the E/N cadherin switch by aEVs in GBM 011 cells (although not so strongly as by bEVs, Figure 5b) additionally points to possible remaining of invasion stimulating effects even after tumor resection.

Interestingly, hEVs down-regulated both N and E cadherins in the astrocytes, suggesting that hEVs may also regulate the formation of intercellular contacts in the normal astrocytes under heathy conditions. It should be noted that up-regulation of E cadherin observed here for aEVs in U251 MG cells (Figure 5c) was previously described in GB patients and xenografts and is associated with tumor invasion [72]. P cadherin drives GB proliferation, migration, and invasion and is considered a biomarker of GB [73]. Its up-regulation in U251 MG cells (Figure 5c) may mediate the pro-invasive effect of bEVS.

GB progression is accompanied by the secretion of many inflammatory and pro-migratory factors in the tumor microenvironment [2]. EVs can stimulate secretion of some cytokines and growth factors by the GB cells and astrocytes [2,15]. Here, we found that all types of EVs influence secretion of many adhesion molecules, some of which regulate GB cell migration (Figure 6, Table S1). In the normal astrocytes, GMB011, and U251 MG cells, all types of EVs activated the secretion of ALCAM-1, the pro-inflammatory factor [74], which stimulates GB invasion in vivo and whose level correlates with a worse survival prognosis for GB patients [75]. CD44, which was up-regulated in the astrocytes and GB cells upon incubation with EVs, induces GB cell growth and invasiveness [76,77]. Secretion of the pro-inflammatory cytokine EpCAM [78], which was up-regulated in the astrocytes and GBM011 cells upon incubation with hEVs, drives carcinoma invasion but its role in GB progression is not well understood [79]. ICAM-1, which was absent in the media of the astrocytes but was up-regulated in the media of the GB cells upon treatment with all types of EVs (Figure 6, Table S1), is a pro-inflammatory factor that stimulates invasiveness of chemotherapy-resistant GB cells in vivo [80]. ICAM-3, whose secretion was up-regulated only by bEVs in U251 MG cells, drives carcinoma cell migration and invasion via the AKT pathway [81,82]. Notably, bEVs stimulated the AKT activity in GB011 cells; although for U251 MG cells, this effect was not found (Figure 3). Nevertheless, we hypothesize that the pro-invasive activity of bEVs in U251 MG cells (which was not observed for aEVs) may be mediated by the ICAM-3-AKT functional interaction. NCAM-1 regulates the extracellular matrix degradation and serves as the inhibitor of GB cell invasion [83]. Its overexpression decreases GB cell motility [84]. Here, we observed either no effects from hEVs and bEVs and stimulation of NCAM-1 secretion by aEVs in the astrocytes or down-regulation of NCAM-1 in the GB cells upon incubation with all types of EVs (Figure 6, Table S1). This agrees well with the data on the stimulation of GB cell invasion by aEVs and bEVs (Figure 2).

VCAM-1 promotes tumor invasion and metastasis through interaction with tumor-associated macrophages [85]. Interestingly, VCAM-1 is also an immunosuppressive and anti-inflammatory factor, in particular, it reduces T-cell infiltration to carcinoma lesions [86]. Thus, it may not only promote GB cell invasion but also may mediate the formation of an immunosuppressive GB environment. Here, EVs differentially regulated VCAM-1 secretion: aEVs and bEVs decreased it in U251 MG cells (while hEVs demonstrated no effect), but in GBM011 cells, all EVs (including hEVs) dramatically increased VCAM-1 secretion. At the same time, only aEVs down-regulated its secretion in the astrocytes (Figure 6, Table S1). Pro-inflammatory E-, L-, and P-selectins [87] regulate leucocyte adhesion, so their up-regulation can be associated with formation of the tumor inflammatory microenvironment [88]. Selectins can mediate tumor cell invasion by facilitating the interaction of tumor cells with the endothelium [88], thus, they may also be involved in GB invasion. In addition, P-selectin induces secretion of anti-inflammatory cytokines by microglia, thus inhibiting anti-tumor immunity and promoting GB cell invasion [89]. In our work, a slight increase in E-selectin secretion was revealed in the astrocytes treated by aEVs and hEVs, while in GB011 cells, we observed its up-regulation by all types of EVs with a simultaneous close-to-zero effect from EVs in U251 MG cells. For L-selectin, dramatic up-regulation by all EVs was detected in both astrocytes and GB011 cells, while for P-selectin, insignificant up-regulation of its secretion was found only upon incubation of U251 MG cells with bEVs (Figure 6, Table S1). Such diverse effects of different EVs on secretion of various regulatory molecules may be associated with different factors (see below) and requires further study. However, in almost all the cases, a tendency to maintain a pro-inflammatory environment is observed.

Similar to plasma GDEVs, GDEVs from CSF can carry mRNA of pro-oncogenic factors such as the mutant variant of the EGFR, -*EGFRvIII* [20], and pro-oncogenic miRNAs [28,37,90]. Although, the effects of GDEVs from CSF on the GB cells were not previously studied, we propose that the effects of GDEVs from CSF on the invasion and regulation of protein expression/secretion by the normal and tumor cells can be similar to those observed here for plasma GDEVs. In line with this, both CSF and plasma GDEVs contain pro-oncogenic miR-21, miR-24, miR-103, and miR-125 [90]. Further study of GDEVs from CSF is necessary.

Different overall effects of GDEVs on the astrocytes, GBM 011 cells, and U251 MG cells should also be emphasized. In GBM011 but not in U251 MG cells, aEVs increased cell invasion. In addition, different MAP kinases were activated by bEVs in these cells: AKT in GBM011 cells and JNK and p38 in U251 MG cells. EVs also differentially regulate the secretion of cytokines and adhesion factors by the GB cells. We propose that the difference between these effects can be explained by several factors such as (i) different molecular characteristics of the GB cells, (ii) different localization of the tumors, (iii) the fact that we studied the effect of all plasma EVs but not of a specific EV population, and (iv) different genetics of tumor cells. High heterogeneity of GB tumors is well known [1]; thus, the effect of EVs may also be mediated by the characteristics of the GB cells.

It should be emphasized that hEVs also affected the normal astrocytes and GB cells: up-regulated SNAI2 level in the nuclei of U251 MG cells (Figure 4), down-regulated cadherins expression in the astrocytes, and up-regulated E and N cadherins expression in U251 MG and GBM011 cells, respectively (Figure 5). hEVs also up-regulated the secretion of cytokines and pro-invasion adhesion factors by the astrocytes and GB cells (Figure 6, Table S1). It was described that hEVs can transfer some pro-migratory factors and be implicated in the regulation of cell growth, migration, and angiogenesis [91]. Additionally, our study points to hEVs as the regulators of intercellular contacts and possible stimulators of pro-oncogenic responses in GB cells. The possible pro-oncogenic activity of hEVs should be further studied to ensure their safety for targeted delivery of therapeutic substances to GB.

In general, we can propose the model of EV activity in the astrocytes and GB cells (Figure 7). In health, hEVs crossing the BBB have very little effect on the normal astrocytes: they do not alter cell motility and MAP kinases' activity. However, they down-regulate the expression of N and E cadherins, thus regulating the intercellular contacts. In GB, before tumor resection, bEVs are secreted by the tumor and surrounding cells providing the tumor progression. As vesicles can cross the BBB in both directions, some bEVs may return back to the tumor and increase GB invasion. This may be mediated by the activation of some invasion-related MAP kinases (such as AKT, ERK, JNK, or p38) and supplemented by increasing the amount of SNAI1 clusters in the tumor cell nucleus. In the nucleus, SNAI1 can repress the E cadherin transcription and promote the E/N cadherin switch,—the marker of EMT. In addition, bEVs increase the expression of pro-invasive P cadherin. Besides the induction of invasion, bEVs up-regulate the secretion of pro-migratory cytokines and adhesion factors. Interestingly, bEVs have no effect on the normal astrocytes. This is difficult to explain, but we can speculate that EVs only activate the astrocytes, making them reactive without malignant transformation. Another possibility is that the time of our in vitro experiments (72 h, chosen so that the cells did not die at the end of the experiment) is not enough for the astrocytic transformation. Moreover, we cannot exclude the existence of possible protective mechanisms in the astrocytes preventing their transformation.

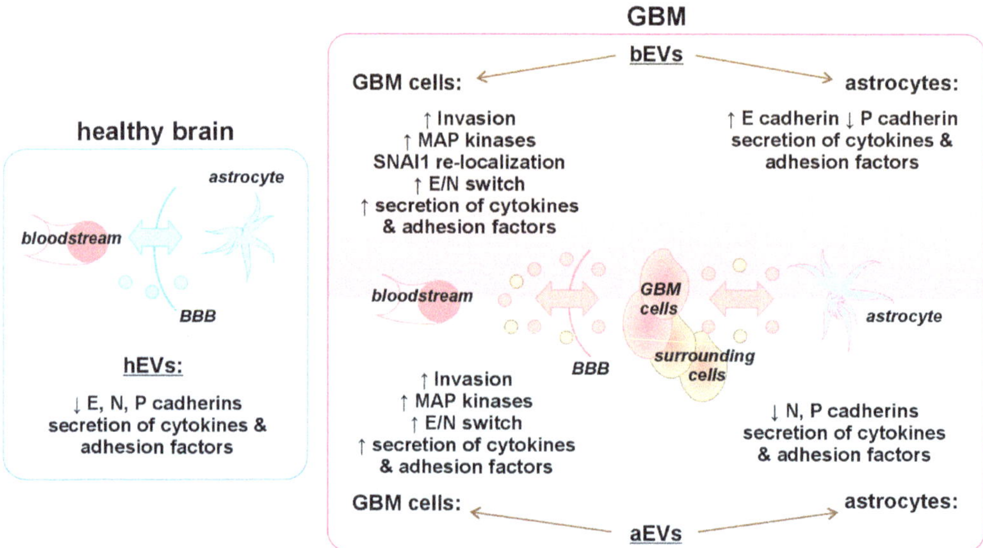

Figure 7. Proposed model of influence of EVs from the plasma of healthy donors and GB patients before and after tumor resection in astrocytes and GB cells. The effects revealed in our work for aEVs, bEVs, and hEVs are listed. ↑ and ↓ indicate up- and down-regulation of protein expression or secretion in different cells upon incubation with EVs.

When GB is resected, EVs previously secreted by the tumor and tumor surrounding cells remain in the bloodstream (aEVs), although their activity can be changed already on the next day after resection. As they can cross the BBB, they can return to the brain and affect the GB cells remaining after tumor resection. aEVs may mediate the invasion of GB cells by the activation of JNK and E/N switch, as well as by the stimulation of the secretion of different pro-migratory cytokines and inflammatory adhesion molecules in the remaining GB cells (Figure 7). Thus, even after tumor resection, aEVs can stimulate intercellular contacts of tumor cells and provide conditions for the tumor progression.

Nevertheless, our work has some limitations. In particular, we used rat astrocytes as a model of the normal astrocytes. It is not clear how many EVs return to the tumor after being secreted into the bloodstream and how fast tumorigenic activity of aEVs changes and in what direction after tumor resection. Some common effects of hEVs and GDEVs may overlap when we choose hEVs as a baseline for the analysis of the GDEVs' effects. Moreover, we analyzed the effect of all EVs isolated from the plasma, including ones secreted by non-GB cells surrounding the tumor. Thus, some effects can be mediated not only by EVs from the GB tissue but also by tumor-surrounding cells. Also, an analysis of EVs isolated after a longer time period after the tumor resection can give us more information about the EV impact in GB recurrence. All mentioned points require additional investigation. Analysis of the content of EVs and study of the mechanisms of their action in the tumor and normal cells would improve our understanding of the EV role in the GB progression and recurrence. Another interesting issue raised from our results is the possible influence of plasma EVs on non-neuronal cells, which may help us to better understand the formation of secondary cancers in GB survivors.

5. Conclusions

Obtained results point to EVs as one of the most important factors in the GB progression and provide possible mechanisms by which EVs may not only promote GB invasion but also cause tumor recurrence. Overall, our study provides a landscape of plasma EV influence in health and during GB progression and shows that even after tumor resection, aEVs from the bloodstream can stimulate the remaining GB cells. This may either lead to GB recurrence or somehow affect other tissues in the body, causing secondary tumors in GB survivors. It is probable that clearing of the patient's bloodstream from EVs after tumor resection may be a new prospective strategy to prevent GB recurrence or secondary cancers. Moreover, stimulation of some pro-oncogenic effects by hEVs in the GB cells, that requires additional attention when using hEVs in therapy and diagnostics, is described.

Supplementary Materials: The following supporting information can be downloaded at: https://www.mdpi.com/article/10.3390/biomedicines12122834/s1. Table S1. Concentrations of adhesion molecules assayed by the 13× adhesion panel LegendPlex immunoassay kit; Figure S1. Comparison of EVs isolated by ultracentrifugation and by the Total Exosome Isolation kit (from plasma); Figure S2. Representative gating strategy flow cytometry analyses; Figure S3. Comparison of action of EVs from U251 MG cells and GDEVs on invasion of U251 MG cells; Figure S4. Whole Western blotting membranes of pAKT, pERK (a), pJNK, and pp38 (b) expression in astrocytes; Figure S5. Whole Western blotting membranes of pAKT, pERK (a), pJNK, and pp38 (b) ex-pression in GBM 011 cells; Figure S6. Whole Western blotting membranes of pAKT, pERK (a), pJNK, and pp38 (b) expression in U251 MG cells.

Author Contributions: Conceptualization, M.L.B. and E.N.L.; methodology, M.L.B. and A.V.K.; software, M.L.B. and A.V.K.; validation, M.L.B.; formal analysis, M.L.B. and A.V.K.; investigation, M.L.B. and A.V.K.; resources, I.A.M. and K.S.Y.; data curation, M.L.B.; writing—original draft preparation, M.L.B. and E.N.L.; writing—review and editing, A.V.K., I.A.M., K.S.Y. and M.P.K.; visualization, M.L.B. and E.N.L.; supervision, E.N.L. and M.P.K.; project administration, M.L.B. and E.N.L.; funding acquisition, M.L.B. and E.N.L. All authors have read and agreed to the published version of the manuscript.

Funding: This research was funded by Russian Science Foundation, grant number 23-74-00040.

Institutional Review Board Statement: Collection of patient's plasma was approved by the ethical committee of Clinic of Privolzhsky Research Medical University (protocol #12 from 25 June 2019). Isolation of primary astrocytes was approved by the ethical committee of IBCH RAS (protocol #379 from 22 January 2024).

Informed Consent Statement: Written informed consent was obtained from all subjects involved in the study.

Data Availability Statement: All datasets generated within the experiment are available upon request.

Acknowledgments: We thank M. S. Pavlyukov for sharing with us the primary glioblastoma GBM 011 cell line. Mikhail P. Kirpichnikov, and Ekaterina N. Lyukmanova are part of an innovative drug development team based on structural biology and bioinformatics at Shenzhen MSU-BIT University (#2022KCXTD034).

Conflicts of Interest: The authors declare no conflicts of interest.

References

1. Barthel, L.; Hadamitzky, M.; Dammann, P.; Schedlowski, M.; Sure, U.; Thakur, B.K.; Hetze, S. Glioma: Molecular Signature and Crossroads with Tumor Microenvironment. *Cancer Metastasis Rev.* **2022**, *41*, 53–75. [CrossRef] [PubMed]
2. Almiron Bonnin, D.A.; Havrda, M.C.; Israel, M.A. Glioma Cell Secretion: A Driver of Tumor Progression and a Potential Therapeutic Target. *Cancer Res.* **2018**, *78*, 6031–6039. [CrossRef] [PubMed]
3. Davidson, C.L.; Vengoji, R.; Jain, M.; Batra, S.K.; Shonka, N. Biological, Diagnostic and Therapeutic Implications of Exosomes in Glioma. *Cancer Lett.* **2024**, *582*, 216592. [CrossRef] [PubMed]
4. Yang, S.; Sun, Y.; Liu, W.; Zhang, Y.; Sun, G.; Xiang, B.; Yang, J. Exosomes in Glioma: Unraveling Their Roles in Progression, Diagnosis, and Therapy. *Cancers* **2024**, *16*, 823. [CrossRef]
5. Guo, X.; Sui, R.; Piao, H. Exosomes-Mediated Crosstalk between Glioma and Immune Cells in the Tumor Microenvironment. *CNS Neurosci. Ther.* **2023**, *29*, 2074–2085. [CrossRef]
6. Osaid, Z.; Haider, M.; Hamoudi, R.; Harati, R. Exosomes Interactions with the Blood-Brain Barrier: Implications for Cerebral Disorders and Therapeutics. *Int. J. Mol. Sci.* **2023**, *24*, 15635. [CrossRef]
7. Spelat, R.; Jihua, N.; Sánchez Triviño, C.A.; Pifferi, S.; Pozzi, D.; Manzati, M.; Mortal, S.; Schiavo, I.; Spada, F.; Zanchetta, M.E.; et al. The Dual Action of Glioma-Derived Exosomes on Neuronal Activity: Synchronization and Disruption of Synchrony. *Cell Death Dis.* **2022**, *13*, 1–15. [CrossRef]
8. Banerjee, S.; Sharma, V.; Das Mukhopadhyay, C. Exploring Emerging Concepts of Exosomes for the Diagnosis, Prognosis, and Therapeutics of Brain Cancers. *Extracell. Vesicle* **2024**, *3*, 100038. [CrossRef]
9. Pancholi, S.; Tripathi, A.; Bhan, A.; Acharya, M.M.; Pillai, P. Emerging Concepts on the Role of Extracellular Vesicles and Its Cargo Contents in Glioblastoma-Microglial Crosstalk. *Mol. Neurobiol.* **2022**, *59*, 2822–2837. [CrossRef]
10. Zeng, A.; Wei, Z.; Rabinovsky, R.; Jun, H.J.; El Fatimy, R.; Deforzh, E.; Arora, R.; Yao, Y.; Yao, S.; Yan, W.; et al. Glioblastoma-Derived Extracellular Vesicles Facilitate Transformation of Astrocytes via Reprogramming Oncogenic Metabolism. *iScience* **2020**, *23*, 101420. [CrossRef]
11. Shi, J.; Zhang, Y.; Yao, B.; Sun, P.; Hao, Y.; Piao, H.; Zhao, X. Role of Exosomes in the Progression, Diagnosis, and Treatment of Gliomas. *Med. Sci. Monit.* **2020**, *26*, e924023. [CrossRef] [PubMed]
12. Skog, J.; Würdinger, T.; van Rijn, S.; Meijer, D.H.; Gainche, L.; Sena-Esteves, M.; Curry, W.T.; Carter, B.S.; Krichevsky, A.M.; Breakefield, X.O. Glioblastoma Microvesicles Transport RNA and Proteins That Promote Tumour Growth and Provide Diagnostic Biomarkers. *Nat. Cell Biol.* **2008**, *10*, 1470–1476. [CrossRef] [PubMed]
13. Musatova, O.E.; Rubtsov, Y.P. Effects of Glioblastoma-Derived Extracellular Vesicles on the Functions of Immune Cells. *Front. Cell Dev. Biol.* **2023**, *11*, 1060000. [CrossRef] [PubMed]
14. Low, J.J.W.; Sulaiman, S.A.; Johdi, N.A.; Abu, N. Immunomodulatory Effects of Extracellular Vesicles in Glioblastoma. *Front. Cell Dev. Biol.* **2022**, *10*, 996805. [CrossRef]
15. Oushy, S.; Hellwinkel, J.E.; Wang, M.; Nguyen, G.J.; Gunaydin, D.; Harland, T.A.; Anchordoquy, T.J.; Graner, M.W. Glioblastoma Multiforme-Derived Extracellular Vesicles Drive Normal Astrocytes towards a Tumour-Enhancing Phenotype. *Philos. Trans. R. Soc. Lond. B Biol. Sci.* **2018**, *373*, 20160477. [CrossRef]
16. Indira Chandran, V.; Gopala, S.; Venkat, E.H.; Kjolby, M.; Nejsum, P. Extracellular Vesicles in Glioblastoma: A Challenge and an Opportunity. *npj Precis. Oncol.* **2024**, *8*, 1–8. [CrossRef]
17. Foster, J.B.; Koptyra, M.P.; Bagley, S.J. Recent Developments in Blood Biomarkers in Neuro-Oncology. *Curr. Neurol. Neurosci. Rep.* **2023**, *23*, 857–867. [CrossRef]
18. Street, J.M.; Barran, P.E.; Mackay, C.L.; Weidt, S.; Balmforth, C.; Walsh, T.S.; Chalmers, R.T.A.; Webb, D.J.; Dear, J.W. Identification and Proteomic Profiling of Exosomes in Human Cerebrospinal Fluid. *J. Transl. Med.* **2012**, *10*, 5. [CrossRef]
19. Chen, W.W.; Balaj, L.; Liau, L.M.; Samuels, M.L.; Kotsopoulos, S.K.; Maguire, C.A.; Loguidice, L.; Soto, H.; Garrett, M.; Zhu, L.D.; et al. BEAMing and Droplet Digital PCR Analysis of Mutant *IDH1* mRNA in Glioma Patient Serum and Cerebrospinal Fluid Extracellular Vesicles. *Mol. Ther. Nucleic Acids* **2013**, *2*, e109. [CrossRef]
20. Figueroa, J.M.; Skog, J.; Akers, J.; Li, H.; Komotar, R.; Jensen, R.; Ringel, F.; Yang, I.; Kalkanis, S.; Thompson, R.; et al. Detection of Wild-Type *EGFR* Amplification and *EGFRvIII* Mutation in CSF-Derived Extracellular Vesicles of Glioblastoma Patients. *Neuro Oncol.* **2017**, *19*, 1494–1502. [CrossRef]

21. Treps, L.; Edmond, S.; Harford-Wright, E.; Galan-Moya, E.M.; Schmitt, A.; Azzi, S.; Citerne, A.; Bidère, N.; Ricard, D.; Gavard, J. Extracellular Vesicle-Transported Semaphorin3A Promotes Vascular Permeability in Glioblastoma. *Oncogene* **2016**, *35*, 2615–2623. [CrossRef] [PubMed]
22. Osti, D.; Del Bene, M.; Rappa, G.; Santos, M.; Matafora, V.; Richichi, C.; Faletti, S.; Beznoussenko, G.V.; Mironov, A.; Bachi, A.; et al. Clinical Significance of Extracellular Vesicles in Plasma from Glioblastoma Patients. *Clin. Cancer Res.* **2019**, *25*, 266–276. [CrossRef] [PubMed]
23. Koch, C.J.; Lustig, R.A.; Yang, X.-Y.; Jenkins, W.T.; Wolf, R.L.; Martinez-Lage, M.; Desai, A.; Williams, D.; Evans, S.M. Microvesicles as a Biomarker for Tumor Progression versus Treatment Effect in Radiation/Temozolomide-Treated Glioblastoma Patients. *Transl. Oncol.* **2014**, *7*, 752–758. [CrossRef] [PubMed]
24. Shao, H.; Chung, J.; Lee, K.; Balaj, L.; Min, C.; Carter, B.S.; Hochberg, F.H.; Breakefield, X.O.; Lee, H.; Weissleder, R. Chip-Based Analysis of Exosomal mRNA Mediating Drug Resistance in Glioblastoma. *Nat. Commun.* **2015**, *6*, 6999. [CrossRef]
25. Akers, J.C.; Ramakrishnan, V.; Kim, R.; Skog, J.; Nakano, I.; Pingle, S.; Kalinina, J.; Hua, W.; Kesari, S.; Mao, Y.; et al. MiR-21 in the Extracellular Vesicles (EVs) of Cerebrospinal Fluid (CSF): A Platform for Glioblastoma Biomarker Development. *PLoS ONE* **2013**, *8*, e78115. [CrossRef]
26. Kucharzewska, P.; Christianson, H.C.; Welch, J.E.; Svensson, K.J.; Fredlund, E.; Ringnér, M.; Mörgelin, M.; Bourseau-Guilmain, E.; Bengzon, J.; Belting, M. Exosomes Reflect the Hypoxic Status of Glioma Cells and Mediate Hypoxia-Dependent Activation of Vascular Cells during Tumor Development. *Proc. Natl. Acad. Sci. USA* **2013**, *110*, 7312–7317. [CrossRef]
27. Tzaridis, T.; Weller, J.; Bachurski, D.; Shakeri, F.; Schaub, C.; Hau, P.; Buness, A.; Schlegel, U.; Steinbach, J.-P.; Seidel, C.; et al. A Novel Serum Extracellular Vesicle Protein Signature to Monitor Glioblastoma Tumor Progression. *Int. J. Cancer* **2023**, *152*, 308–319. [CrossRef]
28. Lunavat, T.R.; Nieland, L.; Vrijmoet, A.B.; Zargani-Piccardi, A.; Samaha, Y.; Breyne, K.; Breakefield, X.O. Roles of Extracellular Vesicles in Glioblastoma: Foes, Friends and Informers. *Front. Oncol.* **2023**, *13*, 1291177. [CrossRef]
29. Ricklefs, F.L.; Alayo, Q.; Krenzlin, H.; Mahmoud, A.B.; Speranza, M.C.; Nakashima, H.; Hayes, J.L.; Lee, K.; Balaj, L.; Passaro, C.; et al. Immune Evasion Mediated by PD-L1 on Glioblastoma-Derived Extracellular Vesicles. *Sci. Adv.* **2018**, *4*, eaar2766. [CrossRef]
30. Serpe, C.; Monaco, L.; Relucenti, M.; Iovino, L.; Familiari, P.; Scavizzi, F.; Raspa, M.; Familiari, G.; Civiero, L.; D'Agnano, I.; et al. Microglia-Derived Small Extracellular Vesicles Reduce Glioma Growth by Modifying Tumor Cell Metabolism and Enhancing Glutamate Clearance through miR-124. *Cells* **2021**, *10*, 2066. [CrossRef]
31. Whitehead, C.A.; Luwor, R.B.; Morokoff, A.P.; Kaye, A.H.; Stylli, S.S. Cancer Exosomes in Cerebrospinal Fluid. *Transl. Cancer Res.* **2017**, *6*, S1352–S1370. [CrossRef]
32. Wang, M.; Cai, Y.; Peng, Y.; Xu, B.; Hui, W.; Jiang, Y. Exosomal LGALS9 in the Cerebrospinal Fluid of Glioblastoma Patients Suppressed Dendritic Cell Antigen Presentation and Cytotoxic T-Cell Immunity. *Cell Death Dis.* **2020**, *11*, 896. [CrossRef] [PubMed]
33. Jafari, D.; Tiyuri, A.; Rezaei, E.; Moradi, Y.; Jafari, R.; Jokar Shoorijeh, F.; Barati, M. Diagnostic Accuracy of Cerebrospinal Fluid and Serum-Isolated Extracellular Vesicles for Glioblastoma: A Systematic Review and Meta-Analysis. *Expert Rev. Mol. Diagn.* **2020**, *20*, 1075–1085. [CrossRef] [PubMed]
34. Del Bene, M.; Osti, D.; Faletti, S.; Beznoussenko, G.V.; DiMeco, F.; Pelicci, G. Extracellular Vesicles: The Key for Precision Medicine in Glioblastoma. *Neuro Oncol.* **2022**, *24*, 184–196. [CrossRef]
35. Simionescu, N.; Zonda, R.; Petrovici, A.R.; Georgescu, A. The Multifaceted Role of Extracellular Vesicles in Glioblastoma: microRNA Nanocarriers for Disease Progression and Gene Therapy. *Pharmaceutics* **2021**, *13*, 988. [CrossRef] [PubMed]
36. Muller, L.; Muller-Haegele, S.; Mitsuhashi, M.; Gooding, W.; Okada, H.; Whiteside, T.L. Exosomes Isolated from Plasma of Glioma Patients Enrolled in a Vaccination Trial Reflect Antitumor Immune Activity and Might Predict Survival. *Oncoimmunology* **2015**, *4*, e1008347. [CrossRef]
37. Papadimitrakis, D.; Perdikakis, M.; Gargalionis, A.N.; Papavassiliou, A.G. Biomarkers in Cerebrospinal Fluid for the Diagnosis and Monitoring of Gliomas. *Biomolecules* **2024**, *14*, 801. [CrossRef]
38. Dobra, G.; Bukva, M.; Szabo, Z.; Bruszel, B.; Harmati, M.; Gyukity-Sebestyen, E.; Jenei, A.; Szucs, M.; Horvath, P.; Biro, T.; et al. Small Extracellular Vesicles Isolated from Serum May Serve as Signal-Enhancers for the Monitoring of CNS Tumors. *Int. J. Mol. Sci.* **2020**, *21*, 5359. [CrossRef]
39. Cunha Silva, L.; Branco, F.; Cunha, J.; Vitorino, C.; Gomes, C.; Carrascal, M.A.; Falcão, A.; Miguel Neves, B.; Teresa Cruz, M. The Potential of Exosomes as a New Therapeutic Strategy for Glioblastoma. *Eur. J. Pharm. Biopharm.* **2024**, *203*, 114460. [CrossRef]
40. Zhan, Q.; Yi, K.; Qi, H.; Li, S.; Li, X.; Wang, Q.; Wang, Y.; Liu, C.; Qiu, M.; Yuan, X.; et al. Engineering Blood Exosomes for Tumor-Targeting Efficient Gene/Chemo Combination Therapy. *Theranostics* **2020**, *10*, 7889–7905. [CrossRef]
41. Verweij, F.J.; Balaj, L.; Boulanger, C.M.; Carter, D.R.F.; Compeer, E.B.; D'Angelo, G.; El Andaloussi, S.; Goetz, J.G.; Gross, J.C.; Hyenne, V.; et al. The Power of Imaging to Understand Extracellular Vesicle Biology in Vivo. *Nat. Methods* **2021**, *18*, 1013–1026. [CrossRef] [PubMed]
42. Li, Y.; Lyu, P.; Ze, Y.; Li, P.; Zeng, X.; Shi, Y.; Qiu, B.; Gong, P.; Yao, Y. Exosomes Derived from Plasma: Promising Immunomodulatory Agents for Promoting Angiogenesis to Treat Radiation-Induced Vascular Dysfunction. *PeerJ* **2021**, *9*, e11147. [CrossRef] [PubMed]
43. Arraud, N.; Linares, R.; Tan, S.; Gounou, C.; Pasquet, J.-M.; Mornet, S.; Brisson, A.R. Extracellular Vesicles from Blood Plasma: Determination of Their Morphology, Size, Phenotype and Concentration. *J. Thromb. Haemost.* **2014**, *12*, 614–627. [CrossRef] [PubMed]

44. Huang, M.-B.; Xia, M.; Gao, Z.; Zhou, H.; Liu, M.; Huang, S.; Zhen, R.; Wu, J.Y.; Roth, W.W.; Bond, V.C.; et al. Characterization of Exosomes in Plasma of Patients with Breast, Ovarian, Prostate, Hepatic, Gastric, Colon, and Pancreatic Cancers. *J. Cancer Ther.* **2019**, *10*, 382–399. [CrossRef]
45. Muller, L.; Hong, C.-S.; Stolz, D.B.; Watkins, S.C.; Whiteside, T.L. Isolation of Biologically-Active Exosomes from Human Plasma. *J. Immunol. Methods* **2014**, *411*, 55–65. [CrossRef]
46. Bychkov, M.L.; Kirichenko, A.V.; Mikhaylova, I.N.; Paramonov, A.S.; Yastremsky, E.V.; Kirpichnikov, M.P.; Shulepko, M.A.; Lyukmanova, E.N. Extracellular Vesicles Derived from Acidified Metastatic Melanoma Cells Stimulate Growth, Migration, and Stemness of Normal Keratinocytes. *Biomedicines* **2022**, *10*, 660. [CrossRef]
47. Holcar, M.; Ferdin, J.; Sitar, S.; Tušek-Žnidarič, M.; Dolžan, V.; Plemenitaš, A.; Žagar, E.; Lenassi, M. Enrichment of Plasma Extracellular Vesicles for Reliable Quantification of Their Size and Concentration for Biomarker Discovery. *Sci. Rep.* **2020**, *10*, 21346. [CrossRef]
48. Chen, X.; Luo, Y.; Zhu, Q.; Zhang, J.; Huang, H.; Kan, Y.; Li, D.; Xu, M.; Liu, S.; Li, J.; et al. Small Extracellular Vesicles from Young Plasma Reverse Age-Related Functional Declines by Improving Mitochondrial Energy Metabolism. *Nat. Aging* **2024**, *4*, 814–838. [CrossRef]
49. Ren, J.; Li, L.; Yu, B.; Xu, E.; Sun, N.; Li, X.; Xing, Z.; Han, X.; Cui, Y.; Wang, X.; et al. Extracellular Vesicles Mediated Proinflammatory Macrophage Phenotype Induced by Radiotherapy in Cervical Cancer. *BMC Cancer* **2022**, *22*, 88. [CrossRef]
50. Albino, D.; Falcione, M.; Uboldi, V.; Temilola, D.O.; Sandrini, G.; Merulla, J.; Civenni, G.; Kokanovic, A.; Stürchler, A.; Shinde, D.; et al. Circulating Extracellular Vesicles Release Oncogenic miR-424 in Experimental Models and Patients with Aggressive Prostate Cancer. *Commun. Biol.* **2021**, *4*, 1–13. [CrossRef]
51. Cao, H.; Abd Aziz, N.H.; Xavier, J.R.; Shafiee, M.N.; Kalok, A.; Jee, B.; Salker, M.S.; Singh, Y. Dysregulated Exosomes Result in Suppression of the Immune Response of Pregnant COVID-19 Convalescent Women. *Front. Mol. Biosci.* **2022**, *9*, 869192. [CrossRef] [PubMed]
52. Zhang, L.; Wang, X.; Chen, J.; Sheng, S.; Kleyman, T.R. Extracellular Intersubunit Interactions Modulate Epithelial Na+ Channel Gating. *J. Biol. Chem.* **2023**, *299*, 102914. [CrossRef] [PubMed]
53. Zhao, H.; Zhao, Z.; Li, D.; Wang, X.; Dai, D.; Fu, H. Effect Study of Exosomes Derived from Platelet-Rich Plasma in the Treatment of Knee Cartilage Defects in Rats. *J. Orthop. Surg. Res.* **2023**, *18*, 160. [CrossRef] [PubMed]
54. Pavlyukov, M.S.; Yu, H.; Bastola, S.; Minata, M.; Shender, V.O.; Lee, Y.; Zhang, S.; Wang, J.; Komarova, S.; Wang, J.; et al. Apoptotic Cell-Derived Extracellular Vesicles Promote Malignancy of Glioblastoma via Intercellular Transfer of Splicing Factors. *Cancer Cell* **2018**, *34*, 119–135.e10. [CrossRef] [PubMed]
55. Schildge, S.; Bohrer, C.; Beck, K.; Schachtrup, C. Isolation and Culture of Mouse Cortical Astrocytes. *J. Vis. Exp.* **2013**, *71*, e50079. [CrossRef]
56. Oeck, S.; Malewicz, N.M.; Hurst, S.; Rudner, J.; Jendrossek, V. The Focinator—A New Open-Source Tool for High-Throughput Foci Evaluation of DNA Damage. *Radiat. Oncol.* **2015**, *10*, 163. [CrossRef]
57. Lyukmanova, E.; Kirichenko, A.; Kulbatskii, D.; Isaev, A.; Kukushkin, I.; Che, Y.; Kirpichnikov, M.; Bychkov, M. Water-Soluble Lynx1 Upregulates Dendritic Spine Density and Stimulates Astrocytic Network and Signaling. *Mol. Neurobiol.* **2024**. [CrossRef]
58. Xu, W.; Yang, Z.; Lu, N. A New Role for the PI3K/Akt Signaling Pathway in the Epithelial-Mesenchymal Transition. *Cell Adh Migr.* **2015**, *9*, 317–324. [CrossRef]
59. Meel, M.H.; Schaper, S.A.; Kaspers, G.J.L.; Hulleman, E. Signaling Pathways and Mesenchymal Transition in Pediatric High-Grade Glioma. *Cell Mol. Life Sci.* **2018**, *75*, 871–887. [CrossRef]
60. Kudaravalli, S.; den Hollander, P.; Mani, S.A. Role of P38 MAP Kinase in Cancer Stem Cells and Metastasis. *Oncogene* **2022**, *41*, 3177–3185. [CrossRef]
61. Kühnöl, C.D.; Würfel, C.; Staege, M.S.; Kramm, C. Snail Homolog 1 Is Involved in Epithelial-Mesenchymal Transition-like Processes in Human Glioblastoma Cells. *Oncol. Lett.* **2017**, *13*, 3882–3888. [CrossRef] [PubMed]
62. Yang, H.W.; Menon, L.G.; Black, P.M.; Carroll, R.S.; Johnson, M.D. SNAI2/Slug Promotes Growth and Invasion in Human Gliomas. *BMC Cancer* **2010**, *10*, 301. [CrossRef] [PubMed]
63. Noronha, C.; Ribeiro, A.S.; Taipa, R.; Castro, D.S.; Reis, J.; Faria, C.; Paredes, J. Cadherin Expression and EMT: A Focus on Gliomas. *Biomedicines* **2021**, *9*, 1328. [CrossRef]
64. Bălașa, A.; Șerban, G.; Chinezu, R.; Hurghiș, C.; Tămaș, F.; Manu, D. The Involvement of Exosomes in Glioblastoma Development, Diagnosis, Prognosis, and Treatment. *Brain Sci.* **2020**, *10*, 553. [CrossRef]
65. Kim, J.-Y.; Jackman, J.G.; Woodring, S.; McSherry, F.; Herndon, J.E.; Desjardins, A.; Friedman, H.S.; Peters, K.B. Second Primary Cancers in Long-Term Survivors of Glioblastoma. *Neurooncol Pract.* **2019**, *6*, 386–391. [CrossRef]
66. Zhou, S.; Niu, R.; Sun, H.; Kim, S.-H.; Jin, X.; Yin, J. The MAP3K1/c-JUN Signaling Axis Regulates Glioblastoma Stem Cell Invasion and Tumor Progression. *Biochem. Biophys. Res. Commun.* **2022**, *612*, 188–195. [CrossRef]
67. Grave, N.; Scheffel, T.B.; Cruz, F.F.; Rockenbach, L.; Goettert, M.I.; Laufer, S.; Morrone, F.B. The Functional Role of P38 MAPK Pathway in Malignant Brain Tumors. *Front. Pharmacol.* **2022**, *13*, 975197. [CrossRef]
68. Muqbil, I.; Wu, J.; Aboukameel, A.; Mohammad, R.M.; Azmi, A.S. Snail Nuclear Transport: The Gateways Regulating Epithelial-to-Mesenchymal Transition? *Semin. Cancer Biol.* **2014**, *27*, 39–45. [CrossRef]
69. Villarejo, A.; Cortés-Cabrera, A.; Molina-Ortíz, P.; Portillo, F.; Cano, A. Differential Role of Snail1 and Snail2 Zinc Fingers in E-Cadherin Repression and Epithelial to Mesenchymal Transition. *J. Biol. Chem.* **2014**, *289*, 930–941. [CrossRef]

70. Loh, C.-Y.; Chai, J.Y.; Tang, T.F.; Wong, W.F.; Sethi, G.; Shanmugam, M.K.; Chong, P.P.; Looi, C.Y. The E-Cadherin and N-Cadherin Switch in Epithelial-to-Mesenchymal Transition: Signaling, Therapeutic Implications, and Challenges. *Cells* **2019**, *8*, 1118. [CrossRef]
71. Iser, I.C.; Lenz, G.; Wink, M.R. EMT-like Process in Glioblastomas and Reactive Astrocytes. *Neurochem. Int.* **2019**, *122*, 139–143. [CrossRef] [PubMed]
72. Lewis-Tuffin, L.J.; Rodriguez, F.; Giannini, C.; Scheithauer, B.; Necela, B.M.; Sarkaria, J.N.; Anastasiadis, P.Z. Misregulated E-Cadherin Expression Associated with an Aggressive Brain Tumor Phenotype. *PLoS ONE* **2010**, *5*, e13665. [CrossRef] [PubMed]
73. Martins, E.P.; Gonçalves, C.S.; Pojo, M.; Carvalho, R.; Ribeiro, A.S.; Miranda-Gonçalves, V.; Taipa, R.; Pardal, F.; Pinto, A.A.; Custódia, C.; et al. Cadherin-3 Is a Novel Oncogenic Biomarker with Prognostic Value in Glioblastoma. *Mol. Oncol.* **2022**, *16*, 2611–2631. [CrossRef] [PubMed]
74. Kim, M.N.; Hong, J.Y.; Shim, D.H.; Sol, I.S.; Kim, Y.S.; Lee, J.H.; Kim, K.W.; Lee, J.M.; Sohn, M.H. Activated Leukocyte Cell Adhesion Molecule Stimulates the T-Cell Response in Allergic Asthma. *Am. J. Respir. Crit. Care Med.* **2018**, *197*, 994–1008. [CrossRef] [PubMed]
75. Kijima, N.; Hosen, N.; Kagawa, N.; Hashimoto, N.; Nakano, A.; Fujimoto, Y.; Kinoshita, M.; Sugiyama, H.; Yoshimine, T. CD166/Activated Leukocyte Cell Adhesion Molecule Is Expressed on Glioblastoma Progenitor Cells and Involved in the Regulation of Tumor Cell Invasion. *Neuro Oncol.* **2012**, *14*, 1254–1264. [CrossRef]
76. Inoue, A.; Ohnishi, T.; Nishikawa, M.; Ohtsuka, Y.; Kusakabe, K.; Yano, H.; Tanaka, J.; Kunieda, T. A Narrative Review on CD44's Role in Glioblastoma Invasion, Proliferation, and Tumor Recurrence. *Cancers* **2023**, *15*, 4898. [CrossRef]
77. Kolliopoulos, C.; Ali, M.M.; Castillejo-Lopez, C.; Heldin, C.-H.; Heldin, P. CD44 Depletion in Glioblastoma Cells Suppresses Growth and Stemness and Induces Senescence. *Cancers* **2022**, *14*, 3747. [CrossRef]
78. Huang, L.; Yang, Y.; Yang, F.; Liu, S.; Zhu, Z.; Lei, Z.; Guo, J. Functions of EpCAM in Physiological Processes and Diseases (Review). *Int. J. Mol. Med.* **2018**, *42*, 1771–1785. [CrossRef]
79. Mohtar, M.A.; Syafruddin, S.E.; Nasir, S.N.; Low, T.Y. Revisiting the Roles of Pro-Metastatic EpCAM in Cancer. *Biomolecules* **2020**, *10*, 255. [CrossRef]
80. Piao, Y.; Henry, V.; Tiao, N.; Park, S.Y.; Martinez-Ledesma, J.; Dong, J.W.; Balasubramaniyan, V.; de Groot, J.F. Targeting Intercellular Adhesion Molecule-1 Prolongs Survival in Mice Bearing Bevacizumab-Resistant Glioblastoma. *Oncotarget* **2017**, *8*, 96970–96983. [CrossRef]
81. Park, J.K.; Park, S.H.; So, K.; Bae, I.H.; Yoo, Y.D.; Um, H.-D. ICAM-3 Enhances the Migratory and Invasive Potential of Human Non-Small Cell Lung Cancer Cells by Inducing MMP-2 and MMP-9 via Akt and CREB. *Int. J. Oncol.* **2010**, *36*, 181–192. [CrossRef] [PubMed]
82. Shen, W.; Xie, J.; Zhao, S.; Du, R.; Luo, X.; He, H.; Jiang, S.; Hao, N.; Chen, C.; Guo, C.; et al. ICAM3 Mediates Inflammatory Signaling to Promote Cancer Cell Stemness. *Cancer Lett.* **2018**, *422*, 29–43. [CrossRef] [PubMed]
83. Seker-Polat, F.; Pinarbasi Degirmenci, N.; Solaroglu, I.; Bagci-Onder, T. Tumor Cell Infiltration into the Brain in Glioblastoma: From Mechanisms to Clinical Perspectives. *Cancers* **2022**, *14*, 443. [CrossRef] [PubMed]
84. Prag, S.; Lepekhin, E.A.; Kolkova, K.; Hartmann-Petersen, R.; Kawa, A.; Walmod, P.S.; Belman, V.; Gallagher, H.C.; Berezin, V.; Bock, E.; et al. NCAM Regulates Cell Motility. *J. Cell Sci.* **2002**, *115*, 283–292. [CrossRef]
85. Zhang, D.; Bi, J.; Liang, Q.; Wang, S.; Zhang, L.; Han, F.; Li, S.; Qiu, B.; Fan, X.; Chen, W.; et al. VCAM1 Promotes Tumor Cell Invasion and Metastasis by Inducing EMT and Transendothelial Migration in Colorectal Cancer. *Front. Oncol.* **2020**, *10*, 1066. [CrossRef]
86. Wu, T.-C. The Role of Vascular Cell Adhesion Molecule-1 in Tumor Immune Evasion. *Cancer Res.* **2007**, *67*, 6003–6006. [CrossRef]
87. Barthel, S.R.; Gavino, J.D.; Descheny, L.; Dimitroff, C.J. Targeting Selectins and Selectin Ligands in Inflammation and Cancer. *Expert Opin. Ther. Targets* **2007**, *11*, 1473. [CrossRef]
88. Tvaroška, I.; Selvaraj, C.; Koča, J. Selectins-The Two Dr. Jekyll and Mr. Hyde Faces of Adhesion Molecules-A Review. *Molecules* **2020**, *25*, 2835. [CrossRef]
89. Yeini, E.; Ofek, P.; Pozzi, S.; Albeck, N.; Ben-Shushan, D.; Tiram, G.; Golan, S.; Kleiner, R.; Sheinin, R.; Israeli Dangoor, S.; et al. P-Selectin Axis Plays a Key Role in Microglia Immunophenotype and Glioblastoma Progression. *Nat. Commun.* **2021**, *12*, 1912. [CrossRef]
90. Akers, J.C.; Ramakrishnan, V.; Kim, R.; Phillips, S.; Kaimal, V.; Mao, Y.; Hua, W.; Yang, I.; Fu, C.-C.; Nolan, J.; et al. miRNA Contents of Cerebrospinal Fluid Extracellular Vesicles in Glioblastoma Patients. *J. Neurooncol.* **2015**, *123*, 205–216. [CrossRef]
91. Exosomes: The Good, The Bad, and The Ugly. Available online: https://www.asra.com/news-publications/asra-newsletter/newsletter-item/asra-news/2023/05/12/exosomes-the-good-the-bad-and-the-ugly (accessed on 6 December 2024).

biomedicines

MDPI

Review

Zonulin as Gatekeeper in Gut–Brain Axis: Dysregulation in Glioblastoma

Hannah Hagemeyer [1], Olaf J. C. Hellwinkel [2] and Julio Plata-Bello [3,*]

[1] Institut für Neuroimmunologie und Multiple Sklerose, University Medical Center Hamburg-Eppendorf, Falkenried 94, 20251 Hamburg, Germany; hannah.hagemeyer@zmnh.uni-hamburg.de
[2] Department of Forensic Medicine, University Medical Center Hamburg-Eppendorf, Martinistraße 52, 20251 Hamburg, Germany
[3] Department of Neurosurgery, Hospital Universitario de Canarias, S/C de Tenerife, 38320 La Laguna, Spain
* Correspondence: jplabel@gobiernodecanarias.org or jplata5@hotmail.com

Abstract: Novel biomarkers and therapeutic strategies for glioblastoma, the most common malignant brain tumor with an extremely unfavorable prognosis, are urgently needed. Recent studies revealed a significant upregulation of the protein zonulin in glioblastoma, which correlates with patient survival. Originally identified as pre-haptoglobin-2, zonulin modulates both the intestinal barrier and the blood–brain barrier by disassembling tight junctions. An association of zonulin with various neuroinflammatory diseases has been observed. It can be suggested that zonulin links a putative impairment of the gut–brain barrier with glioblastoma carcinogenesis, leading to an interaction of the gut microbiome, the immune system, and glioblastoma. We therefore propose three interconnected hypotheses: (I) elevated levels of zonulin in glioblastoma contribute to its aggressiveness; (II) upregulated (serum-) zonulin increases the permeability of the microbiota–gut–brain barrier; and (III) this creates a carcinogenic and immunosuppressive microenvironment preventing the host from an effective antitumor response. The role of zonulin in glioblastoma highlights a promising field of research that could yield diagnostic and therapeutic options for glioblastoma patients and other diseases with a disturbed microbiota–gut–brain barrier.

Keywords: blood–brain barrier; glioblastoma; zonulin; pre-haptoglobin

1. Introduction

Glioblastoma is the most common malignant brain tumor, but also the brain tumor with the lowest median survival of only 8 months and thus the major reason for death from primary cerebral neoplasms [1]. According to the classification delineated by the World Health Organization (WHO), glioblastomas are defined as IDH-wildtype gliomas [2]. Histologically, glioblastomas are characterized by an elevated cell density with high mitotic activity, atypical cell types including hyperchromatic and pleomorphic nuclei, extensive necrotic regions, and robust neovascularization [3,4]. The standard treatment entails maximal safe surgical excision while preserving neurological functionality, followed by concurrent administration of radiation and the DNA alkylating agent temozolomide [5]. Despite ongoing research and these triple therapeutic options, the progression-free survival ranges only from 1.5 to 4.2 months [6], which has not significantly increased within the last years. Merely 6.9% of patients survive beyond five years [1,7,8]. These limited diagnostic and therapeutic options emphasize the urgent need for research in the field of glioblastomas to ameliorate the prognostic outlook.

Recent studies have unveiled a significant upregulation of the protein zonulin exclusively in glioblastoma, correlating negatively with patient survival [9]. Originally identified as pre-haptoglobin-2, zonulin modulates intestinal and blood–brain barrier function through the disassembly of tight junctions [10]. Lately, zonulin has attracted growing attention as it shapes several neuroinflammatory diseases such as Major depressive disorders [11], Alzheimer's disease [12], Multiple Sclerosis [13,14], Myalgic encephalomyelitis/Chronic fatigue syndrome (ME/CFS) [15], Chronic fatigue syndrome in schizophrenia [15], schizophrenia [16], and Parkinson's disease [17–19].

Zonulin represents a potential link between a leaky gut–brain axis and glioblastoma. The interplay of the immune system, the gut microbiome, and glial tumor carcinogenesis is influenced by zonulin. The gut–brain axis (GBA) represents a bidirectional exchange platform between the gastrointestinal tract and the central nervous system (CNS) dedicated to maintaining homeostasis between environmental and internal signals [20]. Based on heightened zonulin production in glioblastoma, three hypotheses can be proposed, potentially enhancing each other in a vicious cycle: (I) zonulin contributes to tumor aggressiveness; (II) the elevated zonulin levels in glioblastoma and the corresponding blood-stream increase the permeability of the microbiota–gut–brain axis; and (III) higher trafficking of microbiota and immune cells subsequently induces a chronic inflammatory and carcinogenic microenvironment. A local immunosuppression impairs the hosts to eliminate glial tumor cells. In this review article, we will endeavor to provide the justifications supporting these hypotheses in the intricate interplay of zonulin and glioblastoma.

2. Zonulin: Regulating Intestinal Barrier Permeability and Beyond

Through what started off as a failed attempt for a vaccination against cholera [21], the discovery of zonulin revolutionized the view of the microbiota–gut–brain axis. Zonulin corresponds to the precursor of haptoglobin-2 (Hp2) [14]. As a multifunctional protein, zonulin can either act in its uncleaved form to regulate the permeability of tight junctions or (after cleavage and bisulfite bridge reassembling) as "mature" Hp2 to build a haptoglobin–hemoglobin complex preventing tissue damage by oxidative stress [14]. Upon formation of mature Hp2, the protein loses its function to induce paracellular permeability (Figure 1) [22].

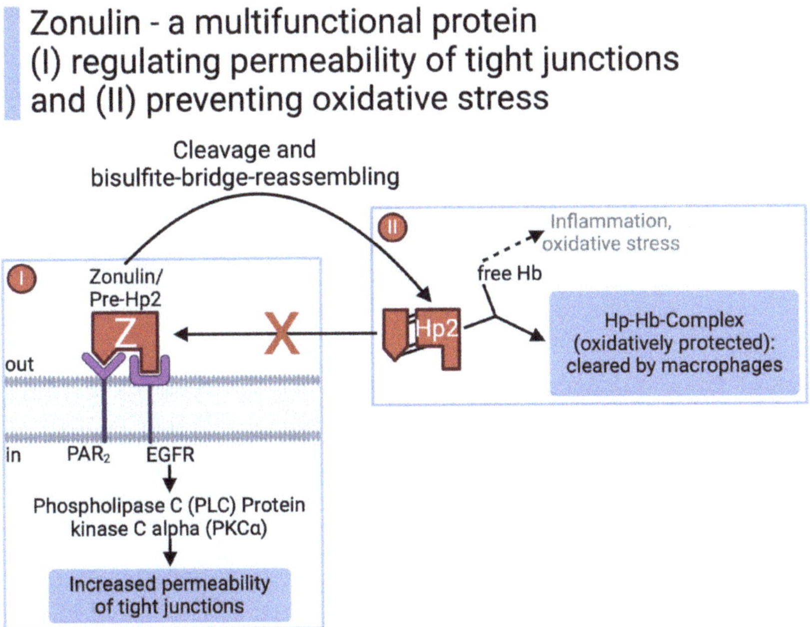

Figure 1. While zonulin (Pre-Hp2) increases permeability of tight junctions, its "mature" form Hp2 prevents oxidative stress [10,14,21–23]. Created with BioRender.com.

The uncleaved 47 kDa human protein zonulin was originally identified as a protein mimicked by zonula occludens toxin (Zot), an enterotoxin by Vibrio cholerae modulating the intestinal barrier [23,24]. The bacterial enterotoxin and the endogenous human zonulin act through the same intracellular pathway to regulate the permeability of intestinal tight junctions [14,23,25]. Tight junctions do not merely consist of the bare link between two cells but are rather a complex network of transmembrane proteins, peripheral membrane proteins, and intracellular regulatory factors [26]. Mechanistically, zonulin transactivates the epidermal growth factor (EGFR) directly or via proteinase-activated receptor 2 (PAR_2). This induces an intracellular cascade of phospholipase C (PLC) and protein kinase C alpha (PKCα) [10,22,23].

EGFR and PAR_2 receptors are expressed on brain endothelial cells and small intestinal epithelial cells. Therefore, zonulin is involved in regulating the segregation of—firstly—pathogens from host tissue in the gut and—secondly—immune cells from the "immune-privileged" CNS [10]. Besides being synthesized in the small intestine and liver, zonulin can be detected in the brain, heart, lungs, adipose tissue, immune cells, kidneys, and skin [23,27,28]. The gut immune barrier, consisting of (entodermal-) epithelial cells, segregates the gut lumen from the host internal space. In contrast, the blood–brain barrier (BBB), composed of (vaso-) endothelial cells, pericytes, and astrocytes, isolates the CNS parenchyma from the lumen of blood vessels [29]. Compared to the leakiness of blood vessels in most human tissue, trafficking of immune cells and pathogens across the BBB is tightly restricted to protect the CNS [29]. Taken together, zonulin shapes the permeability of the intestinal barrier and the BBB.

As the largest interface between the human organism and the environment, the intestinal barrier has to be tightly regulated to prevent pathogen invasion and to flush out microorganisms that already entered the host. Nonetheless, a sufficient nutrient and electrolyte exchange with digested food in the gut is necessary [14,30]. Due to its regulatory function in intestinal epithelial tight junctions [10,31], zonulin plays a crucial role in the control of the gut immune barrier in diseases such as Celiac disease [24] and inflammatory bowel disease [27]. Different stimuli trigger zonulin release in the intestinal epithelium. As a component of gluten in wheat, gliadin induces zonulin release and increases the permeability of the intestinal barrier, which is a postulated mechanism in the pathogenesis of Celiac disease (CD) [32,33]. Another main trigger for intestinal zonulin secretion involves several pathogenic and non-pathogenic enterobacteria such as *E. coli* and *Salmonella typhy* [34]. The high amino acid sequence identity (90%) of gliadin and bacterial proteins may explain their shared ability to induce zonulin release through binding to C-X-C chemokine receptor type 3 (CXCR3) [35]. Elevated zonulin levels are associated with pathogen overgrowth in stool samples [36]. However, zonulin can also flush invading microorganisms back into the intestinal lumen [34], and some microbiota such as *Lactobacillus* even counteract a disruption of the epithelial barrier by preventing zonulin release [37]. In summary, both gliadin and intestinal bacteria can stimulate zonulin release and subsequently increase tight junction permeability.

3. Glioblastoma, Gut Microbiome, and Immune Microenvironment—Interconnected in Tumor Progression and Therapeutic Response

Glioblastomas induce a proangiogenic, inflammatory microenvironment and a more permeable BBB [38]. The compromised barrier function is clinically observed through enhanced gadolinium contrast medium and intense vasogenic edema surrounding glioblastoma in magnetic resonance imaging [9]. The leaky BBB facilitates the invasion of microbiota and immune cells normally absent from the "immune-privileged" CNS [38–41]. For example, bacterial DNA has been detected in glioblastoma samples [42,43]. The relationship between glioblastoma and the gut microbiome appears bidirectional, as glioblastoma seems to influence the gut microbiome composition [44], while a dysbiosis of the gut microbiome could shape glial tumor growth [45].

The load of certain microbiota was increased in glioblastoma mice and patients compared to healthy controls, which was neutralized under temozolomide treatment [44]. Microbiota have also been reported to influence tumor outcome directly by modifying inflammatory transcriptional pathways, tumor carcinogenesis, and tumor-infiltrating immune cells [46]. As a key factor in glial tumor progression, gut microbiota modify neurotransmitters and subsequently influence glioma cell proliferation [47]. Infiltrating immune cells sensitized to pathogenic or commensal bacterial peptides can cross-recognize tumor antigen-derived peptides presented by HLA molecules on glial tumor cells [48]. Consequently, intra-tumoral bacteria may modulate the antitumoral immunological response [48]. Heterogenic opinions exist regarding concrete agents of the microbiome related to gliomas. For instance, gliomas have been associated with increased levels of *Verrucomicrobia*, *Akkermansia*, *Intestinimonas*, and *Lactobacillus* but decreased levels of *Anaerotruncus* [44,49]. Both increased and decreased levels of *Firmicutes* and *Bacteroidia* have been described in the literature [44,45]. These microorganisms can modulate tumor development: coadministration of *Bifidobacterium lactis* with *Lactobacillus plantarum* [50] and compound **K** (a metabolite of ginseng produced by intestinal bacteria [51]) could reduce glioma cell migration and/or proliferation in vitro. In contrast, chronic antibiotic treatment of glioma-bearing mice leads to a higher glial tumor growth with reduced cytotoxic natural killer (NK) cell subsets [52]. Taken together, a disbalanced gut microbiome and glioblastoma seem to influence—and partially enhance—each other bidirectionally.

This interconnection raises the question as to whether the immunosuppressive microenvironment of glioblastoma provides a refuge for locally invading microbiota (favorable for glioblastoma development) without causing a severe cerebral infection [53]. A possible explanation for the intracranial immunosuppressive milieu surrounding glioblastoma [54,55] could be immune exhaustion as a prolonged and insufficient response to chronic pathogen invasion across the BBB. A substantial influx of microglia and tumor-associated macrophages (TAMs) infiltrates glial tumors, compromising approximately 30% of viable cells within glioblastoma [56,57]. While microglia traditionally regulate immune responses in the brain, they fail to launch an effective antitumor response in glioblastoma. Microglia have come under control of the tumor and exert immunosuppressive functions leading to a predominance of Th2 cytokines [58–60]. Immunosuppressive cytokines such as Transforming growth factor-β2 (TGF-β2), Prostaglandin E_2 (PGE_2), and Interleukine-10 (IL-10) within glioblastoma limit phagocytic activity and induce apoptosis in activated lymphocytes [54,61,62]. Elevated levels of these immunosuppressive mediators correlate with glial tumor grade: high-grade gliomas express elevated IL-10 and TGF-β levels [63,64]. TGF-β also downregulates the activating receptor NKG2D on NK cells and CD8-T cells, impairing their efficiency in killing mutated or infected target cells [65]. Altogether, glioblastomas can control infiltrating microglia and tumor-associated macrophages (TAMs) in favor of an immunosuppressive microenvironment.

The source of immunomodulatory cytokines in response to invading microbiota remains unclear, with potential contributors including glioma cells themselves, M2 monocytes, or regulatory T cells (T_{regs}) [66–68]. Glioma cells secrete cytokines that restrict Major Histocompatibility Complex class II (MHCII) production in microglia. The subsequently limited antigen-presenting capability prevents cytotoxic T cell activation against tumor cells [69]. The glioma-shaped microglia also induce T cell apoptosis through FasL and B7-H1-mediated apoptosis [70,71]. While the restriction of immune responses normally serves as a negative feedback mechanism to reduce an overshooting CNS inflammation after pathogen invasion or prevent autoimmunity, glioma cells hijack this mechanism to evade immune surveillance [72]. Invading microbiota and modified immune cells establish local immunosuppression, which presents a major challenge in the development of immune therapies for glioblastoma patients [72–74]. For instance, trials with anti-PD-1 antibodies failed to demonstrate prognostic advantages in glioblastoma [75–77]. Even though the BBB is more permeable in glioblastoma, metastases outside of the CNS are very rare. This restriction to the CNS might be explained through local immunosuppression around glioblastoma and prevention of extracranial spread through a still effective systemic immune response with the glioblastoma-characteristic immunosuppressive factors being absent in systemic circulation [62,78]. Glioblastomas escape from the host immune system through local immunosuppressive milieu.

4. Hypotheses: Zonulin as Dysregulated Gatekeeper of the Microbiota–Gut–Brain Axis in Glioblastoma

Three hypotheses can be proposed explaining the interplay of zonulin and glioblastoma: elevated zonulin levels (I) contribute to glioblastoma aggressiveness, (II) they mechanistically increase the permeability of the microbiota–gut–brain axis in glioblastoma, and (III) they contribute significantly to a tumorigenic microenvironment and the impairment of the host to eliminate tumor cells.

4.1. (I) Zonulin and Its Mature Form Haptoglobin Produced in Glioblastoma Reduce Prognostic Outcome

Zonulin that shapes glioblastoma is not only provided by peripheral tissues, but the tumor itself can also produce zonulin. An in vitro experiment showed that zonulin is produced by three different glioblastoma cell lines. Zonulin was upregulated when the cell lines were cultured in specific conditions for glioma stem cells [9]. Increased zonulin expression in both tumor tissue and the blood-stream of glioblastoma patients correlates with aggressiveness and worse prognosis measured by a short progression-free survival (PFS) [9]. Elevated levels of zonulin correspond to the malignancy of glial tumors [79]. The correlation of zonulin expression and patients' survival suggests zonulin as a specific prognostic biomarker for glioblastoma patients [80]. Pre-haptoglobin, which actually corresponds to zonulin, was already proposed as a possible glioblastoma biomarker [80–83] because it is detected only in glioblastoma plasma but not in the plasma of healthy controls or other oncologic patients (e.g., patients with colon cancer) [80]. In summary, glioblastoma-induced zonulin shapes the malignancy of the tumor.

The modulation of zonulin cleavage remains to be fully explored in the context of glioblastoma. However, we can hypothesize that elevated zonulin levels shift to higher levels of its cleaved product haptoglobin as epiphenomenon in the context of a dynamic equilibrium. Haptoglobin is an acute phase protein [81] with increased concentrations in colorectal cancer [84], Prostate cancer [85], epithelial ovarian cancers [86], triple-negative breast cancer [87], acute myocardial infarction [88], and heart failure [89]. While acute phase proteins are expected to be elevated in stressful metabolic situations, haptoglobin reaches its highest levels in glioblastoma compared to acute phase reactions (not related to cancer) or other cancer [80,90,91]. Being a cleaved and reassembled form of zonulin, haptoglobin also corresponds to therapeutic advances in glioblastoma patients with significantly decreased serum levels after adjuvant therapy [92]. The processed haptoglobin is expressed in different glioma cell lines in vitro, but the failure to detect haptoglobin protein in the cytosol or serum indicates its transient expression or the need of certain stimuli for haptoglobin to be translated [80,93]. Stimuli for this release of the processed haptoglobin include amyloid-β peptides in Alzheimer's disease [94], signals secreted in the surrounding of glial tumors [93], or supposedly elevated zonulin levels. Taken together, glial tumors produce elevated levels of zonulin as well as its downstream product haptoglobin, which correlate with clinical severity (Figure 2).

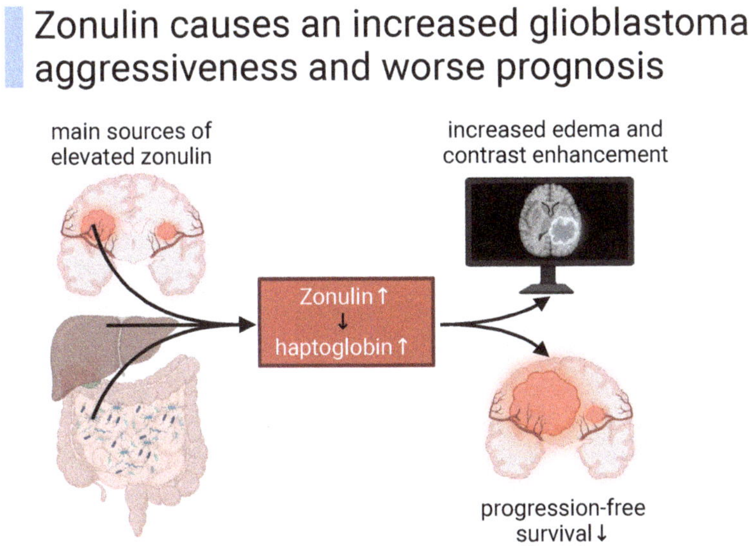

Figure 2. Zonulin induces glioblastoma aggressiveness [9,27,28]. Created with BioRender.com.

4.2. (II) Zonulin Weakens the Blood–Brain Barrier and the Gut Immune Barrier in Glioblastoma

In glioblastoma tissue, zonulin is expressed in a disrupted BBB and colocalizes with Griffonia simplicifolia lectin (GSI), a marker for endothelial cells [79]. Radiologically, higher levels of zonulin are also associated with an increased edema and contrast enhancement in glioblastoma patients, confirming the disrupted BBB [9]. Conditioned media from glioma cells containing high amounts of zonulin make the endothelial cell layer leaky when compared to conditioned media from healthy astrocytes; neuronal stem cells are attracted to brain pathology, thus transmigrating across the BBB and the trans-endothelial electric resistance of the BBB is decreased [30]. An elimination of zonulin from this glioma conditioned media reduces the number of transmigrating neuronal stem cells and completely reverses the decrease in trans-endothelial electric resistance [30]. Similarly, zonulins procaryotic analog ZOT leads to a higher permeability of bovine brain endothelial cells. ZOT has been proposed as a therapeutic agent to increase the delivery of anticancer agents to the brain [95]. Zonulin as well as its analog ZOT induce leakiness of the BBB.

Claudin-5 is a main component of brain endothelial tight junctions [96]. Both zonulin and claudin-5 locate to the boarders of blood vessels in mice gliomas [30,97]. Elevated zonulin levels lead to decreased expression of claudin-5 [30]. In accordance with the essential role of claudin-5 in preserving the integrity of the BBB, a decrease in claudin-5 expression increases BBB permeability, abnormal neoangiogenesis, and progression in glioblastomas [98]. Altered claudin expression is also associated with the control of cell and organ proliferation and thus influences tumorigenesis. Claudin-1 translocation to the nucleus shapes metastatic behavior in colon cancer [26,99]. The complete absence of claudin-5 leads to 100% mortality of newborn mice, highlighting its indispensable function [100]. Taken together, zonulin prevents claudin-5 from maintaining a functional blood–brain axis, serving as a putative mechanism in glioblastoma carcinogenesis.

Zonulin does not only reduce claudin-5 expression at the BBB but also at the intestinal (entodermal-) epithelium [10], leading to an impaired gut immune barrier (GIB). The GIB is the hosts' initial checkpoint against invading microbiota and food antigens, with a tight balance between tolerance and first line of defense [29]. The GIB keeps track of intestinal homeostasis, avoiding chronic inflammation but remaining responsive to acute infectious stressors. A defective GIB may contribute to intestinal inflammation and an invasion of microbiota. Due to the microbiota–gut–brain axis, a deficient GIB also influences brain pathology. In summary, the mutagenic and tumorigenic potential of elevated zonulin levels in glioblastoma could be partly mediated by an increased invasion of microbiota as inflammatory stressors across the impaired GIB and BBB (Figure 3).

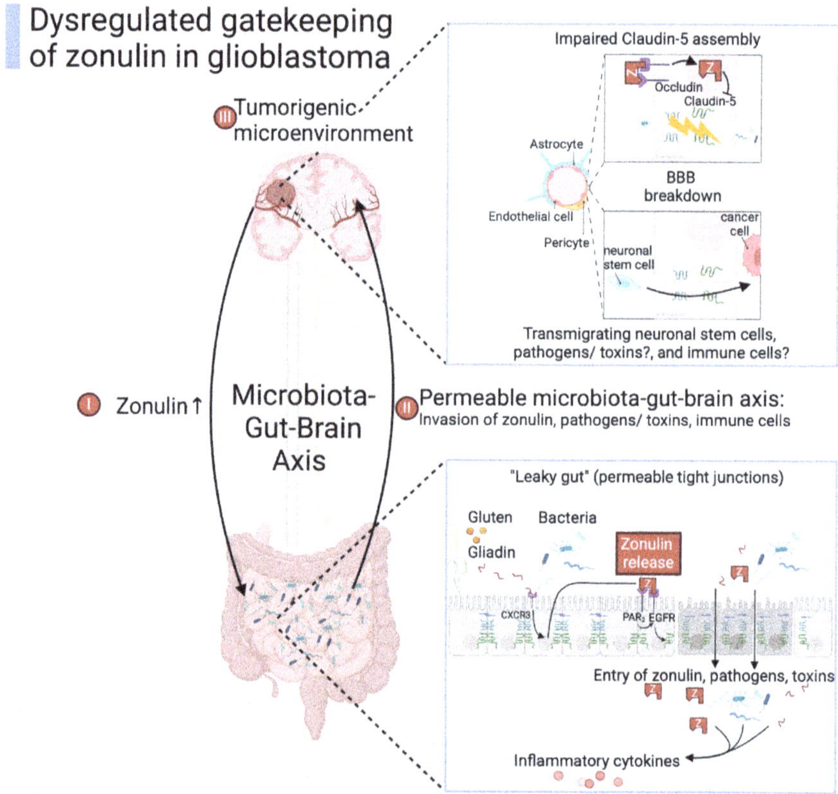

Figure 3. Zonulin as dysregulated gatekeeper of the microbiota–gut–brain axis in glioblastoma [9,10,13,14,23,30,34,42,73]. Created with BioRender.com.

4.3. (III) Immune Cells and Microbiota Cross the Disrupted Blood–Brain Barrier, Influencing the Tumorigenic Microenvironment in a Glioblastoma-Favorable Manner

While microglia are the main cells exerting immune functions within the CNS under physiological conditions, upregulated zonulin can grant access to immune cells from the hematopoietic system which are normally absent in the CNS [72]. Whether these invading immune cells potentially fight against the tumor or immediately come under the immunosuppressive control of the tumor remains to be clarified. The leaky BBB, through elevated zonulin levels, disrupts the balanced immune surveillance of the CNS and entails the risk of a chronic inflammatory state.

Besides a higher exposure to immune cells, an increased number of invading microbiota across the impaired gut immune barrier also fosters an inflammatory state with elevated proliferative signaling [58,72]. The gut–brain axis is more precisely named the microbiota–gut–brain axis. This concept emphasizes a short-term inflammatory interaction as well as a long-term genetic co-evolution of microbiota and the host brain [101]. As environmental stressors, bacteria exert selective pressure on agents involved in host–pathogen interaction [102–104]. Evolutionary adaptation in the evolutionary arms race between the host and pathogens can help the host to fight invading pathogens. However, these adjustments during evolution can also entail adverse mutations or altered gene expression relevant for emerging tumor growth. The high inter- and intraspecies variability and genetic evolution of zonulin hint at its adaptation during this evolutionary arms race [14]. Zonulin could have initially served as key that opens the BBB for immune cells to launch an early immune response against CNS infections. In the long run, a chronically disrupted BBB with invading neuronal stem cells, immune cells, and pathogens/toxins could exert selective pressure on mutagenesis in the CNS and could therefore be partly responsible for emerging glial tumors.

The zonulin pathway is finely tuned and achieves a disassembly of tight junctions within few hours and is mostly reversible afterwards. Nevertheless, zonulin also causes chronic effects on the BBB, evident by an impaired claudin-5 assembly in the long run [10, 29]. More permeable barriers through zonulin permit the immune system to launch an early immune response against pathogens and allergens, but a chronic state of inflammation also entails a risk of DNA damage and tumor development. Chronically elevated zonulin levels might shape tumor development: the incidence of glioblastoma increases in the elderly, with a median age at diagnosis of 66 years [1], and zonulin levels correlate with age-related cytokines TNF-α and IL-6 and gut permeability [105]. The increased exposure of the CNS to inflammatory stressors can help the tumor to acquire capabilities such as (A) tissue invasion with promotion of growth signals and increased cellular replication, (B) evasion of apoptosis and anti-growth signals, and (C) angiogenesis [106].

Besides its disruption of the BBB with indirect changes in the intracerebral immune surveillance, zonulin has also been shown to directly modulate the immune response. Zonulin concentration correlates with higher numbers of neutrophils, functional activity of circulating neutrophils, higher numbers of $CD3^{+}CD8^{+}$ and NK cells, and lower $CD19^{+}$ cells in blood samples of patients with inflammatory bowel disease [107]. Besides cellular immunity, zonulin levels also correlate with serum IL10, IL17, and IL22 in patients with inflammatory bowel disease [108] and with IL6, TNF-α, and lipopolysaccharide in Vitiligo patients [109]. Moreover, the zonulin antagonist *Larazotide* has been shown to alter T cell homeostasis in the spleen with a shift towards anti-inflammatory signaling in a model of arthritis [110]. Taken together, zonulin could enhance the local immunosuppression already established by glioblastomas in a vicious cycle (Figure 4).

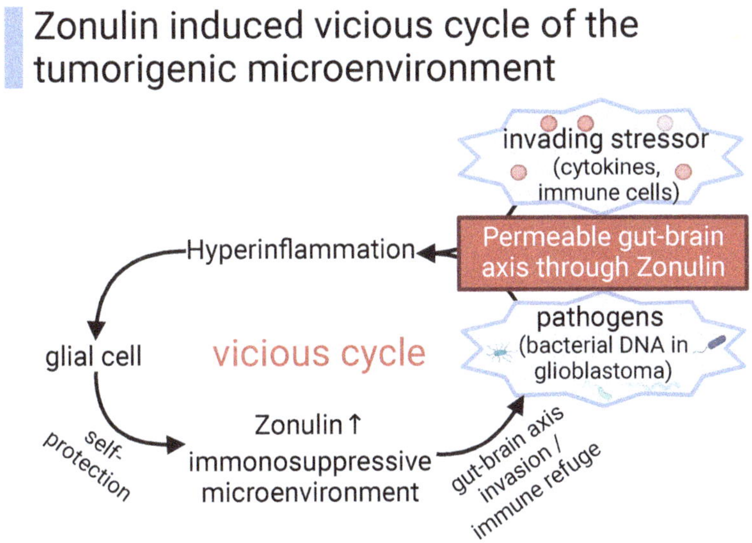

Figure 4. Elevated zonulin levels create a carcinogenic environment in a vicious cycle [9,42,43,55]. Created with BioRender.com.

5. Future Perspectives

Future research is needed to fill the controversies and gaps in knowledge regarding the function of zonulin in glial tumors. The role of zonulin in CNS carcinogenesis needs to be further investigated to improve the prognostic outcome of glioblastoma patients. We propose three ideas to take advantage of zonulin: (I) as a prognostic biomarker, (II) as a therapeutic modulator of tumor progression, and (III) as a target for drug delivery across the BBB.

In particular, relapse rates are extremely high in glioblastoma patients, so close surveillance is necessary to enable early therapeutic intervention. We are currently facing two major difficulties regarding the monitoring of glioblastoma progression. Firstly, imaging modalities may not clearly differentiate between tumor progression and treatment-related "pseudo-progression" in the early phase of follow-up after surgery/radio–chemotherapy [111]. Secondly, tissue biopsies have limitations such as diagnostic follow-up regarding clinical complications, intricate accessibility, and failure to represent the heterogeneity of the whole tumor [112]. Therefore, biomarkers that can be easily assessed in liquid biopsies especially in minimally invasive blood samples are necessary for "real-time" evaluation of tumor growth and therapeutic efficacy [112]. The prognostic potential of zonulin in glioblastoma patients has been investigated with promising data [80–83]. These findings need to be confirmed in bigger cohorts and regarding the response to treatment or relapse.

Zonulin could also improve prognostic outcomes of glioblastoma patients as therapeutic targets. The modulation of different agents of the zonulin pathway has already been proven successful in protecting the BBB [113–115]. Therefore, an inhibition of zonulin itself and all its associated putatively pro-tumoral effects in glioblastoma seem to be reasonable to prevent BBB disruption. The zonulin antagonist Larazotide (also named AT-1001 or FZI/0) reduces antigen and immune cell trafficking across tight junctions [116,117] through a blockade of the zonulin receptor without an alteration of zonulin levels [118,119]. Several clinical studies have already shown the good tolerability and promising therapeutic effects of *Larazotide* on Celiac disease and COVID-19-MIS-C (Multisystem Inflammatory Syndrome in Children) [116,120]. *Larazotide* still remains to be investigated in CNS diseases: *Larazotide* needs to be further modified or administered intravenously/intrathecally to achieve its effects on the CNS [121] because it was originally used only in Celiac disease with intestinal target [122]. Nutritional changes with reduced wheat intake and thus decreased gliadin, as one of the main stimulators for zonulin release, could also modulate zonulin levels. Moreover, changes in the gut microbiome, potentially mediated by altered zonulin levels, may influence the immune environment in glioblastoma and the efficacy of chemotherapeutic treatments [74,123–125]. This raises the question as to what extent nutrition influences microbiota and zonulin levels and how both shape glioblastoma. For example, a probiotic treatment reduces serum zonulin and postoperative infectious complications in patients with colorectal liver metastases [126]. Similarly, *Lactobacillus* has protective effects on the epithelial barrier through reduced zonulin release [37]. The therapeutic applicability of protective microbiota targeting zonulin levels and glioblastoma prognosis needs further investigation regarding optimal pro- and prebiotics. In summary, zonulin antagonists, a modification of gliadin, and nutrition could serve as therapeutic options to influence zonulin-mediated glioblastoma progression.

Finally, effective drugs against glioblastoma require sufficient access to the CNS across the BBB [3,127]. With only a handful of FDA-approved therapies within the last 30 years, it has been proposed that the failure of drug treatment in glioblastoma patients is due to reduced and heterogenous drug delivery across the BBB [40]. The zonulin receptor agonist AT-1002 is already used in drug development for other diseases to increase absorption by opening tight junctions [128]. Already existing therapeutic options could be co-administered with a single-shot dosage of zonulin agonists. Therefore, one of the capacities of zonulin (i.e., BBB disruption) can be its use for more effective drug delivery across the BBB in glioblastoma patients and also putatively in patients with brain metastases.

6. Conclusions

Elevated zonulin levels have been associated with worse prognoses of glioblastoma patients. Higher tumor aggressiveness can be explained mechanistically by a disrupted BBB and a permeable gut immune barrier. Increased invasion of microbiota and immune cells leads to hyperinflammation and reduced immune response against glial tumor cells. The tumorigenic microenvironment grows out of control of the immune system and the rising zonulin levels result in a vicious cycle. If these hypotheses are confirmed in further clinical studies, zonulin could be used as a prognostic biomarker, and the modulation of the zonulin pathway could serve as a therapeutic option in patients with glioblastoma and even other brain tumors. Zonulin is a promising causal, diagnostic, and therapeutic agent in CNS neoplasms with many unresolved questions that should be explored in the near future.

Author Contributions: Conceptualization, H.H. and J.P.-B.; investigation, H.H. and J.P.-B.; resources, H.H. and J.P.-B.; writing—original draft preparation, H.H.; writing—review and editing, all authors; visualization, H.H.; supervision, J.P.-B. and O.J.C.H. All authors have read and agreed to the published version of the manuscript.

Funding: This research received no external funding.

Institutional Review Board Statement: Not applicable.

Data Availability Statement: Any data related to the work are available upon request.

Conflicts of Interest: The authors declare no conflicts of interest.

References

1. Ostrom, Q.T.; Price, M.; Neff, C.; Cioffi, G.; Waite, K.A.; Kruchko, C.; Barnholtz-Sloan, J.S. CBTRUS Statistical Report: Primary Brain and Other Central Nervous System Tumors Diagnosed in the United States in 2016–2020. *Neuro-Oncology* **2023**, *25*, iv1–iv99. [CrossRef] [PubMed]
2. van den Bent, M.J.; Geurts, M.; French, P.J.; Smits, M.; Capper, D.; Bromberg, J.E.C.; Chang, S.M. Primary brain tumours in adults. *Lancet* **2023**, *402*, 1564–1579. [CrossRef] [PubMed]
3. Shergalis, A.; Bankhead, A., 3rd; Luesakul, U.; Muangsin, N.; Neamati, N. Current Challenges and Opportunities in Treating Glioblastoma. *Pharmacol. Rev.* **2018**, *70*, 412–445. [CrossRef] [PubMed]
4. Martin, K.C.; Ma, C.; Yip, S. From Theory to Practice: Implementing the WHO 2021 Classification of Adult Diffuse Gliomas in Neuropathology Diagnosis. *Brain Sci.* **2023**, *13*, 817. [CrossRef] [PubMed]
5. Obrador, E.; Moreno-Murciano, P.; Oriol-Caballo, M.; López-Blanch, R.; Pineda, B.; Gutiérrez-Arroyo, J.L.; Loras, A.; Gonzalez-Bonet, L.G.; Martinez-Cadenas, C.; Estrela, J.M.; et al. Glioblastoma Therapy: Past, Present and Future. *Int. J. Mol. Sci.* **2024**, *25*, 2529. [CrossRef]
6. McBain, C.; Lawrie, T.A.; Rogozińska, E.; Kernohan, A.; Robinson, T.; Jefferies, S. Treatment options for progression or recurrence of glioblastoma: A network meta-analysis. *Cochrane Database Syst. Rev.* **2021**, CD013579. [CrossRef]
7. Louis, D.N.; Perry, A.; Wesseling, P.; Brat, D.J.; Cree, I.A.; Figarella-Branger, D.; Hawkins, C.; Ng, H.K.; Pfister, S.M.; Reifenberger, G.; et al. The 2021 WHO Classification of Tumors of the Central Nervous System: A summary. *Neuro-Oncology* **2021**, *23*, 1231–1251. [CrossRef] [PubMed]
8. Weller, M.; Wick, W.; Aldape, K.; Brada, M.; Berger, M.; Pfister, S.M.; Nishikawa, R.; Rosenthal, M.; Wen, P.Y.; Stupp, R.; et al. Glioma. *Nat. Rev. Dis. Primers* **2015**, *1*, 15017. [CrossRef]
9. Repossi, R.; Martín-Ramírez, R.; Gómez-Bernal, F.; Medina, L.; Fariña-Jerónimo, H.; González-Fernández, R.; Martín-Vasallo, P.; Plata-Bello, J. Evaluation of Zonulin Expression and Its Potential Clinical Significance in Glioblastoma. *Cancers* **2024**, *16*, 356. [CrossRef]
10. Rahman, M.T.; Ghosh, C.; Hossain, M.; Linfield, D.; Rezaee, F.; Janigro, D.; Marchi, N.; van Boxel-Dezaire, A.H.H. IFN-γ, IL-17A, or zonulin rapidly increase the permeability of the blood-brain and small intestinal epithelial barriers: Relevance for neuro-inflammatory diseases. *Biochem. Biophys. Res. Commun.* **2018**, *507*, 274–279. [CrossRef]
11. Wu, H.; Wang, J.; Teng, T.; Yin, B.; He, Y.; Jiang, Y.; Liu, X.; Yu, Y.; Li, X.; Zhou, X. Biomarkers of intestinal permeability and blood-brain barrier permeability in adolescents with major depressive disorder. *J. Affect. Disord.* **2023**, *323*, 659–666. [CrossRef]
12. Wang, X.; Liu, G.J.; Gao, Q.; Li, N.; Wang, R.T. C-type lectin-like receptor 2 and zonulin are associated with mild cognitive impairment and Alzheimer's disease. *Acta Neurol. Scand.* **2020**, *141*, 250–255. [CrossRef]
13. Camara-Lemarroy, C.R.; Silva, C.; Greenfield, J.; Liu, W.Q.; Metz, L.M.; Yong, V.W. Biomarkers of intestinal barrier function in multiple sclerosis are associated with disease activity. *Mult. Scler.* **2020**, *26*, 1340–1350. [CrossRef]
14. Fasano, A. Zonulin and its regulation of intestinal barrier function: The biological door to inflammation, autoimmunity, and cancer. *Physiol. Rev.* **2011**, *91*, 151–175. [CrossRef] [PubMed]

15. Maes, M.; Andrés-Rodríguez, L.; Vojdani, A.; Sirivichayakul, S.; Barbosa, D.S.; Kanchanatawan, B. In Schizophrenia, Chronic Fatigue Syndrome- and Fibromyalgia-Like Symptoms are Driven by Breakdown of the Paracellular Pathway with Increased Zonulin and Immune Activation-Associated Neurotoxicity. *CNS Neurol. Disord. Drug Targets* **2023**, *22*, 215–225. [CrossRef]
16. Wan, C.; La, Y.; Zhu, H.; Yang, Y.; Jiang, L.; Chen, Y.; Feng, G.; Li, H.; Sang, H.; Hao, X.; et al. Abnormal changes of plasma acute phase proteins in schizophrenia and the relation between schizophrenia and haptoglobin (Hp) gene. *Amino Acids* **2007**, *32*, 101–108. [CrossRef]
17. Dumitrescu, L.; Marta, D.; Dănău, A.; Lefter, A.; Tulbă, D.; Cozma, L.; Manole, E.; Gherghiceanu, M.; Ceafalan, L.C.; Popescu, B.O. Serum and Fecal Markers of Intestinal Inflammation and Intestinal Barrier Permeability Are Elevated in Parkinson's Disease. *Front. Neurosci.* **2021**, *15*, 689723. [CrossRef]
18. Schwiertz, A.; Spiegel, J.; Dillmann, U.; Grundmann, D.; Bürmann, J.; Faßbender, K.; Schäfer, K.H.; Unger, M.M. Fecal markers of intestinal inflammation and intestinal permeability are elevated in Parkinson's disease. *Park. Relat. Disord.* **2018**, *50*, 104–107. [CrossRef] [PubMed]
19. Boncuk Ulaş, S.; Güzey Aras, Y.; Irmak Gözükara, S.; Acar, T.; Acar, B.A. Correlates of Zonulin and Claudin-5, markers of intestinal and brain endothelial permeability, in Parkinson's Disease: A pilot study. *Park. Relat. Disord.* **2023**, *110*, 105361. [CrossRef]
20. Agirman, G.; Yu, K.B.; Hsiao, E.Y. Signaling inflammation across the gut-brain axis. *Science* **2021**, *374*, 1087–1092. [CrossRef]
21. Fasano, A.; Baudry, B.; Pumplin, D.W.; Wasserman, S.S.; Tall, B.D.; Ketley, J.M.; Kaper, J.B. Vibrio cholerae produces a second enterotoxin, which affects intestinal tight junctions. *Proc. Natl. Acad. Sci. USA* **1991**, *88*, 5242–5246. [CrossRef]
22. Tripathi, A.; Lammers, K.M.; Goldblum, S.; Shea-Donohue, T.; Netzel-Arnett, S.; Buzza, M.S.; Antalis, T.M.; Vogel, S.N.; Zhao, A.; Yang, S.; et al. Identification of human zonulin, a physiological modulator of tight junctions, as prehaptoglobin-2. *Proc. Natl. Acad. Sci. USA* **2009**, *106*, 16799–16804. [CrossRef]
23. Wang, W.; Uzzau, S.; Goldblum, S.E.; Fasano, A. Human zonulin, a potential modulator of intestinal tight junctions. *J. Cell Sci.* **2000**, *113 Pt 24*, 4435–4440. [CrossRef]
24. Fasano, A.; Not, T.; Wang, W.; Uzzau, S.; Berti, I.; Tommasini, A.; Goldblum, S.E. Zonulin, a newly discovered modulator of intestinal permeability, and its expression in coeliac disease. *Lancet* **2000**, *355*, 1518–1519. [CrossRef] [PubMed]
25. Goldblum, S.E.; Rai, U.; Tripathi, A.; Thakar, M.; De Leo, L.; Di Toro, N.; Not, T.; Ramachandran, R.; Puche, A.C.; Hollenberg, M.D.; et al. The active Zot domain (aa 288–293) increases ZO-1 and myosin 1C serine/threonine phosphorylation, alters interaction between ZO-1 and its binding partners, and induces tight junction disassembly through proteinase activated receptor 2 activation. *FASEB J.* **2011**, *25*, 144–158. [CrossRef] [PubMed]
26. Turner, J.R. Intestinal mucosal barrier function in health and disease. *Nat. Rev. Immunol.* **2009**, *9*, 799–809. [CrossRef]
27. Vanuytsel, T.; Vermeire, S.; Cleynen, I. The role of Haptoglobin and its related protein, Zonulin, in inflammatory bowel disease. *Tissue Barriers* **2013**, *1*, e27321. [CrossRef] [PubMed]
28. Yeung, C.Y.; Chiang Chiau, J.S.; Cheng, M.L.; Chan, W.T.; Jiang, C.B.; Chang, S.W.; Liu, C.Y.; Chang, C.W.; Lee, H.C. Effects of Vitamin D-Deficient Diet on Intestinal Epithelial Integrity and Zonulin Expression in a C57BL/6 Mouse Model. *Front. Med.* **2021**, *8*, 649818. [CrossRef]
29. Daneman, R.; Rescigno, M. The gut immune barrier and the blood-brain barrier: Are they so different? *Immunity* **2009**, *31*, 722–735. [CrossRef]
30. Díaz-Coránguez, M.; Segovia, J.; López-Ornelas, A.; Puerta-Guardo, H.; Ludert, J.; Chávez, B.; Meraz-Cruz, N.; González-Mariscal, L. Transmigration of neural stem cells across the blood brain barrier induced by glioma cells. *PLoS ONE* **2013**, *8*, e60655. [CrossRef]
31. Rahner, C.; Mitic, L.L.; Anderson, J.M. Heterogeneity in expression and subcellular localization of claudins 2, 3, 4, and 5 in the rat liver, pancreas, and gut. *Gastroenterology* **2001**, *120*, 411–422. [CrossRef] [PubMed]
32. Lammers, K.M.; Lu, R.; Brownley, J.; Lu, B.; Gerard, C.; Thomas, K.; Rallabhandi, P.; Shea-Donohue, T.; Tamiz, A.; Alkan, S.; et al. Gliadin induces an increase in intestinal permeability and zonulin release by binding to the chemokine receptor CXCR3. *Gastroenterology* **2008**, *135*, 194–204.e3. [CrossRef] [PubMed]
33. Pizzorno, J. Zonulin! The wheat conundrum solved (well, mostly ...). *Altern. Ther. Health Med.* **2014**, *20* (Suppl. S1), 10–15. [PubMed]
34. El Asmar, R.; Panigrahi, P.; Bamford, P.; Berti, I.; Not, T.; Coppa, G.V.; Catassi, C.; Fasano, A. Host-dependent zonulin secretion causes the impairment of the small intestine barrier function after bacterial exposure. *Gastroenterology* **2002**, *123*, 1607–1615. [CrossRef] [PubMed]
35. Lauxmann, M.A.; Vazquez, D.S.; Schilbert, H.M.; Neubauer, P.R.; Lammers, K.M.; Dodero, V.I. From celiac disease to coccidia infection and vice-versa: The polyQ peptide CXCR3-interaction axis. *Bioessays* **2021**, *43*, e2100101. [CrossRef] [PubMed]
36. Pasini, E.; Corsetti, G.; Assanelli, D.; Testa, C.; Romano, C.; Dioguardi, F.S.; Aquilani, R. Effects of chronic exercise on gut microbiota and intestinal barrier in human with type 2 diabetes. *Minerva Med.* **2019**, *110*, 3–11. [CrossRef] [PubMed]
37. Orlando, A.; Linsalata, M.; Notarnicola, M.; Tutino, V.; Russo, F. Lactobacillus GG restoration of the gliadin induced epithelial barrier disruption: The role of cellular polyamines. *BMC Microbiol.* **2014**, *14*, 19. [CrossRef] [PubMed]
38. Chen, Z.; Hambardzumyan, D. Immune Microenvironment in Glioblastoma Subtypes. *Front. Immunol.* **2018**, *9*, 1004. [CrossRef] [PubMed]
39. Gieryng, A.; Pszczolkowska, D.; Walentynowicz, K.A.; Rajan, W.D.; Kaminska, B. Immune microenvironment of gliomas. *Lab. Investig.* **2017**, *97*, 498–518. [CrossRef]

40. Sarkaria, J.N.; Hu, L.S.; Parney, I.F.; Pafundi, D.H.; Brinkmann, D.H.; Laack, N.N.; Giannini, C.; Burns, T.C.; Kizilbash, S.H.; Laramy, J.K.; et al. Is the blood-brain barrier really disrupted in all glioblastomas? A critical assessment of existing clinical data. *Neuro-Oncology* **2018**, *20*, 184–191. [CrossRef]
41. Wilson, E.H.; Weninger, W.; Hunter, C.A. Trafficking of immune cells in the central nervous system. *J. Clin. Investig.* **2010**, *120*, 1368–1379. [CrossRef] [PubMed]
42. Nejman, D.; Livyatan, I.; Fuks, G.; Gavert, N.; Zwang, Y.; Geller, L.T.; Rotter-Maskowitz, A.; Weiser, R.; Mallel, G.; Gigi, E.; et al. The human tumor microbiome is composed of tumor type-specific intracellular bacteria. *Science* **2020**, *368*, 973–980. [CrossRef] [PubMed]
43. Yust-Katz, S.; Gigi, E.; Rosenberg, D.; Kanner, A.A.; Laviv, Y.; Benouaich-Amiel, A.; Siegal, T.; Barda, A.L.; Straussman, R. TAMI-40. Tumor microbiome and glioblastoma (GBM). *Neuro-Oncology* **2020**, *22*, ii221–ii222. [CrossRef]
44. Patrizz, A.; Dono, A.; Zorofchian, S.; Hines, G.; Takayasu, T.; Husein, N.; Otani, Y.; Arevalo, O.; Choi, H.A.; Savarraj, J.; et al. Glioma and temozolomide induced alterations in gut microbiome. *Sci. Rep.* **2020**, *10*, 21002. [CrossRef] [PubMed]
45. Fan, Y.; Su, Q.; Chen, J.; Wang, Y.; He, S. Gut Microbiome Alterations Affect Glioma Development and Foxp3 Expression in Tumor Microenvironment in Mice. *Front. Oncol.* **2022**, *12*, 836953. [CrossRef] [PubMed]
46. Galeano Niño, J.L.; Wu, H.; LaCourse, K.D.; Kempchinsky, A.G.; Baryiames, A.; Barber, B.; Futran, N.; Houlton, J.; Sather, C.; Sicinska, E.; et al. Effect of the intratumoral microbiota on spatial and cellular heterogeneity in cancer. *Nature* **2022**, *611*, 810–817. [CrossRef] [PubMed]
47. D'Alessandro, G.; Lauro, C.; Quaglio, D.; Ghirga, F.; Botta, B.; Trettel, F.; Limatola, C. Neuro-Signals from Gut Microbiota: Perspectives for Brain Glioma. *Cancers* **2021**, *13*, 2810. [CrossRef] [PubMed]
48. Naghavian, R.; Faigle, W.; Oldrati, P.; Wang, J.; Toussaint, N.C.; Qiu, Y.; Medici, G.; Wacker, M.; Freudenmann, L.K.; Bonté, P.E.; et al. Microbial peptides activate tumour-infiltrating lymphocytes in glioblastoma. *Nature* **2023**, *617*, 807–817. [CrossRef] [PubMed]
49. Li, X.C.; Wu, B.S.; Jiang, Y.; Li, J.; Wang, Z.F.; Ma, C.; Li, Y.R.; Yao, J.; Jin, X.Q.; Li, Z.Q. Temozolomide-Induced Changes in Gut Microbial Composition in a Mouse Model of Brain Glioma. *Drug Des. Dev. Ther.* **2021**, *15*, 1641–1652. [CrossRef]
50. Wang, L.; Li, S.; Fan, H.; Han, M.; Xie, J.; Du, J.; Peng, F. *Bifidobacterium lactis* combined with *Lactobacillus plantarum* inhibit glioma growth in mice through modulating PI3K/AKT pathway and gut microbiota. *Front. Microbiol.* **2022**, *13*, 986837. [CrossRef]
51. Kim, H.; Roh, H.S.; Kim, J.E.; Park, S.D.; Park, W.H.; Moon, J.Y. Compound K attenuates stromal cell-derived growth factor 1 (SDF-1)-induced migration of C6 glioma cells. *Nutr. Res. Pract.* **2016**, *10*, 259–264. [CrossRef] [PubMed]
52. D'Alessandro, G.; Antonangeli, F.; Marrocco, F.; Porzia, A.; Lauro, C.; Santoni, A.; Limatola, C. Gut microbiota alterations affect glioma growth and innate immune cells involved in tumor immunosurveillance in mice. *Eur. J. Immunol.* **2020**, *50*, 705–711. [CrossRef] [PubMed]
53. Dono, A.; Nickles, J.; Rodriguez-Armendariz, A.G.; McFarland, B.C.; Ajami, N.J.; Ballester, L.Y.; Wargo, J.A.; Esquenazi, Y. Glioma and the gut-brain axis: Opportunities and future perspectives. *Neurooncol. Adv.* **2022**, *4*, vdac054. [CrossRef] [PubMed]
54. Parney, I.F. Basic Concepts in Glioma Immunology. In *Glioma: Immunotherapeutic Approaches*; Yamanaka, R., Ed.; Springer: New York, NY, USA, 2012; pp. 42–52.
55. Grabowski, M.M.; Sankey, E.W.; Ryan, K.J.; Chongsathidkiet, P.; Lorrey, S.J.; Wilkinson, D.S.; Fecci, P.E. Immune suppression in gliomas. *J. Neuro-Oncol.* **2021**, *151*, 3–12. [CrossRef] [PubMed]
56. Parney, I.F.; Waldron, J.S.; Parsa, A.T. Flow cytometry and in vitro analysis of human glioma-associated macrophages. Laboratory investigation. *J. Neurosurg.* **2009**, *110*, 572–582. [CrossRef] [PubMed]
57. Badie, B.; Schartner, J.M. Flow Cytometric Characterization of Tumor-associated Macrophages in Experimental Gliomas. *Neurosurgery* **2000**, *46*, 957–962. [PubMed]
58. Mehrian-Shai, R.; Reichardt, J.K.V.; Harris, C.C.; Toren, A. The Gut-Brain Axis, Paving the Way to Brain Cancer. *Trends Cancer* **2019**, *5*, 200–207. [CrossRef] [PubMed]
59. Yang, I.; Han, S.J.; Kaur, G.; Crane, C.; Parsa, A.T. The role of microglia in central nervous system immunity and glioma immunology. *J. Clin. Neurosci.* **2010**, *17*, 6–10. [CrossRef] [PubMed]
60. Hao, C.; Parney, I.F.; Roa, W.H.; Turner, J.; Petruk, K.C.; Ramsay, D.A. Cytokine and cytokine receptor mRNA expression in human glioblastomas: Evidence of Th1, Th2 and Th3 cytokine dysregulation. *Acta Neuropathol.* **2002**, *103*, 171–178. [CrossRef]
61. Siepl, C.; Bodmer, S.; Frei, K.; MacDonald, H.R.; De Martin, R.; Hofer, E.; Fontana, A. The glioblastoma-derived T cell suppressor factor/transforming growth factor-beta 2 inhibits T cell growth without affecting the interaction of interleukin 2 with its receptor. *Eur. J. Immunol.* **1988**, *18*, 593–600. [CrossRef]
62. Rodrigues, J.C.; Gonzalez, G.C.; Zhang, L.; Ibrahim, G.; Kelly, J.J.; Gustafson, M.P.; Lin, Y.; Dietz, A.B.; Forsyth, P.A.; Yong, V.W.; et al. Normal human monocytes exposed to glioma cells acquire myeloid-derived suppressor cell-like properties. *Neuro-Oncology* **2010**, *12*, 351–365. [CrossRef] [PubMed]
63. Kjellman, C.; Olofsson, S.P.; Hansson, O.; Von Schantz, T.; Lindvall, M.; Nilsson, I.; Salford, L.G.; Sjögren, H.O.; Widegren, B. Expression of TGF-beta isoforms, TGF-beta receptors, and SMAD molecules at different stages of human glioma. *Int. J. Cancer* **2000**, *89*, 251–258. [CrossRef] [PubMed]
64. Zhang, Z.; Huang, X.; Li, J.; Fan, H.; Yang, F.; Zhang, R.; Yang, Y.; Feng, S.; He, D.; Sun, W.; et al. Interleukin 10 promotes growth and invasion of glioma cells by up-regulating KPNA 2 in vitro. *J. Cancer Res. Ther.* **2019**, *15*, 927–932. [CrossRef] [PubMed]

65. Crane, C.A.; Han, S.J.; Barry, J.J.; Ahn, B.J.; Lanier, L.L.; Parsa, A.T. TGF-beta downregulates the activating receptor NKG2D on NK cells and CD8+ T cells in glioma patients. *Neuro Oncol.* **2010**, *12*, 7–13. [CrossRef] [PubMed]
66. Qiu, B.; Zhang, D.; Wang, C.; Tao, J.; Tie, X.; Qiao, Y.; Xu, K.; Wang, Y.; Wu, A. IL-10 and TGF-β2 are overexpressed in tumor spheres cultured from human gliomas. *Mol. Biol. Rep.* **2011**, *38*, 3585–3591. [CrossRef]
67. Prosniak, M.; Harshyne, L.A.; Andrews, D.W.; Kenyon, L.C.; Bedelbaeva, K.; Apanasovich, T.V.; Heber-Katz, E.; Curtis, M.T.; Cotzia, P.; Hooper, D.C. Glioma Grade Is Associated with the Accumulation and Activity of Cells Bearing M2 Monocyte Markers. *Clin. Cancer Res.* **2013**, *19*, 3776–3786. [CrossRef] [PubMed]
68. Fecci, P.E.; Mitchell, D.A.; Whitesides, J.F.; Xie, W.; Friedman, A.H.; Archer, G.E.; Herndon, J.E., II; Bigner, D.D.; Dranoff, G.; Sampson, J.H. Increased regulatory T-cell fraction amidst a diminished CD4 compartment explains cellular immune defects in patients with malignant glioma. *Cancer Res.* **2006**, *66*, 3294–3302. [CrossRef]
69. Flügel, A.; Labeur, M.S.; Grasbon-Frodl, E.M.; Kreutzberg, G.W.; Graeber, M.B. Microglia only weakly present glioma antigen to cytotoxic T cells. *Int. J. Dev. Neurosci.* **1999**, *17*, 547–556. [CrossRef]
70. Badie, B.; Schartner, J.; Prabakaran, S.; Paul, J.; Vorpahl, J. Expression of Fas ligand by microglia: Possible role in glioma immune evasion. *J. Neuroimmunol.* **2001**, *120*, 19–24. [CrossRef]
71. Wintterle, S.; Schreiner, B.; Mitsdoerffer, M.; Schneider, D.; Chen, L.; Meyermann, R.; Weller, M.; Wiendl, H. Expression of the B7-related molecule B7-H1 by glioma cells: A potential mechanism of immune paralysis. *Cancer Res.* **2003**, *63*, 7462–7467.
72. Galvão, R.P.; Zong, H. Inflammation and Gliomagenesis: Bi-Directional Communication at Early and Late Stages of Tumor Progression. *Curr. Pathobiol. Rep.* **2013**, *1*, 19–28. [CrossRef] [PubMed]
73. Mangani, D.; Weller, M.; Roth, P. The network of immunosuppressive pathways in glioblastoma. *Biochem. Pharmacol.* **2017**, *130*, 1–9. [CrossRef] [PubMed]
74. Lyu, Y.; Yang, H.; Chen, L. Metabolic regulation on the immune environment of glioma through gut microbiota. *Semin. Cancer Biol.* **2022**, *86*, 990–997. [CrossRef] [PubMed]
75. Omuro, A.; Brandes, A.A.; Carpentier, A.F.; Idbaih, A.; Reardon, D.A.; Cloughesy, T.; Sumrall, A.; Baehring, J.; van den Bent, M.; Bähr, O.; et al. Radiotherapy combined with nivolumab or temozolomide for newly diagnosed glioblastoma with unmethylated MGMT promoter: An international randomized phase III trial. *Neuro-Oncology* **2022**, *25*, 123–134. [CrossRef] [PubMed]
76. Reardon, D.A.; Brandes, A.A.; Omuro, A.; Mulholland, P.; Lim, M.; Wick, A.; Baehring, J.; Ahluwalia, M.S.; Roth, P.; Bähr, O.; et al. Effect of Nivolumab vs Bevacizumab in Patients with Recurrent Glioblastoma: The CheckMate 143 Phase 3 Randomized Clinical Trial. *JAMA Oncol.* **2020**, *6*, 1003–1010. [CrossRef]
77. Lim, M.; Weller, M.; Idbaih, A.; Steinbach, J.; Finocchiaro, G.; Raval, R.R.; Ansstas, G.; Baehring, J.; Taylor, J.W.; Honnorat, J.; et al. Phase III trial of chemoradiotherapy with temozolomide plus nivolumab or placebo for newly diagnosed glioblastoma with methylated MGMT promoter. *Neuro-Oncology* **2022**, *24*, 1935–1949. [CrossRef] [PubMed]
78. Müller, C.; Holtschmidt, J.; Auer, M.; Heitzer, E.; Lamszus, K.; Schulte, A.; Matschke, J.; Langer-Freitag, S.; Gasch, C.; Stoupiec, M.; et al. Hematogenous dissemination of glioblastoma multiforme. *Sci. Transl. Med.* **2014**, *6*, 247ra101. [CrossRef] [PubMed]
79. Skardelly, M.; Armbruster, F.P.; Meixensberger, J.; Hilbig, H. Expression of Zonulin, c-kit, and Glial Fibrillary Acidic Protein in Human Gliomas. *Transl. Oncol.* **2009**, *2*, 117–120. [CrossRef] [PubMed]
80. Naryzhny, S.; Ronzhina, N.; Zorina, E.; Kabachenko, F.; Zavialova, M.; Zgoda, V.; Klopov, N.; Legina, O.; Pantina, R. Evaluation of Haptoglobin and Its Proteoforms as Glioblastoma Markers. *Int. J. Mol. Sci.* **2021**, *22*, 6533. [CrossRef]
81. Naryzny, S.N.; Legina, O.K. Haptoglobin as a Biomarker. *Biochem. (Mosc.) Suppl. B Biomed. Chem.* **2021**, *15*, 184–198. [CrossRef]
82. Gollapalli, K.; Ray, S.; Srivastava, R.; Renu, D.; Singh, P.; Dhali, S.; Bajpai Dikshit, J.; Srikanth, R.; Moiyadi, A.; Srivastava, S. Investigation of serum proteome alterations in human glioblastoma multiforme. *Proteomics* **2012**, *12*, 2378–2390. [CrossRef] [PubMed]
83. Kumar, D.M.; Thota, B.; Shinde, S.V.; Prasanna, K.V.; Hegde, A.S.; Arivazhagan, A.; Chandramouli, B.A.; Santosh, V.; Somasundaram, K. Proteomic identification of haptoglobin α2 as a glioblastoma serum biomarker: Implications in cancer cell migration and tumor growth. *J. Proteome Res.* **2010**, *9*, 5557–5567. [CrossRef] [PubMed]
84. Morishita, K.; Kondo, J.; Sakon, D.; Hayashibara, A.; Tamura, I.; Shimizu, K.; Takamatsu, S.; Murata, K.; Kamada, Y.; Miyoshi, E. Prohaptoglobin is a possible prognostic biomarker for colorectal cancer. *Biochem. Biophys. Res. Commun.* **2023**, *672*, 72–80. [CrossRef] [PubMed]
85. Pang, X.; Tashiro, K.; Eguchi, R.; Komatsu, N.; Sasada, T.; Itoh, K.; Kuhara, S. Haptoglobin proved a prognostic biomarker in peripheral blood of patients with personalized peptide vaccinations for advanced castration-resistant prostate cancer. *Biosci. Biotechnol. Biochem.* **2013**, *77*, 766–770. [CrossRef] [PubMed]
86. Moothanchery, M.; Perumal, J.; Mahyuddin, A.P.; Singh, G.; Choolani, M.; Olivo, M. Rapid and sensitive detection of ovarian cancer biomarker using a portable single peak Raman detection method. *Sci. Rep.* **2022**, *12*, 12459. [CrossRef] [PubMed]
87. Tabassum, U.; Reddy, O.; Mukherjee, G. Elevated serum haptoglobin is associated with clinical outcome in triple-negative breast cancer patients. *Asian Pac. J. Cancer Prev.* **2012**, *13*, 4541–4544. [CrossRef] [PubMed]
88. Haas, B.; Serchi, T.; Wagner, D.R.; Gilson, G.; Planchon, S.; Renaut, J.; Hoffmann, L.; Bohn, T.; Devaux, Y. Proteomic analysis of plasma samples from patients with acute myocardial infarction identifies haptoglobin as a potential prognostic biomarker. *J. Proteom.* **2011**, *75*, 229–236. [CrossRef]
89. Graves, K.L.; Vigerust, D.J. Hp: An inflammatory indicator in cardiovascular disease. *Future Cardiol.* **2016**, *12*, 471–481. [CrossRef]

90. Matsuura, H.; Nakazawa, S. Prognostic significance of serum alpha 1-acid glycoprotein in patients with glioblastoma multiforme: A preliminary communication. *J. Neurol. Neurosurg. Psychiatry* **1985**, *48*, 835–837. [CrossRef]
91. Weiss, J.F.; Morantz, R.A.; Bradley, W.P.; Chretien, P.B. Serum acute-phase proteins and immunoglobulins in patients with gliomas. *Cancer Res.* **1979**, *39*, 542–544.
92. van Linde, M.E.; van der Mijn, J.C.; Pham, T.V.; Knol, J.C.; Wedekind, L.E.; Hovinga, K.E.; Aliaga, E.S.; Buter, J.; Jimenez, C.R.; Reijneveld, J.C.; et al. Evaluation of potential circulating biomarkers for prediction of response to chemoradiation in patients with glioblastoma. *J. Neurooncol.* **2016**, *129*, 221–230. [CrossRef] [PubMed]
93. Sanchez, D.J.; Armstrong, L.; Aguilar, R.; Adrian, G.S.; Haro, L.; Martinez, A.O. Haptoglobin gene expression in human glioblastoma cell lines. *Neurosci. Lett.* **2001**, *303*, 181–184. [CrossRef] [PubMed]
94. Maresca, B.; Spagnuolo, M.S.; Cigliano, L. Haptoglobin Modulates Beta-Amyloid Uptake by U-87 MG Astrocyte Cell Line. *J. Mol. Neurosci.* **2015**, *56*, 35–47. [CrossRef] [PubMed]
95. Karyekar, C.S.; Fasano, A.; Raje, S.; Lu, R.; Dowling, T.C.; Eddington, N.D. Zonula occludens toxin increases the permeability of molecular weight markers and chemotherapeutic agents across the bovine brain microvessel endothelial cells. *J. Pharm. Sci.* **2003**, *92*, 414–423. [CrossRef] [PubMed]
96. Tsukita, S.; Furuse, M. Claudin-based barrier in simple and stratified cellular sheets. *Curr. Opin. Cell Biol.* **2002**, *14*, 531–536. [CrossRef] [PubMed]
97. Liebner, S.; Fischmann, A.; Rascher, G.; Duffner, F.; Grote, E.H.; Kalbacher, H.; Wolburg, H. Claudin-1 and claudin-5 expression and tight junction morphology are altered in blood vessels of human glioblastoma multiforme. *Acta Neuropathol.* **2000**, *100*, 323–331. [CrossRef] [PubMed]
98. Wu, S.; Wang, J.; Liu, J.; Zhu, H.; Li, R.; Wan, X.; Lei, J.; Li, Y.; You, C.; Hu, F.; et al. Programmed cell death 10 increased blood-brain barrier permeability through HMGB1/TLR4 mediated downregulation of endothelial ZO-1 in glioblastoma. *Cell. Signal.* **2023**, *107*, 110683. [CrossRef] [PubMed]
99. Dhawan, P.; Singh, A.B.; Deane, N.G.; No, Y.; Shiou, S.R.; Schmidt, C.; Neff, J.; Washington, M.K.; Beauchamp, R.D. Claudin-1 regulates cellular transformation and metastatic behavior in colon cancer. *J. Clin. Investig.* **2005**, *115*, 1765–1776. [CrossRef] [PubMed]
100. Braniste, V.; Al-Asmakh, M.; Kowal, C.; Anuar, F.; Abbaspour, A.; Tóth, M.; Korecka, A.; Bakocevic, N.; Ng, L.G.; Kundu, P.; et al. The gut microbiota influences blood-brain barrier permeability in mice. *Sci. Transl. Med.* **2014**, *6*, 263ra158. [CrossRef]
101. Cryan, J.F.; O'Riordan, K.J.; Cowan, C.S.M.; Sandhu, K.V.; Bastiaanssen, T.F.S.; Boehme, M.; Codagnone, M.G.; Cussotto, S.; Fulling, C.; Golubeva, A.V.; et al. The Microbiota-Gut-Brain Axis. *Physiol. Rev.* **2019**, *99*, 1877–2013. [CrossRef]
102. Bordenstein, S.R.; Theis, K.R. Host Biology in Light of the Microbiome: Ten Principles of Holobionts and Hologenomes. *PLoS Biol.* **2015**, *13*, e1002226. [CrossRef]
103. Zilber-Rosenberg, I.; Rosenberg, E. Role of microorganisms in the evolution of animals and plants: The hologenome theory of evolution. *FEMS Microbiol. Rev.* **2008**, *32*, 723–735. [CrossRef] [PubMed]
104. Pääbo, S. The human condition-a molecular approach. *Cell* **2014**, *157*, 216–226. [CrossRef] [PubMed]
105. Qi, Y.; Goel, R.; Kim, S.; Richards, E.M.; Carter, C.S.; Pepine, C.J.; Raizada, M.K.; Buford, T.W. Intestinal Permeability Biomarker Zonulin is Elevated in Healthy Aging. *J. Am. Med. Dir. Assoc.* **2017**, *18*, 810.e1–810.e14. [CrossRef]
106. Hanahan, D.; Weinberg, R.A. The hallmarks of cancer. *Cell* **2000**, *100*, 57–70. [CrossRef] [PubMed]
107. Khusainova, G.; Genkel, V.; Kuznetsova, A.; Nikushkina, K.; Saenko, A.; Abramovskikh, O.; Dolgushina, A. The Relationship between Serum Zonulin and Innate Immunity in Patients with Inflammatory Bowel Disease. *Gastroenterol. Insights* **2024**, *15*, 179–190. [CrossRef]
108. Dąbek-Drobny, A.; Kaczmarczyk, O.; Piątek-Guziewicz, A.; Woźniakiewicz, M.; Paśko, P.; Dobrowolska-Iwanek, J.; Woźniakiewicz, A.; Targosz, A.; Ptak-Belowska, A.; Zagrodzki, P.; et al. Application of the Clustering Technique to Multiple Nutritional Factors Related to Inflammation and Disease Progression in Patients with Inflammatory Bowel Disease. *Nutrients* **2022**, *14*, 3960. [CrossRef]
109. Arslan, S.; Altunisik, N.; Turkmen, D.; Uremis, M.M.; Sener, S.; Turkoz, Y. Evaluation of plasma zonulin level and its relationship with inflammatory cytokines in patients with vitiligo. *J. Cosmet. Dermatol.* **2023**, *22*, 1011–1016. [CrossRef] [PubMed]
110. Tajik, N.; Frech, M.; Schulz, O.; Schälter, F.; Lucas, S.; Azizov, V.; Dürholz, K.; Steffen, F.; Omata, Y.; Rings, A.; et al. Targeting zonulin and intestinal epithelial barrier function to prevent onset of arthritis. *Nat. Commun.* **2020**, *11*, 1995. [CrossRef]
111. Thust, S.C.; van den Bent, M.J.; Smits, M. Pseudoprogression of brain tumors. *J. Magn. Reson. Imaging* **2018**, *48*, 571–589. [CrossRef]
112. Müller Bark, J.; Kulasinghe, A.; Chua, B.; Day, B.W.; Punyadeera, C. Circulating biomarkers in patients with glioblastoma. *Br. J. Cancer* **2020**, *122*, 295–305. [CrossRef]
113. Yang, Y.; Thompson, J.F.; Taheri, S.; Salayandia, V.M.; McAvoy, T.A.; Hill, J.W.; Yang, Y.; Estrada, E.Y.; Rosenberg, G.A. Early Inhibition of MMP Activity in Ischemic Rat Brain Promotes Expression of Tight Junction Proteins and Angiogenesis during Recovery. *J. Cereb. Blood Flow Metab.* **2013**, *33*, 1104–1114. [CrossRef]
114. Kuhlmann, C.R.W.; Tamaki, R.; Gamerdinger, M.; Lessmann, V.; Behl, C.; Kempski, O.S.; Luhmann, H.J. Inhibition of the myosin light chain kinase prevents hypoxia-induced blood–brain barrier disruption. *J. Neurochem.* **2007**, *102*, 501–507. [CrossRef] [PubMed]

115. Huang, T.; Gao, D.; Hei, Y.; Zhang, X.; Chen, X.; Fei, Z. D-allose protects the blood brain barrier through PPARγ-mediated anti-inflammatory pathway in the mice model of ischemia reperfusion injury. *Brain Res.* **2016**, *1642*, 478–486. [CrossRef]
116. Yonker, L.M.; Swank, Z.; Gilboa, T.; Senussi, Y.; Kenyon, V.; Papadakis, L.; Boribong, B.P.; Carroll, R.W.; Walt, D.R.; Fasano, A. Zonulin Antagonist, Larazotide (AT1001), As an Adjuvant Treatment for Multisystem Inflammatory Syndrome in Children: A Case Series. *Crit. Care Explor.* **2022**, *10*, e0641. [CrossRef]
117. Troisi, J.; Venutolo, G.; Terracciano, C.; Carri, D.M.; Di Micco, S.; Landolfi, A.; Fasano, A. The Therapeutic use of the Zonulin Inhibitor AT-1001 (Larazotide) for a Variety of Acute and Chronic Inflammatory Diseases. *Curr. Med. Chem.* **2021**, *28*, 5788–5807. [CrossRef] [PubMed]
118. Drago, S.; El Asmar, R.; Di Pierro, M.; Grazia Clemente, M.; Sapone, A.T.A.; Thakar, M.; Iacono, G.; Carroccio, A.; D'Agate, C.; Not, T.; et al. Gliadin, zonulin and gut permeability: Effects on celiac and non-celiac intestinal mucosa and intestinal cell lines. *Scand. J. Gastroenterol.* **2006**, *41*, 408–419. [CrossRef]
119. Clemente, M.G.; Virgiliis, S.D.; Kang, J.S.; Macatagney, R.; Musu, M.P.; Pierro, M.R.D.; Drago, S.; Congia, M.; Fasano, A. Early effects of gliadin on enterocyte intracellular signalling involved in intestinal barrier function. *Gut* **2003**, *52*, 218–223. [CrossRef] [PubMed]
120. Hoilat, G.J.; Altowairqi, A.K.; Ayas, M.F.; Alhaddab, N.T.; Alnujaidi, R.A.; Alharbi, H.A.; Alyahyawi, N.; Kamal, A.; Alhabeeb, H.; Albazee, E.; et al. Larazotide acetate for treatment of celiac disease: A systematic review and meta-analysis of randomized controlled trials. *Clin. Res. Hepatol. Gastroenterol.* **2022**, *46*, 101782. [CrossRef]
121. Veres-Székely, A.; Szász, C.; Pap, D.; Szebeni, B.; Bokrossy, P.; Vannay, Á. Zonulin as a Potential Therapeutic Target in Microbiota-Gut-Brain Axis Disorders: Encouraging Results and Emerging Questions. *Int. J. Mol. Sci.* **2023**, *24*, 7548. [CrossRef]
122. Slifer, Z.M.; Krishnan, B.R.; Madan, J.; Blikslager, A.T. Larazotide acetate: A pharmacological peptide approach to tight junction regulation. *Am. J. Physiol.-Gastrointest. Liver Physiol.* **2021**, *320*, G983–G989. [CrossRef]
123. Viaud, S.; Saccheri, F.; Mignot, G.; Yamazaki, T.; Daillère, R.; Hannani, D.; Enot, D.P.; Pfirschke, C.; Engblom, C.; Pittet, M.J.; et al. The intestinal microbiota modulates the anticancer immune effects of cyclophosphamide. *Science* **2013**, *342*, 971–976. [CrossRef] [PubMed]
124. Liang, J.; Li, T.; Zhao, J.; Wang, C.; Sun, H. Current understanding of the human microbiome in glioma. *Front. Oncol.* **2022**, *12*, 781741. [CrossRef] [PubMed]
125. Iida, N.; Dzutsev, A.; Stewart, C.A.; Smith, L.; Bouladoux, N.; Weingarten, R.A.; Molina, D.A.; Salcedo, R.; Back, T.; Cramer, S.; et al. Commensal bacteria control cancer response to therapy by modulating the tumor microenvironment. *Science* **2013**, *342*, 967–970. [CrossRef] [PubMed]
126. Liu, Z.; Li, C.; Huang, M.; Tong, C.; Zhang, X.; Wang, L.; Peng, H.; Lan, P.; Zhang, P.; Huang, N.; et al. Positive regulatory effects of perioperative probiotic treatment on postoperative liver complications after colorectal liver metastases surgery: A double-center and double-blind randomized clinical trial. *BMC Gastroenterol.* **2015**, *15*, 34. [CrossRef]
127. Agarwal, S.; Sane, R.; Oberoi, R.; Ohlfest, J.R.; Elmquist, W.F. Delivery of molecularly targeted therapy to malignant glioma, a disease of the whole brain. *Expert. Rev. Mol. Med.* **2011**, *13*, e17. [CrossRef]
128. Ding, R.; Zhao, Z.; He, J.; Tao, Y.; Zhang, H.; Yuan, R.; Sun, K.; Shi, Y. Preparation, Drug Distribution, and In Vivo Evaluation of the Safety of Protein Corona Liposomes for Liraglutide Delivery. *Nanomaterials* **2023**, *13*, 540. [CrossRef]

biomedicines

MDPI

Case Report

Expanded Use of Vorasidenib in Non-Enhancing Recurrent CNS WHO Grade 3 Oligodendroglioma

Alexander S. Himstead [1], Jefferson W. Chen [1], Eleanor Chu [2], Mari A. Perez-Rosendahl [3], Michelle Zheng [4], Sherin Mathew [5] and Carlen A. Yuen [6,*]

1 Department of Neurological Surgery, University of California, Irvine, CA 92697, USA; ahimstea@hs.uci.edu (A.S.H.); jeffewc1@hs.uc.edu (J.W.C.)
2 Department of Radiological Sciences, University of California, Irvine, CA 92697, USA; eleanoc@hs.uci.edu
3 Department of Pathology & Laboratory Medicine, University of California, Irvine, CA 92697, USA; mperezro@hs.uci.edu
4 UC Irvine Charlie Dunlop School of Biological Sciences, University of California, Irvine, CA 92697, USA
5 Department of Research, University of California, Irvine, CA 92697, USA
6 Department of Neurology, Division of Neuro-Oncology, University of California, Irvine, CA 92697, USA
* Correspondence: carleny@hs.uci.edu; Tel.: +1-714-456-8000

Abstract: Background/Objectives: Anaplastic oligodendrogliomas (AOs) are central nervous system (CNS) World Health Organization (WHO) grade 3 gliomas characterized by isocitrate dehydrogenase (IDH) mutation (m)IDH and 1p/19q codeletion. AOs are typically treated with surgery and chemoradiation. However, chemoradiation can cause detrimental late neurocognitive morbidities and an accelerated disease course. The recently regulatory-approved vorasidenib, a brain-penetrating oral inhibitor of IDH1/2, has altered the treatment paradigm for recurrent/residual non-enhancing surgically resected CNS WHO grade 2 mIDH gliomas. Though vorasidenib can delay the time to chemoradiation for grade 2 gliomas, the implications for vorasidenib in non-grade 2 mIDH gliomas are not well understood. **Results:** We present a case of a 71-year-old male with a grade 3 non-enhancing oligodendroglioma successfully treated with vorasidenib with an 11% reduction in residual tumor volume. Vorasidenib was well tolerated in our patient with a mild elevation in his liver transaminases that resolved following a brief interruption in treatment. **Conclusions:** Our case suggests that vorasidenib may impart therapeutic benefits in this setting. This case illustrates the need for further investigation into these less commonly addressed scenarios and treatment strategies that extend beyond current guidelines.

Keywords: vorasidenib; anaplastic oligodendroglioma; isocitrate dehydrogenase; IDH inhibitor; glioma

1. Introduction

Anaplastic oligodendrogliomas (AOs) are central nervous system (CNS) World Health Organization (WHO) grade 3 gliomas characterized by isocitrate dehydrogenase mutations (mIDHs) and 1p/19q codeletion [1,2]. The diagnostic criteria for oligodendrogliomas have undergone multiple revisions with the integration of molecular criteria to improve upon diagnostic accuracy. However, the grading criteria in the current classification schema for oligodendrogliomas continues to predominantly rely upon histopathologic examination; the differentiating criterion between grade 2 and grade 3 oligodendrogliomas are the presence of conspicuous microvascular proliferation and/or 6 mitoses per 10 high-power field [3–11]. These criteria are subject to inter-rater variability, and accordingly, the reliability of these benchmarks as a predictor of patient outcome have been called into question [7,12–14]. To ameliorate this variability, molecular alterations, including homozygous loss of cyclin-dependent kinase inhibitor (CDKN)2A and mutations in phosphatase and tensin homolog (PTEN) and NOTCH1 have been investigated as adjunctive markers for risk stratification. Nevertheless, their prognostic role and clinical relevance are yet to be determined [15–17].

The distinction between grade 2 and grade 3 oligodendrogliomas carries therapeutic relevance. While maximal safe resection remains the initial treatment for oligodendrogliomas, the implications for adjuvant chemotherapy and radiation are reliant upon risk stratification [18–22]. To date, consensus has not been reached on the risk stratification criteria for oligodendrogliomas (Table 1). Various risk factors have been identified across multiple trials, including the European Organization for Research and Treatment of Cancer (EORTC) 228445, 228446, and Radiation Therapy Oncology Group (RTOG) 0424 trials. RTOG 9802 and other studies further emphasize the impact of tumor extent of resection (EOR) as a prognostic factor [23–28]. Consequently, there is a growing focus on residual tumor volume (RTV) as a principal prognostic factor [10,27,29,30].

Table 1. Variable criteria for risk stratification for oligodendrogliomas.

Study Title	Age	Lineage	Tumor Size	Tumor Location	Neurological Deficit	Risk
EORTC 22844/5	Age ≥ 40 years	Astrocytic	≥6 cm or crossing midline	NA	Preoperative deficit	Low risk: <3 Risk factors High risk: ≥3 Risk factors
EORTC 22033-26033	Age ≥ 40 years	Progressive disease	≥5 cm	Tumor crossing midline	Preoperative deficit	Low risk: <1 Risk Factor High risk: ≥1 Risk factor
RTOG 0424	Age ≥ 40 years	Astrocytic	≥6 cm	Tumor crossing midline	Preoperative deficit	Low risk: <3 Risk factors High risk: ≥3 Risk factors
RTOG 9802	Age ≥ 40 years OR Age ≥ 18 years with subtotal resection					Low risk: <1 Risk Factor High risk: ≥1 Risk factor

2. Detailed Case Description

Twenty-five years prior to presentation, a 71-year-old ambidextrous male presented to an outside hospital with syncope (Figure 1). He was incidentally found to have a left parietal non-enhancing mass. He underwent resection at a community hospital with a diagnosis of grade 2 oligodendroglioma. The EOR is unknown. He was monitored for 11 years with no evidence of recurrence (Figure 2A,B), and surveillance was discontinued.

At year 24, he presented to our institution for evaluation of right arm numbness. His neurological exam showed decreased upper-right extremity sensation to light touch. Magnetic resonance imaging (MRI) of the brain showed an interval increase in T2/FLAIR hyperintensity surrounding the resection cavity with no correlative enhancement (Figure 2C–F). A functional MRI showed left-sided language lateralization at Broca's area (Figure 3). During lip movement, there was overlap in activation of the left primary motor cortex with T2/FLAIR signal hyperintensity, but foot and hand movements were distant from the lesion. His clinical and radiographic progression warranted re-resection and tissue diagnosis to guide adjuvant therapy. A subtotal resection was achieved with approximately 2 cm of residual disease and an RTV of 45 cm^3 remaining in eloquent structures (arcuate fasciculus, superior longitudinal fasciculus).

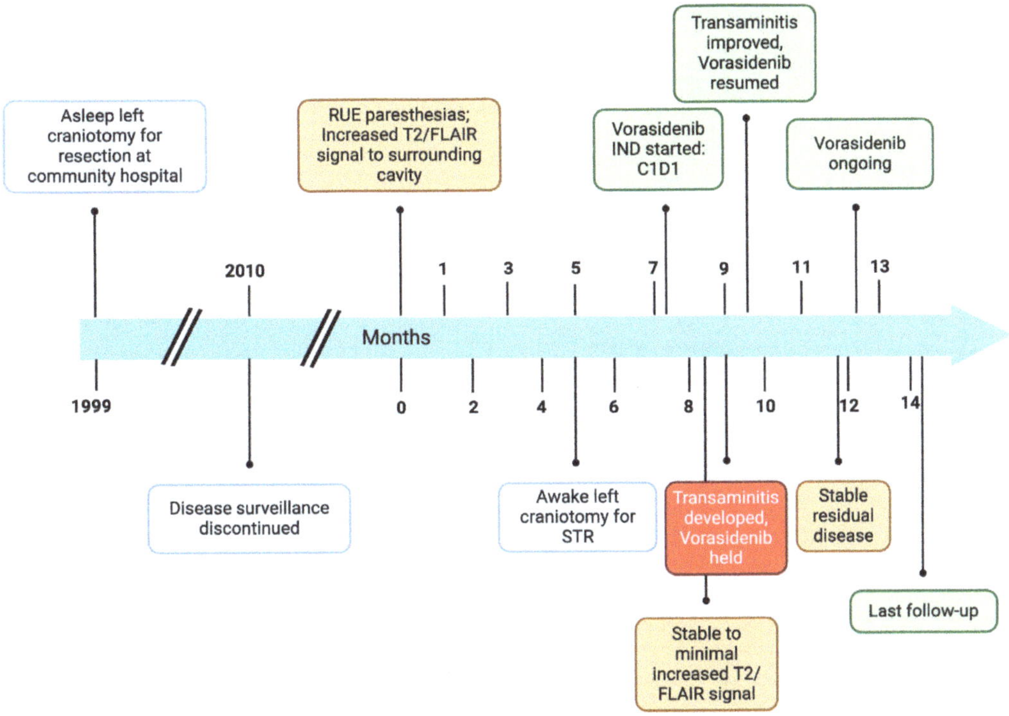

Figure 1. Patient disease course timeline. RUE = right upper extremity; STR = subtotal resection; IND = investigational new drug; FLAIR = fluid attenuated inversion recovery.

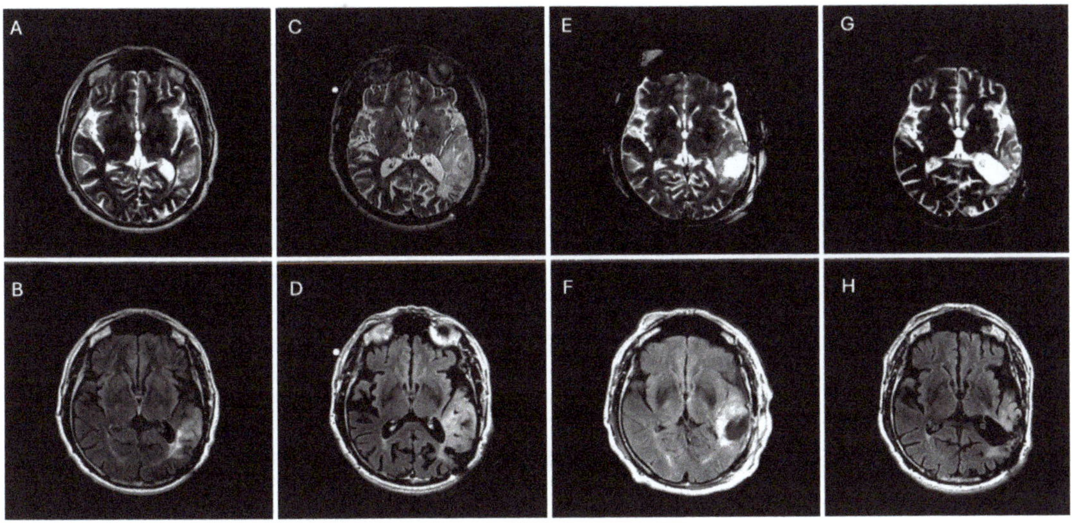

Figure 2. Axial T2 (top panels) and FLAIR (bottom panels) brain MRIs demonstrating an interval increase in left parietal–temporal T2/FLAIR-hyperintensity from 2017 (**A**,**B**) to 2024 (**C**,**D**) with subsequent surgical debulking (residual tumor volume 45 cm^3) (**E**,**F**) followed by 8 months of vorasidenib (residual tumor volume 40 cm^3) (**G**,**H**).

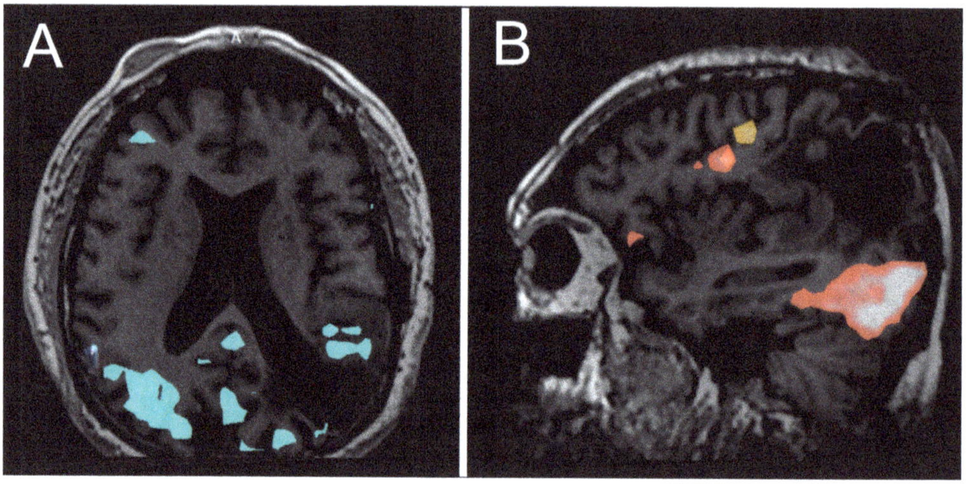

Figure 3. Functional MRI (fMRI) demonstrating areas of activation during lip movement (**A**), word production, and verb comprehension (**B**).

Pathology (reviewed independently by two board-certified, fellowship-trained neuropathologists) showed a widely infiltrative glioma with classic oligodendroglial morphology, including round to oval nuclei, perinuclear halos, and thin intervening capillaries (Figure 4A). High-grade features were also present (Figure 4B), characterized by markedly cellular areas with brisk mitotic activity (up to 10 mitoses in 10 high power fields). No necrosis or microvascular proliferation was seen. Immunohistochemistry demonstrated positivity for IDH1 R132H mutant protein and ATRX expression was retained in tumor nuclei. 1p/19q co-deletion was detected by fluorescence in situ hybridization (FISH) and Tempus xT 648 gene panel reported genomic variants in IDH1, TERT, CIC, and FUBP1, as expected for an oligodendroglioma. These findings yielded a final diagnosis of oligodendroglioma, IDH-mutant and 1p/19q-codeleted, CNS WHO grade 3.

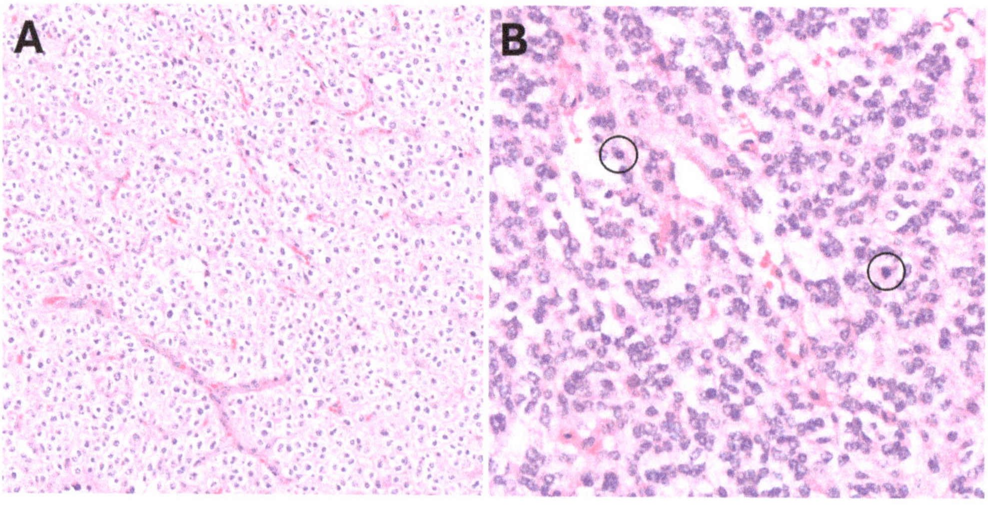

Figure 4. Classic oligodendroglial morphology, 200× (**A**). High-grade areas (**B**) showed brisk mitotic activity (circles) and hypercellularity, 400×.

The patient's postoperative course was uncomplicated. His mild right upper extremity weakness, paresthesia, and incoordination improved. Given his grade 3 tumor designation, chemoradiation versus vorasidenib was discussed. A consensus was reached at our multidisciplinary Neuro-Oncology Tumor Board to recommend vorasidenib. The patient decided to proceed with 40 mg of vorasidenib. Vorasidenib was well-tolerated, with the exception of asymptomatic transaminitis, which subsequently resolved spontaneously after a two-week treatment interruption. At 8-month follow-up, he remains clinically stable with radiographic findings of an 11% reduction in RTV to 40 cm^3 (Figure 2G,H).

3. Discussion

The management of oligodendrogliomas following surgery is influenced by several key factors, including age, tumor grade, and EOR. Together, these components stratify the risk of recurrence (Table 1). The median age of diagnosis for oligodendrogliomas is 49.5 years of age [17], which corroborates with our patient's age of initial diagnosis at 47 years. The role of age as a prognostic indicator for oligodendrogliomas remains a matter of debate with a historical threshold of $\geq$40 years as the benchmark for high-risk classification in grade 2 gliomas [10]. Recent studies suggest that an older age cutoff (45, >50, or $\geq$60) is a more reliable indicator for identifying high-risk LGG patients [8,16,31]. Based on RTOG 9802 and EORTC 22033–26033 criteria, our patient is categorized as high-risk on the basis of his age at diagnosis. On the contrary, he is stratified to a low-risk classification under the EORTC 22844/5 and RTOG 0424 criteria (oligodendroglioma lineage, and absence of pre-operative neurological deficit, unknown preoperative tumor diameter) [10,24,28,32–35].

Our patient defied survival expectations with a disease trajectory that continues over 24 years from diagnosis, and he remains alive at time of publication. Under the "wait-and-see" strategy, the anticipated median OS is 13.2–14.2 years with a median PFS of 3.4 years for grade 2 LGGs [10,33]. His unexpected longevity may stem from the persistent lack of enhancement of his tumor at recurrence, which may indicate a less aggressive glioma compared to an enhancing glioma [36]. Despite historical controversy regarding surgical management of LGGs, early maximal safe resection is now favored over the watchful waiting approach [27,37–40]. In our patient, there was minimal residual tumor observed on his 10-year MRI, suggesting an initial near-total or gross-total resection. Early and maximal surgery offers three related benefits of reducing malignant transformation rate, reducing recurrence rate, and improving OS [23,29,30,39–41]. Results from a 20-year investigation conducted by Hervey-Jumper et al. suggest that $\geq$75% EOR positively influences survival in these tumors [42]. Our patient's tumor also exhibited an insidious growth pattern. Based on his available imaging, his estimated growth rate was 0.27 cm^3 per month, or a volume of diametric expansion (VDE) of 0.87 mm per year. VDE, the rate of change in tumor diameter over time, is an independent predictor of outcome in LGGs [43–45]. This insidious growth rate may have contributed to the protracted quiescent period prior to his tumor's malignant transformation. Gozé et al. showed that LGGs with a VDE of < 8 mm/year are less likely to undergo malignant transformation compared to LGGs with accelerated growth rates (36.1% vs. 73.9%, respectively) and exhibit prolonged time to malignant transformation (71.2 vs. 47.1 months, $p < 0.001$) [43]. Lastly, our patient had a low RTV following his initial surgery. The benefit of a smaller RTV is substantiated in several studies and associated with a decreased risk of recurrence and improved OS [29,30]. RTV > 10–15 cm^3 is associated with earlier progression and decreased survival [29,30]. Following his second resection, our patient's RTV was 45 cm^3 with a 2 cm diameter owing to tumor in eloquent language cortex.

At the time of initial diagnosis, our patient's oligodendroglioma diagnosis was established based on the WHO 1993 grading criteria, which were exclusively based on histomorphology. Though molecular analyses were not obtained for our patient's initial tumor, molecular analyses obtained from his re-resection confirmed that his tumor harbors the canonical IDH1-R132H and codeletion of 1p/19q. Further, our patient's tumor underwent malignant degeneration to grade 3 with findings of brisk mitotic activity, though microvascular proliferation and necrosis were absent and thus fulfilling only one criterion for a grade 3 designation [14]. Our patient's tumor harbored mutations in TERT, FUBP1, and CIC, which are common alterations in oligodendroglioma, but not clinically relevant [46,47]. A rare finding in oligodendrogliomas, CDKN2A/B is the sole molecular marker to distinguish grade 2 from grade 3 oligodendrogliomas [17] but was not present in our patient's tumor. Accordingly, our patient's tumor met the criteria for a grade 3 designation based on a solitary histologic feature alone.

Our patient would have been ineligible for the INDIGO trial and is ineligible for the regulatory-approved drug based on his tumor's grade 3 designation. At the time of recurrence, our patient was elderly, his tumor malignantly transformed, and he had residual tumor. Taken together, adjuvant therapy was warranted. In view of the well-documented grade 3 and 4 hematologic toxicities associated with chemoradiation, we reasoned that vorasidenib was the optimal therapy for our patient due to its low toxicity profile, his non-enhancing residual disease, and a grade 3 determination based on brisk mitotic activity alone in the absence of microvascular proliferation, necrosis, and intact CDKN2A/B. His tumor is conceivably an intermediate-risk oligodendroglioma, a proposed new category of grade 3 oligodendrogliomas [48]. On these bases, vorasidenib was favored over sequential chemoradiation with the goal of halting disease progression and prolonging the time to his next intervention. Arguably, the majority of cases in the INDIGO trial were high-risk gliomas warranting chemoradiation [48]. However, despite this high-risk assignment, PFS was improved in the vorasidenib group [49].

At last follow-up, our patient was clinically stable with radiographic improvement of an 11% reduction in RTV (40 cm^3). Although a defined RTV cutoff for benefit with maintenance vorasidenib has yet to be determined, our case suggests that vorasidenib has a beneficial effect despite a substantial RTV. He continues to tolerate treatment well. His transient grade 1 liver transaminase elevation resolved with a brief interruption in treatment, which can be observed in 9.6% of patients who develop $\geq$ grade 3 elevated alanine aminotransferase [49]. Limited evidence suggests that IDHi responders lack NOTCH1 mutations [50]. Though our patient's tumor lacks NOTCH1 mutations, it is unclear if this is linked to his response to vorasidenib. Vorasidenib is FDA indicated for use in grade 2 oligodendroglioma but may have greater potential, including in non-enhancing grade 3 oligodendrogliomas as substantiated by our case.

We acknowledge that the limitations of this study are the nature of a case report as a single case is not generalizable to all grade 3 oligodendrogliomas. Though a 11% reduction in RTV was demonstrated in our case, we could not evaluate for long-term response given the short follow-up. Subsequent analyses from the INDIGO trial demonstrated decreased tumor growth rate as measured by percent change in volume in 6-month intervals [49]. Given our patient's prolonged disease course, and initial diagnosis during the pre-molecular era, molecular analysis was not performed for the patient's initial tumor tissue. Moreover, DNA methylation profiling was not performed on his tumor tissue, which may have been informative to identify the favorable glioma-CpG island (G-CIMP)-high methylated phenotype from a less favorable G-CIMP-low phenotype [51–53]. Lastly, we could not confirm the initial RTV nor determine his initial preoperative VDE given that he was under active surveillance at an outside institution with irregular monitoring.

Future investigations should be directed at recognition of additional cohorts of LGG patients who may benefit from vorasidenib and identifying the utility of IDHis in non-grade

2 and enhancing gliomas. Accordingly, investigations with safusidenib (DS-1001) and olutasidenib, both of which are oral brain-penetrant IDH inhibitors with activity in enhancing gliomas, are underway. Safusidenib is a selective IDH R132 inhibitor that has explicitly demonstrated benefit in an enhancing grade 3 oligodendroglioma [54]. This is a notable finding, given that there are differences in outcome with vorasidenib in canonical mIDH1 R132H gliomas compared to non-canonical mIDH gliomas [55]. In patients treated with vorasidenib, it is unknown if IDH inhibition and alteration of this pathway will modify the tumor's biology and if this inhibition will confer resistance to future chemoradiation [48]. Conversely, another open area of investigation is the role of maintenance vorasidenib in patients previously treated with chemoradiation. Forthcoming studies should also be directed at identifying epigenetic changes within additional affected signaling pathways, such as RB and PI3K [56]. These studies may detect actionable targets for use in combinatorial therapy with vorasidenib [56,57]. As our understanding of IDH-mutant gliomas tumorigenesis evolve, therapies will also continue to advance.

4. Conclusions

The grading criteria for oligodendrogliomas is predominantly based on subjective histopathologic features. Oligodendrogliomas may be classified as grade 3 based on brisk mitotic activity alone. We present the successful use of vorasidenib in a novel clinical context of an individual with a recurrent malignantly transformed chemoradiation-naïve oligodendroglioma with an acceptable toxicity profile. Vorasidenib may have indications that extend beyond current guidelines.

Author Contributions: C.A.Y.—study concept, data collection, analysis, interpretation, manuscript drafting, revision, and final approval. A.S.H.—data collection, analysis, interpretation, manuscript drafting, revision, and final approval. J.W.C.—data analysis, interpretation, and manuscript final approval. E.C.—data collection, analysis, interpretation, and manuscript final approval. M.A.P.-R.—data collection, analysis, interpretation, and manuscript final approval. M.Z.—data collection and final approval. S.M.—data collection and final approval. All authors have read and agreed to the published version of the manuscript.

Funding: This research received no external funding.

Institutional Review Board Statement: This study was conducted in accordance with the Declaration of Helsinki, and approved by the University of California, Irvine, Institutional Review Board.

Informed Consent Statement: Informed consent was obtained from the subject involved in the study.

Data Availability Statement: The data presented in this study are available on request from the corresponding author due to privacy and ethical restrictions.

Acknowledgments: We would like to thank Servier for their support in production of this work.

Conflicts of Interest: The authors declare no conflicts of interest.

Abbreviations

2-HG	2-hydroxyglutarate
AO	anaplastic oligodendroglioma
CDKN	cyclin-dependent kinase inhibitor
CNS	central nervous system
EOR	extent of resection
EORTC	European Organization for Research and Treatment of Cancer
FLAIR	fluid attenuated inversion recovery
fMRI	functional MRI

G-CIMP	glioma-CpG island
IDH	isocitrate dehydrogenase
IDHis	isocitrate dehydrogenase inhibitors
IND	investigational new drug
LGG	low-grade glioma
mIDH	isocitrate dehydrogenase mutations
MRI	magnetic resonance imaging
OS	overall survival
PCV	procarbazine, CCNU, and vincristine
PFS	progression-free survival
PTEN	phosphatase and tensin homolog
RTOG	Radiation Therapy Oncology Group
RTV	residual tumor volume
RUE	right upper extremity
STR	subtotal resection
TMZ	temozolomide
VDE	volume of diametric expansion
WHO	World Health Organization

References

1. Ostrom, Q.T.; Price, M.; Neff, C.; Cioffi, G.; A Waite, K.; Kruchko, C.; Barnholtz-Sloan, J.S. CBTRUS Statistical Report: Primary Brain and Other Central Nervous System Tumors Diagnosed in the United States in 2016–2020. *Neuro-Oncol.* **2023**, *25*, iv1–iv99. [CrossRef]
2. Jaeckle, K.A.; Ballman, K.V.; Van Den Bent, M.; Giannini, C.; Galanis, E.; Brown, P.D.; Jenkins, R.B.; Cairncross, J.G.; Wick, W.; Weller, M.; et al. CODEL: Phase III study of RT, RT + TMZ, or TMZ for newly diagnosed 1p/19q codeleted oligodendroglioma. Analysis from the initial study design. *Neuro-Oncol.* **2021**, *23*, 457–467. [CrossRef]
3. Aboud, O.; Shah, R.; Vera, E.; Burton, E.; Theeler, B.; Wu, J.; Boris, L.; Quezado, M.; Reyes, J.; Wall, K.; et al. Challenges of imaging interpretation to predict oligodendroglioma grade: A report from the Neuro-Oncology Branch. *CNS Oncol.* **2022**, *11*, CNS83. [CrossRef]
4. Malta, T.M.; Sabedot, T.S.; Morosini, N.S.; Datta, I.; Garofano, L.; Vallentgoed, W.; Varn, F.S.; Aldape, K.; D'Angelo, F.; Bakas, S.; et al. The Epigenetic Evolution of Glioma Is Determined by the IDH1 Mutation Status and Treatment Regimen. *Cancer Res.* **2024**, *84*, 741–756. [CrossRef] [PubMed]
5. Cimino, P.J.; Zager, M.; McFerrin, L.; Wirsching, H.G.; Bolouri, H.; Hentschel, B.; von Deimling, A.; Jones, D.; Reifenberger, G.; Holland, E.C.; et al. Multidimensional scaling of diffuse gliomas: Application to the 2016 World Health Organization classification system with prognostically relevant molecular subtype discovery. *Acta Neuropathol. Commun.* **2017**, *5*, 39. [CrossRef]
6. Dubbink, H.J.; Atmodimedjo, P.N.; Kros, J.M.; French, P.J.; Sanson, M.; Idbaih, A.; Wesseling, P.; Enting, R.; Spliet, W.; Tijssen, C.; et al. Molecular classification of anaplastic oligodendroglioma using next-generation sequencing: A report of the prospective randomized EORTC Brain Tumor Group 26951 phase III trial. *Neuro-Oncol.* **2016**, *18*, 388–400. [CrossRef] [PubMed]
7. Olar, A.; Wani, K.M.; Alfaro-Munoz, K.D.; Heathcock, L.E.; van Thuijl, H.F.; Gilbert, M.R.; Armstrong, T.S.; Sulman, E.P.; Cahill, D.P.; Vera-Bolanos, E.; et al. IDH mutation status and role of WHO grade and mitotic index in overall survival in grade II-III diffuse gliomas. *Acta Neuropathol.* **2015**, *129*, 585–596. [CrossRef] [PubMed]
8. Carstam, L.; Latini, F.; Solheim, O.; Bartek, J.; Pedersen, L.K.; Zetterling, M.; Beniaminov, S.; Sjåvik, K.; Ryttlefors, M.; Jensdottir, M.; et al. Long-term follow up of patients with WHO grade 2 oligodendroglioma. *J. Neuro-Oncol.* **2023**, *164*, 65–74. [CrossRef]
9. van den Bent, M.J. Interobserver variation of the histopathological diagnosis in clinical trials on glioma: A clinician's perspective. *Acta Neuropathol.* **2010**, *120*, 297–304. [CrossRef] [PubMed]
10. van den Bent, M.J.; French, P.J.; Brat, D.; Tonn, J.C.; Touat, M.; Ellingson, B.M.; Young, R.J.; Pallud, J.; von Deimling, A.; Sahm, F.; et al. The biological significance of tumor grade, age, enhancement and extent of resection in IDH mutant gliomas: How should they inform treatment decision in the era of IDH inhibitors? *Neuro-Oncol.* **2024**, *26*, 1805–1822. [CrossRef] [PubMed]
11. Schaff, L.R.; Lassman, A.B. Indications for Treatment: Is Observation or Chemotherapy Alone a Reasonable Approach in the Management of Low-Grade Gliomas? *Semin. Radiat. Oncol.* **2015**, *25*, 203–209. [CrossRef] [PubMed]
12. Figarella-Branger, D.; Mokhtari, K.; Dehais, C.; Jouvet, A.; Uro-Coste, E.; Colin, C.; Carpentier, C.; Forest, F.; Maurage, C.-A.; Vignaud, J.-M.; et al. Mitotic index, microvascular proliferation, and necrosis define 3 groups of 1p/19q codeleted anaplastic oligodendrogliomas associated with different genomic alterations. *Neuro-Oncol.* **2014**, *16*, 1244–1254. [CrossRef] [PubMed]

13. Louis, D.N.; Ohgaki, H.; Wiestler, O.D.; Cavenee, W.K. *WHO Classification of Tumours of the Central Nervous System*, 4th ed.; International Agency for Research on Cancer: Lyon, France, 2016.
14. Giannini, C.; Scheithauer, B.W.; Weaver, A.L.; Burger, P.C.; Kros, J.M.; Mork, S.; Graeber, M.B.; Bauserman, S.; Buckner, J.C.; Altermatt, H.; et al. Oligodendrogliomas: Reproducibility and prognostic value of histologic diagnosis and grading. *J. Neuropathol. Exp. Neurol.* **2001**, *60*, 248–262. [CrossRef] [PubMed]
15. Wijnenga, M.M.J.; French, P.J.; Dubbink, H.J.; Dinjens, W.N.M.; Atmodimedjo, P.N.; Kros, J.M.; Fleischeuer, R.; Dirven, C.M.F.; Vincent, A.J.P.E.; Van Den Bent, M.J. Prognostic relevance of mutations and copy number alterations assessed with targeted next generation sequencing in IDH mutant grade II glioma. *J. Neuro-Oncol.* **2018**, *139*, 349–357. [CrossRef]
16. Aoki, K.; Nakamura, H.; Suzuki, H.; Matsuo, K.; Kataoka, K.; Shimamura, T.; Motomura, K.; Ohka, F.; Shiina, S.; Yamamoto, T.; et al. Prognostic relevance of genetic alterations in diffuse lower-grade gliomas. *Neuro-Oncol.* **2018**, *20*, 66–77. [CrossRef] [PubMed]
17. Appay, R.; Dehais, C.; Maurage, C.A.; Alentorn, A.; Carpentier, C.; Colin, C.; Ducray, F.; Ducray, F.; Idbaih, A.; Figarella-Branger, D.; et al. CDKN2A homozygous deletion is a strong adverse prognosis factor in diffuse malignant IDH-mutant gliomas. *Neuro-Oncol.* **2019**, *21*, 1519–1528. [CrossRef]
18. Lassman, A.B.; Hoang-Xuan, K.; Polley, M.-Y.C.; Brandes, A.A.; Cairncross, J.G.; Kros, J.M.; Ashby, L.S.; Taphoorn, M.J.; Souhami, L.; Dinjens, W.N.; et al. Joint Final Report of EORTC 26951 and RTOG 9402: Phase III Trials With Procarbazine, Lomustine, and Vincristine Chemotherapy for Anaplastic Oligodendroglial Tumors. *J. Clin. Oncol.* **2022**, *40*, 2539–2545. [CrossRef]
19. Van Den Bent, M.J.; Brandes, A.A.; Taphoorn, M.J.; Kros, J.M.; Kouwenhoven, M.C.; Delattre, J.Y.; Bernsen, H.J.J.A.; Frenay, M.; Tijssen, C.C.; Hoang-Xuan, K.; et al. Adjuvant procarbazine, lomustine, and vincristine chemotherapy in newly diagnosed anaplastic oligodendroglioma: Long-term follow-up of EORTC brain tumor group study 26951. *J. Clin. Oncol.* **2013**, *31*, 344–350. [CrossRef]
20. Cairncross, G.; Wang, M.; Shaw, E.; Jenkins, R.; Brachman, D.; Buckner, J.; Fink, K.; Souhami, L.; Laperriere, N.; Mehta, M.; et al. Phase III trial of chemoradiotherapy for anaplastic oligodendroglioma: Long-term results of RTOG 9402. *J. Clin. Oncol.* **2013**, *31*, 337–343. [CrossRef]
21. Weller, M.; Van Den Bent, M.; Tonn, J.C.; Stupp, R.; Preusser, M.; Cohen-Jonathan-Moyal, E.; Henriksson, R.; Le Rhun, E.; Balana, C.; Wick, W.; et al. European Association for Neuro-Oncology (EANO) guideline on the diagnosis and treatment of adult astrocytic and oligodendroglial gliomas. *Lancet Oncol.* **2017**, *18*, e315–e329. [CrossRef]
22. Schiff, D.; Van den Bent, M.; Vogelbaum, M.A.; Wick, W.; Miller, C.R.; Taphoorn, M.; Pope, W.; Brown, P.D.; Platten, M.; Jalali, R.; et al. Recent developments and future directions in adult lower-grade gliomas: Society for Neuro-Oncology (SNO) and European Association of Neuro-Oncology (EANO) consensus. *Neuro-Oncol.* **2019**, *21*, 837–853. [CrossRef]
23. Shaw, E.G.; Berkey, B.; Coons, S.W.; Bullard, D.; Brachman, D.; Buckner, J.C.; Stelzer, K.J.; Barger, G.R.; Brown, P.D.; Gilbert, M.R.; et al. Recurrence following neurosurgeon-determined gross-total resection of adult supratentorial low-grade glioma: Results of a prospective clinical trial. *J. Neurosurg.* **2008**, *109*, 835–841. [CrossRef] [PubMed]
24. Baumert, B.G.; Hegi, M.E.; van den Bent, M.J.; von Deimling, A.; Gorlia, T.; Hoang-Xuan, K.; Brandes, A.A.; Kantor, G.; Taphoorn, M.J.B.; Ben Hassel, M.; et al. Temozolomide chemotherapy versus radiotherapy in high-risk low-grade glioma (EORTC 22033-26033): A randomised, open-label, phase 3 intergroup study. *Lancet Oncol.* **2016**, *17*, 1521–1532. [CrossRef]
25. Pignatti, F.; Van Den Bent, M.; Curran, D.; Debruyne, C.; Sylvester, R.; Therasse, P.; Afra, D.; Cornu, P.; Bolla, M.; Vecht, C.; et al. Prognostic factors for survival in adult patients with cerebral low-grade glioma. *J. Clin. Oncol.* **2002**, *20*, 2076–2084. [CrossRef] [PubMed]
26. Daniels, T.B.; Brown, P.D.; Felten, S.J.; Wu, W.; Buckner, J.C.; Arusell, R.M.; Curran, W.J.; Abrams, R.A.; Schiff, D.; Shaw, E.G. Validation of EORTC prognostic factors for adults with low-grade glioma: A report using intergroup 86-72-51. *Int. J. Radiat. Oncol. Biol. Phys.* **2011**, *81*, 218–224. [CrossRef] [PubMed]
27. Smith, J.S.; Chang, E.F.; Lamborn, K.R.; Chang, S.M.; Prados, M.D.; Cha, S.; Tihan, T.; VandenBerg, S.; McDermott, M.W.; Berger, M.S. Role of extent of resection in the long-term outcome of low-grade hemispheric gliomas. *J. Clin. Oncol.* **2008**, *26*, 1338–1345. [CrossRef]
28. Buckner, J.C.; Shaw, E.G.; Pugh, S.L.; Chakravarti, A.; Gilbert, M.R.; Barger, G.R.; Coons, S.; Ricci, P.; Bullard, D.; Brown, P.D.; et al. Radiation plus Procarbazine, CCNU, and Vincristine in Low-Grade Glioma. *N. Engl. J. Med.* **2016**, *374*, 1344–1355. [CrossRef]
29. Roelz, R.; Strohmaier, D.; Jabbarli, R.; Kraeutle, R.; Egger, K.; Coenen, V.A.; Weyerbrock, A.; Reinacher, P.C. Residual Tumor Volume as Best Outcome Predictor in Low Grade Glioma - A Nine-Years Near-Randomized Survey of Surgery vs. *Biopsy. Sci. Rep.* **2016**, *6*, 32286. [CrossRef]
30. Berger, M.S.; Deliganis, A.V.; Dobbins, J.; Keles, G.E. The effect of extent of resection on recurrence in patients with low grade cerebral hemisphere gliomas. *Cancer* **1994**, *74*, 1784–1791. [CrossRef]
31. Reuss, D.E.; Mamatjan, Y.; Schrimpf, D.; Capper, D.; Hovestadt, V.; Kratz, A.; Sahm, F.; Koelsche, C.; Korshunov, A.; von Deimling, A.; et al. IDH mutant diffuse and anaplastic astrocytomas have similar age at presentation little difference and in survival: A grading problem for, W.H.O. *Acta Neuropathol.* **2015**, *129*, 867–873. [CrossRef]

32. Fisher, B.J.; Hu, C.; Macdonald, D.R.; Lesser, G.J.; Coons, S.W.; Brachman, D.G.; Ryu, S.; Bahary, J.-P.; Chakravarti, A.; Mehta, M.; et al. Phase 2 study of temozolomide-based chemoradiation therapy for high-risk low-grade gliomas: Preliminary results of Radiation Therapy Oncology Group 0424. *Int. J. Radiat. Oncol. Biol. Phys.* **2015**, *91*, 497–504. [CrossRef]
33. Van den Bent, M.J.; Afra, D.; De Witte, O.; Hassel, M.B.; Schraub, S.; Hoang-Xuan, K.; Malmström, P.-O.; Collette, L.; Piérart, M.; Karim, A.B.M.F.; et al. Long-term efficacy of early versus delayed radiotherapy for low-grade astrocytoma and oligodendroglioma in adults: The EORTC 22845 randomised trial. *Lancet* **2005**, *366*, 985–990. [CrossRef]
34. Karim, A.B.; Maat, B.; Hatlevoll, R.; Menten, J.; Rutten, E.H.; Thomas, D.G.; Mascarenhas, F.; Horiot, J.C.; Parvinen, L.M.; van Reijn, M.; et al. A randomized trial on dose-response in radiation therapy of low-grade cerebral glioma: European Organization for Research and Treatment of Cancer (EORTC) Study 22844. *Int. J. Radiat. Oncol. Biol. Phys.* **1996**, *36*, 549–556. [CrossRef] [PubMed]
35. Bell, E.H.; Zhang, P.; Shaw, E.G.; Buckner, J.C.; Barger, G.R.; Bullard, D.E.; Mehta, M.P.; Gilbert, M.R.; Brown, P.D.; Stelzer, K.J.; et al. Comprehensive Genomic Analysis in NRG Oncology/RTOG 9802: A Phase III Trial of Radiation Versus Radiation Plus Procarbazine, Lomustine (CCNU), and Vincristine in High-Risk Low-Grade Glioma. *J. Clin. Oncol.* **2020**, *38*, 3407–3417. [CrossRef]
36. Suchorska, B.; Schüller, U.; Biczok, A.; Lenski, M.; Albert, N.L.; Giese, A.; Kreth, F.-W.; Ertl-Wagner, B.; Tonn, J.-C.; Ingrisch, M. Contrast enhancement is a prognostic factor in IDH1/2 mutant, but not in wild-type WHO grade II/III glioma as confirmed by machine learning. *Eur. J. Cancer* **2019**, *107*, 15–27. [CrossRef]
37. Chaichana, K.L.; McGirt, M.J.; Laterra, J.; Olivi, A.; Quiñones-Hinojosa, A. Recurrence and malignant degeneration after resection of adult hemispheric low-grade gliomas. *J. Neurosurg.* **2010**, *112*, 10–17. [CrossRef] [PubMed]
38. Weller, M.; van den Bent, M.; Preusser, M.; Le Rhun, E.; Tonn, J.C.; Minniti, G.; Bendszus, M.; Balana, C.; Chinot, O.; Wick, W.; et al. EANO guidelines on the diagnosis and treatment of diffuse gliomas of adulthood. *Nat. Rev. Clin. Oncol.* **2021**, *18*, 170–186. [CrossRef]
39. Jakola, A.S.; Myrmel, K.S.; Kloster, R.; Torp, S.H.; Lindal, S.; Unsgñrd, G.; Solheim, O. Comparison of a strategy favoring early surgical resection vs a strategy favoring watchful waiting in low-grade gliomas. *JAMA* **2012**, *308*, 1881–1888. [CrossRef] [PubMed]
40. McGirt, M.J.; Chaichana, K.L.; Attenello, F.J.; Weingart, J.D.; Than, K.; Burger, P.C.; Olivi, A.; Brem, H.; Quinoñes-Hinojosa, A. Extent of surgical resection is independently associated with survival in patients with hemispheric infiltrating low-grade gliomas. *Neurosurgery* **2008**, *63*, 700–707, Author reply 7–8. [CrossRef] [PubMed]
41. Capelle, L.; Fontaine, D.; Mandonnet, E.; Taillandier, L.; Golmard, J.L.; Bauchet, L.; Pallud, J.; Peruzzi, P.; Guyotat, J.; Duffau, H.; et al. Spontaneous and therapeutic prognostic factors in adult hemispheric World Health Organization Grade II gliomas: A series of 1097 cases: Clinical article. *J. Neurosurg.* **2013**, *118*, 1157–1168. [CrossRef] [PubMed]
42. Hervey-Jumper, S.L.; Zhang, Y.; Phillips, J.J.; Morshed, R.A.; Young, J.S.; McCoy, L.; Lafontaine, M.; Luks, T.; Ammanuel, S.; Kakaizada, S.; et al. Interactive Effects of Molecular, Therapeutic, and Patient Factors on Outcome of Diffuse Low-Grade Glioma. *J. Clin. Oncol.* **2023**, *41*, 2029–2042. [CrossRef]
43. Gozé, C.; Blonski, M.; Le Maistre, G.; Bauchet, L.; Dezamis, E.; Page, P.; Varlet, P.; Capelle, L.; Devaux, B.; Pallud, J.; et al. Imaging growth and isocitrate dehydrogenase 1 mutation are independent predictors for diffuse low-grade gliomas. *Neuro-Oncol.* **2014**, *16*, 1100–1109. [CrossRef]
44. Pallud, J.; Blonski, M.; Mandonnet, E.; Audureau, E.; Fontaine, D.; Sanai, N.; Bauchet, L.; Peruzzi, P.; Frénay, M.; Colin, P.; et al. Velocity of tumor spontaneous expansion predicts long-term outcomes for diffuse low-grade gliomas. *Neuro-Oncol.* **2013**, *15*, 595–606. [CrossRef] [PubMed]
45. Pallud, J.; Taillandier, L.; Capelle, L.; Fontaine, D.; Peyre, M.; Ducray, F.; Matthieu, P.; François, D.; Hugues, D.; Mandonnet, E.; et al. Quantitative morphological magnetic resonance imaging follow-up of low-grade glioma: A plea for systematic measurement of growth rates. *Neurosurgery* **2012**, *71*, 729–739; Discussion 39–40. [CrossRef] [PubMed]
46. Baumgarten, P.; Harter, P.N.; Tönjes, M.; Capper, D.; Blank, A.E.; Sahm, F.; von Deimling, A.; Kolluru, V.; Schwamb, B.; Mittelbronn, M.; et al. Loss of FUBP1 expression in gliomas predicts FUBP1 mutation and is associated with oligodendroglial differentiation, IDH1 mutation and 1p/19q loss of heterozygosity. *Neuropathol. Appl. Neurobiol.* **2014**, *40*, 205–216. [CrossRef] [PubMed]
47. Cancer Genome Atlas Research Network; Brat, D.J.; Verhaak, R.G.; Aldape, K.D.; Yung, W.K.; Salama, S.R.; Cooper, L.A.D.; Rheinbay, E.; Miller, C.R.; Vitucci, M.; et al. Comprehensive, Integrative Genomic Analysis of Diffuse Lower-Grade Gliomas. *N. Engl. J. Med.* **2015**, *372*, 2481–2498. [PubMed]
48. Dipasquale, A.; Franceschi, E.; Lombardi, G.; Simonelli, M. Vorasidenib in IDH mutant WHO grade 2 gliomas: Time to stop sitting on the fence? *Neuro-Oncol. Adv.* **2024**, *6*, vdae003. [CrossRef] [PubMed]
49. Mellinghoff, I.K.; van den Bent, M.J.; Blumenthal, D.T.; Touat, M.; Peters, K.B.; Clarke, J.; Mendez, J.; Yust-Katz, S.; Welsh, L.; Mason, W.P.; et al. Vorasidenib in IDH1- or IDH2-Mutant Low-Grade Glioma. *N. Engl. J. Med.* **2023**, *389*, 589–601. [CrossRef]
50. Spitzer, A.; Gritsch, S.; Nomura, M.; Jucht, A.; Fortin, J.; Raviram, R.; Weisman, H.R.; Castro, L.N.G.; Druck, N.; Chanoch-Myers, R.; et al. Mutant IDH inhibitors induce lineage differentiation in IDH-mutant oligodendroglioma. *Cancer Cell* **2024**, *42*, 904–914.e9. [CrossRef] [PubMed]

51. Shirahata, M.; Ono, T.; Stichel, D.; Schrimpf, D.; Reuss, D.E.; Sahm, F.; Koelsche, C.; Wefers, A.; Reinhardt, A.; Huang, K.; et al. Novel, improved grading system(s) for IDH-mutant astrocytic gliomas. *Acta Neuropathol.* **2018**, *136*, 153–166. [CrossRef]
52. de Souza, C.F.; Sabedot, T.S.; Malta, T.M.; Stetson, L.; Morozova, O.; Sokolov, A.; Laird, P.W.; Wiznerowicz, M.; Iavarone, A.; Snyder, J.; et al. A Distinct DNA Methylation Shift in a Subset of Glioma CpG Island Methylator Phenotypes during Tumor Recurrence. *Cell Rep.* **2018**, *23*, 637–651. [CrossRef] [PubMed]
53. Malta, T.M.; de Souza, C.F.; Sabedot, T.S.; Silva, T.C.; Mosella, M.S.; Kalkanis, S.N.; Snyder, J.; Castro, A.V.B.; Noushmehr, H. Glioma CpG island methylator phenotype (G-CIMP): Biological and clinical implications. *Neuro-Oncol.* **2018**, *20*, 608–620. [CrossRef] [PubMed]
54. Natsume, A.; Arakawa, Y.; Narita, Y.; Sugiyama, K.; Hata, N.; Muragaki, Y.; Shinojima, N.; Kumabe, T.; Saito, R.; Motomura, K.; et al. The first-in-human phase I study of a brain-penetrant mutant IDH1 inhibitor DS-1001 in patients with recurrent or progressive IDH1-mutant gliomas. *Neuro-Oncol.* **2023**, *25*, 326–336. [CrossRef]
55. Tesileanu, C.M.S.; Vallentgoed, W.R.; Sanson, M.; Taal, W.; Clement, P.M.; Wick, W.; Brandes, A.A.; Baurain, J.F.; Chinot, O.L.; French, P.J.; et al. Non-IDH1-R132H IDH1/2 mutations are associated with increased DNA methylation and improved survival in astrocytomas, compared to IDH1-R132H mutations. *Acta Neuropathol.* **2021**, *141*, 945–957. [CrossRef] [PubMed]
56. Tesileanu, C.M.S.; Vallentgoed, W.R.; French, P.J.; van den Bent, M.J. Molecular markers related to patient outcome in patients with IDH-mutant astrocytomas grade 2 to 4: A systematic review. *Eur. J. Cancer* **2022**, *175*, 214–223. [CrossRef] [PubMed]
57. Montesinos-Rongen, M.; Schmitz, R.; Brunn, A.; Gesk, S.; Richter, J.; Hong, K.; Wiestler, O.D.; Siebert, R.; Küppers, R.; Deckert, M. Mutations of CARD11 but not TNFAIP3 may activate the NF-kappaB pathway in primary CNS lymphoma. *Acta Neuropathol.* **2010**, *120*, 529–535. [CrossRef] [PubMed]

biomedicines

MDPI

Review

The Role of HDAC6 in Glioblastoma Multiforme: A New Avenue to Therapeutic Interventions?

Francesco Spallotta [1,2] and Barbara Illi [3,*]

1 Department of Biology and Biotechnology Charles Darwin, Sapienza University, 00185 Rome, Italy; francesco.spallotta@uniroma1.it
2 Istituto Pasteur Italia-Fondazione Cenci Bolognetti, Sapienza University, 00185 Rome, Italy
3 Institute of Molecular Biology and Pathology, National Research Council (IBPM-CNR), 00185 Rome, Italy
* Correspondence: barbara.illi@cnr.it

Abstract: Despite the great advances in basic research results, glioblastoma multiforme (GBM) still remains an incurable tumour. To date, a GBM diagnosis is a death sentence within 15–18 months, due to the high recurrence rate and resistance to conventional radio- and chemotherapy approaches. The effort the scientific community is lavishing on the never-ending battle against GBM is reflected by the huge number of clinical trials launched, about 2003 on 10 September 2024. However, we are still far from both an in-depth comprehension of the biological and molecular processes leading to GBM onset and progression and, importantly, a cure. GBM is provided with high intratumoral heterogeneity, immunosuppressive capacity, and infiltrative ability due to neoangiogenesis. These features impact both tumour aggressiveness and therapeutic vulnerability, which is further limited by the presence in the tumour core of niches of glioblastoma stem cells (GSCs) that are responsible for the relapse of this brain neoplasm. Epigenetic alterations may both drive and develop along GBM progression and also rely on changes in the expression of the genes encoding histone-modifying enzymes, including histone deacetylases (HDACs). Among them, HDAC6—a cytoplasmic HDAC—has recently gained attention because of its role in modulating several biological aspects of GBM, including DNA repair ability, massive growth, radio- and chemoresistance, and de-differentiation through primary cilia disruption. In this review article, the available information related to HDAC6 function in GBM will be presented, with the aim of proposing its inhibition as a valuable therapeutic route for this deadly brain tumour.

Keywords: glioblastoma multiforme; glioblastoma stem cells; epigenetics; HDAC6; epidrugs

1. Introduction

The high number of clinical trials (2003 on 10 September 2024) attempting, at least, to increase the life expectancy of patients affected by glioblastoma multiforme (GBM) gives an idea about the effort the scientific community is providing to identify valuable therapies for this neoplasm, which is still neither defeated nor curable. Indeed, whereas living with an increasing number of other cancer types is now possible, a GBM diagnosis is a death sentence in about 15–18 months [1].

The identification of whatever molecule or strategy able to slow or even eradicate any kind of tumour requires a deep understanding of the biology and molecular and metabolic processes that make that specific tumour a unique entity with specific vulnerabilities. A great body of knowledge has been acquired for GBM in the past few years. OMIC studies, even at the single-cell level, shed light on the molecular pathways working in glioblastoma cells, helping with the classification of GBM into subtypes [2–4] and leading to testing a variety of new potential therapeutic strategies, including (i) the administration of monoclonal antibodies, small molecules, and protein kinase inhibitors and (ii) the application of electric fields, intraoperative photodynamic therapy, and CAR-T immunotherapy (see the clinicaltrials.gov website). However, none of these routes have been proven to be really effective in treating this brain cancer, which is still faced with maximal surgical resection, radiotherapy, and temozolomide (TMZ)-based chemotherapy.

GBM may be classified into the proneural, classical, and mesenchymal subtypes [2]. This classification takes into account mostly the transcriptional profile typical of each subtype, which is mirrored by the transcripts output of the glioblastoma stem cells (GSCs) from which each tumour stems. The discovery of GSCs [5] was a milestone, both from a scientific and a clinical point, because, from then on, they represent the major therapeutic target for GBM. Indeed, GSCs are responsible for GBM recurrence and resistance to therapies, as their surgical eradication is always incomplete and engage a series of molecular pathways, including DNA repair mechanisms, to overcome the cell damage occurring upon exposure to radiations and chemotherapy [6–9]. By definition, GSCs hold the characteristics of self-renewing pluripotent stem cells. A small percentage is also capable of asymmetrical cell division, which gives rise to cycling stem cells and differentiated cells which increase the tumour mass [10–12]. As stated above, GSCs mirror the biological, molecular, and genetic characteristics of the tumour subtype they belong to, indicating the requirement of differential therapeutic approaches according to the subtype-specific vulnerability or the identification of a common player, pivotal to GSCs survival, to be explored as a potential candidate for GBM treatment.

Typical epigenetic abnormalities are frequently found in GBM and, as in other tumours, the main outcome is both the silencing of tumour suppressor genes and the activation of DNA damage repair systems, among others [13]. These phenomena depend on the modification of the DNA methylation profile, the aberrant DNA methylation–demethylation cycle, and changes in both the histone modification pattern and chromatin architecture [14] within the regulatory regions of the above-mentioned genes. Each of these processes is ruled by specific enzymes that are variably either overexpressed or downregulated in GBM (see Section 3 below). Among them, histone deacetylases (HDACs) have been found to be heavily deregulated in GBM. Members of class I HDACs (HDAC 1, 2, 3, and 8) are mostly overexpressed. Class IIa HDACs (specifically HDAC 4, 5, and 9) are frequently upregulated, while, among class IIb, HDAC10 is downregulated and HDAC6 is upregulated. Sirtuins, belonging to class III, may be both up- or downregulated [15]. The unique member of class IV HDACs, HDAC11, has been found to decrease along GBM's progression [16]. While a considerable number of preclinical studies report the use of HDAC inhibitors [15] and underly the importance of HDACs' deregulation in GBM malignancy, few clinical trials (22 on 10 September 2024) employed or are employing HDACi, usually as a combo-therapy with TMZ and radiations, suggesting that the use of these small molecules, also called epidrugs, still has to be implemented, and further studies are needed to identify the best therapeutic candidate.

In 2020, the Society of Neuroncology (SNO) and the European Society of Neuroncology (ESNO) provided an extensive consensus review on the current status of knowledge and management of primary GBM [17]. On the front of therapies, the most recent strategies and hypotheses of targeted interventions are reported, including the use of Bevacizumab (not approved by the European Medicines Agency for clinical use), nistrosoureas (lomustine, carmusitne, and fotemustine, the latter of which is not approved by the Food and Drug Administration), and kinase inhibitors already used for other cancer types. Except for a certain degree of efficacy of lomustine in prolonging the overall survival (OS; 7.1–8.6 months) and progression-free survival (PFS; 1.5–3 months), none of these treatments were proved to be efficient. The high heterogeneity of GBM is probably the basis of these failures. Immunotherapy is at the forefront of GBM treatment. Stimulating responses to tumour antigens and overcoming microenvironment immunosuppressive mechanisms and immunotolerance are pivotal to GBM eradication. Different immunotherapeutic approaches are currently ongoing, including chimeric antigen receptor T cells (CAR-T) transfer, immune checkpoint inhibitors (ICs), oncolytic viruses (OVs), and cancer vaccines (CVs). All of these routes showed to be promising, but further refinements and trials are needed [18].

HDAC6 is currently a hot topic in the GBM field. The most recent literature underscores an increasing number of signalling pathways and molecular processes that are affected and controlled by this protein in GBM cells. Significantly, HDAC6 is overexpressed in GSCs, contributing to the maintenance of their stemness and the resistance to chemotherapeutic agents [19,20]. Specifically, HDAC6 has been found to promote proliferation and resistance to TMZ in GBM cells [21–23]. This latter phenomenon depends on its ability to modulate DNA damage repair [20,24,25]. Further, it restricts GSCs differentiation through Sonic Hedgehog (Shh) pathway activation [26,27] and primary cilia disassembly [19], while inducing the epithelial-to-mesenchymal transition (EMT) and autophagy [28].

In light of this evidence, HDAC6 inhibitors (HDAC6i) are now at the forefront of GBM treatment, with some of them having already entered into clinical trials.

In this work, a detailed overview of the aforementioned HDAC6 functions in promoting and sustaining GBM malignancy will be provided. Further, the possibility of employing its pharmacological inhibition as a novel, adjuvant strategy to fight GBM will be discussed.

2. Glioblastoma Multiforme

Primary (i.e, de novo) GBM is a rare brain tumour and is defined as a grade-IV astrocytoma, distinct from secondary GBM arising from low-grade (I-III) astrocytoma. Despite its rarity, GBM represent 14.3% of all the tumours affecting the central nervous system (CNS) and 49% of malignant CNS cancers in adults (>50 years of age [29]). However, GBM may also occur in children with distinct genetic characteristics [30].

Before GBM classification into molecular subtypes, histopathological variants have been defined by the World Health Organization (WHO), including gliosarcoma, GBM with giant cells, and conventional GBM. Additional histotypes were identified later [31], underlying the high heterogeneity of this cancer and explaining the term "multiforme", but the implementation of transcriptomic analyses definitely locked within specific molecular boundaries the GBM subtypes that define the currently accepted classification [2].

2.1. GBM Classification: From (Epi)genetics to Transcriptomic Profiles

GBM classification has been thoroughly discussed in [32]. Here, a concise summary of the concepts and steps that led to the actual GBM classification will be provided.

In addition to the histological characteristics, genetic abnormalities represent the first level of GBM classification. Primary and secondary GBM may be discriminated, for example, by the frequency of genetic alterations, rather than the type [33], and among them, the point mutations in the enzyme encoding isocitrate dehydrogenase (IDH) 1 and 2 were identified as robust markers for these tumours [34]. Indeed, 70% of secondary GBMs carry the R132H mutation in IDH1, which is present only in 5% of primary GBM [35]. The R172K mutation in IDH2 is very rare and is present in only 3% of secondary GBMs, oligodendrogliomas, and grade II-III astrocytomas [35]. Other frequent genetic abnormalities found are the loss of heterozygosity (LOH) of chromosome 10q or the monosomy of chromosome 10, epidermal growth factor receptor (EGFR) gene copy number gain on chromosome 7, deletion of cell cycle inhibitor genes, such as p16INK4a and cyclin-dependent kinase inhibitor (CDKN) 2A and 2B, and TP53 and PTEN mutations [36]. EGFR amplification is typical of highly aggressive primary GBM; about 50% of these tumours present a truncated and constitutively active form of EGFR (EGFRvIII), lacking part of the extracellular domain as a result of exons 2–7 deletion [37]. Other typical mutations are found in genes encoding for CDK4 and 6, hepatocyte growth factor receptor (MET), and murine minute doubles (MDMs) 2 and 4 [35,38]. Secondary GBM may also carryATRX mutations [30].

Chromatin organisation may provide a further level of classification, as changes in epigenetic modifications may parallel genetic abnormalities, although this is not a rule. While pediatric GBM presents mutations in histone-coding genes [39,40], adult GBM mostly present a typical DNA methylation pattern [41] at the promoter regions of both tumour suppressor genes (hypermethylation) [42–44] and genes deputed to cell proliferation, escape from apoptosis, and DNA repair (hypomethylation) [45]. In addition, this modification relies on DNA methyltransferase activity [46]. Abnormalities in the methylation profile of GBM cells also depend on the deregulated activity of DNA demethylating enzymes, namely the ten-to-eleven translocation (TET) family of proteins [47], which typically occurs in GBM carrying IDH1 mutations [48–50]. Indeed, mutated IDH1 transforms isocitrate into D-2-hydroxy-ketoglutarate (D2-HG), which inhibits the dioxygenase activity of TETs, leading to an accumulation of methylated cytosine residues and the occurrence of the so-called glioma hypermethylator phenotype (G-CIMP) [51,52]. In addition, IDH-mutated GBMs present disorganised topological associated domains (TADs), three-dimensional chromatin structures that regulate gene transcription controlling the proximity of regulatory regions, mainly enhancers, with gene bodies [52]. In low-grade gliomas, the N6-methyladenosine (m6A) profile of specific miRNAs has been found to differentiate between low- and high-risk gliomas more than IDH mutation [53]. This aspect will be not further discussed here. For more information, see [32].

In the early 2000s, the first large-scale studies opened the way for the identification of the transcriptional signatures that are able to discriminate between astrocytomas and GBM and, within GBM, among three different subtypes, whose molecular and biological characteristics have been refined over the years.

Microarray studies led first to the identification of 360 genes able to differentiate astrocytomas and GBM [54] and then to the discovery of 35 transcripts specific for three different GBM subtypes [55]. Most of these genes are related to proliferation, migration, and, more importantly, to key neurogenetic steps, supporting the hypotheses that GBM may arise from the re-activation of normal developmental routes in quiescent stem cells resident in the brain [56] or from de-differentiation processes from astrocytes to neural stem cells that derail into GSCs [57,58]. Thus, the first classification of molecular GBM subtypes defined the proliferative (Prolif), mesenchymal (Mes), and proneural (PN) subtypes mirroring the biological and molecular properties of these tumours, with the Prolif subtype characterised by the expression of genes controlling the cell cycle, the aggressive Mes subtype marked by genes involved in neo-angiogenesis, and the PN subtype associated with a more differentiated phenotype, due to the expression of neural differentiation-related genes [59–62]. Each subtype-specific panel was further associated with genetic lesions [38], detailing further GBM subtypes at the molecular level till the definition of the current nomenclature used to classify GBM into classical, mesenchymal, and proneural subtypes [2]. A fourth subtype, called neural and thought to be the result of a contamination of normal brain cells within the samples undergoing RNA sequencing [4], has been recently validated and is the result of the activation of neural developmental programs in GSCs located at the tumour border by signals from surrounding neurons [63].

Classical and mesenchymal subtypes consistently overlap at the transcriptomic level, but the mesenchymal subtype also presents an inactivation of neurofibromin 1 (NF1), overexpression of the YKL-40 gene, and proteins of NF-κB network, which is consistent with the inflammatory features that characterise this tumour. Furthermore, this subtype is associated with the transcripts belonging to tumour-associated glia and microglia, indicating a strict communication between the tumour and the surrounding microenvironment and the possibility of tumour re-shaping according to tissue environmental signals [4]. The proneural subtype invariably bears platelet-derived growth factor receptor alpha (PDGFRA) alterations and hot-spot mutations in IDH1. Moreover, genes involved in oligodendrocyte differentiation are also expressed [2].

A hypermutator phenotype was also uncovered. These GBMs belonged to a cluster of cancers treated with TMZ or lomustine or both and presented mutations in the DNA mismatch repair system and heavy methylation of O-6-methylguanine-DNA methyltransferase (MGMT) promoter [64]. MGMT removes the alkyl residues added by chemotherapeutic agents to the DNA. Therefore, MGMT promoter methylation represents both a prognostic marker and, when hypomethylated, indicates tumours resistant to chemotherapeutic approaches [65,66].

Notably, a shift from the proneural to the mesenchymal subtype has been observed upon tumour recurrence and is associated with the expression of the YKL-40 gene, encoding for a glycoprotein of the extracellular matrix [59–62].

2.2. Glioblastoma Stem Cells (GSCs)

As with most tumours, GBMs possess tumour-initiating cells, named glioblastoma stem cells (GSCs) [67]. Although representing a minority of tumour cells, $CD133^+/CD44^+$ GSCs are the real cells that are responsible for GBM aggressiveness and infiltration, due to the activation of neoangiogenesis, resistance to therapies, and finally, the death of patients, as their complete surgical eradication is not possible without causing severe brain damage. Thus, over the years, they became both a challenge and a major target for scientists and neurooncologists.

GSCs closely resemble normal neural stem cells that are capable of self-renewal due to the activation of the Nanog-Sox2-Oct4-KLF-4 transcriptional circuitry and unlimited proliferative ability due to Myc oncogene overexpression [68–71]. The Sonic Hedgehog (Shh), notch, and Wnt/β-catenin signalling pathways are also active in GSCs but are often heavily deregulated, leading to a transcriptional derailment of the genes involved in the proliferation and differentiation of neural stem cells [7,72–74]. As we will see below, abnormalities in these pathways also depend on the lack of primary cilia, which characterises terminally differentiated neural cells.

It is widely accepted that GSCs recapitulate at the phenotypic and genomic level the tumour subtype of origin. However, in surgical GBM explants, mostly Mes and PN GSCs are found [75,76]. They are believed also to be responsible for GBM intratumoral heterogeneity [77,78], but this phenomenon does not depend on (epi)genetic inheritance in the tumour progenies but rather on growth and cell fate determinants [79]. Among them, the interaction with cells, especially immune cells, in the tumour microenvironment represents a fundamental source of GBM heterogeneity and evolution. Indeed, each GBM subtype-specific transcriptome is typically associated with transcriptional signatures of different immune cell populations. Furthermore, these immune signatures may evolve and change upon the acquisition of a resistant phenotype. Moreover, the genes involved in normal neural development have been detected in GSCs at the outer border of the tumour core as a result of signals from neighbour neurons in brain regions not invaded by cancer cells [4].

2.2.1. GSCs and Resistance to Radio- and Chemotherapy

Resistance to GBM gold-standard therapies, namely radiations and TMZ, is a unique property of GSCs, as tumour cells lacking the CD133 stem marker were proven to be not resistant [12]. To achieve both radio and TMZ resistance, GSCs activate diverse DNA repair systems. Indeed, although both $CD133^-$ and $CD133^+$ GBM cells activate the ataxia-telangiectasia-mutated (ATM), Rad17, Chk1, and Chk2 checkpoint proteins, only CD133+ GSCs potently phosphorylates Chk1 and Chk2 [8]. Other efficient DNA repair mechanisms deployed by GSCs include the single-strand break repair (SSBR) system, activation of poly (ADP-ribose) polymerase (PARP) [6,80], and activation of MGMT due to its promoter hypomethylation [55,56]. Intriguingly, the NF-κB-dependent PN-Mes shift [45] also favours GBM resistance [9], as the cells belonging to the Mes phenotype have been demonstrated to show less γH2AX foci, suggesting efficient DNA repair, and do not accumulate in the G2/M phase of the cell cycle [45].

Specific epigenetic modifications have been shown to be associated with the TMZ resistance of GSCs. In particular, downregulation of the H3.3 histone variant has been demonstrated to discriminate between resistant and nonresistant cells [79,81]. Indeed, histone H3.3 favours the differentiation of GSCs that exploit the mixed-lineage leukaemia 5 (MLL5) methyltransferase to silence its expression [81].

2.2.2. GSCs and the Primary Cilium

The primary cilium is a non-motile, microtubule-based organelle protruding from the cell membrane, serving as an "antenna" for the extracellular signals ruling developmental processes and cellular homeostasis [82]. Its central core is constituted of more than 1000 polypeptides (ref. [82] and https://esbl.nhlbi.nih.gov/Databases/CiliumProteome/, accessed on 15 October 2024), making the primary cilium one of the most complex cell organelles. Typically, the primary cilia are present in terminally differentiated cells and are assembled during the G0/G1 phase of the cell cycle [82]. The importance of the primary cilium in the maintenance of proper cellular development and homeostasis is highlighted by a group of genetic diseases called "ciliopathies", characterised by a wide range of mutations in many different ciliary genes, with a profound impact on the CNS (especially the cerebellum), kidney, eyes [83,84]. It is not surprising that primary cilia loss occurs in several types of cancer (breast, pancreas, and kidney). Representing a brake for cell cycle progression, tumour cells have to devise strategies leading to cilium disassembly.

Brief Overview of the Structure of Motile and Non-Motile (Primary) Cilia

Historically, the structure of motile cilia was found to be constituted by nine microtubule doublets that surround a couple of central microtubules (9+2 axoneme), whereas primary, non-motile cilia have a 9+0 structure [82]. However, a 9+4 axoneme has been identified in rabbits and a 3+0 structure in protozoans [85,86]. Of note, microtubules within the cilia axoneme have to be acetylated to allow the proper assembly and function of the cilium. These hairy-like organelles originate from a basal body formed by two centrioles. The mother centriole represents the cilium root at the cell membrane. The whole basal body is not only the centre of cilium assembly/disassembly but also controls protein entry and exit within the cilium, being in strict connection with the transition zone, a region which houses many proteins that are later transported to the ciliary membrane [87–89]. This latter holds many receptors, transporters, ion channels, and sensory proteins, while the soluble cilioplasm contains signalling molecules. Intraflagellar transport (IFT) motor proteins, which "walk" on the axoneme microtubules, allow the anterograde and retrograde transport of molecules within the cilia [90], whereas Bardet–Biedl syndrome (BBS) proteins (also called the BBSome) function as adaptors between the IFT machinery and the ciliary membrane, allowing for the compartmentalisation of molecules within the cilia [91].

Altered Primary Cilia Signalling in GBM

Primary cilia are the collectors of a wide variety of signalling pathways to a greater extent than thought before [92]. Within the scope of this work, we will discuss the altered cilia-dependent signalling pathways that are relevant to GBM and GSCs biology.

- One of the most important primary cilium-dependent pathways is Shh signalling, which controls the activation of many transcriptional programs, including the differentiation of neuroblasts, cell polarity and patterning, and when deregulated, tumorigenesis. The final players of the Shh cascade are the glioma-associated oncogene homologue (Gli) transcription factors (TFs) [93–95] located within the cilium. In the absence of Shh, the suppressor of fused (Sufu) protein binds and inhibits the nuclear translocation of the Gli family. On the contrary, when Shh is produced, it binds to its receptor PTCH1, which is removed from the cell membrane, releasing the smoothened (SMO) receptor to the cilium where it inhibits the conversion of active Gli transcription factors into repressor forms [92]. In GBM, where the Shh pathway is overactive, Gli proteins promote the transcription of genes involved in stem cell maintenance, tumour progression, and resistance to therapy [73,96];
- Centrosomes play a pivotal role in orchestrating the nucleation of interphase microtubules, are involved in different signalling pathways, and control cell motility and ciliogenesis. The core of the controsome is represented by the centriole, which organises the surrounding pericentriolar material provided with centriolar satellites, whose major component is the pericentriolar material 1 (PCM1) protein [97]. PCM1 has many

functions, including the correct location of centrosomal proteins in the centrosomes. Therefore, PCM1 dysfunction has a remarkable impact on cell physiology and is associated with both primary cilium-related diseases and cancer. Although a functional PCM1 is related to the proper assembly of the cilium (i.e., to a "non-cancer state"), in GBM, it has been reported that PCM1 depletion—and, consequently, primary cilia deprivation—is favourable to GBM cell death and TMZ sensitivity [98];

- The cell cycle-related kinases (CCRK)–intestinal kinase (ICK)–male germ cell-associated kinase (MAK) pathway negatively regulates ciliogenesis, while playing a pivotal role in intraflagellar transport [99–101] and Shh response [102]. CCRK depletion in both fibroblasts and GBM, which presents high levels of CCRK, results in cilia restoration, as a lack of phosphorylation of the CCRK downstream effector ICK inhibits its suppressive effect on ciliogenesis. Consequently, CCRK and ICK depletion produce cell cycle arrest in a cilia-dependent manner [103].

Ciliogenesis in GSCs

The presence and role of the primary cilia in GSCs are controversial. Goranci-Buzhala et al. [104] reported that most of the GSCs do not possess primary cilia, irrespective of their specific subtype of origin, and show accelerated proliferation. This characteristic, typical also of neural precursor cells (NPCs), depends on the high expression of the proteins forming the cilium disassembly complex (CDC), which includes HDAC6 (Figure 1). Depletion or inactivation of one CDC component—the Nek2 kinase, important for the activation of kinesin 24 (Kif24), which depolymerises microtubules—results in cilia restoration and GSC differentiation, but only in the proneural subtype, indicating that putative CDC targets are subtype-specific. Indeed, cilia-dependent differentiation of PN GSCs depends on PDGFRα relocation to the primary cilia [104] Indeed, PDGFRα, that is altered in the PN subtype, is widely diffused in unciliated GSCs [2]. Thus, in GBM, the presence and the function of primary cilia are probably subtype- and context-specific. This phenomenon further confirms the heterogeneity of this tumour and its resident stem cells. More recently, it has been shown that 25% of GSCs possess primary cilia. In these cells, Sox2-dependent Kelch domain-containing 8A (KLHDC8A) is required for primary cilia formation, Shh signalling, and GSC proliferation, whereas KLHDC8A deprivation leads to cilia loss and decreased in vivo tumorigenic properties of GSCs [105]. Further, the multidomain protein BAG3, involved in the suppression of ciliogenesis and cilia homeostasis, is overexpressed in GBM and participates in GSC stemness maintenance [106]. Similarly, ciliogenesis impairment, obtained through PCM1 depletion, results in GSCs' decreased proliferation, induction of apoptosis, and sensitivity to TMZ [98].

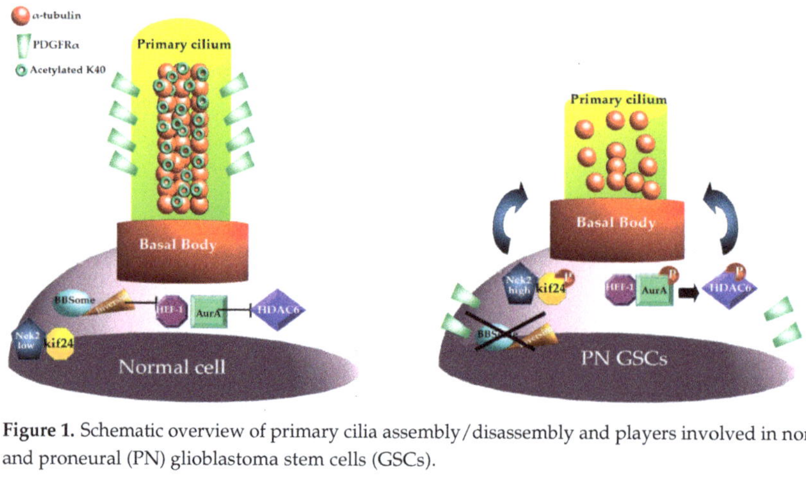

Figure 1. Schematic overview of primary cilia assembly/disassembly and players involved in normal and proneural (PN) glioblastoma stem cells (GSCs).

3. Epigenetics of GBM

Rearrangements of chromatin structure and topology in cancer cells, including GBM cells, frequently lead to the aberrant regulation of transcripts normally ruling basic cell properties, such as proliferation and death, migration, and differentiation.

3.1. DNA Methylation

The most frequent epigenetic abnormality found in GBM is represented by changes in the DNA methylation pattern, mostly at the CpG islands of gene promoters. Methylation of cytosine at position 5 (5mC) is highly stable and, thus, heritable. De novo methylation is catalysed by DNA methylatransferases 3A and 3B [107,108], whereas methylation pattern maintenance across cell generations is ensured by DNA methylatransferase 1 [109]. Although typical of CpG islands, 5mC is found also in non-CpG genomic regions, especially in highly differentiated adult cells, including neurons [110–112]. At the epigenetic level, 5mC content at gene promoters has been definitely associated with gene repression. However, 5mC is highly enriched in the bodies of actively transcribed genes [113], specifically in exons compared to introns. Two possible mechanisms have been proposed to explain this paradoxical role of DNA methylation, namely the regulation of mRNA splicing [114–117] and the repression of intragenic, cryptic promoters [118]. Furthermore, an activating role for the methylation of CpGs within promoters has been also documented [119].

In GBM, the most well-known and characterised gene affected by DNA methylation at its promoter is MGMT, which has a highly prognostic value [120]. By removing alkyl residues from TMZ-modified DNA, its expression strongly predicts patient outcome. Thus, hypomethylation of MGMT promoter results in worst prognosis and reduced median survival, as TMZ is ineffective. Usually, 5mC residues within chromatin act as docking sites for methyl CpG-binding domain (MBD) proteins, which, in turn, recruit other classes of transcriptional co-repressors, such as histone methyltransferases [121]. It has been reported that the polycomb repressor complex (PRC) member enhancer of zeste homologue 2 (EZH2) is capable of conveying DNA methyltransferases onto target regulatory loci, strictly linking DNA methylation with repressive histone modifications and creating highly compacted chromatin regions [122]. Aberrant DNA methylation profiles may also occur upon the dysfunction of demethylating enzymes, such as the TET family of proteins. TETs transform 5mC into unmethylated cytosine through a series of oxidative steps that foresee the formation of 5-hydroxymethylcytosine first (5hmC), 5-formilcytosine (5fC), and 5-carboxylcytosine (5caC) [123,124]. The latter is excised by thymine DNA glycosylase (TDG), leaving an abasic site that is later replaced by the base excision repair (BER) system [125,126]. The IDH1 mutant GBM typically presents a deregulated methylation–demethylation cycle, due to the production of 2D-HG by mutant IDH1 from isocitrate. The 2D-HG cannot serve as a co-factor for TETs, which are inhibited, with the consequent accumulation of 5mC and 5hmC and the occurrence of the so-called glioma CpG methylator phenotype (G-CIMP). This phenotype has been recently found to be also correlated with 5hmC content. The loss of 5hmC corresponds to 5mC enrichment at the chromatin loci, which also present high levels of dimethylated histone H3 on lysine 4 (H3k4me2), providing a novel glioma-specific chromatin signature [127,128]. Specific DNA methylation patterns may alter the binding of TFs and the related co-regulators (both activators and repressors) and even the chromatin architecture (for details see [129]).

3.2. Histone Acetylation

A wide variety of histone modifications have been identified to date, including acetylation, methylation, isomerisation, sumoylation, ubiquitilation, nitration, carbonylation [130], lactylation [131], and glutationylation [130]. According to the scope of this review manuscript, we will focus on acetylation/deacetylation of histones.

With the exception of histone H4 acetylation on lysine 20 (H4K20ac), associated with gene repression [132], the addition of acetyl moieties to the K residues at the N-terminal tail of histones is, probably, the most well-established epigenetic modification leading to transcriptional activation. The presence of high levels of histone acetylation in GBM specimens compared to healthy controls, and the further enhancement along the tumour stages, remarks upon the importance of this modification to the onset and progression of this neoplasm [133]. Specific histone acetylation profiles have been recently related to the single-cell types present within GBM. Thus, cells with high levels of histone acetylation have been found to belong to the oligodendrocyte precursors and myeloid lineages [134], which is consistent with the activation of immune cells in the tumour microenvironment [133,134]. Enrichment analyses showed that histone acetylation is linked to the activation of genes involved in focal and cell adhesion, actin binding, axon development, and differentiation programs [134]. The relative level of histone acetylation has been also used to design a risk model that proved to be as effective as those currently used. High- and low-risk subgroups have been identified, which are able to predict the clinical outcome of patients with overlapping accuracy compared to the other risk models. Acetylation levels have been also related to the efficacy of immuno- and chemotherapy [133]. Moreover, a recent work revealed that, in GSCs, high levels of simultaneous H4K8ac and H4K5ac identify superenhancers that are involved in the regulation of oncogenes pivotal for stemness maintenance [135].

3.3. *HATs and HDACs in GBM*

Acetylation, as well as all the other epigenetic modifications, is reversible. Histone acetyltransferases (HATs) and histone deacetylases (HDACs) are the enzymes that catalyse the addition and the removal, respectively, of histone K acetyl groups. Both are deregulated, to different extents, in GBM.

3.3.1. HATs Deregulation in GBM

HATs are divided into three subgroups, namely (i) the Gcn5-related N-acetyltransferase (GNAT); (ii) the MOZ, Ybf2-Sas3, Sas2, the Tip60 (MYST); and (iii) the CREB binding protein (CBP)/p300 family. Acetylating also a variety of non-histone proteins, such as TP53, Myc, NF-κB, HATs may impact gene transcription either directly, through histone modification, or indirectly, inhibiting or potentiating the activity of the protein they acetylate. Thus, it is not surprising that the deregulation of HATs has been observed in many human diseases, including cancer. Remarkably, the role of HATs in GBM is poorly investigated. It is known that p300 has a tumour suppressor role in GBM, inducing the differentiation of GBM cells into astrocytes and inhibiting migration/invasion [136]. Indeed, the EID3 p300 inhibitor is overexpressed in GBM [137]. Another paper indicated KAT6A as a putative GBM molecular target, as its overexpression activates the PI3K/Akt pathway, leading to increased tumorigenic properties [138]. In rodent models of glioma, KAT8 activity, which mediates H4K16 acetylation, has been related to microglia conversion from an immune tumour counterpart to a tumour-supporting layer. KAT8 recruitment at the microglial gene promoters is Sirt1-dependent, providing an interesting example of cooperation between HATs and HDACs in promoting tumorigenesis [139].

3.3.2. HDACs Deregulation in GBM

Contrary to HATs, HDACs are known to be heavily deregulated in GBM.

- Class I HDACs are ubiquitously expressed, although they may have peculiar roles within cells. Indeed, whereas HDAC1 and 2 are involved in the control of cell proliferation and neurogenesis [140], HDAC3 is associated with lipid metabolism [141] and cardiac [142] and neural development [143], while HDAC8 controls sister chromatid exchange, muscle contractility, microtubule stability, and energy homeostasis [144]. All of them are overexpressed in a wide variety of cancers [15]. In GBM, HDAC 1 and 2 depletion have been demonstrated to reduce GBM cells' proliferation and migration while inducing TMZ sensitisation [145,146]. HDAC3 is mainly overrepresented in aggressive glioma phenotypes and is an unfavourable prognostic marker [147]. HDAC8 is also associated with a block of the cell cycle and decreased levels of MGMT, thus promoting TMZ sensitisation [148];

- Class II HDACs are divided into two subclasses, a and b. Subclass IIa HDACs (4, 5, 7, and 9) are highly tissue specific. HDAC5 and 9 are expressed in neurons and the heart [149]. HDAC4 is mostly expressed in bone [150], neurons [151], and in cells of mesodermal origin, as well as HDAC7 [152]. These HDACs are provided with nuclear localisation (NLS) and nuclear export (NES) signals that control their intracellular location, according to a variety of stimuli [153]. Subclass IIb (HDAC6 and HDAC10) has a mostly cytoplasmic localisation and selective substrate specificity [154,155]. Indeed, HDAC6 deacetylates mainly non-histone proteins, such as tubulin, cortactin, and geat shock protein (HSP)90 ([156], see Section 4), while HDAC10, a polyamine deacetylase, shows selectivity for long *N*8-acetylspermidine, acetylputrescine, and acetylcadaverine [155]. As well as class I HDACs, both class IIa and class IIb HDACs are deregulated in neoplastic malignancies and GBM. Class IIa HDACs are overexpressed in GBM cells and are associated with enhanced proliferation and migration/invasion [15], as well as class IIb HDAC6 [28]. HDAC10 is downregulated in paediatric GBM and astrocytomas [16], but no information are available to date regarding adult GBM;
- The peculiar seven members of class III HDACs (also called Sirtuins) are NAD^+-dependent and do not possess a Zn^{2+} binding domain. They are located in many cellular compartments, including the cytosol, nucleus, and mitochondria [157–160]. Although histones are deacetylated by Sirtuins, these enzymes exert their activity mainly on non-histone substrates, regulating an impressive number of biological processes with a profound impact, especially on metabolism, oxidative stress, and energy homeostasis. Therefore, the deregulation of Sirtuins is found in many human disorders, from cardiovascular diseases to neurodegeneration, from inflammatory disorders to cancer. SIRT1,2,3,6 and 7 have been found to be deregulated in GBM, with conflicting results. SIRT1 has been identified both as an oncogene [161] and a tumour suppressor in GBM cells [162]. SIRT2 is a tumour suppressor in GBM cells and acts through the NF-κB/p21 pathways [163]. SIRT3 has a prognostic value. The higher the SIRT3 expression levels, the worse the life expectancy [164]. SIRT6 inhibits both proliferation and metabolic reprogramming in GBM cells [165], whereas SIRT7 enhances the proliferation of glioma cells via the ERK/STAT3 axis [166];
- HDAC11, representing the sole member of class IV HDACs, is tissue-specific and expressed in a variety of organs, including the heart, kidney, and brain. Its localisation varies from the cytoplasm to the mitochondria to the nucleus, according to the tissue and physiopathological context, and it seems to be involved in the control of DNA synthesis, inflammatory response, and metabolism [167]. It has been recently indicated as a novel therapeutic target for cancer and is downregulated in GBM [16].

3.4. HDAC Inhibitors (HDACi) in GBM

Epigenetic therapy by HDACi is, to date, a well-established strategy attempting to overcome the limits of the standard treatments applied, with impressive results at both the preclinical and clinical stages, even in the presence of genetic mutations. Examples are the results obtained with valproic acid (VPA) on mouse models of recessive dystrophic epidermolysis bullosa (RDEB) [168] and the approval of Givinostat for Duchenne muscular dystrophy (DMD) [169]. With 777 clinical trials, 52 still looking for patients, their application, either alone or in combination with other drugs (e.g., kinase inhibitors, monoclonal antibodies, and standard chemotherapies) in a wide variety of cancers, is a matter of fact. The important role HDACs' deregulation plays in glioblastoma onset and progression and the preclinical evidence of promising, beneficial effects of HDACi administration in restraining GBM growth both in vivo and in vitro provided the background required for their application also for this brain tumour. However, the results of phase I-III clinical trials employing HDACi, mainly in combination with other agents such as TMZ or Bevacizumab, were disappointing [15]. None of the HDACi tested increased the OS or PFS of enrolled patients [15]. HDACi penetration through the blood–brain barrier (BBB) may be one of the key issues in explaining the poor clinical efficacy of these epidrugs. Further, these results may also depend on the different environments and cell–cell interactions GBM cells experience in the human brain, which are extremely different from both 2D in vitro conditions and in vivo mouse brains. The isolation of patients' GSCs, cultured as 3D neurospheres, and, more importantly, the generation of patients' minibrain models of GBM [170] recently enriched the amount of manipulable tools that are useful for designing personalised therapies. However, whereas many works report GSC targeting by HDACi [171], no information has been acquired in GBM organoid models, which may give clues about the influence of the tumour microenvironment and extracellular matrix on HDACi efficacy. In the last 20 years, accumulating evidence provided the proof of principle that HDACs targeting may represent a doable route to fight GBM. In GBM cell lines and GSCs, it has been demonstrated that HDACi affect different pathways that are pivotal to their survival. Class I HDACs inhibitors have been shown to disrupt the chromatin superenhancers deputed to the overexpression of glycolytic genes in a Myc-dependent manner. This results in GBM metabolic reprogramming, with a shift from aerobic glycolysis to the fatty acid oxidation (FAO) metabolic pathway as a strategy to compensate for the high energy demand. Indeed, inhibiting both class I HDACs and FAO reduced cellular density, the mitotic index, and apoptosis in a GBM PDX model in vivo [172]. Similarly, the class I HDACi sodium butyrate and sodium valproate synergise with the inhibitors of glycolysis (WP1122) to reduce GBM cells' viability [173]. HDACi also impair GSCs proliferation [174], promote GSCs differentiation, and decrease GSCs migration by limiting Wnt signalling and rearranging the cytoskeleton [175,176], impairing their self-renewal [177] also in combination with MAPK/ERK kinase (MEK) inhibitors [178] and modulating the immune microenvironment when in combination with BET inhibitors [179].

3.4.1. HDACi and GBM Neoangiogenesis

Restraining GBM neoangiogenesis is another primary target for GBM treatment. Indeed, although not metastatic, GBM relies on the formation of new vessels to invade the whole brain. One of the mechanisms at the basis of GBM angiogenesis is the release of the vascular endothelial growth factor (VEGF) by GSCs and the consequent recruitment of endothelial cells (ECs) from pre-existing vessels [180]. However, anti-angiogenic therapies may not be efficient in counteracting this specific phenomenon, as GSCsc also deployed vasculogenic mimicry (VM) to self-provide a vascular tree in alternative ways compared to endothelial and smooth muscle cell transdifferentiation [181,182]. The VM network consists of tubular structures, anatomically similar to normal blood vessels but with different intrinsic properties, such as specific matrix components and location of the deposed basal lamina [183]. Given the high plasticity of GSCs, the endothelial-like derived cells begin to express true EC markers, such as CD31, VEGF receptors, and VE-cadherin to connect to host blood vessels and forming a percolative system for both nutrient and oxygen demand and the elimination of cells' secretions [182]. These types of structures are resistant to anti-angiogenic therapies. However, it has been demonstrated that class I and II HDACi Suberoyl anilide hydroxamic acid (SAHA) and MC1568 may represent a valuable route to restrain VM in GBM [184]. Similarly, Panobinostat, a hydroxamic acid-derived pan-HDACi, reduces vessel density in GBM mouse subcutaneous xenografts and potently limits angiogenesis by disrupting HDAC6/Hsp90 interaction, promoting hypoxia-inducible factor (HIF) 1α instability and a consequent decrease in VEGF expression [185].

3.4.2. HDACi and GBM Resistance to Therapies

An important property of HDACi is to sensitise GBM cells to chemo- and radiotherapy. In GSCs, Givinostat, a pan-HDACi, enhances the cytotoxic activity of TMZ in GSCs by decreasing the expression of Sp1 required for MGMT expression [186]. Panobinostat has been also shown to induce apoptosis in GBM cells in combination with TMZ and other damaging agents [187,188]. Both Trichostatin-A (TSA) and SAHA synergise with TMZ in reducing spheres formation and the proliferation of U87MG cells, increasing the levels of dual-specificity phosphatase 1 (DUSP1), a MAP kinase phosphatase that positively correlates with patient survival. Indeed, high DUSP1 levels are correlated with increased GBM cell differentiation and reduced tumorigenic ability, both in vitro and in vivo [189]. SAHA also synergises with melatonin in reducing the levels of transcription factor EB (TFEB), which is a master regulator of autophagy and lysosomal biogenesis and is overexpressed in high-grade GBM, and promoting apoptotic gene expression. DNA damage, as demonstrated by the occurrence of DSBs in GBM cells treated with the combination of SAHA and melatonin, and PARP cleavage are part of the mechanism underlying SAHA/melatonin-induced apoptotic GBM cell death [190]. However, SAHA has been also associated with TMZ resistance through MGMT upregulation via a chromatin-based mechanism, including NF-κB, Sp1, Jun, and p300 recruitment at its own promoter in GBM xenograft models [191]. Class I and II HDACi Romidepsin potentiates the effects of TMZ, inducing apoptosis of GBM cells by increasing the expression of pro-apoptotic genes and restraining the PI3K/Akt pathway both in vitro and in vivo [192]. The HDAC8 inhibitor NBM-BMX has been reported to counteract TMZ resistance in GBM cell lines by reducing the level of MGMT and increasing the expression of p53. A decrease in c-Myc and Cyclin D1 levels was also observed. At the biological level, NBM-BMX, in combination with TMZ, inhibits cell viability and proliferation and promotes apoptosis [193]. The HDAC1 and 3 inhibitor RGFP109 alters the binding capacity of NF-κB, blocking the association to its co-activators (P/CAF and p300) and promoting the interaction with the inhibitor of growth 4 (ING4), downregulating the expression of pro-survival genes [194].

3.4.3. HDACi Crossing the BBB

Except for MS-275, a potent class I HDACi [195] and givinostat [177], as stated above, hitherto, the presence of the BBB represents an obstacle to the efficient application of pre-clinically validated epidrugs in humans. Thus, a major effort is ongoing in the design of new molecules capable of penetrating the BBB and reaching the brain at a clinically valuable concentration. Quisinostat, a hydroxamic acid derivative, has been shown to be cytotoxic, to promote the accumulation of DSBs in GSCs, and thus to radiosensitise GSCs in vitro, and to cross the BBB, reducing the tumour mass in vivo [196]. Largazole, a natural, orally bioavailable, class I HDACi from marine cyanobacteria, also crosses the BBB, leading to changes in the gene expression pattern of GBM-affected mouse brains, where the genes involved in neuroprotection become upregulated [197]. Other hydroxamic acid derivatives have been developed to allow BBB crossing. SAHA analogues, with different caps, have been proven to be effective in reducing U87MG cell viability while inducing reactive oxygen species (ROS) accumulation and apoptosis [198]. Further, these molecules have been shown to inhibit HDAC8 activity in GBM and HDAC2 and 3 expression. Importantly, these SAHA analogues downregulate the expression of mTOR signalling components, such as Rictor, whereas p53 and mir143, which targets hexokinase2 (HK2), the first enzyme involved in glycolysis and overexpressed in GBM [199], are upregulated [198]. Panobinostat, when encapsulated into nano-micelles, may cross the BBB in rat models and has anti-proliferative effects in a variety of GBM cell lines in vitro [200]. Piperazine-based HDACi benzamides have been also shown to cross the BBB in mouse models and to potently impair GBM cell lines proliferation by affecting cell cycle-related pathways, such as p16INK4a-CDK4/6-pRb [201].

4. HDAC6

The HDAC6 coding gene is located on chromosome X p.11.22-23 and is about 22 kb long. As a member of class IIb HDACs, the 1215 amino acids corresponding gene product is provided with two catalytic domains (CD1 and 2) and a $Zn^{2+/}$/ubiquitin binding pocket (ZnF-UBP; Figure 2), which makes this deacetylating enzyme unique within the HDACs family. One NLS and one NES (NES1) are located at the N-terminus of the molecule, while NES2 is at the C-terminus. Between the two CDs, a dynein motor proteins binding domain (DMB) is found, whereas a SE14 tetra decapeptide repeat (for a total of eight tetra decapeptides) is located between the second catalytic domain and NES2. This region, which is proper for the sole human HDAC6, is required for cytoplasmic retention [156]. CD1 requires CD2 for its activity, and both require Zn^{2+} to exert their function. The DMB motif provides an anchor for microtubules and the related transport of different cargo along microtubules [202].

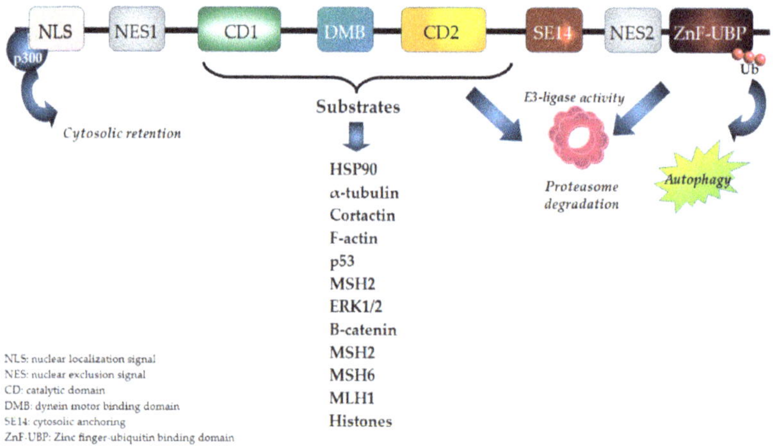

Figure 2. Multidomain HDAC6 structure is shown. Substrates and HDAC6 functions discussed in the present work are indicated.

Different post-translational modifications affect HDAC6 activity. Indeed, p300-dependent acetylation negatively regulates HDAC6, whereas ubiquitination may either not affect [203] or lead to HDAC6 degradation [204,205]. Some residues, when phosphorylated, increase HDAC6 activity, (S1060 targeted by GPCR kinase 2 (GRK2) [205]; T1031, S1035 phosphorylated by extracellular signal-regulated kinase (ERK) [206]; and S22 phosphorylated by glycogen synthase kinase 3β (GSK-3β) [207], while others are detrimental, e.g., Y570, which is a target of epidermal growth factor receptor (EGFR) [208]. Additional HDAC6 activating kinases are Aurora A kinase (AurA) [209], p38α, and protein kinase Cα [210]. Furthermore, HDAC6 has been also found to be S-nitrosylated and inactive in this specific form [211].

4.1. HDAC6 Functions

Located primarily in the cytoplasm, HDAC6 exerts its activity—which includes both the deacetylation, binding, and aggregation of ubiquitinated proteins and the ubiquitination of certain targets, mainly on non-histone targets. However, HDADC6 plays an important role also in the cell nucleus.

4.1.1. Deacetylation-Dependent Functions of Nuclear HDAC6

In cycling cells, HDAC6 is preferentially cytoplasmic. However, in resting cells, a fraction of HDAC6 translocates to the nucleus which participates in the regulation of gene expression by binding to and regulating the activity of transcription factors (TFs) and transcriptional co-repressors/activators. Examples of TFs that recruit HDAC6 into the nucleus are Runx2 and NF-κB [212,213]. These proteins take advantage of HDAC6 to repress genes in a tissue-specific manner. HDAC6-mediated transcriptional repression usually foresees the involvement of co-repressors (e.g., HDAC11 and ligand-dependent nuclear receptor co-repressor (LCoR)) [214] or activators that are modified in order to lose the ability to induce transcription. Indeed, when sumoylated, p300 acts as a transcriptional repressor by HDAC6 recruitment [215–217]. On the other hand, p300 acetylates HDAC6, impairing its tubulin-deacetylating activity [218] and promoting its cytosolic retention by blocking its interaction with importin-α [219]. HDAC6 also controls p53 activity. Indeed, it is responsible for p53 deacetylation at K381/382, strongly limiting the p53-dependent transcription of growth arrest and apoptotic genes [220]. HDAC6 exerts this specific function within the nucleus, as changes in the expression levels of genes controlled by p53 are dependent upon the nuclear HDAC6 amount [220].

Importantly, HDAC6 has been found to deacetylate and regulate the proteins belonging to the DNA mismatch repair system (MMR), including MSH2 [221] and MLH1. This latter, when deacetylated, impairs the formation of the MutSα–MutLα complex, thereby inducing DNA damage tolerance [222]. This specific HDAC6 activity is particularly important in promoting the chemo- and radioresistance of cancer cells (see below).

The nuclear quota of HDAC6 may also deacetylate histones [223–226]. In addition, indirect mechanisms may account for HDAC6 histone deacetylase activity, such as the cytosolic sequestration and the ubiquitination of HATs [227].

4.1.2. Deacetylation-Dependent Functions of Cytosolic HDAC6

It is well established that HDAC6 exerts its activity mainly on cytosolic proteins, being its primary substrate α-tubulin, the principal component of microtubules. α-tubulin is acetylated by α-tubulin acetyltransferase 1 (αTAT1) [228]. The first demonstration of HDAC6-dependent α-tubulin K40 deacetylation dates from 2002 [229], followed by the identification of cortactin, which regulates actin polymerisation and branching through the binding to F-actin, as another HDAC6 substrate [230]. Deacetylation of α-tubulin leads to microtubule depolymerisation and improved cell motility. This activity is enhanced when HDAC6 is phosphorylated onto S1035 by the extracellular regulated kinase 1 (ERK1). In addition, HDAC6 alters the binding capacity of cortactin to F-actin [230], thus affecting not only the microtubule dynamics but also actin-based cell motility. A paradigm of the importance of this specific activity of HDAC6, associated with the presence of a DMB, is represented by its role in both the central and peripheral nervous systems, as axons rely on the transport of molecules and organelles (i.e., mitochondria) along cytoskeletal components for their survival. Specifically, it has been shown that HDAC6 may affect axonal transport deacetylating α-tubulin. Indeed, acetylated α−tubulin provides a docking site for motor proteins, and it has been hypothesised that the dynamic acetylation/deacetylation of α-tubulin may represent a code for specific motor proteins [231]. Kinesins, for example, which are responsible for the anterograde transport along microtubules, preferentially recognise acetylated α-tubulin [232]. Furthermore, HDAC6 may also influence mitochondria axonal transport. In fact, HDAC6 deacetylates Miro1, a calcium-binding outer mitochondrial membrane protein, which, when acetylated on K105, increases mitochondria transport along axons [233,234]. Thus, HDAC6 negatively affects axonal transport by α-tubulin and Miro1 deacetylation and, consequently, impairs axonal outgrowth. The latter is also dependent upon the cortactin–F-actin network [235] at the growth cone. As mentioned before, acetylated cortactin drives F-actin polymerisation [230], which is required for the membrane protrusion that, in turn, fuels the leading edge and axon outgrowth. Therefore, cortactin deacetylation is another mechanism through which HDAC6 severely impairs axonal outgrowth [230,236].

In addition to its role in cytoskeleton dynamics and cargo transport along microtubules, HDAC6 deacetylates also a number of signalling molecules. Indeed, HDAC6 binds and deacetylates ERK 1 and 2, enhancing their activity [237], while, as mentioned above, ERK1 phosphorylates HDAC6, resulting in a self-fuelling circuit that controls both the response to extracellular signals (e.g., growth factors) and, consequently, cell proliferation and motility [206]. In addition, HDAC6 participates in both the PI3K/Akt and the Wnt signalling pathways. By deacetylating HSP90, HDAC6 reinforces Akt/HSP90 binding, providing protection for HSP90 from proteasomal degradation and stabilising Akt phosphorylation [156]. By deacetylating β-catenin, HDAC6 allows its nuclear translocation and activation of Wnt-dependent transcription [238].

4.1.3. ZnF/UBP-Dependent HDCA6 Activity

The ZnF/UBP binding domain of HDAC6 virtually hooks every ubiquitinated protein due to its high affinity for ubiquitin (ub)-residues. This property makes HDAC6 actively involved in the elimination of misfolded protein aggregates through the autophagy pathway when the proteasome is inhibited [239,240]. Indeed, when the proteasome machinery is functional, HDAC6 interacts with valosin containing protein (VCP)/p97. This interaction promotes the dissociation of HDAC6 from the ubiquitinated target and the degradation of the latter through the proteasome [241]. However, when the proteasome is inhibited, HDAC6 moves misfolded aggregates to the perinuclear region at the microtubule organising centre (MTOC) through dynein, which is responsible for retrograde transport in the microtubules, contributing to aggresomes formation, which are further degraded by the autophagy pathway [242]. HDAC6 also impairs the formation of misfolded protein aggregates through the activation of HSPs. Indeed, in physiological conditions, HDAC6 is bound and deacetylates HSP90/heat shock factor 1 (HSF1). When polyubiquitinated proteins are bound by the ZnF/UBP domain of HDAC6, HDAC6 detaches from and releases HSP90, which becomes acetylated, and HSF1, which induces the transcription of HSP70 and 27. These chaperones, together with HSP90, impair the formation of new misfolded aggregates [240].

Very recently, it has been also demonstrated that HDAC6 participates in aggresomes' structure maintenance by interacting with vimentin p72 and locking the aggresome vimentin cage [243], uncovering another intriguing function for HDAC6.

In addition to aggresomes, the ubiquitin binding and motor activities of HDAC6 control also the formation and activation of the NACHT, leucine-rich repeat (LRR), and pyrin domain (PYD)-containing protein 3 (NLRP3) inflammasomes, which protect the cell from endogenous dangerous signals (due to both cell damage and death and a variety of pathogens) employing pro- and activated caspase 1 and pyroptosis and inducing the secretion of interleukins (1 and 18) [244,245]. HDAC6 binds to NLRP3, mediates its reverse transport to the MTOC [242], and activates the NLRP3 inflammasome, a process dependent on the HDAC6 ubiquitin-binding domain. Moreover, HDAC6 interacts with ubiquitinated NLRP3, promoting its degradation in an autophagic manner [246]. In parallel, the prominent affinity for ubiquitin residues makes HDAC6 capable of regulating viral infections, especially of influenza A (IAV), human immunodeficiency 1 (HIV-1), and Coxsackie A16 viruses (CA16). In this regard, HDAC6 exerts both pro-viral and antiviral activities. Indeed, by binding the M1 tag on the IAV capsid, HDAC6 transports IAV particles along the microtubules. After M1 removal and virus uncoating, caspase-3-dependent degradation of the ZnF-UBP domain of HDAC6 allows for viral replication and virion assembly [247]. At the same time, stabilisation of the HDAC6 SE14 domain induces cell apoptosis, spreading the virus outside the dying cell [248]. However, HDAC6 may also block IAV replication and spread by directly inhibiting PA ribonuclease and RNA polymerase and reducing the transport of virions along microtubules by deacetylating α-tubulin [249,250].

HDAC6 is also a "guardian" that monitors infections by HIV-1. Indeed, by binding to and moving Vif and Pr55Gag, two key players in HIV-1 assembly and release, to the autophagosomes, HDAC6 restricts HIV-1 infection [251]. On the other hand, the HIV-1 core helper protein Nef promotes HDAC6 degradation, ensuring HIV-1 dissemination [252].

CA16 is a common enterovirus, causing hand–foot–mouth disease. The PKR/eIF2α pathway is exploited by the cell to form stress granules (SGs) [253,254] that limit viral replication and induce the production of antiviral molecules, such as interferons. The ZnF/UBP domain of HDAC6, together with p62, promotes SGs degradation, inhibiting type I interferon release and allowing viral replication [255].

4.1.4. Ubiquitinating Activity

In addition to binding to ub-residues, HDAC6 has been found to possess a ubiquitin E3 ligase activity. Indeed, HDAC6 ubiquitinates DNA repair enzymes belonging to both the base excision repair (BER) and the mismatch repair systems (MMR). It has been found to ubiquitinate MSH2 [221], Chk1 [256], and p300 [227].

4.2. HDAC6 and Cilia

Both the critical activity of HDAC6 in regulating the assembly of cytoskeletal components (i.e., microtubules and actin fibres) and the ZnF/UBP-dependent functions are linked to the important role this enzyme plays in primary cilium formation/resorption (Figure 1). Although the role of HDAC6 in primary cilia disassembly and signalling is still an active area of investigation, it has been uncovered that the AurA kinase-mediated phosphorylation of HDAC6 results in its activation, axoneme's microtubules deacetylation, and cilia retraction [209]. During this process, HDAC6 is assisted by a wide number of mediators, e.g., human enhancer of filamentation 1, pitchfork, calmodulin, nephrocystin-2/inversin, macro-phage stimulating 1/2 (Mst1/2), and β-catenin, which regulate HDAC6/AurA interaction [257–261]. In parallel, HDAC6 is differentially regulated by the proteins involved in cilia formation and signalling, being either inhibited [262] or activated [263] or intracellularly re-localised [264]. Further, stress signal-dependent cilia shortening relies on the ability of HDAC6 to eliminate the aggregates of misfolded intracellular ciliary proteins that form when cilia are damaged by toxic agents, such as cigarette smoke. In this process, misfolded aggregates are recognised by HDAC6 and moved to the autophagosome in order to be transferred to lysosomes for autophagic degradation [265].

4.3. HDAC6 in GBM

The role of HDAC6 in cancer has been extensively reviewed elsewhere [156,266]. In this paragraph, we will strictly focus on the functions HDAC6 performs in the onset and progression of GBM. It has to be remarked that, to date, very few papers investigated the role of HDAC6 in glioblastoma ontogeny. In addition, most of the findings have been similarly reported in both GBM cell lines and patient-derived GSCs. Thus, in this paragraph, a summary of the whole amount of available data will be provided, summarised, and schemed in Figure 3.

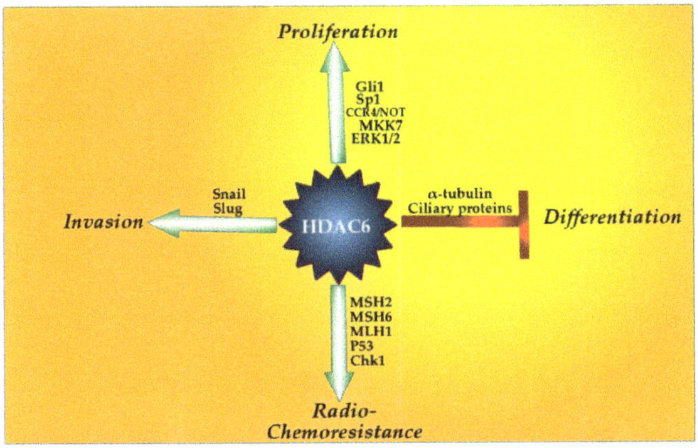

Figure 3. Pathways potentially affected by HDAC6 in GBM. Multifaceted HDAC6 may impact diverse processes pivotal to GBM ontogeny and progression, suggesting HDAC6 to be potentially targeted for therapeutic purposes.

Despite the little piece of information, HDAC6 has been found to be involved in pathways pivotal to GBM cell survival, such as proliferation, spheroid formation, migration, de-differentiation, and resistance to both radio- and chemotherapy, due to its involvement in DNA damage tolerance.

4.3.1. HDAC6 and GBM Cells' Proliferation

It is widely accepted and demonstrated that GBM cells, including GSCs, exhibit high levels of HDAC6. HDAC6 promotes the proliferation of GBM cells in a number of ways, a phenomenon that is classically paralleled by radio- and chemotherapy resistance. First, by potentiating ERK1 and 2 activity, it strongly amplifies EGF receptor mitogenic signalling and potentiates GBM spheroids formation. Further, stabilising EGFR also promotes resistance to TMZ [21]. By interacting with carbon catabolite repression, negative on TATA-less (CCR4-NOT) core exoribonuclease subunit 6 (CNOT6), a typical protein related to mRNA decay, and FUS RNA protecting protein, HDAC6 protects the long non-coding RNA LINC00461 by preserving polyadenylate tail maintenance. This HDAC6-dependent mechanism results in an increase in the proteins related to cell division by a sponging mechanism through which LINC00461 sequesters miR-485-3p [267]. HDAC6 has been also found to increase the activity of TFs deputed to the regulation of cell cycle-related genes. Specifically, HDAC6 increases MAP kinase 7 (MKK7) protein levels and downstream Jun N-terminal kinase (JNK)/c-Jun activities, bursting GBM cell proliferation. In this regard, HDAC6 protects MKK7 from proteasomal degradation [22]. This mechanism of protection could rely on MKK7 deacetylation by HDAC6, as occurs for Flotillin-2 (FLOT2) in nasopharyngeal carcinoma [268]. In addition, in cooperation with HDAC1 and 2, it induces Sp1 transcription by a positive feedback loop in which Sp1 deacetylation is required for its binding to its own promoter. Consequently, enhanced Sp1 activity has been shown to upregulate cell cycle genes, promoting GBM cell proliferation [269]. Gli1 is also controlled by HDAC6 at the transcriptional level. Gli TFs are downstream players of the Shh pathway, which is involved in GBM cell proliferation and GSC stemness maintenance (see also section "Altered Primary Cilia Siganlling in GBM" [73,270,271]). Indeed, it has been found that, upon HDAC6 silencing or chemical inhibition by tubastatin A (see below), Gli1 mRNA decreases in GBM cell lines and that this regulation is transcription-dependent [28,272]. Thus, sustaining Gli1 activity, HDAC6 exploits Shh signalling to propel GBM cell proliferation. Smad2 is another TF affected by HDAC6. Indeed, this latter inhibits Smad2 phosphorylation, impairing its binding to the p21 promoter and inducing GBM cell proliferation [23].

4.3.2. HDAC6 and the Epithelial–Mesenchymal Transition (EMT)

Very little information is available regarding the role HDAC6 plays in GBM EMT. It has been shown that HDAC6 regulates EMT TFs Snail and Slug expression, presumably at the transcriptional level (or via increased mRNA stability), although a molecular mechanism has not been provided [28]. However, given the role that HDAC6 exerts in this process in other cancers [273–275], it is conceivable that GBM spreading and invasion of the surrounding brain tissue would, at least in part, depend on HDAC6 activity.

4.3.3. HDAC6 Action Through GSCs Primary Cilia

Very few reports address the role of HDAC6 in controlling pivotal GSC properties through the modulation of primary cilia assembly/disassembly and signalling. Inhibiting HDAC6 enzymatic activity produces an increase in both the acetylated levels of α-tubulin and in the number of ciliated, patient-derived GSCs, as expected. Intriguingly, in the same experimental conditions, α-tubulin within the cilia axoneme is deacetylated. As a consequence, cilia depletion through KIF3A and ARL13B knockdown does not entail GSC growth arrest upon HDAC6 inhibition, but rather a block of differentiation. Thus, in GSCs, HDAC6 acts through the primary cilia to restrain differentiation programs (see also Section 2.2.2), maintaining their proliferation ability [19]. This phenomenon may be dependent on overactive Shh signalling in HDAC6-overexpressing GSCs. Indeed, in HDAC6-depleted cells, Gli TFs and patched receptors are downregulated and the Shh pathway is inactive, leading to GSC differentiation [18].

4.3.4. HDAC6 and GBM Resistance to Radio- and Chemotherapy

Given the established role of HDAC6 in activating diverse DNA damage response (DDR) pathways [222,276–278], its role in mediating both radio- and chemotherapy resistance in GBM is not surprising. HDAC6 is known to activate multiple DDR genes via Sp1 [20], thus promoting TMZ resistance in GBM cells. It has been reported that, together with HDAC4, HDAC6 promotes double-strand breaks (DSBs) repair in glioblastoma, as interfering with their translation promotes radiosensitivity in the U87MG and U251 GBM cell lines but not in normal astrocytes or cortical neurons. HDAC6 interference not only provided the accumulation of γH2AX spots onto chromatin but also impaired the nuclear translocation of ATM and DNA-Pkcs, two key players involved in DSBs repair, which interact with HDAC6. HDAC6 silencing induces both apoptosis and autophagy in GBM cells and, more importantly, negatively affects GSC's self-renewal [24]. HDAC6 inhibition also promotes the accumulation of MSH2 and 6, as well as the decrease in MGMT and p53, inducing apoptosis in TMZ-resistant GBM cells [273]. In GSCs, HDAC6 inhibition has been shown to promote Chk1 degradation through the downregulation of the X-linked inhibitor of apoptosis (XIAP), thus promoting radiosensitivity [26].

4.3.5. GBM Subtypes: A HDAC6 Point of View

Although no information is available about the selective functions of HDAC6 in the three different GBM subtypes, some insights may be deduced by the HDAC6-dependent regulation of key players identifying a specific GBM subtype. The involvement of HDAC6 in EGFR and Shh signalling amplification [21,73,270,271] suggests a role in the onset and/or maintenance of the classical GBM subtype. In parallel, HDAC6's role in promoting neoangiogenesis and in regulating inflammation and cell migration indicates that deregulation of HDAC6 activity may also influence pathway derangement in mesenchymal GBM cells [4,212,213]. It has been shown that HDAC6 controls VEGF-dependent notch signalling, promoting angiogenesis in lung ECs [279]. Further, by Sp1 deacetylation and the consequent increased transcriptional activity, HDAC6 regulates endoglin, a co-receptor activating transforming growth factor-β (TGF-β) signal transduction, expression and tumour angiogenesis [280,281]. Strikingly, HDAC6-dependent cortactin deacetylation (see Section 4.1.2) initiates ECs migration [281].

The role HDAC6 plays in regulating cilia disassembly directly impacts the tumorigenic properties of the proneural subtype cells, which are characterised by alterations in PDFGRα (focal amplification and mutations [2]). By PDGFRα de-localisation from the ciliary membrane to the cell cytosol, due to cilia disassembly, HDAC6 may contribute to PDFGRα signalling deregulation and proneural GBM cell maintenance [104].

4.4. *HDAC6 Inhibitors*

FDA-approved HDACi for clinical use has the disadvantage of causing consistent side effects when administered to humans [15]. Indeed, vorinostat, panobinostat, belinostat, romidepsin, and chidamide [282–285] are pan-HDACi that impact systemically on diverse organs, provoking asthenia, cardiotoxicity, diarrhoea, fatigue, and a severe decrease in blood cell populations [286–289]. In contrast, selective HDACi may be more well-tolerated, with mitigated side effects. Over the years, different specific HDAC6i have been developed, taking into account the "gold" of the pharmacophore model common to all HDACs, namely the cap, the linker, and the zinc-binding group (ZBG). In general, the cap is an aromatic group connected to the hydrophobic alkyl group representing the linker and the ZBG coordinates the Zn^{2+} ion in the active site. HDAC6i produced are discriminated by the ZBG, which may be a hydroxamic derivative or another ZBG. Among the hydroxamic acid-based HDAC6i, Tubacin was the first to be discovered [290,291] showing an almost 320-fold selectivity over HDAC1 and 2. Tubacin has no severe side effects, but it cannot be used for clinical purposes, as it is highly lipophilic. Based on the tubacin structure, Ricolinostat has been proven to be a better drug. It is the first HDAC6i approved for human use to treat multiple myeloma (MM) [292] and synergises with both bortezominb and carfilzomib (proteasome inhibitors) to induce apoptosis of MM cells [293]. Linear triazolylphenyl–hydroxamic acid derivatives have been shown to be selective HDAC6i with NOC-7 being the most potent (IC_{50} = 0.002 nM) [294]. Also, biaryl hydroxamates possess an nM inhibitor activity over HDAC6 [295]. SAHA (vorinostat) derivatives, with modifications of C_2, C_4, and C_5 in the linker, also showed a certain selectivity for HDAC6 [296].

Considering the wider and almost outward channel of HDAC6, new inhibitors have been developed that replace the alkyl chain linker with aromatic groups and are designed to have larger and stiffer caps, which were supposed to be more effective in inhibiting HDAC6 activity. Tubastatin A, a tetrahydro-γ-carboline derivative, is one of these inhibitors and shows a 1000-fold selectivity for HDAC6 over all of the HDACs, except HDAC8 (57 fold) [297]. Intriguingly, Tubastatin A not only promotes α-tubulin hyperacetylation but also histone acetylation, thus also suggesting an impairment of HDAC6 nuclear function. Second-generation and sulphur analogues of Tubastatin have been developed, showing a ~5000–7000 fold selectivity over class I HDACs and a subnanomolar inhibitory activity over HDAC6 [298,299]

"Y-shaped" HDAC6i also hold potent inhibitor activity over HDAC6 at nanomolar concentrations. Nexurastat is 601-fold more selective for HDAC6 over HDAC8 and possesses a branching element near the ZBG, which accounts for its specificity [300]. Similarly, HPOB is selective for HDAC6, with an IC_{50} 10-fold higher than that of Nexurastat [301].

Many other HDAC6i have been designed, although their efficacies were proven at submicromolar concentrations, and they frequently inhibited not only HDAC6 but also HDAC8 [302,303]. Of note, hydroxamates are genotoxic. Therefore, the recent tendency is to provide HDAC6i with other ZBGs, such as mercaptoacetamide, thicarbonate, trifluoromethylketone, hydrazide, hydroxypyridones, and others. However, these molecules still deserve further improvements [302].

4.4.1. HDAC6 PROTACS

An intriguing novel class of HDAC6i is represented by proteolysis-targeting chimaeras (PROTACs), which are bifunctional molecules provided with a small molecule inhibitor and a ligand of the ubiquitin E3 ligase [304], which promote proteasome degradation of the protein of interest. This technology fully revolutionised the field of small molecules based exclusively on the chemical inhibition of the catalytic pocket, as they provide the complete elimination of the protein of interest (POI). Further, they showed high versatility with respect to small molecules targeting POI active sites, as they may be transiently linked to any fissure present in their target. First reported at the beginning of the XXI century, PROTACs research has skyrocketed in the past 5 years and is applied to different POIs, including TFs, chromatin remodelling enzymes, and nuclear and membrane receptors, among others [305]. Importantly, two entered clinical trials, namely ARV-110 (clinical trial identifier NCT NCT03888612) and ARV-471 (clinical trial identifier NCT04072952), targeting the androgen and the estrogen receptor, respectively. PROTACs present several advantages compared to small molecule inhibitors, including isoform selectivity, disruption of enzymatic and scaffolding activities, and degradation of members of multimolecular complexes [305]. Different PROTACs having HDAC6 as a POI have been developed. Hydroxamate-based, cereblon-based and PROTACs designed onto Y-shaped HDAC6s [306–308] have been demonstrated to potently degrade HDAC6 and to be efficient in restraining HDAC6-dependent inflammatory events and impair cancer cells' proliferation [309–311].

4.4.2. Dual Inhibitors

A characteristic of most of the HDACis is that their efficacy is basically limited to haematologic malignancies. Thus, dual inhibitors have been designed to be applied also to solid cancers. 6-(4-((5-Chloro-4-((4-chlorophenyl) amino) pyrimidin-2-yl) amino)-1H-pyrazol-1-yl)-N-hydroxyhexanamide is a JAK/HDAC inhibitor. When the 4-chlorophenyl moiety is substituted by pyridine or other phenyl groups, the selectivity for HDAC6 increases, together with the anti-tumour properties [312]. Derivatives of VEGFR and HDAC inhibitors were also produced and showed anticancer activity [313]. GSK3β/HDAC6 dual inhibitors and HDAC6/tubulin inhibitors have been also developed and showed significant efficacy both as anticancer agents and neuroprotective drugs [314,315].

4.4.3. HDAC6i in Clinical Trials

To date, eight clinical trials employing HDAC6 inhibitors, alone and in combination with other drugs, for cancer treatment have been launched. Half were completed. Two stopped early. One was withdrawn, and one is still recruiting. The results from the completed trials are encouraging, as the therapies were safe and well-tolerated. Further, responses, although partial, were observed. Ricolinostat (ACY1215) in combination with bortezomib, a proteasome inhibitor, and dexamethasone has been proven to be relatively efficient in relapsed MM patients (37%) and, most importantly, in a small percentage of bortezomib refractory patients (14%) [292]. Citarinostat (ACY241), either in combination with nivolumab or paclitaxel, has been tested in patients affected by solid tumours. In 17 non-small cell lung cancer (NSCLC) patients, no dose-limiting toxicity was reported, and either partial response or stable disease was achieved with increased infiltrating $CD3^+$ lymphocytes [316]. The same promising results were obtained in 20 patients affected by non-hematologic malignancies. No dose-limiting toxicity, partial responses, and stable diseases were observed together with decreased paclitaxel-induced neutropenia [317]. KA2507 (IC_{50} = 2.5 nM) similarly showed no dose-limiting toxicity in patients with PD-L1-expressing tumours. The best response detected was a stable disease in patients with relapsed and/or refractory solid tumours [318]. Overall, these results strongly suggest the use of HDAC6i, alone or in combination, as a powerful strategy to treat advanced and refractory cancers. Moreover, the lack of considerable side effects, which are, instead, provided by pan-HDACi, makes HDAC6i a more advisable strategy for cancer treatment.

4.5. HDAC6i Application in GBM

HDAC6i application for GBM therapy is still an unexplored field of investigation. Few works have reported the use of HDAC6i in GBM models. However, the available literature is unanimous in suggesting HDAC6 inhibition as a valuable tool to counteract GBM progression and, more importantly, resistance to therapy. A variety of mechanisms and biological effects are at the basis of HDAC6i efficacy in both GBM cells and GSCs and in animal models. Tubastatin A has been demonstrated to inhibit migration, the Shh pathway, and to accelerate apoptosis in TMZ-treated GBM cell lines [272]. Dual inhibition of Shh and HDAC6 by tubastatin A and cyclopamine significantly inhibits GBM cells' proliferation in vitro and in orthotopic transplants in zebrafish hindbrain ventricles. Mechanistically, the combo treatment results in lysosomal stress with an impaired fusion of lysosomes and autophagosomes and derailment of sphingolipids catabolism in GBM cell lines and zebrafish embryos [27]. Additional evidence has been provided regarding the impairment of the autophagic pathway by HDAC6i as a route to induce GBM cell apoptosis. Indeed, tubastatin A and TMZ reverse the endoplasmic reticulum stress tolerance (ERST), a phenomenon that accounts, at least in part, for TMZ resistance and induces pro-apoptotic signals by activating the unfolded protein system (UPS) and harmful ER stress. Tubastatin A alone reduced the HDAC6 levels in autophagosomes of GBM cells, whereas the combination treatment promotes the association of HDAC6 to VCP/p97, resulting in defects in the clearance of misfolded proteins through the HDAC6-dependent autophagic pathway while promoting UPS [319]. Similarly, tubacin promotes autophagosome accumulation, growth arrest, and death in patient-derived glioma cells. In combination with TMZ, these effects were greatly enhanced, suggesting that fusion impairment of autophagosomes with lysosomes could be a common mechanism of action of HDAC6i [320]. In TMZ-resistant GBM cells, tubastatin A and different HDAC6i induce MMR genes and promote apoptosis. Additionally, a decrease in EGFR phosphorylation is observed. HDAC6i also induce wild-type p53 in TMZ-sensitive patients and decrease mutant p53 expression in TMZ-resistant GBM cells [25].

HDAC6 PROTACS have been also proven to be a useful strategy to inhibit GBM growth. The J22352 compound promotes the degradation of aberrantly expressed HDAC6 in GBM, with the consequent autophagic-dependent cell death, block of cell migration, and tumour growth inhibition in mouse subcutaneous xenografts. More importantly, J22352 reduced the level of immunosuppressive PD-L1 while dramatically recruiting $CD8^{+}T$ lymphocytes at the tumour site in vivo [321].

Dual inhibitors have been also designed and tested as efficient in the reduction of GBM growth. Adducts of donepezil, a drug approved for Alzheimer's disease, and different linkers and hydroxamate ZBGs have been produced. One of them, with an IC_{50} of 2.7nM for HDAC6 and 710nM for HDAC2, showed the greatest efficacy in limiting GBM cell growth in vitro and in vivo and in overcoming TMZ resistance [322]. A dual inhibitor of cytochrome P450 17A1 (CYP17A1), which is correlated with a poor prognosis in GBM patients and resistance to TMZ [323], and HDAC6 has been also produced. This abiraterone [324] (CYP17A1 inhibitor)/hydroxamic acid inhibitor also showed a potent antiproliferative effect on GBM both in vitro and in vivo, enhanced ROS production, activated DDR, and reversed TMZ resistance [325].

5. Conclusions

As outlined in the present work, HDAC6 appears as a multifaceted molecule ruling a plethora of biological mechanisms, spanning through the regulation of cytoskeleton-dependent processes until transcriptional regulation [156]. As a consequence, its inhibition has to be carefully evaluated when considering HDAC6 inhibition to treat human disorders. However, several pieces of evidence effectively suggest HDAC6 targeting as a route to face different diseases.

5.1. *From NDs to Cancer: Blocking Deacetylating and ZnF-UBP-Related Functions of HDAC6*

The fundamental role HDAC6 plays in controlling the polymerisation/depolymerisation of α-tubulin and actin implies a major involvement in CNS and PNS proper functionality. Defects in axonal transport are typical of neurodegenerative disorders (NDs), as well as the presence of aggregates of misfolded proteins and neuroinflammation due to inflammasome activation [326–328]. The involvement of HDAC6 in the axonal transport and regulation of misfolded aggregates and inflammasomes links HDAC6 to NDs, such as Alzheimer's disease (AD), Parkinson's Disease (PD) [328], and peripheral neuropathies such as Charcot Marie Tooth (CMT) syndrome [329] and chemotherapy-induced peripheral neuropathy [330]. Further, HDAC6 inhibition has been shown to reverse transactive response DNA-binding protein-43 (TDP-43)-related axonal defects [331,332], suggesting HDAC6 targeting as a still-unexplored treatment for NDs.

Similarly, its role in regulating primary cilia disassembly may envisage HDAC6 as a molecular target for the treatment of ciliopathies, a family of diseases presenting both genotypic and phenotypic heterogeneity, primarily affecting the CNS [83,84]. In this context, HDAC6 functions are not yet fully investigated, but it is highly probable that, in addition to its role in controlling microtubule depolymerisation, HDAC6-dependent deacetylation of ciliary proteins or adaptors/mediators may participate in both the structural and signalling complexity of this cellular antenna. Different HDAC6 functions may be clinically targeted in an attempt to counteract primary cilia dysfunction. Inhibiting its deacetylation activity against α-tubulin could be the primary objective, as this should result in cilia restoration [209,257–261]. Also, the inhibition of HDAC6 ZnF-UBP-dependent autophagic activity could represent a potential goal to restrain cilia shortening [265]. Although a link between cilia and autophagy has been clearly established, we are still at the dawn of this emerging field of investigation, and further studies are necessary to dissect this complex circuitry [332]. Indeed, studies reporting the role of the autophagic process in ciliogenesis have been contradictory. It has been observed that autophagic degradation of the oral–facial–digital type 1 (OFD1) protein promotes ciliogenesis [333], whereas an autophagy-dependent depletion of ITF20 causes the opposite [334].

The involvement in viral infections (see Section 4.1.3) indicates HDAC6 as another potential weapon to prevent and/or treat viral diseases. With regard to inflammation-related disorders, it has to be noted that, depending on the specific context, HDAC6's role in regulating the inflammasome may be beneficial or detrimental. Thus, while in NDs blocking inflammation and HDAC6-dependent inflammasome activation may be exploited as a strategy to prevent, treat, and/or ameliorate NDs symptoms [326], in cancer, the inhibition of this specific HDAC6 function is a double-edged sword. Indeed, chronic inflammation activates the NLRP3 inflammasome, which triggers an immunosuppressive response, tumour progression, and metastasis formation [335]. However, the opposite has been also observed. In colorectal cancer, NLRP3 inflammasome activation is associated with natural killer cells recruitment and tumour suppression [336]. Furthermore, inflammation-associated IL-18 production has been proven to possess tumoricidal activity [337]. Thus, the efficacy of the inhibition of inflammasome-associated HDAC6 functions is highly context-dependent.

5.2. *HDAC6 Inhibition: A Novel Strategy Against GBM?*

HDAC inhibitor application for GBM treatment surprisingly results in failure when administered mainly as a combo therapy in clinical trials. Multiple reasons may account for HDACi's inefficacy in GBM. One of major importance is the presence of the BBB, which preserves the brain from insults. In addition, tumour heterogeneity and the surrounding microenvironment may provide a further level of complexity, which may strongly limit HDACi's success. Over the years, the drug discovery field moved to the design of novel hybrid molecules able to cross the BBB [200,201] and to simultaneously target HDACs and other players pivotal to glioblastomagenesis [322,338,339]. However, thorough preclinical investigations are required to determine the effectiveness of these molecules.

Despite the paucity of information, inhibiting HDAC6 is emerging as a potential novel tool to enrich the extremely poor arsenal of treatments available against GBM. Indeed, high HDAC6 levels are constantly associated with (i) enhanced GBM cell proliferation and migration; (ii) increased resistance to radio- and chemotherapy; and (iii) self-renewal of GSCs. The amplification of Shh signalling and the resorption of primary cilia are characteristic of both HDAC6 activity [73,270,271] and GSCs, further strengthening the importance of GSCs targeting to the treatment of GBM. In this regard, resistance to current therapies is a specific trait of GSCs, capable of tolerating high levels of DNA damage [340]. Notably, HDAC6 has been found to interact with a plethora of DNA repair proteins, including PARP9, XRCC6, and TP53 [341], inducing DNA damage tolerance and TMZ resistance. Thus, HDAC6 inhibition may not only counteract GBM cells' tumorigenic properties but also overcome resistance to therapies. Derailment of the autophagic pathway and inhibition of autophagosome–lysosome fusion have been observed as an action mechanism of HDAC6i. Interestingly, starvation-induced TDP-43, whose insoluble aggregates are associated with NDs such as amyotrophic lateral sclerosis, frontotemporal dementia (FTD), and ADs, activates autophagy in an HDAC6-dependent manner in GBM, blocking apoptosis. Consequently, HDAC6 inhibition reverses the TDP-43 autophagic process and the anti-apoptotic effect [342].

To date, three HDAC6i, namely ricolinostat, citarinostat, and KA2507, entered clinical trials for multiple myelomas [343] and solid cancers [316–318,344]. HDACi have been proven to be inefficient in synergising with the current therapeutic approaches for GBM and promote considerable side effects, and most of them do not cross the BBB. Thus, treatments able to block tumour progression or to induce sensitisation to radio- and chemotherapy are extremely urgent. Affecting different HDAC6 functions may be a useful strategy to target different GBM properties. The design of inhibitors that hit the diverse domains involved in the execution of the activities HDAC6 exert in GBM cells could greatly enhance selectivity, whereas potency could be powered by adducts targeting GBM subtype-specific molecular signatures while penetrating the BBB. Inclusion into nanomicelles or the design of piperazine-based HDAC6i [200,201] may pave the way to the production of more efficient brain-penetrative drugs. This strategy may foster the design of personalised therapies aimed first at increasing the life expectancy of GBM patients, who are currently without an effective cure.

Author Contributions: F.S. wrote Sections 3, 3.1, 4.4, 4.4.1 and 4.4.2. B.I. wrote all the other sections. All authors have read and agreed to the published version of the manuscript.

Funding: This work was partially supported by the Consiglio Nazionale delle Ricerche—CNR (project DBA.AD005.225-NUTRAGE-FOE2021) and MFAG grant number 23099 to F.S.

Institutional Review Board Statement: Not applicable.

Informed Consent Statement: Not applicable.

Data Availability Statement: Not applicable.

Conflicts of Interest: The authors declare no conflicts of interest.

References

1. Preusser, M.; de Ribaupierre, S.; Wohrer, A.; Erridge, S.C.; Hegi, M.; Weller, M.; Stupp, R. Current concepts and management of glioblastoma. *Ann. Neurol.* **2011**, *70*, 9–21. [CrossRef] [PubMed]
2. Verhaak, R.G.; Hoadley, K.A.; Purdom, E.; Wang, V.; Qi, Y.; Wilkerson, M.D.; Miller, C.R.; Ding, L.; Golub, T.; Mesirov, J.P.; et al. Integrated genomic analysis identifies clinically relevant subtypes of glioblastoma characterized by abnormalities in PDGFRA, IDH1, EGFR, and NF1. *Cancer Cell* **2010**, *17*, 98–110. [CrossRef] [PubMed]
3. Patel, A.P.; Tirosh, I.; Trombetta, J.J.; Shalek, A.K.; Gillespie, S.M.; Wakimoto, H.; Cahill, D.P.; Nahed, B.V.; Curry, W.T.; Martuza, R.L.; et al. Single-cell RNA-seq highlights intratumoral heterogeneity in primary glioblastoma. *Science* **2014**, *344*, 1396–1401. [CrossRef] [PubMed]
4. Wang, Q.; Hu, B.; Hu, X.; Kim, H.; Squatrito, M.; Scarpace, L.; deCarvalho, A.C.; Lyu, S.; Li, P.; Li, Y.; et al. Tumor Evolution of Glioma-Intrinsic Gene Expression Subtypes Associates with Immunological Changes in the Microenvironment. *Cancer Cell* **2017**, *32*, 42–56.e46. [CrossRef] [PubMed]
5. Gimple, R.C.; Bhargava, S.; Dixit, D.; Rich, J.N. Glioblastoma stem cells: Lessons from the tumor hierarchy in a lethal cancer. *Genes. Dev.* **2019**, *33*, 591–609. [CrossRef]
6. Venere, M.; Hamerlik, P.; Wu, Q.; Rasmussen, R.D.; Song, L.A.; Vasanji, A.; Tenley, N.; Flavahan, W.A.; Hjelmeland, A.B.; Bartek, J.; et al. Therapeutic targeting of constitutive PARP activation compromises stem cell phenotype and survival of glioblastoma-initiating cells. *Cell Death Differ.* **2014**, *21*, 258–269. [CrossRef]
7. Wang, J.; Wakeman, T.P.; Lathia, J.D.; Hjelmeland, A.B.; Wang, X.F.; White, R.R.; Rich, J.N.; Sullenger, B.A. Notch promotes radioresistance of glioma stem cells. *Stem Cells* **2010**, *28*, 17–28. [CrossRef]
8. Bao, S.; Wu, Q.; McLendon, R.E.; Hao, Y.; Shi, Q.; Hjelmeland, A.B.; Dewhirst, M.W.; Bigner, D.D.; Rich, J.N. Glioma stem cells promote radioresistance by preferential activation of the DNA damage response. *Nature* **2006**, *444*, 756–760. [CrossRef]
9. Bhat, K.P.L.; Balasubramaniyan, V.; Vaillant, B.; Ezhilarasan, R.; Hummelink, K.; Hollingsworth, F.; Wani, K.; Heathcock, L.; James, J.D.; Goodman, L.D.; et al. Mesenchymal differentiation mediated by NF-kappaB promotes radiation resistance in glioblastoma. *Cancer Cell* **2013**, *24*, 331–346. [CrossRef]
10. Adams, J.M.; Strasser, A. Is tumor growth sustained by rare cancer stem cells or dominant clones? *Cancer Res.* **2008**, *68*, 4018–4021. [CrossRef]
11. Diehn, M.; Cho, R.W.; Clarke, M.F. Therapeutic implications of the cancer stem cell hypothesis. *Semin. Radiat. Oncol.* **2009**, *19*, 78–86. [CrossRef] [PubMed]
12. Tamura, K.; Aoyagi, M.; Ando, N.; Ogishima, T.; Wakimoto, H.; Yamamoto, M.; Ohno, K. Expansion of CD133-positive glioma cells in recurrent de novo glioblastomas after radiotherapy and chemotherapy. *J. Neurosurg.* **2013**, *119*, 1145–1155. [CrossRef]
13. Dawson, M.A.; Kouzarides, T. Cancer epigenetics: From mechanism to therapy. *Cell* **2012**, *150*, 12–27. [CrossRef] [PubMed]
14. Uddin, M.S.; Mamun, A.A.; Alghamdi, B.S.; Tewari, D.; Jeandet, P.; Sarwar, M.S.; Ashraf, G.M. Epigenetics of glioblastoma multiforme: From molecular mechanisms to therapeutic approaches. *Semin. Cancer Biol.* **2022**, *83*, 100–120. [CrossRef] [PubMed]
15. Kunadis, E.; Lakiotaki, E.; Korkolopoulou, P.; Piperi, C. Targeting post-translational histone modifying enzymes in glioblastoma. *Pharmacol. Ther.* **2021**, *220*, 107721. [CrossRef]
16. Lucio-Eterovic, A.K.; Cortez, M.A.; Valera, E.T.; Motta, F.J.; Queiroz, R.G.; Machado, H.R.; Carlotti, C.G., Jr.; Neder, L.; Scrideli, C.A.; Tone, L.G. Differential expression of 12 histone deacetylase (HDAC) genes in astrocytomas and normal brain tissue: Class II and IV are hypoexpressed in glioblastomas. *BMC Cancer* **2008**, *8*, 243. [CrossRef]
17. Wen, P.Y.; Weller, M.; Lee, E.Q.; Alexander, B.M.; Barnholtz-Sloan, J.S.; Barthel, F.P.; Batchelor, T.T.; Bindra, R.S.; Chang, S.M.; Chiocca, E.A.; et al. Glioblastoma in adults: A Society for Neuro-Oncology (SNO) and European Society of Neuro-Oncology (EANO) consensus review on current management and future directions. *Neuro Oncol.* **2020**, *22*, 1073–1113. [CrossRef]
18. Agosti, E.; Zeppieri, M.; De Maria, L.; Tedeschi, C.; Fontanella, M.M.; Panciani, P.P.; Ius, T. Glioblastoma Immunotherapy: A Systematic Review of the Present Strategies and Prospects for Advancements. *Int. J. Mol. Sci.* **2023**, *24*, 15037. [CrossRef]

19. Shi, P.; Hoang-Minh, L.B.; Tian, J.; Cheng, A.; Basrai, R.; Kalaria, N.; Lebowitz, J.J.; Khoshbouei, H.; Deleyrolle, L.P.; Sarkisian, M.R. HDAC6 Signaling at Primary Cilia Promotes Proliferation and Restricts Differentiation of Glioma Cells. *Cancers* **2021**, *13*, 1644. [CrossRef]
20. Yang, W.B.; Wu, A.C.; Hsu, T.I.; Liou, J.P.; Lo, W.L.; Chang, K.Y.; Chen, P.Y.; Kikkawa, U.; Yang, S.T.; Kao, T.J.; et al. Histone deacetylase 6 acts upstream of DNA damage response activation to support the survival of glioblastoma cells. *Cell Death Dis.* **2021**, *12*, 884. [CrossRef]
21. Wang, Z.; Hu, P.; Tang, F.; Lian, H.; Chen, X.; Zhang, Y.; He, X.; Liu, W.; Xie, C. HDAC6 promotes cell proliferation and confers resistance to temozolomide in glioblastoma. *Cancer Lett.* **2016**, *379*, 134–142. [CrossRef]
22. Huang, Z.; Xia, Y.; Hu, K.; Zeng, S.; Wu, L.; Liu, S.; Zhi, C.; Lai, M.; Chen, D.; Xie, L.; et al. Histone deacetylase 6 promotes growth of glioblastoma through the MKK7/JNK/c-Jun signaling pathway. *J. Neurochem.* **2020**, *152*, 221–234. [CrossRef] [PubMed]
23. Li, S.; Liu, X.; Chen, X.; Zhang, L.; Wang, X. Histone deacetylase 6 promotes growth of glioblastoma through inhibition of SMAD2 signaling. *Tumour Biol.* **2015**, *36*, 9661–9665. [CrossRef] [PubMed]
24. Marampon, F.; Megiorni, F.; Camero, S.; Crescioli, C.; McDowell, H.P.; Sferra, R.; Vetuschi, A.; Pompili, S.; Ventura, L.; De Felice, F.; et al. HDAC4 and HDAC6 sustain DNA double strand break repair and stem-like phenotype by promoting radioresistance in glioblastoma cells. *Cancer Lett.* **2017**, *397*, 1–11. [CrossRef] [PubMed]
25. Kim, G.W.; Lee, D.H.; Yeon, S.K.; Jeon, Y.H.; Yoo, J.; Lee, S.W.; Kwon, S.H. Temozolomide-resistant Glioblastoma Depends on HDAC6 Activity Through Regulation of DNA Mismatch Repair. *Anticancer. Res.* **2019**, *39*, 6731–6741. [CrossRef] [PubMed]
26. Yang, W.; Liu, Y.; Gao, R.; Yu, H.; Sun, T. HDAC6 inhibition induces glioma stem cells differentiation and enhances cellular radiation sensitivity through the SHH/Gli1 signaling pathway. *Cancer Lett.* **2018**, *415*, 164–176. [CrossRef] [PubMed]
27. Pezzotta, A.; Brioschi, L.; Carbone, S.; Mazzoleni, B.; Bontempi, V.; Monastra, F.; Mauri, L.; Marozzi, A.; Mione, M.; Pistocchi, A.; et al. Combined Inhibition of Hedgehog and HDAC6: In Vitro and In Vivo Studies Reveal a New Role for Lysosomal Stress in Reducing Glioblastoma Cell Viability. *Int. J. Mol. Sci.* **2023**, *24*, 5771. [CrossRef]
28. Urdiciain, A.; Erausquin, E.; Zelaya, M.V.; Zazpe, I.; Lanciego, J.L.; Melendez, B.; Rey, J.A.; Idoate, M.A.; Riobo-Del Galdo, N.A.; Castresana, J.S. Silencing of Histone Deacetylase 6 Decreases Cellular Malignancy and Contributes to Primary Cilium Restoration, Epithelial-to-Mesenchymal Transition Reversion, and Autophagy Inhibition in Glioblastoma Cell Lines. *Biology* **2021**, *10*, 467. [CrossRef]
29. Ostrom, Q.T.; Cioffi, G.; Waite, K.; Kruchko, C.; Barnholtz-Sloan, J.S. CBTRUS Statistical Report: Primary Brain and Other Central Nervous System Tumors Diagnosed in the United States in 2014–2018. *Neuro Oncol.* **2021**, *23*, iii1–iii105. [CrossRef]
30. Sturm, D.; Witt, H.; Hovestadt, V.; Khuong-Quang, D.A.; Jones, D.T.; Konermann, C.; Pfaff, E.; Tonjes, M.; Sill, M.; Bender, S.; et al. Hotspot mutations in H3F3A and IDH1 define distinct epigenetic and biological subgroups of glioblastoma. *Cancer Cell* **2012**, *22*, 425–437. [CrossRef]
31. Miller, C.R.; Perry, A. Glioblastoma. *Arch. Pathol. Lab. Med.* **2007**, *131*, 397–406. [CrossRef] [PubMed]
32. Cencioni, C.; Scagnoli, F.; Spallotta, F.; Nasi, S.; Illi, B. The "Superoncogene" Myc at the Crossroad between Metabolism and Gene Expression in Glioblastoma Multiforme. *Int. J. Mol. Sci.* **2023**, *24*, 4217. [CrossRef]
33. Ohgaki, H.; Dessen, P.; Jourde, B.; Horstmann, S.; Nishikawa, T.; Di Patre, P.L.; Burkhard, C.; Schuler, D.; Probst-Hensch, N.M.; Maiorka, P.C.; et al. Genetic pathways to glioblastoma: A population-based study. *Cancer Res.* **2004**, *64*, 6892–6899. [CrossRef]
34. Hartmann, C.; Meyer, J.; Balss, J.; Capper, D.; Mueller, W.; Christians, A.; Felsberg, J.; Wolter, M.; Mawrin, C.; Wick, W.; et al. Type and frequency of IDH1 and IDH2 mutations are related to astrocytic and oligodendroglial differentiation and age: A study of 1,010 diffuse gliomas. *Acta Neuropathol.* **2009**, *118*, 469–474. [CrossRef]
35. Brennan, C.W.; Verhaak, R.G.; McKenna, A.; Campos, B.; Noushmehr, H.; Salama, S.R.; Zheng, S.; Chakravarty, D.; Sanborn, J.Z.; Berman, S.H.; et al. The somatic genomic landscape of glioblastoma. *Cell* **2013**, *155*, 462–477. [CrossRef]
36. Appin, C.L.; Brat, D.J. Molecular pathways in gliomagenesis and their relevance to neuropathologic diagnosis. *Adv. Anat. Pathol.* **2015**, *22*, 50–58. [CrossRef] [PubMed]
37. Yamazaki, H.; Ohba, Y.; Tamaoki, N.; Shibuya, M. A deletion mutation within the ligand binding domain is responsible for activation of epidermal growth factor receptor gene in human brain tumors. *Jpn. J. Cancer Res.* **1990**, *81*, 773–779. [CrossRef] [PubMed]
38. The Cancer Genome Atlas Research Network. Comprehensive genomic characterization defines human glioblastoma genes and core pathways. *Nature* **2008**, *455*, 1061–1068. [CrossRef]
39. Mackay, A.; Burford, A.; Carvalho, D.; Izquierdo, E.; Fazal-Salom, J.; Taylor, K.R.; Bjerke, L.; Clarke, M.; Vinci, M.; Nandhabalan, M.; et al. Integrated Molecular Meta-Analysis of 1,000 Pediatric High-Grade and Diffuse Intrinsic Pontine Glioma. *Cancer Cell* **2017**, *32*, 520–537.e525. [CrossRef]
40. Lewis, P.W.; Muller, M.M.; Koletsky, M.S.; Cordero, F.; Lin, S.; Banaszynski, L.A.; Garcia, B.A.; Muir, T.W.; Becher, O.J.; Allis, C.D. Inhibition of PRC2 activity by a gain-of-function H3 mutation found in pediatric glioblastoma. *Science* **2013**, *340*, 857–861. [CrossRef]
41. Portela, A.; Esteller, M. Epigenetic modifications and human disease. *Nat. Biotechnol.* **2010**, *28*, 1057–1068. [CrossRef] [PubMed]
42. Lambiv, W.L.; Vassallo, I.; Delorenzi, M.; Shay, T.; Diserens, A.C.; Misra, A.; Feuerstein, B.; Murat, A.; Migliavacca, E.; Hamou, M.F.; et al. The Wnt inhibitory factor 1 (WIF1) is targeted in glioblastoma and has a tumor suppressing function potentially by induction of senescence. *Neuro Oncol.* **2011**, *13*, 736–747. [CrossRef] [PubMed]

43. Gotze, S.; Wolter, M.; Reifenberger, G.; Muller, O.; Sievers, S. Frequent promoter hypermethylation of Wnt pathway inhibitor genes in malignant astrocytic gliomas. *Int. J. Cancer* **2010**, *126*, 2584–2593. [CrossRef] [PubMed]
44. Horiguchi, K.; Tomizawa, Y.; Tosaka, M.; Ishiuchi, S.; Kurihara, H.; Mori, M.; Saito, N. Epigenetic inactivation of RASSF1A candidate tumor suppressor gene at 3p21.3 in brain tumors. *Oncogene* **2003**, *22*, 7862–7865. [CrossRef] [PubMed]
45. Martinez, R.; Esteller, M. The DNA methylome of glioblastoma multiforme. *Neurobiol. Dis.* **2010**, *39*, 40–46. [CrossRef]
46. Mattei, A.L.; Bailly, N.; Meissner, A. DNA methylation: A historical perspective. *Trends Genet.* **2022**, *38*, 676–707. [CrossRef]
47. Zhang, X.; Zhang, Y.; Wang, C.; Wang, X. TET (Ten-eleven translocation) family proteins: Structure, biological functions and applications. *Signal Transduct. Target. Ther.* **2023**, *8*, 297. [CrossRef]
48. Muller, T.; Gessi, M.; Waha, A.; Isselstein, L.J.; Luxen, D.; Freihoff, D.; Freihoff, J.; Becker, A.; Simon, M.; Hammes, J.; et al. Nuclear exclusion of TET1 is associated with loss of 5-hydroxymethylcytosine in IDH1 wild-type gliomas. *Am. J. Pathol.* **2012**, *181*, 675–683. [CrossRef]
49. Hughes, L.A.; Melotte, V.; de Schrijver, J.; de Maat, M.; Smit, V.T.; Bovee, J.V.; French, P.J.; van den Brandt, P.A.; Schouten, L.J.; de Meyer, T.; et al. The CpG island methylator phenotype: What's in a name? *Cancer Res.* **2013**, *73*, 5858–5868. [CrossRef]
50. Ohba, S.; Hirose, Y. Biological Significance of Mutant Isocitrate Dehydrogenase 1 and 2 in Gliomagenesis. *Neurol. Med. Chir.* **2016**, *56*, 170–179. [CrossRef]
51. Ichimura, K. Molecular pathogenesis of IDH mutations in gliomas. *Brain Tumor Pathol.* **2012**, *29*, 131–139. [CrossRef] [PubMed]
52. Xu, W.; Yang, H.; Liu, Y.; Yang, Y.; Wang, P.; Kim, S.H.; Ito, S.; Yang, C.; Wang, P.; Xiao, M.T.; et al. Oncometabolite 2-hydroxyglutarate is a competitive inhibitor of alpha-ketoglutarate-dependent dioxygenases. *Cancer Cell* **2011**, *19*, 17–30. [CrossRef] [PubMed]
53. Yuan, F.; Wang, Y.; Cai, X.; Du, C.; Zhu, J.; Tang, C.; Yang, J.; Ma, C. N6-methyladenosine-related microRNAs risk model trumps the isocitrate dehydrogenase mutation status as a predictive biomarker for the prognosis and immunotherapy in lower grade gliomas. *Explor. Target. Antitumor Ther.* **2022**, *3*, 553–569. [CrossRef] [PubMed]
54. Rickman, D.S.; Bobek, M.P.; Misek, D.E.; Kuick, R.; Blaivas, M.; Kurnit, D.M.; Taylor, J.; Hanash, S.M. Distinctive molecular profiles of high-grade and low-grade gliomas based on oligonucleotide microarray analysis. *Cancer Res.* **2001**, *61*, 6885–6891.
55. Phillips, H.S.; Kharbanda, S.; Chen, R.; Forrest, W.F.; Soriano, R.H.; Wu, T.D.; Misra, A.; Nigro, J.M.; Colman, H.; Soroceanu, L.; et al. Molecular subclasses of high-grade glioma predict prognosis, delineate a pattern of disease progression, and resemble stages in neurogenesis. *Cancer Cell* **2006**, *9*, 157–173. [CrossRef]
56. Pollen, A.A.; Nowakowski, T.J.; Chen, J.; Retallack, H.; Sandoval-Espinosa, C.; Nicholas, C.R.; Shuga, J.; Liu, S.J.; Oldham, M.C.; Diaz, A.; et al. Molecular identity of human outer radial glia during cortical development. *Cell* **2015**, *163*, 55–67. [CrossRef]
57. Friedmann-Morvinski, D.; Bushong, E.A.; Ke, E.; Soda, Y.; Marumoto, T.; Singer, O.; Ellisman, M.H.; Verma, I.M. Dedifferentiation of neurons and astrocytes by oncogenes can induce gliomas in mice. *Science* **2012**, *338*, 1080–1084. [CrossRef]
58. Liu, C.; Sage, J.C.; Miller, M.R.; Verhaak, R.G.; Hippenmeyer, S.; Vogel, H.; Foreman, O.; Bronson, R.T.; Nishiyama, A.; Luo, L.; et al. Mosaic analysis with double markers reveals tumor cell of origin in glioma. *Cell* **2011**, *146*, 209–221. [CrossRef]
59. Kastrup, J. Can YKL-40 be a new inflammatory biomarker in cardiovascular disease? *Immunobiology* **2012**, *217*, 483–491. [CrossRef]
60. Johansen, J.S.; Schultz, N.A.; Jensen, B.V. Plasma YKL-40: A potential new cancer biomarker? *Future Oncol.* **2009**, *5*, 1065–1082. [CrossRef]
61. Nutt, C.L.; Betensky, R.A.; Brower, M.A.; Batchelor, T.T.; Louis, D.N.; Stemmer-Rachamimov, A.O. YKL-40 is a differential diagnostic marker for histologic subtypes of high-grade gliomas. *Clin. Cancer Res.* **2005**, *11*, 2258–2264. [CrossRef] [PubMed]
62. Pelloski, C.E.; Mahajan, A.; Maor, M.; Chang, E.L.; Woo, S.; Gilbert, M.; Colman, H.; Yang, H.; Ledoux, A.; Blair, H.; et al. YKL-40 expression is associated with poorer response to radiation and shorter overall survival in glioblastoma. *Clin. Cancer Res.* **2005**, *11*, 3326–3334. [CrossRef] [PubMed]
63. Varn, F.S.; Johnson, K.C.; Martinek, J.; Huse, J.T.; Nasrallah, M.P.; Wesseling, P.; Cooper, L.A.D.; Malta, T.M.; Wade, T.E.; Sabedot, T.S.; et al. Glioma progression is shaped by genetic evolution and microenvironment interactions. *Cell* **2022**, *185*, 2184–2199 e2116. [CrossRef] [PubMed]
64. Pegg, A.E.; Dolan, M.E.; Moschel, R.C. Structure, function, and inhibition of O6-alkylguanine-DNA alkyltransferase. *Prog. Nucleic Acid. Res. Mol. Biol.* **1995**, *51*, 167–223. [CrossRef] [PubMed]
65. Stommel, J.M.; Kimmelman, A.C.; Ying, H.; Nabioullin, R.; Ponugoti, A.H.; Wiedemeyer, R.; Stegh, A.H.; Bradner, J.E.; Ligon, K.L.; Brennan, C.; et al. Coactivation of receptor tyrosine kinases affects the response of tumor cells to targeted therapies. *Science* **2007**, *318*, 287–290. [CrossRef]
66. Esteller, M.; Garcia-Foncillas, J.; Andion, E.; Goodman, S.N.; Hidalgo, O.F.; Vanaclocha, V.; Baylin, S.B.; Herman, J.G. Inactivation of the DNA-repair gene MGMT and the clinical response of gliomas to alkylating agents. *N. Engl. J. Med.* **2000**, *343*, 1350–1354. [CrossRef]
67. Ignatova, T.N.; Kukekov, V.G.; Laywell, E.D.; Suslov, O.N.; Vrionis, F.D.; Steindler, D.A. Human cortical glial tumors contain neural stem-like cells expressing astroglial and neuronal markers in vitro. *Glia* **2002**, *39*, 193–206. [CrossRef]
68. Ignatova, T.N.; Chaitin, H.J.; Kukekov, N.V.; Suslov, O.N.; Dulatova, G.I.; Hanafy, K.A.; Vrionis, F.D. Gliomagenesis is orchestrated by the Oct3/4 regulatory network. *J. Neurosurg. Sci.* **2021**, *68*, 148–156. [CrossRef]
69. Guo, G.; Yang, J.; Nichols, J.; Hall, J.S.; Eyres, I.; Mansfield, W.; Smith, A. Klf4 reverts developmentally programmed restriction of ground state pluripotency. *Development* **2009**, *136*, 1063–1069. [CrossRef]

70. Akberdin, I.R.; Omelyanchuk, N.A.; Fadeev, S.I.; Leskova, N.E.; Oschepkova, E.A.; Kazantsev, F.V.; Matushkin, Y.G.; Afonnikov, D.A.; Kolchanov, N.A. Pluripotency gene network dynamics: System views from parametric analysis. *PLoS ONE* **2018**, *13*, e0194464. [CrossRef]
71. Galardi, S.; Savino, M.; Scagnoli, F.; Pellegatta, S.; Pisati, F.; Zambelli, F.; Illi, B.; Annibali, D.; Beji, S.; Orecchini, E.; et al. Resetting cancer stem cell regulatory nodes upon MYC inhibition. *EMBO Rep.* **2016**, *17*, 1872–1889. [CrossRef] [PubMed]
72. Wang, J.; Wang, H.; Li, Z.; Wu, Q.; Lathia, J.D.; McLendon, R.E.; Hjelmeland, A.B.; Rich, J.N. c-Myc is required for maintenance of glioma cancer stem cells. *PLoS ONE* **2008**, *3*, e3769. [CrossRef] [PubMed]
73. Liu, Y.; Luan, Y.; Ma, K.; Zhang, Z.; Liu, Y.; Chen, X. ISL1 Promotes Human Glioblastoma-Derived Stem Cells' Self-Renewal by Activation of Sonic Hedgehog/GLI1 Function. *Stem Cells Dev.* **2022**, *31*, 258–268. [CrossRef] [PubMed]
74. Kanwar, S.S.; Yu, Y.; Nautiyal, J.; Patel, B.B.; Majumdar, A.P. The Wnt/beta-catenin pathway regulates growth and maintenance of colonospheres. *Mol. Cancer* **2010**, *9*, 212. [CrossRef]
75. Marziali, G.; Signore, M.; Buccarelli, M.; Grande, S.; Palma, A.; Biffoni, M.; Rosi, A.; D'Alessandris, Q.G.; Martini, M.; Larocca, L.M.; et al. Metabolic/Proteomic Signature Defines Two Glioblastoma Subtypes with Different Clinical Outcome. *Sci. Rep.* **2016**, *6*, 21557. [CrossRef]
76. Wang, L.; Babikir, H.; Muller, S.; Yagnik, G.; Shamardani, K.; Catalan, F.; Kohanbash, G.; Alvarado, B.; Di Lullo, E.; Kriegstein, A.; et al. The Phenotypes of Proliferating Glioblastoma Cells Reside on a Single Axis of Variation. *Cancer Discov.* **2019**, *9*, 1708–1719. [CrossRef]
77. Snuderl, M.; Fazlollahi, L.; Le, L.P.; Nitta, M.; Zhelyazkova, B.H.; Davidson, C.J.; Akhavanfard, S.; Cahill, D.P.; Aldape, K.D.; Betensky, R.A.; et al. Mosaic amplification of multiple receptor tyrosine kinase genes in glioblastoma. *Cancer Cell* **2011**, *20*, 810–817. [CrossRef]
78. Piccirillo, S.G.M.; Colman, S.; Potter, N.E.; van Delft, F.W.; Lillis, S.; Carnicer, M.J.; Kearney, L.; Watts, C.; Greaves, M. Genetic and functional diversity of propagating cells in glioblastoma. *Stem Cell Rep.* **2015**, *4*, 7–15. [CrossRef]
79. Lan, X.; Jorg, D.J.; Cavalli, F.M.G.; Richards, L.M.; Nguyen, L.V.; Vanner, R.J.; Guilhamon, P.; Lee, L.; Kushida, M.M.; Pellacani, D.; et al. Fate mapping of human glioblastoma reveals an invariant stem cell hierarchy. *Nature* **2017**, *549*, 227–232. [CrossRef]
80. Lesueur, P.; Chevalier, F.; El-Habr, E.A.; Junier, M.P.; Chneiweiss, H.; Castera, L.; Muller, E.; Stefan, D.; Saintigny, Y. Radiosensitization Effect of Talazoparib, a Parp Inhibitor, on Glioblastoma Stem Cells Exposed to Low and High Linear Energy Transfer Radiation. *Sci. Rep.* **2018**, *8*, 3664. [CrossRef]
81. Gallo, M.; Coutinho, F.J.; Vanner, R.J.; Gayden, T.; Mack, S.C.; Murison, A.; Remke, M.; Li, R.; Takayama, N.; Desai, K.; et al. MLL5 Orchestrates a Cancer Self-Renewal State by Repressing the Histone Variant H3.3 and Globally Reorganizing Chromatin. *Cancer Cell* **2015**, *28*, 715–729. [CrossRef] [PubMed]
82. Lancaster, M.A.; Gleeson, J.G. The primary cilium as a cellular signaling center: Lessons from disease. *Curr. Opin. Genet. Dev.* **2009**, *19*, 220–229. [CrossRef] [PubMed]
83. Sattar, S.; Gleeson, J.G. The ciliopathies in neuronal development: A clinical approach to investigation of Joubert syndrome and Joubert syndrome-related disorders. *Dev. Med. Child. Neurol.* **2011**, *53*, 793–798. [CrossRef] [PubMed]
84. Reiter, J.F.; Leroux, M.R. Genes and molecular pathways underpinning ciliopathies. *Nat. Rev. Mol. Cell Biol.* **2017**, *18*, 533–547. [CrossRef] [PubMed]
85. Feistel, K.; Blum, M. Three types of cilia including a novel 9+4 axoneme on the notochordal plate of the rabbit embryo. *Dev. Dyn.* **2006**, *235*, 3348–3358. [CrossRef]
86. Prensier, G.; Vivier, E.; Goldstein, S.; Schrevel, J. Motile flagellum with a "3 + 0" ultrastructure. *Science* **1980**, *207*, 1493–1494. [CrossRef]
87. Schou, K.B.; Pedersen, L.B.; Christensen, S.T. Ins and outs of GPCR signaling in primary cilia. *EMBO Rep.* **2015**, *16*, 1099–1113. [CrossRef]
88. Jin, D.; Ni, T.T.; Sun, J.; Wan, H.; Amack, J.D.; Yu, G.; Fleming, J.; Chiang, C.; Li, W.; Papierniak, A.; et al. Prostaglandin signalling regulates ciliogenesis by modulating intraflagellar transport. *Nat. Cell Biol.* **2014**, *16*, 841–851. [CrossRef]
89. Berbari, N.F.; Lewis, J.S.; Bishop, G.A.; Askwith, C.C.; Mykytyn, K. Bardet-Biedl syndrome proteins are required for the localization of G protein-coupled receptors to primary cilia. *Proc. Natl. Acad. Sci. USA* **2008**, *105*, 4242–4246. [CrossRef]
90. Rosenbaum, J.L.; Witman, G.B. Intraflagellar transport. *Nat. Rev. Mol. Cell Biol.* **2002**, *3*, 813–825. [CrossRef]
91. Lechtreck, K. Cargo adapters expand the transport range of intraflagellar transport. *J. Cell Sci.* **2022**, *135*, jcs260408. [CrossRef] [PubMed]
92. Pala, R.; Alomari, N.; Nauli, S.M. Primary Cilium-Dependent Signaling Mechanisms. *Int. J. Mol. Sci.* **2017**, *18*, 2272. [CrossRef] [PubMed]
93. Huangfu, D.; Liu, A.; Rakeman, A.S.; Murcia, N.S.; Niswander, L.; Anderson, K.V. Hedgehog signalling in the mouse requires intraflagellar transport proteins. *Nature* **2003**, *426*, 83–87. [CrossRef] [PubMed]
94. Goetz, S.C.; Ocbina, P.J.; Anderson, K.V. The primary cilium as a Hedgehog signal transduction machine. *Methods Cell Biol.* **2009**, *94*, 199–222. [CrossRef]
95. Bai, C.B.; Stephen, D.; Joyner, A.L. All mouse ventral spinal cord patterning by hedgehog is Gli dependent and involves an activator function of Gli3. *Dev. Cell* **2004**, *6*, 103–115. [CrossRef]
96. Ji, M.; Wang, L.; Chen, J.; Xue, N.; Wang, C.; Lai, F.; Wang, R.; Yu, S.; Jin, J.; Chen, X. CAT(3), a prodrug of 13a(S)-3-hydroxyl-6,7-dimethoxyphenanthro[9,10-b]-indolizidine, circumvents temozolomide-resistant glioblastoma via the Hedgehog signaling

pathway, independently of O(6)-methylguanine DNA methyltransferase expression. *Onco Targets Ther.* **2018**, *11*, 3671–3684. [CrossRef]
97. Vasquez-Limeta, A.; Loncarek, J. Human centrosome organization and function in interphase and mitosis. *Semin. Cell Dev. Biol.* **2021**, *117*, 30–41. [CrossRef]
98. Hoang-Minh, L.B.; Deleyrolle, L.P.; Nakamura, N.S.; Parker, A.K.; Martuscello, R.T.; Reynolds, B.A.; Sarkisian, M.R. PCM1 Depletion Inhibits Glioblastoma Cell Ciliogenesis and Increases Cell Death and Sensitivity to Temozolomide. *Transl. Oncol.* **2016**, *9*, 392–402. [CrossRef]
99. Moon, H.; Song, J.; Shin, J.O.; Lee, H.; Kim, H.K.; Eggenschwiller, J.T.; Bok, J.; Ko, H.W. Intestinal cell kinase, a protein associated with endocrine-cerebro-osteodysplasia syndrome, is a key regulator of cilia length and Hedgehog signaling. *Proc. Natl. Acad. Sci. USA* **2014**, *111*, 8541–8546. [CrossRef]
100. Broekhuis, J.R.; Verhey, K.J.; Jansen, G. Regulation of cilium length and intraflagellar transport by the RCK-kinases ICK and MOK in renal epithelial cells. *PLoS ONE* **2014**, *9*, e108470. [CrossRef]
101. Chaya, T.; Maeda, Y.; Tsutsumi, R.; Ando, M.; Ma, Y.; Kajimura, N.; Tanaka, T.; Furukawa, T. Ccrk-Mak/Ick signaling is a ciliary transport regulator essential for retinal photoreceptor survival. *Life Sci. Alliance* **2024**, *7*, e202402880. [CrossRef] [PubMed]
102. Snouffer, A.; Brown, D.; Lee, H.; Walsh, J.; Lupu, F.; Norman, R.; Lechtreck, K.; Ko, H.W.; Eggenschwiler, J. Cell Cycle-Related Kinase (CCRK) regulates ciliogenesis and Hedgehog signaling in mice. *PLoS Genet.* **2017**, *13*, e1006912. [CrossRef] [PubMed]
103. Yang, Y.; Roine, N.; Makela, T.P. CCRK depletion inhibits glioblastoma cell proliferation in a cilium-dependent manner. *EMBO Rep.* **2013**, *14*, 741–747. [CrossRef] [PubMed]
104. Goranci-Buzhala, G.; Mariappan, A.; Ricci-Vitiani, L.; Josipovic, N.; Pacioni, S.; Gottardo, M.; Ptok, J.; Schaal, H.; Callaini, G.; Rajalingam, K.; et al. Cilium induction triggers differentiation of glioma stem cells. *Cell Rep.* **2021**, *36*, 109656. [CrossRef] [PubMed]
105. Lee, D.; Gimple, R.C.; Wu, X.; Prager, B.C.; Qiu, Z.; Wu, Q.; Daggubati, V.; Mariappan, A.; Gopalakrishnan, J.; Sarkisian, M.R.; et al. Superenhancer activation of KLHDC8A drives glioma ciliation and hedgehog signaling. *J. Clin. Investig.* **2023**, *133*, e163592. [CrossRef]
106. Roth, C.; Paulini, L.; Hoffmann, M.E.; Mosler, T.; Dikic, I.; Brunschweiger, A.; Korschgen, H.; Behl, C.; Linder, B.; Kogel, D. BAG3 regulates cilia homeostasis of glioblastoma via its WW domain. *Biofactors* **2024**. [CrossRef]
107. Okano, M.; Xie, S.; Li, E. Cloning and characterization of a family of novel mammalian DNA (cytosine-5) methyltransferases. *Nat. Genet.* **1998**, *19*, 219–220. [CrossRef]
108. Qiu, C.; Sawada, K.; Zhang, X.; Cheng, X. The PWWP domain of mammalian DNA methyltransferase Dnmt3b defines a new family of DNA-binding folds. *Nat. Struct. Biol.* **2002**, *9*, 217–224. [CrossRef]
109. Hermann, A.; Goyal, R.; Jeltsch, A. The Dnmt1 DNA-(cytosine-C5)-methyltransferase methylates DNA processively with high preference for hemimethylated target sites. *J. Biol. Chem.* **2004**, *279*, 48350–48359. [CrossRef]
110. Guo, J.U.; Su, Y.; Shin, J.H.; Shin, J.; Li, H.; Xie, B.; Zhong, C.; Hu, S.; Le, T.; Fan, G.; et al. Distribution, recognition and regulation of non-CpG methylation in the adult mammalian brain. *Nat. Neurosci.* **2014**, *17*, 215–222. [CrossRef]
111. Schultz, M.D.; He, Y.; Whitaker, J.W.; Hariharan, M.; Mukamel, E.A.; Leung, D.; Rajagopal, N.; Nery, J.R.; Urich, M.A.; Chen, H.; et al. Human body epigenome maps reveal noncanonical DNA methylation variation. *Nature* **2015**, *523*, 212–216. [CrossRef] [PubMed]
112. Jang, H.S.; Shin, W.J.; Lee, J.E.; Do, J.T. CpG and Non-CpG Methylation in Epigenetic Gene Regulation and Brain Function. *Genes* **2017**, *8*, 148. [CrossRef] [PubMed]
113. Lister, R.; Pelizzola, M.; Dowen, R.H.; Hawkins, R.D.; Hon, G.; Tonti-Filippini, J.; Nery, J.R.; Lee, L.; Ye, Z.; Ngo, Q.M.; et al. Human DNA methylomes at base resolution show widespread epigenomic differences. *Nature* **2009**, *462*, 315–322. [CrossRef] [PubMed]
114. Laurent, L.; Wong, E.; Li, G.; Huynh, T.; Tsirigos, A.; Ong, C.T.; Low, H.M.; Kin Sung, K.W.; Rigoutsos, I.; Loring, J.; et al. Dynamic changes in the human methylome during differentiation. *Genome Res.* **2010**, *20*, 320–331. [CrossRef]
115. Gelfman, S.; Cohen, N.; Yearim, A.; Ast, G. DNA-methylation effect on cotranscriptional splicing is dependent on GC architecture of the exon-intron structure. *Genome Res.* **2013**, *23*, 789–799. [CrossRef]
116. Shayevitch, R.; Askayo, D.; Keydar, I.; Ast, G. The importance of DNA methylation of exons on alternative splicing. *RNA* **2018**, *24*, 1351–1362. [CrossRef]
117. Yang, X.; Han, H.; De Carvalho, D.D.; Lay, F.D.; Jones, P.A.; Liang, G. Gene body methylation can alter gene expression and is a therapeutic target in cancer. *Cancer Cell* **2014**, *26*, 577–590. [CrossRef]
118. Maunakea, A.K.; Nagarajan, R.P.; Bilenky, M.; Ballinger, T.J.; D'Souza, C.; Fouse, S.D.; Johnson, B.E.; Hong, C.; Nielsen, C.; Zhao, Y.; et al. Conserved role of intragenic DNA methylation in regulating alternative promoters. *Nature* **2010**, *466*, 253–257. [CrossRef]
119. Bahar Halpern, K.; Vana, T.; Walker, M.D. Paradoxical role of DNA methylation in activation of FoxA2 gene expression during endoderm development. *J. Biol. Chem.* **2014**, *289*, 23882–23892. [CrossRef]
120. Della Monica, R.; Cuomo, M.; Buonaiuto, M.; Costabile, D.; Franca, R.A.; Del Basso De Caro, M.; Catapano, G.; Chiariotti, L.; Visconti, R. MGMT and Whole-Genome DNA Methylation Impacts on Diagnosis, Prognosis and Therapy of Glioblastoma Multiforme. *Int. J. Mol. Sci.* **2022**, *23*, 7148. [CrossRef]
121. Li, Y.; Chen, X.; Lu, C. The interplay between DNA and histone methylation: Molecular mechanisms and disease implications. *EMBO Rep.* **2021**, *22*, e51803. [CrossRef] [PubMed]

122. Vire, E.; Brenner, C.; Deplus, R.; Blanchon, L.; Fraga, M.; Didelot, C.; Morey, L.; Van Eynde, A.; Bernard, D.; Vanderwinden, J.M.; et al. The Polycomb group protein EZH2 directly controls DNA methylation. *Nature* **2006**, *439*, 871–874. [CrossRef] [PubMed]
123. Maiti, A.; Drohat, A.C. Thymine DNA glycosylase can rapidly excise 5-formylcytosine and 5-carboxylcytosine: Potential implications for active demethylation of CpG sites. *J. Biol. Chem.* **2011**, *286*, 35334–35338. [CrossRef] [PubMed]
124. Ito, S.; Shen, L.; Dai, Q.; Wu, S.C.; Collins, L.B.; Swenberg, J.A.; He, C.; Zhang, Y. Tet proteins can convert 5-methylcytosine to 5-formylcytosine and 5-carboxylcytosine. *Science* **2011**, *333*, 1300–1303. [CrossRef] [PubMed]
125. Kohli, R.M.; Zhang, Y. TET enzymes, TDG and the dynamics of DNA demethylation. *Nature* **2013**, *502*, 472–479. [CrossRef]
126. Volkenandt, S.; Beierlein, F.; Imhof, P. Interaction of Thymine DNA Glycosylase with Oxidised 5-Methyl-cytosines in Their Amino- and Imino-Forms. *Molecules* **2021**, *26*, 5728. [CrossRef]
127. Noushmehr, H.; Weisenberger, D.J.; Diefes, K.; Phillips, H.S.; Pujara, K.; Berman, B.P.; Pan, F.; Pelloski, C.E.; Sulman, E.P.; Bhat, K.P.; et al. Identification of a CpG island methylator phenotype that defines a distinct subgroup of glioma. *Cancer Cell* **2010**, *17*, 510–522. [CrossRef]
128. Fernandez, A.F.; Bayon, G.F.; Sierra, M.I.; Urdinguio, R.G.; Torano, E.G.; Garcia, M.G.; Carella, A.; Lopez, V.; Santamarina, P.; Perez, R.F.; et al. Loss of 5hmC identifies a new type of aberrant DNA hypermethylation in glioma. *Hum. Mol. Genet.* **2018**, *27*, 3046–3059. [CrossRef]
129. Dabrowski, M.J.; Wojtas, B. Global DNA Methylation Patterns in Human Gliomas and Their Interplay with Other Epigenetic Modifications. *Int. J. Mol. Sci.* **2019**, *20*, 3478. [CrossRef]
130. Garcia-Gimenez, J.L.; Roma-Mateo, C.; Pallardo, F.V. Oxidative post-translational modifications in histones. *Biofactors* **2019**, *45*, 641–650. [CrossRef]
131. Lv, X.; Lv, Y.; Dai, X. Lactate, histone lactylation and cancer hallmarks. *Expert. Rev. Mol. Med.* **2023**, *25*, e7. [CrossRef] [PubMed]
132. Kaimori, J.Y.; Maehara, K.; Hayashi-Takanaka, Y.; Harada, A.; Fukuda, M.; Yamamoto, S.; Ichimaru, N.; Umehara, T.; Yokoyama, S.; Matsuda, R.; et al. Histone H4 lysine 20 acetylation is associated with gene repression in human cells. *Sci. Rep.* **2016**, *6*, 24318. [CrossRef] [PubMed]
133. Jin, X.; Qin, Z.; Zhao, H. Histone acetylation risk model predicts prognosis and guides therapy selection in glioblastoma: Implications for chemotherapy and anti-CTLA-4 immunotherapy. *BMC Immunol.* **2024**, *25*, 51. [CrossRef] [PubMed]
134. Yan, X.; Feng, L.; Xu, Z.; Chen, W.; Yan, H.; Wu, P.; Ding, C.; Zhu, X.; Lu, Y. Histone acetylation gene-based biomarkers as novel markers of the immune microenvironment in glioblastoma. *J. Gene Med.* **2023**, *25*, e3511. [CrossRef]
135. Das, N.D.; Chang, J.C.; Hon, C.C.; Kelly, S.T.; Ito, S.; Lizio, M.; Kaczkowski, B.; Watanabe, H.; Katsushima, K.; Natsume, A.; et al. Defining super-enhancers by highly ranked histone H4 multi-acetylation levels identifies transcription factors associated with glioblastoma stem-like properties. *BMC Genom.* **2023**, *24*, 574. [CrossRef]
136. Panicker, S.P.; Raychaudhuri, B.; Sharma, P.; Tipps, R.; Mazumdar, T.; Mal, A.K.; Palomo, J.M.; Vogelbaum, M.A.; Haque, S.J. p300- and Myc-mediated regulation of glioblastoma multiforme cell differentiation. *Oncotarget* **2010**, *1*, 289–303. [CrossRef]
137. Diao, P.Y.; Li, S.X.; Peng, J.; Yang, J.H.; Pan, Y.C.; Xu, X.P.; Tang, H.; Hu, J.X.; Zhao, H.F.; Huang, G.D. Overexpression of EP300-interacting inhibitor of differentiation 3 predicts poor prognosis in patients with glioblastoma multiforme. *Int. J. Clin. Exp. Pathol.* **2020**, *13*, 979–988.
138. Lv, D.; Jia, F.; Hou, Y.; Sang, Y.; Alvarez, A.A.; Zhang, W.; Gao, W.Q.; Hu, B.; Cheng, S.Y.; Ge, J.; et al. Histone Acetyltransferase KAT6A Upregulates PI3K/AKT Signaling through TRIM24 Binding. *Cancer Res.* **2017**, *77*, 6190–6201. [CrossRef]
139. Saidi, D.; Cheray, M.; Osman, A.M.; Stratoulias, V.; Lindberg, O.R.; Shen, X.; Blomgren, K.; Joseph, B. Glioma-induced SIRT1-dependent activation of hMOF histone H4 lysine 16 acetyltransferase in microglia promotes a tumor supporting phenotype. *Oncoimmunology* **2018**, *7*, e1382790. [CrossRef]
140. Jurkin, J.; Zupkovitz, G.; Lagger, S.; Grausenburger, R.; Hagelkruys, A.; Kenner, L.; Seiser, C. Distinct and redundant functions of histone deacetylases HDAC1 and HDAC2 in proliferation and tumorigenesis. *Cell Cycle* **2011**, *10*, 406–412. [CrossRef]
141. Paluvai, H.; Shanmukha, K.D.; Tyedmers, J.; Backs, J. Insights into the function of HDAC3 and NCoR1/NCoR2 co-repressor complex in metabolic diseases. *Front. Mol. Biosci.* **2023**, *10*, 1190094. [CrossRef] [PubMed]
142. Jang, J.; Bentsen, M.; Kim, Y.J.; Kim, E.; Garg, V.; Cai, C.L.; Looso, M.; Li, D. Endocardial HDAC3 is required for myocardial trabeculation. *Nat. Commun.* **2024**, *15*, 4166. [CrossRef] [PubMed]
143. Li, L.; Jin, J.; Yang, X.J. Histone Deacetylase 3 Governs Perinatal Cerebral Development via Neural Stem and Progenitor Cells. *iScience* **2019**, *20*, 148–167. [CrossRef] [PubMed]
144. Chakrabarti, A.; Oehme, I.; Witt, O.; Oliveira, G.; Sippl, W.; Romier, C.; Pierce, R.J.; Jung, M. HDAC8: A multifaceted target for therapeutic interventions. *Trends Pharmacol. Sci.* **2015**, *36*, 481–492. [CrossRef] [PubMed]
145. Li, S.; Chen, X.; Mao, L.; Zahid, K.R.; Wen, J.; Zhang, L.; Zhang, M.; Duan, J.; Duan, J.; Yin, X.; et al. Histone deacetylase 1 promotes glioblastoma cell proliferation and invasion via activation of PI3K/AKT and MEK/ERK signaling pathways. *Brain Res.* **2018**, *1692*, 154–162. [CrossRef]
146. Zhang, Z.; Wang, Y.; Chen, J.; Tan, Q.; Xie, C.; Li, C.; Zhan, W.; Wang, M. Silencing of histone deacetylase 2 suppresses malignancy for proliferation, migration, and invasion of glioblastoma cells and enhances temozolomide sensitivity. *Cancer Chemother. Pharmacol.* **2016**, *78*, 1289–1296. [CrossRef]
147. Zhong, S.; Fan, Y.; Wu, B.; Wang, Y.; Jiang, S.; Ge, J.; Hua, C.; Zhao, G.; Chen, Y.; Xu, H. HDAC3 Expression Correlates with the Prognosis and Grade of Patients with Glioma: A Diversification Analysis Based on Transcriptome and Clinical Evidence. *World Neurosurg.* **2018**, *119*, e145–e158. [CrossRef]

148. Santos-Barriopedro, I.; Li, Y.; Bahl, S.; Seto, E. HDAC8 affects MGMT levels in glioblastoma cell lines via interaction with the proteasome receptor ADRM1. *Genes. Cancer* **2019**, *10*, 119–133. [CrossRef]
149. Chang, S.; McKinsey, T.A.; Zhang, C.L.; Richardson, J.A.; Hill, J.A.; Olson, E.N. Histone deacetylases 5 and 9 govern responsiveness of the heart to a subset of stress signals and play redundant roles in heart development. *Mol. Cell Biol.* **2004**, *24*, 8467–8476. [CrossRef]
150. Liu, J.; You, Y.; Sun, Z.; Zhang, L.; Li, X.; Dai, Z.; Ma, J.; Chen, Y.; Jiao, G. WTAP-Mediated m6A RNA Methylation Regulates the Differentiation of Bone Marrow Mesenchymal Stem Cells via the miR-29b-3p/HDAC4 Axis. *Stem Cells Transl. Med.* **2023**, *12*, 307–321. [CrossRef]
151. Chen, B.; Cepko, C.L. HDAC4 regulates neuronal survival in normal and diseased retinas. *Science* **2009**, *323*, 256–259. [CrossRef] [PubMed]
152. Spallotta, F.; Rosati, J.; Straino, S.; Nanni, S.; Grasselli, A.; Ambrosino, V.; Rotili, D.; Valente, S.; Farsetti, A.; Mai, A.; et al. Nitric oxide determines mesodermic differentiation of mouse embryonic stem cells by activating class IIa histone deacetylases: Potential therapeutic implications in a mouse model of hindlimb ischemia. *Stem Cells* **2010**, *28*, 431–442. [CrossRef] [PubMed]
153. Asfaha, Y.; Schrenk, C.; Alves Avelar, L.A.; Hamacher, A.; Pflieger, M.; Kassack, M.U.; Kurz, T. Recent advances in class IIa histone deacetylases research. *Bioorg. Med. Chem.* **2019**, *27*, 115087. [CrossRef] [PubMed]
154. Seidel, C.; Schnekenburger, M.; Dicato, M.; Diederich, M. Histone deacetylase 6 in health and disease. *Epigenomics* **2015**, *7*, 103–118. [CrossRef]
155. Lambona, C.; Zwergel, C.; Fioravanti, R.; Valente, S.; Mai, A. Histone deacetylase 10: A polyamine deacetylase from the crystal structure to the first inhibitors. *Curr. Opin. Struct. Biol.* **2023**, *82*, 102668. [CrossRef]
156. Kaur, S.; Rajoria, P.; Chopra, M. HDAC6: A unique HDAC family member as a cancer target. *Cell Oncol.* **2022**, *45*, 779–829. [CrossRef]
157. Chang, H.C.; Guarente, L. SIRT1 and other sirtuins in metabolism. *Trends Endocrinol. Metab.* **2014**, *25*, 138–145. [CrossRef]
158. Ji, Z.; Liu, G.H.; Qu, J. Mitochondrial sirtuins, metabolism, and aging. *J. Genet. Genom.* **2022**, *49*, 287–298. [CrossRef]
159. Jaiswal, A.; Xudong, Z.; Zhenyu, J.; Saretzki, G. Mitochondrial sirtuins in stem cells and cancer. *FEBS J.* **2022**, *289*, 3393–3415. [CrossRef]
160. Watroba, M.; Dudek, I.; Skoda, M.; Stangret, A.; Rzodkiewicz, P.; Szukiewicz, D. Sirtuins, epigenetics and longevity. *Ageing Res. Rev.* **2017**, *40*, 11–19. [CrossRef]
161. Chen, H.; Lin, R.; Zhang, Z.; Wei, Q.; Zhong, Z.; Huang, J.; Xu, Y. Sirtuin 1 knockdown inhibits glioma cell proliferation and potentiates temozolomide toxicity via facilitation of reactive oxygen species generation. *Oncol. Lett.* **2019**, *17*, 5343–5350. [CrossRef]
162. Yao, Z.Q.; Zhang, X.; Zhen, Y.; He, X.Y.; Zhao, S.; Li, X.F.; Yang, B.; Gao, F.; Guo, F.Y.; Fu, L.; et al. A novel small-molecule activator of Sirtuin-1 induces autophagic cell death/mitophagy as a potential therapeutic strategy in glioblastoma. *Cell Death Dis.* **2018**, *9*, 767. [CrossRef]
163. Li, Y.; Dai, D.; Lu, Q.; Fei, M.; Li, M.; Wu, X. Sirt2 suppresses glioma cell growth through targeting NF-kappaB-miR-21 axis. *Biochem. Biophys. Res. Commun.* **2013**, *441*, 661–667. [CrossRef]
164. Luo, K.; Huang, W.; Tang, S. Sirt3 enhances glioma cell viability by stabilizing Ku70-BAX interaction. *Onco Targets Ther.* **2018**, *11*, 7559–7567. [CrossRef]
165. Feng, J.; Yan, P.F.; Zhao, H.Y.; Zhang, F.C.; Zhao, W.H.; Feng, M. SIRT6 suppresses glioma cell growth via induction of apoptosis, inhibition of oxidative stress and suppression of JAK2/STAT3 signaling pathway activation. *Oncol. Rep.* **2016**, *35*, 1395–1402. [CrossRef]
166. Mu, P.; Liu, K.; Lin, Q.; Yang, W.; Liu, D.; Lin, Z.; Shao, W.; Ji, T. Sirtuin 7 promotes glioma proliferation and invasion through activation of the ERK/STAT3 signaling pathway. *Oncol. Lett.* **2019**, *17*, 1445–1452. [CrossRef]
167. Liu, S.S.; Wu, F.; Jin, Y.M.; Chang, W.Q.; Xu, T.M. HDAC11: A rising star in epigenetics. *Biomed. Pharmacother.* **2020**, *131*, 110607. [CrossRef]
168. Primerano, A.; De Domenico, E.; Cianfarani, F.; De Luca, N.; Floriddia, G.; Teson, M.; Cristofoletti, C.; Cardarelli, S.; Scaglione, G.L.; Baldini, E.; et al. Histone deacetylase inhibition mitigates fibrosis-driven disease progression in recessive dystrophic epidermolysis bullosa. *Br. J. Dermatol.* **2024**, *191*, 568–579. [CrossRef]
169. Lamb, Y.N. Givinostat: First Approval. *Drugs* **2024**, *84*, 849–856. [CrossRef]
170. Pawlowski, K.D.; Duffy, J.T.; Babak, M.V.; Balyasnikova, I.V. Modeling glioblastoma complexity with organoids for personalized treatments. *Trends Mol. Med.* **2023**, *29*, 282–296. [CrossRef]
171. Reddy, R.G.; Bhat, U.A.; Chakravarty, S.; Kumar, A. Advances in histone deacetylase inhibitors in targeting glioblastoma stem cells. *Cancer Chemother. Pharmacol.* **2020**, *86*, 165–179. [CrossRef]
172. Nguyen, T.T.T.; Zhang, Y.; Shang, E.; Shu, C.; Torrini, C.; Zhao, J.; Bianchetti, E.; Mela, A.; Humala, N.; Mahajan, A.; et al. HDAC inhibitors elicit metabolic reprogramming by targeting super-enhancers in glioblastoma models. *J. Clin. Investig.* **2020**, *130*, 3699–3716. [CrossRef]
173. Pajak, B.; Siwiak-Niedbalska, E.; Jaskiewicz, A.; Soltyka, M.; Zielinski, R.; Domoradzki, T.; Fokt, I.; Skora, S.; Priebe, W. Synergistic Anticancer Effect of Glycolysis and Histone Deacetylases Inhibitors in a Glioblastoma Model. *Biomedicines* **2021**, *9*, 1749. [CrossRef]
174. Was, H.; Krol, S.K.; Rotili, D.; Mai, A.; Wojtas, B.; Kaminska, B.; Maleszewska, M. Histone deacetylase inhibitors exert anti-tumor effects on human adherent and stem-like glioma cells. *Clin. Epigenetics* **2019**, *11*, 11. [CrossRef]

175. Rampazzo, E.; Manfreda, L.; Bresolin, S.; Cani, A.; Mariotto, E.; Bortolozzi, R.; Della Puppa, A.; Viola, G.; Persano, L. Histone Deacetylase Inhibitors Impair Glioblastoma Cell Motility and Proliferation. *Cancers* **2022**, *14*, 1897. [CrossRef]
176. Perez, T.; Berges, R.; Maccario, H.; Oddoux, S.; Honore, S. Low concentrations of vorinostat decrease EB1 expression in GBM cells and affect microtubule dynamics, cell survival and migration. *Oncotarget* **2021**, *12*, 304–315. [CrossRef]
177. Marampon, F.; Leoni, F.; Mancini, A.; Pietrantoni, I.; Codenotti, S.; Ferella, L.; Megiorni, F.; Porro, G.; Galbiati, E.; Pozzi, P.; et al. Histone deacetylase inhibitor ITF2357 (givinostat) reverts transformed phenotype and counteracts stemness in in vitro and in vivo models of human glioblastoma. *J. Cancer Res. Clin. Oncol.* **2019**, *145*, 393–409. [CrossRef]
178. Essien, E.I.; Hofer, T.P.; Atkinson, M.J.; Anastasov, N. Combining HDAC and MEK Inhibitors with Radiation against Glioblastoma-Derived Spheres. *Cells* **2022**, *11*, 775. [CrossRef]
179. Gusyatiner, O.; Bady, P.; Pham, M.D.T.; Lei, Y.; Park, J.; Daniel, R.T.; Delorenzi, M.; Hegi, M.E. BET inhibitors repress expression of interferon-stimulated genes and synergize with HDAC inhibitors in glioblastoma. *Neuro Oncol.* **2021**, *23*, 1680–1692. [CrossRef]
180. Maniotis, A.J.; Folberg, R.; Hess, A.; Seftor, E.A.; Gardner, L.M.; Pe'er, J.; Trent, J.M.; Meltzer, P.S.; Hendrix, M.J. Vascular channel formation by human melanoma cells in vivo and in vitro: Vasculogenic mimicry. *Am. J. Pathol.* **1999**, *155*, 739–752. [CrossRef]
181. Ricci-Vitiani, L.; Pallini, R.; Biffoni, M.; Todaro, M.; Invernici, G.; Cenci, T.; Maira, G.; Parati, E.A.; Stassi, G.; Larocca, L.M.; et al. Tumour vascularization via endothelial differentiation of glioblastoma stem-like cells. *Nature* **2010**, *468*, 824–828. [CrossRef]
182. Angara, K.; Borin, T.F.; Arbab, A.S. Vascular Mimicry: A Novel Neovascularization Mechanism Driving Anti-Angiogenic Therapy (AAT) Resistance in Glioblastoma. *Transl. Oncol.* **2017**, *10*, 650–660. [CrossRef]
183. Folberg, R.; Maniotis, A.J. Vasculogenic mimicry. *APMIS* **2004**, *112*, 508–525. [CrossRef]
184. Pastorino, O.; Gentile, M.T.; Mancini, A.; Del Gaudio, N.; Di Costanzo, A.; Bajetto, A.; Franco, P.; Altucci, L.; Florio, T.; Stoppelli, M.P.; et al. Histone Deacetylase Inhibitors Impair Vasculogenic Mimicry from Glioblastoma Cells. *Cancers* **2019**, *11*, 747. [CrossRef]
185. Yao, Z.G.; Li, W.H.; Hua, F.; Cheng, H.X.; Zhao, M.Q.; Sun, X.C.; Qin, Y.J.; Li, J.M. LBH589 Inhibits Glioblastoma Growth and Angiogenesis Through Suppression of HIF-1alpha Expression. *J. Neuropathol. Exp. Neurol.* **2017**, *76*, 1000–1007. [CrossRef]
186. Nakagawa-Saito, Y.; Mitobe, Y.; Togashi, K.; Suzuki, S.; Sugai, A.; Kitanaka, C.; Okada, M. Givinostat Inhibition of Sp1-dependent MGMT Expression Sensitizes Glioma Stem Cells to Temozolomide. *Anticancer. Res.* **2023**, *43*, 1131–1138. [CrossRef]
187. De La Rosa, J.; Urdiciain, A.; Zazpe, I.; Zelaya, M.V.; Melendez, B.; Rey, J.A.; Idoate, M.A.; Castresana, J.S. The synergistic effect of DZ-NEP, panobinostat and temozolomide reduces clonogenicity and induces apoptosis in glioblastoma cells. *Int. J. Oncol.* **2020**, *56*, 283–300. [CrossRef]
188. De La Rosa, J.; Urdiciain, A.; Zelaya, M.V.; Zazpe, I.; Melendez, B.; Rey, J.A.; Idoate, M.A.; Castresana, J.S. APR-246 combined with 3-deazaneplanocin A, panobinostat or temozolomide reduces clonogenicity and induces apoptosis in glioblastoma cells. *Int. J. Oncol.* **2021**, *58*, 312–330. [CrossRef]
189. Arrizabalaga, O.; Moreno-Cugnon, L.; Auzmendi-Iriarte, J.; Aldaz, P.; Ibanez de Caceres, I.; Garros-Regulez, L.; Moncho-Amor, V.; Torres-Bayona, S.; Pernia, O.; Pintado-Berninches, L.; et al. High expression of MKP1/DUSP1 counteracts glioma stem cell activity and mediates HDAC inhibitor response. *Oncogenesis* **2017**, *6*, 401. [CrossRef]
190. Sung, G.J.; Kim, S.H.; Kwak, S.; Park, S.H.; Song, J.H.; Jung, J.H.; Kim, H.; Choi, K.C. Inhibition of TFEB oligomerization by co-treatment of melatonin with vorinostat promotes the therapeutic sensitivity in glioblastoma and glioma stem cells. *J. Pineal Res.* **2019**, *66*, e12556. [CrossRef]
191. Kitange, G.J.; Mladek, A.C.; Carlson, B.L.; Schroeder, M.A.; Pokorny, J.L.; Cen, L.; Decker, P.A.; Wu, W.; Lomberk, G.A.; Gupta, S.K.; et al. Inhibition of histone deacetylation potentiates the evolution of acquired temozolomide resistance linked to MGMT upregulation in glioblastoma xenografts. *Clin. Cancer Res.* **2012**, *18*, 4070–4079. [CrossRef]
192. Wu, Y.; Dong, L.; Bao, S.; Wang, M.; Yun, Y.; Zhu, R. FK228 augmented temozolomide sensitivity in human glioma cells by blocking PI3K/AKT/mTOR signal pathways. *Biomed. Pharmacother.* **2016**, *84*, 462–469. [CrossRef]
193. Tsai, C.Y.; Ko, H.J.; Chiou, S.J.; Lai, Y.L.; Hou, C.C.; Javaria, T.; Huang, Z.Y.; Cheng, T.S.; Hsu, T.I.; Chuang, J.Y.; et al. NBM-BMX, an HDAC8 Inhibitor, Overcomes Temozolomide Resistance in Glioblastoma Multiforme by Downregulating the beta-Catenin/c-Myc/SOX2 Pathway and Upregulating p53-Mediated MGMT Inhibition. *Int. J. Mol. Sci.* **2021**, *22*, 5907. [CrossRef]
194. Li, Z.Y.; Li, Q.Z.; Chen, L.; Chen, B.D.; Wang, B.; Zhang, X.J.; Li, W.P. Histone Deacetylase Inhibitor RGFP109 Overcomes Temozolomide Resistance by Blocking NF-kappaB-Dependent Transcription in Glioblastoma Cell Lines. *Neurochem. Res.* **2016**, *41*, 3192–3205. [CrossRef]
195. Eyupoglu, I.Y.; Hahnen, E.; Trankle, C.; Savaskan, N.E.; Siebzehnrubl, F.A.; Buslei, R.; Lemke, D.; Wick, W.; Fahlbusch, R.; Blumcke, I. Experimental therapy of malignant gliomas using the inhibitor of histone deacetylase MS-275. *Mol. Cancer Ther.* **2006**, *5*, 1248–1255. [CrossRef]
196. Lo Cascio, C.; Margaryan, T.; Luna-Melendez, E.; McNamara, J.B.; White, C.I.; Knight, W.; Ganta, S.; Opachich, Z.; Cantoni, C.; Yoo, W.; et al. Quisinostat is a brain-penetrant radiosensitizer in glioblastoma. *JCI Insight* **2023**, *8*, e167081. [CrossRef]
197. Al-Awadhi, F.H.; Salvador-Reyes, L.A.; Elsadek, L.A.; Ratnayake, R.; Chen, Q.Y.; Luesch, H. Largazole is a Brain-Penetrant Class I HDAC Inhibitor with Extended Applicability to Glioblastoma and CNS Diseases. *ACS Chem. Neurosci.* **2020**, *11*, 1937–1943. [CrossRef]
198. Mekala, J.R.; Ramalingam, P.S.; Mathavan, S.; Yamajala, R.; Moparthi, N.R.; Kurappalli, R.K.; Manyam, R.R. Synthesis, in vitro and structural aspects of cap substituted Suberoylanilide hydroxamic acid analogs as potential inducers of apoptosis in Glioblastoma cancer cells via HDAC /microRNA regulation. *Chem. Biol. Interact.* **2022**, *357*, 109876. [CrossRef]

199. Wolf, A.; Agnihotri, S.; Micallef, J.; Mukherjee, J.; Sabha, N.; Cairns, R.; Hawkins, C.; Guha, A. Hexokinase 2 is a key mediator of aerobic glycolysis and promotes tumor growth in human glioblastoma multiforme. *J. Exp. Med.* **2011**, *208*, 313–326. [CrossRef]
200. Singleton, W.G.; Collins, A.M.; Bienemann, A.S.; Killick-Cole, C.L.; Haynes, H.R.; Asby, D.J.; Butts, C.P.; Wyatt, M.J.; Barua, N.U.; Gill, S.S. Convection enhanced delivery of panobinostat (LBH589)-loaded pluronic nano-micelles prolongs survival in the F98 rat glioma model. *Int. J. Nanomed.* **2017**, *12*, 1385–1399. [CrossRef]
201. Lu, Y.; Feng, Y.; Li, Z.; Li, J.; Zhang, H.; Hu, X.; Jiang, W.; Shi, T.; Wang, Z. Novel piperazine based benzamide derivatives as potential anti-glioblastoma agents inhibiting cell proliferation and cell cycle progression. *Eur. J. Med. Chem.* **2022**, *227*, 113908. [CrossRef]
202. Roberts, A.J.; Kon, T.; Knight, P.J.; Sutoh, K.; Burgess, S.A. Functions and mechanics of dynein motor proteins. *Nat. Rev. Mol. Cell Biol.* **2013**, *14*, 713–726. [CrossRef]
203. Hook, S.S.; Orian, A.; Cowley, S.M.; Eisenman, R.N. Histone deacetylase 6 binds polyubiquitin through its zinc finger (PAZ domain) and copurifies with deubiquitinating enzymes. *Proc. Natl. Acad. Sci. USA* **2002**, *99*, 13425–13430. [CrossRef]
204. Ran, J.; Liu, M.; Feng, J.; Li, H.; Ma, H.; Song, T.; Cao, Y.; Zhou, P.; Wu, Y.; Yang, Y.; et al. ASK1-Mediated Phosphorylation Blocks HDAC6 Ubiquitination and Degradation to Drive the Disassembly of Photoreceptor Connecting Cilia. *Dev. Cell* **2020**, *53*, 287–299.e285. [CrossRef]
205. Lafarga, V.; Aymerich, I.; Tapia, O.; Mayor, F., Jr.; Penela, P. A novel GRK2/HDAC6 interaction modulates cell spreading and motility. *EMBO J.* **2012**, *31*, 856–869. [CrossRef]
206. Williams, K.A.; Zhang, M.; Xiang, S.; Hu, C.; Wu, J.Y.; Zhang, S.; Ryan, M.; Cox, A.D.; Der, C.J.; Fang, B.; et al. Extracellular signal-regulated kinase (ERK) phosphorylates histone deacetylase 6 (HDAC6) at serine 1035 to stimulate cell migration. *J. Biol. Chem.* **2013**, *288*, 33156–33170. [CrossRef]
207. Chen, S.; Owens, G.C.; Makarenkova, H.; Edelman, D.B. HDAC6 regulates mitochondrial transport in hippocampal neurons. *PLoS ONE* **2010**, *5*, e10848. [CrossRef]
208. Deribe, Y.L.; Wild, P.; Chandrashaker, A.; Curak, J.; Schmidt, M.H.H.; Kalaidzidis, Y.; Milutinovic, N.; Kratchmarova, I.; Buerkle, L.; Fetchko, M.J.; et al. Regulation of epidermal growth factor receptor trafficking by lysine deacetylase HDAC6. *Sci. Signal* **2009**, *2*, ra84. [CrossRef]
209. Pugacheva, E.N.; Jablonski, S.A.; Hartman, T.R.; Henske, E.P.; Golemis, E.A. HEF1-dependent Aurora A activation induces disassembly of the primary cilium. *Cell* **2007**, *129*, 1351–1363. [CrossRef]
210. Du, Y.; Seibenhener, M.L.; Yan, J.; Jiang, J.; Wooten, M.C. aPKC phosphorylation of HDAC6 results in increased deacetylation activity. *PLoS ONE* **2015**, *10*, e0123191. [CrossRef]
211. Okuda, K.; Ito, A.; Uehara, T. Regulation of Histone Deacetylase 6 Activity via S-Nitrosylation. *Biol. Pharm. Bull.* **2015**, *38*, 1434–1437. [CrossRef]
212. Westendorf, J.J.; Zaidi, S.K.; Cascino, J.E.; Kahler, R.; van Wijnen, A.J.; Lian, J.B.; Yoshida, M.; Stein, G.S.; Li, X. Runx2 (Cbfa1, AML-3) interacts with histone deacetylase 6 and represses the p21(CIP1/WAF1) promoter. *Mol. Cell Biol.* **2002**, *22*, 7982–7992. [CrossRef]
213. Yu, Z.; Zhang, W.; Kone, B.C. Histone deacetylases augment cytokine induction of the iNOS gene. *J. Am. Soc. Nephrol.* **2002**, *13*, 2009–2017. [CrossRef]
214. Fernandes, I.; Bastien, Y.; Wai, T.; Nygard, K.; Lin, R.; Cormier, O.; Lee, H.S.; Eng, F.; Bertos, N.R.; Pelletier, N.; et al. Ligand-dependent nuclear receptor corepressor LCoR functions by histone deacetylase-dependent and -independent mechanisms. *Mol. Cell* **2003**, *11*, 139–150. [CrossRef]
215. Girdwood, D.; Bumpass, D.; Vaughan, O.A.; Thain, A.; Anderson, L.A.; Snowden, A.W.; Garcia-Wilson, E.; Perkins, N.D.; Hay, R.T. P300 transcriptional repression is mediated by SUMO modification. *Mol. Cell* **2003**, *11*, 1043–1054. [CrossRef]
216. Ling, L.; Lobie, P.E. RhoA/ROCK activation by growth hormone abrogates p300/histone deacetylase 6 repression of Stat5-mediated transcription. *J. Biol. Chem.* **2004**, *279*, 32737–32750. [CrossRef]
217. Ma, H.; Nguyen, C.; Lee, K.S.; Kahn, M. Differential roles for the coactivators CBP and p300 on TCF/beta-catenin-mediated survivin gene expression. *Oncogene* **2005**, *24*, 3619–3631. [CrossRef]
218. Han, Y.; Jeong, H.M.; Jin, Y.H.; Kim, Y.J.; Jeong, H.G.; Yeo, C.Y.; Lee, K.Y. Acetylation of histone deacetylase 6 by p300 attenuates its deacetylase activity. *Biochem. Biophys. Res. Commun.* **2009**, *383*, 88–92. [CrossRef]
219. Liu, Y.; Peng, L.; Seto, E.; Huang, S.; Qiu, Y. Modulation of histone deacetylase 6 (HDAC6) nuclear import and tubulin deacetylase activity through acetylation. *J. Biol. Chem.* **2012**, *287*, 29168–29174. [CrossRef]
220. Ryu, H.W.; Shin, D.H.; Lee, D.H.; Choi, J.; Han, G.; Lee, K.Y.; Kwon, S.H. HDAC6 deacetylates p53 at lysines 381/382 and differentially coordinates p53-induced apoptosis. *Cancer Lett.* **2017**, *391*, 162–171. [CrossRef]
221. Zhang, M.; Xiang, S.; Joo, H.Y.; Wang, L.; Williams, K.A.; Liu, W.; Hu, C.; Tong, D.; Haakenson, J.; Wang, C.; et al. HDAC6 deacetylates and ubiquitinates MSH2 to maintain proper levels of MutSalpha. *Mol. Cell* **2014**, *55*, 31–46. [CrossRef] [PubMed]
222. Zhang, M.; Hu, C.; Moses, N.; Haakenson, J.; Xiang, S.; Quan, D.; Fang, B.; Yang, Z.; Bai, W.; Bepler, G.; et al. HDAC6 regulates DNA damage response via deacetylating MLH1. *J. Biol. Chem.* **2019**, *294*, 5813–5826. [CrossRef]
223. Sun, J.; Liu, Q.; Lv, L.; Sun, R.; Li, Z.P.; Huang, B.; Cui, K.; Shi, D. HDAC6 Is Involved in the Histone Deacetylation of In Vitro Maturation Oocytes and the Reprogramming of Nuclear Transplantation in Pig. *Reprod. Sci.* **2021**, *28*, 2630–2640. [CrossRef]
224. Sui, L.; Huang, R.; Yu, H.; Zhang, S.; Li, Z. Inhibition of HDAC6 by tubastatin A disrupts mouse oocyte meiosis via regulating histone modifications and mRNA expression. *J. Cell Physiol.* **2020**, *235*, 7030–7042. [CrossRef]

225. Zhang, S.; Sui, L.; Kong, X.; Huang, R.; Li, Z. HDAC6 decreases H4K16 and alpha-tubulin acetylation during porcine oocyte maturation. *Cell Cycle* **2023**, *22*, 2057–2069. [CrossRef]
226. Kai, H.; Wu, Q.; Yin, R.; Tang, X.; Shi, H.; Wang, T.; Zhang, M.; Pan, C. LncRNA NORAD Promotes Vascular Endothelial Cell Injury and Atherosclerosis Through Suppressing VEGF Gene Transcription via Enhancing H3K9 Deacetylation by Recruiting HDAC6. *Front. Cell Dev. Biol.* **2021**, *9*, 701628. [CrossRef]
227. Zamperla, M.G.; Illi, B.; Barbi, V.; Cencioni, C.; Santoni, D.; Gagliardi, S.; Garofalo, M.; Zingale, G.A.; Pandino, I.; Sbardella, D.; et al. HDAC6 inhibition disrupts HDAC6-P300 interaction reshaping the cancer chromatin landscape. *Clin. Epigenetics* **2024**, *16*, 109. [CrossRef]
228. Fernandez-Barrera, J.; Bernabe-Rubio, M.; Casares-Arias, J.; Rangel, L.; Fernandez-Martin, L.; Correas, I.; Alonso, M.A. The actin-MRTF-SRF transcriptional circuit controls tubulin acetylation via alpha-TAT1 gene expression. *J. Cell Biol.* **2018**, *217*, 929–944. [CrossRef]
229. Hubbert, C.; Guardiola, A.; Shao, R.; Kawaguchi, Y.; Ito, A.; Nixon, A.; Yoshida, M.; Wang, X.F.; Yao, T.P. HDAC6 is a microtubule-associated deacetylase. *Nature* **2002**, *417*, 455–458. [CrossRef]
230. Zhang, X.; Yuan, Z.; Zhang, Y.; Yong, S.; Salas-Burgos, A.; Koomen, J.; Olashaw, N.; Parsons, J.T.; Yang, X.J.; Dent, S.R.; et al. HDAC6 modulates cell motility by altering the acetylation level of cortactin. *Mol. Cell* **2007**, *27*, 197–213. [CrossRef]
231. Dompierre, J.P.; Godin, J.D.; Charrin, B.C.; Cordelieres, F.P.; King, S.J.; Humbert, S.; Saudou, F. Histone deacetylase 6 inhibition compensates for the transport deficit in Huntington's disease by increasing tubulin acetylation. *J. Neurosci.* **2007**, *27*, 3571–3583. [CrossRef]
232. Reed, N.A.; Cai, D.; Blasius, T.L.; Jih, G.T.; Meyhofer, E.; Gaertig, J.; Verhey, K.J. Microtubule acetylation promotes kinesin-1 binding and transport. *Curr. Biol.* **2006**, *16*, 2166–2172. [CrossRef]
233. Kalinski, A.L.; Kar, A.N.; Craver, J.; Tosolini, A.P.; Sleigh, J.N.; Lee, S.J.; Hawthorne, A.; Brito-Vargas, P.; Miller-Randolph, S.; Passino, R.; et al. Deacetylation of Miro1 by HDAC6 blocks mitochondrial transport and mediates axon growth inhibition. *J. Cell Biol.* **2019**, *218*, 1871–1890. [CrossRef]
234. Van Den Bosch, L. HDAC6 and Miro1: Another interaction causing trouble in neurons. *J. Cell Biol.* **2019**, *218*, 1769–1770. [CrossRef]
235. Wu, H.; Parsons, J.T. Cortactin, an 80/85-kilodalton pp60src substrate, is a filamentous actin-binding protein enriched in the cell cortex. *J. Cell Biol.* **1993**, *120*, 1417–1426. [CrossRef]
236. Dent, E.W.; Gupton, S.L.; Gertler, F.B. The growth cone cytoskeleton in axon outgrowth and guidance. *Cold Spring Harb. Perspect. Biol.* **2011**, *3*, a001800. [CrossRef]
237. Wu, J.Y.; Xiang, S.; Zhang, M.; Fang, B.; Huang, H.; Kwon, O.K.; Zhao, Y.; Yang, Z.; Bai, W.; Bepler, G.; et al. Histone deacetylase 6 (HDAC6) deacetylates extracellular signal-regulated kinase 1 (ERK1) and thereby stimulates ERK1 activity. *J. Biol. Chem.* **2018**, *293*, 1976–1993. [CrossRef]
238. Li, Y.; Zhang, X.; Polakiewicz, R.D.; Yao, T.P.; Comb, M.J. HDAC6 is required for epidermal growth factor-induced beta-catenin nuclear localization. *J. Biol. Chem.* **2008**, *283*, 12686–12690. [CrossRef]
239. Jiang, Q.; Ren, Y.; Feng, J. Direct binding with histone deacetylase 6 mediates the reversible recruitment of parkin to the centrosome. *J. Neurosci.* **2008**, *28*, 12993–13002. [CrossRef]
240. Boyault, C.; Zhang, Y.; Fritah, S.; Caron, C.; Gilquin, B.; Kwon, S.H.; Garrido, C.; Yao, T.P.; Vourc'h, C.; Matthias, P.; et al. HDAC6 controls major cell response pathways to cytotoxic accumulation of protein aggregates. *Genes. Dev.* **2007**, *21*, 2172–2181. [CrossRef]
241. Pernet, L.; Faure, V.; Gilquin, B.; Dufour-Guerin, S.; Khochbin, S.; Vourc'h, C. HDAC6-ubiquitin interaction controls the duration of HSF1 activation after heat shock. *Mol. Biol. Cell* **2014**, *25*, 4187–4194. [CrossRef]
242. Magupalli, V.G.; Negro, R.; Tian, Y.; Hauenstein, A.V.; Di Caprio, G.; Skillern, W.; Deng, Q.; Orning, P.; Alam, H.B.; Maliga, Z.; et al. HDAC6 mediates an aggresome-like mechanism for NLRP3 and pyrin inflammasome activation. *Science* **2020**, *369*, eaas8995. [CrossRef]
243. Chen, J.M.; Chuang, C.Y.; Cheng, C.Y.; Liao, Y.A.; Liao, Y.C.; Pan, C.M.; Huang, Y.J.; Wei, T.W.; Tsai, J.R.; Lee, L.W.; et al. NF-small ka, CyrillicB promotes aggresome formation via upregulating HDAC6 and in turn maintaining Vimentin cage. *Am. J. Physiol. Cell Physiol.* **2024**, *369*, eaas8995. [CrossRef]
244. Broz, P.; Dixit, V.M. Inflammasomes: Mechanism of assembly, regulation and signalling. *Nat. Rev. Immunol.* **2016**, *16*, 407–420. [CrossRef]
245. Lamkanfi, M.; Dixit, V.M. Mechanisms and functions of inflammasomes. *Cell* **2014**, *157*, 1013–1022. [CrossRef]
246. Chang, P.; Li, H.; Hu, H.; Li, Y.; Wang, T. The Role of HDAC6 in Autophagy and NLRP3 Inflammasome. *Front. Immunol.* **2021**, *12*, 763831. [CrossRef]
247. Rajsbaum, R.; Garcia-Sastre, A. Virology. Unanchored ubiquitin in virus uncoating. *Science* **2014**, *346*, 427–428. [CrossRef]
248. Husain, M.; Harrod, K.S. Influenza A virus-induced caspase-3 cleaves the histone deacetylase 6 in infected epithelial cells. *FEBS Lett.* **2009**, *583*, 2517–2520. [CrossRef]
249. Husain, M.; Cheung, C.Y. Histone deacetylase 6 inhibits influenza A virus release by downregulating the trafficking of viral components to the plasma membrane via its substrate, acetylated microtubules. *J. Virol.* **2014**, *88*, 11229–11239. [CrossRef]
250. Chen, H.; Qian, Y.; Chen, X.; Ruan, Z.; Ye, Y.; Chen, H.; Babiuk, L.A.; Jung, Y.S.; Dai, J. HDAC6 Restricts Influenza A Virus by Deacetylation of the RNA Polymerase PA Subunit. *J. Virol.* **2019**, *93*, e01896. [CrossRef]

251. Valera, M.S.; de Armas-Rillo, L.; Barroso-Gonzalez, J.; Ziglio, S.; Batisse, J.; Dubois, N.; Marrero-Hernandez, S.; Borel, S.; Garcia-Exposito, L.; Biard-Piechaczyk, M.; et al. The HDAC6/APOBEC3G complex regulates HIV-1 infectiveness by inducing Vif autophagic degradation. *Retrovirology* **2015**, *12*, 53. [CrossRef]
252. Marrero-Hernandez, S.; Marquez-Arce, D.; Cabrera-Rodriguez, R.; Estevez-Herrera, J.; Perez-Yanes, S.; Barroso-Gonzalez, J.; Madrid, R.; Machado, J.D.; Blanco, J.; Valenzuela-Fernandez, A. HIV-1 Nef Targets HDAC6 to Assure Viral Production and Virus Infection. *Front. Microbiol.* **2019**, *10*, 2437. [CrossRef]
253. Protter, D.S.W.; Parker, R. Principles and Properties of Stress Granules. *Trends Cell Biol.* **2016**, *26*, 668–679. [CrossRef]
254. Kwon, S.; Zhang, Y.; Matthias, P. The deacetylase HDAC6 is a novel critical component of stress granules involved in the stress response. *Genes. Dev.* **2007**, *21*, 3381–3394. [CrossRef]
255. Zheng, Y.; Zhu, G.; Tang, Y.; Yan, J.; Han, S.; Yin, J.; Peng, B.; He, X.; Liu, W. HDAC6, A Novel Cargo for Autophagic Clearance of Stress Granules, Mediates the Repression of the Type I Interferon Response During Coxsackievirus A16 Infection. *Front. Microbiol.* **2020**, *11*, 78. [CrossRef]
256. Moses, N.; Zhang, M.; Wu, J.Y.; Hu, C.; Xiang, S.; Geng, X.; Chen, Y.; Bai, W.; Zhang, Y.W.; Bepler, G.; et al. HDAC6 Regulates Radiosensitivity of Non-Small Cell Lung Cancer by Promoting Degradation of Chk1. *Cells* **2020**, *9*, 2237. [CrossRef]
257. Kinzel, D.; Boldt, K.; Davis, E.E.; Burtscher, I.; Trumbach, D.; Diplas, B.; Attie-Bitach, T.; Wurst, W.; Katsanis, N.; Ueffing, M.; et al. Pitchfork regulates primary cilia disassembly and left-right asymmetry. *Dev. Cell* **2010**, *19*, 66–77. [CrossRef]
258. Plotnikova, O.V.; Nikonova, A.S.; Loskutov, Y.V.; Kozyulina, P.Y.; Pugacheva, E.N.; Golemis, E.A. Calmodulin activation of Aurora-A kinase (AURKA) is required during ciliary disassembly and in mitosis. *Mol. Biol. Cell* **2012**, *23*, 2658–2670. [CrossRef]
259. Mergen, M.; Engel, C.; Muller, B.; Follo, M.; Schafer, T.; Jung, M.; Walz, G. The nephronophthisis gene product NPHP2/Inversin interacts with Aurora A and interferes with HDAC6-mediated cilia disassembly. *Nephrol. Dial. Transpl. Transplant.* **2013**, *28*, 2744–2753. [CrossRef]
260. Kim, M.; Kim, M.; Lee, M.S.; Kim, C.H.; Lim, D.S. The MST1/2-SAV1 complex of the Hippo pathway promotes ciliogenesis. *Nat. Commun.* **2014**, *5*, 5370. [CrossRef]
261. Dere, R.; Perkins, A.L.; Bawa-Khalfe, T.; Jonasch, D.; Walker, C.L. β-catenin links von Hippel-Lindau to aurora kinase A and loss of primary cilia in renal cell carcinoma. *J. Am. Soc. Nephrol.* **2015**, *26*, 553–564. [CrossRef]
262. Yang, Y.; Ran, J.; Liu, M.; Li, D.; Li, Y.; Shi, X.; Meng, D.; Pan, J.; Ou, G.; Aneja, R.; et al. CYLD mediates ciliogenesis in multiple organs by deubiquitinating Cep70 and inactivating HDAC6. *Cell Res.* **2014**, *24*, 1342–1353. [CrossRef]
263. Wang, G.; Chen, Q.; Zhang, X.; Zhang, B.; Zhuo, X.; Liu, J.; Jiang, Q.; Zhang, C. PCM1 recruits Plk1 to the pericentriolar matrix to promote primary cilia disassembly before mitotic entry. *J. Cell Sci.* **2013**, *126*, 1355–1365. [CrossRef]
264. Sanchez de Diego, A.; Alonso Guerrero, A.; Martinez, A.C.; van Wely, K.H. Dido3-dependent HDAC6 targeting controls cilium size. *Nat. Commun.* **2014**, *5*, 3500. [CrossRef]
265. Lam, H.C.; Cloonan, S.M.; Bhashyam, A.R.; Haspel, J.A.; Singh, A.; Sathirapongsasuti, J.F.; Cervo, M.; Yao, H.; Chung, A.L.; Mizumura, K.; et al. Histone deacetylase 6-mediated selective autophagy regulates COPD-associated cilia dysfunction. *J. Clin. Investig.* **2013**, *123*, 5212–5230. [CrossRef]
266. Aldana-Masangkay, G.I.; Sakamoto, K.M. The role of HDAC6 in cancer. *J. Biomed. Biotechnol.* **2011**, *2011*, 875824. [CrossRef]
267. Wu, A.C.; Yang, W.B.; Chang, K.Y.; Lee, J.S.; Liou, J.P.; Su, R.Y.; Cheng, S.M.; Hwang, D.Y.; Kikkawa, U.; Hsu, T.I.; et al. HDAC6 involves in regulating the lncRNA-microRNA-mRNA network to promote the proliferation of glioblastoma cells. *J. Exp. Clin. Cancer Res.* **2022**, *41*, 47. [CrossRef]
268. Luo, C.; Wen, B.; Liu, J.; Yang, W. HDAC6-mediated deacetylation of FLOT2 maintains stability and tumorigenic function of FLOT2 in nasopharyngeal carcinoma. *Zhong Nan Da Xue Xue Bao Yi Xue Ban* **2024**, *49*, 687–697. [CrossRef]
269. Yang, W.B.; Hsu, C.C.; Hsu, T.I.; Liou, J.P.; Chang, K.Y.; Chen, P.Y.; Liu, J.J.; Yang, S.T.; Wang, J.Y.; Yeh, S.H.; et al. Increased activation of HDAC1/2/6 and Sp1 underlies therapeutic resistance and tumor growth in glioblastoma. *Neuro Oncol.* **2020**, *22*, 1439–1451. [CrossRef]
270. Skora, B.; Masicz, M.; Nowak, P.; Lachowska, J.; Soltysek, P.; Biskup, J.; Matuszewska, P.; Szychowski, K.A. Suppression of sonic hedgehog pathway-based proliferation in glioblastoma cells by small-size silver nanoparticles in vitro. *Arch. Toxicol.* **2023**, *97*, 2385–2398. [CrossRef]
271. Torrisi, F.; Alberghina, C.; Lo Furno, D.; Zappala, A.; Valable, S.; Li Volti, G.; Tibullo, D.; Vicario, N.; Parenti, R. Connexin 43 and Sonic Hedgehog Pathway Interplay in Glioblastoma Cell Proliferation and Migration. *Biology* **2021**, *10*, 767. [CrossRef]
272. Urdiciain, A.; Erausquin, E.; Melendez, B.; Rey, J.A.; Idoate, M.A.; Castresana, J.S. Tubastatin A, an inhibitor of HDAC6, enhances temozolomide-induced apoptosis and reverses the malignant phenotype of glioblastoma cells. *Int. J. Oncol.* **2019**, *54*, 1797–1808. [CrossRef]
273. Gu, S.; Liu, Y.; Zhu, B.; Ding, K.; Yao, T.P.; Chen, F.; Zhan, L.; Xu, P.; Ehrlich, M.; Liang, T.; et al. Loss of alpha-Tubulin Acetylation Is Associated with TGF-beta-induced Epithelial-Mesenchymal Transition. *J. Biol. Chem.* **2016**, *291*, 5396–5405. [CrossRef]
274. Shi, Y.; Tao, M.; Ni, J.; Tang, L.; Liu, F.; Chen, H.; Ma, X.; Hu, Y.; Zhou, X.; Qiu, A.; et al. Requirement of Histone Deacetylase 6 for Interleukin-6 Induced Epithelial-Mesenchymal Transition, Proliferation, and Migration of Peritoneal Mesothelial Cells. *Front. Pharmacol.* **2021**, *12*, 722638. [CrossRef]
275. Hu, Y.; Dai, M.; Zheng, Y.; Wu, J.; Yu, B.; Zhang, H.; Kong, W.; Wu, H.; Yu, X. Epigenetic suppression of E-cadherin expression by Snail2 during the metastasis of colorectal cancer. *Clin. Epigenetics* **2018**, *10*, 154. [CrossRef]

276. Xu, W.; Yan, P.; Zhou, Z.; Yao, J.; Pan, H.; Jiang, L.; Bo, Z.; Ni, B.; Sun, M.; Gao, S.; et al. HDAC6 Triggers the ATM-Dependent DNA Damage Response to Promote PRV Replication. *Microbiol. Spectr.* **2023**, *11*, e0213222. [CrossRef]
277. Qiu, L.; Xu, W.; Lu, X.; Chen, F.; Chen, Y.; Tian, Y.; Zhu, Q.; Liu, X.; Wang, Y.; Pei, X.H.; et al. The HDAC6-RNF168 axis regulates H2A/H2A.X ubiquitination to enable double-strand break repair. *Nucleic Acids Res.* **2023**, *51*, 9166–9182. [CrossRef]
278. Ozaki, T.; Wu, D.; Sugimoto, H.; Nagase, H.; Nakagawara, A. Runt-related transcription factor 2 (RUNX2) inhibits p53-dependent apoptosis through the collaboration with HDAC6 in response to DNA damage. *Cell Death Dis.* **2013**, *4*, e610. [CrossRef]
279. Xia, S.; Menden, H.L.; Mabry, S.M.; Sampath, V. HDAC6 and ERK/ADAM17 Regulate VEGF-Induced NOTCH Signaling in Lung Endothelial Cells. *Cells* **2023**, *12*, 2231. [CrossRef]
280. Sun, C.; Xie, K.; Yang, L.; Cai, S.; Wang, M.; Zhu, Y.; Tao, B.; Zhu, Y. HDAC6 Enhances Endoglin Expression through Deacetylation of Transcription Factor SP1, Potentiating BMP9-Induced Angiogenesis. *Cells* **2024**, *13*, 490. [CrossRef]
281. Kaluza, D.; Kroll, J.; Gesierich, S.; Yao, T.P.; Boon, R.A.; Hergenreider, E.; Tjwa, M.; Rossig, L.; Seto, E.; Augustin, H.G.; et al. Class IIb HDAC6 regulates endothelial cell migration and angiogenesis by deacetylation of cortactin. *EMBO J.* **2011**, *30*, 4142–4156. [CrossRef]
282. Duvic, M.; Vu, J. Vorinostat: A new oral histone deacetylase inhibitor approved for cutaneous T-cell lymphoma. *Expert. Opin. Investig. Drugs* **2007**, *16*, 1111–1120. [CrossRef]
283. Whittaker, S.J.; Demierre, M.F.; Kim, E.J.; Rook, A.H.; Lerner, A.; Duvic, M.; Scarisbrick, J.; Reddy, S.; Robak, T.; Becker, J.C.; et al. Final results from a multicenter, international, pivotal study of romidepsin in refractory cutaneous T-cell lymphoma. *J. Clin. Oncol.* **2010**, *28*, 4485–4491. [CrossRef]
284. Garnock-Jones, K.P. Panobinostat: First global approval. *Drugs* **2015**, *75*, 695–704. [CrossRef]
285. Ning, Z.Q.; Li, Z.B.; Newman, M.J.; Shan, S.; Wang, X.H.; Pan, D.S.; Zhang, J.; Dong, M.; Du, X.; Lu, X.P. Chidamide (CS055/HBI-8000): A new histone deacetylase inhibitor of the benzamide class with antitumor activity and the ability to enhance immune cell-mediated tumor cell cytotoxicity. *Cancer Chemother. Pharmacol.* **2012**, *69*, 901–909. [CrossRef]
286. Duvic, M.; Vu, J. Vorinostat in cutaneous T-cell lymphoma. *Drugs Today* **2007**, *43*, 585–599. [CrossRef]
287. Rivers, Z.T.; Oostra, D.R.; Westholder, J.S.; Vercellotti, G.M. Romidepsin-associated cardiac toxicity and ECG changes: A case report and review of the literature. *J. Oncol. Pharm. Pract.* **2018**, *24*, 56–62. [CrossRef]
288. Smith, N.; Nucera, C. Personalized therapy in patients with anaplastic thyroid cancer: Targeting genetic and epigenetic alterations. *J. Clin. Endocrinol. Metab.* **2015**, *100*, 35–42. [CrossRef]
289. Van Veggel, M.; Westerman, E.; Hamberg, P. Clinical Pharmacokinetics and Pharmacodynamics of Panobinostat. *Clin. Pharmacokinet.* **2018**, *57*, 21–29. [CrossRef]
290. Haggarty, S.J.; Koeller, K.M.; Wong, J.C.; Butcher, R.A.; Schreiber, S.L. Multidimensional chemical genetic analysis of diversity-oriented synthesis-derived deacetylase inhibitors using cell-based assays. *Chem. Biol.* **2003**, *10*, 383–396. [CrossRef]
291. Haggarty, S.J.; Koeller, K.M.; Wong, J.C.; Grozinger, C.M.; Schreiber, S.L. Domain-selective small-molecule inhibitor of histone deacetylase 6 (HDAC6)-mediated tubulin deacetylation. *Proc. Natl. Acad. Sci. USA* **2003**, *100*, 4389–4394. [CrossRef]
292. Vogl, D.T.; Raje, N.; Jagannath, S.; Richardson, P.; Hari, P.; Orlowski, R.; Supko, J.G.; Tamang, D.; Yang, M.; Jones, S.S.; et al. Ricolinostat, the First Selective Histone Deacetylase 6 Inhibitor, in Combination with Bortezomib and Dexamethasone for Relapsed or Refractory Multiple Myeloma. *Clin. Cancer Res.* **2017**, *23*, 3307–3315. [CrossRef]
293. Amengual, J.E.; Johannet, P.; Lombardo, M.; Zullo, K.; Hoehn, D.; Bhagat, G.; Scotto, L.; Jirau-Serrano, X.; Radeski, D.; Heinen, J.; et al. Dual Targeting of Protein Degradation Pathways with the Selective HDAC6 Inhibitor ACY-1215 and Bortezomib Is Synergistic in Lymphoma. *Clin. Cancer Res.* **2015**, *21*, 4663–4675. [CrossRef]
294. Chen, Y.; Lopez-Sanchez, M.; Savoy, D.N.; Billadeau, D.D.; Dow, G.S.; Kozikowski, A.P. A series of potent and selective, triazolylphenyl-based histone deacetylases inhibitors with activity against pancreatic cancer cells and Plasmodium falciparum. *J. Med. Chem.* **2008**, *51*, 3437–3448. [CrossRef]
295. Kozikowski, A.P.; Chen, Y.; Gaysin, A.M.; Savoy, D.N.; Billadeau, D.D.; Kim, K.H. Chemistry, biology, and QSAR studies of substituted biaryl hydroxamates and mercaptoacetamides as HDAC inhibitors-nanomolar-potency inhibitors of pancreatic cancer cell growth. *ChemMedChem* **2008**, *3*, 487–501. [CrossRef]
296. Negmeldin, A.T.; Knoff, J.R.; Pflum, M.K.H. The structural requirements of histone deacetylase inhibitors: C4-modified SAHA analogs display dual HDAC6/HDAC8 selectivity. *Eur. J. Med. Chem.* **2018**, *143*, 1790–1806. [CrossRef]
297. Butler, K.V.; Kalin, J.; Brochier, C.; Vistoli, G.; Langley, B.; Kozikowski, A.P. Rational design and simple chemistry yield a superior, neuroprotective HDAC6 inhibitor, tubastatin A. *J. Am. Chem. Soc.* **2010**, *132*, 10842–10846. [CrossRef]
298. Kalin, J.H.; Butler, K.V.; Akimova, T.; Hancock, W.W.; Kozikowski, A.P. Second-generation histone deacetylase 6 inhibitors enhance the immunosuppressive effects of Foxp3+ T-regulatory cells. *J. Med. Chem.* **2012**, *55*, 639–651. [CrossRef]
299. De Vreese, R.; Verhaeghe, T.; Desmet, T.; D'Hooghe, M. Potent and selective HDAC6 inhibitory activity of N-(4-hydroxycarbamoylbenzyl)-1,2,4,9-tetrahydro-3-thia-9-azafluorenes as novel sulfur analogues of Tubastatin A. *Chem. Commun.* **2013**, *49*, 3775–3777. [CrossRef]
300. Bergman, J.A.; Woan, K.; Perez-Villarroel, P.; Villagra, A.; Sotomayor, E.M.; Kozikowski, A.P. Selective histone deacetylase 6 inhibitors bearing substituted urea linkers inhibit melanoma cell growth. *J. Med. Chem.* **2012**, *55*, 9891–9899. [CrossRef]
301. Lee, J.H.; Mahendran, A.; Yao, Y.; Ngo, L.; Venta-Perez, G.; Choy, M.L.; Kim, N.; Ham, W.S.; Breslow, R.; Marks, P.A. Development of a histone deacetylase 6 inhibitor and its biological effects. *Proc. Natl. Acad. Sci. USA* **2013**, *110*, 15704–15709. [CrossRef]
302. Liang, T.; Fang, H. Structure, Functions and Selective Inhibitors of HDAC6. *Curr. Top. Med. Chem.* **2018**, *18*, 2429–2447. [CrossRef]

303. Zhao, Y.; Liang, T.; Hou, X.; Fang, H. Recent Development of Novel HDAC6 Isoform-selective Inhibitors. *Curr. Med. Chem.* **2021**, *28*, 4133–4151. [CrossRef]
304. Li, X.; Song, Y. Proteolysis-targeting chimera (PROTAC) for targeted protein degradation and cancer therapy. *J. Hematol. Oncol.* **2020**, *13*, 50. [CrossRef]
305. Nalawansha, D.A.; Crews, C.M. PROTACs: An Emerging Therapeutic Modality in Precision Medicine. *Cell Chem. Biol.* **2020**, *27*, 998–1014. [CrossRef]
306. Darwish, S.; Heimburg, T.; Ridinger, J.; Herp, D.; Schmidt, M.; Romier, C.; Jung, M.; Oehme, I.; Sippl, W. Synthesis, Biochemical, and Cellular Evaluation of HDAC6 Targeting Proteolysis Targeting Chimeras. *Methods Mol. Biol.* **2023**, *2589*, 179–193. [CrossRef]
307. Sinatra, L.; Yang, J.; Schliehe-Diecks, J.; Dienstbier, N.; Vogt, M.; Gebing, P.; Bachmann, L.M.; Sonnichsen, M.; Lenz, T.; Stuhler, K.; et al. Solid-Phase Synthesis of Cereblon-Recruiting Selective Histone Deacetylase 6 Degraders (HDAC6 PROTACs) with Antileukemic Activity. *J. Med. Chem.* **2022**, *65*, 16860–16878. [CrossRef]
308. Yang, H.; Lv, W.; He, M.; Deng, H.; Li, H.; Wu, W.; Rao, Y. Plasticity in designing PROTACs for selective and potent degradation of HDAC6. *Chem. Commun.* **2019**, *55*, 14848–14851. [CrossRef]
309. Xia, K.; Qiu, T.; Jian, Y.; Liu, H.; Chen, H.; Liu, X.; Chen, Z.; Wang, L. Degradation of histone deacetylase 6 alleviates ROS-mediated apoptosis in renal ischemia-reperfusion injury. *Biomed. Pharmacother.* **2023**, *165*, 115128. [CrossRef]
310. Cao, Z.; Gu, Z.; Lin, S.; Chen, D.; Wang, J.; Zhao, Y.; Li, Y.; Liu, T.; Li, Y.; Wang, Y.; et al. Attenuation of NLRP3 Inflammasome Activation by Indirubin-Derived PROTAC Targeting HDAC6. *ACS Chem. Biol.* **2021**, *16*, 2746–2751. [CrossRef]
311. Bockstiegel, J.; Wurnig, S.L.; Engelhardt, J.; Enns, J.; Hansen, F.K.; Weindl, G. Pharmacological inhibition of HDAC6 suppresses NLRP3 inflammasome-mediated IL-1beta release. *Biochem. Pharmacol.* **2023**, *215*, 115693. [CrossRef]
312. Liang, X.; Zang, J.; Li, X.; Tang, S.; Huang, M.; Geng, M.; Chou, C.J.; Li, C.; Cao, Y.; Xu, W.; et al. Discovery of Novel Janus Kinase (JAK) and Histone Deacetylase (HDAC) Dual Inhibitors for the Treatment of Hematological Malignancies. *J. Med. Chem.* **2019**, *62*, 3898–3923. [CrossRef]
313. Xue, X.; Zhang, Y.; Liao, Y.; Sun, D.; Li, L.; Liu, Y.; Wang, Y.; Jiang, W.; Zhang, J.; Luan, Y.; et al. Design, synthesis and biological evaluation of dual HDAC and VEGFR inhibitors as multitargeted anticancer agents. *Investig. New Drugs* **2022**, *40*, 10–20. [CrossRef]
314. De Simone, A.; La Pietra, V.; Betari, N.; Petragnani, N.; Conte, M.; Daniele, S.; Pietrobono, D.; Martini, C.; Petralla, S.; Casadei, R.; et al. Discovery of the First-in-Class GSK-3beta/HDAC Dual Inhibitor as Disease-Modifying Agent to Combat Alzheimer's Disease. *ACS Med. Chem. Lett.* **2019**, *10*, 469–474. [CrossRef]
315. Wu, Y.W.; Hsu, K.C.; Lee, H.Y.; Huang, T.C.; Lin, T.E.; Chen, Y.L.; Sung, T.Y.; Liou, J.P.; Hwang-Verslues, W.W.; Pan, S.L.; et al. A Novel Dual HDAC6 and Tubulin Inhibitor, MPT0B451, Displays Anti-tumor Ability in Human Cancer Cells in Vitro and in Vivo. *Front. Pharmacol.* **2018**, *9*, 205. [CrossRef]
316. Awad, M.M.; Le Bruchec, Y.; Lu, B.; Ye, J.; Miller, J.; Lizotte, P.H.; Cavanaugh, M.E.; Rode, A.J.; Dumitru, C.D.; Spira, A. Selective Histone Deacetylase Inhibitor ACY-241 (Citarinostat) Plus Nivolumab in Advanced Non-Small Cell Lung Cancer: Results from a Phase Ib Study. *Front. Oncol.* **2021**, *11*, 696512. [CrossRef]
317. Gordon, M.S.; Shapiro, G.I.; Sarantopoulos, J.; Juric, D.; Lu, B.; Zarotiadou, A.; Connarn, J.N.; Le Bruchec, Y.; Dumitru, C.D.; Harvey, R.D. Phase Ib Study of the Histone Deacetylase 6 Inhibitor Citarinostat in Combination with Paclitaxel in Patients with Advanced Solid Tumors. *Front. Oncol.* **2021**, *11*, 786120. [CrossRef]
318. Tsimberidou, A.M.; Beer, P.A.; Cartwright, C.A.; Haymaker, C.; Vo, H.H.; Kiany, S.; Cecil, A.R.L.; Dow, J.; Haque, K.; Silva, F.A.; et al. Preclinical Development and First-in-Human Study of KA2507, a Selective and Potent Inhibitor of Histone Deacetylase 6, for Patients with Refractory Solid Tumors. *Clin. Cancer Res.* **2021**, *27*, 3584–3594. [CrossRef]
319. Li, Z.Y.; Zhang, C.; Zhang, Y.; Chen, L.; Chen, B.D.; Li, Q.Z.; Zhang, X.J.; Li, W.P. A novel HDAC6 inhibitor Tubastatin A: Controls HDAC6-p97/VCP-mediated ubiquitination-autophagy turnover and reverses Temozolomide-induced ER stress-tolerance in GBM cells. *Cancer Lett.* **2017**, *391*, 89–99. [CrossRef]
320. Yin, C.; Li, P. Growth Suppression of Glioma Cells Using HDAC6 Inhibitor, Tubacin. *Open Med. (Wars)* **2018**, *13*, 221–226. [CrossRef]
321. Liu, J.R.; Yu, C.W.; Hung, P.Y.; Hsin, L.W.; Chern, J.W. High-selective HDAC6 inhibitor promotes HDAC6 degradation following autophagy modulation and enhanced antitumor immunity in glioblastoma. *Biochem. Pharmacol.* **2019**, *163*, 458–471. [CrossRef] [PubMed]
322. Nepali, K.; Wu, A.C.; Lo, W.L.; Chopra, B.; Lai, M.J.; Chuang, J.Y.; Liou, J.P. Rationally designed donepezil-based hydroxamates modulate Sig-1R and HDAC isoforms to exert anti-glioblastoma effects. *Eur. J. Med. Chem.* **2023**, *248*, 115054. [CrossRef]
323. Yang, W.B.; Chuang, J.Y.; Ko, C.Y.; Chang, W.C.; Hsu, T.I. Dehydroepiandrosterone Induces Temozolomide Resistance Through Modulating Phosphorylation and Acetylation of Sp1 in Glioblastoma. *Mol. Neurobiol.* **2019**, *56*, 2301–2313. [CrossRef] [PubMed]
324. Petrunak, E.M.; Bart, A.G.; Peng, H.M.; Auchus, R.J.; Scott, E.E. Human cytochrome P450 17A1 structures with metabolites of prostate cancer drug abiraterone reveal substrate-binding plasticity and a second binding site. *J. Biol. Chem.* **2023**, *299*, 102999. [CrossRef] [PubMed]
325. Sharma, R.; Chiang, Y.H.; Chen, H.C.; Lin, H.Y.; Yang, W.B.; Nepali, K.; Lai, M.J.; Chen, K.Y.; Liou, J.P.; Hsu, T.I. Dual inhibition of CYP17A1 and HDAC6 by abiraterone-installed hydroxamic acid overcomes temozolomide resistance in glioblastoma through inducing DNA damage and oxidative stress. *Cancer Lett.* **2024**, *586*, 216666. [CrossRef]

326. Feng, Y.S.; Tan, Z.X.; Wu, L.Y.; Dong, F.; Zhang, F. The involvement of NLRP3 inflammasome in the treatment of Alzheimer's disease. *Ageing Res. Rev.* **2020**, *64*, 101192. [CrossRef]
327. Pulya, S.; Amin, S.A.; Adhikari, N.; Biswas, S.; Jha, T.; Ghosh, B. HDAC6 as privileged target in drug discovery: A perspective. *Pharmacol. Res.* **2021**, *163*, 105274. [CrossRef]
328. Zhu, Y.; Feng, M.; Wang, B.; Zheng, Y.; Jiang, D.; Zhao, L.; Mamun, M.A.A.; Kang, H.; Nie, H.; Zhang, X.; et al. New insights into the non-enzymatic function of HDAC6. *Biomed. Pharmacother.* **2023**, *161*, 114438. [CrossRef]
329. Rossaert, E.; Van Den Bosch, L. HDAC6 inhibitors: Translating genetic and molecular insights into a therapy for axonal CMT. *Brain Res.* **2020**, *1733*, 146692. [CrossRef]
330. English, K.; Barton, M.C. HDAC6: A Key Link Between Mitochondria and Development of Peripheral Neuropathy. *Front. Mol. Neurosci.* **2021**, *14*, 684714. [CrossRef]
331. Fazal, R.; Boeynaems, S.; Swijsen, A.; De Decker, M.; Fumagalli, L.; Moisse, M.; Vanneste, J.; Guo, W.; Boon, R.; Vercruysse, T.; et al. HDAC6 inhibition restores TDP-43 pathology and axonal transport defects in human motor neurons with TARDBP mutations. *EMBO J.* **2021**, *40*, e106177. [CrossRef]
332. Lee, S.; Kwon, Y.; Kim, S.; Jo, M.; Jeon, Y.M.; Cheon, M.; Lee, S.; Kim, S.R.; Kim, K.; Kim, H.J. The Role of HDAC6 in TDP-43-Induced Neurotoxicity and UPS Impairment. *Front. Cell Dev. Biol.* **2020**, *8*, 581942. [CrossRef]
333. Tang, Z.; Lin, M.G.; Stowe, T.R.; Chen, S.; Zhu, M.; Stearns, T.; Franco, B.; Zhong, Q. Autophagy promotes primary ciliogenesis by removing OFD1 from centriolar satellites. *Nature* **2013**, *502*, 254–257. [CrossRef] [PubMed]
334. Pampliega, O.; Orhon, I.; Patel, B.; Sridhar, S.; Diaz-Carretero, A.; Beau, I.; Codogno, P.; Satir, B.H.; Satir, P.; Cuervo, A.M. Functional interaction between autophagy and ciliogenesis. *Nature* **2013**, *502*, 194–200. [CrossRef] [PubMed]
335. Bruchard, M.; Mignot, G.; Derangere, V.; Chalmin, F.; Chevriaux, A.; Vegran, F.; Boireau, W.; Simon, B.; Ryffel, B.; Connat, J.L.; et al. Chemotherapy-triggered cathepsin B release in myeloid-derived suppressor cells activates the Nlrp3 inflammasome and promotes tumor growth. *Nat. Med.* **2013**, *19*, 57–64. [CrossRef] [PubMed]
336. Dupaul-Chicoine, J.; Arabzadeh, A.; Dagenais, M.; Douglas, T.; Champagne, C.; Morizot, A.; Rodrigue-Gervais, I.G.; Breton, V.; Colpitts, S.L.; Beauchemin, N.; et al. The Nlrp3 Inflammasome Suppresses Colorectal Cancer Metastatic Growth in the Liver by Promoting Natural Killer Cell Tumoricidal Activity. *Immunity* **2015**, *43*, 751–763. [CrossRef] [PubMed]
337. Zaki, M.H.; Vogel, P.; Body-Malapel, M.; Lamkanfi, M.; Kanneganti, T.D. IL-18 production downstream of the Nlrp3 inflammasome confers protection against colorectal tumor formation. *J. Immunol.* **2010**, *185*, 4912–4920. [CrossRef]
338. Meng, W.; Wang, B.; Mao, W.; Wang, J.; Zhao, Y.; Li, Q.; Zhang, C.; Ma, J. Enhanced efficacy of histone deacetylase inhibitor panobinostat combined with dual PI3K/mTOR inhibitor BEZ235 against glioblastoma. *Nagoya J. Med. Sci.* **2019**, *81*, 93–102. [CrossRef]
339. Romanelli, A.; Stazi, G.; Fioravanti, R.; Zwergel, C.; Di Bello, E.; Pomella, S.; Perrone, C.; Battistelli, C.; Strippoli, R.; Tripodi, M.; et al. Design of First-in-Class Dual EZH2/HDAC Inhibitor: Biochemical Activity and Biological Evaluation in Cancer Cells. *ACS Med. Chem. Lett.* **2020**, *11*, 977–983. [CrossRef]
340. Salvatori, L.; Malatesta, S.; Illi, B.; Somma, M.P.; Fionda, C.; Stabile, H.; Fontanella, R.A.; Gaetano, C. Nitric Oxide Prevents Glioblastoma Stem Cells' Expansion and Induces Temozolomide Sensitization. *Int. J. Mol. Sci.* **2023**, *24*, 11286. [CrossRef]
341. Duda, J.M.; Thomas, S.N. Interactions of Histone Deacetylase 6 with DNA Damage Repair Factors Strengthen its Utility as a Combination Drug Target in High-Grade Serous Ovarian Cancer. *ACS Pharmacol. Transl. Sci.* **2023**, *6*, 1924–1933. [CrossRef] [PubMed]
342. Lin, T.W.; Chen, M.T.; Lin, L.T.; Huang, P.I.; Lo, W.L.; Yang, Y.P.; Lu, K.H.; Chen, Y.W.; Chiou, S.H.; Wu, C.W. TDP-43/HDAC6 axis promoted tumor progression and regulated nutrient deprivation-induced autophagy in glioblastoma. *Oncotarget* **2017**, *8*, 56612–56625. [CrossRef] [PubMed]
343. Laubach, J.P.; San-Miguel, J.F.; Hungria, V.; Hou, J.; Moreau, P.; Lonial, S.; Lee, J.H.; Einsele, H.; Alsina, M.; Richardson, P.G. Deacetylase inhibitors: An advance in myeloma therapy? *Expert. Rev. Hematol.* **2017**, *10*, 229–237. [CrossRef] [PubMed]
344. Zeleke, T.Z.; Pan, Q.; Chiuzan, C.; Onishi, M.; Li, Y.; Tan, H.; Alvarez, M.J.; Honan, E.; Yang, M.; Chia, P.L.; et al. Network-based assessment of HDAC6 activity predicts preclinical and clinical responses to the HDAC6 inhibitor ricolinostat in breast cancer. *Nat. Cancer* **2023**, *4*, 257–275. [CrossRef]

biomedicines

MDPI

Article

Neuronal Differentiation of Human Glioma Cells Induced by Parthenolide Under In Vitro Conditions

Zhaoqi Tang [1,2,*], Chang Cao [1,2], Weiwei Tang [3,4,5], Yanrong Ye [1,6], Zhenhui Chen [1,2] and Yun Shen [1,6,*]

1 Department of Pharmacy, Zhongshan Hospital (Xiamen), Fudan University, Xiamen 361015, China
2 Xiamen Clinical Research Center for Cancer Therapy, Xiamen 361015, China
3 Department of Medical Oncology, The First Affiliated Hospital of Xiamen University, School of Medicine, Xiamen University, Xiamen 361003, China
4 Department of Medical Oncology, The First Affiliated Hospital of Xiamen University, School of Clinical Medicine, Fujian Medical University, Xiamen 361003, China
5 Xiamen Key Laboratory of Antitumor Drug Transformation Research, The First Affiliated Hospital of Xiamen University, Xiamen 361003, China
6 Department of Pharmacy, Zhongshan Hospital, Fudan University, Shanghai 200032, China
* Correspondence: TangZaoqi@hotmail.com (Z.T.); shenyun.zhongshan@outlook.com (Y.S.)

Abstract: Objective: Previous drug repositioning studies have suggested that parthenolide may be a differentiation-inducing agent for glioma cells. This study aimed to experimentally verify the neuronal differentiation-inducing effects and proliferative impact of parthenolide on human glioma cells and explore its potential mechanisms. **Methods:** HE staining was used to observe the morphological changes in human glioma cell lines U87 and A172 induced by parthenolide. Immunocytochemistry was conducted to detect the expression of differentiation markers. The Ki-67 detection and CCK-8 assay were used to assess the effects of parthenolide on cell proliferation. The sphere formation assay was conducted to evaluate the self-renewal. Glioma stem cells (GSCs) derived from U87 cells were utilized to assess the ability of parthenolide to induce differentiation in GSCs. Western blot was used to detect the expression of histone deacetylase 1 (HDAC1). Bioinformatics analysis based on the CGGA database was conducted to evaluate the role of HDAC1 in glioma. **Results:** Parthenolide (4 μM) altered the morphology of U87 and A172 cells, as elongated cell projections were observed. Parthenolide induced glioma cells to express neuronal markers NeuN, MAP2, SYP, and NEFL, but not astrocyte or oligodendrocyte markers. Parthenolide significantly inhibited proliferation and self-renewal in glioma cells. Similar effects were observed in U87 GSCs. Furthermore, parthenolide downregulated HDAC1 expression in glioma cells, and the bioinformatics analysis revealed a potential relationship between neuronal characteristics and low expression of HDAC1 in glioma. **Conclusion:** Parthenolide induced neuronal differentiation and inhibited the cell proliferation in human glioma cells, which might be associated with the inhibition of HDAC1.

Keywords: parthenolide; glioma; differentiation; neuron; proliferation; histone deacetylase

1. Introduction

Glioma is the most common primary malignant brain tumor in adults. Glioblastoma multiforme (GBM), the most prevalent type of glioma, is a highly malignant grade 4 diffuse glioma. The median survival for untreated patients is 3–4.5 months, and maximal treatment with debulking surgery followed by chemoradiotherapy only increases the median survival to 15–16 months, with a 2-year survival rate of 27–31% and a 5-year survival rate of 7–10% [1]. Therefore, more effective treatment strategies for glioma are needed. Owing to the infiltrative nature of glioma, complete surgical resection is difficult. Residual glioma stem cells (GSCs) are characterized by self-renewal and heterogeneity, as well as resistance to chemotherapeutic agents such as temozolomide, leading to tumor recurrence, which is a significant cause of treatment failure [2]. The induction of glioma cell differentiation and attenuation of stemness in GSCs may play crucial roles in the treatment of glioma and prevention of postoperative recurrence. Some scholars have researched the induction of glioma cell differentiation. For example, cyclic adenosine monophosphate (cAMP) activators can induce the neuronal differentiation of GSCs [3], the upregulation of the expression of the transcription factors nuclear factor 1 A (NFIA) and nuclear factor 1 B (NFIB) can induce the differentiation of GBM cells into astrocytes [4], and the downregulation of zinc finger protein 117 (ZNF117) expression can induce the differentiation of GSCs into oligodendrocytes [5]. These differentiation induction treatments significantly inhibited the proliferation of glioma cells, indicating that differentiation induction is a promising therapeutic strategy for glioma.

Parthenolide is a natural sesquiterpene lactone produced as secondary metabolite by plants of the Asteraceae/Compositae (daisies) and Magnoliaceae family (magnolias), and is the main biologically active ingredient of feverfew. It exhibits promising anti-inflammatory and anti-tumor properties [6]. Parthenolide has been shown to inhibit nuclear transcription factor-κB (NF-κB) signaling and other prosurvival signaling pathways, induce apoptosis, and reduce a subpopulation of cancer stem-like cells in several cancers [7]. In our previous study of drug repositioning via the Connectivity Map database, we reported that parthenolide may have a differentiation-inducing effect on glioma cells [8], but there are currently no relevant experimental research reports on this topic. This study aimed to experimentally verify the differentiation-inducing and proliferation-inhibiting effects of parthenolide on glioma cells and explore its potential mechanism.

2. Materials and Methods

2.1. Cell Culture and Reagents

Human glioma cell lines U87 and A172 were purchased from the Cell Bank of Chinese Academy of Sciences and cultured in DMEM (HyClone, Logan, UT, USA) supplemented with 10% fetal bovine serum (ExCell, Shanghai, China) and 1% penicillin/streptomycin (BasalMedia, Shanghai, China). Cells were maintained at 37 °C in a humidified atmosphere containing 5% CO_2. The drug treatment group was cultured with complete culture medium containing parthenolide (Macklin, Shanghai, China), while the control group was cultured with complete culture medium containing DMSO solvent.

U87 GSCs were isolated from the U87 cell line. U87 cells were cultured in ultra-low attachment culture dishes using DMEM/F12 (HyClone, USA) medium supplemented with 2% B27 supplement (iCell, Shanghai, China), 20 ng/mL epidermal growth factor (EGF) (Novoprotein, Beijing, China), and 20 ng/mL basic fibroblast growth factor (bFGF) (Novoprotein, China). After 5 days, the cell spheres were collected using a 70 mm cell strainer. The cell spheres were digested and dispersed with trypsin and then cultured in the same manner. The cell spheres collected for the third time were used as GSCs. For differentiation, poly-L-Lysine-coated cell crawling slides were used.

2.2. Hematoxylin-Eosin (HE) Staining

Cells were cultured in 6-well plates and subsequently treated with parthenolide for 3 days. Then, cells were fixed using 4% paraformaldehyde for 10 min and stained with hematoxylin (Biosharp, Hefei, China) for 5 min and eosin (Biosharp, China) for 10 s. The images were captured via an inverted microscope (Nikon, Tokyo, Japan).

2.3. Immunocytochemistry

Cells were cultured in 6-well plates and subsequently treated with parthenolide (4 μM) for 3 days. Then, cells were fixed using 4% paraformaldehyde for 10 min, permeabilized with methanol at 4 °C for 10 min, blocked with 5% bull serum albumin for 1 h, then incubated with primary antibodies at 4 °C overnight. After that, cells were incubated with secondary antibody at room temperature for 1 h, followed by staining with DAPI for 10 min, and finally mounted with antifade mounting medium. The images were captured via an inverted microscope (Nikon, Tokyo, Japan). The primary antibodies used included the following: microtubule-associated protein 2 (MAP2) antibody (Abcam, Cambridge, UK), neuronal nuclei antigen (NeuN) antibody (Abcam, Cambridge, UK), synaptophysin (SYP) antibody (Beyotime, Shanghai, China), neurofilament light chain (NEFL) antibody (Proteintech, Shanghai, China), glial fibrillary acidic protein (GFAP) antibody (CST, Peachtree City, GA, USA), S100 calcium binding protein B (S100B) antibody (ABclonal, Wuhan, China), oligodendrocyte transcription factor 2 (Olig2) antibody (CST, USA), myelin basic protein (MBP) antibody (Novus, Chesterfield, MO, USA), and Ki-67 antibody (CST, USA).

2.4. Ki-67 Positive Rate Calculation

For each sample, five fields of view were randomly selected and photographed under 200× magnification. The Image-Pro Plus 6.0 software was used to count Ki-67 stained cells and DAPI-stained cells in the same field of view. The experiment was repeated three times, and the positive rate of each field of view was calculated and averaged.

2.5. Cell Viability Assay

Cells were cultured in 96-well plates and subsequently treated with parthenolide (4 μM) for 3 days. Then, 10 μL of CCK-8 (Glpbio, Montclair, CA, USA) reagent was added to each well of the plates, and the cells were incubated at 37 °C for 1 h. The optical density at 450 nm was read with a microplate reader (Thermo Scientific, Waltham, MA, USA). Four replicate wells were set for each group. The experiment was repeated three times.

2.6. Sphere Formation Assay

Cells were cultured in ultra-low attachment 12-well plates with DMEM/F12 medium supplemented with 2% B27 supplement, 20 ng/mL EGF, and 20 ng/mL bFGF for 5 days. For each sample, three random fields of view were photographed under 100× magnification. The diameters of the neurospheres were measured using ImageJ 1.51j8 software. The total number of neurospheres with diameters greater than 75 μm in the three fields of view was also calculated. The experiment was repeated three times.

2.7. Western Blot

Cells were cultured in 6-well plates and subsequently treated with parthenolide (4 μM) for 3 days. Protein samples were separated by SDS-PAGE and then transferred to an NC membrane. The membrane was blocked with 5% BSA on a shaker at room temperature for 1 h. The antibody was diluted with blocking solution, and the membrane was incubated with primary antibody overnight at 4 °C. After that, the membrane was washed with PBST three times, each for 10 min, and then incubated with the secondary antibody at room temperature in the dark for 1 h. This was followed by washing the membrane with PBST three times, each for 10 min. After adding the ECL agent, the membrane was imaged. The images were analyzed via ImageJ software.

2.8. Chinese Glioma Genome Atlas (CGGA) Analysis

The mRNAse_325 dataset was downloaded from the CGGA database (http://www.cgga.org.cn/, accessed on 28 September 2023). The samples were grouped according to the quartile of target gene expression, and those above the quartile were divided into the high group and those below the quartile were divided into the low group. Genes with |Log2FC| values greater than 3 and p values less than 0.05 were considered as the differentially expressed genes (DEGs) between the high and low groups. The differences in gene expression, tumor grade, and survival between groups were analyzed.

2.9. Enrichment Analysis

The gene symbols were uploaded to the Search Tool for Retrieval for Interaction Gene/Proteins (STRING) database (https://cn.string-db.org/, accessed on 7 October 2023) for protein–protein interaction (PPI) network creation and to the Database for Annotation,

Visualization, and Integrated Discovery (DAVID, https://david.ncifcrf.gov/, accessed on 7 October 2023) for Gene Ontology (GO) enrichment analysis.

2.10. Statistical Analysis

Statistical analysis was performed using SPSS (International Business Machines Corporation, Armonk, NY, USA) 16.0 software. A *t* test was used to compare the mean values between groups. The log-rank test was used to compare the survival curves. The chi-square test was used to compare tumor grade compositions between groups. A *p* value less than 0.05 was considered statistically significant.

3. Results

3.1. Parthenolide Induced Morphological Changes in Glioma Cells

Cell microscopy images showed the cell morphology, and HE staining was performed to enhance the visualization of cell morphology. Cell microscopy images and HE staining results revealed that parthenolide had a relatively minor effect on the morphology of U87 and A172 cells at a concentration of 2 μM. At a concentration of 4 μM, some dead cells were observed, and surviving cells exhibited some morphological changes, such as the development of elongated cell projections. At a concentration of 8 μM, all the cells died (Figure 1). Therefore, a concentration of 4 μM was chosen for subsequent experiments.

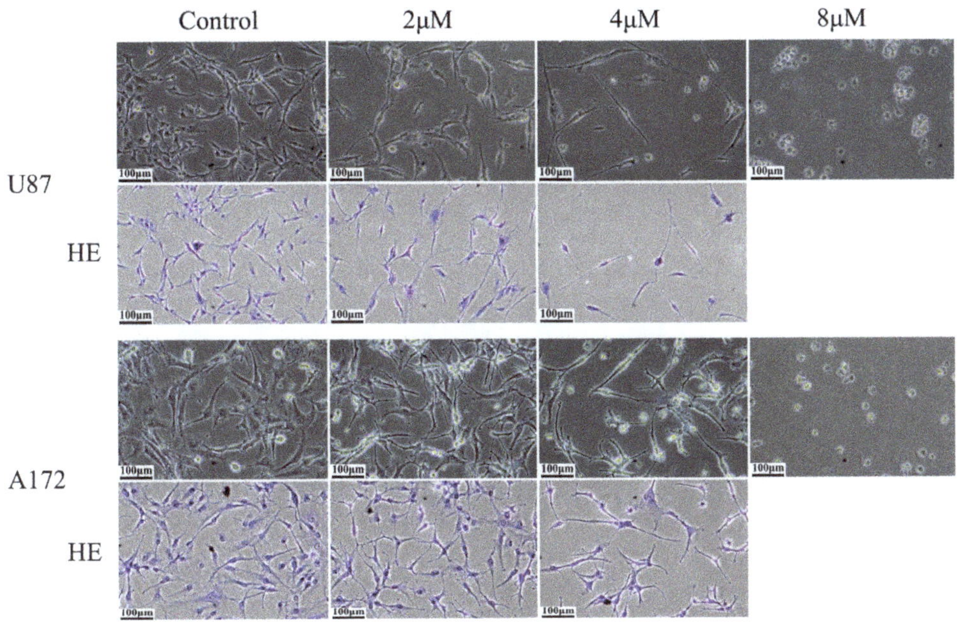

Figure 1. Effects of parthenolide on the morphology of glioma cells (200×), scale bar = 100 μm. Elongated cell projections appeared after parthenolide (4 μM) treatment for 3 days.

3.2. Parthenolide Induced the Expression of Neuronal Markers in Glioma Cells

The immunocytochemistry results showed that the expression of neuronal markers NeuN, MAP2, SYP, and NEFL was detected in the parthenolide treatment group, but not in the control group (Figure 2A,B). Additionally, no expression of astrocyte markers GFAP and S100B or oligodendrocyte markers MBP and Olig2 was detected after parthenolide treatment (Figure 2C).

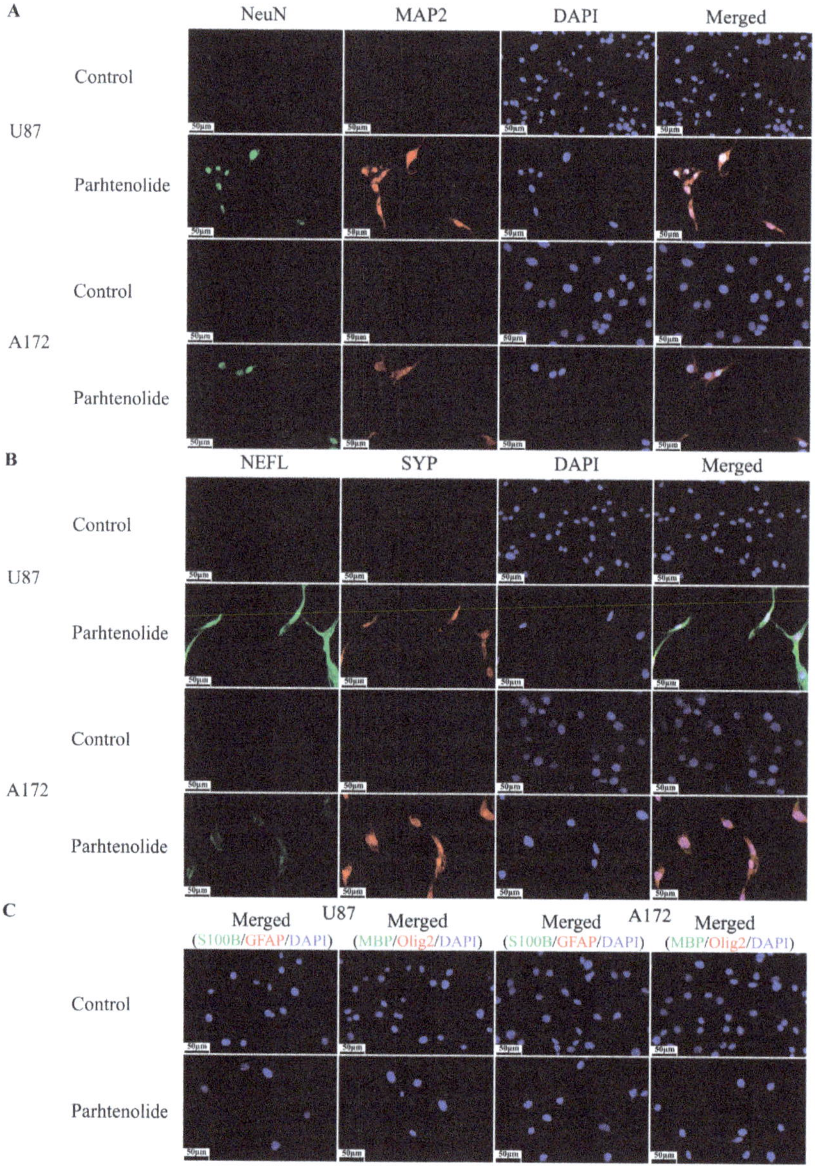

Figure 2. Effects of parthenolide on the expression of differentiation markers in glioma cells (400×), scale bar = 50 μm. Cells expressed neuronal markers, but not astrocyte or oligodendrocyte markers, after parthenolide (4 μM) treatment for 3 days. (**A**) Expression of neuronal markers NeuN and MAP2; (**B**) expression of neuronal markers SYP and NEFL; (**C**) expression of astrocyte and oligodendrocyte markers.

3.3. Parthenolide Inhibited the Proliferation of Glioma Cells

The immunocytochemistry of Ki-67 showed that the Ki-67 positive rates of U87 and A172 cells in the parthenolide treatment groups were significantly lower than those in the corresponding groups (Figure 3A,B). Additionally, the results of the CCK-8 assay indicated that the viability of U87 and A172 cells significantly decreased after parthenolide treatment (Figure 3C). These findings suggested that parthenolide significantly inhibited the proliferation of glioma cells.

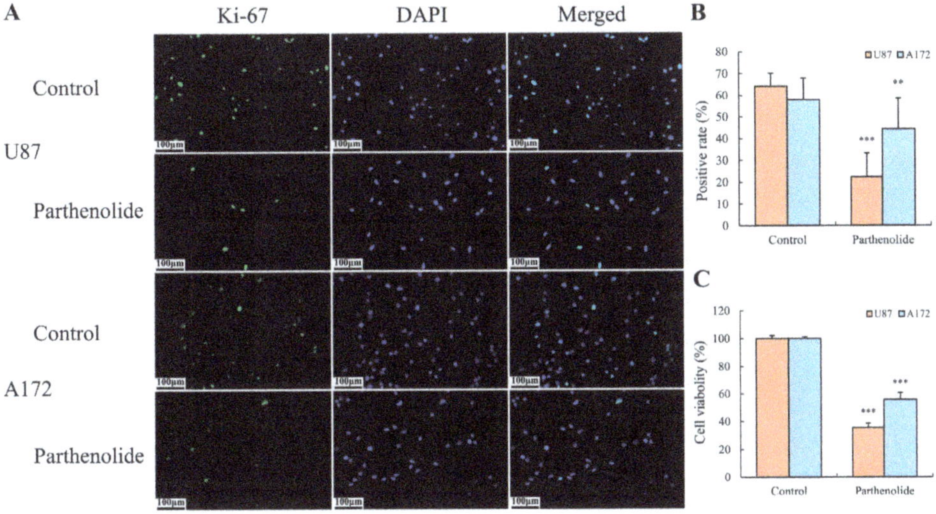

Figure 3. Effects of parthenolide on the proliferation of glioma cells. Parthenolide (4 μM) significantly inhibited the proliferation of U87 and A172 cells. (**A**) Immunocytochemistry detection of Ki-67 (200×), scale bar = 100 μm; (**B**) positive rates of Ki-67 ($n = 3$); (**C**) cell viability detected by the CCK-8 assay ($n = 3$). ** $p < 0.01$ vs. control group, *** $p < 0.001$ vs. control group.

3.4. Parthenolide Inhibited the Self-Renewal of Glioma Cells

The results of the sphere formation assay show that, in the control groups of U87 and A172 cells, clear neurospheres were formed, whereas in the parthenolide groups, no neurospheres with a diameter greater than 75 μm were observed (Figure 4), indicating that parthenolide significantly inhibits the self-renewal of glioma cells.

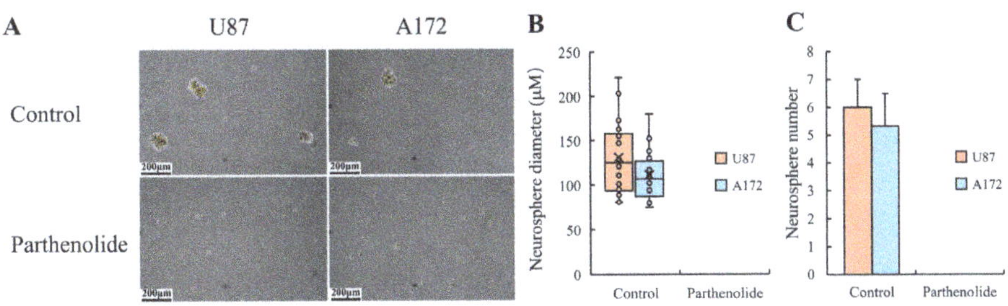

Figure 4. Effects of parthenolide on the self-renewal of glioma cells ($n = 3$). Parthenolide (4 μM) significantly inhibited the sphere formation. (**A**) Microscopy images of neurosphere formation (100×), scale bar = 200 μm; (**B**) neurosphere diameters; (**C**) neurosphere numbers.

3.5. Parthenolide Induced the Differentiation and Proliferation Inhibition of GSCs

The immunocytochemistry results showed that NSC markers nestin and CD133 were expressed in U87 GSCs (Figure 5A). Under microscopic observation, U87 GSCs appeared approximately round, and after parthenolide treatment, they developed neuron-like elongations (Figure 5B). Additionally, cell proliferation was inhibited as well (Figure 5C). Sphere formation assays demonstrated that, compared with the control group, the parthenolide group presented significantly fewer and smaller neurospheres, indicating that parthenolide attenuated the stemness of U87 GSCs.

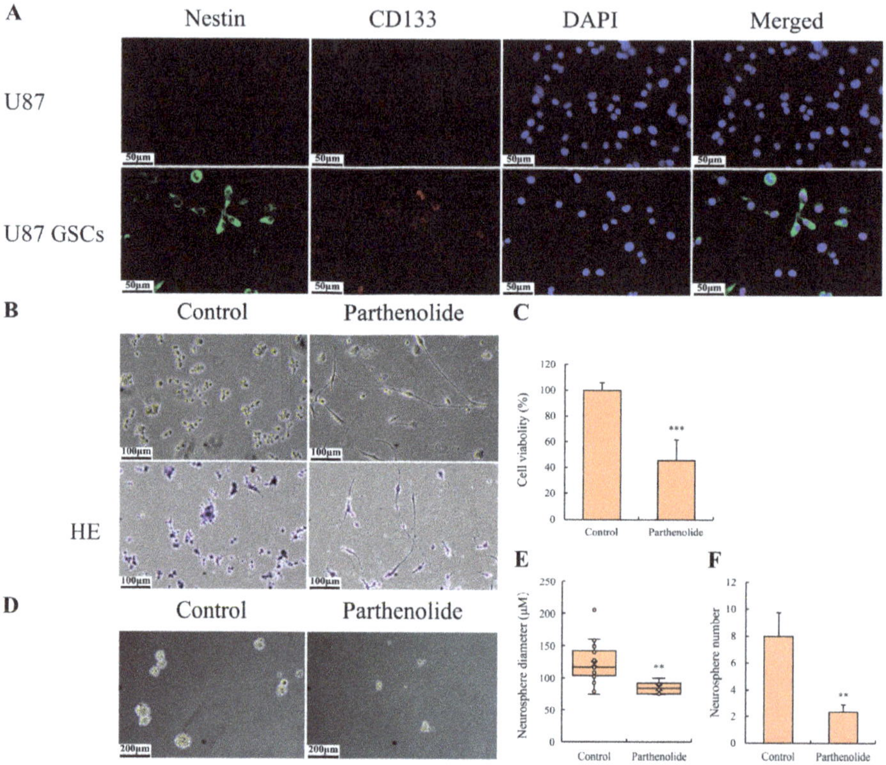

Figure 5. Effects of parthenolide on the differentiation and proliferation of U87 GSCs. Parthenolide (4 μM) induced differentiation and inhibited the cell proliferation in U87 GSCs. (**A**) NSC markers detected by immunocytochemistry (400×), scale bar = 50 μm; (**B**) morphological changes induced by parthenolide (200×), scale bar = 100 μm; (**C**) cell viability detected by a CCK-8 assay (n = 3); (**D**) microscopy images of neurosphere formation (100×), scale bar = 200 μm; (**E**) neurosphere diameters (n = 3); (**F**) neurosphere numbers (n = 3). ** $p < 0.01$ vs. control group, *** $p < 0.001$ vs. control group.

3.6. Inhibition of Histone Deacetylase 1 (HDAC1) Is a Potential Mechanism

It is reported that HDAC inhibitors can induce neuron-like differentiation in glioma cells [9,10]. Additionally, parthenolide was found to be a HDAC1 inhibitor [6]. Therefore, we hypothesized that the differentiation-inducing effect exhibited by parthenolide may be associated with HDAC1. To further investigate, we explored the potential role of HDAC1 in glioma.

The Western blot results demonstrated that parthenolide significantly downregulated the expression of HDAC1 in U87 and A172 cells (Figure 6A,B). Differences in gene expression between glioma samples with high and low HDAC1 expression were analyzed via the CGGA database. There was a statistically significant difference in HDAC1 expression between the high and low expression groups (Figure 6C). The PPI network revealed that the upregulated and downregulated genes in the high-HDAC1 group could be roughly divided into two clusters (Figure 6D), so enrichment analysis was performed on these genes separately. For the upregulated genes, the biological processes (BP), cellular components (CC), and molecular functions (MF) in which the genes were enriched were mainly related to the extracellular matrix (ECM) (Figure 6E). For the downregulated genes, the enrichment terms were mainly related to synapses (Figure 6F). Moreover, the proportion of tumor grade was significantly different between the two groups, with the high-HDAC1 group having a higher proportion of WHO grade 4 (GBM) (80.25%) than the low-HDAC1 group did (9.88%) (Figure 6G). Overall survival was lower in the high-HDAC1 group than in the low-HDAC1 group (Figure 6H).

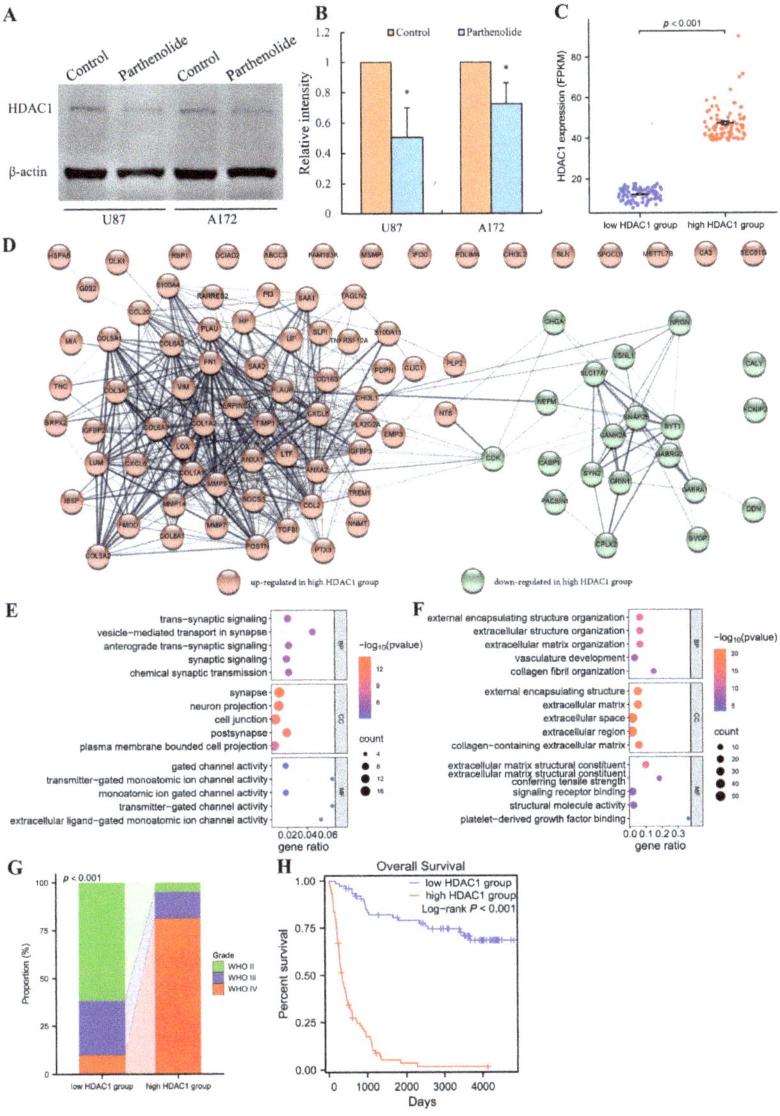

Figure 6. Potential role of HDAC1 in neuronal differentiation induced by parthenolide. (**A**) Western blot bands showing the effects of parthenolide on the expression of HDAC1 in glioma cells; (**B**) relative expression level of HDAC1 based on Western blot bands ($n = 3$), * $p < 0.5$ vs. control group; (**C**) expression level of HDAC1 in the high- and low-HDAC1 groups of glioma samples in the CGGA database; (**D**) PPI network of the DEGs between the high and low groups; (**E**) GO enrichment analysis of the upregulated genes in the high-HDAC1 group; (**F**) GO enrichment analysis of the downregulated genes in the high-HDAC1 group; (**G**) tumor grade composition of the two groups; (**H**) comparison of survival between the two groups, n (low-HDAC1 group) = 81, n (high-HDAC1 group) = 81.

4. Discussion

This study investigated the differentiation-inducing effects of parthenolide on human glioma cells and its impact on cell proliferation, as well as the potential mechanisms. The results showed that treatment with a 4 μM concentration of parthenolide for three days significantly altered the morphology of U87 and A172 cells; induced the expression of neuronal markers NeuN, MAP2, SYP, and NEFL; and inhibited their proliferation and self-renewal. Furthermore, parthenolide also suppressed the expression of HDAC1 in glioma cells, and bioinformatics analysis suggested that this effect may be related to its ability to induce neuronal differentiation.

Due to the lack of proliferative capacity in terminally differentiated neurons, some studies have focused on inducing the differentiation of glioma cells into neurons in recent years. For example, Chen et al. [3] demonstrated that cAMP activators induced the neuronal differentiation of GSCs and inhibited glioma growth in mouse xenograft models. Liu et al. [9] reported that the HDAC inhibitor MS-275, in combination with cAMP activators, could induce U87 cells and GSCs to differentiate into neuron-like cells, and these neuronal transformations significantly inhibited the proliferation of glioma cells. Liu et al. [10] reported that the HDAC inhibitor sodium butyrate induced U87 cells to differentiate into cholinergic neurons and inhibited their proliferation. Our study revealed that parthenolide treatment changed the morphology of U87 and A172 cells and induced the expression of neuronal markers without the expression of astrocyte or oligodendrocyte markers, indicating that parthenolide induced U87 and A172 cells to differentiate into neuron-like cells. Further research revealed that after parthenolide treatment, in addition to a significant decrease in overall cell viability, the Ki-67 positivity rates of surviving cells also decreased significantly, indicating that the induction of differentiation by parthenolide attenuated the proliferative capacity of glioma cells. Inducing neuronal-like differentiation of glioma cells and thereby inhibiting their proliferation is involved in the anti-glioma mechanism of parthenolide.

The clinical course of GBM is characterized by almost inevitable recurrence within the first year of treatment and significant resistance to chemotherapy and radiotherapy. Low proliferative activity, treatment resistance, and associations with tumor recurrence are typical characteristics of GSCs [11]. To investigate whether parthenolide has a differentiation-inducing effect on GSCs, U87 GSC-like cells were utilized in this study. The results indicated that parthenolide induced the differentiation of GSC-like cells and inhibited their proliferation and self-renewal, suggesting that parthenolide has the potential to prevent glioma recurrence.

Previous studies have shown that the molecular mechanisms underlying the antiglioma effects of parthenolide are related mainly to the inhibition of Akt and NF-κB. Additionally, it reduces temozolomide resistance by downregulating O-6-Methylguanine-DNA Methyltransferase (MGMT) expression [12,13]. In other cancers, the anticancer mechanism of parthenolide is believed to be mainly related to the inhibition of NF-κB, and other mechanisms include the inhibition of mouse double minute 2 homolog (MDM2), HDAC1, transcription protein 3 (STAT3), and glutathione (GSH) [7]. Since HDAC inhibitors have been found to induce neuronal-like differentiation in glioma cells [9,10], and there are currently no reports on such effects related to the drug targets of parthenolide except HDAC1, we focused our attention on HDAC1. HDACs are important chromatin-modifying enzymes that catalyze the deacetylation of lysine residues in histone. Deacetylated histones maintain their positive charge and remain tightly bound to negatively charged DNA, thus limiting the accessibility of transcription factors and suppressing gene expression. HDAC1 belongs to class I HDACs [14]. Most HDAC inhibitors are not specific, while parthenolide selectively depletes HDAC1 in micromolar concentrations through ataxia telangiectasia mutated (ATM) activation, leaving other HDACs unaffected [15]. This study confirms the inhibitory effect of parthenolide on HDAC1 in glioma cells. Recent studies on HDAC1 in glioma have shown that HDAC1 is a necessary class I HDAC in GSCs that maintains the malignant phenotype of GSCs and promotes the progression of GBM [16,17]. Furthermore, HDAC1 is an important component of the RE-1 silencing transcription factor (REST) complex. REST is an inhibitory transcription factor that targets multiple neuronal genes. NSCs express high levels of REST, which inhibits the expression of neuronal genes and helps maintain the stem cell state, but its expression is downregulated during neuronal development, allowing for extensive transcription of neuron-specific genes [18]. These findings suggest a potential association of HDAC1 with neuronal differentiation. Bioinformatics analysis in this study indicated that high expression of HDAC1 in glioma was associated with the extracellular matrix (ECM) and poor prognosis. The ECM is a non-cellular component of tissues that provides biochemical and structural support to cells and has been shown to guide cell migration and proliferation [19]. In glioma cells, the synthesis of the ECM is upregulated, thereby inducing the expression of invasion-related molecules [20]. After surgery, residual glioma cells after surgery actively create and remodel a more abundant, denser, and stiffer ECM, promoting glioma recurrence and progression through stemness or aggression [21]. These findings suggest that high expression of HDAC1 may be associated with the high invasiveness and recurrence of glioma. Samples with low HDAC1 expression were associated with more neuronal features and better prognosis, indicating that inhibiting HDAC1 may be associated with the neuronal-like differentiation of glioma cells induced by parthenolide.

5. Conclusions

In summary, this study suggested that parthenolide induced the differentiation of glioma cells into neuron-like cells and inhibited cell proliferation. The inhibition of HDAC1 expression in glioma cells may potentially be associated with these effects, although further investigation is needed to confirm the underlying mechanism. We will continue to explore the role of HDAC1 in the neuronal differentiation induced by parthenolide and the molecular mechanisms involved in this process in subsequent studies. This study confirmed the anti-glioma effect of parthenolide and supplemented the understanding of its anti-glioma mechanism, which has the potential to inform future clinical trials and the development of new therapeutic strategies for glioma patients. This study also verified the reliability of using the Connectivity Map database for drug repositioning.

Author Contributions: Conceptualization, Z.T. and Y.S.; methodology, Z.T. and W.T.; software, Z.C.; validation, W.T.; formal analysis, Y.Y.; investigation, Z.T.; resources, Z.T.; data curation, C.C.; writing—original draft preparation, Z.T.; writing—review and editing, Y.S.; visualization, C.C.; supervision, Y.S.; project administration, Z.T.; funding acquisition, Z.T. All authors have read and agreed to the published version of the manuscript.

Funding: This research was funded by Natural Science Foundation of Xiamen, China, grant number 3502Z202372068.

Institutional Review Board Statement: Not applicable.

Informed Consent Statement: Not applicable.

Data Availability Statement: The original data presented in the study are openly available in FigShare at 10.6084/m9.figshare.27088660.

Acknowledgments: We are grateful to the colleagues who helped in the bioinformatics analysis and experiments.

Conflicts of Interest: The authors declare no conflicts of interest.

References

1. McKinnon, C.; Nandhabalan, M.; Murray, S.A.; Plaha, P. Glioblastoma: Clinical presentation, diagnosis, and management. *BMJ* **2021**, *374*, n1560. [CrossRef] [PubMed]
2. Grek, C.L.; Sheng, Z.; Naus, C.C.; Sin, W.C.; Gourdie, R.G.; Ghatnekar, G.G. Novel approach to temozolomide resistance in malignant glioma: Connexin43-directed therapeutics. *Curr. Opin. Pharmacol.* **2018**, *41*, 79–88. [CrossRef] [PubMed]

3. Chen, Z.; Zhong, Y.; Chen, J.; Sun, S.; Liu, W.; Han, Y.; Liu, X.; Guo, C.; Li, D.; Hu, W.; et al. Disruption of β-catenin-mediated negative feedback reinforces cAMP-induced neuronal differentiation in glioma stem cells. *Cell Death Dis.* **2022**, *13*, 493. [CrossRef] [PubMed]
4. Chen, K.S.; Bridges, C.R.; Lynton, Z.; Lim, J.W.C.; Stringer, B.W.; Rajagopal, R.; Wong, K.T.; Ganesan, D.; Ariffin, H.; Day, B.W.; et al. Transcription factors NFIA and NFIB induce cellular differentiation in high-grade astrocytoma. *J. Neurooncol.* **2020**, *146*, 41–53. [CrossRef]
5. Liu, J.; Wang, X.; Chen, A.T.; Gao, X.; Himes, B.T.; Zhang, H.; Chen, Z.; Wang, J.; Sheu, W.C.; Deng, G.; et al. ZNF117 regulates glioblastoma stem cell differentiation towards oligodendroglial lineage. *Nat. Commun.* **2022**, *13*, 2196. [CrossRef]
6. Freund, R.R.A.; Gobrecht, P.; Fischer, D.; Arndt, H.D. Advances in chemistry and bioactivity of parthenolide. *Nat. Prod. Rep.* **2020**, *37*, 541–565. [CrossRef]
7. Sztiller-Sikorska, M.; Czyz, M. Parthenolide as Cooperating Agent for Anti-Cancer Treatment of Various Malignancies. *Pharmaceuticals* **2020**, *13*, 194. [CrossRef]
8. Tang, Z.Q.; Ye, Y.R. Predicting Glioma Cell Differentiation-inducing Drugs Using a Drug Repositioning Strategy. *Comb. Chem. High Throughput Screen.* **2023**, *26*, 339–346.
9. Jiang, B.; Sai, K.; Yang, W.; Gu, J.; Wang, J.; Sun, S.; Chen, Z.; Zhong, Y.; Liang, X.; Chen, C.; et al. Differential regulation of H3K9/H3K14 acetylation by small molecules drives neuron-fate-induction of glioma cell. *Cell Death Dis.* **2023**, *14*, 142.
10. Liu, H.; Xia, J.; Wang, T.; Li, W.; Song, Y.; Tan, G. Differentiation of human glioblastoma U87 cells into cholinergic neuron. *Neurosci. Lett.* **2019**, *704*, 1–7. [CrossRef]
11. Biserova, K.; Jakovlevs, A.; Uljanovs, R.; Strumfa, I. Cancer Stem Cells: Significance in Origin, Pathogenesis and Treatment of Glioblastoma. *Cells* **2021**, *10*, 621. [CrossRef] [PubMed]
12. Nakabayashi, H.; Shimizu, K. Involvement of Akt/NF-κB pathway in antitumor effects of parthenolide on glioblastoma cells in vitro and in vivo. *BMC Cancer* **2012**, *12*, 453. [CrossRef] [PubMed]
13. Yu, Z.; Chen, Y.; Wang, S.; Li, P.; Zhou, G.; Yuan, Y. Inhibition of NF-κB results in anti-glioma activity and reduces temozolomide-induced chemoresistance by down-regulating MGMT gene expression. *Cancer Lett.* **2018**, *428*, 77–89. [CrossRef]
14. King, J.; Patel, M.; Chandrasekaran, S. Metabolism, HDACs, and HDAC Inhibitors: A Systems Biology Perspective. *Metabolites* **2021**, *11*, 792. [CrossRef] [PubMed]
15. Gopal, Y.N.; Arora, T.S.; Van Dyke, M.W. Parthenolide specifically depletes histone deacetylase 1 protein and induces cell death through ataxia telangiectasia mutated. *Chem. Biol.* **2007**, *14*, 813–823. [CrossRef]
16. Song, Y.; Jiang, Y.; Tao, D.; Wang, Z.; Wang, R.; Wang, M.; Han, S. NFAT2-HDAC1 signaling contributes to the malignant phenotype of glioblastoma. *Neuro-Oncol.* **2020**, *22*, 46–57. [CrossRef]
17. Bastola, S.; Pavlyukov, M.S.; Yamashita, D.; Ghosh, S.; Cho, H.; Kagaya, N.; Zhang, Z.; Minata, M.; Lee, Y.; Sadahiro, H.; et al. Glioma-initiating cells at tumor edge gain signals from tumor core cells to promote their malignancy. *Nat. Commun.* **2020**, *11*, 4660. [CrossRef]
18. Garcia-Manteiga, J.M.; D'Alessandro, R.; Meldolesi, J. News about the Role of the Transcription Factor REST in Neurons: From Physiology to Pathology. *Int. J. Mol. Sci.* **2019**, *21*, 235. [CrossRef]
19. Walker, C.; Mojares, E.; Del Río Hernández, A. Role of Extracellular Matrix in Development and Cancer Progression. *Int. J. Mol. Sci.* **2018**, *19*, 3028. [CrossRef]
20. Ferrer, V.P.; Moura Neto, V.; Mentlein, R. Glioma infiltration and extracellular matrix: Key players and modulators. *Glia* **2018**, *66*, 1542–1565. [CrossRef]
21. Wei, R.; Zhou, J.; Bui, B.; Liu, X. Glioma actively orchestrate a self-advantageous extracellular matrix to promote recurrence and progression. *BMC Cancer* **2024**, *24*, 974. [CrossRef] [PubMed]

MDPI AG
Grosspeteranlage 5
4052 Basel
Switzerland
Tel.: +41 61 683 77 34

Biomedicines Editorial Office
E-mail: biomedicines@mdpi.com
www.mdpi.com/journal/biomedicines

www.ingramcontent.com/pod-product-compliance
Lightning Source LLC
Chambersburg PA
CBHW040746250926
51850CB00007BB/1419